UR III TEXTS IN THE SCHØYEN COLLECTION

The publication of
CORNELL UNIVERSITY STUDIES IN ASSYRIOLOGY AND SUMEROLOGY
Volume 39

was made possible thanks to a generous subvention from an anonymous donor

Cornell University Studies in Assyriology and Sumerology (CUSAS)

Volume 39

MANUSCRIPTS IN THE SCHØYEN COLLECTION

CUNEIFORM TEXTS XIII

Ur III Texts in the Schøyen Collection

by

Jacob L. Dahl

Eisenbrauns
University Park, Pennsylvania
2020

Library of Congress Cataloging-in-Publication Data

Names: Dahl, Jacob L., author.
Title: Ur III texts in the Schøyen Collection / by Jacob L. Dahl.
Other titles: Cornell University studies in Assyriology and Sumerology ; v. 39.
Description: University Park, Pennsylvania : Eisenbrauns, 2020. | Series: Cornell University studies in Assyriology and Sumerology (CUSAS) ; volume 39 | Includes bibliographical references and indexes. | English with cuneiform texts in transliterated Sumerian with English translation.
Summary: "A comprehensive study of the workings of the administrative machinery of the Ur III state (ca. 2100–2000 BC), based on approximately 250 cuneiform tablets translated into English"—Provided by publisher.
Identifiers: LCCN 2020007417 | ISBN 9781575067384 (cloth)
Subjects: LCSH: Schøyen Collection. | Sumerian language—Texts. | Cuneiform inscriptions, Sumerian—Iraq. | Cuneiform inscriptions, Sumerian—Translations into English. | Ur (Extinct city)—Politics and government.
Classification: LCC PJ4081 .D34 2020 | DDC 899/.95—dc23
LC record available at https://lccn.loc.gov/2020007417

Printed in the United States of America
Published by The Pennsylvania State University Press,
University Park, PA 16802-1003

Eisenbrauns is an imprint of The Pennsylvania State University Press.

The Pennsylvania State University Press is a member of the Association of University Presses.

It is the policy of The Pennsylvania State University Press to use acid-free paper. Publications on uncoated stock satisfy the minimum requirements of American National Standard for Information Sciences—Permanence of Paper for Printed Library Material, ANSI Z39.48-1992.

Contents

Statement of Provenance

THE NEAR EASTERN PICTOGRAPHIC TABLETS, CUNEIFORM TABLETS, AND SEALS

A. Ownership History

The holdings of pictographic tablets, cuneiform tablets and seals in The Schøyen Collection were collected mainly in the late 1980s, with further items in the 1990s. They derive from a great variety of former collections and sources. It would not have been possible to collect so many items, of such major textual importance, if it had not been based on the endeavour of some of the greatest collectors in earlier times. Collections that once held tablets, and seals now in The Schøyen Collection are:

Institute of Antiquity and Christianity, Claremont Graduate School, Claremont, California (1970–94)

Erlenmeyer Collection and Foundation, Basel (1943–88)

Cumberland Clark Collection, Bournemouth, UK (1920s–1941)

Lord Amherst of Hackney, UK (1894–1909)

Crouse Collection, Hong Kong and New England (1920s–80s)

Dring Collection, Surrey, UK (1911–90)

Rihani Collection, Irbid (*ca.* 1935) and Amman, Jordan (before 1965–88) and London (1988–)

Lindgren Collection, San Francisco, California (1965–85)

Rosenthal Collection, San Francisco, California (1953–88)

Kevorkian Collection, New York (*ca.* 1930–59) and Fund (1960–77)

Kohanim Collection, Tehran, Paris and London (1959–85)

Simmonds Collection, UK (1944–87)

Schaeffer Collection, Collège de France, Zürich (1950s)

Henderson Collection, Boston, Massachusetts (1930s–50s)

Pottesman Collection, London (1904–78)

Geuthner Collection, France (1960s–80s)

Harding Smith Collection, UK (1893–1922)

Rev. Dr. W. F. Williams, Mosul (*ca.* 1850–60)

Frida Hahn Collection, Berlin (1925–73)

Mixon Collection, California and UK (1920s–1967) and heirs

These collections are the source of almost all the tablets and seals. Other items were acquired through Christie's and Sotheby's, where in a few cases the names of their former owners were not revealed.

The sources of the oldest collections, such as Amherst, Harding Smith, and Cumberland Clark, were antiquities' dealers who acquired tablets and seals in the Near East in the 1890s–1930s. During this period many tens of thousands of tablets came on the market: in the summers of 1893–94 alone some 30,000 tablets. While most of these were bought by museums, others were acquired by private collectors. In this way some of the older of these collections were the source of some of the later collections. For instance, a large number of the tablets in the Crouse Collection came from the Cumberland Clark, Kohanim, Amherst, and Simmonds collections. The Claremont tablets came from the Schaeffer Collection, and the Dring tablets came from the Harding Smith Collection.

B. Archaeological Provenance, Findspots

In most cases the original findspots of tablets that came on the market in the 1890s–1930s and later are unknown. Therefore great parts of the holdings of most major museums in Europe and the United States are without archaeological provenance. This also applies to The Schøyen Collection. Based on the texts of the tablets themselves the following provenances can nevertheless be identified:

About 85% of the Early Dynastic and Old Akkadian tablets come from palace and temple archives in Adab and Umma.

About 90% of the Old Babylonian tablets come from Larsa.

The Old Assyrian tablets all come from Kanesh (Kültepe) excavation level II, mostly from Bedřich Hrozný's findspots 2, 3, 4 and 10, unearthed 1890–1925.

All Ugaritic tablets come from Ras Shamra, excavation level I, excavated under the direction of Claude Schaeffer, 1957–58.

Most Neo-Assyrian tablets come from Assur, unearthed during the German excavations under Walter Andrae, 1903–14.

From Lagash and its vicinity there are tablets from the E-Ninnu temple, Ninkar temple in Nimin, Ningishzida temple, Nindara and Ningirsu temples in Girsu, the Ur-Bau temple in Urukug, and the Inanna and Emush temples in Bad-Tibira.

From Nineveh: The Royal Library of Ashurbanipal, and the Ezida temple of Nabu.

From Nimrud: North-west palace of Ashurnasirpal II, the library of Nabû-zuqup-kena, and the palace of Sargon II.

In addition to other major sites like Ur, Uruk, Eridu, Isin, Babylon, Nippur, Susa, Persepolis, there are tablets and seals from at least thirty further sites.

Martin Schøyen

MANUSCRIPTS IN THE SCHØYEN COLLECTION

CUNEIFORM TEXTS

Vol. I. Jöran Friberg, *A Remarkable Collection of Babylonian Mathematical Texts*
Sources and Studies in the History of Mathematics and Physical Sciences
New York: Springer, 2007

Vol. II. Bendt Alster, *Sumerian Proverbs in the Schøyen Collection*
Cornell University Studies in Assyriology and Sumerology 2
Bethesda, Md.: CDL Press, 2007

Vol. III. Stephanie Dalley, *Babylonian Tablets from the First Sealand Dynasty in the Schøyen Collection*
Cornell University Studies in Assyriology and Sumerology 9
Bethesda, Md.: CDL Press, 2009

Vol. IV. A. R. George, *Babylonian Literary Texts in the Schøyen Collection*
Cornell University Studies in Assyriology and Sumerology 10
Bethesda, Md.: CDL Press, 2009

Vol. V. Miguel Civil, *Lexical Texts in the Schøyen Collection*
Cornell University Studies in Assyriology and Sumerology 12
Bethesda, Md.: CDL Press, 2010

Vol. VI. A. R. George, *Cuneiform Royal Inscriptions in the Schøyen Collection*
with contributions by M. Civil, G. Frame, P. Steinkeller, F. Vallat, K. Volk, M. Weeden, and C. Wilcke
Cornell University Studies in Assyriology and Sumerology 17
Bethesda, Md.: CDL Press, 2011

Vol. VII. A. R. George, *Babylonian Divinatory Texts Chiefly in the Schøyen Collection*
with an appendix of materials from the papers of W. G. Lambert†
Cornell University Studies in Assyriology and Sumerology 18
Bethesda, Md.: CDL Press, 2013

Vol. VIII. A. R. George, *Mesopotamian Incantations and Related Texts in the Schøyen Collection*
Cornell University Studies in Assyriology and Sumerology 32
Bethesda, Md.: CDL Press, 2016

Vol. IX. A. R. George, T. Hertel, J. Llop-Raduà, K. Radner, and W. H. van Soldt, *Assyrian Archival Texts in the Schøyen Collection and Other Documents from North Mesopotamia and Syria*
Cornell University Studies in Assyriology and Sumerology 34
Bethesda, Md.: CDL Press, 2017

Vol. X. Vitali Bartash, *Sumerian Administrative and Legal Documents ca. 2900–2200 BC in the Schøyen Collection*
Cornell University Studies in Assyriology and Sumerology 35
Bethesda, Md.: CDL Press, 2017

Vol. XI. A. R. George, *Old Babylonian Texts in the Schøyen Collection, Part One: Selected Letters*
Cornell University Studies in Assyriology and Sumerology 36
Bethesda, Md.: CDL Press, 2018

Vol. XII. Christopher Metcalf, *Sumerian Literary Texts in the Schøyen Collection, Vol. 1: Literary Sources on Old Babylonian Religion*
Cornell University Studies in Assyriology and Sumerology 38
University Park: Eisenbrauns, 2019

Vol. XIII. Jacob L. Dahl, *Ur III Texts in the Schøyen Collection*
Cornell University Studies in Assyriology and Sumerology 39
University Park: Eisenbrauns, 2020

Vol. XIV. A. R. George and Gabriella Spada, *Old Babylonian Texts in the Schøyen Collection, Part Two: School Letters, Model Contracts, and Related Texts*
Cornell University Studies in Assyriology and Sumerology 43
University Park: Eisenbrauns, 2019

Other volumes are in preparation

Series Editor's Preface

Jacob L. Dahl's publication of the Ur III texts of the Schøyen Collection concludes the study of the remaining unpublished Ur III economic texts from the late third millennium in the collection. As is often the case with Ur III collections, the texts are representative of archives from both well-known and undetermined sites. While the bulk of the collection stems from Umma, a significant addition to the lesser known corpus of texts from Adab is also represented. Dahl's publication of the texts goes beyond the more traditional presentations of economic tablets and provides extensive commentary and accurate translations that make the volume an important contribution to the study of the Ur III period, in particular for Assyriology but also for scholars and students in general. Extensive new data on prosopography, economy, accounting procedures, letters, contracts, technical terminology, agriculture, etc., add significantly to our knowledge of society and the economy during the Third Dynasty of Ur. As such, the volume serves as an up-to-date and broad survey of the range of detailed documentation for this period that these frequently laconic sources often do not provide. Coupled with extensive commentary and exhaustive indexes, the volume will serve also as a useful handbook for scholars and students alike. We are most grateful to Jacob L. Dahl for undertaking the comprehensive study of these texts, to Andrew George for his editorial supervision, and to Martin Schøyen for his enthusiastic and generous support of the many volumes of texts from his unique collection that are appearing in the CUSAS series.

David I. Owen
Curator of Tablet Collections
Jonathan and Jeannette Rosen
Ancient Near Eastern Studies Seminar
Cornell University, Ithaca, New York
February 2020

Preface

Innovation and playfulness are displayed in the very earliest written records known to us—new sign forms were devised with no practical application (Damerow 2006: §8.3 and Fig. 5), and mathematical exercises with difficult or extraordinary numbers were set (Nissen, Englund, and Damerow 1990: 98)—but we should not forget the darker sides of our history. In the texts published here, all from the time of the Third Dynasty of Ur (c. 2100–2000 BC), as well as throughout the combined extant records from that period, by far the greatest effort invested by the ancient administrators was in the excessively long monthly and yearly rosters assigning tiny parcels of land to countless prebend holders, or starvation rations to even more numerous estate slaves. Forget private enterprise, forget literature, forget mathematics—judging from the sheer amount of textual material left us, the ancient rulers were above all obsessed with keeping track of their subjects, and recording with frightening detail the whereabouts of the poorest individuals making up the majority of the population under their jurisdiction. They did this year after year, noting even minute changes in the staffing of their teams. Take, for example, the following excerpt from the monthly roster of cattle hands on a state-run estate, text No. 130 (edited in Chapter 8). This excerpt is found at the beginning of the second column of the obverse: "One prebend plot (for) Lugal-ezem (and for) Šeš-kala (and for) Ur-Sukkal. They (Šeš-kala and Ur-Sukkal) are his children, returned from flight." While we know all too well the circumstances surrounding flight, pursuit, and punishment from much later New World slavery, the full picture from ancient Mesopotamia is only now being revealed (Reid 2015).

This book presents editions of 244 cuneiform tablets from the period of the Third Dynasty of Ur. The vast majority of them are previously unpublished. For the more recent collection history, see the collector's statement prefixed to this study. The ancient provenience is for the most part the province Umma, whereas the other core provinces are represented in smaller numbers. In addition, the collection provides notable contributions of texts from ancient Adab, otherwise under-represented in the published record. In order to provide a fuller picture of the administration of the Ur III state, many texts from other collections, both published and unpublished, have been included in this book.

I wish to thank Martin Schøyen for his permission to study these tablets in the Schøyen Collection, and for his gracious hospitality during my visits to the collection. My work in Norway was also supported by Jens E. Braarvig and Elizabeth Sørenssen.

Naturally, a project of this sort does not occur in a vacuum, and I would like to thank the following persons for their assistance at various stages of the work (in alphabetical order): B. Alster (†), S. Dahl, P. Damerow (†), R. K. Englund, A. R. George, B. Lafont, T. Ozaki, D. I. Owen, J. N. Reid, K. Wagensonner, and M. Widell. Finally, I wish to thank Axel Theodore Dahl and James Lawrence Dahl for their help with the final editing of this book.

I am grateful also for the financial support I have received over the years for my work on the Schøyen Collection, including funding from the Danish Research Academy (now defunct), and the Faculty of Oriental Studies, the University of Oxford.

Since my first visit to the Schøyen Collection in 2001, I have kept all the core records concerning the Ur III texts in the collection up to date and and made them freely accessible to other researchers through the web-pages of the Cuneiform Digital Library Initiative (CDLI, see https://cdli.ucla.edu). Thus, my publication of the tablets has benefited over time from comments from colleagues, and it is my understanding that the work of others has benefited from unhindered access to these documents.

Given the nature of the sources, I have refrained from making hand copies of the tablets and refer the reader to the photographs available online. Several generations of images are available, varying from hand copies of some of those tablets that were previously published, scanned images made by myself, photographs made by the team of Braarvig, and most recently HDR photos and RTI images made by Klaus Wagensonner for the CDLI.

Jacob L. Dahl
Oxford, 2020.

Conventions

Transliterations

All text transliterations follow CDLI conventions; all readings not in Borger (1978) and Ellermeier (1979–80) are explained. Akkadian and Sumerian are transliterated with the same font and type. Signs with unknown readings are transliterated using capitals. The sign-name is given in parenthesis when a new reading is proposed. Signs not in Borger or Ellermeier are numbered following Schneider (1935), and prefixed KWU. Index numbers are always given with numerals. Broken signs are indicated with half-brackets. Breaks are indicated by square brackets: square brackets are never placed inside a sign. If it is useful to indicate in the transliteration which part of a sign is broken, this is done in the notes to the texts. Standard Assyriological fonts are used in both transliterations and transcriptions. However, sade (ṣ), tet (ṭ), and nasalized g (ŋ) are not rendered in the transliterations. Although the sign *ze*$_2$ in some cases is to be read *ṣe* it is always transliterated *ze*$_2$; similarly, although *ga*$_2$ is always used for *ŋa* it is transliterated *ga*$_2$, etc. Transliterations within the body of the text are spaced for Sumerian and italicized for Akkadian.

When texts or text excerpts are transliterated in the footnotes, they are, as a rule, given in a running format, using / as a line separator, and // as a surface separator (for example, obv. l. 1 / obv. l. 2 // rev. l. 1 / rev. l. 2 // seal l. 1, etc.).

Translations

All texts are translated into English, except those appearing only in the Appendix. Sexagesimal numerical notations are transcribed into the decimal system; all other notations are given using the original system of values. Numerical notations have been translated only when a one-to-one semantic correspondence with an English term can be found (gi = reed; kuš$_3$ = cubit; gu$_2$ = talent; gin$_2$ = shekel; še = grain). Capacity notations have been translated into liters in the discussions only. Sumerian words have been translated throughout this study, whenever possible. The Sumerian form and any necessary discussion are to be found either in the notes or between brackets in the main text (not in repeated instances). Certain words such as *sukkalmaḫ* (sukkal-maḫ, a high-ranking title in the imperial administration), or *nam-šatam* (nam-ša$_3$-tam, a certain administrative function or office) have been left untranslated, but pseudo-transcribed, for the sake of convention.

Personal Names

Names are not distinguished in the transliterations. Names are transcribed in the translations and in the body of the text with attention to the presumed language of that name. Akkadian and Sumerian names are transcribed with the same font and type. Names are capitalized in the transcriptions but not in the transliterations. Akkadian names have been transcribed as closely as possible to the standard conventions of Akkadian (see, for example, von Soden 1952: 8–9 §6c–d). Sumerian names are transcribed in a reader-friendly way that does not attempt to render any phonetic qualities of the names. All personal names presumably had a meaning to their owners, whether we understand them or not. The system of transcribing names in this book intends to render them in a way that illustrates the meaning of the name. I will not attempt to translate any names, many of which were abbreviated forms. In ambiguous cases footnotes are used to explain the choice of transcription. The name lu$_2$-kal-la has thus been transcribed Lu-kala, since it is understood to mean something like "the precious man," and since the double writing of the final "l" is understood to be a result of scribal conventions rather than an expression of the phonetic value of the signs. ur-e$_{11}$-e has been transcribed Ur-E'e, since E'e is a divine name (a god in the local pantheon of Umma). The apostrophe does not relate to pronunciation; it is inserted only to indicate that the name is spelled with two signs, each transliterated "e" (similarly in the transliteration of the numerical signs geš'u and bur'u, see below). A name such as gu-du-du has simply been transcribed Gududu, since it remains impossible to isolate the meanings of components of such names beyond reasonable doubt. Names of unknown reading have not been transcribed.

Numbers and Metrology

Numerical notations are transliterated using CDLI standards (digits or fractions followed by a qualifier between brackets). Apart from sexagesimal notations, no numerical notations are transcribed into modern systems except in the discussion. Below is a quick reference for conversion of the numerical notations found in the texts published here.

The basic unit in the sexagesimal system, used when counting discrete objects is 1(diš).

1 $šar_2$ = 6 geš'u
1 geš'u = 10 $geš_2$
1 $geš_2$ = 6 u
1 u = 10 diš

Fractions of the smallest unit are expressed by either subdividing 1(diš) into 60 gin_2, and further by subdividing each gin_2 into 180 še, or by a system of reciprocal notations referred to as the "igi-*n*-gal_2" system.

igi-6(diš)-gal = 1/6
igi-4(diš)-gal = ¼
etc.

The basic unit in the capacity system is 1(diš) $sila_3$. Notations of 300 $sila_3$ or larger were recorded in the sexagesimal system. 300 $sila_3$ equal 1 gur, which was recorded with a horizontal wedge (aš) rather than a vertical wedge (diš). Notations above 6(geš'u) are notated with 1 ($guru_7$) and so forth (lit. one granary), rather than 1 ($šar_2$).

1 gur = 5 barig
1 barig = 6 ban_2
1 ban_2 = 10 diš

As with the smallest notation in the sexagesimal system, so too the $sila_3$ can be subdivided, first into 60 gin_2 and further each gin_2 into 180 še.

The basic unit of the weights system is 1(diš) gin_2 (Akkadian *šiqlum*):

1 gu_2 = 60 ma-na
1 ma-na = 60 gin_2
1 gin_2 (shekel) = 180 še

The basic unit of the area measure system is 1(diš) iku. The iku can be subdivided into 100 sar. Fractions of the iku can be expressed with ½(iku) (written with the U sign) and ¼(iku) (written with the DIŠ sign).

1 $šar_2$ = 6 bur_3
1 bur'u = 10 bur_3
1 bur_3 = 3 $eše_3$
1 $eše_3$ = 6 iku
1 iku = 100 sar

Below is a list of the approximate conversions of the basic units to units in the metric system:

1(diš) $sila_3$ = 1 liter
1(aš) gur = 300 liters
1(diš) gin_2 = 8 ½ grams
1(diš) ma-na = ½ kilogram
1(diš) sar = 36 square meters
1(bur_3) = 6.48 hectares

In transliterations the notations are described as multiples of the numerical sign. For example, the following notation, from text No. 91 obv. 5:

1(aš) 1(barig) 1(ban_2) 2(diš) ⅔(diš) $sila_3$ 8(diš) gin_2 gur

Represents 1 gur, 1 barig, 1 ban_2, 2 ⅔ $sila_3$ and 8 shekel (of lard). This notation can be converted into a notation of 372 4/5 $sila_3$ or about 372 4/5 liters of lard.

Or in the following example, from text No. 155 obv. iv 12–13:

2(bur_3) 1($eše_3$) 5(iku) ½(iku) GAN_2 geš a-ra2 3($aš_{45}$) ⸢4(iku)⸣ ½(iku) GAN_2-ta / a_2 $erin_2$-na-bi ⸢u_4⸣ 1($geš_2$) 3(u) 5(diš)

Here 2 bur_3, 1 $eše_3$ and 5 ½ iku of field is harrowed three times at a rate of 4 ½ iku daily, by a team of three workers, resulting in an expenditure of workdays of 1 geš$_2$ and 3 u and 5 diš, or 95 workdays in a decimal notation.

Calendrical Information

Dates, mostly the terminal dates of administrative documents, are given in the following format: (1) abbreviated ruler-name (Š = Šulgi, AS = Amar-Suen, ŠS = Šu-Suen, IS = Ibbi-Suen) followed by (2) a year-count in Arabic numerals, (3) the month number in Latin numerals, and (4) the day number in Arabic numerals.

Examples:

AS 5–v–12 = Amar-Suen, year 5, month 5, day 12.

ŠS 9 = Šu-Suen, year 9, no month or day information.

X vi = Unknown ruler, month 6.

Question marks and comments are added when necessary.

Catalog Information

Catalog information concerning texts published in this volume is provided in the following form, where the first number represents the publication number of the text when it is published here for the first time:

n. MS nnnn(/nn) (provenience, date)

The first text published in this volume is therefore described in the following way:

1. MS 1719 (Drehem, ŠS 4–i to ŠS 6–xiii)

Abbreviations

A list of the text identifications used in this book can be found online at the CDLI project at: http://cdli.ox.ac.uk/wiki/doku.php?id=abbreviations_for_assyriology.

As far as it has been deemed necessary museum numbers have been added to text IDs of cited texts for clarification.

The following additional abbreviations are used in this study:

AbZ	R. Borger, *Assyrisch-babylonische Zeichenliste* (AOAT 33–33A; Neukirchen-Vluyn 1981)
AhW	W. von Soden, *Akkadisches Handwörterbuch* (Wiesbaden 1959–81)
CAD	*The Assyrian Dictionary of the University of Chicago* (Chicago 1956–2010)
CDLI	Cuneiform Digital Library Initiative (joint project of the University of California, Los Angeles, and the Max Planck Institute for the History of Science, Berlin, see https://cdli.ucla.edu)
Ellermeier	F. Ellermeier, *Sumerisches Glossar* 1/1/1–2 (Nörten-Hardenberg 1979–80)
KWU	Schneider, N. *Die Keilschriftzeichen der Wirtschaftsurkunden von Ur III nebst ihren charakteristischsten Schreibvarianten, systematisch zusammengestellt* (Rome 1935).
Lagaš I	First Dynasty of Lagaš (pre-Sargonic Lagash)
Lagaš II	Second Dynasty of Lagaš (the dynasty of Gudea, also called the dynasty of Ur-Ba'u)
MSCT 1	J. Friberg, *A Remarkable Collection of Babylonian Mathematical Texts* (New York 2007)
RAI	Rencontre Assyriologique Internationale
SKL	Sumerian King-List
Ur III	Third Dynasty of Ur
USKL	Ur III recension of the Sumerian King-List

Catalog

Archival Documents

No.	Collection ID	Provenience	Date	Measurement (in mm)	CDLI	Ch.
1	MS 1719	Drehem	ŠS 4 i to ŠS 6 xiii	38×32×17	P250470	2
2	MS 2020/10	Umma	—	34×34×16	P250771	2
3	MS 5047/1	Umma?	—	30×31×16	P254136	2
4	MS 1942/3	Umma	Š 44	32(diam.)×38(h)	P250614	2
5	MS 1942/4	Umma	Š 34 to Š 36	24(diam)×38(h)	P250615	2
6	MS 2077	Umma	IS 1–xi	67(h)×95(side A)×95(B)×95(C)	P250827	2
7	MS 1942/1	Umma	—	62×56×19	P250612	2
8	MS 1942/2	Umma	—	54×56×30	P250613	2
9	MS 1942/6	Umma	—	51×41×23	P250617	2
10	MS 1942/7	Umma	—	49×45×24	P250618	2
11	MS 1942/8	Umma	—	46×36×20	P250619	2
12	MS 2023	—	—	22×34×15	P250795	2
13	MS 4715/19	—	—	32×50×15	P253743	2
14	MS 1942/12	Umma	—	24×25×13	P250623	2
15	MS 1943/7	—	—	28×34×12	P250630	2
16	MS 1943/1	—	—	24×30×10	P250624	2
17	MS 1943/9	—	—	26×32×11	P250632	2
18	MS 1943/2	—	—	27×41×10	P250625	2
19	MS 1943/3	—	—	23×34×10	P250626	2
20	MS 1943/8	—	—	26×32×10	P250631	2
21	MS 1943/10	—	—	27×32×10	P250633	2
22	MS 1943/4	—	—	25×32×10	P250627	2
23	MS 1943/6	—	—	25×38×10	P250629	2
24	MS 1943/5	Umma	—	25×30×11	P250628	2
168	MS 1942/5	Umma	—	50×38×25	P250616	10
169	MS 1942/9	Umma	ŠS 6	55×45×36	P250620	10

Accounts

No.	Collection ID	Provenience	Date	Measurement (in mm)	CDLI	Ch.
28	MS 2019/2	Umma	IS 4?	48×43×17	P250754	4
29	MS 2020/3	Umma	Š 44	43×35×16	P250764	4
30	MS 4310	Umma	ŠS 5	80×50×20	P253383	4
31	MS 2016	Umma	ŠS 3 to 4	110×75×24	P250742	4
34	MS 2019/1	Umma	Š 44	51×43×17	P250753	4
35	MS 4343	—	IS 2	79×47×25	P253496	4
36	MS 1983	Umma	Š 36–ix	208×212×45	P127665	4
37	MS 4675	Garšana	—	138×82×30	P253686	4
40	MS 4356	Umma	AS 7	49×48×23	P253509	6
41	MS 4679	Umma	AS 5–xii	137×146×32	P253689	6
42	MS 4744	Umma	ŠS 3	110×79×29	P253774	6
155	MS 4712	Umma	—	197×178×38	P253723	8
156	MS 4713	Umma	—	188×187×30	P253724	8
157	MS 4699	Umma	—	96×50×24	P253709	8
158	MS 4089	Garšana	ŠS 6	78×50×21	P253186	8
234	MS 4715/11	Umma	IS 1	68×50×25	P253735	12
235	MS 4518	Umma	—	70(h)×68(w)	P253618	12

Receipts

No.	Collection ID	Provenience	Date	Measurement (in mm)	CDLI	Ch.
27	MS 1947/1	Umma	IS 3 i to IS 3–xiii	58×60×14	P250639	3
32	MS 1947/5	Umma	IS 1	46×45×14	P250643	4
33	MS 2020/12	Umma	AS 7	36×33×16	P250773	4
39	MS 1947/16	Umma	X 2–x	19×18×12	P250654	5
43	MS 4715/9	Adab?	IS 1–vii	43×38×16	P253733	7
44	MS 4040	Drehem	ŠS 6–iv	35×32×16	P253137	7
45	MS 2020/16	Umma	AS 8	30×27×15	P250777	7
46	MS 2018/5	Umma	ŠS 7–xi	44×47×15	P250748	7
47	MS 4692	Umma	ŠS 8–x	61×51×20	P253702	7
48	MS 4688	Garšana	ŠS 8–iii	50×45×22	P253698	7
49	MS 4715/2	Adab?	AS 2	38×35×16	P253726	7
50	MS 4715/3	Adab?	ŠS 3–x	48×39×19	P253727	7
51	MS 4715/6	Adab?	ŠS 4–ix	45×43×16	P253730	7
52	MS 1712	Umma	Š 45	34×35×15	P250463	7
53	MS 4715/7	Adab?	IS 2	43×36×16	P253731	7
54	MS 4715/8	Adab?	IS 1?	49×42×22	P253732	7
55	MS 4715/12	Adab?	AS 3	43×44×18	P253736	7
56	MS 2018/9	Umma	AS 7–xii	49×41×16	P250752	7
57	MS 4338/27	Ur?	X–v	38×38×17	P253437	7

No.	Collection ID	Provenience	Date	Measurement (in mm)	CDLI	Ch.
58	MS 4715/10	Adab?	IS 10?	43×37×18	P253734	7
59	MS 1947/13	Umma	Š 34?–vi	32×33×12	P250651	7
60	MS 4715/15	Adab?	IS 2	55×46×20	P253739	7
61	MS 4715/18	Adab?	ŠS 2	47×40×19	P253742	7
62	MS 4715/16	Adab?	IS 2–iv	54×44×21	P253740	7
63	MS 1947/6	Umma	ŠS 9	49×46×15	P250644	7
64	MS 1947/12	Umma	AS 4–xi	29×28×14	P250650	7
65	MS 1789/1	Umma	AS 5	33×30	P250492	7
66	MS 2021/9	Umma	AS 7–vii	23×23×11	P250787	7
67	MS 4686	Umma	AS 8	41×38×16	P253696	7
68	MS 4715/17	Umma	AS 8	48×44×19	P253741	7
69	MS 2018/8	Umma	IS 2–xi to IS 2–xii	54×43×18	P250751	7
70	MS 1947/7	Umma	Š 44	47×41×13	P250645	7
71	MS 2018/4	Garšana	ŠS 2	44×38×14	P250747	7
72	MS 2018/3	Umma	IS 3	37×35×13	P250746	7
73	MS 2018/2	Umma	AS 1–x	37×40×13	P250745	7
74	MS 1723/1	Umma	IS 3–xi	39×37×13	P250472	7
75	MS 1723/2	Umma	IS 3	37×36×11	P250473	7
76	MS 1698/2	Umma	ŠS 1	56×45×11	P250459	7
77	MS 1724	Umma	Š 46	34×36×14	P250474	7
78	MS 1725	Umma	AS 7–viii	43×42×14	P250475	7
79	MS 2018/6	Umma	ŠS 6–x	47×46×15	P250749	7
80	MS 1726	Girsu	ŠS 8	41×38×18	P114422	7
81	MS 4971	Irisagrig?	ŠS 9–x	49×49×29	P254002	7
82	MS 1949/5	Umma	Š 33–vi	48×43×24	P250662	7
83	MS 1739/2	—	—	Tablet: 32×28×13 Envelope: 41×41×11	P250481	7
84	MS 4696	—	ŠS 9–iii	45×40×19	P253706	7
85	MS 2021/1	Umma	Š 37–xii	26×26×16	P250779	7
86	MS 2021/7	Umma	Š 47	25×23×12	P250785	7
87	MS 2019/8	Umma	IS 2–i	47×40×17	P250760	7
88	MS 2021/4	Umma	Š 44	27×26×12	P250782	7
89	MS 2021/10	Umma	X–vii	23×20×13	P250788	7
90	MS 1947/17	Umma	Š 44–ii	39×37×19	P250655	7
91	MS 3990	Umma	Š 48 to AS 1	40×37×17	P253087	7
92	MS 4700	Garšana	ŠS 7–ii	40×39	P253710	7
93	MS 4424	Garšana	ŠS 7–iii–10	39×35×16	P253577	7
94	MS 2020/9	Umma	ŠS 1–v	36×32×15	P250770	7
95	MS 1653/2	Drehem	IS 1–iv–22	36×32×15	P250455	7
96	MS 1947/9	Umma	AS 6–ii	36×34×15	P250647	7
97	MS 2020/6	Umma	AS 7–xii	35×33×13	P250767	7
98	MS 2020/8	Umma	ŠS 4	33×32×15	P250769	7
99	MS 2020/11	Umma	AS 8–i	35×30×13	P250772	7
100	MS 4709	Garšana	ŠS 8–vi	75×52×21	P253720	7

No.	Collection ID	Provenience	Date	Measurement (in mm)	CDLI	Ch.
101	MS 4454	Garšana	ŠS 7–iii	35×31×17	P253607	7
102	MS 4036	Garšana?	IS 1–xi	42×42×17	P253133	7
103	MS 1916	Umma	AS 1–v	41×35×??	P250593	7
104	MS 2021/6	Umma?	X–ii	26×23×13	P250784	7
105	MS 2020/4	Umma	ŠS 3–xiii	41×36×17	P250765	7
106	MS 2021/3	Umma	AS 7–iv	26×25×14	P250781	7
107	MS 1947/10	Umma	AS 7–vi	32×31×14	P250648	7
108	MS 4706	Drehem	ŠS 8–ix		P253717	7
109	MS 4715/4	Adab?	X–x	50×38×18	P253728	7
110	MS 4702	Garšana	ŠS 9–iii	50×47×20	P253712	7
111	MS 4970	Drehem	ŠS 7–ii	44×41×25	P254001	7
112	MS 1740	Nippur	X–vii	80×50×17	P250482	7
113	MS 4711	Garšana	ŠS 7–vi	68×51×20	P253722	7
114	MS 4698	Garšana	ŠS 7–xii	42×39×17	P253708	7
115	MS 4689	Garšana	ŠS 8–iv	50×45×22	P253699	7
116	MS 4690	Garšana	ŠS 8–iv	50×46×19	P253700	7
117	MS 4650	Garšana	ŠS 6–v	46×38×18	P253661	7
118	MS 2021/8	Umma	Š–xi	24×23×12	P250786	7
119	MS 4708	—	ŠS 2–?–6	86×51×23	P253719	7
120	MS 4695	—	ŠS 2 ?–12	92×58×24	P253705	7
121	MS 4693	—	ŠS 2–?–24	98×51×24	P253703	7
122	MS 4385	Garšana	ŠS 8–i	38×38×18	P253538	7
123	MS 1947/2	Umma	ŠS 7–viii	79×51×16	P250640	7
124	MS 1722	Umma	AS 4–vi	47×43×15	P114248	7
148	MS 2018/7	Umma	ŠS 3–iv–5	49×44×15	P250750	8
149	MS 4707	Umma	ŠS 9?	69×50×22	P253718	8
150	MS 1653/1	Umma	ŠS 3	49×44×15	P114293	8
151	MS 2021/5	Umma	AS 1–vii	29×26×12	P250783	8
152	MS 1879	Umma	ŠS 4–i	42×42×14	P112174	8
153	MS 1741	Umma	Š 48–xi	40×36×15	P250483	8
154	MS 1942/11	Umma	Š 36–vi	36×34×14	P250622	8

Lists and Inventories

No.	Collection ID	Provenience	Date	Measurement (in mm)	CDLI	Ch.
125	MS 4324	Umma	ŠS 7 v	113×65×25	P253397	8
126	MS 1884	Umma	X–v to xii	187×190×35	P250546	8 & Appx
127	MS 4705	Umma	AS 5 vii 15	134×99×29	P253716	8 & Appx
128	MS 2369	Umma	AS 3	176×123×25	P251598	8 & Appx
129	MS 1883	Umma	AS 5	211×222×46	P250545	8 & Appx
130	MS 4739	Drehem?	AS 6–xi	118×86×30	P253769	8 & Appx
131	MS 4764	Umma	AS 3–v	87×61×25	P253794	8 & Appx

No.	Collection ID	Provenience	Date	Measurement (in mm)	CDLI	Ch.
132	MS 2015	—	—	128×71×24	P250741	8
133	MS 1975	Umma	AS 5–vii–15	192×163×??	P250730	8 & Appx
134	MS 1846/2	Umma	AS 3–v	118×74×20	P250520	8
135	MS 1908	Umma	AS 6	223×227×37	P250589	8 & Appx
136	MS 1846/1	Umma	AS 4–vii–15	107×50×23	P250519	8
137	MS 4691	Umma	—	83×45×21	P253701	8
138	MS 2012	Umma	—	180×300×50	P250739	8 & Appx
139	MS 4357	Umma	—	66×64×15	P253510	8
140	MS 4332	Umma	AS 5–vii	157×97×35	P253405	8 & Appx
141	MS 2017	Umma	—	114×55×22	P250743	8
142	MS 4756	—	—	57×41×20	P253786	8
143	MS 1947/15	—	—	24×22×12	P250653	8
144	MS 2020/14	Umma	AS 6–iv	31×31×12	P250775	8
145	MS 2028	Umma	X–xii–24	39×33×17	P250799	8
146	MS 2020/15	Umma	—	34×31×14	P250776	8
147	MS 4340	—	Š 38	58×45×22	P253493	8
209	MS 4694	Umma?	AS 7	79×46×21	P253704	12
210	MS 1845	Umma	AS 6–xii	117×76×30	P250518	12
211	MS 2011	Umma	AS 7	152×135×25	P250738	12

Letters

No.	Collection ID	Provenience	Date	Measurement (in mm) h = height, w = width	CDLI	Ch.
159	MS 4738	Garšana	—	47×43×17	P253768	9
160	MS 4715/14	Adab	—	39×37×14	P253738	9
161	MS 2020/5	Girsu	—	38×36×14	P250766	9
162	MS 4715/21	Adab	—	47×38×17	P253745	9
163	MS 4715/13	Adab	—	43×40×19	P253737	9
164	MS 2019/3	Umma	—	52×39×20	P250755	9
165	MS 2020/2	—	—	47×39×20	P250763	9
166	MS 4730	Adab	—	42×46×21	P253760	9
167	MS 4760	—	—	49×37×19	P253790	9

Messenger Texts

For the two archival documents discussed in Ch. 10, see the catalog of archival documents above.

No.	Collection ID	Provenience	Date	Measurement (in mm) h = height, w = width	CDLI	Ch.
170	MS 1871/2	Umma	ŠS 2–iv–5	33×26×12	P250530	10
171	MS 1871/5	Umma	ŠS 2–ii–25	27×22×11	P250533	10

No.	Collection ID	Provenience	Date	Measurement (in mm) h = height, w = width	CDLI	Ch.
172	MS 1871/1	Umma	ŠS 2–vi–20	32×25×12	P250529	10
173	MS 1871/6	Umma	ŠS 2–ix–8	30×26×11	P250534	10
174	MS 1871/4	Umma	ŠS 3–x–12	27×25×10	P250532	10
175	MS 2022/2	Umma	ŠS 4–iii–18	21×19×09	P250790	10
176	MS 2022/3	Umma	ŠS 6–ii–8	26×24×13	P250791	10
177	MS 1871/3	Umma	AS 7–i–10	26×23×10	P250531	10
178	MS 1746	Umma	X–iv–1	26×21×11	P250489	10
179	MS 1871/7	Umma	X–o–20?	34×27×13	P250535	10
180	MS 1871/8	Umma	X–ix–23	36×31×13	P250536	10
181	MS 1944/1	Umma	X–iii–14	24×19×10	P250634	10
182	MS 1944/2	Umma	X–o–17	19×18×08	P250635	10
183	MS 1944/3	Umma	X–o–18	22×19×10	P250636	10
184	MS 4987	Umma	—	26×24×09	P254018	10
185	MS 4988	Umma	—	23×26×14	P254019	10
186	MS 4989	Umma	—	33×22×13	P254020	10
187	MS 4990	Umma	X–xi–11	30×25×13	P254021	10
188	MS 4992	Umma	—	28×24×08	P254023	10
189	MS 4993	Umma	—	31×27×08	P254024	10
190	MS 2022/1	Umma	ŠS 6–xi–21	28×26×13	P250789	10
191	MS 2022/5	Umma	ŠS 6–xii–13	23×21×09	P250793	10
192	MS 1709/1	Umma	X–vii–23	28×26×15	P250461	10
193	MS 1709/2	Umma	X–vi–1	30×26×15	P250462	10
194	MS 2022/6	Umma		33×25×14	P250794	10
195	MS 4734	Umma	—	29×26×08	P253764	10

Legal Texts

No.	Collection ID	Provenience	Date	Measurement (in mm) h = height, w = width	CDLI	Ch.
196	MS 1716/2	Umma	Š 40	58×42×20	P250468	11
197	MS 5010	Adab	—	110×55×28	P254041	11
198	MS 4096	Umma	ŠS 4–vi	82×47×23	P253193	11
199	MS 1743	Nippur	ŠS 7–viii	40×33×15	P250486	11
200	MS 1745	Nippur	X–xii	38×40×15	P250488	11
201	MS 4687	Nippur	Š 43–10	50×41×20	P253697	11
202	MS 1744	Nippur	X–iii	45×38×17	P250487	11
203	MS 1946	Umma?	—	95×62×25	P250638	11
204	MS 2018/1	Umma	Š 44–i	49×45×15	P250744	11
205	MS 2020/7	Umma	ŠS 4	34×32×15	P250768	11
206	MS 4997	Adab	—	57×50×27	P254028	11
207	MS 4422	Umma	Š 44	76×46×21	P253575	11
208	MS 4685	Umma	ŠS 4	51×46×19	P253695	11

Miscellaneous Texts

No.	Collection ID	Provenience	Date	Measurement (in mm) h = height, w = width	CDLI	Ch.
25	MS 1915	Umma	AS 1 to IS 4	90×49×19	P250592	3
26	MS 1939	Umma?	Š 33–Š 34	diam. 105; thickness 25		3
38	MS 1947/4	Umma	AS 6	54×45×16	P250642	5
212	MS 4898	—	IS 2	54×41×17	P253928	12
213	MS 4715/5	—	ŠS 3	62×48×24	P253729	12
214	MS 1938/1	Umma	Š 33	96×66×27	P250599	12
215	MS 2019/9	Umma	ŠS 9–v	47×40×15	P250761	12
216	MS 2019/6	—	—	59×37×19	P250758	12
217	MS 1947/3	Umma?	IS 3	58×46×20	P250641	12
218	MS 1942/10	—	—	82×35×32	P250621	12
219	MS 1747	Umma	AS 5–vii	30×25×14	P250490	12
220	MS 4451	—	—	41×38×18	P253604	12
221	MS 1947/11	—	ŠS 2–vi	35×32×13	P250649	12
222	MS 2019/4	—	—	37×44×18	P250756	12
223	MS 1742/1	Nippur	IS 3	42×35×15	P250484	12
224a	MS 4704/1	Umma	IS 1–ii	48×45×20	P253714	12
224b	MS 4704/2	Umma	IS 1	27×45×20	P253715	12
225	MS 1945	—	—	112×58×20	P250637	12
226	MS 1947/14	—	—	29×26×15	P250652	12
227	MS 2019/7	—	—	45×38×16	P250759	12
228	MS 2021/2	—	ŠS 3–iii	27×26×15	P250780	12
229	MS 2020/13	—	—	35×33×14	P250774	12
230	MS 2364	Umma	X–viii	19×17×11	P251577	12
231	MS 1947/8	Umma	ŠS–vii	35×36×15	P250646	12
232	MS 2020/17	—	—	31×28×18	P250778	12
233	MS 4294	Umma	—	100×85×32	P253367	12
236	MS 1792/2	—	X–iv or vi–20	c. 30×20×10	P250498	12
237	MS 2022/4	—	X–?–20	25×22×12	P250792	12
238	MS 2019/5	Umma	—	48×38×16	P250757	12
239	MS 4697	—	AS 5–X–11	60×46×18	P253707	12
240	MS 4667	Umma	Š 25 or 32 or 44–vi	80×48×22	P253678	12
241	MS 4701	Umma	IS 1–i	50×40×19	P253711	12
242	MS 2772	—	—	45×43×15	P251795	12
243	MS 1742/2	—	—	36×36×13	P250485	11
244	MS 2893	Garšana	—	85×53×22	P252000	12

Concordances

1. Index of Previously Published Ur III Tablets in the Schøyen Collection

Publication ID	No.	Collection ID	CDLI	Ch.
CUSAS 3, 494	100	MS 4709	P253720	7
CUSAS 3, 550	244	MS 2893	P252000	12
CUSAS 3, 1514	71	MS 2018/4	P250747	7
CUSAS 3, 1515	93	MS 4424	P253577	7
CUSAS 3, 1516	92	MS 4700	P253710	7
CUSAS 3, 1517	113	MS 4711	P253722	7
CUSAS 3, 1518	114	MS 4698	P253708	7
CUSAS 3, 1519	122	MS 4385	P253538	7
CUSAS 3, 1520	48	MS 4688	P253698	7
CUSAS 3, 1521	115	MS 4689	P253699	7
CUSAS 3, 1522	116	MS 4690	P253700	7
CUSAS 3, 1523	117	MS 4650	P253661	7
CUSAS 3, 1524	84	MS 4696	P253706	7
CUSAS 3, 1525	110	MS 4702	P253712	7
CUSAS 3, 1526	159	MS 4738	P253768	9
CUSAS 3, 1527	37	MS 4675	P253686	4
CUSAS 17, 101	25	MS 1915	P250592	3
Friberg, MSCT 1, 137	—	MS 1984	P115981	not published here
Friberg, MSCT 1, 140	—	MS 1850	P250525	not published here
JCS 37, 108	152	MS 1879	P112174	8
MVN 5, 28	124	MS 1722	P114248	8
MVN 5, 73	150	MS 1653/1	P114293	8
MVN 5, 131	95	MS 1653/2	P114351	7
MVN 5, 202	80	MS 1726	P114422	7
MVN 10, 214	—	MS 1984	P115981	not published here
RA 16, 19	36	MS 1983	P127665	4
SET 66	—	MS 1714	P129476	not published here*

2. Index of Tablets from Other Collections Edited Here in Full

Publication ID	Museum number	Provenience	Date	CDLI	Ch.
Aleppo 119	NMSA 3727	Umma	Š 35–vii	P100451	7

* See Jones and Snyder 1961, Owen 1997: 391; also Liu Changyu 2015, Yoshikawa 1992: 428. A collated transliteration is available on CDLI.

Publication ID	Museum number	Provenience	Date	CDLI	Ch.
Aleppo 122	NMSA 4156	Umma	Š 37–vi	P100454	7
Aleppo 482	NMSA 3789	Umma	Š 46	P100814	5
Aleppo 495	NMSA 4064	Umma	Š 44	P100827	7
Amherst 119	(dispersed)	Girsu	AS 9	P100958	7
AnOR 1, 28	BNUS 159	Drehem	IS 1–v	P101019	7
ASJ 19, 215 43	UMNH 1812	Umma	AS 3	P102734	7
AUCT 1, 750	AUAM 73.1680	Drehem	IS 1–v–27	P103595	7
AUCT 2, 392	AUAM 73.0566	Umma	ŠS 3–iii	P104210	5
AUCT 3, 279	AUAM 73.0868	Umma	AS 7 i	P104493	7
BCT 1, 120	A.1251_1982	Drehem	AS 6–v to AS 6–xii	P105222	2
BIN 3, 354	NBC 592	Drehem	ŠS 3–i to ŠS 3–xi (diri)	P106160	2
BIN 3, 356	NBC 359	Drehem	ŠS 5–vii–28	P106162	7
BIN 5, 114	NBC 1919	Umma	Š 34 to Š 47	P106548	4
BPOA 1, 1234	BM 107574	Umma	—	P339889	9
BPOA 1, 309	BM 102168	Girsu	AS 1–vi	P206646	10
BRM 3, 31	MLC 2338	Drehem	AS 5–xi	P107253	2
BRM 3, 44	MLC 2310	Umma	AS 8–iv	P107261	2
CHEU 14	HE 14	Umma	Š 35–iii	P107447	7
Georgica 1.1.3	OIM A 5923	Umma	AS 7	P109386	7
JCS 2, 187 NBC 3500	NBC 3500	Umma	AS 4	P111827	8
MCS 1, 54, BM 113107	BM 113107	Umma	AS 1–vii	P112584	7
MVN 14, 2	Ist Um 2	Umma	AS 1–i to AS 1–viii	P117683	8
MVN 14, 87	Ist Um 87	Umma	AS 4–xii	P117768	8
MVN 2, 11	MAH 15870	Girsu	Š 40	P113310	7
MVN 2, 273	MAH 16553	Umma	Š 45	P113572	2
MVN 21, 212	Erm 14497	Umma	AS 6–i to AS 6–xiii	P120449	3
MVN 4, 173	IB 165	Umma	ŠS 2–iv–30	P114125	10
MVN 4, 257	CPO 6	Umma	ŠS 1–viii–4	P114209	7
MVN 5, 98	Pinches 54 (dispersed)	Drehem	Š 44–iii–2	P114318	7
Nisaba 15, 127	—	Irisagrig	AS 8–?–1	P453652	10
Nisaba 15, 96	—	Irisagrig	AS 8–?–8	P453636	10
Nisaba 22, 59	BM 22920	Girsu	ŠS 1–vii–14	P320142	10
Nisaba 8, 314	BM 117383	Drehem	AS 7–ix–20	P320908	7
OIP 115, 189	A 3124	Drehem	Š 46–viii–15	P123337	7
Ontario 2, 219	ROM 925.062.306	Umma	Š 45	P209590	2
Ontario 2, 297	ROM 925.062.445	Umma	ŠS 1–vi	P209680	7
Princeton 1, 277	PTS 1299	Umma	ŠS 5	P126966	7
Princeton 1, 301	PTS 358	Umma	AS 7–viii	P126990	7
Princeton 1, 308	PTS 547	Umma	ŠS 2–iv	P126997	7
SANTAG 6, 20	Erm 7694	Umma	Š 33 to Š 45	P211552	4

Publication ID	Museum number	Provenience	Date	CDLI	Ch.
TCNU 646	MAT 646	Umma	ŠS 3	P135492	7
TLB 3, 157–58	LB 270 & 414	Girsu	AS 7–vi	P134298	7
unpublished	ICP 1295	Umma	X–x	P275245	10
unpublished	ICP 1227	Girsu	X–v	P275204	10
unpublished	DIA 19.024.13	Drehem	Š 47–viii–3	P461506	7
unpublished	KM 89206	Drehem	Š 46–vii–1	P234973	7
UTI 3, 1916	Ist Um 1916	Umma	AS 7–i to AS 7–viii	P139935	8
UTI 4, 2660	Ist Um 2660	Umma	ŠS 3	P140679	8

3. Concordances of Text Numbers and Collection Numbers

A. Sorted by Text Numbers

Text No.	Collection No.	CDLI No.	Text No.	Collection No.	CDLI No.
1	MS 1719	P250470	30	MS 4310	P253383
2	MS 2020/10	P250771	31	MS 2016	P250742
3	MS 5047/1	P254136	32	MS 1947/5	P250643
4	MS 1942/3	P250614	33	MS 2020/12	P250773
5	MS 1942/4	P250615	34	MS 2019/1	P250753
6	MS 2077	P250827	35	MS 4343	P253496
7	MS 1942/1	P250612	36	MS 1983	P127665
8	MS 1942/2	P250613	37	MS 4675	P253686
9	MS 1942/6	P250617	38	MS 1947/4	P250642
10	MS 1942/7	P250618	39	MS 1947/16	P250654
11	MS 1942/8	P250619	40	MS 4356	P253509
12	MS 2023	P250795	41	MS 4679	P253689
13	MS 4715/19	P253743	42	MS 4744	P253774
14	MS 1942/12	P250623	43	MS 4715/9	P253733
15	MS 1943/7	P250630	44	MS 4040	P253137
16	MS 1943/1	P250624	45	MS 2020/16	P250777
17	MS 1943/9	P250632	46	MS 2018/5	P250748
18	MS 1943/2	P250625	47	MS 4692	P253702
19	MS 1943/3	P250626	48	MS 4688	P253698
20	MS 1943/8	P250631	49	MS 4715/2	P253726
21	MS 1943/10	P250633	50	MS 4715/3	P253727
22	MS 1943/4	P250627	51	MS 4715/6	P253730
23	MS 1943/6	P250629	52	MS 1712	P250463
24	MS 1943/5	P250628	53	MS 4715/7	P253731
25	MS 1915	P250592	54	MS 4715/8	P253732
26	MS 1939	P250601	55	MS 4715/12	P253736
27	MS 1947/1	P250639	56	MS 2018/9	P250752
28	MS 2019/2	P250754	57	MS 4338/27	P253437
29	MS 2020/3	P250764	58	MS 4715/10	P253734

Text No.	Collection No.	CDLI No.
59	MS 1947/13	P250651
60	MS 4715/15	P253739
61	MS 4715/18	P253742
62	MS 4715/16	P253740
63	MS 1947/6	P250644
64	MS 1947/12	P250650
65	MS 1789/1	P250492
66	MS 2021/9	P250787
67	MS 4686	P253696
68	MS 4715/17	P253741
69	MS 2018/8	P250751
70	MS 1947/7	P250645
71	MS 2018/4	P250747
72	MS 2018/3	P250746
73	MS 2018/2	P250745
74	MS 1723/1	P250472
75	MS 1723/2	P250473
76	MS 1698/2	P250459
77	MS 1724	P250474
78	MS 1725	P250475
79	MS 2018/6	P250749
80	MS 1726	P114422
81	MS 4971	P254002
82	MS 1949/5	P250662
83	MS 1739/2	P250481
84	MS 4696	P253706
85	MS 2021/1	P250779
86	MS 2021/7	P250785
87	MS 2019/8	P250760
88	MS 2021/4	P250782
89	MS 2021/10	P250788
90	MS 1947/17	P250655
91	MS 3990	P253087
92	MS 4700	P253710
93	MS 4424	P253577
94	MS 2020/9	P250770
95	MS 1653/2	P250455
96	MS 1947/9	P250647
97	MS 2020/6	P250767
98	MS 2020/8	P250769
99	MS 2020/11	P250772
100	MS 4709	P253720
101	MS 4454	P253607
102	MS 4036	P253133

Text No.	Collection No.	CDLI No.
103	MS 1916	P250593
104	MS 2021/6	P250784
105	MS 2020/4	P250765
106	MS 2021/3	P250781
107	MS 1947/10	P250648
108	MS 4706	P253717
109	MS 4715/4	P253728
110	MS 4702	P253712
111	MS 4970	P254001
112	MS 1740	P250482
113	MS 4711	P253722
114	MS 4698	P253708
115	MS 4689	P253699
116	MS 4690	P253700
117	MS 4650	P253661
118	MS 2021/8	P250786
119	MS 4708	P253719
120	MS 4695	P253705
121	MS 4693	P253703
122	MS 4385	P253538
123	MS 1947/2	P250640
124	MS 1722	P114248
125	MS 4324	P253397
126	MS 1884	P250546
127	MS 4705	P253716
128	MS 2369	P251598
129	MS 1883	P250545
130	MS 4739	P253769
131	MS 4764	P253794
132	MS 2015	P250741
133	MS 1975	P250730
134	MS 1846/2	P250520
135	MS 1908	P250589
136	MS 1846/1	P250519
137	MS 4691	P253701
138	MS 2012	P250739
139	MS 4357	P253510
140	MS 4332	P253405
141	MS 2017	P250743
142	MS 4756	P253786
143	MS 1947/15	P250653
144	MS 2020/14	P250775
145	MS 2028	P250799
146	MS 2020/15	P250776

Text No.	Collection No.	CDLI No.
147	MS 4340	P253493
148	MS 2018/7	P250750
149	MS 4707	P253718
150	MS 1653/1	P114293
151	MS 2021/5	P250783
152	MS 1879	P112174
153	MS 1741	P250483
154	MS 1942/11	P250622
155	MS 4712	P253723
156	MS 4713	P253724
157	MS 4699	P253709
158	MS 4089	P253186
159	MS 4738	P253768
160	MS 4715/14	P253738
161	MS 2020/5	P250766
162	MS 4715/21	P253745
163	MS 4715/13	P253737
164	MS 2019/3	P250755
165	MS 2020/2	P250763
166	MS 4730	P253760
167	MS 4760	P253790
168	MS 1942/5	P250616
169	MS 1942/9	P250620
170	MS 1871/2	P250530
171	MS 1871/5	P250533
172	MS 1871/1	P250529
173	MS 1871/6	P250534
174	MS 1871/4	P250532
175	MS 2022/2	P250790
176	MS 2022/3	P250791
177	MS 1871/3	P250531
178	MS 1746	P250489
179	MS 1871/7	P250535
180	MS 1871/8	P250536
181	MS 1944/1	P250634
182	MS 1944/2	P250635
183	MS 1944/3	P250636
184	MS 4987	P254018
185	MS 4988	P254019
186	MS 4989	P254020
187	MS 4990	P254021
188	MS 4992	P254023
189	MS 4993	P254024
190	MS 2022/1	P250789
191	MS 2022/5	P250793
192	MS 1709/1	P250461
193	MS 1709/2	P250462
194	MS 2022/6	P250794
195	MS 4734	P253764
196	MS 1716/2	P250468
197	MS 5010	P254041
198	MS 4096	P253193
199	MS 1743	P250486
200	MS 1745	P250488
201	MS 4687	P253697
202	MS 1744	P250487
203	MS 1946	P250638
204	MS 2018/1	P250744
205	MS 2020/7	P250768
206	MS 4997	P254028
207	MS 4422	P253575
208	MS 4685	P253695
209	MS 4694	P253704
210	MS 1845	P250518
211	MS 2011	P250738
212	MS 4898	P253928
213	MS 4715/5	P253729
214	MS 1938/1	P250599
215	MS 2019/9	P250761
216	MS 2019/6	P250758
217	MS 1947/3	P250641
218	MS 1942/10	P250621
219	MS 1747	P250490
220	MS 4451	P253604
221	MS 1947/11	P250649
222	MS 2019/4	P250756
223	MS 1742/1	P250484
224a	MS 4704/1	P253714
224b	MS 4704/2	P253715
225	MS 1945	P250637
226	MS 1947/14	P250652
227	MS 2019/7	P250759
228	MS 2021/2	P250780
229	MS 2020/13	P250774
230	MS 2364	P251577
231	MS 1947/8	P250646
232	MS 2020/17	P250778
233	MS 4294	P253367

Text No.	Collection No.	CDLI No.
234	MS 4715/11	P253735
235	MS 4518	P253618
236	MS 1792/2	P250498
237	MS 2022/4	P250792
238	MS 2019/5	P250757
239	MS 4697	P253707
240	MS 4667	P253678
241	MS 4701	P253711
242	MS 2772	P251795
243	MS 1742/2	P250485
244	MS 2893	P252000

B. Sorted by Collection Numbers

Collection No.	Text No.	CDLI No.
MS 1653/1	150	P114293
MS 1653/2	95	P250455
MS 1698/2	76	P250459
MS 1709/1	192	P250461
MS 1709/2	193	P250462
MS 1712	52	P250463
MS 1716/2	196	P250468
MS 1719	1	P250470
MS 1722	124	P114248
MS 1723/1	74	P250472
MS 1723/2	75	P250473
MS 1724	77	P250474
MS 1725	78	P250475
MS 1726	80	P114422
MS 1739/2	83	P250481
MS 1740	112	P250482
MS 1741	153	P250483
MS 1742/1	223	P250484
MS 1742/2	243	P250485
MS 1743	199	P250486
MS 1744	202	P250487
MS 1745	200	P250488
MS 1746	178	P250489
MS 1747	219	P250490
MS 1789/1	65	P250492
MS 1792/2	236	P250498
MS 1845	210	P250518
MS 1846/1	136	P250519
MS 1846/2	134	P250520
MS 1871/1	172	P250529
MS 1871/2	170	P250530
MS 1871/3	177	P250531
MS 1871/4	174	P250532
MS 1871/5	171	P250533
MS 1871/6	173	P250534
MS 1871/7	179	P250535
MS 1871/8	180	P250536
MS 1879	152	P112174
MS 1883	129	P250545
MS 1884	126	P250546
MS 1908	135	P250589
MS 1915	25	P250592
MS 1916	103	P250593
MS 1938/1	214	P250599
MS 1939	26	P250601
MS 1942/1	7	P250612
MS 1942/2	8	P250613
MS 1942/3	4	P250614
MS 1942/4	5	P250615
MS 1942/5	168	P250616
MS 1942/6	9	P250617
MS 1942/7	10	P250618
MS 1942/8	11	P250619
MS 1942/9	169	P250620
MS 1942/10	218	P250621
MS 1942/11	154	P250622
MS 1942/12	14	P250623
MS 1943/1	16	P250624
MS 1943/2	18	P250625
MS 1943/3	19	P250626
MS 1943/4	22	P250627
MS 1943/5	24	P250628
MS 1943/6	23	P250629
MS 1943/7	15	P250630
MS 1943/8	20	P250631
MS 1943/9	17	P250632

Collection No.	Text No.	CDLI No.
MS 1943/10	21	P250633
MS 1944/1	181	P250634
MS 1944/3	183	P250636
MS 1944/2	182	P250635
MS 1945	225	P250637
MS 1946	203	P250638
MS 1947/1	27	P250639
MS 1947/2	123	P250640
MS 1947/3	217	P250641
MS 1947/4	38	P250642
MS 1947/5	32	P250643
MS 1947/6	63	P250644
MS 1947/7	70	P250645
MS 1947/8	231	P250646
MS 1947/9	96	P250647
MS 1947/10	107	P250648
MS 1947/11	221	P250649
MS 1947/12	64	P250650
MS 1947/13	59	P250651
MS 1947/14	226	P250652
MS 1947/15	143	P250653
MS 1947/16	39	P250654
MS 1947/17	90	P250655
MS 1949/5	82	P250662
MS 1975	133	P250730
MS 1983	36	P127665
MS 2011	211	P250738
MS 2012	138	P250739
MS 2015	132	P250741
MS 2016	31	P250742
MS 2017	141	P250743
MS 2018/1	204	P250744
MS 2018/2	73	P250745
MS 2018/3	72	P250746
MS 2018/4	71	P250747
MS 2018/5	46	P250748
MS 2018/6	79	P250749
MS 2018/7	148	P250750
MS 2018/8	69	P250751
MS 2018/9	56	P250752
MS 2019/3	164	P250755
MS 2019/5	238	P250757
MS 2019/6	216	P250758
MS 2019/9	215	P250761

Collection No.	Text No.	CDLI No.
MS 2019/1	34	P250753
MS 2019/2	28	P250754
MS 2019/4	222	P250756
MS 2019/7	227	P250759
MS 2019/8	87	P250760
MS 2020/2	165	P250763
MS 2020/3	29	P250764
MS 2020/4	105	P250765
MS 2020/5	161	P250766
MS 2020/6	97	P250767
MS 2020/7	205	P250768
MS 2020/8	98	P250769
MS 2020/9	94	P250770
MS 2020/10	2	P250771
MS 2020/11	99	P250772
MS 2020/12	33	P250773
MS 2020/13	229	P250774
MS 2020/14	144	P250775
MS 2020/15	146	P250776
MS 2020/16	45	P250777
MS 2020/17	232	P250778
MS 2021/1	85	P250779
MS 2021/2	228	P250780
MS 2021/3	106	P250781
MS 2021/4	88	P250782
MS 2021/5	151	P250783
MS 2021/6	104	P250784
MS 2021/7	86	P250785
MS 2021/8	118	P250786
MS 2021/9	66	P250787
MS 2021/10	89	P250788
MS 2022/1	190	P250789
MS 2022/2	175	P250790
MS 2022/3	176	P250791
MS 2022/4	237	P250792
MS 2022/5	191	P250793
MS 2022/6	194	P250794
MS 2023	12	P250795
MS 2028	145	P250799
MS 2077	6	P250827
MS 2364	230	P251577
MS 2369	128	P251598
MS 2772	242	P251795
MS 2893	244	P252000

Collection No.	Text No.	CDLI No.
MS 3990	91	P253087
MS 4036	102	P253133
MS 4040	44	P253137
MS 4089	158	P253186
MS 4096	198	P253193
MS 4294	233	P253367
MS 4310	30	P253383
MS 4324	125	P253397
MS 4332	140	P253405
MS 4338/27	57	P253437
MS 4340	147	P253493
MS 4343	35	P253496
MS 4356	40	P253509
MS 4357	139	P253510
MS 4385	122	P253538
MS 4422	207	P253575
MS 4424	93	P253577
MS 4451	220	P253604
MS 4454	101	P253607
MS 4518	235	P253618
MS 4650	117	P253661
MS 4667	240	P253678
MS 4675	37	P253686
MS 4679	41	P253689
MS 4685	208	P253695
MS 4686	67	P253696
MS 4687	201	P253697
MS 4688	48	P253698
MS 4689	115	P253699
MS 4690	116	P253700
MS 4691	137	P253701
MS 4692	47	P253702
MS 4693	121	P253703
MS 4694	209	P253704
MS 4695	120	P253705
MS 4696	84	P253706
MS 4697	239	P253707
MS 4698	114	P253708
MS 4699	157	P253709
MS 4700	92	P253710
MS 4701	241	P253711
MS 4702	110	P253712
MS 4704/1	224a	P253714
MS 4704/2	224b	P253715
MS 4705	127	P253716
MS 4706	108	P253717

Collection No.	Text No.	CDLI No.
MS 4707	149	P253718
MS 4708	119	P253719
MS 4709	100	P253720
MS 4711	113	P253722
MS 4712	155	P253723
MS 4713	156	P253724
MS 4715/2	49	P253726
MS 4715/3	50	P253727
MS 4715/4	109	P253728
MS 4715/5	213	P253729
MS 4715/6	51	P253730
MS 4715/7	53	P253731
MS 4715/8	54	P253732
MS 4715/9	43	P253733
MS 4715/10	58	P253734
MS 4715/11	234	P253735
MS 4715/12	55	P253736
MS 4715/13	163	P253737
MS 4715/14	160	P253738
MS 4715/15	60	P253739
MS 4715/16	62	P253740
MS 4715/17	68	P253741
MS 4715/18	61	P253742
MS 4715/19	13	P253743
MS 4715/21	162	P253745
MS 4730	166	P253760
MS 4734	195	P253764
MS 4738	159	P253768
MS 4739	130	P253769
MS 4744	42	P253774
MS 4756	142	P253786
MS 4760	167	P253790
MS 4764	131	P253794
MS 4898	212	P253928
MS 4970	111	P254001
MS 4971	81	P254002
MS 4987	184	P254018
MS 4988	185	P254019
MS 4989	186	P254020
MS 4990	187	P254021
MS 4992	188	P254023
MS 4993	189	P254024
MS 4997	206	P254028
MS 5010	197	P254041
MS 5047/1	3	P254136

4. *Concordances of Text Numbers and Seal Numbers*

There are seventy-five sealed tablets in the collection published here. Ten of these are entirely illegible, and six are poorly preserved and do not allow for a reconstruction. Twenty-three of the tablets from other collections edited here are sealed. S-numbers are CDLI seal numbers.

A. Seal Impressions on Ur III Tablets in the Schøyen Collection, Sorted by Text Number

Text No.	Collection No.	CDLI No.	Text No.	Collection No.	CDLI No.
4	MS 1942/03	S002825	77	MS 1724	—
5	MS 1942/04	illegible	78	MS 1725	S003732
6	MS 2077	S005940	79	MS 2018/6	S005506
7	MS 1942/01	1: S002014	80	MS 1726	S003076a
		2: S005354	81	MS 4971	illegible
8	MS 1942/02	S000223	82	MS 1949/5	S005821
9	MS 1942/06	S000493.2	83	MS 1739/2	S005990
10	MS 1942/07	S004448	84	MS 4696	illegible
11	MS 1942/08	S004065	103	MS 1916	S004972
32	MS 1947/05	S005940	108	MS 4706	S004199
43	MS 4715/09	S002127	110	MS 4702	S006035
46	MS 2018/5	S004361	111	MS 4970	illegible
47	MS 4692	S004361	113	MS 4711	illegible
48	MS 4688	illegible	114	MS 4698	S004199
49	MS 4715/02	S001800	115	MS 4689	S004199
50	MS 4715/03	S004274	116	MS 4690	S004199
51	MS 4715/06	S005378	117	MS 4650	illegible
52	MS 1712	illegible	124	MS 1722	S005354
53	MS 4715/07	S002469	128	MS 2369	S001829
54	MS 4715/08	S002469	131	MS 4764	S003612
55	MS 4715/12	—	132	MS 2015	S000306
56	MS 2018/9	illegible	134	MS 1846/2	—
57	MS 4338/27	illegible	148	MS 2018/7	S002175
58	MS 4715/10	illegible	149	MS 4707	S003102
59	MS 1947/13	—	150	MS 1653/1	S002124
60	MS 4715/15	S004738	152	MS 1879	S002124
61	MS 4715/18	—	154	MS 1942/11	S002175
62	MS 4715/16	S005960	162	MS 4715/2	S003322
63	MS 1947/06	S004986	168	MS 1942/05	S005881
67	MS 4686	S002054	169	MS 1942/09	S000493.2
68	MS 4715/17	S004250	197	MS 5010	illegible
69	MS 2018/8	—	198	MS 4096	S004311
71	MS 2018/4	S000033	200	MS 1745	S002889
72	MS 2018/3	S003812	201	MS 4687	S003057
73	MS 2018/2	S006150	204	MS 2018/1	S005278
74	MS 1723/1	S003341	207	MS 4422	illegible
75	MS 1723/2	S003813	217	MS 4451	illegible
76	MS 1698/2	S000493.1	242	MS 2772	S006049

B. Seal Impressions on Ur III Tablets from Other Collections Edited Here in Full

Publication ID	CDLI No.
Aleppo 119	S005355
Aleppo 122	S003230
Aleppo 495 (NMSA 4064)	S005354
Amherst 119	S005168
ASJ 19, 215 43	S001779
AUCT 3, 279	S004974
BIN 3, 356	S000563
BRM 3, 31	S000302
BRM 3, 44	S005907
CHEU 14	S002893
Georgica 1.1.3	S002533
JCS 2, 187 NBC 3500	S002932
MCS 1, 54, BM 113107	S002533
MVN 14, 2	S003565

Publication ID	CDLI No.
MVN 14, 87	S003673
MVN 2, 11	S005787
MVN 2, 273	S002825?
MVN 4, 173	1: S000493.2
	2: S002932
MVN 4, 257	S000033
Ontario 2, 219	S002825
Princeton 1, 277	S004065.2
TCNU 646	S004663
TLB 3, 157–58	1: S003154
	2: S003153
	3: S002392
UTI 3, 1916	S003415
UTI 4, 2660	S002813

C. Seal Impressions Sorted by CDLI Number

CDLI No.	Text No. Collection No. or	Publication ID
S000033	71	MS 2018/4
S000033	—	MVN 4, 257
S000223	8	MS 1942/02
S000302	—	BRM 3, 31
S000306	132	MS 2015
S000493.1	76	MS 1698/2
S000493.2	9	MS 1942/06
S000493.2	169	MS 1942/09
S000493.2	—	MVN 4, 173
S000563	—	BIN 3, 356
S001779	—	ASJ 19, 215 43
S001800	49	MS 4715/02
S001829	128	MS 2369
S002014	7	MS 1942/01
S002054	67	MS 4686
S002124	150	MS 1653/1
S002124	152	MS 1879
S002127	43	MS 4715/09
S002175	148	MS 2018/7
S002175	154	MS 1942/11
S002392	—	TLB 3, 157–58
S002469	53	MS 4715/07

CDLI No.	Text No. Collection No. or	Publication ID
S002469	54	MS 4715/08
S002533	—	Georgica 1.1.3
S002533	—	MCS 1, 54,
		BM 113107
S002813	—	UTI 4, 2660
S002825	4	MS 1942/03
S002825	—	MVN 2, 273
S002825	—	Ontario 2, 219
S002889	200	MS 1745
S002893	—	CHEU 14
S002932	—	JCS 2, 187
		NBC 3500
S002932	—	MVN 4, 173
S003057	201	MS 4687
S003076a	80	MS 1726
S003102	149	MS 4707
S003153	—	TLB 3, 157–58
S003154	—	TLB 3, 157–58
S003230	—	Aleppo 122
S003322	162	MS 4715/2
S003341	74	MS 1723/1
S003415	—	UTI 3, 1916

CDLI No.	Text No. Collection No. or	Publication ID
S003565	—	MVN 14, 2
S003612	131	MS 4764
S003673	—	MVN 14, 87
S003732	78	MS 1725
S003812	72	MS 2018/3
S003813	75	MS 1723/2
S004065	11	MS 1942/08
S004065.2	—	Princeton 1, 277
S004199	108	MS 4706
S004199	114	MS 4698
S004199	115	MS 4689
S004199	116	MS 4690
S004250	68	MS 4715/17
S004274	50	MS 4715/03
S004311	198	MS 4096
S004361	46	MS 2018/5
S004361	47	MS 4692
S004448	10	MS 1942/07
S004663	—	TCNU 646
S004738	60	MS 4715/15
S004972	103	MS 1916
S004974	—	AUCT 3, 279
S004986	63	MS 1947/06
S005168	—	Amherst 119
S005278	204	MS 2018/1
S005354	7	MS 1942/01
S005354	124	MS 1722
S005354	—	Aleppo 495 (NMSA 4064)
S005355	—	Aleppo 119
S005378	51	MS 4715/06

CDLI No.	Text No. Collection No. or	Publication ID
S005506	79	MS 2018/6
S005787	—	MVN 2, 11
S005821	82	MS 1949/5
S005881	168	MS 1942/05
S005907	—	BRM 3, 44
S005940	6	MS 2077
S005940	32	MS 1947/05
S005960	62	MS 4715/16
S005990	83	MS 1739/2
S006035	110	MS 4702
S006049	242	MS 2772
S006150	73	MS 2018/2
—	55	MS 4715/12
—	59	MS 1947/13
—	61	MS 4715/18
—	69	MS 2018/8
—	77	MS 1724
—	134	MS 1846/2
illegible	5	MS 1942/04
illegible	48	MS 4688
illegible	52	MS 1712
illegible	56	MS 2018/9
illegible	57	MS 4338/27
illegible	58	MS 4715/10
illegible	81	MS 4971
illegible	84	MS 4696
illegible	111	MS 4970
illegible	113	MS 4711
illegible	117	MS 4650
illegible	197	MS 5010
illegible	207	MS 4422
illegible	217	MS 4451

Shukhov never overslept. He was always up at the call. That way he had an hour and a half all to himself before work parade—time for a man who knew his way around to earn a bit on the side.

—Alexander Solzhenitsyn, *One Day in the Life of Ivan Denisovich*

1
INTRODUCTION

Neo-Sumerian administrative documents, which understandably contain a rich array of technical terminology, can only be read when their inner structure is understood. In other words, the technical terms will often seem meaningless, or even contradictory, when the structure of the documents remains unclear. It is therefore deceptive to translate such loaded terms literally, as is of course most often the case when translating from any language, whether ancient or modern. In addition, the documents that form the core of this book, the administrative records of the Third Dynasty of Ur (henceforth Ur III), often appear trivial when considered individually or without reference to the society which produced them, and a holistic approach to the ancient administration of the period is therefore helpful to decipher them.

The Ur III kingdom was a centralized, expansive polity based on the old city-states of southern Babylonia. The state was ruled by a dynasty of five kings from the capital city, Ur, and lasted approximately one hundred years (c. 2100–2000 BC). These five kings successfully monopolized succession (Dahl 2004) and power over the previously independent city-states of Sumer, and apart from Ur-Namma, founder and first king of the dynasty, each was deified during his lifetime.[1] Whereas the eastern periphery was controlled to a large extent by the military (Steinkeller 1987a), relations to the north and north-east were more determined by political alliances than through subjection by force.[2] Some of the kings were glorified in court poetry known to us from Old Babylonian texts whose composition dates remain unknown.[3] A corpus of letters that may contain remnants of the correspondence of the kings of Ur,[4] or be simply an apocryphal collection,[5] was produced in the scribal academies during the Old Babylonian period, presumably for educational and/or political purposes.[6]

This book is not directly concerned with the power and politics of the Ur III state or its successors, or with the memory of this state and the literary production pertaining to its rulers, whether real or constructed. Rather, it seeks to shed light on the bookkeeping system of the Ur III state.[7] It is, of course, superfluous to remind anyone that this system reflects back on the power and politics of the realm altogether. This book therefore seeks to offer a comprehensive discussion of both the structure and terminology of Ur III administrative documents, as well as a description of the administrative system which fostered them. It is also the primary publication of a group of 244 Ur III texts in the Schøyen Collection. Fortunately, the texts in this collection cover almost all known genres and are therefore used to illustrate a majority of the points made in this book. Occasionally, documents from other collections have been included to complete or complement the picture provided.

---

1 See Michalowski 2013 for an attempt at assessing the importance of the Girsu state prior to, and during the Ur III period and its subsequent incorporation into the Ur III state: the author suggests that the governors of Girsu were powerful enough to retain certain privileges.

2 See also Dahl 2007: 13–32 for an introduction to the period.

3 For a positivistic viewpoint, see Rubio 2005.

4 Hallo 2006.

5 Most notably Huber 2001.

6 See Michalowski 2011 for a recent study of this corpus. There is no scholarly consensus as to whether these letters were composed during the Ur III period or the Old Babylonian period or how the transmission of Ur III chancery documents into Old Babylonian school texts could have taken place, if indeed the corpus retains a core of historically correct information.

7 See, e.g., Grégoire 1970, Hrozny 1913, Englund 1990, for studies particularly devoted to the administrative history of the ancient Near East.

The texts published here never constituted an archive in ancient times, although a sizeable number of the texts appear to originate from Adab.[8] Generally speaking, the core sites of Drehem and Girsu are underrepresented among the texts in the collection, while Umma features prominently. A few texts in the collection originating from ancient Garšana were included in David I. Owen's edition of the Garšana archive (Owen and Mayr 2007) and are published here too.

Ur III administrative documents can be divided into two main groups: (1) texts documenting the assets of the state, and (2) documents relating to the running of the administrative machinery. The latter include letters, legal texts, certain lists, messenger texts, tags, and sealings, whereas the former include accounts, primary documents such as receipts, lists, inventories, and so forth. The royal inscriptions from the Ur III period in the Schøyen Collection are not included in this book, since they have recently been published (George 2011: nos. 34–36, 101, 107).

In essence, there is no structural difference between a document recording a specific transaction in, for example, the agricultural sector or the manufacturing sector of the economy, but there may exist types of documents within one sector that are not mirrored in the other. Likewise, documents from any level of the administrative hierarchy appear to conform to the same format and to use the same terminology. This is exemplified in the use of certain titles across all levels of the administration. Most illustrative, probably, is the use of the title ugula, usually translated as "overseer." In the Ur III state anyone could be an overseer, both low-ranking supervisors of work crews and high-ranking officials. A vestige of this is perhaps seen in the way in which the title ugula was incorporated among the titles of the ruler of the Old Assyrian city state Assur (Larsen 1976: 109 ff.). Extensive prosopographical studies are therefore needed to determine the administrative level of many documents (McGuiness 1982b).

Theoretically, all goods were recorded at least twice, encoded as either "debits" or "credits" in the accounts of a person or an institution. On another level, this can be described as the documentation of the expectations, and the documentation of the rate of fulfillment of obligations within a "planned" economy. We shall return to a discussion of these terms throughout this book.

The Sumerian word for goods, nig_2-gur_{11}, is perhaps derived from Akkadian, *makkūrum*,[9] although the similarity may be a mere coincidence.[10] The distinction between private and public property in third-millennium BC Mesopotamia is not always clear, and nig_2-gur_{11} could be used to describe private as well as public property.[11] Work was thought to be commensurable with movable property, and it could be translated into movable goods by means of standardized equivalencies. Unparalleled in ancient history, work in itself was treated as a commodity that could be transferred, accumulated, or dissipated. The accountants of the Ur III administration were the first in recorded history to implement a system of man-days tied to a set of fixed equivalencies.[12]

A sophisticated system of equivalences was used throughout the administration. Some scholars have equated this system with a monetary system.[13] However, since the equivalences were used in a "planned"

---

[8] See Widell 2002 §3 and n. 3, and note in particular the seal of Lu-Utu, "scribe, child of Ur-Ašgi, governor of Adab," rolled on text No. 162.

[9] MSL 17, 190: nig_2-gur_{11} = *ma-ak-ku-ru*.

[10] See also n. 20 below where an equation of GA = gur_{11} = *kamārum*, "to add up," may signify that the gur_{11} element of nig_2-gur_{11} is not a phonetic rendering of the second half of the Akkadian word *makkūru(m)* but a "native" term for adding stuff up, making plausible a translation of nig_2-gur_{11} as "piled up stuff" = "goods."

[11] See the discussion in Heimpel 1997. See further Maekawa 1996a and b.

[12] See already Struve 1969: 128 "... From this I inferred that the Sumerian accountants had a notion of man-day, and that the formula 'so many labourers for one day' used in the primary documentation is not meant to indicate the number of labourers who actually worked for one day but means the number of man-days."

[13] See, e.g., Hallo and Curtis 1959: 103–39.

economy, centrally organized in a system lacking most elements of a market economy,[14] it seems justified to explain the fixed rates used by the administrators to estimate the value of a product or a work as equivalences and not "prices." We shall return to this, in depth, below.

The accounts, or the "year-end's" accounts, are perhaps the most famous documents from the Ur III period. They have been designated "balanced accounts" by some because they can contain a remainder, positive as well as negative.[15] These accounts were not, however, balanced, but rather records of the "credits" and the "debits" of individuals and institutions. The negative or positive remainder can be compared to the modern accounting term "operating balance" which describes a (positive) "remainder" carried forward in a sequence of running accounts. Whereas the accounts have received much attention in scholarly publications, the receipts have not. However, receipts are the most numerous Ur III documents, and perhaps the most numerous type of document from the ancient world altogether. This book therefore includes a substantial discussion of the receipts of the Ur III period (Chapter 7).

It appears helpful to order the following presentation of the Ur III administrative documents in a virtual hierarchy, starting with the archival documents used to label other documents, before describing the accounts and the primary documents used when drawing up the accounts, then lists and inventories which served as building blocks for the accounts, and finally texts relating to the running of the administration (letters, contracts, etc.). For typological reasons I will treat the commodity tags together with the archival tags rather than with letters and contracts. I will also separate the administration of work from that of commodities.

---

[14] For a discussion of Mesopotamian societies without a market(-place) in the classical sense (~agora) and the subsequent social and historical implications, see, above all, Polanyi 1957: 12–27, and Clancier *et al.* (eds.) 2005. See also the discussion in Englund 1990: 14–18.

[15] See, e.g., Snell 1982.

2

ARCHIVAL DOCUMENTS

The archival context of most Ur III documents is reconstructed entirely using internal arguments based on the content of the documents themselves, as they were almost all found either in trash deposits, floor fillings, by illicit excavators, or during the large-scale "plunder" of ancient Iraq during the last decades of the nineteenth century and the first decades of the twentieth century AD, all of which were conducted almost entirely without reference to archaeological standards.[16]

At most sites and during most periods, the scant evidence concerning archival practice seems to suggest that tablets were stored in special containers for certain amounts of time. At some sites and during some periods these containers could be clay vessels,[17] at others they could be reed baskets or wooden containers.[18]

Although we lack physical information about the arrangement of Ur III tablets within their original archives, we can suggest a possible system of ordering the documents based on internal evidence (Van De Mieroop 1999–2000). For example, the content of some ancient tablet containers can be reconstructed, since such containers often had a tag attached to them that provided an indication of the contents. However, the information on these tags is usually insufficient to identify which specific tablets were stored together. Tags were probably also attached directly to goods, although this cannot be proven.

Archival Tags

The most common type of archival tag is the so-called pisan-dub-ba (Nelson 1976, id. 1979; Sallaberger 1999a: 214–16). In the Ur III period, the pisan-dub-ba is a small squarish tablet that once was attached to a box or basket (pisan) holding documents. The Ur III pisan-dub-ba document was formed around the string with which it was attached to the container. The two ends of the string were joined inside the clay document. The string entered the document in one or two places on the left edge. pisan-dub-ba documents are thus easily recognizable by the one or two holes on the left edge left by the decayed cord. The document hung from its left side, providing a clue to the original direction of writing at this point in time (Fitzgerald 2003). The content of the container is described in the text of the pisan-dub-ba. Whereas the technical term pisan dub-ba introduces the document, it is terminated by the finite verb i_3-gal, "is present."[19] The time covered by the documents in the container is often given in the text. Most pisan-dub-ba documents conform to the format of text No. 1:

---

[16] Note the 19 recently published Ur III texts from the Šara temple in Umma (Al-Mutawalli 2010: 45 ff.). These administrative texts, all related to the leather workshop of Aya-kala, chief of the leather workers (ašgab gal), and his son Lu-Šara (who never held the same title: see Dahl 2007: 132 for this apparent systemic taboo against using one's father's title), were found in "room 10" in the temple. The texts are all dated between Šu-Suen's 9th and final year and Ibbi-Suen's 3rd year. The temple of Šara was rebuilt in Šu-Suen's 8th year with the following 9th year being named after this event. The last Ur III texts from Umma were written in Ibbi-Suen's 3rd year. It may therefore be possible that all of our Umma texts (more than 32,000 known to date) originally came from the Šara temple, but that the vast majority of these were discarded already in antiquity when the temple was rebuilt in Šu-Suen's 8th year. See Tsouparopoulou 2013 for a discussion of the archival context of tablets from Drehem reconstructed entirely from information in the documents themselves.

[17] See Radner 2004 for an excavated example from a Middle Assyrian provincial town, and references to the widespread use of clay vessels as archival containers (p. 51). It is reasonable to suggest that this practice existed in earlier periods as well.

[18] This is suggested, for example, by the reed impressions on the reverse of several ED IIIb archival tags from Girsu (Nik 1, 128; 129; 165; 205; 215; 216; 275; TSA 49 [all with digital images available on CDLI search for Provenience = Girsu; Period = ED IIIb; and Sub-genre = pisan]). There is sporadic archaeological evidence that documents could be kept on shelves. Little is otherwise known about this form of archival storage.

[19] In the ED IIIb pisan-dub-ba documents we find instead pisan pisan dub . . . e-da-gal_2.

No. 1. *MS 1719 (Drehem, ŠS 4–i to ŠS 6–xiii)*

obv.

1.	pisan dub-ba	Tablet container:
2.	gur$_{11}$-gur$_{11}$-ra-a	(Tablets concerning) the total(?)[20]
3.	ki ur-ku$_{3}$-nun-na	of (the account of) the place of Ur-kununa,
4.	iti še-sag$_{11}$-ku$_{5}$	from month: "Harvest,"
5.	mu bad$_{3}$ mar-tu ba-du$_{3}$-ta	(in the) year: "When the Martu wall was built,"

rev.

1.	iti diri ezem-me-ki-gal$_{2}$	to the extra month (following month): "Festival of Mekigal,"
2.	mu na-ru$_{2}$-a maḫ ba-ru$_{2}$-še$_{3}$	(in the) year: "The lofty stela was erected"—
3.	mu 3(diš)-kam	that is (a period of) 3 years—
4.	i$_{3}$-gal$_{2}$	are present.
	(blank line)	

BIN 3, 354 is a close parallel to text No. 1, and is included here for the sake of clarity:

BIN 3, 354 (Drehem, ŠS 3–i to xi dirig)

obv.

1.	pisan dub-ba	Tablet container:
2.	sag-nig$_{2}$-gur$_{11}$-ra u$_{3}$ zi-ga	(Tablets concerning) the "credits" and "debits"
3.	gur$_{11}$-gur$_{11}$-ra-a	of the total(?),
4.	ki in-ta-e$_{3}$-a	of (the account of) the place of Inta'ea,
5.	iti maš-da$_{3}$-gu$_{7}$-ta	from month: "Eating the gazelle,"

[20] The term gur$_{11}$-gur$_{11}$-ra(-a) has at least two different meanings: (a) a technical term for "total" (perhaps a passive participle of gur$_{11}$, corresponding to Akkadian *kamārum, kumurrûm* [Kraus 1966: 125]), and (b) a technical term indicating that a total has been transferred by means of leather sacks (du$_{10}$-gan, perhaps itself a technical term similar to the Old Assyrian *naruqqum* denoting some sort of investment [see Oppenheim 1948: 79 n. 98]). For meaning (a), see MCS 4, 21 19 rev. 12–13: [*n* animals / slaughtered] gur$_{11}$-gur$_{11}$-ra, "Total: n slaughtered animals" (Gomi did not discuss this term but described the text as "Total of dead animals from Abaenlilgi in Nippur" in his 1980 collations article of the Manchester texts [Gomi 1981, 1985, 1986]; Fish referred the reader to Oppenheim 1948: 79 without being convinced by Oppenheim's translation of "established account"); and AAICAB 1/1, pl. 78, 1924–2162 left edge: gur$_{11}$- gur$_{11}$-ra-a ba-a-gar, "placed on the total." For meaning (b), see, e.g., HLC 35 (pl. 45) rev. i 6–ii 1: [total of beer-bread and butter-oil / … / … /] ^{kuš}du$_{10}$-gan gur$_{11}$- gur$_{11}$-ra, "(for) placing in leather sacks"; MVN 17, 4 rev. ii 9–10: [large total of barley /] $^{kuš!}$du$_{10}$-gan gur$_{11}$- gur$_{11}$-ra-a-še$_{3}$, "for placing in leather sacks"; and the pisan-dub-ba TUT 164-04: pisan dub-ba / im gaba zum / u$_{3}$ ^{kuš}du$_{10}$-gan / gur$_{11}$- gur$_{11}$-ra-a nin-dingir-ra // ⸢i$_{3}$-gal$_{2}$⸣, "Tablet container holding gaba-zum tablets [type of archival copies?] and transfers to the leather sack of Nindingir." The term also occurs in texts from Garšana with an application similar to meaning (a). Note that the editors of the Garšana archive read ga-ga-ra(-a), and translated "capital, total" (CUSAS 4: 53). Leather bags (^{kuš}du$_{10}$-gan) could be used to store or transport certain administrative documents (Tsouparopoulou 2017: 617 ff.), allowing for the possible overlap of meanings (a) and (b). Tsouparopoulou speculates that certain polyhedral bullae were used to close such bags (2017: 619 ff.). For examples of this group, see PPAC 4, 121 + 122 or BRM 3, 37. None of the texts from this group makes any reference to archival procedures.

rev.

1.	iti diri ezem-me-ki-gal$_2$-e us$_2$-sa-še$_3$	to the extra month (following month): "Festival of Mekigal"
2.	iti 1(u) 2(diš)-kam	—that is (a period of) twelve months—
3.	mu si-ma-num$_2$^{ki} ba-ḫul	(in the) year: "Simanum was destroyed,"
4.	i$_3$-gal$_2$	are present.

There are two further pisan-dub-ba texts in the Schøyen Collection, Nos. 2 and 3:

No. 2. *MS 2020/10 (Umma, —)*

obv.

1.	pisan dub-ba	Tablet container:
2.	im i$_7$ guruš-gin$_7$-DU ba-al-la	Tablets[21] (concerning) the excavation of the Gurušgin-DU-canal,
3.	u$_3$ kin e ra-a	and work (at) striking the levee(?),
4.	a-ba-gal-^{d}en-lil$_2$-la$_2$	(in the?) Abagal-Enlila (field?),[22]

rev.

1.	i$_3$-gal$_2$	are present.
	(*blank space*)	

Two administrative documents, both from Umma and Šu-Suen's sixth year, record work performed on the levee of the Gurušgin-DU-canal (MVN 16, 912 and 961), but there is no evidence that they are the actual ones recorded by our tablet container.

No. 3. *MS 5047/1 (Umma?, —)*

obv.

1.	pisan dub-ba	Tablet container:
2.	kišib$_3$ aš-a[23] x-x ugula uš-bar	Sealed tablets (receipts?) of . . . , overseer of the weaving mill,
3.	i$_3$-gal$_2$	are present.

rev. (*blank*)

Another type of archival tablet is the mace-head shaped tag that appears to have been attached to top-level documents. Where accounts usually have two main sections, first the "debits," followed by the technical term sag-nig$_2$-gur$_{11}$-ra-kam, and second the "credits," framed by ša$_3$-bi-ta . . . . zi-ga, the mace-head tags mention the sag-nig$_2$-gur$_{11}$-ra and the ša$_3$-bi su-ga (see Chapter 4 for more on the Ur III accounts). Usually, su-ga indicates repaid deficits (la$_2$-ia$_3$ su-ga). ša$_3$-bi su-ga in the mace-head tags

---

[21] For im (lit. "clay") meaning tablets, see, for example, the pisan-dub-ba AOAT 25, 437 BM 14440 (AS 6): pisan dub-ba / im di til-la / ^{d}šara$_2$-kam ensi$_2$-ka // i$_3$-gal$_2$ / mu ša-aš-ru^{ki} ba-hul, "Tablet container holding tablets (with/concerning) the verdicts of Šarakam, governor. Year: 'Šašrum was destroyed.'"

[22] The proper noun Abagal-Enlila is attested only as a name of a field or an associated installation (threshing floor, levee, etc.).

[23] The terminology kišib$_3$ aš-a is frequent in administrative documents from the Ur III period (close to a hundred attestations known to the author). It may relate to the number of primary documents behind a certain entry in a summary account, in which case it may refer to either one receipt or "more" (didli).

remains difficult to explain but may indicate that the "credits" have been settled, as they were seen as something that the person whose accounts were being drawn up had to fulfill in order to avoid a deficit. Two examples of this sort of archival tag are found in the Schøyen Collection, texts Nos. 4 and 5:

No. 4. *MS 1942/3 (Umma, Š 44)*

1.	sag-nig$_2$-gur$_{11}$-ra	(Tablets concerning) the "debits"
2.	ša$_3$-bi su-ga	(and) fulfilled "credits"
3.	[i$_3^?$]-⸢gal$_2^?$⸣	are present(?).
4.	da-⸢da$^?$-ga$^?$⸣	(Concerning) Dadaga(?).
5.	mu si-mu-ru-⸢um⸣ lu-lu-bu^{ki} a-ra$_2$ 1(u) la$_2$ 1(diš$_{tenû}$)-kam [ba]-ḫul	Year: "Simurum and Lulubu(m) were destroyed for the ninth time."

seal (S002825)

1.	lu$_2$-du$_{10}$-ga	Lu-duga,
2.	dub-sar	scribe,
3.	dumu ur-nigar^{gar}	child of Ur-nigar.

Two closely related, and well-preserved, parallels from the following year exist. One is in the Musée d'Art et d'Histoire, Geneva, Switzerland, the other in the Royal Ontario Museum of Archaeology, Toronto, Ontario, Canada. They are included here in support of the reconstruction of the very damaged text No. 4:

MVN 2, 273 (Umma, Š 45)

1.	sag-nig$_2$-gur$_{11}$-ra	(Tablets concerning) the "debits"
2.	ša$_3$-bi su-ga da-da-ga	(and) fulfilled "credits." (Concerning) Dadaga.
3.	mu ur-bi$_2$-lum^{ki} ba-ḫul	Year "Urbilum was destroyed."
	(blank space with seal impression)	

seal (S002825)

1.	lu$_2$-du$_{10}$-ga	Lu-duga,
2.	dub-sar	scribe,
3.	dumu ur-nigar^{gar}	child of Ur-nigar.

Ontario 2, 219 (Umma, Š 45)

1.	sag-nig$_2$-gur$_{11}$-ra	(Tablets concerning) the "debits"
2.	ša$_3$-bi su-ga	(and) fulfilled "credits,"
3.	ku$_3$ dam-gar$_3$	of the silver of the trade agent(s),
4.	da-da-ga	(concerning) Dadaga.
5.	mu ur-bi$_2$-lum^{ki} ba-ḫul	Year: "Urbilum was destroyed."

seal (S002825)

1.	lu$_2$-du$_{10}$-ga	Lu-duga,
2.	dub-sar	scribe,
3.	dumu ur-nigar^{gar}	child of Ur-nigar.

The other mace-head tag in the Schøyen Collection does not record the name of the person whose accounts were being archived:

No. 5. *MS 1942/4 (Umma, Š 34 to Š 36)*

1.	sag-nig$_2$-[gur$_{11}$-ra]	(Tablets concerning) the "debits"
2.	⸢ša$_3$-bi su-ga⸣	(and) fulfilled "credits,"
3.	mu 3(diš)-⸢kam⸣	of three years.
4.	mu an-ša-[an]^{ki}-⸢ta⸣	From the year: "Anšan (was destroyed),"
5.	mu ^{d}⸢nanna$^{?}$⸣ [. . .] kar-⸢zi⸣-[da . . .]	to the year: "Nanna of Karzida [. . .]."

seal (*illegible*)

The exact function of these documents is unknown, but their consistent relation to accounts and their standard format may provide a clue to their original use. It is the hypothesis here that texts from this group of archival documents in Umma were used to seal special boxes containing top-level accounts.[24]

A group of archival documents from Drehem, that include the key-term e$_2$-tum, are shaped similarly to the mace-head tags described above.[25] However, the Drehem tags were penetrated by the string with which they were originally attached to a tablet container, whereas the Umma mace-head tags were not penetrated by a string or stick and attached to a tablet container. Perhaps they were placed in the container with the tablets.

The key-terminology, e$_2$-tum, probably to be transcribed *bītum*,[26] terminates the text of most of the Drehem tags and acts also as a header in a few.[27] The same term is also found in other archival documents next to administrative terms such as "credits," "debits," or the like. The key to understanding this and other similar technical terms may lie in the broad use of this terminology: both the specific administrative functions and the containers holding the documents pertaining to the same functions, could be labeled with one and the same term. It is even possible that administrative terminology could have been deduced originally from the names of containers or actions involving containers.

Although these Drehem mace-head tags may be archival documents that seal sub-groups of tablets later entered into accounts, that remains difficult to prove. BRM 3, 31 serves as an example of a round Drehem tag:

BRM 3, 31 (Drehem, AS 5–xi)

obv.

1.	4(u) 7(diš) gu$_4$ ab$_2$ ḫi-a	47 oxen and cows, various,
2.	1(geš'u) 4(geš$_2$) 2(u) udu maš$_2$ ḫi-a	860 sheep and goats, various,
3.	5(geš$_2$) 4(u) la$_2$ 1(diš) maš-da$_3$	339 gazelles,
4.	7(diš) az	7 bears.
5.	mu$^{!}$-ku$_x$(DU) lugal	mu-ku$_x$(DU) deliveries[28] of the king.
6.	ab-ba-sa$_6$-ga ⸢i$_3$⸣-dab$_5$	Abba-saga seized.
7.	iti ezem-me-ki-gal$_2$	Month: "Festival of Mekigal."
8.	mu en-unu$_6$-gal ^{d}inanna unu^{ki} ba-ḫun	Year: "Enungal(-Anna) was installed (as En-priest) of Inana of Uruk."
9.	e$_2$-tum	"House."

---

[24] See also BRM 3, 14a and UTI 5, 3257.

[25] See Tsouparopoulou 2017: 620, with literature.

[26] See first Maeda 1996, later Hilgert 2003: 76 n. 255. Note in particular the syllabic writing bi$_2$-tum attested in three archival documents (CUSAS 3, 1483; MVN 15, 288; Nisaba 15, 1152).

[27] E.g., CDLJ 2008/2 §2.21, translated by its editor, Hilgert, as "House" (-container with tablets recording), see Hilgert 2008, with reference to Hilgert 2003 (see above).

[28] See Ch. 7 below.

seal (S000302)

col. i

1.	^{d}šul-gi	Šulgi,
2.	nita kal-ga	strong man,
3.	lugal uri$_5$^{ki}-ma	king of Ur:

col. ii

1.	na-sa$_6$	Nasa,
2.	kurušda	(chief) fattener,
3.	ARAD$_2$-[zu]	(is) your slave.

As mentioned above, the term e$_2$-tum or *bītum* can also be found in archival tags listed among other and better-known administrative terms such as sag-nig$_2$-gur$_{11}$-ra-kam. As such it has been interpreted as representing a physical sub-division of the archival container. However, structurally it could well represent an administrative key-term. Typologically, this formation of terminology would be similar to the use of "book" in modern bookkeeping. BCT 1, 120 is an example of an archival container including the term e$_2$-tum/*bītum*:

BCT 1, 120 (Drehem, AS 6–v)

obv.

1.	pisan dub-ba	Tablet container:
2.	e$_2$-tum	"house(s),"
3.	sag-nig$_2$-gur$_{11}$-ra	(tablets relating to the) "debits,"
4.	u$_3$ zi-ga	and (tablets relating to the) "credits."
5.	ta$_2$-ḫi-iš-a-tal	(Concerning) Tahiš-atal.
6.	iti ezem-^{d}nin-a-zu u$_4$ 1(u) 8(diš) zal-la-ta	From the month: "Festival of Nin-azu," the 18th day has passed,

rev.

1.	iti še-sag$_{11}$-ku$_5$-še$_3$	until month: "Harvest."
2.	iti 7(diš) u$_4$ 1(u) 2(diš)-kam	It is 7 months and 12 days.
3.	mu ša-aš-ru^{ki} ba-ḫul	Year: "Šašru was destroyed."
	(*blank space*)	

In summary, the term e$_2$-tum/*bītum* represents either a special container for documents, sometimes placed inside another archival container, or a bookkeeping term, on par with "credits" or "debits," which perhaps received its name from the particular type of container used to keep the documents. The two interpretations are not mutually exclusive.

Sealed Tags with Inscriptions

There are one complete and two fragments of triangular tags from Umma in the Schøyen Collection. Triangular tags in Umma served two different purposes. One purpose was monthly summaries of the expenditures for the messengers; two tags in the collection fall into this group and will be dealt with in Chapter 10 (texts Nos. 168 and 169). The other purpose, exemplified by text No. 6, was summaries of regular deliveries for various deities (No. 6 side C l. 3: sa$_2$-du$_{11}$ dingir-re-ne). These Umma documents were usually sealed by members of one branch of the ruling family of Umma, namely Ur-E'e and his sons Lu-kala and Lu-Ḫaya, sometimes together with the chief archivist Ur-Nungal.[29] However, text No. 6 is sealed by Gududu, the cousin of Lu-kala and Lu-Ḫaya.

No. 6. *MS 2077 (Umma, IS 1–xi)*

side A

1.	3(u) 8(diš) udu niga 2(u) 4(diš) ⸢udu⸣	38 fattened sheep, 24 sheep,
2.	7(diš) sila$_4$ ga 1(diš) maš$_2$ niga 9(diš) maš$_2$	7 suckling lambs, 1 fattened goat, 9 goats,
3.	sa$_2$-du$_{11}$	regular (deliveries).[30]
4.	1(diš) udu geš ^{d}pa$_4$-u$_2$-e	1 mature(?)[31] sheep (for) Pa'u'e.[32]
5.	7(diš) udu 1(diš) sila$_4$ ga 2(diš) maš$_2$	7 sheep, 1 suckling lamb, 2 goats,
6.	nig$_2$-^{geš}tag-ga ⸢lugal⸣	(for) the nig$_2$-tag-offerings[33] of the king.
7.	⸢giri$_3$?⸣ [...]	Conveyor: [...].
8.	[x udu] niga 1(diš) udu u$_2$ ^{d}⸢šara$_2$⸣ KI.AN^{ki}	*n* fattened sheep, 1 sheep (for) Šara of KIAN.
9.	[n] ⸢udu⸣ bara$_2$ gir$_{13}$-geš^{ki}	*n* fattened sheep (for) the dais of Girgeš.
10.	[n] udu 1(diš) sila$_4$ 4(diš) maš$_2$ ^{d}nin-ur$_4$-ra	*n* sheep, 1 lamb, 1 goat (for) Nin-Urra.
11.	[n udu] niga 8(diš) udu u$_2$ ^{d}gu-la	*n* fattened sheep, 8 grass(-fed) sheep (for) Gula.
12.	[x] sa$_2$-du$_{11}$ 3(diš) udu gu$_2$-gu$_2$ mu-e$_3$	... regular (deliveries). 3 sheep, (for) the clothing
13.	[^{d}]en-lil$_2$	of Enlil[34].
14.	[n] maš$_2$ sa$_2$-du$_{11}$	*n goats, regular (deliveries)*
15.	[a]-⸢tu$_5$⸣-a ^{d}nin-eb-[gal]	(for) the bathing of Nin-Ebgal.

side B

1.	x x-[...]	...
2.	[a] ⸢šed$_{12}$⸣-de$_2$-a ^{d}dumu-zi URUxA^{a} ⸢^{ki}⸣	(for) the cold water libation of Dumuzi of Urua.
3.	[... ^{d}nin]-⸢e$_{11}$⸣-e	... (for) Nin-E'e.
4.	[... ^{d}nin-]da-lagaš^{ki}	... (for) Nin-Da-Lagaš.
5.	[... ^{d}]⸢kar?⸣-ra-⸢du?⸣	... (for) Karadu.
6.	[n udu] niga 3(diš) udu u$_2$ 1(diš) maš$_2$	*n* fattened sheep, 3 grass(-fed) sheep, 1 goat
7.	[^{d}šul?]-gi	(for) Šulgi.
8.	[n udu] ⸢niga⸣ 3(diš) udu u$_2$ 1(diš) maš$_2$	*n* fattened sheep, 3 grass(-fed) sheep, 1 goat
9.	[x ^{d}]⸢amar⸣-^{d}suen	(for) Amar-Suen.
10.	⸢4(diš)⸣ udu niga 2(diš) udu u$_2$ 1(diš) ⸢sila$_4$⸣	4 fattened sheep, 2 grass(-fed) sheep,
11.	^{d}šu-^{d}suen	(for) Šu-Suen.
12.	1(diš) udu 1(diš) maš	1 lamb, 1 goat

---

[29] Note the failure in Dahl 2007: 102 to differentiate between the two groups of Umma triangular tags.

[30] sa$_2$-du$_{11}$ is commonly translated as "regular offerings" in the literature (Sigrist 1992: 199), but a translation "regular (deliveries)" may be preferable to highlight the frequent use of the term for purposes other than offerings, and to indicate that the literary meaning of the term itself relates to the regularity of the delivery rather than the act of giving or transferring (sa$_2$, "to be, make straight").

[31] Probably an error for udu geš-du$_3$, which in Ur III texts is a phonetic writing for udu geš$_3$-du$_3$, a "sheep which has been mounted," but cf. gu$_4$ geš, possibly to be interpreted as a yoke-ox (e.g., No. 31 obv. i 15).

[32] pa$_4$-u$_2$-e is an Umma divine name (here transcribed Pa'u'e), frequently written without divine determinative (Krebernik 2004: 367).

[33] Sallaberger 1993: 230–31.

[34] See, e.g., Attinger 1998: 170–71 and n. 24. The term gu$_2$-gu$_2$ mu-e$_3$ is used very infrequently in Ur III records (the receipt SA 125 [Umma, X–xi]; the three large accounts P315448 [unpublished] [Umma, covering the years AS 8 to ŠS 1–xii], Nisaba 24, 25 [Umma, no date], and YOS 4, 207 [Umma, date broken]).

13.	^{d}šu-^{d}suen min-kam	(for) Šu-Suen, the second time.
13.	1(diš) udu	1 sheep

side C

1.	siskur$_2$ e$_2$ maš	(for) the offerings of the Emaš.
2.	1(u) 4(diš) udu 3(diš) sila$_4$ 5(diš) maš$_2$	14 sheep, 3 lamb, 5 goats
3.	eš$_3$-eš$_3$ ša$_3$ nig$_2$-^{geš}tag-ga dingir-re-ne	(for) the shrines of the nig$_2$-tag-offerings of the gods.
3.	udu sa$_2$-du$_{11}$ dingir-re-ne	Sheep (of the) regular (deliveries) for the gods.
4.	ki a-lu$_5$-lu$_5$-ta	From Alulu.
5.	⸢kišib$_3$ gu⸣-du-du	Sealed tablet of Gududu.
6.	iti ^{d}pa$_4$-u$_2$-e	Month: "Pa'u'e."
7.	mu ^{d}i-bi$_2$-^{d}suen ⸢lugal⸣	Year: "Ibbi-Suen (was) king."
8.	lugal-nesag-e u$_3$ lu$_2$-⸢du$_{10}$⸣-[ga] im-gi-⸢ne$^{?}$⸣-[eš]	Lugal-nesage and Lu-duga confirmed it.

seal (S005940)

col. i

1.	^{d}i-bi$_2$-^{d}suen	Ibbi-Suen,
2.	lugal kal-ga	strong king,
3.	lugal uri$_5$^{ki}-ma	king of Ur,
4.	lugal an-ub-da limmu-ba	king of the four corners (of the world):

col. ii

1.	gu-du-du	Gududu,
2.	dub-sar	scribe,
3.	dumu da-da-ga	child of Dadaga,
4.	ensi$_2$	governor
5.	umma^{ki}	of Umma,
6.	ARAD$_2$-zu	(is) your slave.

BRM 3, 44 from AS 8 is very similar to text No. 6; however, it is sealed by Ur-Lisi, governor of Umma, and uncle of Lu-kala and Lu-Ḫaya:

BRM 3, 44 (Umma, AS 8–iv)

side A

1.	1(u) 7(diš) udu niga 5(u) udu u$_2$	17 fattened sheep, 50 grass-fed sheep,
2.	2(u) la2 1(diš) udu bar-ba zi-ga	19 sheep without fleece,[35]
3.	1(u) 3(diš) sila$_4$ bar-ba zi-ga	13 lamb without fleece,
4.	1(diš) maš$_2$ niga 2(diš) ⸢maš$_2$⸣ [x]	1 fattened goat, 2 . . . goats,
5.	sa$_2$-du$_{11}$	regular (deliveries).
6.	1(diš) maš$_2$ PA	1 . . . goat,
7.	7(diš) udu u$_2$ 3(diš) sila$_4$ bar-ba zi-ga	7 grass-fed sheep, 3 lambs without fleece,

[35] Presumably a local (Umma) variant of b a r s u $_{(3)}$ - g a (see Steinkeller 1995: 56, and Heimpel 1993: 127–29), used at Umma between AS 6 and ŠS 4.

8.	nig$_2$-^{geš}tag-ga lugal	(for) the nig$_2$-tag-offerings of the king.
9.	giri$_3$ sagi-ne	Conveyor: The cupbearers.
10.	^{d}šara$_2$ umma^{ki}	(For) Šara of Umma.
11.	2(diš) udu niga 5(diš) udu u$_2$ 6(diš) udu bar-ba zi-ga	2 fattened sheep, 5 grass(-fed) sheep, 6 sheep without fleece,
12.	1(diš) sila$_4$ bar-ba zi-ga 3(diš) maš$_2$	1 lamb without fleece, 3 goats,
13.	^{d}šara$_2$ KI.AN^{ki}	(for) Šara of KIAN.
14.	6(diš) udu niga 2(diš) udu u$_2$	6 fattened sheep, 2 grass(-fed) sheep,

side B

1.	3(diš) sila$_4$ bar-ba zi-ga 1(diš) [x]	3 lambs without fleece, 1. . . . ,
2.	^{d}šul-gi	(for) Šulgi.
3.	5(diš) udu niga 1(diš) udu u$_2$ 1(diš) maš$_2$	5 fattened sheep, 1 grass(-fed) sheep, 1 goat,
4.	1(diš) sila$_4$ bar-ba zi-ga	1 lamb without fleece,
5.	^{d}amar-^{d}suen	(for) Amar-Suen.
6.	3(diš) udu x bara$_2$ gir$_{13}$-geš^{ki}	3 sheep . . . (for) the dais at/in Girgeš.
7.	1(diš) udu ^{d}en-lil$_2$	1 sheep (for) Enlil.
8.	1(diš) udu balag u$_4$ nu$_2$-a	1 sheep (for the) “Harp of the disappearance (of the moon).”
9.	3(diš) udu ^{d}gu-la umma^{ki}	3 sheep (for) Gula of Umma.
10.	1(diš) maš$_2$ šu-nir gu$_2$-de$_3$-na	1 goat (for) the emblem of Gu(e)dena.
11.	1(diš) udu siskur$_2$ e$_2$ maš	1 sheep (for) the offerings of the Emaš.
12.	1(diš) udu 1(diš) udu bar-ba zi-ga	1 sheep, 1 sheep without fleece,
13.	1(diš) maš$_2$ ^{d}nin-eb-gal	1 goat, (for) Nin-ebgal.

side C

1.	2(diš) udu 1(diš) sila$_4$ bar-⌜ba⌝ [zi]-ga	2 sheep, 1 lamb without fleece,
2.	^{d}en-[ki]	(for) Enki.
3.	1(diš) udu ^{d}kar-ra-⌜du⌝	1 sheep (for) Karadu.
4.	1(diš) maš$_2$ a de$_2$-a ^{d}dumu-[zi]	1 goat, libations (for) Dumuzi.
5.	1(diš) udu ^{d}nin-e$_{11}$-e	1 sheep (for) Nin-E'e.
6.	1(diš) udu ^{d}nin-^{d}da-⌜lagaš⌝[^{ki}]	1 sheep (for) Nin-Da-Lagaš.
7.	1(u) 2(diš) udu 1(diš) udu bar-ba zi-ga	12 sheep, 1 sheep without fleece,
8.	4(diš) sila$_4$ bar-ba zi-ga	4 lambs without fleece,
9.	eš$_3$-eš$_3$ ša$_3$ nig$_2$-^{geš}tag-[ga] dingir-re-ne	(for) the shrines of the nig$_2$-tag-offerings of the gods.
10.	1(diš) udu niga 1(diš) udu siskur$_2$	1 fattened sheep, 1 sheep, offerings.
11.	⌜giri$_3$⌝ du-u$_2$-du$_{11}$ igi-du$_8$	Conveyor: Du-udu, the igi-du$_8$.[36]

[36] Sallaberger (1993: 92) suggested that Du-udu (D U - u$_2$ - K A) was a “seer,” employed as a cultic technician in the agricultural administration and knowledgeable about the correct timing of offerings. See also Heimpel 2009 for the term i g i - n u - d u$_8$ and workers who have been blinded. i g i - d u$_8$ is also read p a l i l (Akkadian *pālilu*, guard from *palālu*, to watch over) in some contexts (especially divine epithets). A title a i g i - d u$_8$, possibly a water inspector, is also attested, primarily in Girsu and occasionally in Umma.

side D

1.	sa$_2$-du$_{11}$ dingir-re-ne ki a-lu$_5$-lu$_5$-ta	Regular (deliveries for) the gods. From Alulu.
2.	kišib$_3$ ensi$_2$-ka	Sealed tablet of the Governor.
3.	iti nesag	Month "First Fruits."
4.	mu en eridu^{ki} ba-hun	Year: "The En-priest of Eridu was installed."

seal (S005907)

col. i

1.	^{d}amar-^{d}suen	Amar-Suen,
2.	nita kal-ga	strong man,
3.	lugal uri$_5$^{ki}-ma	king of Ur,
4.	lugal an ub-da limmu$_2$-ba	king of the four corners (of the world):

col. ii

1.	ur-^{d}li$_9$-si$_4$	Ur-Lisi,
2.	ensi$_2$	governor
3.	umma^{ki}	of Umma,
4.	ARAD$_2$-zu	(is) your slave.

Other Sealed Tags

Five tags in the collection have no inscription but only one or two seal impressions (Nos. 7–11). The purpose of these documents remains unclear.

No. 7. *MS 1942/1 (Umma, —)*

seal 1 (S002014)[37]

1.	ba-sa$_6$	Basa,
2.	dub-sar	scribe,
3.	dumu lugal-sa$_6$-⸢ga⸣	child of Lugal-saga.

seal 2 (S005354)

1.	ur-^{d}šara$_2$	Ur-Šara,
2.	dub-sar	scribe,
3.	dumu lugal-ušur$_4$	child of Lugal-ušur.

Both seals on text No. 7 have the typical Ur III-period presentation scene of a worshipper being introduced into the presence of a seated divine being (possibly the king) by a personal deity. However, whereas the worshipper in Ur-Šara's seal, most likely Ur-Šara himself, is being led by the hand by a deity in front of him, Basa is being blessed by a deity standing immediately behind him. Since Basa had another seal, where he was introduced in the same way as Ur-Šara, in use until Š 45 (see Mayr n.d.: 183, seal 113A), this tag most likely dates to somewhere between Š 46 and the last attested use of this seal in ŠS 8. The reverse is true for Ur-Šara, whose seal with a deity standing behind him is attested between Š 31 and Š 43, while his seal depicting him led by a deity, as on this tag, is dated from Š 43 to AS 5. Both persons also had other seals mentioning the governors of Umma (see Mayr n.d.: 429–31 for Ur-Šara's seals).

[37] Basa, child of Lugal-saga had 4 different seals, according to Mayr (n.d.: 182–83); the one on this tablet is Mayr's seal 113D.

No. 8. *MS 1942/2 (Umma, —)*

seal (S000223)

1.	lugal-nesag-e	Lugal-nesage,
2.	dub-sar	scribe,
3.	dumu da-a-gi$_{4}$	child of Dayagi.

The seal has a standard presentation scene, with an additional divine figure behind the throne.[38]

No. 9. *MS 1942/6 (Umma, —)*

seal (S000493.2)[39]

1.	[ur-^{d}]⸢nun⸣-gal	Ur-Nungal,
2.	[dub]-⸢sar⸣	scribe,
3.	[dumu] ur-^{d}šara$_{2}$	child of Ur-Šara,
4.	ša$_{13}$-dub-ba-⸢ka⸣	chief archivist.

The seal has a standard presentation scene, with a lion depicted under the inscription. This is the seal that Ur-Nungal used when sealing most of the bullae together with Lu-kala (discussed above, see also Mayr n.d.: 419).

No. 10. *MS 1942/7 (Umma, —)*

seal (S004448)

1.	ur-e$_{2}$-maḫ	Ur-Emaḫ,
2.	dub-sar	scribe,
3.	dumu ur-^{d}⸢šara$_{2}$⸣	child of Ur-Šara,
4.	ša$_{13}$-dub-⸢ba-ka⸣	chief archivist.

The seal has a standard presentation scene. It is only attested on three tablets, only one of which is published: CST 574 (ŠS 7). Of the two unpublished tablets, OIM A02753 is dated to ŠS 8, and RBC 447 lacks a date.

No. 11. *MS 1942/8 (Umma, —)*

seal (S004065)[40]

1.	⸢ša$_{3}$⸣-ku$_{3}$-ge	Ša-kuge,
2.	dumu ḫe-sa$_{6}$-ge	child of Ḫesage,
3.	[išib ^{d}šara$_{2}$-ka]	išib-priest of Šara.

The seal has a standard presentation scene.

Commodity Tags

There are thirteen small tags in the Schøyen Collection, which can be assumed once to have been attached to commodities (Nos. 12–24). Three of these, Nos. 12–14, have perforations in the left side where a string once connected the tag to the commodities listed in the text.

[38] The impressions used by Mayr (n.d.) do not include a standing figure behind the throne (see p. 323).

[39] See Mayr n.d.: 419 (seal no. 1025B).

[40] According to Mayr (n.d.: 349), Šakuge had three seals, but it is not clear which one was rolled on text No. 11.

No. 12. *MS 2023 (Umma?, —)*

obv.

1.	siki tug$_2$ nig$_2$-lam$_2$ 4(diš)-kam us$_2$	Wool for nig$_2$-lam$_2$ garments,[41] 4th class, lesser (quality);
2.	nig$_2$-du$_{10}$-ga-mu na-gada[42]	Nigdugamu, herdsman.

rev. (*blank*)

No. 13. *MS 4715/19 (—)*

obv.

1.	sa$_{10}$ gi	Barter with reed.
2.	kišib$_3$ ur-ba-ba	Sealed tablet of Ur-Baba.

rev. (*blank*)

No. 14. *MS 1942/12 (Umma, —)*

obv.

1.	kišib$_3$ lugal-ḫe$_2$-gal$_2$ gu-za-la$_2$	Sealed tablet of Lugal-ḫegal, "throne-bearer,"[43]
2.	u$_3$ la-ni-mu dub-sar	and Lanimu, scribe.

rev. (*blank*)

The remaining nine small tags are without perforations, and it cannot therefore be established beyond doubt whether they were physically attached to the commodities described in the text. They are all concerned with textiles. Since none of these tags records any quantities it is likely that they were wrapped in the textiles they describe. All of the textiles mentioned in these documents are low grade. None of the nine documents is sealed.

No. 15. *MS 1943/7 (—)*

obv.

1.	tug$_2$ uš-bar	Weaver(-quality) textiles.

rev. (*blank*)

No. 16. *MS 1943/1 (—)*

obv.

1.	tug$_2$ aktum 3(diš)-kam us$_2$	aktum textiles of third class, lesser (quality).

rev. (*blank*)

---

[41] Equivalent to Akkadian *lamaḫuššû*; see Waetzoldt 1980–83: 22.

[42] For this personal name, see also BPOA 2, 2404 (BM 112160) from Umma.

[43] Although perhaps originally a cultic title, the gu-za-la$_2$ of the Ur III period can hardly be regarded as anything but an ordinary client of the state doing manual labor.

No. 17. *MS 1943/9 (—)*

obv.

1. tug$_2$ aktum 4(diš)-kam us$_2$	aktum textiles of fourth class, lesser (quality).

rev. (*blank*)

No. 18. *MS 1943/2 (—)*

obv.

1. tug$_2$ gu$_2$-e$_3$ 3(diš)-kam us$_2$	gu$_2$-e textiles of third class, lesser (quality).

rev. (*blank*)

No. 19. *MS 1943/3 (—)*

obv.

1. tug$_2$ bar-dul$_5$ [. . . *n*(diš)]-kam us$_2$	bar-dul$_5$ textiles[44] of nth class, lesser (quality).

rev. (*blank*)

No. 20. *MS 1943/8 (—)*

obv.

1. tug$_2$ bar-si šu	bar-si textiles, hand-quality(?).

rev. (*blank*)

No. 21. *MS 1943/10 (—)*

1. tug$_2$ bar-si us$_2$ nin	bar-si textiles, lesser (quality), lady(?).

rev. (*blank*)

No. 22. *MS 1943/4 (—)*

1. tug$_2$ ba-tab du$_8$-ḫu-um 4(diš)-kam ⌜us$_2$⌝	ba-tab du$_8$-ḫu-um textiles of fourth class, lesser (quality).[45]

rev. (*blank*)

No. 23. *MS 1943/6 (—)*

obv.

1. gada us$_2$	Flax, lesser (quality).

rev. (*blank*)

One further document is grouped with the tags in this study, although it has no perforations. Text No. 24 is not sealed and does not list any commodities. Its purpose remains obscure.

---

[44] Equivalent to Akkadian *kusītu*. See Waetzoldt 1980–83: 21.

[45] See, e.g., Waetzoldt 1972: 157 discussing UET 3, 1616: 9.

No. 24. *MS 1943/5 (Umma, —)*

1.	lugal-ušur$_x$(LAL$_2$.TUG$_2$)	Lugal-ušur,
2.	dumu ur-šul	child of Ur-Šul.

rev. (*blank*)

One other possible tag has been included with the miscellaneous texts in Chapter 12 as text No. 226.

3
TIMEKEEPING

The task of managing and administrating the Ur III state was facilitated by a fairly standardized administrative calendar that was based on the already centuries-old tradition of a division of the year into twelve administrative months of thirty days each (Englund 1988). Intercalation was used to keep the administrative calendar synchronized with the solar year. Regional calendars, ultimately based on cultic calendars rooted in local traditions, often varied. The task of bringing these into agreement was ongoing throughout the Ur III period.

Each year was named according to an important event which had taken place in the preceding year. Since the calendars of the various provinces of the Ur III state were never fully synchronized, the new year would be reached at different times across the state. When a city reached the new year ahead of the capital, administrators would be forced to call the new year "year following x" until the capital city also reached new year and proclaimed its name (Dahl 2010b).

Although year-name lists were almost certainly kept for administrative purposes, few of these are known. The following text (first discussed in Dahl 2007: 5 n. 18, published by George 2011 as CUSAS 17 no. 101) lists abbreviated year-names from Amar-Suen's first year to Ibbi-Suen's fourth year. Although nothing is known for certain about the provenience of this text, it is possible to speculate that it was written in Umma, where no text is dated to after Ibbi-Suen's fourth year, the final year of this list. The last year-name of Amar-Suen and Šu-Suen is followed by a double ruling.

No. 25. *MS 1915 = CUSAS 17, 101 (Umma$^?$, AS 1 to IS 4)*

obv.

1.	mu ^{d}amar-^{d}suen lugal	Year: "Amar-Suen (was) king."
2.	mu ^{d}amar-^{d}suen lugal-e ur-bi$_2$-lum mu-ḫul	Year: "Amar-Suen, king, destroyed Urbilum."
3.	mu ^{geš}gu-za ^{d}en-lil$_2$-la$_2$ ba-dim$_2$	Year: "The throne of Enlil was fabricated."
4.	mu en-maḫ-gal-an-na ba-ḫun	Year: "En-maḫgalana was installed."
5.	mu en unu$_6$-gal ^{d}inanna ba-ḫun	Year: "Enunugal (the En-priest of) Inanna was installed."
6.	mu ša-aš-šu$_2$-ru$^{⸢ki⸣}$ ba-ḫul	Year: "Šašru was destroyed."
7.	mu ḫu-ḫu-nu-ri^{ki} ba-⸢ḫul⸣	Year: "Ḫuḫnuri was destroyed."
8.	mu en eridu^{ki} ba-ḫun	Year: "The En-priest of Eridu was installed."
9.	mu en ga-eš$_3$ ba-ḫun *(double ruling)*	Year: "The En-priest of Ga'eš was installed."
10.	⸢mu $^{d⸣}$šu-^{d}suen lugal	Year: "Šu-Suen (was) king."
11.	mu ma$_2$ dara$_3$ abzu ⸢ba⸣-ab-du$_8$	Year: "The boat 'the ibex of the Abzu' was caulked."
12.	⸢mu⸣ si-ma-num$^{⸢ki⸣}$ ba-ḫul	Year: "Simanum was destroyed."
13.	mu bad$_3$ mar-tu ba-du$_3$	Year: "The Martu wall was built."
14.	mu us$_2$-sa bad$_3$ mar-tu ba-du$_3$	Year following: "The Martu wall was built."
15.	mu na-ru$_2$-a maḫ ba-ru$_2$	Year: "The lofty stela was erected."
16.	mu ma-⸢da⸣ za-ba-ša-li^{ki} ba-ḫul	Year: "The territory of Zabšali was destroyed."
17.	mu ma$_2$-gur$_8$ maḫ ba-dim$_2$	Year: "The lofty barge was fashioned."

rev.

1.	mu e$_2$ ^{d}šara$_2$ ba-du$_3$	Year: "The house of Šara was built."
	(*double ruling*)	
2.	mu ^{d}i-bi$_2$-^{d}suen lugal	Year: "Ibbi-Suen (was) king."
3.	mu en ^{d}inanna unug^{ki} maš-e i$_3$-pa$_3$	Year: "The En-priest of Inanna of Uruk was chosen by omen."
4.	mu si-mu-ru-um^{ki} ba-ḫul	Year: "Simurum was destroyed."
	(*blank space*)	

Other texts, provisionally classified as school texts, record annual events that either drew from known lists of year-names or served to reinforce their memorization. One such text, No. 26, presumably lists offerings of oxen for three major festivals in eleven consecutive years (Cohen 2015: 166 n. 11). It is one of a pair of near-identical documents, the other being SNAT 274 (BM 106413).[46] Since both copies of this text lack the usual administrative terminology, and since the unusual format (lenticular) was otherwise reserved in Ur III times for the so-called "cadaster" texts from the Girsu province, they have been classified as school texts (for other examples of Ur III practice texts, see Chapter 12). The year-names listed in the two texts are exceedingly abbreviated; they are expanded in the translation to the usual forms found in the administrative texts.

No. 26. *MS 1939 (Umma?, Š 33 to Š 44)*

obv. col. i

1.	⸢3(diš)⸣ gu$_4$ ezem 3(diš) ku$_3$	3 oxen, (for) the 3 shiny festivals,
2.[47]	mu us$_2$-sa si-mu-<ru-um> a-ra$_2$ 3(diš$_{tenû}$)-kam	(of the) year following: "Simurrum (was destroyed) for the third time."
3.	3(diš) gu$_4$ ezem 3(diš) ku$_3$	3 oxen, (for) the three shiny festivals,
4.	mu an-ša-an^{ki}	(of the) year: "Anšan (was destroyed)."
5.	⸢3(diš)⸣ gu$_4$ ezem 3(diš) ku$_3$	3 oxen, (for) the three shiny festivals,
6.	mu us$_2$-sa an-ša-an^{ki}	(of the) year following: "Anšan (was destroyed)."
7.	⸢3(diš)⸣ gu$_4$ ezem 3(diš) ⸢ku$_3$⸣	3 oxen, (for) the three shiny festivals,
8.	mu ^{d}nanna kar-⸢zi⸣-da	(of the) year: "Nanna of Karzida (was brought into his house)."[48]
9.	3(diš) gu$_4$ ezem 2(diš) ⸢ku$_3$⸣	3 oxen, (for) the two shiny festivals,
10.	mu bad$_3$ ba-du$_3$	(of the) year: "The wall was built."
11.	3(diš) gu$_4$ ezem 3(diš) ⸢ku$_3$⸣	3 oxen, (for) the three shiny festivals,
12.	mu us$_2$-sa bad$_3$ [ba-du$_3$]	(of the) year following: "The wall was built."
13.	3(diš) gu$_4$ ezem ⸢3(diš)?⸣ [ku$_3$]	3 oxen, (for) the three shiny festivals,
14.	⸢mu e$_2$ puzur$_4$⸣ -da-[gan]	(of the) year: "The house of Puzriš-Dagan (was built)."

---

[46] A further copy seems to exist at Yale (personal communication Verderame); Cohen 2015: 166 n. 11 draws attention to SNAT 403, which also mentions three festivals (rev. 3: ezem 3(diš)-a-ba).

[47] SNAT 274 obv. 2: mu us$_2$-sa mu a-ra$_2$ 3(diš)-kam.

[48] Note that the brevity of the year formula excludes a conclusion as to the origin of the document: the year formula for Šulgi 36 differs slightly between all the major sites in the Ur III state.

obv. col. ii

1.	3(diš) gu$_4$ ezem 3(diš) ku$_3$	3 oxen, (for) the three shiny festivals,
2.[49]	mu us$_2$-sa e$_2$	(of the) year following: "The house (of Puzriš-Dagan was built)."
3.	3(diš) ⸢gu$_4$⸣ ezem 2(diš) ku$_3$	3 oxen, (for) the two shiny festivals,
4.[50]	mu us$_2$-sa e$_2$ puzur$_4^!$(PU$_3$.<ŠA>) mu us$_2$-sa-bi	(of the) second year following the year: "The house of Puzriš-Dagan (was built)."
5.	2(diš) ⸢gu$_4$⸣ ezem 3(diš) ku$_3$	2 oxen, (for) the three shiny festivals,
6.	mu ša-aš-ru^{ki} ba-hul	(of the) year: "Šašrum was destroyed."
7.	⸢3(diš) gu$_4$⸣ ezem 2(diš) ku$_3$	3 oxen, (for) the two shiny festivals,
8.	mu en ^{d}nanna	(of the) year: "The En-priestess of Nanna (was chosen by omen)."
9.	⸢3(diš)⸣ gu$_4$ ezem 3(diš) ku$_3$	3 oxen, (for) the three shiny festivals,
10.	⸢mu⸣ si-mu-ru-um^{ki}	(of the) year: "Simurum (was destroyed)."
	(blank space)	

rev. *(blank)*

These school texts, together with real administrative documents spanning several years or giving the distance in years and months between two accounting points, have been used to establish the correct sequence of the years of the Ur III rulers and to sort out, as far as possible, the intercalations at various locations.[51] It is important to remember that this was not the original purpose of these texts. Due to the scarcity of texts from the early part of the Ur III period, some uncertainty remains concerning the ordering of the years of Ur-Namma, and also some of the early years of Šulgi.

These interesting documents aside, it is noteworthy that no year-name proclamations or official documents, giving the full names and not the abbreviated forms, have been recovered from the Ur III period.[52]

Similarly, official month-name lists are not known from the Ur III period, but many documents list the monthly progression of, for example, work crews. Such lists can be used to reconstruct the administrative calendar of the Ur III state. A set of Umma texts list the monthly progression of work crews and conclude with calculations of the average number of man-days available each month and the total man-days for the accounting period. Apart from showcasing the arithmetical skills of the Ur III accountants, these texts highlight the pre-planned nature of the amounts and numbers in the Ur III bookkeeping documents.

MVN 21, 212 (Umma, AS 6 i to xiii)

obv.

1.	2(geš$_2$) 5(u) 7(diš) ⸢geme$_2$⸣ [3(ban$_2$)]	177 female dependent workers (receiving) 3 ban$_2$ (each a month).
2.	1(u) 5(diš) geme$_2$ [a$_2$ ½(diš)]	15 female dependent workers working at half (output).
3.	iti še-sag$_{11}$-ku$_5$	Month: "Harvest."

[49] SNAT 274 obv. 16: mu us$_2$-sa e$_2$ puzur$_{4\text{puzur}4}$-da-gan.

[50] SNAT 274 rev. 1: mu us$_2$-sa e$_2$ puzur$_4$-da-gan mu us$_2$-sa-bi.

[51] See in particular Gomi 1984a. Gomi discussed the key-text AnOr 12, 314, misunderstood by Schneider to suggest that intercalation was not standardized even within discrete administrative units such as the city of Umma.

[52] See, e.g., the bilingual Old Babylonian tablet OECT 13, 147 recording the year-name of Ammi-ditana 14(b/c) in Sumerian on the obverse and Akkadian on the reverse.

4.	2(geš$_2$) 5(u) 7(diš) geme$_2$ 3(ban$_2$)	177 female dependent workers (receiving) 3 ban$_2$ (each a month).
5.	1(u) 5(diš) geme$_2$ a$_2$ ½(diš)	15 female dependent workers working at half (output).
6.	iti sig$_4$-^{geš}i$_3$-šub-ba-gar	Month: "Brick placed in the mold."
7.	2(geš$_2$) 5(u) 9(diš) geme$_2$ 3(ban$_2$)	179 female dependent workers (receiving) 3 ban$_2$ (each a month).
8.	1(u) 5(diš) geme$_2$ a$_2$ ½(diš)	15 female dependent workers working at half (output).
9.	iti še-kar-ra-gal$_2$-la	Month: "Barley brought to the harbor."
10.	2(geš$_2$) 5(u) 9(diš) geme$_2$ 3(ban$_2$)	179 female dependent workers (receiving) 3 ban$_2$ (each a month).
11.	1(u) 5(diš) geme$_2$ a$_2$ ½(diš)	15 female dependent workers working at half (output).
12.	iti nesag	Month: "First fruit."
13.	3(geš$_2$) geme$_2$ 3(ban$_2$)	180 female dependent workers (receiving) 3 ban$_2$ (each a month).
14.	1(u) 5(diš) geme$_2$ a$_2$ ½(diš)	15 female dependent workers working at half (output).
15.	iti dal	Month: "Flight."
16.	3(geš$_2$) la$_2$ 2(diš) geme$_2$ 3(ban$_2$)	178 female dependent workers (receiving) 3 ban$_2$ (each a month).
17.	1(u) 5(diš) geme$_2$ a$_2$ ½(diš)	15 female dependent workers working at half (output).
18.	iti šu-numun	Month: "Seeding."
19.	2(geš$_2$) 5(u) 7(diš) geme$_2$ 3(ban$_2$)	177 female dependent workers (receiving) 3 ban$_2$ (each a month).
20.	1(u) 5(diš) geme$_2$ a$_2$ ½(diš)	15 female dependent workers working at half (output).
21.	iti min-eš$_3$	Month: "Double sanctuary."
22.	3(geš$_2$) [3(diš)] ⸢geme$_2$⸣ 3(ban$_2$)	183 female dependent workers (receiving) 3 ban$_2$ (each a month).

rev.

1.	1(u) 5(diš) geme$_2$ a$_2$ ½(diš)	15 female dependent workers working at half (output).
2.	iti e$_2$-iti-6(diš)	Month: "House-month-six."
3.	3(geš$_2$) 4(diš) geme$_2$ 3(ban$_2$)	184 female dependent workers (receiving) 3 ban$_2$ (each a month).
4.	1(u) 5(diš) geme$_2$ a$_2$ ½(diš)	15 female dependent workers working at half (output).
5.	iti ^{d}li$_9$-si$_4$	Month: "Lisi."
6.	3(geš$_2$) 2(diš) geme$_2$ 3(ban$_2$)	182 female dependent workers (receiving) 3 ban$_2$ (each a month).
7.	1(u) 5(diš) geme$_2$ a$_2$ ½(diš)	15 female dependent workers working at half (output).

8.	iti ezem-^{d}šul-gi	Month: "Festival of Šulgi."
9.	3(geš$_2$) 1(diš) geme$_2$ 3(ban$_2$)	181 female dependent workers (receiving) 3 ban$_2$ (each a month).
10.	1(u) 5(diš) geme$_2$ a$_2$ ½(diš)	15 female dependent workers working at half (output).
11.	iti pa$_4$-u$_2$-e	Month: "Pa'u'e."
12.	3(geš$_2$) geme$_2$ 3(ban$_2$)	180 female dependent workers (receiving) 3 ban$_2$ (each a month).
13.	1(u) 5(diš) geme$_2$ a$_2$ ½(diš)	15 female dependent workers working at half (output).
14.	iti ^{d}dumu-zi	Month: "Dumuzi."
15.	2(geš$_2$) 5(u) la$_2$ 1(diš) geme$_2$ 3(ban$_2$)	169 female dependent workers (receiving) 3 ban$_2$ (each a month).
16.	1(u) 5(diš) geme$_2$ a$_2$ ½(diš)	15 female dependent workers working at half (output).
17.	iti diri	Month: "Extra."
	(*blank line*)	
18.	šunigin[53] 3(geš'u) 8(geš$_2$) 4(u) 6(diš) geme$_2$ 3(ban$_2$)	Total: 2326 female dependent workers (receiving) 3 ban$_2$ (each a month).
19.	šunigin 3(geš$_2$) 1(u) 5(diš) geme$_2$ a$_2$ ½(diš)	Total: 195 female dependent workers working at half (output).
20.	3(ban$_2$) igi 1(u) 3(diš)-gal$_2$-bi 2(geš$_2$) 5(u) [9(diš)]	(The female dependent workers receiving) 3 ban$_2$ (monthly) its 13th is 179.
21.	½(diš) igi 1(u) 3(diš)-gal$_2$-bi 1(u) 5(diš)	(The female) half (output workers) its 13th is 15.
22.	iti 1(u) 3(diš)-kam ur-^{d}nin-tu i$_3$-[dab$_5$]	It is of 13 months. Ur-Nintu seized.
23.	mu ša-aš-ru-um^{ki}	Year: "When Šašrum (was destroyed)."

In this well-preserved example of the genre (discussed again in Chapter 8, under work-crew lists), the accountant listed the progression in numbers of a work crew consisting of two categories of female dependent workers—those receiving three ban$_2$ (c. 30 liters) a month, and those working at half output—over one year with an intercalated month. The extra month is placed after the final month of the year, the month "Dumuzi."[54] Over the thirteen months covered by the text the numbers of female dependent workers receiving three ban$_2$ a month—the standard ration for female dependent workers during the Ur III period[55]—fluctuated between a minimum of 169 (in the extra month) and a maximum of 184 (in the month "Lisi"). Usually, texts such as this one will see a steady slow reduction in the numbers of workers over the period of accounting. The fate of the women exiting or entering the record is unknown. They may have fallen ill, died, fled, or retired from the workforce, some may have recovered from illness or new workers may have been added in their place, others may have been returned from flight. In this particular example, the number (15) of half-output dependent female workers stayed the same during the thirteen months. Following a total of first the women receiving three ban$_2$, and then the half-output women, the accountant calculated the average monthly numbers available to the overseer. In the case of the regular workers the result is unfortunately partly broken but was probably 179, which is 0.1 away from the actual 13th fraction of 2326 (178.923). Obviously, the 13th of the total of the half-output workers was fifteen, as this number remained constant over the thirteen months of the text. It

---

[53] Following CDLI conventions, the compound ŠU + LAGAB is here given the reading šunigin.

[54] Before Šulgi's 40th year the intercalendrical month was placed after the first month of the year in Umma: see Gomi 1984a.

[55] Gelb 1965: 236.

was these two final numbers which would be inserted into the debits of the running account of the overseer. There they would be expressed as "x female dependent workers for thirteen months."

For the less well-established calendars of smaller settlements, painstaking reconstructions, based sometimes on only pairs of month names in overlapping texts, must be used to establish the calendar.[56] For an overview of the calendars of the Ur III period, see the list of Ur III month names at the CDLI.[57]

Intercalation was not used with any strict regularity but out of a need to synchronize calendars with the cultic solar year and the regional calendars with one another.

Text No. 27 is a short administrative receipt from Umma, recording the total expenditure of barley for a group of slaves over a period of one year with thirteen months. Many such documents exist.

No. 27. *MS 1947/1 (Umma, IS 3–i to xiii)*

obv.

1.	3(geš'u) 7(geš$_2$) 1(u) 5(aš) 3(barig) 1(ban$_2$) 5(diš) sila$_3$ še gur	2235 gur, 3 barig, 1 ban$_2$, 5 sila$_3$ of barley.
2.	še-ba geme$_2$ ARAD$_2$-da	Barley rations for male and female slaves.
3.	ša$_3$ umma^{ki}	Within Umma.
4.	iti 1(u) 3(diš)-kam	For 13 months.
5.	iti še-sag$_{11}$-ku$_5$-ta	From month "Harvest,"

rev.

1.	iti diri-še$_3$	to month "Extra."
2.	ki gu-du-du-ta	From Gududu.
3.	kišib$_3$ ur-^{d}nun-gal	Sealed tablet of Ur-Nungal.
	(*blank space*)	
4.	mu ^{d}i-bi$_2$-^{d}suen lugal-e si-mu-ru-um^{ki} mu-ḫul	Year: "Ibbi-Suen, king, destroyed Simurum."

The amount of barley recorded in this text is very large (670,695 sila$_3$, probably around four hundred tonnes), enough to feed about 1,700 persons for one year.

The distinctiveness of the local calendars is often helpful in assigning an ancient text to its original provenience.

There is no indication in the administrative texts that the months were further subdivided, as was the case in the slightly younger Old Assyrian texts (see, e.g., Dercksen 2011).

---

[56] The calendar of the Turam-ili archive, first reconstructed by Widell 2003, is now understood to have been the calendar of the settlement Irisagrig, also read Āl-Šarrākī (Owen 2013: 64).

[57] https://cdli.ucla.edu/tools/ur3months/month.html.

4
ACCOUNTS

The standard word for an account in Sumerian is nig$_2$-ka$_9$ ("things counted").[58] Although most accounts are multi-column documents, some are very short. There are two examples of short accounts in the Schøyen Collection, texts Nos. 28 and 29. Text No. 28 is an account concerning a certain Ur-Šulpa'e. It consists of only thirteen lines.

Short Accounts

No. 28. *MS 2019/2 (Umma, IS 4?)*

obv.

1.	2(u) 1(aš) 2(barig)$^{!}$[59] še gur	21 gur, 2 barig of barley,
2.	ki-su$_7$ ^{geš}asal$_2$-du$_3$-a-ta	from the threshing floor of (the field) Asal-dua.
3.	1(aš) 2(barig) 3(ban$_2$) gur ša$_3$-gal anše iti še-sag$_{11}$-ku$_5$	1 gur, 2 barig, 3 ban$_2$ (of barley) fodder for the onagers (in the) month: "Harvest."
4.	1(barig) še-ba šeš-kal-la-ka iti še-sag$_{11}$-ku$_5$	1 barig of barley-rations for Šeš-kala (in the) month "Harvest."
5.	2(u) 2(aš) 4(barig) 3(ban$_2$) gur	(Total:) 22 gur, 4 barig, 3 ban2 (of barley ~the "debits").

rev.

1.	ša$_3$-bi-⸢ta⸣	Out of it:
2.	1(u) 8(aš) gur	18 gur (barley),
3.	ša$_3$-gal anše iti 1(u) 2(diš)-kam	fodder for onagers for 12 months.
4.	2(aš) ⸢1(barig) še⸣-ba šeš-kal-la	2 gur, 1 barig of barley-rations for Šeš-kala.
5.	⸢2(aš)⸣ 1(barig) še-ba ur-am$_3$-ma	2 gur, 1 barig of barley-rations for Ur-amma.
	(blank space)	
6.	šunigin 2(u) 2(aš) 4(barig) še gur	Total: 22 gur, 4 barig (~the "credits").
7.	nig$_2$-ka$_9$ ak ⸢ur-^{d}šul⸣-pa-⸢e$_3$⸣	Account of Ur-Šulpa'e.
8.	mu si-mu-ru-um^{ki} ba-ḫul	Year: "Simurum was destroyed."

Text No. 28 should have terminated with a small deficit, since the total of the debits is larger than that of the credits. The document may have been invalidated in antiquity, as suggested by the scratching across the reverse.

Most short accounts lack many of the technical terms that denote the various sections of the account. These have been hinted at in parentheses in the translation above and will be discussed below.

Whereas text No. 28 is balanced, the following short account No. 29 is not. It also lacks key terminology, and the total of the "credits" is written in the blank space separating the "credits" from the negative balance, the "deficit."

---

[58] Earlier read nig$_2$-ŠID or nig$_2$-kas$_7$. Although the short reading nig$_2$-ka$_9$ is retained here, nig$_2$-kas$_7$, based on the Akkadian borrowing *nikkassu*, might in the end prove more correct. The reading ka$_9$ is based on a late Babylonian entry in MSL 14: 451, Ea VII 6': ka$_9$$^{ka-a}$ | ŠID | *ša* NIG$_2$.ŠID *ni-ka-as-su*, and Reciprocal Ea l. 123 (p. 526): MIN(= ka-a) | ŠID | *ni-ka-as-su*. See also Englund 1990: 26 with n. 93.

[59] This notation almost certainly contains an error, and the 1(barig) written should be emended to 2(barig), to conform with total written in obv. 5: although 2(barig) is written in an odd way in l. 3 (diš over diš), the notation in l. 1 is most certainly 1(diš).

No. 29. *MS 2020/3 (Š 44)*

obv.

1.	3(aš) ninda gur	3 gur of bread,
2.	ninda nig$_2$-gal$_2$-la iti 5(diš)-kam	nig$_2$-gal$_2$-la[60] bread of 5 months (~the "debits").
3.	ša$_3$-bi-ta	Out of it:
4.	3(barig) ur-^{d}dumu-zi-da gu-za-la$_2$	3 barig, (for) Ur-Dumuzida, "throne-bearer."
5.	1(barig) 3(ban$_2$) ama-šim	1 barig, 3 ban$_2$, (for) Ama-šim.
6.	3(barig) lu$_2$-$^{d⌜}$nin-ur$_4$-ra⌝	3 barig, (for) Lu-Nin-ura.

rev.

1.	šu-a-gi-na	Regular[61] (deliveries)
2.	iti 6(diš)-kam	for 6 months.
3.	2(barig) 5(ban$_2$) kišib$_3$ ur-^{d}dumu-zi-da	2 barig, 5 ban$_2$, sealed tablet of Ur-Dumuzida.
	(*blank space with computations*):	
	2(aš) 2(ban$_2$) gur	(Total:) 2 gur, 2 ban$_2$.
4.	zi-ga-am$_3$	is booked out (~the "credits").
5.	la$_2$-ia$_3$ 4(barig) 4(ban$_2$) še	Deficit: 4 barig, 4 ban$_2$ of barley.
6.	nig$_2$-ka$_9$ ak ^{geš}guzza-ni	Account of Guzzani.

left edge

1.	mu si-mu-ru-um^{ki}	Year: "Simurum."

We shall see below how the deficit is dealt with.

Text No. 30, another small account in the collection, also lacks some key terminology and it too did not produce a balance. It records transfers of barley, including long-headed barley (sag-bi gid$_2$-da), for regular (deliveries) (sa$_2$-du$_{11}$). The debits are made up of smaller deliveries from individuals and fields. It has a close parallel in MVN 21, 333.

No. 30. *MS 4310 (Umma, ŠS 5)*

obv.

1.	[1(aš) 2(barig) 3(ban$_2$) še gur sag-bi] gid$_2$-da	1 gur, 2 barig, 3 ban$_2$ of long-headed barley.
2.	[. . . mu ^{d}]⌜šu⌝-^{d}suen lugal-e bad$_3$ mar-tu mu-du$_3$	. . . Year: "Šu-Suen, king, built the Martu wall."
3.	2(aš) gur a-ša$_3$ ^{geš}ma-nu-ta	2 gur, from the Manu field.
4.	2(aš) gur 4(diš) sila$_3$ še gur	2 gur, 4 sila$_3$ of barley,
5.	1(aš) 2(barig) gur 4(diš) sila$_3$ ziz$_2$ gur	1 gur, 2 ban$_2$, 4 sila$_3$ of emmer,
6.	⌜uku$_2$⌝-nu-ti-ta?	From the Ukunuti (field).[62]
7.	4(aš) gur a-ša$_3$ ^{d}nin-ur$_4$-ra-⌜ta$^{?}$⌝	4 gur from the Nin-ura field.
8.	2(aš) 2(barig) 1(ban$_2$) 8(diš) sila$_3$ ziz$_2$ gur	2 gur, 2 barig, 5 ban$_2$, 8 sila$_3$ of emmer,

---

60 It is unclear how nig$_2$-gal$_2$-la, describing bread (ninda) here and elsewhere in the Ur III corpus, is related to nig$_2$-(e$_2$-a)-gal$_2$-la meaning household utensils (see Salonen 1972–75: 225).

61 For šu-a-gi-na, see Sallaberger 1993: 83 and 64 with n. 277 with literature. Sallaberger juxtaposes šu-a-gi-na, "regular" (*regelmäßige*), with nig$_2$-diri, "extraordinary" (*zusätzlige besondere*), deliveries of animals.

62 A field by the name uku$_2$-nu-ti is well attested in Ur III Umma, but whether it had any relation to an institution concerned with "poor" people (uku$_2$) is not known.

9.	kar-ta	From the harbor.
10.	1(aš) 3(ban$_2$) gur ki šeš-kal-la-ta	1 gur, 3 ban$_2$, from Šeš-kala.
11.	5(aš) 2(barig) gur ki e$_2$-gal-e-si-ta	5 gur, 2 barig, from Egal-esi.
12.	1(aš) ⌜4(barig)⌝ x[63] gur še kaš$^?$ nig$_2$ gal$_2$-la iti 1(u) la$_2$ 1(diš$_{tenû}$)-kam	1 gur, 4 barig barley for beer of the possessions(?), for 9 months.
13.	4(ban$_2$) 5(diš) sila$_3$ še ninda iti 3(diš)$^?$-kam	4 ban$_2$, 5 sila$_3$ barley for bread, for 3 months.
14.	⌜4(ban$_2$)$^?$⌝ 5(diš) sila$_3$ u$_4$-de$_3$ gid$_2$-da u$_4$ 1(diš)-kam	4 ban$_2$, 5 sila$_3$ for the uddagiddû[64] of 1 day.

rev.

	(*blank space*)	
1.	šunigin 2(u) 2(aš) 1(ban$_2$) 6(diš) sila$_3$ gur	Total: 22 gur, 1 ban$_2$, 5 sila$_3$ (~the "debits").
2.	ša$_3$-bi-ta	Out of it:
3.	1(u) 8(aš) 2(barig) 3(ban$_2$) 7(diš) sila$_3$ gur	18 gur, 2 barig, 3 ban$_2$, 7 sila$_3$.
4.	sa$_2$-du$_{11}$ iti 3(diš)-kam nig$_2$-diri pa$_4$-u$_2$-e ib$_2$-gar	Regular (deliveries) for 3 months, placed on the "surplus" of Pa'u'e.
5.	3(aš) 2(barig) 3(ban2) ⌜9(diš)[65]⌝ sila$_3$ gur	3 gur, 2 barig, 3 ban$_2$, 9 sila$_3$.
6.	sag-bi gid$_2$-da	Long-headed (grain).
7.	nig$_2$-ka$_9$ ak ^{d}en-ki	Account of Enki,
8.	nigar^{gar}-ki-du$_{10}$	(concerning) Nigar-kidu.
9.	mu-us$_2$-sa ^{d}šu-^{d}suen lugal-e ⌜bad$_3$ mar-tu⌝ mu-⌜du$_3$⌝	Year after: "Šu-Suen, king, built the Martu wall."

References to accounts occur with some frequency in the economic records documenting different administrative activities (e.g., nig$_2$-ka$_9$ PN-ta, "from the account concerning PN").[66] To "draw up an account" and subsequently the technical term "account concerning PN," are expressed using the verb ak, "to do": /nig.ka(s) ak-a/ > nig$_2$-ka$_9$ ak. Consequently nig$_2$-ka$_9$ is here understood as "an account" and nig$_2$-ka$_9$ ak as a "finished account."[67] This term appears as an explicit or implied subscript in all accounts.[68] A product or an administrative function can take the place of the personal name in this formula. Such non-personal

---

[63] Erasure after 4(barig).

[64] The omitted day(s) making up the difference between the lunar month and the administrative 30-day month (Sallaberger 1993: 11 n. 34).

[65] 9(diš) sila$_3$ is needed, but possibly erased here.

[66] See, e.g., NATN 805 (from AS 7) rev. 21: ugu$_2$ nig$_2$-ka$_9$ dam-gar$_3$ ⌜ga$_2$⌝-ga$_2$-dam, "It is to be placed on the 'debits' (ugu = "front-side": see below for an explanation of this term) of the account concerning the 'trade agents.'" OrSP 47–49, 411 (from ŠS 3) obv. 1–6: 1(geš$_2$) 1(aš) 3(barig) 1(ban$_2$) še gur / sa$_{10}$-am$_3$ urudu / ugu$_2$ lu$_2$-kal-la / ba-a-gar / nig$_2$-ka$_9$ KA-guru$_7$-ka / ba-an-zi, "61 gur and 190 sila of barley, exchange for copper, has been transferred to the 'debits' of Lu-kala, it was booked out of the account concerning the chief of the granary."

[67] Compare also MSL 5, 64 (ḪAR-ra II 167): nig$_2$-ka$_9$ | *nik-kas$_2$-[su]*, and l. 168: nig$_2$-ka$_9$ ak-a | MIN(= *nik-kas$_2$-su*) *ep-[šu]*. See also Calvot 1969: 106.

[68] Accounts kept in (archival) tablet containers (pisan dub-ba, see above) were mostly described as nig$_2$-ka$_9$ ak. This suggests that applying the non-finite form of the verb ak to the word nig$_2$-ka$_9$ refers to a completed account. See, e.g., BRM 3, 166, a "tablet container holding the finished account(s) of Abbagina (from the) year AS 6" (pisan dub-ba / nig$_2$-ka$_9$ ak / ab-ba-gi-na / i$_3$-gal$_2$ // (blank space) / mu ša-aš-šu$_2$-ru^{ki} a-ra$_2$ 2(diš)-kam ba-ḫul), and MVN 16, 709, a "tablet container holding the finished account(s) of ARAD$_2$(mu), the chief of the granary (KA-guru$_7$) (in Umma) for four years" (Š 43–46) (pisan dub-ba / nig$_2$-ka$_9$ ak / ARAD$_2$ KA-guru$_7$ / mu 4(diš)-kam / i$_3$-⌜gal$_2$⌝ // mu en ^{d}nanna [maš$_2$]-e i$_3$-pa$_3$-ta / mu ki-maš^{ki} ba-ḫul-še$_3$). Compare the reference to non-finalized accounts in SANTAG 6, 20 (see below, p. 49–50).

accounts may have a colophon reading "silver-account concerning the governor" (nig$_2$-ka$_9$ ak ku$_3$-babbar ensi$_2$-ka),[69] or "wool-account" (nig$_2$-ka$_9$ ak siki).[70]

Several texts can be quoted that refer to the process of drawing up an account. For example: BPOA 2, 2549 (BM 105354, from ŠS 2) rev. 13: nig$_2$-ka$_9$-bi nu-ak kišib$_3$ ur-kalam, "its account has not been made, sealed tablet of Ur-Kalam"; Ledgers pl. 13, 8 (from AS 6) obv. 39: ur-^{d}nun-gal u$_3$ ur-^{d}gu$_2$-nu$_2$-a-ke$_4$ nig$_2$-ka$_9$-bi ib$_2$-ak, "Ur-Nungal and Ur-Gunu'a made the account"; and finally, the inscription on the left edge of the account MVN 10, 102 (from ŠS 2 i to ŠS 2 xii): [nig$_2$]-ka$_9$-bi ur-e$_2$-maḫ-ke$_4$ in-ak "Ur-Emaḫ made its account." It was presumably the job of the chief accountant (ša$_{13}$-dub-ba) to "draw up" the account. At Umma, the office of the chief accountant was not in the hands of the ruling family.[71] However, the exact responsibilities of the accountant are hard to isolate.

Text No. 31 is an account of the cattle of a number of cowhands (gu$_4$-laḫ$_5$, lit. "ox-drivers") under the supervision of Atu the chief cattle-administrator (šuš$_3$).[72] It is one of the few Ur III accounts with an inscription on the left edge. The short note reads: lu$_2$-du$_{10}$-ga ⌜u$_3$⌝ lu$_2$-kar-zi-da im-da-ab-zi, "Lu-duga and Lu-karzida booked it out."[73]

No. 31. *MS 2016 (Umma, ŠS 3 to ŠS 4)*

obv. col. i

1.	1(u) 7(diš) gu$_4$ ab$_2$ ḫi-a	17 mixed oxen and cows,
2.	si-i$_3$-tum ⌜mu si⌝-ma-num$_2$^{ki} ba-ḫul	remainder from the (account of the) year: "Simanum was destroyed."
3.	3(u) 3(diš) gu$_4$ ab$_2$ ḫi-a	33 oxen and cows, mixed,
4.	ki lu$_2$-zabala$_4$^{ki}-ta	from Lu-Zabala.
5.	7(diš) gu$_4$ ab$_2$ ḫi-a	7 oxen and cows, mixed,
6.	ki lugal-ezem-ta	from Lugal-ezem.
7.	3(u) 4(diš) gu$_4$ ab$_2$ ḫi-a	34 oxen and cows, mixed,
8.	ki ab-ba-gi-na-ta	from Abba-gina.
9.	5(diš) gu$_4$ ab$_2$ ḫi-a	5 oxen and cows, mixed,
10.	ki ^{d}šara$_2$-kam-ta	from Šarakam.
11.	1(u) ⌜la$_2$ 1(diš*tenû*)⌝ gu$_4$ ab$_2$ ḫi-a	9 oxen and cows, mixed,
12.	ki ^{d}šara$_2$-a-mu-ta	from Šara-a(ya)mu.
13.	2(diš) gu$_4$ mu 3(aš)	2 oxen, 3-year old,
14.	ki ur-^{d}a-šar$_2$-ta	from Ur-Ašar.
15.	[1(diš)] gu$_4$ geš	[1] yoke-ox,[74]
16.	ki lu$_2$-^{d}šara$_2$-ta	from Lu-Šara.
17.	1(u) 4(diš) gu$_4$ ab$_2$ ḫi-a	14 oxen and cows, mixed,
18.	ki ur-⌜^{d}⌝su$_4$-da-ta	from Ur-Suda.

---

[69] See, e.g., YNER 8, 13 (from ŠS 1 to ŠS 5).

[70] See, e.g., AnOr 7, 262 (from ŠS 2 iii); also AAICAB 1, 1924-666 (from AS 3), an "account concerning the wool of the governor" (rev. viii 4–5: nig$_2$-ka$_9$ ak siki ensi$_2$-ka), discussed in Dahl 2007: 88–90 and fig. 7.

[71] In Umma, the status of the family of Ur-Šara, the chief accountant, is perhaps clearest seen in their involvement in certifying weights and measures for the metal industry (see Dahl 2007: 76–77 and n. 279).

[72] For the title šuš$_3$, see most recently Dahl 2007: 85 ff. For the reading of SAḪAR = šuš$_3$, see Beal 1992: 48.

[73] Compare MCS 1, 54, BM 106045 with a similar inscription on the left edge: start of line broken followed by lu$_2$-du$_{10}$-ga im-da-ab-zi, "Lu-duga booked it out."

[74] Heimpel 1995: 86. Or perhaps (phonetic) for breeding ox, gu$_4$ geš$_3$-du$_3$ (cf. n. 31 above).

col. ii

1.	9(diš) gu$_4$ ab$_2$ ⸢ḫi⸣-[a]	9 oxen and cows, mixed,
2.	ki uš-<mu$^?$>- ⸢ta⸣	from Ušmu(?).[75]
3.	7(diš) gu$_4$ ab$_2$ ḫi-[a]	7 oxen and cows, mixed,
4.	ki lugal-mes-ta	from Lugal-mes.
5.	1(diš) ab$_2$ maḫ$_2$	1 cow, adult,
6.	ki lu$_2$-du$_{10}$-ga-ta	from Lu-duga.
7.	4(diš) gu$_4$ ab$_2$ ḫi-a	4 oxen and cows, mixed,
8.	ki ab-ba-gi-na-ta	from Abba-gina.
9.	3(diš) gu$_4$ ab$_2$ ḫi-a	3 oxen and cows, mixed,
10.	ki al-la-li$_2$-ta	from Allali.
11.	6(diš) gu$_4$ ab$_2$ ḫi-a	6 oxen and cows, mixed.
12.	ki ur-^{geš}gigir unu$_3$ ensi$_2$-ta	from Ur-gigir, cowherd of the governor.
	(blank space)	
13.	ki unu$_3$-de$_3$-ne	(The above is) from the cowherds.
14.	2(u) 1(diš) ab$_2$ maḫ$_2$	21 cows, adult,
15.	8(diš) ab$_2$ mu 3(aš)	8 cows, 3-year old,
16.	1(diš) ab$_2$ mu 2(aš)	1 cow, 2-year old,
17.	7(diš) gu$_4$ ga	7 oxen, suckling (calves),
18.	ki ur-^{d}ba-ba$_6$-ta	from Ur-Baba.

rev. col. i

	(blank space)	
1.	šunigin 3(geš$_2$) 9(diš) gu$_4$ ab$_2$ ḫi-a	Total 189 oxen and cows, mixed.
2.	sag-nig$_2$-gur$_{11}$-ra-kam	(That is) the "debits."
3.	ša$_3$-bi-ta	Out of it:
4.	2(geš$_2$) 5(u) 2(diš) gu$_4$ ab$_2$ ⸢ḫi-a⸣	152 oxen and cows, mixed,
5.	kišib$_3$ uš-mu	sealed tablet of Ušmu.
6.	6(diš) gu$_4$ mu 2(aš)$^?$	6 oxen, 2-year old,
7.	mu-ku$_x$(DU) i$_3$-dab$_5$	seized mu-ku$_x$(DU) delivery,
8.	kišib$_3$ ur-^{d}ba-ba$_6$	sealed tablet of Ur-Baba.
	(blank space)	

col. ii

	(blank space)	
1.	šunigin ⸢2(geš$_2$) 5(u)⸣ 8(diš) gu$_4$ ab$_2$ ḫi-a	Total: 178 oxen and cows, mixed,
2.	zi-ga-am$_3$	are booked out (~the "credits").
3.	la$_2$-ia$_3$ 1(u) 1(diš) gu$_4$ ab$_2$ ḫi-a	"Deficit": 11 oxen and cows, mixed.
	(blank space)	
4.	⸢nig$_2$-ka$_9$ ak⸣ gu$_4$-laḫ$_5$	Finished account of the cowhands (under the supervision of)
5.	a-tu šuš$_3$	Atu, chief cattle-administrator.

---

[75] One should expect to find the Umma fattener Ušmu here. The text has uš followed by what looks like the beginning of a broken ta. However, some space would remain after the ta and the end of the line.

6. mu ^{d}šu-^{d}suen lugal uri$_5$^{ki}-ma-ke$_4$ bad$_3$ mar-tu mu-ri-iq-ti-id-ni-im mu-du$_3$ (*blank space*) — Year: "Šu-Suen, king of Ur, built the Martu wall called Muriq-tidnim."

left edge

1. lu$_2$-du$_{10}$-ga ⸢u$_3$⸣ lu$_2$-kar-zi-da im-da-ab-zi — Lu-duga and Lu-karzida booked it out.

It is the subscript, or colophon, of an account which holds the vital calendar information, and information concerning the person or institution whose activities were being recorded.[76] The date recorded in the colophon is believed to be the terminal date of the accounting period. When the date is only a year-name it is considered an account covering that entire year, completed at the very end of the year, or even during the beginning of the next. Sometimes, the date of accounting is explicitly recorded, and sometimes the duration of the accounting period was also computed and entered into the colophon.[77]

Structure of the Neo-Sumerian Account

The neo-Sumerian account had three sections.[78] The first section can be described as the "debits" of the person whose transactions were recorded and evaluated, i.e., "the accounted," and the second as his "credits." In a third section, between the "credits" section and the colophon recording the date and the account information, the "operating balance" would be recorded. The "credits" and "debits" sections could be further sub-divided. Both sections were summaries of the primary documents recording the transactions of "the accounted" during the period of accounting. During that period, all of the receipts were presumably kept in tablet containers (such as the pisan dub-ba documents discussed above in Chapter 2). The following text lists a number of such containers. It is uncertain whether it is a delivery note or an inventory. Since the text names several different types of tablet container, it may help us to understand how the ancients archived their documents, information otherwise lost due to the inadequate excavation methods and the perishable organic materials used for the tablet containers. The text reads as follows:

SANTAG 6, 20 (Umma?, Š 33 to Š 45):

obv.

1. 1(diš) ^{gi}pisan dub la$_2$-ia$_3$ — One reed-container for tablets recording "arrears."
2. 1(diš) ^{gi}pisan dub nig$_2$-ka$_9$ nu-ak — One reed-container for non-finalized account-tablets.
3. 1(diš) ^{gi}pisan dub ensi$_2$ ma-da — One reed-container for tablets of the governor of the territory.[79]

---

[76] It is important to note that because colophons were inscribed on the upper left corner of the reverse of tablets (according to the original orientation of the tablets, but the lower left corner according to our publications), they have often been damaged. Presumably when archived a tablet would rest on its lower edge (according to the original orientation of the tablets, but the right edge according to our publications), allowing for easy access to the information in its colophon, but also exposing it to wear and tear.

[77] Some accounts state the duration of the accounting period, see, e.g., SNAT 375 (covering AS 6 and AS 7) rev. iv 6: mu 2(diš)-kam, an account of 2 years; and JAOS 90, 268 (an account spanning 12 years, Š 43 through AS 6) rev. iv 6: mu 1(u) 2(diš)-kam.

[78] Englund 2003: §8 fig. 2. See also Neumann 1999: 45–46.

[79] The term ma-da is most likely a loan from Akkadian *mātum*, "land, country." It is often used to refer to areas outside of the core, the old provinces, as in gu$_2$ ma-da, "tribute of the land," a special tax paid by foreign lands (see Steinkeller 1987a). A number of texts from both Umma and Ur mention an area called ma-da umma^{ki}. It is unclear how this relates to the well-known agricultural district in the Umma province called da-umma^{ki}, but it is possible that the latter was shorthand for ma-da umma^{ki}.

rev.

1.	1(diš) ^{gi}pisan dub ugu$_2$-a ga$_2$-ra	One reed-container for tablets transferred to the "debits."
2.	kišib$_3$ da-da-ga	Sealed tablet(s) of Dadaga.
3.	kišib$_3$ ša$_{13}$-dub-ba	Sealed tablet(s) of the accountant.[80]
4.	mu us$_2$-sa a-ra$_2$ 3(diš*tenû*)-kam si-mu-ru-um ba-ḫul-ta	From the year following "The third time Simurum was destroyed,"
5.	mu ur-bi$_2$-lum^{ki}-še$_3$	to the year: "Urbilum (was destroyed)."
6.	1(diš) ^{gi}pisan dub en$_8$-tar	One reed-container for the tablets of the diviner.[81]
7.	1(diš) ^{gi}ma-ad-li$_2$-um kišib$_3$ lu$_2$-dingir-ra	One reed-madlûm;[82] sealed tablet(s) of Lu-dingira.

We shall use this text in the following discussion of the sections of the account, which are each signified here by their own basket for primary documents. The first tablet container mentioned in SANTAG 6, 20 was intended to hold the documents that recorded arrears. The second container was to hold the non-finalized accounts. The content of the third container remains speculative (see n. 79), whereas the fourth container was to hold the receipts of goods to be entered into the "debits" of the account. For the remainder of the objects, see the notes to the text.

"Debits" (sag-nig$_2$-gur$_{11}$-ra-kam)

The Sumerian term used to describe the first section of the neo-Sumerian account is sag-nig$_2$-gur$_{11}$-ra-kam. This term appears after the total of the first section, conforming to the overall textual structure of Sumerian documents, placing the "header" at the end of the section it describes. A literal translation of the term sag-nig$_2$-gur$_{11}$-ra-kam, "it is the head of the goods" (/sag-nig$_2$.gur$_{11}$-ak-am$_3$/), is not very useful for decoding the administrative meaning of the term. A translation "it is the goods that are in the first section of the account," based on the Sumerian names for the different sections of a cuneiform tablet, is certainly much more correct.[83]

---

80 The information in this and the preceding line perhaps indicates that tablets sealed by Dadaga and the (chief)-accountant were kept in these containers, or that special containers for their tablets were recorded with the other ones listed here. This information situates the document in a historical reality when Dadaga held a high office in the administration of the governor of Umma, to whom he was also related (see Dahl 2007).

81 According to Koslova 2000: 70, (notes to the text) read en$_8$(ŠA)-tar for en$_3$(LI)-tar.

82 Possibly a reed stand or hanger for the baskets. See MSL 6, 60, ḪAR-ra VI 102: ^{geš}gur$_2$-ba-an-du$_8$ | MIN(= *kip-pa-tum*) *mad-li-e*, l. 103: ^{geš}gur$_2$-ba-an-du$_8$-du$_8$ | MIN(= *kip-pa-tum*) MIN(= *mad-li-e*). See also Salonen 1965–66: 263: ^{geš}gur$_2$-ba-an-du$_8$ = *kippatu ša napāti* "Bügel des napātu-Eimers." Cf. *CAD* M/I 19: *madlû*, and Gelb 1957: 292 who, following Bezold, suggested a bucket perhaps for drawing water (for that meaning, see also Koslova's notes to the text (Koslova 2000: 70), "zu ^{gi}ma-ad-li$_2$-um s. MVN 3:231 (^{gi}ma-ad-li$_2$-um pu$_2$-še$_3$)"). The translation "bucket" was accepted by Hasselbach (2005: 275, index).

83 See Kraus 1966: 124–26 for the reading of gur$_{11}$(GA), and evidence for an early equation of sag-nig$_2$-gur$_{11}$-ra with *re-eš na-am-ku-ri* (i.e., "head of the goods") based on VS 7, 202: 31 and 25. See also *AHw* 975 *rēšu(m)* C ("Vorderseite") and esp. D ("Beginn, Anfang"): *i-na re-eš$_{15}$ nikkassē*. sag-dub "head of the tablet" is frequently used as a technical term for goods (particularly slaves) of the best quality listed at the beginning of the document: see, e.g., or CUSAS 3, 280 where geme$_2$ sag-dub is listed at the head of a list of female workers of diminishing "quality"; MVN 2, 39 where one guruš engar sag-dub is listed before a "half-output" worker (see below on worker categories). Note that the same terminology is found in texts Nos. 93 and 126 (see n. 386); see also Yoshikawa 1985. See further Englund 2003: §11 and n. 15 (edition of Erlenmeyer 152), where sag-ba is understood as an abbreviation of sag-nig$_2$-gur$_{11}$-ra-kam (/sag-<nig$_2$-gur$_{11}$-ak-am>-bi-ak/).

To transfer goods to the first section of an account is in Sumerian called to "place it on the 'ugu$_2$' of the person."[84]

Many primary documents (see below) record the transfer of goods, often staples, to the "debits" of an account. In rare instances the corresponding entry in an account has been identified (Englund 2003: §10), but so far no examples using the terminology ugu$_2$ . . . ba-a-gar have been identified in this way. The receipt given below would correspond to an entry within the "debits" of the account of Lu-Nanna from the year "when Ibbi-Suen (was) king." Unfortunately, that account has not been recovered.

No. 32. *MS 1947/5 (Umma, IS 1)*

obv.

1.	2(barig) 4(ban$_2$) 5(diš) sila$_3$ še	2 barig, 4 ban$_2$, 5 sila$_3$ of barley,
2.	ki mu-ni-ta	from Muni.
3.	ugu$_2$ lu$_2$-^{d}nanna ba-a-gar	Transferred to the "debits" of Lu-Nanna.
4.	kišib$_3$ gu-du-du	Sealed tablet of Gududu.

rev.

	(*seal impression*)	
1.	mu ^{d}i-bi$_2$-^{d}suen lugal	Year: "Ibbi-Suen (was) king."

seal (S005940)

col. i

1.	^{d}i-bi$_2$-^{d}suen	Ibbi-Suen,
2.	lugal kal-ga	strong king,
3.	lugal uri$_5$^{ki}-ma	king of Ur,
4.	lugal an ub-da limmu$_2$-ba	king of the four corners (of the world):

col. ii

1.	gu-du-du	Gududu,
2.	dub-sar	scribe,
3.	dumu da-da-ga	child of Dadaga,
4.	ensi$_2$	governor
5.	umma^{ki}	of Umma,
6.	ARAD$_2$-zu	(is) your slave.

Among its many (semantically related) lexical meanings, "ugu" is found to be the equivalent of Akkadian *panu(m)*, which in addition to "face," etc., can be translated as the "obverse" of a tablet.[85] Likewise, sag is another word for the "head" of a tablet or the first part of the front side of a tablet. It is used as such in an

---

[84] This is expressed with either the "imperfect" (*marû*) state (+ copula) of the verb gar (e.g., /ugu-a PN ga.ga-ed-am/ > ugu$_2$-(a) PN ga$_2$-ga$_2$-dam, "to be placed on the 'debits' of PN)" (see, e.g., YOS 18, 123 [from AS 9] rev. viii 33: ugu$_2$ a-kal-la ga$_2$-ga$_2$-dam; Princeton 1, 126 [no date], without enclitic copula (am$_3$), rev. 2: ugu$_2$-a ga$_2$-ga$_2$-de$_3$; and finally Princeton 1, 404 [from AS 5 viii] obv. 4: ugu$_2$ lugal-e$_2$-mah-e ga$_2$-ga$_2$-dam), or with the same verb in the "perfect" (*hamṭu*) state (e.g., /ugu-a PN.ak-ak ba-a$^{?}$-gar/ > ugu$_2$-(a) PN-(ka) ba-a-gar) (see, e.g., BIN 5, 322 [from Š 32? xii] rev. 8: ugu$_2$ šeš-a-ni-ka ba-a-gar; L'uomo 47 [from IS 3] obv. 14: ugu$_2$ nu-banda$_3$-gu$_4$ GAN$_2$ gibil ba-a-gar), depending on the administrative activity recorded. See also MVN 16, 843 (from AS 8) rev. 1: ugu$_2$-a nu-ga$_2$-ga$_2$, "it shall not be placed on the 'ugu.'"

[85] See *AHw* 820 *pānu(m)* C 2.

independent context.[86] The reason for calling the "debits" by one word (ugu$_2$) when describing the act of transferring valuables to that section, while naming that same section otherwise (sag(-nig$_2$-gur$_{11}$-ra-kam)) in the account, is obscure to me; however, a solution might be found that is analogous to the juxtaposing of la$_2$-ia$_3$ with si-i$_3$-tum described below. It is worthwhile to note that among the containers in the text quoted above (SANTAG 6, 20) we find a particular box destined for the texts termed "tablets transferred to the debits" (rev. 1: dub ugu$_2$-a ga$_2$-ra).

The sag-nig$_2$-gur$_{11}$-ra-kam can begin with a remainder, si-i$_3$-tum, from the previous account (usually from the previous year), if such a remainder exists.[87] si-i$_3$-tum is an Akkadian loanword in Sumerian, presumably borrowed during the Old Akkadian period.[88] The "remainder" (si-i$_3$-tum) is always expressed in the medium of equivalence of the particular type of account in which it appears.[89]

If a "remainder" (si-i$_3$-tum) is present, it will always occupy the first slot of the "debits" (sag-nig$_2$-gur$_{11}$-ra-kam). A number of documents further specify the "remainder" (si-i$_3$-tum) by calling it the "remainder (of the account) of the Y(ear) N(ame)" (si-i$_3$-tum (nig$_2$-ka$_9$ ak) mu YN), just as we saw in text No. 31,[90] thus further clarifying the administrative nature of the si-i$_3$-tum as the remainder of the account (from the previous accounting period).[91] The first basket in the receipt quoted above (SANTAG 6, 20) was destined to hold the "deficit" (la$_2$-ia$_3$) tablets, presumably so that these could be entered into the accounts of the following accounting period. We know that a la$_2$-ia$_3$ had to be fulfilled (la$_2$-ia$_3$ su-ga),[92] and it is therefore hard to understand it as other than an arrear. I will translate si-i$_3$-tum with "remainder" and la$_2$-ia$_3$ with "arrear," except when la$_2$-ia$_3$ is found in the colophon of accounts indicating a negative balance, where I will translate it as "deficit."

Text No. 33 records the repayment of such an arrear. It is a tablet copy, and as such not sealed (see Chapter 7).

---

86 See n. 83 above.

87 The accounting period was normally one year. Irregularities could appear either due to a change of power in Ur (an external reason), or due to the early settlement of a deficit, either in the case of the death of the "accounted," or (presumably) following his wish or ability to settle a large deficit (an internal reason). Several examples of accounts running for several years, constantly carrying forward a negative remainder can be found from the Umma sources; see in that regard Snell 1982: 103–8.

88 See Gelb 1957: 262 s.v. *šītum*.

89 An exception is TCL 5, 6036, where no equivalence was used for raw materials such as wooden beams that also make up the "remainder."

90 No. 31 (ŠS 3 to 4) obv. i 2: si-i$_3$-tum ⸢mu si⸣-ma-num^{ki} ba-ḫul. See also the wool-account of the governor: AAICAB 1, 1924-666 (from AS 3) obv. i 2: si-i$_3$-tum mu ^{d}amar-^{d}suen lugal-e ur-bi$_2$-lum^{ki} mu-ḫul; Erlenmeyer 152 obv. i 2: si-i$_3$-tum mu ^{d}šu-^{d}suen lugal; and finally the "damgar"-account concerning Ur-Dumuzida from AS 4, YNER 8, 3 obv. i 2: si-i$_3$-tum mu gu-za ^{d}en-lil$_2$-la$_2$ ba-dim$_2$. An account recording a substantial deficit (more than 11 mana of silver) of Ur-Dumuzida, the trade-agent, from the year AS 3 has recently been published (SANTAG 6, 119 [from AS 3 x]). Since the "remainder" recorded in YNER 8, 3 is less than one-third of a mana, we can speculate that Ur-Dumuzida in the meanwhile had dealt with his deficit. This is in part proven by the account concerning Ur-Dumuzida from AS 4 i, STA 22, which reduces a deficit of 2 ⅓ mana to the same deficit later entered into the year-end's account YNER 8, 3. Several other records deal with the activities of Ur-Dumuzida around this year. See also Neumann 1999: 48–50.

91 Note that S. Langdon in 1912 correctly observed that the si-i$_3$-tum (which he read si-ni-tum) was "an original sum left over from a transaction" (Langdon 1912: 42)

92 See, e.g., STA 3 (from AS 8) obv. i 26–28: 4(u) 5(aš) 1(ban$_2$) še gur / la$_2$-ia$_3$ su-ga lu$_2$ lunga-ke$_4$-ne / nig$_2$-ka$_9$ ak si-i$_3$-tum bi$_2$-du$_{11}$-ga-ta, "45 gur and 1 ban of barley, repaid deficit of the fullers, from the account of the 'remainder' of Biduga."

No. 33. *MS 2020/12 (Umma, AS 7)*

obv.

1.	1(aš) 4(barig) še gur[93]	1 gur, 4 barig of barley.
2.	la$_2$-ia$_3$ su-ga siki	Repaid arrear (of) wool.
3.	ša$_3$ še dingir-mu-ta zi-zi-dam	To be booked out of the barley of Dingirmu.
4.	ki KAŠ$_4$-ta	From KAS.
5.	gaba-ri kišib$_3$ lu$_2$-^{d}šul-gi-ra	Copy of sealed tablet of Lu-Šulgira.

rev.

	(blank space)	
1.	mu ḫu-uḫ$_2$-nu-ri^{ki} ba-ḫul	Year: "Ḫuḫnuri was destroyed."

In addition to settling a deficit through a simple transfer (recorded in a receipt such as No. 33), an account could be drawn up for the sole purpose of detailing how a deficit was settled. The following text, No. 34, is indeed a short account of the running deficit of a certain Lugal-nir:

No. 34. *MS 2019/1 (Umma, Š 44)*

obv.

1.	3(u) dabin gur	30 gur of flour (~ the "debits").
2.	ša$_3$-bi-ta	Out of it,
3.	5(diš) gin$_2$ ku$_3$-babbar	5 shekels of silver,
4.	kišib$_3$ gu-du-du	sealed tablet of Gududu;
5.	1(u) 5(aš) še numun gur	15 gur of seed-barley,
6.	kišib$_3$ lugal-^{d}nanna	sealed tablet of Lugal-Nanna;
7.	8(aš) 3(barig) še šuku-ra gur	8 gur, 3 barig of sustenance barley,

rev.

1.	kišib$_3$ lugal-nir	sealed tablet of Lugal-nir;
2.	1(barig) 4(ban$_2$) kišib$_3$ ša$_3$-nin-ga$_2$	1 barig, 4 ban$_2$ (of barley) sealed tablet of Ša-ninga;
3.	1(aš) gur lu$_2$-du$_{10}$-ga	1 gur (of barley sealed tablet of) Lu-duga,
	(blank space with computation: 2(u) ⌜8(aš) 1(barig)⌝ 4(ban$_2$) gur zi-ga)	(a total of:) 28 gur, 1 barig, 4 ban$_2$, is torn out (~the "credits").
4.	la$_2$-ia$_3$ 1(aš) ⌜3(barig) 2(ban$_2$)⌝ gur	"Deficit": 1 gur, 3 barig, 2 ban$_2$ (of barley).
5.	nig$_2$-ka$_9$ ak si-i$_3$-tum	Account concerning the "remainder"
6.	lugal-nir	of (the account of) Lugal-nir.
7.	mu si-mu-ru-um^{ki} ba-ḫul	Year: "Simurum was destroyed."

BPOA 1, 1434 (Umma) also refers to the account of Lugal-nir, who may have been an agricultural or workshop overseer.[94] It is difficult to prove, but possible, that our Lugal-nir may be identical to Lugal-nir son of Ur-Šara, the chief accountant of Umma. A four-column account concerning a person named Lugal-nir from Šu-Suen's fourth year has been published (UTI 5, 3467), but it appears to be unrelated to text No. 34.

---

[93] Erasure after gur.

[94] That text, BPOA 1, 1434, records the transfer of one person, Giri-Šara-idab, belonging to the "dedicatees" (a-ru-a) of a certain Lugal-itida. He is said to be booked out (obv. 6: zi-zi-dam) of the account of Lugal-nir.

Text No. 35, an account with only one item in the "debits" and only one item in the "credits," may also record the fulfillment of a special obligation or left-over deficit, although this is not mentioned. The layout of No. 35 is unusual, with both the "debits" and the "credits" as well as the balance and parts of the colophon recorded on the obverse. The year-name is separated from the rest of the colophon, which is written in the first two lines of the reverse and at the very bottom of the reverse.

No. 35. *MS 4343 (X, IS 2)*

obv.

1.	5(u) ⸢7(aš)⸣ 3(barig) 3(ban$_2$) ziz$_2$ ⸢gur⸣	57 gur, 3 barig, 3 ban$_2$ of emmer (~the "debits").
2.	ša$_3$-bi-ta	Out of it,
3.	4(u) 8(aš) ziz$_2$ gur	48 gur of emmer.
4.	kišib$_3$ šu-^{d}nin-šubur-⸢ra$^{?}$⸣	Sealed tablet of Šu-Ninšubur.
	(*blank space*)	
5.	šunigin 4(u) 8(aš) ziz$_2$ ⸢gur⸣	Total: 48 gur of emmer,
6.	zi-⸢ga⸣-[am$_3$]	is booked out (~the "credit").
7.	la$_2$-ia$_3$ 9(aš) 3(barig) 3(ban$_2$) ⸢ziz$_2$⸣ [gur]	Deficit: 9 gur, 3 barig, 3 ban$_2$ of emmer.
8.	ma-na-[x]	. . .

rev.

1.	in-da-[x][95]	. . .
2.	nig$_2$-ka$_9$ ak ur-[. . .]	Account concerning Ur- . . .
	(*blank space*)	
3.	mu en $^{d⸢}$inanna unug$^{⸣ki}$-ga maš$_2$-e ⸢in⸣-[pa$_3$]	Year: "The En-priest of Inanna of Uruk was chosen by omen."

The sag-nig$_2$-gur$_{11}$-ra-kam was typically made up of stock goods or the work-days of a regular work crew. In the case of an account concerning the trade agents, or any other account concerned with staple goods such as the barley accounts, the first section consists mostly of durable goods.[96] Such goods were usually transferred to the debits section by officials of central households or workshops, or by other trade-agents.[97] In the accounts concerning work, the first section commonly consisted of the work-days of a permanent work crew with various additions.[98] Equivalences were used throughout the Ur III accounting system in order to compute totals. These will be discussed in the next chapter. We find the total immediately preceding the

---

[95] One would expect a verb here, such as gal$_2$, which is frequently found following the prefix chain in-da-, but it is difficult to see how that would fit here.

[96] See, e.g., YNER 8, 3, an account of Ur-Dumuzida from AS 4 (Umma), which lists barley, dates, and wool in the "debits" section; AAICAB 1/1, pls. 67–68, 1924-667, an account of Pada from AS 5–xi (Umma) which lists wool, silver, and lard in the "debits"; CT 5, pls. 38–39, BM 17752, an account of Ikṣur from Š 43 x (Girsu), which lists only barley and silver in the "debits."

[97] See, e.g., the following entries in the three texts cited in the previous footnote: YNER 8, 3 (AS 4, Umma) obv. i 7–13: 1(u) 6(aš) gu$_2$ 1(u) 6(diš) ma-na siki / ku$_3$-bi 1(diš) ⅔(diš) ma-na 8(diš) ⅓(diš) gin$_2$ 2(u) še / a-ra$_2$ 1(diš)-kam / 2(u) gu$_2$ siki / ku$_3$-bi 2(diš) ma-na 1(u) gin$_2$ / a-ra$_2$ 2(diš)-kam / ki ensi$_2$-ka-ta, "16 talents and 16 ma-na of wool, its silver is 1 ⅔ ma-na 8 ⅓ shekels and 20 grains, the first time; 20 talents wool, its silver 2 ma-na 10 shekels, the second time, from the governor"; AAICAB 1/1, pls. 67–68, 1924-667 (AS 4, Umma) obv. i 9: 2(diš) gin$_2$ ku$_3$ giri$_3$ ur-^{d}nun-gal, "2 shekels of silver via Ur-Nungal." This Ur-Nungal is perhaps identical to the son of Ur-Šara the chief accountant, who likely himself functioned as chief accountant in Umma; CT 5, pls. 38–39, BM 17752 (Girsu SH 43–x) obv. i 3–5: 2(u) 7(aš) 1(barig) 3(ban$_2$) zu$_2$-lum gur lugal / ku$_3$-bi ⅓(diš)^{ša} 7(diš) gin$_2$ igi 3(diš)-gal$_2$ la$_2$ 6(diš) še / ki šabra-ta, "27 gur 1 barig 3 ban$_2$ dates, royal (measure), its silver: ⅓ (ma-na) 7 ⅓ shekels less 6 grains, from the chief administrator."

[98] See, e.g., the accounts concerning the pottery workers discussed in Dahl 2010a.

header, sag-nig$_2$-gur$_{11}$-ra-kam. No medium of equivalence was used when the account included very distinct materials such as wood; text No. 36 (previously published as RA 16, 19) is an example of an account with a very complex total.[99]

Since the sag-nig$_2$-gur$_{11}$-ra-kam section consisted of the "remainder" (si-i$_3$-tum) carried forward from the previous account, and the staple goods or work-days of a permanent work crew transferred to the account (ugu$_2$-a ba-a-gar) by state officials, it is justifiable to propose that the sag-nig$_2$-gur$_{11}$-ra-kam represented the "debits" of "the accounted."[100]

In this connection it may be advantageous to consider the following short account BIN 5, 114 (from Š 47), in which the remainder is not called the "deficit" (la$_2$-ia$_3$) but rather the "remainder" (si-i$_3$-tum) of "the accounted":

BIN 5, 114 (Š 43 to Š 47)

obv.

1.	4(geš'u) 6(geš$_2$) 2(u) 9(aš) 4(barig) še gur	2,789 gur, 4 barig of barley, (~the "debits").
2.	ša$_3$-bi-ta	Out of it:
3.	1(geš'u) 9(geš$_2$) 1(ban$_2$) 5(diš) sila$_3$ še-ba gur	1,140 gur, 1 ban$_2$, 5 sila$_3$ of barley as rations,
4.	2(geš$_2$) zi$_3$ ba-ba gur	120 gur of flour porridge,
5.	mu en ^{d}nanna maš-e i$_3$-pa$_3$	(in the) year: "the En-priest of Nanna was chosen by omen."
7.	1(geš'u) 4(geš$_2$) 3(u) 3(aš) 3(barig) 2(ban$_2$) še-ba gur	873 gur, 3 barig, 2 ban$_2$ of barley as rations,
8.	mu si-mu-ru-um^{ki} lu-lu-bu-um^{ki} a-ra$_2$ 1(u) la$_2$ 1(diš$_{tenû}$)[101]-kam ba-ḫul	(in the) year: "Simurum and Lulubum were destroyed for the ninth time."
9.	2(geš$_2$) 6(aš) 3(barig) še gur	126 gur, 3 barig of barley,

rev.

1.	kišib$_3$ lugal-ušur$_x$(LAL$_2$.TUG$_2$)-ra	sealed tablet of Lugal-ušura,
2.	mu ki-maš^{ki} ba-hul	(in the) year: "Kimaš was destroyed."
3.	⸢šunigin⸣ [3(geš'u)] ⸢5(geš$_2$)⸣ 4(u) 1(barig) 3(ban$_2$)![102] 5(diš) sila$_3$ še gur	Total: 2,140 gur, 1 barig, 3 ban$_2$, 5 sila$_3$ of barley,
4.	šunigin 2(geš$_2$) dabin gur	(and) total: 120 gur flour
5.	zi-ga-am$_3$	is booked out. (~the "credits").
6.	8(geš$_2$) 4(u) 9(aš) 2(barig) 2(ban$_2$)![103] 5(diš) sila$_3$ še gur	529 gur, 2 barig, 2 ban$_2$, 5 sila$_3$ of barley,

---

[99] Comparable to TCL 5, 6036 (AS 4), see also AAS 135 (AS 3 i to xii), where wool of varying qualities are listed separately.

[100] Historically, this has not been well understood; as late as 1982 B. Foster wrote (dealing with the Old Akkadian accounts) (Foster 1982: 11): "In its fullest form, a balanced account (níg-kas$_7$ ak) consisted of an amount on hand (sag níg-GA-ra), disbursements (zi-ga), and amounts due or carried over (là(l)›u)." See the texts MCS 9, 236; Nik 2, 76 and SP 22, 55, for examples of "balanced" accounts from the Old Akkadian period. D. Snell believed that the first section of the large accounts (which he also called balanced) was the credit, or as he writes "capital," of the "accounted." He translated the term sag-nig$_2$-gur$_{11}$-ra-kam as the "head of what has been deposited," and based on the similarity of this translation, and the Latin root for capital, he gave another translation: "It is the capital" (Snell 1982: 25). M. Powell understood the sag-nig$_2$-gur$_{11}$-ra-kam as being the property of the merchant, and translated the term as "that which is over and above the basic *makkūru*" (Powell 1977: 23–29, esp. 27). Note however, that Snell did not question that the la$_2$-ia$_3$ was a negative asset, although its inclusion in the "capital" logically would make this a negative asset too.

[101] In numerical notations with la$_2$ the deducted number is mostly tilted 45° clockwise (in the lexical tradition referred to as *tenû*, see Gong 2000: 32–35 with previous literature).

[102] Copy has 1 (ban$_2$), the calculations suggest that the tablet has 3 (ban$_2$).

[103] Copy has 4 (ban$_2$), the calculations suggest that the tablet has 2 (ban$_2$).

7. si-i$_3$-tum	(is the) "remainder"
8. lu$_2$-dingir-ra šabra	(of the account concerning) Lu-dingira, the chief administrator.
9. mu-us$_2$-sa ki-maš^{ki} ba-ḫul	Year following: "Kimaš was destroyed."

"Credits" (ša$_3$-bi-ta zi-ga-am$_3$)

The second section of an account was called ša$_3$-bi-ta . . . zi-ga-am$_3$ (literally "from its middle . . . is torn out"). It represented the "credits" of the accounted. ša$_3$-bi-ta introduced the section and zi-ga-am$_3$ terminated it, following immediately upon the total of the section. zi(g)-a is understood as "to book out"; its Akkadian equivalent *elû*, "to raise," has in *CAD* the meaning "to debit" with particularly reference to accounts. However, zi.g can also be equivalent to Akakdian *nasāhu*, "to tear out," which may make better sense in this respect, since we see, literally, that the goods are torn out of the middle of the "debits."

The "credits" section recorded the actual deliveries, or work-performance of the work crew, as these were recorded in the primary documents.[104] The section was split in two when the transactions recorded involved a complex production.[105] The second half of the "split-credits" was used to calculate the equivalencies of the manufactured products. The first half recounted only the individual receipts. By "booking out" and meeting his requirements, the agent of the state took part in a "planned" economy. Most deliveries and work-tasks followed "standing orders."[106]

The best-known such complex accounts are the accounts of the Umma basketry and carpentry workshop, TCL 5, 6036, and the three large accounts of Umma potters, MVN 1, 231, 232, and MVN 21, 203 (see in particular Dahl 2010a). The accountant of the basketry and carpentry workshop employed a highly sophisticated system of equivalencies to compute the value of the basketry objects, including both work-time and materials (Englund 1988: 170 n. 43), whereas the equivalence values used to compute the value of the production of the pottery workshop was solely work-time.

Text No. 36, published in 1919 by Alotte de la Fuÿe (*RA* 16: 1–20),[107] is a unique large account of timber, reed, reed mats, and reed products, and several other products. In his 2002 edition of the tablets in the Ashmolean Museum (particularly the former collections of the Bodleian Library) J.-J. Grégoire included a number of tablets in private and for the most part anonymous collections, among them our text No. 36; Grégoire's copy, which is superior to that of Alotte de la Fuÿe, has now been superseded by the photos available on the CDLI. Heimpel used Grégoire's edition of No. 36 for his study of the "Trees Growing in Sumer" (Heimpel 2011: 106–7). Neither scholar offered a full study of the text, and the transliteration and translation below represents the first complete edition to appear. Many of the products remain difficult to translate. The text dates to Šulgi's 36th year. It uses no equivalencies at all, probably because the materials are unique, resulting in a very long summary of products making up both the "debits" and the "credits." However, whereas the entries in the debits section list the length of the individual pieces of wood, as a system of classification, the totals of

---

[104] Struve, who was the first to realize that the primary documents were summarized in the large accounts (Struve 1969: 156–57, showing the relationship between BIN 5, 262 and BIN 5, 272 obv. vi 17–22), was among the few scholars during the first three quarters of the 20th century who understood the "planned economy" nature of neo-Sumerian accounts. I draw attention in particular to the treatment of the account TCL 5, 6036 by Landsberger 1967: 7–10, as an example of the then current, erroneous understanding of the structure of the neo-Sumerian account, but see also, e.g., Sharlach 2004, or Steinkeller 1996.

[105] See, e.g., TCL 5, 6036 or MVN 1, 231.

[106] See also Snell 1982: 96–99 and Appendix 2 (270–78).

[107] Note that Alotte de la Fuÿe understood the structure of the text quite well, although he identified the first section as the "income" (*entrées*), and the second section as the "expenditures" (*sorties*).

the debits calculate the total combined length of each type of wood, using the formulation, "its total length is" (šunigin gid-bi x kuš$_3$).

The colophon of text No. 36 (rev. vii 17–18) reads:

17.	nig$_2$-ka$_9$ ak mu-zu-da	Account concerning Muzuda.
18.	ša$_3$ tum-ma-al^{ki}	Within Tummal.

The location of Tummal, some 20–25 km south of Nippur, is discussed in Steinkeller 2001a: 70–71, and Yoshikawa 1989: 285–91, with reference to Wilcke 1973: 5 (*pace* Sigrist 1992: 381). Most of the texts mentioning Tummal are assigned to Drehem, but this text can be confidently assigned to Umma due to the use of the Umma calendar in the colophon (rev. vii 19: iti ^{d}li$_9$-si$_4$). mu-zu-da is likely a personal name; it is also found in obv. ii 18 as the name of a conveyor (giri$_3$-official, see Chapter 7), and in a few other texts as well.[108] Text No. 36 will serve as an example of a large account with a complex total and is transliterated and translated in full here.

The "debits" section lists first a number of beams and an amount of bitumen received from the "palace":

No. 36. *MS 1983 = RA 16, 19 (Umma, Š 36–ix)*

obv. col. i

1.	3(u) geš-ur$_3$ [*n* kuš$_3$]-ta	30 beams (n cubit?) each.
2.	1(aš) 2(barig) 3(ban$_2$) esir$_2$ E$_2$-A gur lugal	10 gur, 1 barig, 3 ban$_2$ of E$_2$-A bitumen (according to the) king('s standard).
	(*blank space*)	
3.	e$_2$-gal-ta	from the "palace."

This is followed by number of pieces of timber delivered by the governor of Babylon:

obv. col. i

4.	8(diš) ^{geš}šinig gal 1(u) 1(diš) kuš$_3$-ta	8 (pieces of) tamarisk wood, large, 11 cubits each.
5.	1(geš'u) geš gal 1(u) 2(diš) kuš$_3$-ta	600 (pieces of) wood, large, 12 cubits each.
6.	ki ensi$_2$ babila^{ki}-ta	From the governor of Babylon.

The remainder of the "debits" lists other deliveries of the sort one would expect for a storehouse of various industries, and is terminated with a long summary of totals of the various kinds of products.

obv. col. i

7.	⸢4(geš$_2$)⸣ geš gal 1(u) 2(diš) kuš$_3$-ta	240 (pieces of) wood, large, 12 cubits each.
8.	2(geš$_2$) 1(u) geš 7(diš) kuš$_3$-ta	130 (pieces of) wood, 7 cubits each.
9.	3(u) ^{geš}u$_3$-suh$_5$ 1(u) 1(diš) kuš$_3$-ta	30 (pieces of) pine wood, 11 cubits each.
	(*blank space*)	
10.	giri$_3$ šu-ni-an-nam	Conveyor: Šuni-annam.
11.	4(diš) ^{geš}u$_3$-suh$_5$ 1(u) 1(diš) kuš$_3$-ta	4 (pieces of) pine wood, 11 cubits each.
	(*blank space*)	
12.	giri$_3$ ur-^{d}šara$_2$	Conveyor: Ur-Šara,
13.	lu$_2$ lugal-sa$_6$-ga-ni	the man (~subordinate) of Lugal-sagani.
14.	1(diš) ^{geš}šinig 1(u) 3(diš) kuš$_3$	1 (piece of) tamarisk wood, 13 cubits.

[108] A half-output worker (CDLJ 2003/1 no. 1 [Umma, ŠS 2] obv. i 28); an assistant (šeš-tab-ba) (Nisaba 23, 50 [Umma] obv. i 19); recipient (kišib$_3$) of reeds (Nisaba 24, 18 [Umma, AS 5–iii] rev. i 4); a messenger (OrSP 47–49, 280 [Umma, ŠS 4–i] obv. 16); recipient (kišib$_3$) of dried bitumen (SANTAG 6, 19 [Umma, Š 33/38] rev. ii 13); recipient (kišib$_3$) of dried bitumen (TLB 3, 169 [Umma] rev. ii 10').

15.	1(diš) ^{geš}šinig 1(u) 2(diš) kuš$_3$	1 (piece of) tamarisk wood, 12 cubits.
16.	2(diš) ^{geš}šinig 6(diš) kuš$_3$-ta	2 (pieces of) tamarisk wood, 6 cubits each.
17.	1(u) geš-ur$_3$ sumun 1(u) kuš$_3$-ta	10 beams, old, 10 cubits each.
18.	6(diš) geš sumun 8(diš) kuš$_3$-ta	6 (pieces of) wood, old, 8 cubits each.
19.	6(diš) geš sumun 7(diš) kuš$_3$-ta	6 (pieces of) wood, old, 7 cubits each.
20.	4(diš) ^{geš}u$_3$-suḫ$_5$ ^{geš}a-ra sumun 1(u) 1(diš) kuš$_3$-ta	4 (pieces of) pine wood (for) a-ra wood,[109] old, 11 cubits each.
	(blank space)	
21.	geš sumun-am$_3$	It is old wood.
22.	1(geš$_2$) 3(u) geš-ur$_3$ 7(diš) kuš$_3$-ta	90 beams, 7 cubits each.
23.	1(geš$_2$) 2(u) geš-ur$_3$ 6(diš) kuš$_3$-ta	80 beams, 6 cubits each.
24.	geš gibil-am$_3$	It is new wood.
25.	1(u) 2(diš) ^{geš}kun$_5$	12 ladders.
26.	8(diš) dug gur-TUL$_2$	8 gur-vessels of the well.
	(blank space)	
27.	giri$_3$ ḫa-lu$_5$-lu$_5$	Conveyor: Ḫalulu.

The "old" (sumun) and "new" (gibil) wood is listed here in two distinct groups (summarized as "it is old wood" (geš sumun-am$_3$) and "it is new wood" (geš gibil-am$_3$). In the second part of the "debits," listing the combined totals of all the materials, new and old are grouped with their type of wood and not according to the age.

obv. col. i

28.	2(diš) ^{geš}u$_3$-suḫ$_5$ gal 1(u) 2(diš) kuš$_3$-ta	2 (pieces of) pine wood, large, 12 cubits each.
29.	1(u) ^{geš}u$_3$-suḫ$_5$ apin u$_3$-sar 7(diš) kuš$_3$-ta	10 (pieces of) pine wood (for) the u$_3$-sar[110] (of the) plow, 7 cubits each.
30.	2(u) ^{geš}hašḫur erin$_2$	20 (pieces of) apple wood, for balance beams (?).[111]
31.	1(u) ^{geš}asal$_2$ ša$_3$-si ig	10 (pieces of) poplar wood, (for) door filler.[112]
32.	2(u) ^{geš}u$_3$-suḫ$_5$ mi-ri$_2$-za 6(diš) kuš$_3$-ta	20 (pieces of) pine wood for mi-ri$_2$-za planks, 6 cubits each.
33.	1(diš) ^{geš}x gid$_2$ 1(u) kuš$_3$	1 (piece of) ... wood, 10 cubits.[113]
34.	3(geš'u) gi ŠID	1800 (bundles[114] of) ŠID[115] reed.
35.	1(geš'u) gi NE	600 (bundles of) NE[116] reed.
	(blank space)	
36.	ki šeš-a-ni-ta	From Šešani.
37.	5(diš) ^{geš}kun$_5$	4 ladders.
38.	6(diš) dub-<la$_2$> mangaga[117]	6 "towers"[118] of raffia (?).

[109] A type of wood used for shipbuilding, see also comments to text No. 107 in Ch. 7.

[110] See Heimpel 2011: 106 for a translation as "point plow" pines without further discussion.

[111] See discussion of CUSAS 3, 1327 in Heimpel 2011: 118.

[112] See Heimpel 2011: 107.

[113] This item seems not to be included in the total section.

[114] In the total of the "credits" the quantity of both types of reed is specified as bundles.

[115] According to Sallaberger 1989: 315 and Waetzoldt 1992: 130–32 reed used for basketry production.

[116] According to Sallaberger 1993: 77 n. 336 "reed for firing"; according to Waetzoldt 1992: 134–35 "unsorted reed."

[117] Note the erasure between dub and mangaga; dub-la$_2$ restored from the total of the "credits," obv. iv 15.

[118] "Tower" here probably a measure.

39.	1(u) ^{geš}me-te-num$_2$	10 narrow planks.
40.	2(diš) eš$_2$ geš zi-<da>[119]	2 ropes for "straight" (?) wood.

obv. col. ii

1.	[. . .]	. . .
	(blank space)	
2.	ki nig$_2$-u$_2$-rum-ta	From Nig-urum.
3.	4(diš) ^{geš}kun$_5$	4 ladders.
4.	½(diš) ma-na ⸢še⸣-gin$_3$	½ ma-na of glue.
5.	giri$_3$ bi$_2$-da	Conveyor: Bida.
6.	8(diš) eš$_2$ ma$_2$ gid$_2$	8 ropes for punting (?) boats.
7.	2(u) dub-la$_2$ mangaga	20 "towers" of raffia.
8.	1(u)$^?$ la$_2$ 1(aš) esir$_2$ had$_2$ gur	9 gur of dried bitumen.
	(blank space)	
9.	giri$_3$ ur-^{d}suen dumu lugal-dalla	Conveyor: Ur-Suen, child of Lugal-dalla.

This section (obv. i 28–ii 9) deals with materials that could have been destined for the shipyard; both mi-ri$_2$-za and me-te-num$_2$ planks were used in shipbuilding.[120] The ropes in obv. ii 6 are explicitly said to be for boats. Ladders (^{geš}kun$_5$) might also be for boarding the boats, and the "towers" of raffia (?) (dub-la$_2$ mangaga) may be related to some sort of water installation (weir, see Nissen 1976: 26).

The next section records objects for a domestic storehouse:

obv. col. ii

10.	1(u) dug gur-TUL$_2$	10 gur-vessels of the well.
11.	3(diš) dug du-du sig$_{15}$	3 du-du vessels, sig$_{15}$ (quality).[121]
12.	1(diš) dug du-du sig$_{15}$ gid$_2$-da	1 du-du vessel, sig$_{15}$ (quality), long.
13.	1(ban$_2$) i$_3$-geš	1 ban$_2$ of sesame oil.
14.	5(diš) sila$_3$ i$_3$-šah$_2$	5 sila$_3$ of lard.
	(blank space)	
15.	ki dingir-ra-ta	From Dingira.
16.	1(geš$_2$) 4(u) geš 4(diš) kuš$_3$-ta	100 (pieces of) wood, 4 cubits each.
17.	1(barig) esir$_2$ E$_2$-A lugal	1 barig of E$_2$-A bitumen (according to the) king('s standard).
	(blank space)	
18.	giri$_3$ mu-zu-da	Conveyor: Muzuda.
19.	5(diš) eš$_2$ GAN$_2$	5 field ropes (?).[122]
20.	5(diš) murgu$_2$ peš	5 date-palm ribs.

[119] Restored from total of "credits," obv. iv 18.

[120] See *CAD* M/2 43, *metenu*, and Salonen 1939: 85ff. for the meaning "narrow planks." Note ePSD links to *meṭenum*, "flour bin," but the association here with planks (mi-ri$_2$-za) and the fact that me-te-num$_2$ is written with the determinative for wood (geš) rather than that for reed (gi) make the former interpretation most likely.

[121] du-du vessels are very infrequently attested; they are usually qualified by sig$_{15}$(KAL). sig$_{15}$(KAL) is used as a qualifier about various cereals and cereal products, and it is not certain how to interpret this in relation to clay vessels (see Powell 1984: 54, who discusses its interpretation as either a colour or quality designation, based on the lexical evidence).

[122] This product is perhaps also attested in MVN 20, 25 (AS 6 i), where it qualifies sheep(?); see also PPAC 5, 51 (Girsu, Š 42).

21.	2(aš) gu$_2$ mangaga[123]	2 talents of raffia.
22.	1(geš$_2$) ^{geš}i$_3$-šub	60 molds (for regular bricks).
23.	3(geš$_2$) ^{geš}dusu$^?$	180 dusu-baskets.
24.	1(geš$_2$) geš al	60 (pieces of) wood for hoe (handles).
25.	2(geš$_2$) geš zu$_2$ al	120 (pieces of) wood for hoe tines.[124]
26.	8(diš) ^{geš}šinig 8(diš) kuš$_3$-ta	8 (pieces of) tamarisk wood, 8 cubits each.
27.	1(ban$_2$) esir$_2$ E$_2$-A lugal	1 ban$_2$ of E$_2$-A bitumen (according to the) king('s standard).
	(*blank space*)	
28.	ki a-kal-la-ta	From A(ya)-kala.
29.	2(geš$_2$) dug ḫi-a	120 vessels, various (kinds).
30.	4(diš) dug sila$_3$ banda$_3$^{da}	4 sila$_3$-vessels, junior (size).
31.	ki u$_2$-da-ta	From Uda.
32.	8(geš$_2$) in-u gur	480 gur of straw.
33.	giri$_3$ ur-^{d}da-mu	Conveyor: Ur-Damu.
34.	1(geš$_2$) gur giri$_3$ ḫa-lu$_5$-lu$_5$	60 gur (of straw?), conveyor: Halulu.
35.	1(geš$_2$) eš$_3$-tum gur	60 gur of chaff.[125]
36.	giri$_3$ bi$_2$-da	Conveyor: Bida.
37.	4(geš$_2$) in-u gur	240 gur of straw.
38.	giri$_3$ an-gu-gu	Conveyor: Angugu.
39.	2(geš$_2$) še-ta sa$_{10}$-a	120 <gur> bartered from barley.
40.	2(geš$_2$) gur ki ensi$_2$ adab^{ki}-ta	120 gur (of barley) from the governor of Adab.
41.	1(geš$_2$) gur ki ensi$_2$ gu$_2$-du$_8$-a^{ki}-ta	60 gur (of barley) from the governor of Gudua.

obv. col. iii

1.	[...]	...
2.	[...]	...
3.	[x] x x [...]	...
4.	2(šar$_2$) 4(geš'u) 2(geš$_2$) gi NE	6120 (bundles? of) NE reeds.
5.	ki bi$_2$-du$_{11}$-ga-ta	From Biduga.
6.	2(diš) ^{geš}sag-kul gal	2 bolts, large.
7.	1(diš) ^{geš}šu-a-sa$_2$	1 šu-a-sa$_2$.[126]
	(*blank space*)	
8.	ki ARAD$_2$-ta	From ARAD(mu).
9.	5(diš) kuš ḫi-a	5 hides, various.
10.	⅓(diš) <ma-na> kuš gu$_4$	⅓ (ma-na) of ox hide.
11.	ki ur-^{d}šara$_2$ ašgab-ta	From Ur-Šara, the leather-worker.

[123] Note the erased sign before mangaga; for the reading mangaga (KA×SA = SU$_6$), see Volk 2004: 287, and note the Ur III syllabic writing in, e.g., YOS 4, 238.

[124] It is unclear what exactly zu$_2$ al "tooth of the hoe" refers to, as one would expect a hoe's blade to be made of metal (or even stone), and zu$_2$ al is here classified as a wooden object. See Heimpel 2011: 78.

[125] The difference between in-u and eš$_3$-tum is not clear. Both denote chaff or straw, see Steinkeller 2001b.

[126] A wooden object. Attested only in two other texts (BIN 5, 274 [Umma, ŠS 1] obv. 4, and TSU 108 [uncertain] rev. v 11') and always in connection with deliveries of bolts (^{geš}sag-kul).

12.	2(diš) ma-na u$_2$-ḫab$_2$	2 ma-na of oak apples.[127]
13.	2(diš) sila$_3$ al-la-ḫa-ru	2 sila$_3$ of allaharu dye.[128]
14.	⅓(diš) ma-na še-⸢gin$_3$⸣	⅓ ma-na of glue.
15.	3(u) ma-na siki ud$_5$	30 ma-na of goat hair.
16.	2(diš) murgu$_2$ ba	2 turtle shells.
	(*blank space*)	
17.	ki ur-^{d}lamma-ta	from Ur-Lamma.
18.	3(diš) ⅓(diš) ma-na uruda	3 ⅓ ma-na of copper.
19.	3(diš) gin$_2$ su-ḫe$_2$	3 shekels of borax.[129]
20.	ki da-da-ga-ta	From Dadaga.
	(*blank space*)	

Immediately before the key-term sag-nig$_2$-gur$_{11}$-ra-kam, "debits" (obv. v 5), labeling the preceding section, is a list of at least forty-three products (the first lines of obv. iv and v are broken; the list could have been forty-five items long). Several products found in the first part of the debits are not listed in the preserved summary of the debits (tamarisk, ^{geš}šinig, beams, ur$_3$, and ordinary wood, all of various lengths). I reconstruct these in the first two lines of obv. iv.

In those cases where the total is a combination of two or more entries in the preceding debits section, or in uncertain cases where parts of the original entries may be missing, I give the references in the footnotes.

obv. col. iv

1.	[šunigin *n* ^{geš}šinig x x hi-a . . . šunigin gid$_2$-bi *n* kuš$_3$]	[Total: *n* (pieces of) tamarisk wood . . . Their total length: *n* cubit]
2.	[šunigin *n* geš ur$_3$ šunigin gid$_2$-bi *n* kuš$_3$]	[Total: *n* beams. Their total length: *n* cubit]
3.	šunigin 1(geš'u) 4(geš$_2$) ⸢geš gal⸣ ḫi-a	Total: 840 pieces of wood, large, various.[130]
4.	šunigin gid$_2$-bi 1(šar$_2$) 4(geš'u) 4(geš$_2$) 2(u) kuš$_3$	Their total length is 6,260 cubits.[131]
5.	šunigin 4(u) ^{geš}u$_3$-suh$_5$ ḫi-a	Total: 40 (pieces of) pine wood, various.[132]
6.	šunigin gid$_2$-bi 8(geš$_2$) 3(u) 2(diš) kuš$_3$	Their total length is 512 cubits.
7.	šunigin 2(u) ^{geš}u$_3$-suḫ$_5$ mi-ri$_2$-za	Total: 20 (pieces of) pine wood for miriza-planks.
8.	šunigin gid$_2$-bi 2(geš$_2$) kuš$_3$	Their total length is 120 cubits.
9.	šunigin 1(aš) 3(barig) 4(ban$_2$) esir$_2$ E$_2$-A gur lugal	Total: 10 gur, 3 barig, 4 ban$_2$ E$_2$-A bitumen (according to the) king('s standard).[133]
10.	šunigin 3(u) dug gur-TUL$_2$	Total: 30 gur-vessels of the well.[134]
11.	šunigin 1(u)$^?$ la$_2$ 1(aš) esir$_2$ ḫad$_2$ gur	Total: 9 gur of dried bitumen.
12.	šunigin 2(u) 1(diš) ^{geš}kun$_5$	Total: 21 ladders.[135]

[127] Oak apples (German *Gallapfel*) were used in leather production due to their very high content of tannin (Stol 1980–83: 532).

[128] See *CAD* A 359–60.

[129] A product used in metal smelting; see Heimpel 2011: 107 with n. 45.

[130] See obv. i 5 and 7.

[131] This is presumably not a measured but a calculated length.

[132] See col. i 9, 11, 20, 28, 29. The debits lists 50 pieces of pine wood, for a total combined length of exactly 512 kuš$_3$. The text is clear, only 40 pieces are recorded in obv. iv 5 (total of the "credits").

[133] See obv. i 2, ii 17, ii 27.

[134] See obv. i 26, ii 10. Only 18 of these vessels are found in the preserved sections of the "debits."

[135] See obv. i 25, 37, ii 3.

13.	šunigin 2(u) ^{geš}ḫašḫur erin$_2$	Total: 20 (pieces of) apple wood, for balance beams (?).
14.	šunigin 1(u) ⌈^{geš}<asal$_2$>[136] ša$_3$⌉-si ig	Total: 10 (pieces of) poplar wood, for door filler (?).
15.	šunigin 2(u) 6(diš) dub-la$_2$ mangaga	Total: 26 "towers" of raffia.[137]
16.	šunigin 1(u) ^{geš}me-te-num$_2$	Total: 10 narrow planks.
17.	šunigin 8(diš) eš$_2$ ma$_2$ gid$_2$	Total: 8 ropes for punting boats(?).
18.	šunigin 2(diš) eš$_2$ geš zi-da	Total: 2 ropes for "straight"(?) wood.
19.	šunigin 3(diš) dug du-du sig$_{15}$	Total: 3 du-du vessels, sig$_{15}$ (quality).
20.	šunigin 1(barig) i$_3$-geš	Total: 1 ban$_2$ of sesame oil.
21.	šunigin 5(diš) sila$_3$ i$_3$-šaḫ$_2$	Total: 5 sila$_3$ of lard.
22.	šunigin 5(diš) eš$_2$ GAN$_2$	Total: 5 field ropes(?).
23.	šunigin 5(diš) murgu$_2$ peš	Total: 5 date-palm ribs.
24.	šunigin 2(aš) gu$_2$ mangaga	Total: 2 talents of raffia.
25.	šunigin 3(geš$_2$) ^{geš}dusu	Total: 180 dusu-baskets.
26.	šunigin 1(geš$_2$) geš al	Total: 60 (pieces of) wood for hoe (handles).
27.	šunigin 2(geš$_2$) dug ḫi-a	Total: 120 pots, various (kinds).
28.	šunigin 2(geš'u) in-u gur	Total: 1200 gur of straw.[138]
29.	šunigin 1(geš$_2$) eš$_3$-tum gur	Total: 60 gur of chaff
30.	šunigin 3(geš'u) sa gi ŠID	Total: 1,800 bundles of reed,
31.	šunigin 2(šar$_2$) 5(geš'u) 2(geš$_2$) sa gi NE	Total: 10,180 bundles of ŠID and NE reed,[139]
32.	šunigin 2(geš$_2$) geš zu$_2$ al	Total: 120 (pieces of) wood for hoe tines.
33.	šunigin 2(diš) ^{geš}sag-kul gal	Total: 2 bolts, large.
34.	šunigin 1(diš) ^{geš}šu-a-sa$_2$	Total: 1 šu-a-sa$_2$.
35.	šunigin 5(diš) kuš ḫi-a	Total: 5 hides, various.
36.	šunigin ⅓(diš) ma-na ⌈kuš gu$_4$⌉	Total: ⅓ ma-na of ox hide.
37.	šunigin ⅚(diš) ma-na še-gin$_3$	Total: ⅚ ma-na of glue.[140]
38.	šunigin 2(diš) ma-na u$_2$-ḫab$_2$	Total: 2 ma-na of oak apples.
39.	šunigin 2(diš) sila$_3$ al-la-ḫa-ru	Total: 2 sila$_3$ of *allaharu* dye.
40.	šunigin 3(diš) ⅓(diš) ma-na uruda	Total: 3 ⅓ ma-na of copper.
41.	šunigin 2(diš) murgu$_2$ ba	Total: 2 turtle shells.

obv. col. v[141]

1.	[...]	...
2.	[...]	...
3.	[...]	...
4.	šunigin 1(diš) [...]	Total: 1 ...

[136] The break in the text hardly leaves place for any additional signs following the broken geš and before the broken ša$_3$.

[137] See obv. i 38, ii 7.

[138] See obv. ii 32, 37, 39, 40, 41.

[139] See obv. i 35, iii 4.

[140] See obv. ii 4, iii 14.

[141] Among the products once written in the missing lines of col. v are probably borax (obv. iii 19); brick molds (obv. ii 22); and goat hair (obv. iii 15).

The totals of the "debits" section are followed by the technical term s a g - n i g$_2$ - g u r$_{11}$ - r a - k a m, discussed above. Immediately after that we find the term š a$_3$ - b i - t a introducing the "credits" section of the account. z i - g a - a m$_3$, found in rev. vi 17, finishes it.

obv. col. v

	(blank space)	
5.	sag-nig$_2$-gur$_{11}$-ra-⌈kam⌉	It is the "debits."
6.	ša$_3$-bi-ta	Out of it,

The first part of the credits section gives unusual detail about the destination of many of the objects. A majority of these were used to construct various objects or structures of a palatial complex, presumably located in Tummal. These can be summarized according to the headers found in the following lines:

obv. vi 12	(for) the dwelling place of the king.
obv. vi 28	(for the) palace of the king (in Tummal?).
rev. i 11	for three bath houses.
rev. i 19	for the lofty gate.
rev. ii 5	(for) the courtyard of the king.

obv. col. v

7.	4(diš) ^{geš}u$_3$-suh$_5$ gal 1(u) kuš$_3$-ta	4 (pieces of) pine wood, large, 10 cubits each,
8.	dal ugula nar-gu-la	(for the) racks(?),[142] overseer Nargula.[143]
9.	8(diš) geš-ur$_3$ gal 1(u) kuš$_3$-ta	8 beams, large, 10 cubits each,
10.	8(diš) ^{geš}u$_3$-suh$_5$ 1(u) kuš$_3$-ta	8 (pieces of) pine wood, 10 cubits each,
11.	dub ab-ba 1(diš) ½(diš)-še$_3$ ba-dim$_2$	were fashioned into 1 ½ roof-vent covers(?).[144]
12.	3(diš) ma-na 1(u) gin$_2$ uruda	3 ma-na, 10 shekels of copper,
13.	bi$_2$-gu$_7$-bi 1(u) gin$_2$	its reduction: 10 shekels,
14.	5(diš) gin$_2$ su-ḫe$_2$	5 shekels borax,
15.	har dub ab-ba-ka-še$_3$ ba-dim$_2$	were fashioned into the ring of the roof-vent cover(?).
16.	1(u) la$_2$ 1(diš) ^{geš}u$_3$-suh$_5$ 2(diš) kuš$_3$-ta	9 (pieces) of pine wood, 2 cubits each,
17.	dub ka ab-ba-ka-ke$_4$ ba-ab-gi-ib	were placed crosswise on the cover of the roof vent(?).[145]
18.	⌈½(diš)⌉ ma-na še-gin$_3$	½ ma-na glue,
19.	x sag dub-ba-še$_3$	for the . . . of the top of the cover(?).
20.	½(diš)$^?$ [ma$^?$-na še-gin$_3$ ^{geš}sag-kul x]-ra-kukku$_2$	½ ma-na glue to . . . the bolt(?).
21.	8(diš) ^{geš}u$_3$-suḫ$_5$ 7(diš) kuš$_3$-ta	8 (pieces of) pine wood, 7 cubits each,
22.	4(diš) geš 6(diš) kuš$_3$-ta	4 (pieces of) wood, 6 cubits each,
23.	1(u) 6(diš) ^{geš}ḫašḫur ša$_3$-si ig	16 (pieces of) apple wood, (for) door filler,
24.	ig e$_2$ saga za-še$_3$ ba-dim$_2$	were fashioned into the door of the good house of . . . .
25.	1(diš) ^{geš}šinig gal 6(diš) kuš$_3$	1 (piece of) tamarisk wood, large, 6 cubits,
26.	sag-kul ub a$_2$-dar x-za-še$_3$ ba-dim$_2$	was fashioned into the bolts of x ibex horn(?).

[142] See Heimpel 2011: 106 with n. 41.

[143] See Heimpel 2011: 106 with n. 42.

[144] See Heimpel 2011: 106 with n. 44.

[145] See Heimpel 2011: 107.

27.	1(diš) ^{geš}šinig 5(diš) kuš$_3$	1 (piece of) tamarisk wood, 5 cubits,
28.	nu-kuš$_2$ za-še$_3$ ba-dim$_2$	was fashioned into the hinges of . . . .
29.	1(diš) ^{geš}asal$_2$ 4(diš) kuš$_3$	1 (piece of) poplar wood, 4 cubits,
30.	eš$_2$ ig za-še$_3$ ba-dim$_2$	was fashioned into the door of . . . .
31.	1(diš) ^{geš}šinig 3(diš) kuš$_3$ i$_3$-si-nam 3(diš)-še$_3$ ba-dim$_2$	1 (piece of) tamarisk wood, 3 cubits, was fashioned into three. . . .
32.	1(geš$_2$) 2(u) geš 3(diš) kuš$_3$-ta	80 (pieces of) wood, 3 cubits each,
33.	2(u) ^{geš}u$_3$-suh$_5$ bi$_2$-i$_3$-tum 7(diš) kuš$_3$-ta	20 (pieces of) pine wood for a bitum,[146] 7 cubits each,
34.	8(diš) geš gal! 1(u) kuš$_3$-ta mi-sir$_2$ bi$_2$-i$_3$ -tum-še$_3$	8 pieces of wood, large, 10 cubits each, for a . . . .
35.	4(diš) geš 6(diš) kuš$_3$-ta dal e$_2$-da-še$_3$	4 (pieces of) wood, 6 cubits each, for the racks(?) of the house.
36.	1(u) la$_2$ 1(diš) geš 7(diš) kuš$_3$-ta	9 (pieces of) wood, 7 cubits each,
37.	ka ugula nar-gu-la	(for the) openings(?), overseer Nargula.
38.	6(diš) geš 4(diš) kuš$_3$-ta ^{geš}bala ugula nar-gu-la	6 (pieces of) wood, 4 cubits each, for the pestle(?), overseer Nargula.
39.	4(u) la$_2$ 1(diš) geš 2(diš) kuš$_3$-ta geš ka ab-ba-ka [x]	39 (pieces of) wood, 2 cubits each, wood . . .-ed at opening of the roof vent(?).

obv. col. vi

1.	[. . .]	. . .
2.	[. . .]	. . .
3.	[. . .]	. . .
4.	[. . .]	. . .
5.	[. . .]	. . .
	(*blank space*)	. . .
6.	3(u) x [. . .]	30 . . .
7.	geš ka$_2$ a x [. . .]	Wood (for the) gate . . .
8.	4(diš) geš gal 8(diš) kuš$_3$-[ta]	4 (pieces of) wood, large, 8 cubits each,
9.	dab$_x$(LAGABxGU$_4$)$^?$ ab-it-ti-⌜še$_3$$^?$ ba⌝-dim$_2$	were fashioned into . . .[147]
10.	2(u) geš ⌜3(diš)$^?$⌝ kuš$_3$-ta za-x-LUM e$_2$-da	20 (pieces of) wood, 3(?) cubits each, . . . (?)
11.	2(diš) geš gal 1(u) 3(diš) kuš$_3$-ta	2 (pieces of) wood, large, 13 cubits each,
12.	ki-tuš lugal	(for) the dwelling place of the king.
13.	1(u) geš ša$_3$-si mun mun ab-ba-ka ba-a-da-da[148]	10 (pieces of) wood, filling the middle, was . . . .-ed with/in salt of the sea.
14.	1(u) ma-na siki ud$_5$	10 ma-na of goat hair,
15.	im ba-an-gar	was placed on clay.
16.	1(diš) ^{geš} u$_3$-suh$_5$ 3(diš) kuš$_3$ geš-[x]-a-sa$_2$-še$_3$ ba-dim$_2$	1 (piece of) pine wood, cubits, was fashioned into a . . . .
17.	1(aš) 3(barig) esir$_2$ E$_2$-A gur lugal	1 gur, 3 barig of E$_2$-A bitumen (according to the) king('s standard),

[146] Possibly a type of container, see pp. 28–29 above.

[147] For the term a b - i t - t i, see Ontario 2, 383 obv. 4.

[148] Syllabic for t a g$_4$?

18.	1(u)$^{?}$ la$_2$ 1(aš) esir$_2$ ḫad$_2$ gur	9 gur of dried bitumen,
19.	4(u) 5(diš) dug gur-TUL$_2$	45 gur-vessels of the well.
20.	1(ban$_2$) i$_3$-geš	1 ban$_2$ of sesame oil,
21.	5(diš) sila$_3$ i$_3$-šaḫ$_2$	5 sila$_3$ of lard,
22.	du$_{10}$-us$_2$ u$_3$ kun gu-la ba-ra-ab-du$_8$	was caulked onto bathtubs and large(?) drains.
23.	2(geš'u) in-u gur	1,200 gur of straw,
24.	1(geš$_2$) eš$_3$-⸢tum⸣ gur	60 gur of chaff,
25.	3(geš'u) gi ŠID	1,800 (bundles of) ŠID reed.
26.	2(šar$_2$) 5(geš'u) 2(geš$_2$) gi NE	10,120 (bundles of) NE reed.
27.	2(diš) murgu$_2$ ⸢ba⸣	2 turtle shells,
	(*blank space*)	
28.	e$_2$-gal lugal	(for the) palace of the king (in Tummal?).
29.	2(u) la$_2$ 1(diš) geš gal 1(u) kuš$_3$-ta	19 (pieces of) wood, large, 10 cubits each.
30.	6(diš) geš 3(diš) kuš$_3$-ta za-ḫa-num$_2$-še$_3$	6 (pieces of) wood, 3 cubits each, for the zahanum.[149]
31.	5(diš) ^{geš}u$_3$-suḫ$_5$ 2(diš) kuš$_3$-ta ka$^{?}$ ab-ba-še$_3$	5 (pieces of) wood, 2 cubits each, for the opening (?) of the roof vent (?).
	(*blank space*)	

rev. col. i

	(*blank space*)	
1.	x [x] x x x	. . .
2.	[. . .] 7(diš) kuš$_3$-ta	. . . 7 cubits each.
3.	[. . .] x ⸢3(diš)⸣ kuš$_3$-ta	. . . (pieces of) wood, 3 cubits each.
4.	egir e$_2$	The old house.
5.	3(diš) geš ⸢6(diš)⸣ [kuš$_3$]-ta	3 (pieces of) wood, 6 cubits each.
6.	e$_2$ še-ri-[. . .]	The house . . .
7.	2(diš) geš 6(diš) kuš$_3$-[ta]	2 (pieces of) wood, 6 cubits each.
8.	2(diš) geš ka$_2$ 3(diš) kuš$_3$-ta	2 (pieces of) wood for/from a door, 3 cubits each
9.	e$_2$ du$_{10}$-us$_2$ e$_2$ šu us$_2$ *E$_2$*	House of baths . . . .
10.	5(diš) ^{geš}šinig 2(diš) [kuš$_3$]-ta	5 (pieces of) tamarisk wood, 2 cubits each
11.	e$_2$ du$_{10}$-us$_2$ 3(diš)$^{?}$ -še$_3$	For three bath-houses.
12.	2(diš) geš 7(diš) kuš$_3$-[ta]	2 (pieces of) wood, 7 cubits each.
13.	6(diš) geš 3(diš) kuš$_3$-[ta]	6 (pieces of) wood, 3 cubits each.
14.	e$_2$-da [x] gal x [x]	with the house . . . . large . . .
15.	1(diš) ^{geš}u$_3$-suh$_5$ 7(diš) ⸢kuš$_3$⸣	1 (piece of) pine wood, 7 cubits,
16.	2(diš) geš ša$_3$-si ig [. . .]	2 (pieces of) wood, (for) door filler . . . ,
17.	ig-še$_3$ ba-dim$_2$	into a door was fashioned.
18.	1(diš) geš 1(diš) kuš$_3$-<<ta>> ḫu$^{?}$ x	1 (piece of) wood, 1 cubit,
19.	ka$_2$ maḫ-še$_3$	for the lofty gate.
20.	1(diš) ^{geš}u$_3$-suḫ$_5$ 4(diš) kuš$_3$-[ta]	1 (piece of) pine wood, 4 cubits each,
21.	^{geš}ar-gi$_4$-bil-lu kun-še$_3$ ba-dim$_2$	into stair steps was fashioned.[150]

---

[149] A wooden structure, see *CAD* Z 13 s.v. *zaḫānu*.

[150] See Heimpel 2011: 107.

22.	6(diš) ^{geš}ḫašḫur	6 (pieces of) apple wood,
23.	5(u) ^{geš}e-la 1(diš) kuš$_3$-ta	50 (pieces of) e-la[151] wood, 1 cubit each,
24.	1(u) geš al	10 (pieces of) wood for hoe (handles),
25.	ki di-AŠ	. . .
26.	1(diš) ^{geš}šinig 2(diš) kuš$_3$	1 (piece of) tamarisk, 3 cubits,
27.	sag-kul kun-še$_3$ ba-dim$_2$	was fashioned into a bolt-tail (?).
28.	1(u) ^{geš}e-la šu x e-še$_3$ ba-⸢dim$_2$⸣	19 (pieces of) e-la wood were fashioned into a . . .
29.	2(diš) geš gal 1(u) [kuš$_3$]-ta	2 (pieces of) wood, large, 10 cubits each,
30.	geš-ur$_3$ UD šu x [x] ba-a-x-ak-a	were made(?) into . . . beams.
31.	1(diš) geš mi-ri$_2$-za [8(diš)] kuš$_3$	1 (piece of) wood for a mi-ri$_2$-za plank, 6 cubits,
32.	ur$_3$-ur$_3$-še$_3$ ba-⸢dim$_2$⸣	was fashioned into beams.
33.	1(u) geš gal 1(u) 2(diš) kuš$_3$-ta	10 (pieces of) wood, large, 12 cubits each,
34.	1(u) geš 6(diš) kuš$_3$-ta	10 (pieces of) wood, 6 cubits each,
35.	en-dingir-mu šu ba-⸢ti?⸣	Endingirmu received.
36.	5(geš$_2$) 5(u) 2(diš) geš 6(diš) [kuš$_3$-ta]	352 (pieces of) wood, 6 cubits each,
37.	1(u) 2(diš) geš ka$_2$ 2(diš) kuš$_3$-[ta]	12 (pieces of) wood for/from a door, 2 cubits each,
38.	4(diš) ^{geš}u$_3$-suḫ$_5$ 4(diš) [kuš$_3$-ta]	4 (pieces of) pine wood, 4 cubits each,
39.	2(u) 4(diš) ^{geš}dib 1(diš) ½(diš) [kuš$_3$-ta]	24 boards (for doors), 1 ½ cubits each,
40.	6(diš) ^{geš}dib 3(diš) kuš$_3$-[ta]	6 boards (for doors), 3 cubits each,
41.	4(diš) geš ša$_3$-si [ig]	4 (pieces of) wood, door fillers,
42.	ig 2(diš)-še$_3$ ba-dim$_2$	were fashioned into two doors.
43.	4(diš) ^{geš}u$_3$-suh$_5$ 5(diš) ⸢kuš$_3$⸣-[ta]	4 (pieces of) pine wood, 5 cubits each,
44.	1(u) 6(diš) geš mi-ri$_2$-za [6(diš) kuš$_3$-ta]	16 (pieces of) wood for mi-ri$_2$-za planks, 6 cubits each.
45.	3(diš) geš x 3(diš) kuš$_3$-[ta]	3 (pieces of) wood, . . . , 3 cubits each.
	(*rest broken*)	

rev. col. ii

1.	2(diš) ^{geš}u$_3$!-suḫ$_5$ 2(diš) kuš$_3$-ta	2 (pieces of) pine wood, 2 cubits each,
	(*blank space*)	
2.	[. . .]	. . .
3.	zi-ga e$_2$ udu-ka	Booked out of the sheepfold.
4.	1(diš) dug du-du sig$_{15}$ gid$_2$-da 2(aš) gur	1 du-du vessel, sig$_{15}$ (quality), long, 2 gur (capacity)
5.	kisal lugal	(for) the courtyard of the king.
6.	1(u) 5(diš) eš$_2$ GAN$_2$	15 field ropes,
7.	ig-a ba-a-da-da	were . . . .-ed onto the door.
8.	5(diš) murgu$_2$ peš	5 palm ribs.
9.	1(aš) gu$_2$ 4(u) 5(diš) ma-na mangaga	1 talent, 45 ma-na of raffia.
10.	1(u) 5(diš) geš al	15 (pieces of) wood for hoe (handles).
11.	1(geš$_2$) 1(u) 5(diš) ^{geš}dusu	75 dusu-baskets.

[151] A type of wood not otherwise attested.

12.	4(u) dug ḫi-a	40 vessels, various.
13.	2(geš$_2$) <geš> zu$_2$ al	120 (pieces of) wood for hoe tines.
14.	5(diš) kuš ḫi-a	5 hides, various.
15.	⅓(diš) ma-na kuš gu$_4$	⅓ ma-na ox hide.
16.	2(diš) ma-na u$_2$-ḫab$_2$	2 ma-na oak apples.
17.	2(diš) sila$_3$ al-la-ḫa-ru	2 sila$_3$ allaharu dye.
	(blank space)	
18.	zi-ga ša$_3$ tum-ma-al^{ki}	Booked out in Tummal.
19.	3(u) geš 5(diš) kuš$_3$-ta	30 (pieces of) wood, 5 cubits each,
20.	ensi$_2$ babila^{ki}	(for the) governor of Babylon.
21.	2(diš) geš 8(diš) kuš$_3$-ta	2 (pieces of) wood, 8 cubits each.
22.	5(diš) geš 6(diš) kuš$_3$-ta	5 (pieces of) wood, 6 cubits each.
23.	šu-tum ensi$_2$ [. . .]	Storeroom of the governor (of . . .)
	(rest broken)	

The second part of the credit section (following the materials for the courtyard of the king, rev. col. ii 5) is listed as booked out in Tummal for the governor of Babylon, and the storeroom of the governor of another place (name broken). The third and final part of the credits (rev. iii), on the other hand, lists large numbers of pieces of wood, followed by some additional products, all said to have been brought into the palace and received by a certain Aya-kala, child of Lugal-nesage. This is followed by two entries of beams received by two trade-agents.

rev. col. iii

1.	1(diš) geš ur$_3$ sumun 6(diš) kuš$_3$	1 beam, old, 6 cubits,
2.	6(diš) geš ur$_3$ sumun 8(diš) kuš$_3$-ta	6 beams, old, 8 cubits each,
3.	2(diš) geš ur$_3$ sumun 1(u) 1(diš) kuš$_3$-[ta]	2 beams, old, 11 cubits each,
4.	⸢geš sumun-am$_3$⸣ [x]	It is old wood . . .
5.	2(diš) ^{geš}šinig 8(diš) kuš$_3$-ta	2 (pieces of) tamarisk wood, 8 cubits each.
6.	3(diš) ^{geš}šinig 1(u) kuš$_3$-ta	3 (pieces of) tamarisk wood, 10 cubits each.
7.	4(diš) ^{geš}šinig 6(diš) kuš$_3$-ta	4 (pieces of) tamarisk wood, 6 cubits each.
8.	2(diš) ^{geš}šinig 1(u) la$_2$ 1(diš) kuš$_3$-ta	2 (pieces of) tamarisk wood, 9 cubits each.
9.	1(diš) ^{geš}šinig 1(u) 3(diš) kuš$_3$	1 (piece of) tamarisk wood, 13 cubits.
10.	1(diš) ^{geš}šinig 1(u) 2(diš) kuš$_3$	1 (piece of) tamarisk wood, 12 cubits.
11.	1(diš) ^{geš}šinig 1(u) 1(diš) kuš$_3$	1 (piece of) tamarisk wood, 11 cubits.
12.	^{geš}šinig-am$_3$	It is tamarisk
13.	1(diš) ^{geš}da 1(u) kuš$_3$	1 (piece of) DA wood, 10 cubits,
14.	2(diš) geš 1(u) 1(diš) kuš$_3$-ta	2 (pieces of) wood, 11 cubits each.
15.	1(diš) geš 1(u) 2(diš) kuš$_3$	1 (piece of) wood, 12 cubits.
16.	1(geš$_2$) 1(u) geš 6(diš) kuš$_3$-ta	70 (pieces of) wood, 6 cubits each.
17.	1(u) geš 5(diš) kuš$_3$-ta	10 (pieces of) wood, 5 cubits each.
18.	6(diš) geš 7(diš) kuš$_3$-ta	6 (pieces of) wood, 7 cubits each.
19.	8(diš) geš 8(diš) kuš$_3$-ta	6 (pieces of) wood, 8 cubits each.
20.	4(diš) ^{geš}u$_3$-suh$_5$ ^{geš}a-ra sumun 1(u) 1(diš) kuš$_3$-ta	4 (pieces) of pine wood, for a-ra-wood, old, 11 cubits each.
21.	3(diš) ^{geš}u$_3$-suh$_5$ 6(diš) kuš$_3$-ta	3 (pieces of) pine wood, 6 cubits each.
22.	2(diš) ^{geš}u$_3$-suḫ$_5$ 1(u) la$_2$ 1(diš) kuš$_3$-ta	2 (pieces of) pine wood, 9 cubits each.
23.	1(diš) ^{geš}pa-ku$_5$ geš gal 4(diš) kuš$_3$	1 cut-branch, large tree, 4 cubits.

24.	6(diš) ^{geš}sag-ku$_5$ 3(diš) kuš$_3$-ta	6 cut-tops[152], 3 cubits each.
25.	1(u) 2(diš) ^{geš}pa-ku$_5$ 2(diš) ½(diš) kuš$_3$-ta	12 cut-branches, 2 ½ cubits each.
26.	2(u) 4(diš) ^{geš}pa-ku$_5$ 1(diš) ½(diš) kuš$_3$-ta	24 cut-branches, 1 ½ cubits each.
27.	1(u) 6(diš) ^{geš}pa-ku$_5$ 1(diš) kuš$_3$-ta	16 cut-branches, 1 cubit each.
28.	8(diš) ^{geš}sag-ku$_5$ ½(diš) kuš$_3$-ta	8 cut-tops, ½ cubit each.
29.	4(diš) ^{geš}sag-ku$_5$ geš/nigin[153] 1(diš) kuš$_3$-ta	4 cut-tops . . . , 1 cubit each.
30.	4(diš) ^{geš}sag-ku$_5$ 1(diš) ½(diš) kuš$_3$-ta	4 cut-tops, 1 ½ cubits each.
31.	1(diš) ^{geš}sag-ku$_5$ geš gal 2(diš) kuš$_3$	1 cut-top, large tree, 2 cubits.
32.	5(u) ^{geš}e-la [x] kuš$_3$-ta	50 (pieces of) e-la wood, *n* cubits each.
33.	3(u) 4(diš) ^{geš}pa-ku$_5$ tur-tur ½(diš) kuš$_3$-ta	34 cut-branches, small, ½ cubit each.
34.	1(diš) ^{geš}ḪAR-ḪAR	1 ḪAR-ḪAR.[154]
35.	1(diš) ^{geš}sag-keš$_2$	1 sag-keš$_2$.[155]
36.	1(diš) ^{geš}u$_3$-suḫ$_5$ 1(diš) kuš$_3$	1 (piece of) pine wood, 1 cubit.
37.	1(diš) ^{geš}u$_3$-suḫ$_5$ 2(diš) kuš$_3$	1 (piece of) pine wood, 2 cubits.
38.	1(diš) ^{geš}mar im	1 spade (for) clay.
39.	1(diš) ig tur e$_2$-še$_3$/šu du$_7$	1 door, small, for a house completed.
40.	3(u) 1(diš) ^{geš}ab-ba 3(diš) kuš$_3$-ta	31 (pieces of) ab-ba wood, 3 cubits each.
41.	2(diš) ^{geš}sag-kul gal	2 bolts, large.
42.	1(diš) ^{geš}šu-a-sa$_2$	1 šu-a-sa$_2$.
43.	1(diš) ^{geš}šinig al-la-ra 3(diš) kuš$_3$	1 (piece of) tamarisk wood, al-la-ra, 3 cubits.
44.	1(diš) ^{geš}šinig pa ḫal-a 3(diš) kuš$_3$	1 (piece of) tamarisk wood, distributed branches(?), 3 cubits.
45.	1(diš) ^{geš}asal$_2$ pa ḫal-a 2(diš) kuš$_3$	1 (piece of) poplar wood, distributed branches(?), 2 cubits.
46.	5(u) la$_2$ 2(diš) ^{geš}i$_3$-šub si-sa$_2$	48 molds for regular (bricks),
47.	8(diš) ^{geš}i$_3$-šub ar-ḫa	8 molds for half-bricks,
48.	1(u) la$_2$ 1(diš) ^{geš}me-te-num$_2$	9 narrow planks,
	(*rest broken*)	

rev. col. iv

1.	1(diš) ^{gi}ḫal gid$_2$-da in-u	1 ḫal-basket, long, of straw.
2.	1(diš) geš mi-ri$_2$-za 8(diš) kuš$_3$	1 (piece of) wood for a mi-ri$_2$-za plank, 8 cubits,
3.	1(diš) ^{geš}ub a$_2$-da	1 (piece of) ub wood, . . .
4.	[x] ⸢^{gi}⸣gur a bala-e	n gur-baskets (for) water-drawing.
5.	3(diš) gir-ga gal	3 ropes,[156] large,
6.	1(diš) eš$_2$ GAN$_2$	1 field rope (?),
7.	2(u) 5(diš) dub-la$_2$ mangaga	25 "towers" of raffia,
8.	2(u) 1(diš) ^{geš}kun$_5$	21 ladders,

---

[152] Heimpel 2011: 90 with n. 23.

[153] It is not clear if geš or nigin is meant here. Neither is easy to explain.

[154] A wooden tool, probably unrelated to the musical instrument by the same name (see *Enki's Journey to Nippur* l. 63). Since it occurs together with the sag-keš$_2$ it is perhaps related to the plow as well. See Hruška 2005: 512 for technical terms related to the plow.

[155] Part of a plow, see Sallaberger 1999c: 383 n. 15.

[156] Made from raffia (mangaga), see Volk 2004: 287.

9.	1(geš$_2$) 2(u) dug ḫi-a	80 vessels, various,
10.	4(u) ma-na esir$_2$ ḫad$_2$	40 ma-na bitumen, dried,
11.	3(diš) eš$_2$ ma$_2$ gid$_2$ gibil	3 ropes for punting (?) boats, new,
12.	1(u) 5(diš) ma-na mangaga	15 ma-na of raffia,
13.	1(u) 4(diš) dug gur-TUL$_2$	14 gur-vessels of the well.
14.	2(diš) kid ig	2 mats for doors,
15.	1(diš) kid gu-za kuš si-ga	1 reed mat for a chair, "filled" with leather,
16.	4(aš) gu$_2$ gi NE	4 talents of NE reed,
17.	5(diš) ^{gi}gur in-u gibil	5 gur-baskets of straw, new,
18.	4(diš) ^{gi}gur in-u sumun	4 gur-baskets of straw, old,
19.	4(ban$_2$) esir$_2$ E$_2$-A lugal	4 ban$_2$ E$_2$-A bitumen, (according to the) king('s standard),
20.	3(u) ma-na siki ud$_5$	30 ma-na of goat hair,
21.	3(diš) dug du-du sig$_{15}$	3 du-du vessels, sig$_{15}$ (quality),
22.	4(diš) dug sila$_3$ banda$_3$^{da}	3 sila$_3$-vessels, junior (size),
	(*blank space*)	
23.	e$_2$-gal-a ku$_x$(KWU147)-ra	Brought into the palace.
24.	a-kal-la dumu lugal-nesag-e	A(ya)-kala, child of Lugal-nesage,
25.	šu ba-ti	received.
26.	4(u) 3(diš) geš-ur$_3$ 6(diš) kuš$_3$-ta	43 beams, 6 cubits each,
27.	ur-^{geš}gigir dam-gar$_3$ šu ba-ti	Ur-gigir, trade-agent, received.
28.	3(u) geš-ur$_3$ 8(diš) kuš$_3$-ta	30 beams, 8 cubits each,
29.	ur-^{d}a-šar$_2$ dam-gar$_3$ šu ba-ti	Ur-Asar, trade-agent, received.
	(*blank space*)	
	(*rest broken*)	

As expected the debits section is totaled, and as with the credits section this is very complex as no universal medium of equivalence could be applied:

rev. col. v

1.	[šunigin] 2(geš'u) geš ḫi-a	Total: 1,200 (pieces of) wood, various.
2.	[šunigin] ⸢gid$_2$⸣-bi 1(šar$_2$) 4(geš'u) 3(geš$_2$) 2(u) 4(diš) ⸢kuš$_3$⸣	Its total length: 6,204+*n* cubits.
	(*blank space*)	
3.	[šunigin x geš x]	[Total . . .]
4.	[šunigin gid$_2$-bi] 8(geš$_2$) 1(u) 5(diš) kuš$_3$	[Its total length]: 495 cubits.
5.	šunigin 2(u) la$_2$ 2(diš) geš mi-ri$_2$-za	Total: 18 (pieces of) wood for mi-ri$_2$-za planks.[157]
6.	šunigin gid$_2$-bi 2(geš$_2$) la$_2$ 8(diš) kuš$_3$	Its total length: 120 minus 8 cubits.[158]
7.	šunigin 1(aš) 3(barig) 4(ban$_2$) esir$_2$ E$_2$-A gur lugal	Total: 1 gur, 4 barig, 4 ban$_2$ of E$_2$-A bitumen, (according to the) king('s standard).[159]

[157] See rev. i 31, 44, iv 2.

[158] The total length of the mi-ri$_2$-za planks aids the reconstruction of the preceding entries. Note also the unusual notation "120 minus 8" for 112.

[159] See obv. vi 17, rev. iv 19.

8.	šunigin 1(u) la$_2$ 1(aš) esir$_2$ ḫad$_2$ gur	Total: 9 gur of bitumen, dried.[160]
9.	šunigin 1(geš$_2$) la$_2$ 1(diš) dug gur-TUL$_2$	Total: 59 gur-vessels of the well.[161]
10.	šunigin 2(u) 1(diš) ^{geš}kun$_5$!	Total: 21 ladders.
11.	šunigin 2(u) 3(diš) ^{geš}ḫašḫur erin$_2$	Total: 23 (pieces of) apple wood, for balance beams(?).
12.	šunigin 1(u) ^{geš}asal$_2$ ša$_3$-si ig	Total: 10 pieces of poplar wood (for) door filler.
13.	šunigin 2(u) 5(diš) dub-la$_2$ mangaga	Total: 25 "towers" of raffia.
14.	šunigin 1(u) la$_2$ 1(diš) ^{geš}me-te-num$_2$	Total: 9 narrow planks.
15.	šunigin 3(diš) eš$_2$ ma$_2$ gid$_2$	Total: 3 ropes for punting(?) boats,
16.	šunigin 3(diš) dug du-du sig$_{15}$	Total: 3 du-du vessels, sig$_{15}$ (quality).
17.	šunigin 1(diš) dug du-du sig$_{15}$ gid$_2$-da	Total: 1 du-du vessel, sig$_{15}$ (quality), long.
18.	šunigin 1(ban$_2$) i$_3$-geš	Total: 1 ban$_2$ of sesame oil.
19.	šunigin 5(diš) sila$_3$ i$_3$-šah$_2$	Total: 5 sila$_3$ of lard.
20.	šunigin 1(u) 6(diš) eš$_2$ GAN$_2$	Total: 16 field ropes(?).[162]
21.	šunigin 5(diš) murgu$_2$ peš	Total: 5 palm ribs.
22.	šunigin 2(aš) gu$_2$ mangaga	Total: 2 talents of raffia.[163]
23.	šunigin 3(geš$_2$) ^{geš}dusu	Total: 180 dusu-baskets.[164]
24.	šunigin 1(geš$_2$) geš al	Total: 60 (pieces of) wood for hoe (handles).[165]
25.	šunigin 2(geš$_2$) dug ḫi-a	Total: 120 vessels, various.
26.	šunigin 2(geš'u) in-u gur	Total: 1200 gur of straw.
27.	šunigin 1(geš$_2$) eš$_3$-tum gur	Total: 60 gur of chaff.
28.	šunigin 3(geš'u) sa gi ŠID	Total: 1,800 bundles of ŠID reed.
29.	šunigin 2(šar$_2$) 5(geš'u) 2(geš$_2$) sa gi NE	Total: 10,120 bundles of NE reed.
30.	šunigin 2(geš$_2$) geš zu$_2$ al	Total: 120 (pieces of) wood for hoe tines.[166]
31.	šunigin 2(diš) ^{geš}sag-kul gal	Total: 2 bolts, large.
32.	šunigin 1(diš) ^{geš}šu-a-sa$_2$	Total: 1 šu-a-sa$_2$.
33.	šunigin 5(diš) kuš ḫi-a	Total: 5 hides, various.
34.	šunigin ⅓(diš) ma-na kuš gu$_4$	Total: ⅓ ma-na of ox hide.
35.	šunigin 2(diš) ma-na u$_2$-ḫab$_2$	Total: 2 ma-na of oak apples.
36.	šunigin 2(diš) sila$_3$ al-la-ḫa-ru	Total: 2 sila$_3$ of allaharu dye.
37.	šunigin 3(diš) ⅓(diš) ma-na uruda	Total: 3 ⅓ ma-na of copper.[167]
38.	šunigin 5(diš) gin$_2$ su-ḫe$_2$	Total: 5 shekels of borax.

[160] But note that the credits include another amount of dried bitumen, counted in the weights system (ma-na) and not in the capacity system (gur). That amount, 40 ma-na, was subsequently entered into totals of the credits (rev. vi 8), and then into the surplus section (rev. vii 9)

[161] See obv. vi 19, rev. iv 13.

[162] See rev. ii 6, rev. iv 6.

[163] See rev. ii 9, rev. iv 12.

[164] The total lists 5 more dusu baskets than are found in the "credits" section of the account; unfortunately these are not found in the preserved part of the "surplus" section.

[165] See rev. i 24, rev. ii 10. Only 25 hoes are found in the preserved sections of the "credits." However, that number means that the notation in the totals of both the "debits" and "credits" must be read 1(geš$_2$) and not 1(diš).

[166] Based on a comparison with the number of hoe handles recorded in the account it is likely that the account recorded 120 hoe tines rather than two.

[167] The total found here in the credits section is 10 shekels less than the total of the debits, but copper is not found among in the preserved parts of the deficit section.

39.	šunigin 5(u) la$_2$ 2(diš) ^{geš}i$_3$-šub si-sa$_2$	Total: 48 molds for regular (bricks).
40.	šunigin 8(diš) ^{geš}i$_3$-šub ar-ḫa	Total: 8 molds for half-bricks.
41.	šunigin 1(diš) ^{geš}ḪAR-ḪAR	Total: 1 ḪAR-ḪAR.
42.	šunigin 1(diš) ^{geš}sag-keš$_2$	Total: 1 sag-keš$_2$.[168]
43.	[. . .] x	
	(*rest broken*)	

rev. col. vi

1.	šunigin 3(u) 1(diš) ^{geš}ab-ba 3(diš) kuš$_3$-ta	Total: 31 (pieces of) ab-ba wood, 3 cubits each.
2.	šunigin 2(diš) ^{gi}dag$_x$(KWU844)	Total: 2 dag-baskets.[169]
3.	šunigin 2(diš) ^{gi}mun mun ab-ba	Total: 2 salt-baskets for sea salt.[170]
4.	šunigin 1(diš) ^{gi}ḫal gid$_2$-da in-u	Total: 1 hal-basket, long, of straw.
5.	šunigin 1(diš) ^{geš}ub a$_2$-da	Total: 1 (piece of) ub wood, . . .
6.	[šunigin x] ^{gi}gur a bala-e	Total: n gur-baskets (for) water-drawing.
7.	šunigin 3(diš) gir-ga gal	Total: 3 ropes, large.
8.	šunigin 4(u) ma-na esir$_2$ ḫad$_2$	Total: 40 ma-na of bitumen, dried.
9.	šunigin 2(diš) kid ig	Total: 2 mats for doors.
10.	šunigin 1(diš) kid gu-za kuš si-ga	Total: 1 reed mat for a chair, "filled" with leather.
11.	šunigin 4(aš) gu$_2$ gi NE	Total: 4 talents of NE reed.
12.	šunigin 5(diš) ^{gi}gur in-u gibil	Total: 5 gur-baskets of straw, new.
13.	šunigin 4(diš) ^{gi}gur in-u sumun	Total: 4 gur-baskets of straw, old.
14.	šunigin 4(u) ma-na siki ud$_5$	Total: 40 ma-na of goat hair.[171]
15.	šunigin 4(diš) dug sila$_3$ banda$_3$^{da}	Total: 4 sila$_3$-vessels, junior (size).
16.	šunigin 2(diš) murgu$_2$ ba	Total: 2 turtle shells.

The totals of the "credits" are followed by the technical term z i - g a - a m$_3$ concluding the sentence, "out of it . . . is torn" (š a$_3$ - b i - t a . . . z i - g a - a m$_3$) marking the credits.

rev. col. vi

	(*blank space*)	
17.	zi-ga-am$_3$	Is booked out (~the "credits").

The "debits" is followed by a list of eight products classified as "deficit" (l a$_2$ - i a$_3$, see below), and at least eighteen products that are classified as "surplus" (d i r i g - g a, see also below). The colophon with the date terminates the account.

rev. col. vi

18.	la$_2$-ia$_3$ 1(u) 1(diš) geš-ur$_3$ 7(diš) kuš$_3$-ta	"Deficit": 11 beams, 7 cubits each.
19.	1(u) 7(diš) kuš$_3$ ^{geš}u$_3$-suḫ$_5$	17 cubits of pine wood.
20.	8(diš) kuš$_3$ geš mi-ri$_2$-za	8 cubits of wood for mi-ri$_2$-za planks.[172]
21.	1(diš) dub-la$_2$ mangaga	1 "tower" of raffia.

---

[168] Neither the Ḫ A R—Ḫ A R nor the s a g - k e š$_2$ is found in the preserved parts of the debits section, but since no deficit of these two products is listed we can assume that they were.

[169] See Maekawa 1993: 118–20 for the reading d a g$_x$. A ^{gi}d a g$_x$ is otherwise not attested.

[170] Probably originally listed in the broken section of the credits at the end of rev iii.

[171] See obv. vi 14, rev. iv 20.

[172] In both this and the preceding line the total length of wood falls short of the total length recorded in the "debits."

22.	1(diš) ^{geš}me-te-num$_2$	1 narrow plank.
23.	5(diš) eš$_2$ ma$_2$ gid$_2$	5 ropes for punting(?) boats.
24.	1(u) 2(diš) ^{geš}i$_3$-šub si-sa$_2$	12 molds for regular (bricks).
25.	2(diš) eš$_2$ geš zi-da	2 ropes for "straight"(?) wood.
	(*blank space*)	
26.	la$_2$-ia$_3$-am$_3$	(That) is the "deficit."
27.	diri 3(u) la$_2$ 1(diš) dug gur-TUL$_2$	"Surplus": 29 gur-vessels of the well.
28.	2(diš) ^{geš}ḫašḫur erin$_2$	2 (pieces of) apple wood, for balance beams(?).
29.	2(diš) eš$_3$ GAN$_2$	2 field ropes.
30.	8(diš) ^{geš}i$_3$-šub ar-ḫa	8 molds for half-bricks.
	(*rest broken*)[173]	

rev. col. vii

1.	1(diš) ^{geš}ig e$_2$ gibil til-la	1 door, new house, complete.
2.	3(u) 1(diš) ^{geš}ab-ba 3(diš) kuš$_3$-ta	31 (pieces of) ab-ba wood, 3 cubits each.
3.	2(diš) ^{gi}dag$_x$(KWU844)	2 dag-baskets.
4.	2(diš) ^{gi}[mun]-mun ab-ba	2 salt-baskets for sea (salt).
5.	[. . . ^{gi}]gur in-u	*n* gur-baskets of straw.
6.	[x] ^{geš}ub a$_2$-dar	*n* (pieces of) ub wood, . . .
7.	[x] ^{gi}gur a bala-e	*n* gur-baskets (for) water-drawing.
8.	3(diš) gir-ga gal	3 ropes, large.
9.	4(u) ma-na esir$_2$ ḫad$_2$	40 ma-na of bitumen, dried.
10.	2(diš) kid ig	2 mats for doors.
11.	1(diš) kid gu-za kuš si-ga	1 reed mat for a chair, "filled" with leather.
12.	4(aš) gu$_2$ gi NE	4 talent of NE reed.
13.	5(diš) ^{gi}gur in-u gibil	5 gur-baskets of straw, new.
14.	4(diš) ^{gi}gur in-u sumun	4 gur-baskets of straw, old.
15.	1(u) ma-na siki ud$_5$	10 ma-na of goat hair.
	(*blank space*)	
16.	diri-ga-am$_3$	(That) is the surplus.
17.	nig$_2$-ka$_9$ ak mu-zu-da	Account (concerning) Muzuda.
18.	ša$_3$ tum-ma-al^{ki}	Within Tummal.
19.	iti ^{d} li$_9$-si$_4$	Month: "Lisi."
20.	mu ^{d}nanna ga-eš^{ki} e$_2$-a-na ba-an-ku$_x$(KWU147)	Year: "Nanna of Ga'eš was brought into her house."

Operating Balance

As already mentioned at the outset of our discussion of the structure of the neo-Sumerian account, the third and final section of an account may hold its "operating balance." An "operating balance" occurred if the total values of the first and the second sections of the account were not of equal size. If the total value of the first section, the sag-nig$_2$-gur$_{11}$-ra-kam, or the "debits" of the accounted, exceeded the total value of the second section, the ša$_3$-bi-ta . . . zi-ga, or the "credits" of the accounted, a negative "operating balance" would be recorded. A negative "operating balance" or a "deficit" or "arrears" (Sumerian

[173] Among the products probably listed in the broken section of the "surplus" is borax. Only 3 shekels were listed in the "debits," totaled in the broken part, but 5 shekels were found in the "debits."

la₂-ia₃[174]) could, as we have seen, be transferred to the "debits" section of the following account. Eventually, "deficits" could be collected by the state, and we have abundant evidence for the fulfillment, or redemption, of "deficits" (la₂-ia₃ su(-ga)). If the total value of the second section of the account, on the other hand, exceeded the total value of the first section, then a positive "operating balance" would be recorded. A positive "operating balance" or a "surplus" (Sumerian diri(g)) could be transferred to the "credits" section of the following account.[175] If the accounted met the requirements of the "debits" section and the total values of each of the two sections were of equal size, no "operating balance" would be recorded.[176] Since the primary documents testify to the production-related nature of the accounts, there is little evidence to favor a classification of the neo-Sumerian account as a balanced account. No attempts were made to balance the accounts; instead the actual activities of the "accounted" were recorded. The work of the accountant was described by Van De Mieroop (1999–2000). We may repeat his reconstruction here: at the end of the accounting period the tablet containers were emptied and their contents arranged chronologically (when dealing with agricultural accounts), or hierarchically (when dealing with all other accounts), recording the largest, most important receipts first. By working in this way the accountant would instantly know the format of the account, and the job of drawing up the account would be reduced to copying the receipts, reformulating the wording slightly, and adding up the totals. Often the scribes would use edges or blank spaces to scribble numerical notations used for the computation of the totals.[177]

Text No. 37 is a four-column account of barley and bread. The colophon is broken, but one name can be reconstructed, that of Ili-bilanni, who has the title muḫaldim, or kitchen administrator. The text belongs to the archive of Garšana.

This text illustrates well the basic structure of the neo-Sumerian account, and is transliterated and translated here in full.[178]

No. 37. *MS 4675 = CUSAS 3, 1527*[179] *(Garšana, —)*

obv. col. i

1.	[6(aš) 2(barig) ninda gur]	6 gur and 2 barig of bread,
2.	[...[180]]	...
3.	[2(barig) 2(ban₂) ...[181]]	2 barig and 2 ban₂ (of bread), ...

---

[174] On the reading of la₂-ia₃ (LAL-NI), see Steinkeller 1984 (/la'a/); Powell 1977: 26 (/la-a/); Civil [in Steinkeller 1984] (/la-i/ or /la-ia/). A reading /la-ia/ is retained here.

[175] For example the Girsu account of copper concerning a certain Nimgir-ša-kuš, (chief) smith (simug), BPOA 1, 280 (AS 1–i to AS 1–xii), where a surplus from the 12th month of the previous year (Š 48) is entered into the "credits" (first entry: obv. ii 5–6); or the account of Lu-kala concerning the Umma pottery workshop MVN 1, 231 (AS 4), where a "surplus" from the previous year (AS 3) is entered into the "credits" (the account has a split "credits" section, and the "surplus" is first recorded as the last entry of the first part of the "credits": rev. i 1–2, before being recaptured at the end of the second half of the credits: rev. ii 29).

[176] For example the short Umma account concerning slave girls from Nippur (geme₂ nibru[ki]), with the conveyor (giri₃, see below) Ur-Suen, AAICAB 1/2, pl. 153, 1971-391 (from AS 6); or the large Umma account concerning Lugal-gu'e, BIN 5, 272 from AS 3, where credits and debits are exact matches: (2(šar₂) 5(geš'u) 5(geš₂) 1(u) 3(diš) ⅔(diš) guruš u₄ 1(diš)-še₃, or 10,513 ⅔ work-days).

[177] See, e.g., BIN 5, 272; also Ouyang and Proust *forthcoming*.

[178] The translation in CUSAS 3, based on the reconstructions of Heimpel (2009: 93–94), is only partly followed here. We differ in the understanding of certain bookkeeping terms (for Heimpel's capital, "debits" is used here, etc.); I remain unconvinced by Heimpel's reconstruction of the first four lines. Only one of the texts Heimpel uses to reconstruct the first three entries includes barley deliveries for the statue of the king (CUSAS 3, 1024, see obv. 8: sa₂ du₁₁ alam lugal), matching the only entry which can be partly reconstructed in text No. 37. Heimpel's reconstruction of the barley and bread amounts, the colophon and the totals are all accepted here.

[179] For the reconstructions, see Heimpel 2009: 92–93.

[180] Heimpel has: sa₂-du₁₁ [d]nin-an-si₄-an-na ("regular (deliveries) for Nin-Ansianna").

[181] Heimpel has: sa₂-du₁₁ za₃-gu-la₂ [d]nin-an-si₄-an-na ("regular (deliveries) for the Zagula (shrine/container) of Nin-Ansianna").

4.	[2(barig) 4(ban$_2$) . . .[182]] alam lugal	2 barig, 4 ban$_2$ (of bread) for the statue of the king.
5.	[iti] 6(diš)-kam	For six months.
6.	2(u) 3(diš) ⸢⅓(diš)⸣ ma-na bappir saga	23 ⅓ ma-na of good beer-bread,
7.	še-bi 3(ban$_2$) 5(diš) sila$_3$	its barley (equivalency): 3 ban$_2$, 5 sila$_3$.
8.	sa$_2$-du$_{11}$ ku$_5$-ra$_2$ iti 6(diš)-kam	"Cut"[183] regular (deliveries) of the sixth month.
	(*blank space*)	
9.	[šunigin 1(u)] 1(aš) 3(barig) 3(ban$_2$) 5(diš) sila$_3$ še ninda gur	Total: 11 gur, 3 barig, 3 ban$_2$ 5 sila$_3$ of barley bread.
	(*blank space*)	
10.	[sag-nig$_2$]-gur$_{11}$-ra-kam	It is the "debits."
11.	[ša$_3$-bi]-⸢ta⸣	Out of it:

obv. col. ii

1.	[1(aš) 1(barig) 4(diš) sila$_3$ gur]	1 gur, 1 barig, 4 sila$_3$ (of bread),
	(*blank space*)	
2.	zi-ga [x][184]	booked out for x.
3.	7(aš) 1(barig) ninda [gur]	7 gur, 1 barig of bread,
4.	še-ba si$_{12}$(SIG$_7$)-a ⸢ḪA?⸣.[A?]	barley rations for "blind" (workers)[185] x.
5.	1(aš) 1(barig) ⸢ninda gur⸣	1 gur, 1 barig of bread,
6.	še-ba ḫa-la-ša e$_2$?-[a?] gub-ba	barley rations for Ḫalaša, remaining in the house.
7.	1(aš) ninda gur	1 gur of bread,
8.	še-ba ad-da-kal-la	barley rations for Adda-kala.
9.	1(aš) ninda gur	1 gur of bread,
10.	še-ba aḫ-dam-i$_3$-li$_2$	barley rations for Aḫdam-ili.
11.	⸢4(barig)⸣ ninda	4 barig of bread,
12.	nig$_2$-dab$_5$ um-mi-kab-ta$_2$	"take" of Ummi-kabta.
13.	1(barig) ⸢ninda⸣	1 barig of bread,
14.	nig$_2$-dab$_5$ ur-^{d}nin-an-si$_4$-an-na nar	"take" of Ur-Nin-sianna, singer.
15.	1(aš) 1(barig) dabin gur	1 gur, 1 barig of barley flour,
16.	še-ba in-ga-⸢la⸣	barley rations for Ingala.
17.	⸢2(barig)⸣ dabin	2 barig of barley flour,
18.	⸢a⸣-da-lal$_3$	Adalal,

bottom

1.	iti 6(diš)-kam	for six months,

[182] Heimpel has sa$_2$-du$_{11}$.

[183] See discussion in Heimpel 2009: 93, without any conclusive suggestion to the meaning of the term.

[184] Owen and Mayr 2007: 426 reconstruct zi-ga-⸢am$_3$⸣, but I find it unlikely that the "credits" section should already end here.

[185] Heimpel 2009 suggesting the reading si$_{12}$ and proposing a semantic relationship to ze$_x$(SIG$_7$)-a, "to cut." See Greco 2015: 49 and n. 161 for a return to understanding the term as standing for unskilled workers, based on a metaphorical association between unskilled and not seeing.

rev. col. i

1.	šu ba-ti	received.
2.	9(geš$_2$) sa gi NE	540 bundles of NE reed,
3.	sa$_{10}$ še 1(ban$_2$) 2(u) sa gi-ta	barter for barley: 1 ban$_2$ for each 20 bundles of reed,
4.	še-bi 4(barig) 3(ban$_2$)	its barley (equivalency): 4 barig, 3 ban$_2$.
5.	^{d}iškur-illat šabra	Adad-tillatī, chief (household) administrator,
6.	šu ba-ti	received.
	(blank space)	
7.	šunigin 1(u) 5(aš) 3(ban$_2$) 4(diš) sila$_3$ še ninda ⸢gur⸣	Total: 15 gur, 3 ban$_2$, 4 sila$_3$ of barley (and) bread.
	(blank space)	
8.	zi-ga-[am$_3$]	Is booked out. (~the "credits")
9.	diri 3(aš) 1(barig) ⸢5(ban$_2$)⸣ [9(diš) sila$_3$]	Surplus: 3 gur, 1 barig, 5 ban$_2$, 9 sila$_3$ (of bread).
10.	diri-[ga-am$_3$]	It is the "surplus."
	(rest broken)	

rev. col. ii

	(start of column blank)	
1.	[nig$_2$-ka$_9$] ak	Account (concerning)
2.	[i$_3$-li$_2$]-bi-la-ni muḫaldim	Ili-bilanni, kitchen administrator.
3.	[ša$_3$ gar-ša]-an-na^{ki}	In Garshana.
	(rest broken)	

The calculations are easy to follow:

The "debits" ends with a total:

1(u) 1(aš) 3(barig) 3(ban$_2$) 5(diš) sila$_3$ še ninda gur
= 3515 sila$_3$

The "credits" ends with a total:

1(u) 5(aš) 3(ban$_2$) 4(diš) sila$_3$ še ninda gur
= 4534 sila$_3$

Resulting in a surplus:

3(aš) 1(barig) 5(ban$_2$) 9(diš) sila$_3$ (še ninda gur)
= 1019 sila$_3$

Because of my understanding of key administrative terminology, my interpretation of the text differs from that of Heimpel (2009: 92 ff.). Whereas Heimpel understood the first section of the account as the "capital" of the accounted, the cook Ili-bilanni, I understand the same as a negative asset of the accounted. I therefore translate this with "debits," and interpret it as what Ili-bilanni was given by the state, and for which he would therefore be held accountable. The origin of that barley and bread, which according to Heimpel were returned offerings from certain divine households, is left blank in my reconstruction. Based on his reconstruction, Heimpel saw in this text evidence for redistribution of the income of divine households to slaves and other staff.

The second section, in my interpretation the "credits" of the accounted, represents the actual spending of that barley and bread. Should Heimpel's reconstruction of the first four lines of the text prove correct, it is evidence that the barley and bread nominally destined for cultic offerings were given to staff as rations. This would not be surprising, of course, since divine beings do not eat and drink, and it is unlikely that foodstuffs would be left in front of divine images to go to waste.

Colophon

All accounts end with a colophon. As colophons would usually be written in the upper left corner, according to the original direction of writing—and thus presumably in a place which would be exposed—they are often damaged.

The colophons of all accounts contain information about the person or institution being accounted, as well as calendrical information. The colophon of text No. 36 will serve as an example of the colophon of an account:

No. 36. *MS 1983 = RA 16, 19 (Umma, Š 35–39)*

rev. col. vii

15.	nig$_2$-ka$_9$ ak mu-zu-da	Account concerning Muzuda.
16.	ša$_3$ tum-ma-al^{ki}	Within Tummal.
17.	iti ^{d}li$_9$-si$_4$	Month: "Lisi."
18.	mu ^{d}nanna ga-eš^{ki} e$_2$-a-na ba-an-ku$_x$(KWU147)	Year: "Nanna of Ga'eš was brought into her house."

5
EQUIVALENCIES

Equivalencies—the general term used in both ethno-economics and historical economics for sets of (fixed) conversion rates[186]—were widely employed in ancient Mesopotamia, where they are perhaps best known from the accounts of the dam-gar$_3$.[187] The equivalencies, however, were not restricted to the accounts of the dam-gar$_3$ or trade-agents; rather, they were applied throughout the Ur III administration. The implementation of the equivalencies seems to be the result of a "planned" economy and can be studied as a characteristic of state control. As long as the Ur III state was a well-functioning administrative machine, the equivalency rates remained almost completely fixed. Coinciding with the economic troubles early in the reign of Ibbi-Suen, after the breakaway of the provinces, a serious inflation in the equivalency rates can be observed.[188]

The fractional relationship between products (including work) and the medium of equivalency was expressed in the following terms: "Product x: its equivalence: y units of product z" (e.g., 1(aš) še gur / ku$_3$-bi 1(diš) gin$_2$).[189] There are no accounts of trade-agents (dam-gar$_3$) or receipts relating to these in the Schøyen Collection, so the following two texts are included to exemplify the principle of equivalencies:

AUCT 2, 392 (Umma, ŠS 3 iii)

obv.

1.	8(diš) ½(diš) ma-na siki kur-ra du	8 ½ ma-na of kur[190] wool, ordinary (quality).
2.	ku$_3$-bi 1(diš) gin$_2$	Its silver: 1 shekel.
3.	ki ur$_4$-ša$_3$-ki-du$_{10}$-ta	From Uršakidu.[191]
4.	ti-e$_2$-maḫ-ta	Ti-Emaḫta,

rev.

1.	lu$_2$ lukur gal	the man of the great concubine,
2.	šu ba-ti	received.
	(blank space)	
3.	iti še-kar-ra-gal$_2$-la	Month: "Barley brought to the harbor."
4.	mu us$_2$-sa ma$_2$ ^{d}en-ki [ba-ab]-du$_8$	Year after: "The boat of Enki was caulked."

The equivalency rate of kur wool in this text can therefore easily be described as one shekel silver fetching 8 ½ ma-na of kur wool.

Remaining in the domain of wool accounting, the equivalency value of the product recorded in the first line of the second example below is not very easily discernible to the modern scholar:

---

[186] See Halperin 1993 and Polanyi 1957: 20–22.

[187] See Ch. 4 for a discussion of these texts and the unfortunate application of the term "balanced" to them.

[188] See Jacobsen 1953 and Gomi 1984b.

[189] See also Englund 2012a: 435, 437.

[190] According to Steinkeller 1995: 57 denoting wool from "foreign sheep."

[191] Uršakidu is known making similar deliveries in 8 texts dating to between ŠS 1 and ŠS 3. The recipients are unusual and not well attested in the textual record (lu$_2$-[dingir-ra dumu] ⸢ŠID⸣-lu$_5$-ge$_2$ in AUCT 3, 251 from ŠS 1–xii; a-kal-la dumu ur-mes nam-la$_2$ lu$_2$-ša-lim-ke$_4$ in Princeton 1, 300 from ŠS 2–vi; ma-aš$_2$ šu ba-an-ti kišib$_3$ za-an-na-za-an-na dam ^{d}nu-muš-da-an-du$_{13}$ in AUCT 3, 373 from ŠS 3–iv; and dam lugal-[^{d}]⸢ištaran⸣-[ke$_4$$^{?}$] in AAICAB 1/1, pl. 30, 1911-212 from ŠS 3–iv). Furthermore, most of the texts employ a grammatically more complete form of the technical term "to receive" than usual (šu ba-an-ti, see also Chapter 7).

Aleppo 482 (NMSA 3789) (Umma, Š 46)

obv.

1.	2(u) 5(aš) gu$_2$ 3(u) 5(diš) ⅔(diš) ma-na siki GI	25 talents, 35 ⅔ ma-na of GI[192] wool.
2.	ku$_3$-bi 2(diš) ½(diš) ma-na 3(diš) ½(diš) gin$_2$ 1(u) 2(diš) še	Its silver: 2 ½ ma-na, 3 ½ shekel, 12 grains.
3.	ki ensi$_2$-ta	From the Governor.

rev.

1.	⌜ur$^{?}$-$^{[d?]}$dumu⌝-zi-⌜da⌝	Ur-Dumuzida
2.	šu ba-ti	received.
3.	mu ki-maš^{ki} ba-ḫul	Year: "Kimash was destroyed."
	(*blank space*)	

In this text one shekel of silver fetches almost exactly ten ma-na of wool. When converting the amounts into decimal notations of shekel of silver and ma-na of wool this becomes clear to us: 135 ⅔ ma-na of wool is equivalent to 153 ½ shekel of silver, with a remainder of 12 še of silver. Adding that small amount we see that the scribe was off only 18 še from a perfect 1:10 ratio between the products. That is less than one barleycorn of silver for each 100 ma-na of wool.[193]

The high number of instances where the relationship of product and its equivalency value can be expressed as a round number of the product, when set against one shekel of silver, strongly suggests that this was also the way the ancients learned these equivalencies.[194] No lists of equivalency values have been found, and any suggestions as to how these rates were learned and distributed across the realm remains speculation.[195]

The main reason for hypothesizing that the equivalencies were state-imposed rests on the fact that most of them represented a nearly perfect fractional relationship between product and equivalency. The fact that these fixed conversion rates were employed by the administrators with a certain rigidity is thought to be good confirmation of this. The best-known neo-Sumerian medium of equivalency, silver, has from time to time

---

192 According to Steinkeller (1995: 57) siki GI denotes wool from native sheep (udu eme-gir$_x$(GI)). However, he also considers two other interpretations of GI in relation to sheep, that GI denoted the colour of the animal (gi, "yellow" in Sumerian), or wool from sheep fed on a special diet consisting of reed (gi, "reed" in Sumerian) (p. 56). Steinkeller rejects the latter meaning, and reserves the designation "yellow" for the animals, not the wool.

193 Instead of writing 1(u) 2(diš) še the scribe should have written 3(u) to reach the perfect relationship of 1-to-10 between the GI wool and silver. Whether this was a mistake or the result of an actual minor fluctuation in "prices" is unclear. The text, in the Aleppo Museum, Syria, was imaged and collated by Bertrand Lafont and the author in 2006 and 2008. The current state of that collection is unknown.

194 See in particular Englund 2012a: 440 ff. Note, therefore, that this is opposite to Snell's understanding of the equivalency rates (Snell 1982). In Snell's system the equivalency rates become prices, since he translated them into the amount the basic unit of the good it equates to, e.g., one unit of product x, equals y units of the medium of equivalency (in Snell's analysis mostly silver). Snell discussed what he called the two options faced by the ancients when trying to express what he termed "prices" (p. 116): the "a" option conforming with the one expressed in this study, rejected by Snell as a viable way of presenting the equivalencies, and the "b" option giving the number of units one "unit" of the product/work could fetch. Snell's argument for this solution is hard to follow. He seems to base it on the few instances where the equivalence does not represent a nice fraction, and the few cases where the "product" was equated with more than one unit of the media of equivalency. Such an argument is not convincing when considered in light of the many instances of explicitly stated equivalencies in the texts themselves, all of which were expressed as "how much one unit of the media of equivalency can fetch."

195 It may be possible to consider the first eleven paragraphs of, e.g., the Laws of Eshnunna such a codified list of equivalencies (see Roth 1997: 59–60); see now in particular Englund 2012a.

been understood as money.[196] Subsequently, it has been suggested that the silver equivalencies recorded the amounts of silver used to purchase the products listed in the accounts concerning the "trade-agents."[197] Silver was only one among many products that, together with the concept of man-days, could function as a medium of equivalency. These equivalencies were applied to the counted objects of the account with a double purpose. First of all, the equivalencies were introduced to ease the computation of the valuables recorded in the account. When adding numerous discrete objects, the equivalencies made the calculation of the total an easy task. Secondly, supplying each product with a set conversion rate, which presumably resembled an expected value, the administrators hoped to maximize the production.

Sometimes the equivalencies were explicitly stated in the text, as for example in ZA 95, 191 (BM 106050) rev. iii 5–6: 4(diš) gin$_2$ ku$_3$-sig$_{17}$ ḫuš-a 1(u) 5(diš)-ta / ku$_3$-bi 1(diš) ma-na, "four shekels of red gold, (at a rate of) fifteen (shekels silver for) each (shekel gold), its silver: one ma-na." The text Fs. Jones 216 (from AS 3 i) provides a clue as to why the accountants would specify the equivalency rate of gold; we read, obv. ii 1(diš) gin$_2$ ku$_3$-sig$_{17}$ 7(diš)-ta / ku$_3$-bi 7(diš) gin$_2$, and translate: "one shekel of gold, at a rate of seven (shekels silver for each shekel gold), its silver: seven shekels." The rates for gold varied greatly, corresponding to the quality of the gold, and the specific quality of the gold could be described by its equivalency value.[198] Another way to translate the previous example is thus "one shekel of seven-shekel gold," and to treat this explicit equivalency as a quality marker, comparable to the modern unit carat.

Text No. 38, an odd receipt without any recipient or delivering agent, gives the explicit equivalency to red gold on two occasions. In both cases red gold is written simply ku$_3$ ḫuš-a, and not as is most common, ku$_3$-sig$_{17}$ ḫuš-a.

No. 38. *MS 1947/4 (Umma, AS 6)*

obv.

1.	1(diš) tug$_2$ bar-dul$_5$ šar$_3$	1 bar-dul$_5$ textile, šar$_3$ quality.[199]
2.	1(diš) tug$_2$ nig$_2$-lam$_2$ šar$_3$	1 nig$_2$-lam$_2$ textile, šar$_3$ quality.
3.	tum-mal$_x$(TUR$_3$)^{ki}-še$_3$	For Tummal.
4.	a-ra$_2$ 1(diš)-kam	For the first time.
5.	2(diš) gin$_2$ ku$_3$ huš-a 1(u) 5(diš)-ta	2 shekel of red gold, 15 (shekel silver) each (shekel gold)
6.	1(diš) tug$_2$ bar-dul$_5$ šar$_3$	1 bar-dul$_5$ textile, šar$_3$ quality.
7.	1(diš) tug$_2$ nig$_2$-lam$_2$ šar$_3$	1 nig$_2$-lam$_2$ textile, šar$_3$ quality.
8.	ezem-maḫ-še$_3$	For the lofty festival.

---

[196] Hallo and Curtis 1959: 105, 108, 112.

[197] See also Ouyang 2011.

[198] When the equivalency value was not specified, gold was normally exchanged at a rate of 7 shekels of silver, or less, to each shekel of gold. See AUCT 2, 173 (from Š 40 v), where 1 shekel of gold is equivalent to 6 ⅔ shekels of silver; MVN 4, 147 (from Š 45), where the rate is 6 ½ shekels of silver for 1 shekel of gold; and MVN 11, 165 (from Š 39), where the rate is 7 shekels of silver for 1 shekel of gold. This text mentions a bracelet (ḪAR) weighing 1 ma-na (rev. 1) with an equivalency value of a little more than 7 ma-na of silver. AAICAB 1, 1911-483 (from ŠS 6 x) 1–2 has a very high exchange rate of more than 30 shekels of silver for 1 shekel of gold. Finally, note that in SACT 2, 119 (from AS 5), the exchange rate is 8: see ll. 1–2: igi-4(diš)-gal$_2$ ku$_3$-sig$_{17}$ / ku$_3$-bi 2(diš) gin "¼ (shekel) gold, its silver is 2 shekels."

[199] For šar$_3$ as a quality marker, see Waetzoldt 1980–83: 585.

rev.

1.	ša$_3$ uri$_5$^{ki}-ma[200]	Within Ur.
2.	a-ra$_2$ 2(diš)-kam	For the second time.
3.	1(diš) gin$_2$ ku$_3$-ḫuš-a 1(u) 5(diš)-ta	1 shekel of red gold, 15 (shekel silver) each (shekel gold)
4.	1(diš) tug$_2$ bar-dul$_5$ šar$_3$	1 bar-dul$_5$ textile, šar$_3$ quality.
5.	1(diš) tug$_2$ nig$_2$-lam$_2$ šar$_3$	1 ni$_3$-lam$_2$ textile, šar$_3$ quality.
6.	a$_2$-ki-ti ^{d}en-lil$_2$-la$_2$-še$_3$	For the "New Year's" (festival) of Enlil.
7.	a-ra$_2$ 3(diš)-kam	For the third time.
8.	giri$_3$ in-za-an	Conveyor: Inzan.
9.	mu ša-aš-šu$_2$-ru-um^{ki} ba-ḫul	Year: "Šaš(u)rum was destroyed."

The accountant who wrote MVN 11, 101, an account concerning Ur-Šulpa'e the "trade-agent," from Š 43 xii to Š 44 i, applied a set of explicit conversion rates to calculate the equivalencies of all the products in the text.[201] It begins with a "debits" section as follows:

MVN 11, 101

obv.

1.	3(u) 9(aš) 3(ban$_2$) še gur lugal	39 gur 3 ban$_2$ of barley, (according to the) king('s standard),
2.	ku$_3$ 1(diš) gin$_2$-a 1(aš) še gur lugal	in 1 shekel of silver, 1 gur of barley (according to the) king('s standard),
3.	ku$_3$-bi ½(diš) ma-na 9(diš) gin$_2$ 1(u) 8(diš) še	its silver: ½ ma-na, 9 shekels, 18 grains.

The calculations are easily reproduced, since it is a one-to-one conversion: 1 gur of barley to one shekel of silver. This is the standard conversion rate of barley to silver. 39 gur equals 39 shekels, written ½ ma-na (= 30 shekels) and nine shekels, and three ban$_2$ is one tenth of a gur, as 18 še is one tenth of a shekel (holding 180 še).

The first entry of the "credits" section reads:

MVN 11, 101

obv.

7.	3(aš) esir E$_2$-A gur	3 gur of E$_2$-A bitumen,
8.	ku$_3$ 1(diš) gin$_2$-a 1(barig) esir E$_2$-A lugal-ta	in 1 shekel of silver, 1 barig E$_2$-A bitumen each, (according to the) king('s standard),
9.	1 (gur) 4(barig) 2(ban$_2$) 8(diš) sila$_3$ esir E$_2$-A gur 1(barig) 3(ban$_2$)-ta	1 gur, 4 barig, 2 ban$_2$, 8 sila$_3$ of E$_2$-A bitumen, 1 barig, 3 ban$_2$ each,
10.	ku$_3$-bi ⅓(diš)$^{ša!}$ 1(diš) ⅓(diš) gin$_2$ la$_2$ 4(diš) še	its silver: ⅓ (ma-na), 1 ⅓ shekel minus 4 grains.

That is, in other words, three gur of E$_2$-A bitumen, at a rate of 60 sila$_3$ E$_2$-A bitumen for one shekel of silver, and one gur and 268 sila$_3$ of E$_2$-A bitumen, (at a rate of 1 shekel of silver) for each ninety sila$_3$ (of

[200] Written ma ki.

[201] Englund already cited the text OrSP 47–49, 196 (from Š 37 xi) in Englund 1990: 52 with n. 177. Several other examples are found in the Girsu text TUT 122 (from Š 39 to Š 40), see, e.g., iv 4'–7': 8(diš) sila$_3$ šim gig 8(diš) sila$_3$-ta / ku$_3$-bi 1(diš) gin$_2$ / 1(ban$_2$) 5(diš) sila$_3$ i$_3$ ⸢šaḫ$_2$⸣ 1(ban$_2$) 5(diš) sila$_3$-ta / ku$_3$-bi 1(diš) gin$_2$, "8 sila$_3$ of šim gig, at a rate of 8 sila$_3$ each (shekel), its silver: 1 shekel. 15 sila$_3$ lard, at a rate of 15 sila$_3$ each (shekel), its silver: 1 shekel."

E$_2$-A bitumen).[202] It is interesting here to note how the full equivalency rate is written in the first case, but the second time only an abbreviated statement is set down. The entire text of MVN 11, 101 states the equivalency rates in a similar fashion.

In some of the texts published in UET 3, the equivalency rates were also stated explicitly. This may be explained by the fact that all of these texts originate from Ur during the reign of Ibbi-Suen, and therefore fall within the period of time when we expect to find an inflation in the equivalency rates. The phenomenon of explicitly stated equivalency rates may well be a symptom of a degrading economic system.[203]

Although all goods could be furnished with equivalencies like the ones described above, there are notable exceptions. In particular animals both rare and domesticated, as well as plants and trees were rarely, if ever, assigned equivalencies. This is perhaps most clear in the important account of the Umma basketry and carpentry workshop TCL 5, 6036 and the equally important account of trees and plant products text No. 36 (RA 16, 19), both also discussed in Chapter 4. In TCL 5, 6036 the work is furnished with equivalencies but not the raw products. In text No. 36 there is no recording of work-time for refined products, and the raw products are not furnished with equivalencies. In both texts the resulting summaries of both debits and credits are very long.

The equivalency rates, however, were as a rule not explicitly stated in the texts. The fact that equivalencies were almost never written in the primary documents suggests that the equivalencies were not prices, but rather state-imposed conversion rates, applied with the sole purpose of aiding the computation of the rate of fulfillment of the obligations, as expressed when subtracting the "credits" from the "debits."

Barley could function as a medium of equivalency, and could also be transferred into workdays. In the accounts concerning overseers of the mill, barley would be converted into the workdays of female workers.[204] The workdays of "hirelings," who were added to almost all work teams concerned with agricultural work, were recorded in the books as an amount of barley—the conversion was always specified according to the category of the "hireling," who normally worked at a rate of 6–7 liters per day (expressed with the standard formula a$_2$ lu$_2$ ḫun-ga$_2$ n sila$_3$-ta, "work of each hireling *n* sila$_3$ (of barley)").[205]

Text No. 155 is a large account concerning a team of agricultural workers. Although the colophon is missing, it can be surmised, based on parallel texts such as TCL 5, 5675, that the team was supervised by a "captain of plow oxen" (nu-banda$_3$ gu$_4$). The text will be discussed in Chapter 8. In the excerpt below the daily barley rate of the hirelings (six sila$_3$ each) is not used to equate the workdays with barley: in TCL 5, 5675 an amount of barley in the "debits" section is converted into workdays of hirelings (obv. i 6–13).

No. 155. *MS 4712 (Umma, X–xii)*

obv. col. vi

23.	3(geš'u) 6(geš$_2$) sar ^{u2}erin$_x$(KWU896)-na ze$_x$(SIG$_7$)-a 1(u) 5(diš) sar-ta	Cutting 2160 sar of (prickly) cedar(?)[206], 15 sar each (workday).
24.	a$_2$-bi u$_4$ 2(geš$_2$) 2(u) 4(diš)	Its work: 144 days.
25.	a$_2$ lu$_2$ hun-ga$_2$ 6(diš) sila$_3$-ta	Work of hireling 6 sila$_3$ (of barley) each.

[202] Note that this is written /ku(g) diš gin-a(loc.) aš še gur lugal/, literally "in 1 shekel: 1 gur barley." Compare to MVN 11, 102 (from AS 3), where the equivalency rate of E$_2$-A bitumen is expressed in a similar fashion. Further, see also TUT 121 (from AS 9), where 5 shekels of silver fetch 1 gur of E$_2$-A bitumen (see rev. iii 5'–6'); that text also uses explicitly stated equivalency rates throughout.

[203] The texts are UET 3, 1165 (from IS 7 xi), 1198 (from IS 3), 1207 (no date), 1309 (from IS 8 vii), 1377 (from IS 6 viii), 1422 (from IS 8 xi), and 1514 (from IS 3).

[204] See Englund 1990: 81–90.

[205] Maekawa 1989: 47–48. See also Dahl 2002: 333, and most recently Englund 2012a and b.

[206] If KWU 896 is to be read erin (see Ferwerda 1985: 6 with literature, see also n. 342 below) then it may be possible to suggest that a sub-species of cedar is meant here, perhaps the prickly cedar (*Juniperus oxycedrus*) which can grow like a shrub on bad land.

Workdays could function as a medium of equivalency, applied in a very similar fashion to barley or silver equivalencies. The amount of work required as a satisfactory equivalency of one workday seems to have been rigorously established. Departures from the standard equivalencies were based on extraneous circumstances such as the condition of the soil.[207]

The system of equivalencies used for work can usually be described in the following way: task x, given its equivalency value being y units of x per man-day, its work: z days. Text No. 156, a large fragmentary account of work (dealt with separately in Chapter 8) records multiple distinct work tasks that are expressed in the above-mentioned format.[208]

No. 156. *MS 4713 (Umma, X–xii)*

rev. col. ii

11.	2(geš$_2$) 5(u) 7(diš) sar al 6(diš) sar-ta	177 sar (of land) hoed at a rate of 6 sar (each workday),
12.	a$_2$-bi u$_4$ 2(u) 9(diš) ½(diš)	its work: 29 ½ days.

The extraordinary fact that work was in this way commodified has been discussed in the literature (most recently Englund 2012a and b). Apart from field work, the work of "skilled" workers employed in workshops could also be furnished with equivalencies. Most prominent are perhaps the complicated equivalencies used in the mills, mentioned above, where certain qualities of flour were furnished with equivalent amounts of workdays.[209] But also in the basketry and pottery workshops finished products could be assigned a value in both raw materials and workdays.[210]

Equivalencies were also used in the administration of animal husbandry. The herders were responsible for delivering a certain amount of the products from their flocks each year, calculated according to the size of the herd. The products from sheep and goats were wool and meat, as well as dairy products from goats, while the products obtained from large cattle were primarily dairy products. Cattle were herded as a source of traction as well, but only to a lesser extent for their meat, horns, hides, and tendons. Also the fodder for herded animals was computed using equivalancies. Most animals were fed according to standard rates, so for example a fattened sheep would receive 1 sila$_3$ of barley each day, as stated in text No. 39:

No. 39. *MS 1947/16 (Umma, X–ii)*

obv.

1.	6(geš$_2$) 3(u) 6(diš) udu 1(diš) sila$_3$-ta	396 sheep, 1 sila$_3$ (barley) each.
2.	še-bi 1(aš) 1(barig) 3(ban$_2$) 6(diš) sila$_3$ gur	Its barley: 1 gur and 96 sila$_3$ (= 396 sila$_3$).
3.	sa$_2$-du$_{11}$ u$_4$ 1(diš)-kam	Regular (delivery) of the first day.

---

[207] A workday was the equivalent of, e.g., a volume of earth to be excavated of the approximate size of 3 m^3. See, e.g., Aegyptus 8, 264 11 (from AS 3) obv. 4–7: 5(u) 4(diš) sar kin saḫar / guruš 1(u) gin$_2$-ta / a$_2$-bi u$_4$ 5(geš$_2$) 2(u) 4(diš) / i$_7$ a-du$_{10}$-ga ba-al-la, "an area of 54 (cubic) sar (ca. 972 m^3) to be excavated, each worker (each day) 1/6 (unit of 36 cubic sar, ca. 3 m^3), its work: 324 days, excavating the Sweet-water-canal." It seems as if the area an "unskilled" state-dependent worker was required to hoe was between 144 and 180 m^2, daily. The hirelings (lu$_2$-ḫun-ga$_2$), on the other hand, were apparently required to hoe an area considerably larger, perhaps corresponding to their larger daily provisions: whereas the guruš generally received 2 sila$_3$ of barley each day, the hireling received approximately 6 sila$_3$.

[208] However, in none of the preserved entries of either text No. 156 or No. 155, the other large account of field work in the collection, is the full form of this relationship given. BIN 5, 258 will serve here as an example of that: obv. 3–5: 3(u) 9(diš) sar al ak / guruš-e ½(diš) sar-ta/ a$_2$-bi u$_4$ 1(geš$_2$) 5(u)-kam, "39 sar (= c. 1404 m^2) hoed, each worker (hoeing at a rate of) 1⁄2 sar (= c. 18 m^2) (per day), its work is 110 days." Note the surprising low rate of hoeing recorded in this text, presumably due to the conditions of the ground of this particular plot.

[209] Englund 1991.

[210] Englund 1988: 169–70 n. 43 for reed mats; Waetzoldt 1970–71 and Dahl 2010a for pots.

rev.

1. udu niga bala-a — Fattened sheep of the bala (obligation).[211]
   (blank line)
2. iti sig$_4$-$^{ge\check{s}}$i$_3$-šub-ga$_2$-ra — Month: "Brick placed in the mold."

Typically, the administrative records bundled all the animals of a shepherd together and calculated the amount of wool that he was obliged to produce according to the size of the entire herd. Accordingly, it has proven impossible to establish whether the accountants used a specific set of equivalencies when computing the amounts listed in these texts. The products from cattle, in particular the dairy production and the increase in the herds, are well understood. The administration used a set of equivalencies, resembling estimates, when planning the production and growth of each herd of cattle.[212] Other products from cattle, such as hides, meat, horns, and tendons, also entered the economy, but no equivalency rates between the herds and these products have been found.[213]

Silver was furnished with an equivalency in rare cases.[214] In these cases, silver is likely to have existed as a commodity with a set value. An explanation should probably be sought in the system of obligations and deficits and their replacement or fulfillment. It is likely that an obligation expressed in any specific product could be redeemed by an equivalence of silver.[215]

The system of equivalencies used by the Ur III administration was an efficient means of exploiting the producing population and the land. It seems that the equivalencies mostly corresponded to a rate of production which the producers could not achieve, accumulating deficits each year.[216] R. K. Englund has described this process, and the liability of the debtor, in some detail (1990). It is most likely that the state employee mentioned in the colophon of an account was liable for the "operating balance," in extreme cases threatening his own life as well as that of his family.[217] Ample evidence exists that suggests that the state vigorously collected outstanding debts and any unsettled "operating balance," even claiming these assets from the households of deceased agents.[218]

The examples of explicit equivalency rates discussed here represent only a sample of exceptional references.[219] The majority of the equivalencies were simply calculated and written in the books, almost always applying the same rates for the same products. No lists of such rates have ever been recovered from Mesopotamia, but they almost certainly existed, although it is of course possible that the accountants would memorize the many rates.

---

[211] See also BPOA 1, 1539 (BM 107911).

[212] Englund 1995: 377–429.

[213] Englund 2003:1 §§18–21.

[214] See, e.g., CHEU 51 (no date) obv. 5: 7(diš) gin$_2$ ku$_3$-babbar siki-bi 1(diš) gu$_2$ 1(u) ma-na, "7 shekels of silver, its wool is 1 gu$_2$ and 10 ma-na."

[215] See, e.g., CHEU 51 obv. 6: ḫe$_2$-sa$_6$-ge na-gada . . . etc. . . . , rev. 17–19: la$_2$-ia$_3$-ta su-ga / sipa-de$_3$-ne / mu-ku$_x$(DU), "Ḫesage, shepherd, etc., replaced from the deficit, the shepherds brought in."

[216] D. Snell, on the other hand, is of the conviction that "From comparison of prices for different volumes of the same commodity, one can see that the agency was not interested in maximizing return on the money spent; it was interested only in making sure that the bureau were properly supplied." (Snell 1977: 50).

[217] Englund 1990: 38–48.

[218] See, firstly, the evidence presented by Englund 1990: 38–43, 46–48, and compare with BE 3-1, 13 (from ŠS 8 ii), a short text from north Mesopotamia suggesting the hard penalties that could befall an agent who failed to make good on his deficit (in this case documented in clauses of a legal record). SANTAG 7, 172, a silver / barley loan seemingly with a 100% interest rate also presents evidence of this.

[219] Sometimes the equivalency rate and medium are stated, but not the actual equivalency, as in BSA 3, 40 1 (from AS 2 xi) rev. iii 1: 1(u) 5(diš) sa sum sikil 8(diš) gin$_2$-ta, "15 bundles of onions, at a rate of 8 shekels each." Compare to TUT 121 (from AS 9), where the equivalence rate for "crushed" (gaz) onions is stated to be 6 shekels each. No equivalency value is recorded there either.

6
ACCOUNTABILITY

A rigid system of accountability permeated all levels of the Ur III social hierarchy. Anyone entrusted with valuables, whether labor (e.g., in form of a work crew) or property (in form of the yield of a field, a herd of animals, content of a storeroom, etc.), was held accountable by the state administration. The value of the grant and the rate of fulfillment were calculated by means of equivalences. This can to some extent be shown by sampling Ur III accounts. The king and the innermost circles of the imperial court were perhaps excluded from the system of accountability, although some accounts concerning members of the royal clan have been found, and more undoubtedly will be recovered after an extensive search in Ur.[220] The people at the bottom of the social pyramid were people who with some right can be described as being entirely state-property were presumably devoid of land-ownership and access to any means of production. They were, as a result, not held accountable in the same way as their overseers, rather they were the "goods" accounted for in the books.

At the top of a local administrative hierarchy we find the city governor. Several accounts have been published that record transactions of the city governor of Umma.[221] The governor was held accountable by the state for the values entrusted to him. It appears as if what was entrusted the governor was the entire province, and that this province had a value.[222]

The following text, No. 40, is an example of an account of an institution rather than a person, in this case the elusive Tummal:[223]

No. 40. *MS 4356 (Umma, AS 7)*

obv.

1.	1(u) 6(diš) guruš u_4 4(u)-še$_3$	16 workers for 40 days.
2.	a_2-bi u_4 1(geš'u) 4(u)-kam	Their work-days: 640 (~ the "debits").
	(blank space)	
3.	ša$_3$-bi-ta	Out of it:
4.	6(geš$_2$) 1(u) 8(diš) guruš u_4 1(diš)-še$_3$	378 workers for one day (~ work-days).
5.	giri$_3$ lugal-x	Conveyor: Lugal-x
6.	1(u) 6(diš) guruš u_4 ⸢1(u)⸣ la$_2$ 1(diš$_{tenû}$)-še$_3$ giri$_3$ ur-^{d}šara$_2$	16 workers for 9 days. Conveyor: Ur-Šara.
7.	e$_2$ tum-mal$_x$(TUR$_3$)^{ki} du$_3$-a	(For) building the House of Tummal.
8.	[...]	...
	(rest broken)	

---

220 Two texts hint at the existence of accounts concerning the members of the royal family: ASJ 2, 31 87 (from Š 42), and CT 7, 27 (= BM 18376, from Š 42). See also the "account of the overseers of the textile factory and of the fullers of the household of Šulgi-simti in Ur," Orient 16, 107 174 (from Š 43): nig$_2$-ka$_9$ ak / ugula uš-bar-ra u$_3$ ^{lu2}azlag$_2$-e-ne / e$_2$ ^{d}šul-gi-zi-im-ti / ša$_3$ urim$_5$^{ki}-ma. Our knowledge of the households of the members of the royal family has greatly improved with the publication of the newly discovered archives of the provincial city Garšana, which was the (semi)-private estate of a daughter of Amar-Suen and her husband (see Owen 2011; Owen and Mayr 2007).

221 Among these we find MVN 21, 334 (from ŠS 8), an account concerning the subsistence barley of the governor (rev. 6: nig$_2$-ka$_9$ ak še šuku-ra ensi$_2$); Ledgers pl. 23, 13 (from ŠS 1 to ŠS 5), an silver account concerning the governor (rev. 9: nig$_2$-ka$_9$ ak ku$_3$ ensi$_2$-ka); and AAICAB 1, 1924-666 (from AS 3), a wool account concerning the governor (rev. viii 4–5: nig$_2$-ka$_9$ ak siki / ensi$_2$-ka). See also Dahl 2002: 337–38.

222 See, e.g., the account of the bala of Ur-Lamma, the governor of Girsu; RTC 305 (from Š 44 xi to Š 44 xiii) rev. iv 9–10: nig$_2$-ka$_9$ ak / bala ur-^{d}lamma ensi$_2$ gir$_2$-su^{ki}.

223 For the writings of Tummal (tum-ma-al and tum-TUR$_3$, now tum-immal/mal$_x$), see Steinkeller 2001a: 69–70.

rev.

	(beginning broken)	
	(blank space)	
1'.	nig$_2$-ka$_9$ ak e$_2$ tum-mal$_x$(TUR$_3$)^{ki}	Account concerning the House of Tummal.
2'.	mu ḫu-ḫu-nu-ri^{ki} ba-ḫul	Year: "Ḫuḫnuri was destroyed."

Whereas the previous account gives only a partial view of the size of the institution Tummal (in particular labor involved in constructing the main administrative building there), the following account, text No. 41, is an account of the cereals levied from the three districts of Apisal, Gu'edina and Mushbianna in the Umma province in one year. The responsible official is named Egale-si. At first, one could be tempted to suggest that Egale-si was somehow the owner of these districts, but a brief prosopographical investigation will reveal that he was the son of Lu-Šara the field-surveyor, and that he himself inherited that office from his father. He is nowhere listed as owner of this or any other field.

No. 41. *MS 4679 (Umma, X[224]–i to xii)*

obv. col. i

	(start of column broken)	
1'.	[. . .] x x-ta	. . .
	(blank space)	
2'.	⸢še sumun⸣ 1(eše$_3$) GAN$_2$ gu$_4$ mu en-maḫ-gal-an-na ba-ḫun	Old barley (from ?) the domain land, year: "En-maḫgalanna was installed." (= AS 4)
3'.	6(geš$_2$) 3(u) 2(aš) 4(barig) 4(ban$_2$) 9(diš) sila$_3$ gur	(Yield levied): 392 gur, 4 barig, 4 ban$_2$, 9 sila$_3$,
4'.	gur še ma$_2$-a si-ga-ta	load(?) (levied) from the filled boats(?).
5'.	1(geš$_2$) 5(u) 1(barig) še gur	110 gur, 1 barig of barley,
6'.	gur še numun-ta	load(?) (levied) from seed-barley.
7'.	2(geš$_2$) 2(u) 3(aš) 4(barig) 4(diš) sila$_3$ še gur	143 gur, 4 barig, 4 sila$_3$ of barley,
8'.	7(aš) 1(barig) ziz$_2$ gur	7 gur, 1 barig of emmer,
9'.	gur sa$_2$-du$_{11}$-ta	load(?) (levied) from regular (deliveries).
10'.	9(aš) 3(barig) 4(ban$_2$) 5(diš) sila$_3$ [še gur]	9 gur, 3 barig, 4 ban$_2$, 5 sila$_3$ of barley,
11'.	a$_2$ lu$_2$ ḫun-ga$_2$-[ta]	(levied) from the work of hirelings.
12'.	ša$_3$ še gub-ba-ta	Of the available barley.
13'.	1(geš$_2$) 1(u) ⸢4(barig)⸣ 1(ban$_2$) gur	70 gur, 4 barig, 1 ban$_2$,
14'.	⸢gur še⸣ ma$_2$-a si-ga-ta	load(?) (levied) from the filled boats(?).
15'.	2(geš$_2$) 6(aš) 3(barig) 5(ban$_2$) 5(diš) sila$_3$ še <gur>	126 gur, 3 barig, 5 ban$_2$, 5 sila$_3$,
16'.	gur sa$_2$-du$_{11}$-ta	load(?) (levied) from the regular (deliveries).
17'.	4(u) 3(aš) 1(barig) 5(ban$_2$) še gur	43 gur, 1 barig, 5 ban$_2$ of barley,
18'.	gur a$_2$ lu$_2$ ḫun-ga$_2$-ta	load(?) (levied) from the work of hirelings.
19'.	še sumun libir-a	Old barley, old(?).
	(blank line)	
20'.	guru$_7$ a-pi$_4$-sal$_4$^{ki}-ta	(Levied) from the granary of Apisal.
21'.	5(aš) 2(barig) še gur ma$_2$-a si-ga-ta	5 gur, 2 barig of barley, (load levied) from the filled boats(?).

[224] The text mentions the years AS 2, 4, and 5.

obv. col. ii

	(*start of column broken*)	
1'.	1(aš) 1(barig) ⸢gur⸣ a$_2$ ḫun-ga$_2$-ta	1 gur, 1 barig (load levied) from the work of hirelings.
	(*blank space*)	
2'.	še gub-ba u$_3$ še ar$_3$-ra	Available barley and ground barley.
3'.	e$_2$-duru$_5$ a-pu$_3$-ta	(Levied) from the hamlets of Apu(?).
4'.	1(geš$_2$) 6(aš) 2(ban$_2$) gur	66 gur, 2 ban$_2$,
5'.	gur sa$_2$-du$_{11}$-ta	load(?) (levied) from regular (deliveries)
6'.	ša$_3$ še gub-ba	Of the available barley.
7'.	e$_2$ nam-ḫa-ni-ta	From the "House of Namḫani."
8'.	e$_2$-duru$_5$ ku$_5$-da-a	The hamlet of Kudaya.
9'.	5(geš$_2$) 1(u) 8(aš) 2(barig) 3(ban$_2$) še gur še ma$_2$-a si-ga-ta	318 gur, 2 barig, 3 ban$_2$ of barley, barley (load levied) from the filled boats(?).
10'.	⸢4(geš$_2$)⸣ še[225]	240 (gur) of barley,
11'.	gur sa$_2$-du$_{11}$-ta	load(?) (levied) from regular (deliveries).
12'.	še sumun	Old barley.
13'.	4(geš$_2$) 4(u) 2(aš) 4(barig) 3(ban$_2$) 4(diš) sila$_3$ [še gur]	282 gur, 4 barig, 3 ban$_2$, 4 sila$_3$ of barley,
14'.	gur še ma$_2$-a si-[ga-ta]	load(?) (levied) from the filled boats(?).
15'.	[. . .]-ta	. . .
16'.	[. . .]	. . .
17'.	ki-⸢su$_7$⸣ [^{d}]⸢šul⸣-pa-e$_3$-ta	(Levied) from the threshing floor of Šulpa'e.
18'.	9(aš) 2(barig) gur še numun-ta	9 gur, 2 barig (load levied) from the seed-barley.
19'.	2(geš$_2$) 1(u) 3(aš) 2(barig) 5(ban$_2$) gur	133 gur, 2 barig, 5 ban$_2$ (or barley),
20'.	gur sa$_2$-du$_{11}$-ta	load(?) (levied) from the regular (deliveries).
21'.	1(geš$_2$) 4(u) 6(aš) še gur a$_2$ lu$_2$ ḫun-ga$_2$-ta	106 gur of barley (load levied) from the work of hirelings.
22'.	še sumun lu$_2$-dingir-ra dumu inim-^{d}šara$_2$	Old barley, (from?) Lu-Dingira child of Inim-Šara.
23'.	4(aš) gur še gur še ma$_2$-a si-⸢ga⸣-ta	4 gur of barley, load (levied) from the filled boats,
24'.	2(aš) 3(barig) ⸢še gur⸣	2 gur, 3 barig of barley,
25'.	1(barig) 3(ban$_2$) ziz$_2$	1 barig, 3 ban$_2$ of emmer,
26'.	gur še numun-ta	load (levied) from the seed barley.
27'.	4(geš$_2$) 4(u) 4(aš) 4(barig) 4(ban$_2$) 1(diš) sila$_3$ še gur	284 gur, 4 barig, 4 ban$_2$, 1 sila$_3$ of barley.

obv. col. iii

	(*start of column broken*)	
1'.	⸢2(u) 3(aš)⸣ [. . .]	23 (gur?) . . .
2'.	1(geš$_2$) 6(aš) 2(barig) [. . .] gur sa$_2$-[du$_{11}$-ta]	66 gur, 2 barig . . . . load (levied) from the regular (deliveries).
3'.	3(aš) 3(barig) še [gur . . .] x	3 gur, 3 barig of barley. . . .
	(*blank space*)	

[225] Line partly erased.

4'.	⸢še⸣ sumun u$_3$ a e$_2$ x x-ta	Old barley . . . .
5'.	ša$_3$ a-pi$_4$-sal$_4$^{ki}	Within Apisal.
6'.	1(geš$_2$) 1(u) 8(aš) 3(ban$_2$) še gur	78 gur, 3 ban$_2$ of barley,
7'.	gur sa$_2$-du$_{11}$-ta	load (levied) from the regular (deliveries).
8'.	1(geš$_2$) 8(aš) 1(barig) še gur ⸢a$_2$⸣ lu$_2$ ḫun-ga$_2$-ta	86 gur, 1 barig of barley, (load levied) from the hirelings.
9'.	3(aš) 4(barig) gur še sumun [x]	3 gur, 4 barig of old barley . . .
10'.	⸢2(aš)⸣ [. . .]	2 gur . . .
11'.	še sumun ⸢mu⸣ [amar-^{d}]⸢suen⸣-ke$_4$ ur-bi$_2$-⸢lum⸣ mu-ḫul	Old barley from the year: "Amar-Suen destroyed Urbilum" (= AS 2).
12'.	1(geš$_2$) 5(u) 7(aš) 1(barig) gur še [x]	117 gur 1 barig of barley . . . ,
13'.	1(aš) 3(barig) gur še ⸢ma$_2$⸣-a [si-ga]-⸢ta$^?$⸣	1 gur, 3 barig of barley (load levied) from the filled boats(?).
14'.	5(geš$_2$) 6(aš) 2(barig) 3(ban$_2$) 8(diš) [sila$_3$ še] gur ⸢sa$_2$⸣-du$_{11}$-⸢ta⸣	306 gur, 2 barig, 3 ban$_2$, 8 sila$_3$ of barley, (load levied) from the regular (deliveries).
15'.	1(geš$_2$) 5(u) 1(aš) ⸢4(barig) 3(ban$_2$) gur a⸣ lu$_2$ ḫun-[ga$_2$]-⸢ta⸣	111 gur, 4 barig, 3 ban$_2$, (load levied) from the hirelings.
16'.	še sumun mu en-⸢unu$_6$-gal⸣-an-na [ba-ḫun]	Old barley (from) the year: "En-unugal-anna was installed." (= AS 5)
17'.	⸢1(geš$_2$)⸣ 4(aš) 4(barig) 3(ban$_2$) gur sa$_2$-[du$_{11}$-ta]	64 gur, 4 barig, 3 ban$_2$ (of barley, load levied) from the regular deliveries.
18'.	1(u) 5(aš) gur ⸢a$_2$ lu$_2$ ḫun⸣-ga$_2$-ta	15 gur (of barley, load levied) from the work of hirelings.
19'.	še gibil GAN$_2$-⸢ta⸣	New barley, from the field.
20'.	5(u) 1(barig) gur sa$_2$-⸢du$_{11}$-ta⸣	50 gur, 1 barig of barley (load levied) from the regular (deliveries).
21'.	6(aš) 3(ban$_2$) gur še ma$_2$-a si-ga-ta	6 gur, 3 ban$_2$ of barley (load levied) from the filled boats(?).
22'.	še apin-la$_2$ gu$_2$-⸢edin⸣-na u$_3$ muš-bi-an-na	Barley from the tillers of Gu'edina and Mušbianna.

obv. col. iv

	(start of column broken)	
1'.	[. . .] 2(ban$_2$) [. . . še gur ma$_2$]-a si-[ga-ta]	. . . 2 ban$_2$, (of barley, load levied) from the filled boats(?).
2'.	⸢4(u) 1(aš)⸣ 4(ban$_2$) gur x [. . .]	41 gur, 4 ban$_2$. . . ,
3'.	⸢7(aš)⸣ gur sa$_2$-du$_{11}$-⸢ta⸣	7 gur (of barley levied) from the regular (deliveries)
4'.	še gibil e$_2$-ta	Barley, new, from the house.
5'.	4(aš) ziz$_2$ sumun gur sa$_2$-du$_{11}$-ta	4 gur of emmer, old, (load levied) from the regular (deliveries).
	(blank space)	
6'.	ki-⸢su$_7$?⸣ gu$_2$-edin-na-⸢ta⸣	(From) the threshing floor of Gu'edina.
7'.	4(u) 7(aš) 2(barig) gur sa$_2$-du$_{11}$-ta	47 gur, 2 barig, (load levied) from the regular deliveries.

8'.	3(u) 2(aš) 2(barig) 1(ban$_2$) gur a$_2$ lu$_2$ ḫun-ga$_2$-ta	32 gur, 2 barig, 1 ban$_2$, (load levied) from the work of hirelings.
9'.	še sumun GAN$_2$ gu$_4$ guru$_7$ ^{d}anzu^{mušen}-babbar$_2$-ta	Barley, old, from the domain unit of the granary of the white Anzu-bird.
10'.	3(geš$_2$) 5(u) 1(barig) 1(ban$_2$) gur še ma$_2$-a si-ga-ta	230 gur, 1 barig, 1 ban$_2$ of barley, (load levied) from the filled boats(?).
11'.	7(aš) gur še numun-ta	7 gur, (load levied) from the seed-barley.
12'.	še gibil GAN$_2$ gu$_4$	Barley, new, from the domain unit.
13'.	šu-nu-kuš$_2$-ta	From Šunukuš.
14'.	6(geš$_2$) 5(aš) 4(barig) 2(ban$_2$) 5(diš) sila$_3$ gur sa$_2$-du$_{11}$-ta	305 gur, 4 barig, 2 ban$_2$, 5 sila$_3$, (load levied) from the regular (deliveries).
15'.	še sumun GAN$_2$ gu$_4$	Barley, old, (from) the domain unit.
16'.	ki-su$_7$ i$_7$ lugal-ta	From the threshing floor of the "King's Canal."

obv. col. v

(start of column broken)
(several lines erased)

1'.	3(u) 1(aš) x [. . .]	31 gur . . .
2'.	3(geš$_2$) 2(u) ⸢8(aš)⸣ [. . .]	208 gur . . .
3'.	4(u) 1(aš) 1(ban$_2$) [. . .]	41 gur, 1 ban$_2$ . . .
4'.	ša$_3$ gu$_2$-edin-⸢na⸣ [u$_3$] muš-bi-[an-na]	Of Gu'edina and Mušbianna.
5'.	1(geš$_2$) 2(u) 5(aš) 3(barig) 3(ban$_2$) x [. . .]	85 gur 3 barig, 3 ban$_2$ . . .
6'.	6(geš$_2$) 5(u) 5(aš) 3(barig) 2(ban$_2$) ⸢2(diš) sila$_3$⸣ še [. . .]	355 gur, 3 barig, 2 ban$_2$, 2 sila$_3$ of barley . . .
7'.	5(u) 3(aš) 5(ban$_2$) 6(diš) 1/3(diš) sila$_3$ maš$_2$ še gur	53 gur, 5 ban$_2$ 6 1/3 sila$_3$ of "interest" barley.
8'.	7(aš) 1(ban$_2$) še ⸢gur⸣	7 gur, 1 ban$_2$ of barley.
9'.	⸢a$_2$⸣ [. . .]	Work . . .

(rest of obverse broken)

rev. col. i'

1.	2(u) 1(barig) ⸢3(ban$_2$)?⸣ [. . .] x [. . .]	20 gur, 1 barig, 3 ban$_2$ . . .
2.	1(geš$_2$) 1(u) x [. . .]	70 gur . . .
3.	še ⸢ba?⸣ [. . .]	Barley rations (?) . . .
4.	⸢giri$_3$⸣ [. . .]	Conveyor: . . .
5.	2(geš'u)⸣ [. . .]	1200 gur . . .

(rest of column broken)

rev. col. ii'

1.	sa$_2$-du$_{11}$ dingir-e-ne	Regular (deliveries) of the gods.
2.	3(geš$_2$) gur še i$_3$-sah$_2$ u$_3$ sa$_{10}$-am$_3$ siki-ba	180 gur of barley for lard and for barter for wool rations.
3.	ur-^{d}dumu-zi-da	(From?) Ur-Dumuzida.
4.	1(geš$_2$) 3(u) gur	90 gur.
5.	uri$_5$^{ki}-ma x-ba ba-a-zi	Of Ur . . . was levied.

(rest of column broken)

rev. col. iii’

1.	5(aš) ⸢3(barig) 1(ban$_2$)$^?$⸣ la$_2$ 1(diš$_{tenû}$) sila$_3$ gur	5 gur, 3 barig, 1 ban$_2$ minus 1 sila$_3$.
2.	sa$_2$-du$_{11}$ ^{d}lama-lugal ša$_3$ a-pi$_4$-sal$_4$^{ki}	Regular (deliveries) of Lamma-lugal of Apisal.
3.	⸢2(u) ⸣ 6(aš) gur ⸢sa$_2$-du$_{11}$⸣ x	26 gur regular (deliveries) of . . .
4.	x x x[226]	. . .
5.	[x x] 4(ban$_2$) la$_2$ 1(diš$_{tenû}$) sila$_3$ gur	. . . 4 ban$_2$ minus 1 sila$_3$.
6.	[sa$_2$-du$_{11}$] ^{d}lama-lugal	Regular (deliveries) of Lamma-lugal
7.	[. . .] anzu^{mušen} babbar	(of the . . . of) the white Anzu-bird.
	(several lines erased)	
8’.	1(barig) ⸢1(ban$_2$) 5(diš)⸣ sila$_3$ še-ba lugal-i$_3$-sa$_6$	1 barig, 1 ban$_2$, 5 sila$_3$ of barley rations for Lugal-isa.
9’.	3(ban$_2$) si$_{12}$-a lugal-x-[x]	3 ban$_2$ (barley rations) for Lugal-x, blind.
10’.	3(ban$_2$) si$_{12}$-a geme$_2$-^{d}en-[. . .]	3 ban$_2$ (barley rations) for Geme-x, blind.
11’.	[x]-me	They are . . .
	(rest of column broken)	

rev. col. iv’

1.	⸢3(u) 6(aš)⸣ še ar$_3$-ra gur [. . .] gal kam$^?$ APIN x	36 gur of milled barley . . .
	(several lines broken)	
3’.	[šunigin . . .] ⸢6(geš$_2$) 4(aš)⸣ x [. . .] ⸢dabin⸣ [. . .]	Total: +364 gur . . . flour.
4’.	[šunigin . . .] ⸢*n*(barig) 4(ban$_2$) *n*(diš) sila$_3$ zi$_3$ gur⸣	Total: . . . *n* barig, 4 ban$_2$, *n* sila$_3$ of flour.
5’.	[. . .] NA KA [. . .]	. . .
6’.	[šunigin . . .] 5(geš$_2$) 3(u) ⸢5(aš) 2(barig)⸣ [. . .] sila$_3$ gur ŠE$_3$ [. . .]	Total: . . . +335 gur 2 barig . . . sila$_3$ emmer?
7’.	šunigin 5(geš$_2$) [. . .] še gur	Total: 300 gur . . . of barley.
8’.	šunigin ⸢2(u)⸣ [. . .] ⸢zi$_3$⸣ gur	Total: 20 gur . . . of flour.
9’.	[. . .] KA	. . .
	(rest of column broken)	

rev. col. v’

	(start of column blank)	
1.	še-bi *n*(diš) guru$_7$ 2(geš$_2$) 4(u) 4(barig) [. . .] sila$_3$ gur	Its barley: *n* guru$_7$, 160 gur, 4 barig, ...
2.	zi-ga-[am$_3$]	Is booked out (~the “credits”)
3.	la$_2$-ia$_3$ 2(geš$_2$) 1(u) n(aš) [. . . gur]	“Deficit”: 130+*n* gur
4.	nig$_2$-ka$_9$ ak še zi-[ga][227]	Account concerning levied barley,
5.	a-pi$_4$-sal$_4$^{ki} gu$_2$-edin-[na^{ki}] u$_3$ muš-bi-an-na^{ki}	(from the fields of) Apisal, Gu’edina, and Mušbianna.
6.	e$_2$-gal-e-si	(concerning) Egale-si.
7.	iti 1(u) 2(diš)-kam	It is of 12 months.
8.	⸢iti⸣ ^{d}dumu-zi	Month: “Dumuzi.”
	(rest of column blank)	

---

[226] Line and last half of previous line perhaps erased.

[227] Lines 4–8 written on dry clay.

Accounts concerning high-level administrators, often summaries of accounts of their subordinates, are identical in structure to all other accounts. However, identification of the person being held accountable is challenging. Some persons were only rarely identified by title, whereas others were identified by title only.[228] A system of "quick identification" permeated the Ur III scribal code. The shortest possible identifier was always used. A text gave the name or the title of a person, but rarely both, and only if necessary.

The accounts of the trade-agents (Sumerian dam-gar) of the Ur III state have received much attention.[229] These accounts are entirely similar to other Ur III accounts, the agent himself being a low-level state-official. Other low-level officials include both agricultural and workshop overseers.

The agricultural workforce was managed by overseers (ugula) and captains of the (plow-)oxen ($nu-banda_3$ gu_4).[230] The accounts concerning the overseers of the agricultural workforce regularly referred to either of these two officials. These accounts concerned only the work on the land, not the land itself and its crops. Other accounts and summary tablets recorded the size and expected produce from the fields, as well as the ratio of fulfillment.[231]

Texts Nos. 155 and 156 are examples of accounts concerning agricultural overseers. Although both lack a colophon and most of the "debits" section, they can be identified as accounts concerning Lugal-gu'e, a well-known Umma overseer. These two accounts will be discussed in detail in Chapter 8, on administration of work.

Although numerous accounts record the activities of work crews active in the Ur III workshops that produced household utensils and fabrics and processed grain, none is found in the Schøyen Collection.

The grain-processing workshop, in the following referred to as the mill, was of great importance for the economy, and several accounts concerning the work of the females[232] employed there have survived.[233]

Other accounts relate to more specific areas of the economy, such as SNAT 375 (from AS 6 to AS 7), an account concerning an individual shepherd,[234] or Nisaba 6, 31 (from ŠS 6), an account concerning groups of shepherds.[235] Animal products such as hides or dairy products were accounted for in a similar fashion.[236] The

---

[228] As an example we may consider the accounts relating to the chief of the granary (Sumerian $KA-guru_7$), several of which have been published. The person who held this position in Umma, $ARAD_2$(mu), was so famous that he was either referred to as the $KA-guru_7$ or simply by his name, and very rarely with both name and title.

[229] See above all Snell 1982 with literature.

[230] K. Maekawa 1987: 36, translates $nu-banda_3$ gu_4 with "inspector of plow oxen." He also recognized the fluid nature of the title ugula (p. 39).

[231] See, e.g., the account concerning the field of the governor of Girsu (TUT 4), and the account concerning the subsistence barley of the governor of Umma mentioned above (n. 221). Fields allotted to members of the ruling elite were also recorded in the books, but no private fields have ever been found in the published record of Ur III Umma texts. See also Dahl 2002: 333. The land-allotments given to the staff of the household of Inanna at Nippur hardly represent privately owned fields. See Zettler 1989: 305–13.

[232] However, see the account of the work of female and male workers of the mill concerning Ur-Engaldudu; RA 47, 141 (from Š 47 x 5 to Š 48 vi 15) rev. viii 1–2: nig_2-ka_9-ak a_2 $geme_2$ guruš $kikken_2$ / ur-en-gal-du-du.

[233] See, e.g., the account concerning Dingira, regarding the work of the female workers; TCL 5, 5668 (from Š 48 iv to xii) rev. iv 10–12: nig_2-ka_9 ak / dingir-ra-ka / a_2 $geme_2$-ka; and the barley account sealed by the overseers of the mill, SET 241 (from Š 25) l.e. 1: nig_2-⸢ka_9 ak⸣ še $kišib_3$ ugula $kikken_2-ke_4$-ne.

[234] Rev. iv 5: nig_2-ka_9 ak lu_2-eb-gal sipa udu kur-ra-ka, "account concerning Lu-Ebgal shepherd of kur (~ foreign?) sheep."

[235] Rev. v 13–14: nig_2-ka_9 ak / sipa-de_3-ne, "account concerning the shepherds."

[236] See the treatment of the dairy production by Englund 1995: 377–429, and his discussion of the other products from large cattle in Englund 2003.

state also kept records concerning another low-level administrator, the "fattener."[237] Other accounts record different "domestic" activities, such as brewing,[238] cooking,[239] baking,[240] oil making,[241] among others.[242]

Accounts concerning the goods and the staff of the divine households appear frequently in the published record,[243] with most originating from Girsu.[244] At the top level we find SNAT 273 (from Š 32 i to xiii), an account concerning the divine household dedicated to Šulgi.[245] Others record the activities of lower-level officials. CT 7, 46 (BM 17772, from Š 48), an account concerning bartered copper, via the sanga-official of Ninmar, suggests that the divine households partook in the bartering activities of the trade-agents.[246] In a similar way, ASJ 15, 123 94 (from Š 42) can be used to demonstrate that divine households (at least in Lagaš) engaged in agricultural activities.[247] The exact nature of the relationship between divine households and state has yet to be clearly defined.

Occasionally, documents were said to be validated by a third party. This is quite frequently the case in the triangular tags (e.g., text No. 6 in Chapter 2), which probably sealed bags holding other documents, but validation occurs occasionally in accounts. Usually, a short inscription on the left edge of the tablet indicates this process.

In the following inspection of fruits, text No. 42, the total is said to be validated by Ur-Gepar and Ḫuwawa.[248] It is interesting to note here that the document, which itself is said to be an inspection or measure (kab$_2$—du$_{11}$, see Civil 1994: 153–58), is also validated (gin).

The first three columns of the text list various amounts of four types of fruits. Two of these can be identified (figs, ^{geš}peš$_3$ and grapes, geštin), but the other two cannot be translated (^{geš}ge$_6$-par$_4$ and ^{geš}nir$_x$(MIR.ZA)).

---

[237] See MVN 13, 568 (from AS 8 viii), an "account concerning Ušmu, the fattener," rev. 14: nig$_2$-ka$_9$ ak uš-mu kurušda. See also the "account concerning Allamu the fattener" (MVN 6, 287 [from Š 43 ii to viii] rev. vi 9–10: nig$_2$-ka$_9$-ak / al-la-mu kurušda); the "account concerning Lugal-ezem shepherd of the fattening house" (RA 10, 209 [= BM 103423, from AS 7 xii] rev. 26: [nig$_2$]-ka$_9$ ak lugal-ezem sipa e$_2$ kurušda); and the "account of the shepherd(s) (and) fattener(s) concerning the overseer Urnigar" (PDT 2, 802 [from Š 47 v] l.e. 1: nig$_2$-ka$_9$-ak sipa kurušda ugula ur-nigar^{gar}). Accounts concerning the fodder for the animals were also kept, see, e.g., TSU 85 (from Š 45 i to iii 15), an "account concerning the fodder for the sheep in the new sheep house, via Katar-Baba, and Ur-Bagara" (rev. vi 2–6: nig$_2$-ka$_9$-ak / še udu gu$_7$-a / ša$_3$ e$_2$ udu gibil / giri$_3$ ka-tar-^{d}ba-ba$_6$ / u$_3$ ur-ba-gara$_2$).

[238] See the beer account concerning Ur-Baba, son of Šešturtur, CT 3, 48 (= BM 21340, from Š 46 iv to v) rev. vi 15–16: nig$_2$-ka$_9$-ak kaš / ur-^{d}ba-ba$_6$ dumu šeš-tur-tur.

[239] The account concerning Ur-Igimaše, the kitchen administrator, TUT 104 (from Š 47) rev. 7–8: nig$_2$-ka$_9$-ak / ur-^{d}igi-ma-še$_3$ muḫaldim. See now also Allred 2006.

[240] The bread account concerning Urtur, son of Anana the kitchen administrator, TUT 116 (from Š 44 xi to xii) rev.vi 1–2: [nig$_2$]-ka$_9$-ak ninda / [ur]-⸢tur⸣ dumu a$_2$-[na]-na muḫaldim.

[241] The oil account concerning Ur-abba son of Bazi, IISS 4, 3 (from AS 1 i to xii) rev. xii 6–8: nig$_2$-ka$_9$-ak i$_3$ / ur-ab-ba / dumu ba-zi.

[242] See, e.g., the account concerning Lu-Ningirsu, the singer, TMH NF 1–2, 123 (from ŠS 9) rev. 8–9: nig$_2$-ka$_9$-ak / ⸢lu$_2$⸣-^{d}nin-gir$_2$-su nar; or the account concerning Urmes, the fuller, ASJ 3, 160 no. 128 (from Š 44 i to xiii) rev. iv 4–5: nig$_2$-ka$_9$-ak / ur-mes ^{lu2}lunga.

[243] See, e.g., the account concerning the gudu$_4$-priest Ur-sasa, SNAT 284 (from Š 40 to Š 43) rev. 10: nig$_2$-ka$_9$-ak ur-sa$_6$-sa$_6$ gudu$_4$; also the "account concerning Lugal-ezem, gudu$_4$-priest of (the god) Lugaluda," ASJ 2, 17 no. 47 (from IS 3) rev. 3: nig$_2$-ka$_9$-ak lugal-ezem ⸢gudu$_4$⸣ ⸢d⸣lugal-u$_4$<-da>.

[244] See, e.g., the account concerning Ur-Nigar, the sanga-official of Nindara, CT 9, 38 (= BM 13657, from Š 40 iv) rev. iv 8–9: nig$_2$-ka$_9$-ak / ur-nigar^{gar} sanga ^{d}nin-dar-a.

[245] Obv. ii 11–12: nig$_2$-ka$_9$-ak / e$_2$ ^{d}šul-gi.

[246] Rev. 13–14: nig$_2$-ka$_9$-ak urudu sa$_{10}$-a / giri$_3$ sanga ^{d}nin-mar^{ki}.

[247] Account of the cultivators concerning the overseers Alla and Ur-Šugalama of the divine household of Šulgi, dated to the time when Ur-Lamma was governor: rev. xii 13–19: nig$_2$-ka$_9$-ak / engar-re-ne / ugula al-la / ⸢u$_3$⸣ ur-šu-ga-lam-ma / [e$_2$] ^{d}⸢šul⸣-⸢gi⸣ / ⸢ur⸣-^{d}lamma / ensi$_2$. The subscript PN ensi$_2$ is often found in accounts from the Lagaš province. No comparable system was used in Umma, perhaps indicative of the greater independence enjoyed by the governors of Girsu.

[248] The pair act in the same capacity in the very different text UTI 6, 3777 (Umma, ŠS 5–v–30), a triangular tag recording the deliveries of small amounts of foodstuffs for messengers (see Chapter 10).

Except for the n i r fruit, the three other fruits are described as wet or green (d u r u$_5$). In the summary an equivalence of dried (ḫ a d$_2$) fruits is computed for each of these, but not for the n i r fruits.

The body of the text is divided into three sections. An overseer (u g u l a) is listed at the end of each section:

Šara-amu (section 1: obv. i 1–22)
Agudu (section 2: obv. i 23–rev. i 2)
PN (section 3: rev. i 3–?)

Both Šara-amu and Agudu are known to have held the title "orchard administrator" (š a n d a n a).[249] The other persons mentioned in the text were probably subordinates responsible for the deliveries, and perhaps themselves picking the fruit.

Below is a full transliteration and translation of text No. 42:

No. 42. *MS 4744 (Umma, ŠS 3)*

obv. col. i

1.	2(aš) ^{geš}peš$_3$ duru$_5$ ⸢gur⸣	2 gur of "wet" figs,
2.	me-pa-e$_3$ dumu lu$_2$-[bara$_2$]	Mepa'e child of Lu-Bara.
3.	1(barig) 5(ban$_2$) 9(diš) sila$_3$ ^{geš}ge$_6$-⸢par$_4$⸣ duru$_5$	1 barig, 5 ban$_2$, 9 sila$_3$ of "wet" ge$_6$-par$_4$-fruits,
4.	4(aš) 4(barig) ^{geš}peš$_3$ duru$_5$ gur	4 gur, 4 barig of "wet" figs,
5.	lu$_2$-ga	Luga.
6.	6(aš) 1(barig) 2(ban$_2$) 4(diš) sila$_3$ ^{geš}nir$_x$(MIR.ZA) gur	6 gur, 1 barig, 2 ban$_2$, and 4 sila$_3$ of nir-fruits,
7.	5(ban$_2$) geštin duru$_5$	5 ban$_2$ of "wet" grapes,
8.	4(barig) 4(ban$_2$) ^{geš}peš$_3$ duru$_5$	4 barig, 4 ban$_2$ of "wet" figs,
9.	lu$_2$-^{d}nin-šubur	Lu-Ninšubur.
10.	1(barig) ^{geš}ge$_6$-par$_4$ duru$_5$	1 barig of "wet" ge$_6$-par$_4$-fruits,
11.	u$_2$-ar-tum	U-artum.
12.	⸢5(ban$_2$)⸣ 6(diš) sila$_3$ ^{geš}peš$_3$ duru$_5$	5 ban$_2$, 6 sila$_3$ of "wet" figs,
13.	lu$_2$-^{d}šara$_2$	Lu-Šara.
14.	1(barig) ^{geš}peš$_3$ duru$_5$	1 barig of "wet" figs,
15.	ur-^{d}šara$_2$	Ur-Šara.
16.	2(aš) 2(barig) ^{geš}peš$_3$ duru$_5$ gur	2 gur, 2 barig of "wet" figs,
17.	a-gu-gu	Agugu.
18.	1(barig) ^{geš}peš$_3$ duru$_5$	1 barig of "wet" figs,
19.	ur-^{d}ab-u$_2$	Ur-Ab'u.
20.	2(ban$_2$) ^{geš}peš$_3$ duru$_5$	2 ban$_2$ of "wet" figs,
21.	a-na-lu$_2$	Analu.
	(*blank line*)	
22.	ugula ^{d}šara$_2$-a-mu	Overseer: Šara-a(ya)mu.
23.	1(aš) ^{geš}ge$_6$-par$_4$ duru$_5$ gur	1 gur of "wet" ge$_6$-par$_4$-fruits,
24.	1(aš) ^{geš}peš$_3$ duru$_5$ gur	1 gur of "wet" figs,
25.	⸢dam⸣ lugal-nesag-e	wife of Lugal-nesage
26.	3(ban$_2$) ^{geš}ge$_6$-par$_4$ duru$_5$	3 ban$_2$ of "wet" ge$_6$-par$_4$-fruits,

[249] See, e.g., the Garšana text CUSAS 3, 1375, the Girsu text CUSAS 6: 85–87 (BM 14309), discussed by Heimpel 2011, or the unpublished text LB 538, where a person with the title š a n d a n a appears to be in charge of orchards, supporting a translation of š a n d a n a as "gardener" or, perhaps better, "orchard supervisor."

obv. col. ii

	(*start missing*)	
1'.	1(barig) ⸢2(ban$_2$)⸣ [. . .]	1 barig 2 ban$_2$. . . ,
2'.	ur-⸢e$_2$⸣-[an-na]	Ur-E'anna.
3'.	1(barig) 3(ban$_2$) ⸢^{geš}⸣ge$_6$-[par$_4$ duru$_5^{?}$]	1 barig, 3 ban$_2$ of "wet" ge$_6$-par$_4$-fruits,
4'.	1(barig) ^{geš}⸢peš$_3$⸣ [duru$_5^{?}$]	1 barig of "wet" figs,
5'.	ur-⸢kun⸣	Urkun.
6'.	1(aš) 2(barig) ^{geš}ge$_6$-par$_4$ ⸢duru$_5$⸣ [gur]	1 gur, 2 barig of "wet" ge$_6$-par$_4$-fruits,
7'.	dam i$_3$-li$_2$-mu	wife of Ilimu.
8'.	3(aš) 1(barig) ^{geš}nir$_x$(MIR.ZA) gur	3 gur, 1 barig of nir-fruits,
9'.	ur-^{d}šul-pa-e$_3$	Ur-Šulpa'e.
10'.	1(barig) 5(ban$_2$) ^{geš}ge$_6$-par$_4$ duru$_5$	1 barig, 5 ban$_2$ of "wet" ge$_6$-par$_4$-fruits,
11'.	a-gu-du	Agudu.
12'.	⸢1(barig)$^{?}$⸣ 5(ban$_2$) ^{geš}ge$_6$-par$_4$ duru$_5$	1 barig, 5 ban$_2$ of "wet" ge$_6$-par$_4$-fruits,
13'.	šeš-a-ni	Šešani.
14'.	5(ban$_2$) ^{geš}ge$_6$-par$_4$ duru$_5$	5 ban$_2$ of "wet" gepar-fruits,
15'.	lu$_2$-eb-gal	Lu-ebgal.
16'.	1(barig) ^{geš}peš$_3$ duru$_5$ 1(barig) ^{geš}ge$_6$-par$_4$ duru$_5$	1 barig of "wet" figs, 1 barig of "wet" ge$_6$-par$_4$-fruits,
17'.	3(barig) ^{geš}nir$_x$(MIR.ZA)	3 barig of nir-fruits,
18'.	ur-eš$_3$-bar-ra	Ur-ešbara.
19'.	1(aš) 2(barig) geštin duru$_5$ gur	1 gur, 2 barig of "wet" grapes,
20'.	^{d}en-lil$_2$-la$_2$-i$_3$-sa$_6$	Enlila-isa.
21'.	1(barig) ^{geš}ge$_6$-par$_4$ duru$_5$	1 barig of "wet" ge$_6$-par$_4$-fruits,
22'.	a-a-lu$_2$-du$_{10}$	Aya-ludu.
23'.	2(ban$_2$) ^{geš}peš$_3$ duru$_5$	2 ban$_2$ of "wet" figs,
24'.	ba-ga	Baga.
25'.	2(ban$_2$) ^{geš}peš$_3$ duru$_5$	2 ban$_2$ of "wet" figs,

rev. col. i

1.	^{d}šara$_2$-mu-DU	Šara-muDU.
	(*blank line*)	
2.	ugula a-gu-du	Overseer: Agudu.
3.	1(barig) ^{geš}peš$_3$ duru$_5$ an-dul$_3$	1 barig of "wet" figs, Andul.
4.	1(barig) ^{geš}ge$_6$-par$_4$ duru$_5$ a-da-lal$_3$	1 barig of "wet" ge$_6$-par$_4$-fruits, Adalal.
5.	1(aš) 1(barig) ^{geš}peš$_3$ duru$_5$ gur	1 gur, 1 barig of "wet" figs,
6.	1(aš) ⸢^{geš}nir$_x$(MIR.ZA)⸣ gur	1 gur of nir-fruits,
7.	ur-li	Urli.
8.	3(ban$_2$) ^{geš}ge$_6$-par$_4$ duru$_5$ u$_3$	3 ban$_2$ of "wet" ge$_6$-par$_4$-fruits and
9.	1(ban$_2$) ^{geš}[x] duru$_5$	1 ban$_2$ of "wet" x,
10.	2(ban$_2$) ^{geš}[ge$_6$]-⸢par$_4$⸣ duru$_5$	2 ban$_2$ of "wet" ge$_6$-par$_4$-fruits,
11.	da-a-[da]-mu	Dayadamu.
12.	1(barig) ^{geš}ge$_6$-par$_4$ duru$_5$ ur-^{d}šul-pa-e$_3$	1 barig of "wet" gepar-fruits, Ur-Šulpa'e.
13.	1(aš) 1(barig) ^{geš}nir$_x$(MIR.ZA) gur	1 gur, 1 barig of nir-fruits,
14.	da-da igi-du$_8$	Dada, blind(?).

15.	1(u) 2(aš) x [. . .] *(rest of column missing)*	12 [gur of . . .]

rev. col. ii

	(blank space)	
1.	šunigin 1(aš) 2(barig) 5(ban$_2$) geštin duru$_5$ gur	Total: 1 gur, 2 barig, 5 ban$_2$ of "wet" grapes.
2.	geštin had$_2$-bi 1(barig) 3(ban$_2$) 4(diš) sila$_3$	Its (equivalency of) dried grapes: 1 barig, 3 ban$_2$, 4 sila$_3$.
3.	šunigin 1(u) 2(aš) 3(barig) 5(ban$_2$) 6(diš) sila$_3$ ^{geš}peš$_3$ duru$_5$ gur	Total: 12 gur, 3 barig, 5 ban$_2$, 6 sila$_3$ of "wet" figs.
4.	^{geš}peš$_3$ še-er-gu-bi 3(geš$_2$) 1(u) 1(diš) ⅓(diš)	Its (equivalency of) cords of figs: 191 ⅓.
5.	šunigin 6(aš) 1(barig) 5(ban$_2$) la$_2$ 1(diš$_{tenû}$) sila$_3$ ^{geš}ge$_6$-par$_4$ duru$_5$ gur	Total: 6 gur, 1 barig, 5 ban$_2$ minus 1 sila$_3$ of "wet" ge$_6$-par$_4$-fruits.
6.	^{geš}ge$_6$-par$_4$ had$_2$-bi 1(aš) 3(barig) 5(ban$_2$) 6(diš) ⅓(diš) sila$_3$ gur	Its (equivalency of) dried ge$_6$-par$_4$-fruits: 1 gur, 3 barig, 5 ban$_2$, 6 ⅓ sila$_3$.
7.	šunigin 2(u) 7(aš) 4(barig) 2(ban$_2$) 4(diš) sila$_3$ ^{geš}nir$_x$(MIR.ZA) gur	Total: 27 gur, 4 barig, 2 ban$_2$, 4 sila$_3$ of nir-fruits.
	(blank space)	
8.	geštin ^{geš}peš$_3$ ⸢kab$_2$⸣ [du$_{11}$-ga]	Measure of grapes and figs.
9.	mu si-ma-num$_2$⸢ki⸣ [ba]-⸢ḫul⸣	Year: "Simanum . . ."

left edge

1.	šunigin-bi ur-ge$_6$-par$_4$ u$_3$ ḫu-wa-wa ib$_2$-gi-in	Its total was made firm (~ validated) by Ur-Gepar and Ḫuwawa.

The totals convert the value of grapes, "wet" figs, and ge$_6$-par$_4$-fruit into dried grapes, strings of figs, and dried ge$_6$-par$_4$-fruits. The relationship between "wet" grapes and dried grapes is 5:1, corresponding very well with the modern ratio between grapes and rasins (Christensen 2000: 194). A translation "raisin" for geštin had$_2$ is therefore very likely. The strings of figs (see Gelb 1982) held almost exactly 20 sila$_3$ each. The ratio between "wet" and "dry" ge$_6$-par$_4$-fruits is close to 3.5:1. nir-fruits are not furnished with an equivalency value, nor are they described as "wet" or "dry."

7
RECEIPTS: THE PRIMARY DOCUMENTS

Whereas the accounts were top-level administrative documents, summarizing all other documents (except, of course, the archival documents discussed in Chapter 2), the primary documents, the receipts, were the building blocks of the administrative machinery. These documents are also the most numerous of all of the neo-Sumerian texts, and quite possibly, of all cuneiform tablets. As noted repeatedly above, all primary documents were summarized in either the "debits" or the "credits" of the accounts. This can be proven in many instances, but unfortunately in none of the texts in the collection published here.

Primary documents were as a rule sealed, but the practices of sealing varied from case to case, from place to place, and probably over time as well. This is in stark contrast to earlier corpora where tablets were only occasionally sealed (Old Akkadian), or where seals were never impressed on tablets (Early Dynastic periods). In most cases the recipient sealed the transaction; in particular corpora other parties to the transaction could also seal.

Sealed Receipts

The simple receipt, used for goods eventually booked in or out in the so-called "damgar" accounts, is sometimes called a "šu ti-a" document, using the Old Babylonian form of the Ur III technical term šu ba-ti, "(PN) received." However, many such "šu ti-a" documents include the technical term kišib$_3$,[250] "sealed document (of PN)," and some documents with the technical term kišib$_3$ lack the term "šu ti-a" but may be classified more broadly with these. Some structural differences have led me to separate primary documents concerning work from those concerning goods, workers and animals. Documents concerning work will be treated in the next chapter (Chapter 8).

The typical sealed receipt takes the following form, illustrated by text No. 43:

No. 43. *MS 4715/9 (Adab?, IS 1–vii)*

Outline		Transliteration	Translation
	obv.		
Product	1.	2(u) ma-na siki	20 ma-na of wool.
ki PN$_1$-ta	2.	ki ur-ba-ba-ta	From Ur-Baba.
PN$_2$	3.	da-da-mu	Dadamu
"šu ba-ti"	4.	šu ba-ti	received.
	rev.		
(blank space)			
Date	1.	iti du$_6$-ku$_3$	Month: "Shiny mound."
	2.	mu ^{d}i-bi$_2$-^{d}suen lugal	Year: "Ibbi-Suen (was) king."
Seal (S002127)	1.	da-da-mu	Dadamu,
	2.	dub-sar	scribe,
	3.	dumu a-lu$_5$-lu$_5$	child of Alulu.

[250] In Ur III texts DUB (kišib$_3$) and MES (kišib) are clearly distinguished: DUB has two small vertical wedges in the head of the sign whereas MES has only one. MES is used only with the value mes, whereas DUB is used with the values dub and kišib$_3$. When kišib$_3$ is found alone and as an object it is translated as "seal," but when it is part of the compound kišib$_3$—ra, it is translated "to seal" (see below n. 285). Preceding a personal name, and denoting some form of receipt or transfer of ownership, kišib$_3$ is here understood to stand for the sealed document.

The vast majority of receipts follow this simple format, although additional information about the origin or destination of the goods is often supplied. If the tablet itself was not sealed we must suspect that it was once encased in an envelope which was sealed (see below). In many cases the tablet was sealed by a different person from the individual cited as receiving the goods; in those cases a line, kišib$_3$ PN, "seal(ed tablet of) PN," was added. In still other cases, another person, whose exact responsibilities remain unclear, was introduced with the phrase giri$_3$ PN. Conventionally this is understood as representing someone conveying the goods, based on the meaning of the term giri$_3$ (lit. "foot," see also below). Finally, some primary documents concerning the control and transfer of metal and metal objects, or textiles, were formatted differently, as were a group of texts concerning deliveries for the cult (mu-ku$_x$(DU) documents), or used for the transfer of specific objects (zi-ga, ba-zi and i$_3$-dab$_5$ documents). These will be treated below.

The majority of receipts in the Schøyen Collection come from Adab and Umma, with only a few examples from other sites (Drehem, Garšana, Irisagrig$^?$, Girsu).[251] The collection is therefore not representative of the Ur III administrative machinery, and to compensate for this I have added to my discussion previously published texts from the main provinces.

Occasionally the terse style of the simple sealed receipt, outlined above, is broken, and additional grammatical elements are expressed. The relatively few texts which give the complete prefix chain of the composite verb šu—ti are mostly unusual documents such as the legal text No. 201, the tablet copy No. 101, or texts from outside of the core provinces such as No. 92, all of which are dealt with below.[252]

Text No. 44, a receipt from Drehem, gives the fuller grammatical form šu ba-an-ti, presumably for /šu ba-n-ti/, where -n- cross-references the subject.[253]

No. 44. *MS 4040 (Drehem, ŠS 6–iv)*

obv.

1.	1(diš) kuš udu niga	1 hide of a fattened sheep.
2.	1(diš) kuš maš$_2$ niga	1 hide of a fattened goat.
3.	ba-uš$_2$	Dead.
4.	⌜ki⌝ ^{d}iškur-illat-ta	From Adad-tillatī.

rev.

1.	a-na-aḫ-i$_3$-li$_2$	Anaḫ-ili
2.	šu ba-an-ti	received.
	(blank space)	
3.	iti u$_5$-bi$_2$-gu$_7$	Month: "Eating the goose(?)."
4.	mu us$_2$-sa ^{d}šu-^{d}suen lugal uri$_5$^{ki}-ma bad$_3$ mar-tu mu-du$_3$ mu-us$_2$-sa-bi	Year following: "Šu-Suen, king of Ur, built the Martu Wall." Year following that.

Among the more interesting exceptions we find šu ba-ab-ti in the following text, No. 45, where the recipients of rations receive them directly from a superior:[254]

---

[251] Note that receipts from the Schøyen Collection are also published in Ch. 2, 3, 4, 8, and 12.

[252] See further AUCT 3, 248/249 (from AS 7 xii) rev. 1–2; MVN 21, 162 (from Š 48 ii) obv. 5–6; and YOS 4, 39 (from ŠS 9 ix) obv. 6–7. Since most Ur III personal names were genitive constructions the case marker on the ergative subject is usually expressed with ke$_4$(note Powell's reservations [1978: 171 n. 5] against adopting the reading ke$_4$ for KID, based on the lack of supporting lexical evidence; ge$_2$ is perhaps to be preferred).

[253] See also text No. 92 below.

[254] See also AAS 183 with plural subject and the following verbal form šu ba-ti$^!$-eš (rev. 2). Note that both recipients seal the tablet.

No. 45. *MS 2020/16 (Umma, AS 8)*

obv.

1.	4(ban$_2$) še-ba	4 ban$_2$ of barley rations
2.	inim-^{d}šara$_2$	(for) Inim-Šara;
3.	4(ban$_2$) ab-ba-gi-na	4 ban$_2$ (of barley rations for) Abbagina;
4.	4(ban$_2$) lugal-ezem	4 ban$_2$ (of barley rations for) Lugal-ezem.
5.	še-ba er$_2$-dingir-ka ku$_5$-dam	The barley rations of Er-Dingir will be cut(?).

rev.

1.	še-bi ki gu-du-du-⸢ta⸣	The barley from Gududu
2.	šu ba-ab-ti	was received.
	(*blank space*)	
3.	iti ^{d}li$_9$-⸢si$_4$⸣	Month: "Lisi."
4.	mu en eridu^{ki} ba-ḫun	Year: "The En-priest of Eridu was installed."

Texts Nos. 44 and 45 are both unsealed, and were probably originally encased in envelopes (see below).

Sealed receipts mostly carried the seal-impression of the person who received the goods, as was the case with the sample document presented above (No. 43). There are a further fifteen documents in the Schøyen Collection which can be classified as simple receipts sealed by the person who is said to have received the goods.[255]

No. 46. *MS 2018/5 (Umma, ŠS 7–xi)*

obv.

1.	*n*(u) tug$_2$ uš-bar	*n* textiles, weaver (quality).[256]
2.	ki i$_3$-kal-la-ta	From I-kala.
3.	ur-am$_3$-ma	Ur-Amma
4.	šu ba-ti	received.

rev.

1.	iti pa$_4$-u$_2$-e	Month: "Pa'u'e."
	(*seal impression*)	
2.	mu ma-da za-ab-ša-li^{ki} ba-ḫul	Year: "The territory of Zabšali was destroyed."

seal (S004361)[257]

1.	ur-am$_3$-ma	Ur-Amma,
2.	dumu ur-^{geš}gigir	child of Ur-Gigir,
3.	lu$_2$ azlag$_2$	(chief) fuller.[258]

---

[255] Nos. 46–60, of which five have illegible seal legends, Nos. 48, 52, 56, 57, and 58.

[256] For the different qualities of wool and textiles, see Waetzoldt 1972 and Firth and Nosch 2012.

[257] This seal, which was rolled on at least 11 texts, is not included in Mayr n.d. See, e.g., Rochester 134 and Fs Hruška 161 no. 3. The same seal was rolled on our text No. 47.

[258] The title here translated "(chief) fuller," lu$_2$ azlag, is literally just "fuller." However, those members of the crafts teams who carried seals were often also those who oversaw production, at a very basic level at least, and who would receive and deliver products in the absence of the nominal manager of the workshop (see Dahl 2010a). This vertical terminology is found in many different areas of the administration and, together with the widespread horizontal terminology (an overseer of either army or plow teams would be called nu-banda$_3$, here translated captain), makes identifications sometimes very difficult.

The following text, No. 47, is an even more elaborate example of a similar transaction. It is also received and sealed by Ur-Amma.

No. 47. *MS 4692 (Umma, ŠS 8–x)*

obv.

1.	1(diš) tug$_2$ nig$_2$-lam$_2$ 3(diš$_{tenû}$)-kam us$_2$	1 nig$_2$-lam textile, 3rd class, lesser (quality);
2.	4(diš) tug$_2$ nig$_2$-lam$_2$ 4(diš)-kam us$_2$	4 nig$_2$-lam textiles, 4th class, lesser (quality);
3.	4(diš) tug$_2$ nig$_2$-lam$_2$ du	4 nig$_2$-lam textiles, running (quality);
4.	1(geš$_2$) 1(diš) tug$_2$ uš-bar tug$_2$ ⸢du⸣	61 textiles, weaver (quality), running (quality) textiles;
5.	8(diš) sila$_3$ i$_3$-šaḫ$_2$	8 sila$_3$ of lard.

rev.

1.	ki i$_3$-kal-la-ta	From I-kala.
2.	ur-am$_3$-ma šu ba-ti	Ur-Amma received.
3.	iti ezem-^{d}šul-gi	Month: "Festival of Šulgi."
	(seal impression)	
4.	mu ma$_2$ gur$_8$-maḫ ba-dim$_2$	Year: "The lofty barge was fashioned."

seal (S004361)

1.	ur-am$_3$-ma	Ur-Amma,
2.	dumu ur-^{geš}gigir	child of Ur-Gigir,
3.	lu$_2$ azlag$_2$	(chief) fuller.

The occurrence of lard (i$_3$-šaḫ$_2$) together with textiles in the same receipt is not unusual. The lard, or another oil, was used after the walking of the textiles. Although the amounts of oil needed for each and every category of textile are not known, the amount in text No. 47 rather nicely agrees with the amounts listed in Firth 2013 (17 ½ shekels for one nig$_2$-lam textile of third class, lesser [quality], and presumably even less for the other textiles listed in the text).

The following text, No. 48 from Garšana, is a receipt of a small amount of lard and glue, both products used in various kinds of manufacturing, such as boat-building, tool-making, etc.

No. 48. *MS 4688 = CUSAS 3, 1520 (Garšana, ŠS 8–iii)*

obv.

1.	3(diš) sila$_3$ i$_3$-šah$_2$	3 sila$_3$ of lard.
2.	½(diš) ma-na še-gin$_2$	½ ma-na of glue.
3.	ki ^{d}iškur-⸢illat⸣-ta	From Adad-tillatī.
4.	a-na-aḫ-i$_3$-li$_2$	Anaḫ-Ili,
5.	šu ba-ti	Received.

rev.

1.	⸢iti ses⸣-da-⸢gu$_7$⸣	Month: "Eating the piglet."
	(blank space)	
2.	mu ma$_2$-gur$_8$ mah ⸢^{d}en-lil$_2$ ^{d}nin-lil$_2$⸣-[ra] mu-ne-dim$_2$	Year: "He fashioned the lofty barge for Enlil and Ninlil."

seal (*illegible*)

As mentioned above, receipts often include comments about the purpose or origin of the goods being recorded. In the first example below, text No. 49, approximately nine hundred liters of barley are received by a certain Akini from an Ur-Baba. The barley is further qualified as compensation for the labor of men hired to thresh barley.[259]

No. 49. *MS 4715/2 (Adab?, AS 2)*

obv.

1.	3(aš) še gur	3 gur of barley,
2.	a$_2$ lu$_2$ ḫun-ga$_2$	(compensation) for work of hirelings
3.	še geš ra-ra	threshing the barley.
4.	ki ur-ba-ba	From Ur-Baba.
5.	a-ki-a-ni	Akiani

rev.

1.	šu ba-ti	received.
	(seal impression)	
2.	mu us$_2$-sa ^{d}amar-^{d}suen lugal	Year following: "Amar-Suen (was) king."

seal (S001800)[260]

1.	a-ki-a-ni	Akiani,
2.	dub-sar	scribe,
3.	dumu ur-^{d}[x]-MUŠ$_3$?	child of Ur-x-MUŠ.

In the second example, text No. 50, a large amount of barley is received from the same(?) Ur-Baba by a royal soldier with the foreign name Tiginibaš.[261] The barley is specified as rations for the soldiers.

No. 50. *MS 4715/3 (Adab?, ŠS 3–x)*

obv.

1.	5(u) 6(aš) 3(barig) 4(ban$_2$)	56 gur, 3 barig 4 ban$_2$,
2.	še-ba aga$_3$-us$_2$	of barley rations for soldiers.
3.	ki ur-ba-ba-ta	From Ur-Baba.
4.	ti-gi-ni-ba-aš	Tiginibaš
5.	šu ba-ti	received.

rev.

1.	ugula ur-^{d}nin-zu	Overseer: Ur-Ninzu.
2.	iti ezem-maḫ	Month: "Lofty Festival."
	(seal impression)	
3.	mu <<a>> si-ma-num$_2$ ba-ḫul	Year: "Simanum was destroyed."

---

[259] Englund 2012a and b.

[260] The seal is otherwise not attested. The patronymic is partly illegible.

[261] Both the name of the seal owner and that of his father are hapax. Etymologically, the name of the owner of the seal may be related to that of Libanukšabaš, the name of a ruler of Marhashi mentioned in Ur III documents (see, e.g., TRU 344 obv. 10: li-ba-an-aš-gu-bi lu$_2$ kin-gi$_4$-a li-ba-nu-uk-ša-ba-aš ensi$_2$ mar-ha-ši^{ki}, "Libanašgubi, messenger of Libanukšabaš, governor of Marhaši.").

seal (S004274)

1.	ti-gi-ni-ba-aš	Tiginibaš,
2.	aga$_3$-us$_2$ lugal	soldier of the king,
3.	dumu ḫu-zi$^{?}$-ti$^{?}$	child of Ḫuziti(?).

In the next example, text No. 51, a large number of reed bundles are received by Ur-Šuba from Ur-Baba, perhaps the same person met in the previous texts. The transaction is said to take place in Nippur, but like the previous two, the document is likely to originate from ancient Adab. The seal is only attested on this tablet.

No. 51. *MS 4715/6 (Adab$^{?}$, ŠS 4–ix)*

obv.

1.	2(geš'u) sa gi	1200 bundles of reed.
2.	ša$_3$ nibru^{ki}	Within Nippur.
3.	ki ur-ba-ba-ta	From Ur-Baba.
4.	ur-^{d}šuba$_3$	Ur-Šuba
5.	šu ba-ti	received.

rev.

1.	iti ezem-^{d}šu-^{d}suen	Month: "Festival of Šu-Suen."
	(seal impression)	
2.	mu bad$_3$ mu-ri-iq-ti-id-ni-im mu-du$_3$	Year: "The wall Muriq-Tidnim was built."

seal (S005378)

1.	ur-^{d}šuba$_3$	Ur-Šuba,
2.	dub-sar	scribe,
3.	dumu ur-si-gar	child of Ur-Sigar.

In the next text, No. 52, a delivery of reed bundles is further specified to be for the production of mats. Unfortunately, the seal is illegible.

No. 52. *MS 1712 (Umma, Š 45)*

obv.

1.	⸢1(geš'u)$^{?}$ sa gi⸣ ^{gi}muru$_x$(KID.ŠU$_2$.MA$_2$)-še$_3$	600 bundles of reed for muru-mats.
2.	ki ab-ba-ta	From Abba.
3.	lugal-e-ba-an-sa$_6$	Lugal-ebansa
4.	šu ba-ti	received.

rev.

	(seal impression)	
1.	[mu-us$_2$]-⸢sa⸣ si-mu-[ru]-⸢um^{ki} lu-lu-bu^{ki} a-ra$_2$ 1(u) la$_2$ 1(diš$_{tenû}$) ba⸣-ḫul	Year following: "Simurum and Lulubu were destroyed for the 9th time."

seal (*illegible*)

In the next two texts, both fragmentary, Ilaknuid receives an amount of barley for barter for reed. In the first, No. 53, the delivering agent is Ur-Baba—this time written with the divine determinative, suggesting that the theophoric element of his name is a syllabic writing of the goddess Baba/Bau.[262] In the second, No. 54, a Lu-Utu is the delivering agent.

No. 53. *MS 4715/7 (Adab$^?$, IS 2)*

obv.

1.	3(aš) še gur	3 gur of barley
2.	⸢sa$_{10}$⸣ gi u$_3$ gi x-⸢ta$^?$⸣	for barter for reed and . . .-reed.
3.	ki ur-^{d}ba-ba-ta	From Ur-Baba.
4.	i-la-ak-nu-id	Ilaknuid
5.	šu ba-ti	received.

rev.

1.	giri$_3$ šu-[. . .]	Conveyor: . . . .
2.	še lu$_2$-^{d}x-x-x	Barley of . . .
	(*seal impression*)	
3.	mu en ^{d}inanna maš$_2$-e in-pa$_3$	Year: "The En-priest of Inanna was chosen by means of omen."

seal (S002469)

1.	i-la-ak-nu-id	Ilaknuid,
2.	dub-sar	scribe,
3.	dumu šu-ma$^?$-[ma$^?$]	child of Šu-Mama.

Texts Nos. 53 and 54 are the only extant examples of the seal of Ilaknuid. The seal legend of No. 54 is reconstructed from No. 53. A seal of Šu-Mama, perhaps the father of Ilaknuid, is partly preserved on No. 55.

No. 54. *MS 4715/8 (Adab$^?$, IS 1?)*

obv.

1.	3(aš) še gur	3 gur of barley,
2.	a$_2$ lu$_2$ ḫun-ga$_2$	(compensation for) work of hirelings
3.	saḫar-c-⸢si$^?$⸣^{ki}-ta	(coming) from Saḫar-esi.[263]
4.	ki lu$_2$-^{d}utu	From Lu-Utu.
5.	i-la-ak-nu-id	Ilaknuid
6.	šu ba-ti	received.

rev.

1.	giri$_3$ ur-ba-ba	Conveyor: Ur-Baba.
	(*seal impression*)	
2.	⸢mu⸣ [us$_2$$^?$-sa$^?$ en ^{d}]⸢nanna kar⸣-[zi-da ba]-⸢ḫun⸣	Year following: "The En-priestess of Nanna of Karzida was installed."

---

[262] See Marchesi 2002 for the reading ^{d}ba-u$_2$, and Richter 2004: 118–19, for the reading ^{d}ba-ba$_6$ of the divine name ^{d}ba-U$_2$. ^{d}ba-ba may here of course be a different deity altogether. See also comments to the text No. 60 below.

[263] This geographical name is otherwise unknown.

seal (S002469)

1.	i-la-ak-nu-id	Ilaknuid,
2.	dub-sar	scribe,
3.	[dumu šu-ma-ma]	child of Šu-Mama.

Šu-Mama, perhaps the father of Ilaknuid, seals the next document, text No. 55. He is also the recipient of the barley recorded in the document. Unfortunately the final line of the seal is illegible. Šu-Mama was a rather common name during the Ur III period, with several hundred attestations. The most famous Šu-Mama was a governor of Kazallu.[264] The seal impression on text No. 55 is, as far as I know, the only extant example of the seal of any person named Šu-Mama from the Ur III period.

No. 55. *MS 4715/12 (Adab$^?$, AS 3)*

obv.

1.	3(aš) 3(barig) še gur	3 gur, 3 barig of barley,
2.	še lugal-ušur$_4$	(it is the) barley of Lugal-Ušur;
3.	9(aš) še gur	9 gur of barley,
4.	du$_6$-ḫe$_2$-gal$_2$	(it is the barley of) Du-ḫegal;
5.	numun$^?$-⸢še$_3$⸣	for seedcorn

rev.

1.	u$_3$ x [...]	and ...
2.	ki ur-ba-[ba$^?$]-⸢ta⸣	From Ur-Baba.
3.	šu-ma-ma ⸢šu⸣ ba-ti	Šu-Mama received.
	(*blank space*)	
4.	mu ^{geš}gu-za ba-dim$_2$-ma	Year: "The throne was fashioned."

seal (—)[265]

1.	[šu]-ma-ma	Šu-Mama,
2.	dub-sar	scribe,
3.	[...]	...

Ordinary receipts, following the outline discussed above, can be very complex, as seen in the next example, text No. 56, which records the transfer of barley for "rent" of seven boats for ten days.

No. 56. *MS 2018/9 (Umma, AS 7–xii)*

obv.

1.	4(diš) ma$_2$ 4(u) gur 1(ban$_2$) 1(diš) sila$_3$-ta	4 boats, each (holding) 40 gur, 1 ban$_2$, 1 sila$_3$.
2.	ma$_2$ ^{geš}u$_2$-bil$_2$-⸢la⸣	Charcoal boat(s).
3.	2(diš) ma$_2$ 4(u) gur 5(diš) ⅔(diš) sila$_3$-ta	2 boats, each (holding) 40 gur 5 ⅔ sila$_3$.
4.	ma$_2$ ninda en-na tuš-e-da unu^{ki}	Until the bread boats are "moored" (at) Uruk.
5.	1(diš) ma$_2$ 1(geš$_2$) gur 1(ban$_2$) 5(diš) sila$_3$-ta	1 boat, each(!) (holding) 60 gur 1 ban$_2$, 5 sila$_3$.

[264] For Šu-Mama, governor of Kazallu, and his possible co-regency with Apilaša, see Goetze 1963 and Kutscher 1968.

[265] See perhaps the seal on Nisaba 15, 153 and 368 (S004245), although that would suggest a provenience of Irisagrig/Al-Šarraki for this and many of the other "Adab" texts published here.

rev.

1.	ma$_2$ x-zi$_3$-zu-a-ma$_2$-še$_3$	Boats for. . . .
2.	u$_4$ 1(u)-še$_3$	For 10 days.
3.	še-bi 2(aš) 1(barig) 4(ban$_2$) gur	Its barley: 2 gur, 1 barig, 4 ban2.[266]
4.	ki lu$_2$-^{d}šul-gi-ta	From Lu-Šulgi.
5.	lugal-e-ba-an-sa$_6$	Lugal-ebansa
6.	šu ba-ti	received.
7.	iti ^{d}dumu-zi	Month: "Dumuzi."

left edge

1.	mu ḫu-uḫ$_2$-nu-ri^{ki} ba-ḫul	Year: "Ḫuḫnuri was destroyed."

seal (*illegible*)

However, simple receipts that, like text No. 57, record the transfer of one or a few objects, remain the most numerous in almost all collections.

No. 57. *MS 4338/27 (Ur$^?$, X–v)*

obv.

1.	1(diš) ^{uruda}gur$_{10}$	1 plowshare of copper.
2.	ki ur-ku$_3$-nun-na-ta	From Ur-Kununa.
3.	e-lu$_2$-sa$_6$	Elusa
4.	šu ba-ti	received.

rev.

1.	iti ki siki ^{d}nin-a-zu (*seal impression*)	Month: "Weaving-place(?) of Ninazu."

seal (*illegible*)

A person named Elusa (e$_2$-lu$_2$-sa$_6$) is not attested in any other text, and it is important to note that text No. 57 lacks a year-name, and therefore might be classified with the practice documents from the Ur III period (see Chapter 12).

The next receipt, text No. 58, introduces a conveyor (see below). This text is discussed here due to its close relationship to several texts discussed above (Nos. 53, 55, etc.), and the fact that it presents problems that are very similar to the following text, No. 59. Since the seal impression is illegible it is not possible to say whether the recipient, Ea-šar, also sealed the text, but that is likely. The delivering agent is the same as in No. 55, and the content is also similar: barley for or from named individuals. Ilaknuid, whom we encountered in Nos. 53 and 54, acts as conveyor.

---

[266] The total overshoots by 2 extra ban$_2$ and 1/3 sila$_3$.

Calculations: 4×(40;0,1,1) = 160;0,4,4
+ 2×(40;0,0,5 2/3) = 80;0,1,1 1/3
+ 60;0,1,5
= 300;1,2,0 1/3.

No. 58. *MS 4715/10 (Adab?, IS 10)*

obv.

1.	6(aš) še gur	6 gur of barley,
2.	še lu_2-dingir-ra	(it is the) barley of Lu-Dingira,
3.	mu zi_3-da-$še_3$	instead of flour.
4.	ki ur-ba-ba-ta	From Ur-Baba.
5.	e_2-a-šar	Ea-šar

rev.

1.	šu ba-ti	received.
2.	$giri_3$ i-la-ak-nu-id (*seal impression*)	Conveyor: Ilaknuid.
3.	[mu en-nir]-⌜KI?⌝-an-na en ^{d}inanna $maš_2$-e i_3-pa_3	Year: "Ennirzianna was chosen by omen as En-priest of Inanna."

seal (*illegible*)

The reconstruction of the year-name of No. 58 is not entirely certain. Amar-Suen's sixth year mentions an En-priest of Inanna chosen by omen ($maš_2$-e i_3-pa_3), but his name, en-nun-gal-an-na hardly fits in the last line of No. 58. Ibbi-Suen's tenth year also mentions the En-priest of Inanna, but his name is en-nir-zi-an-na, which is also not a perfect fit as the broken sign in No. 58 (rev. 3) looks more like a KI than a ZI. The year-name of text No. 59 is also uncertain. Only Šulgi's year 34 mentions the destruction of Anšan, and ḫul, to destroy, is clearly visible at rev. 2. However, the sign preceding this ḫul, interpreted as $ḪUB_2$, makes little sense here.

With more than 100,000 extant Ur III texts is may seem puzzling that dating a document can present such problems. However, two factors continue to hinder our efforts. Firstly, we have an incomplete understanding of provincial calendars, in which local traditions influenced the menologies, year-names were often highly abbreviated, and unusual variants of year-names could be used. Secondly, the year-names of Ur-Namma and the early reign of Šulgi are primarily known from later, unreliable sources.[267]

No. 59. *MS 1947/13 (Umma, Š 34?–vi)*

obv.

1.	4(u) x	40 . . . ,
2.	ki šeš-kal-la-ta	From Šeš-kala.
3.	lugal-^{geš}gigir	Lugal-gigir
4.	šu ba-ti	received.

[267] E.g., BE 1/2, 125, an Old Babylonian list of Ur III year-names which preserves Šulgi years 5–43. In comparison Šulgi years 5–12 are only known from a few handfuls of Girsu texts, see Steinkeller 1988. Šulgi years 13–15 and 20 are not attested in extant Ur III sources, and years 16–19 are attested in a few texts only; significant numbers of texts are only available from Šulgi's year 30 onwards. Attesting to its late date, BE 1/2, 125 does not use the standard Ur III writing of the name of the city Ur (uri_5), but rather the variant known from later Old Babylonian sources (uri_2). The writing of uri_2(ŠEŠ.$AB_{gunû}$) is slightly more complicated than uri_5(ŠEŠ.AB) and may have been seen by Old Babylonian scribes as more archaic. Old Akkadian texts are split more or less evenly between the two forms, whereas all extant Ur III texts use the simple form, except for a few texts of uncertain date, e.g., 6N–T0147 (supposedly an Ur III text, but see Zettler and Sallaberger 2011: 4ff., for a discussion of the archaising script of that and many other 6N–T Ur III texts); NATN 109, a Nippur text from Š 48; and NYPL 390, a Nippur text from Šu-Suen 6.

rev.

1.	⸢iti šu-numun⸣	Month: "Seeding."
2.	⸢mu⸣ an-ša-⸢an$^{?}$⸣^{ki} ḪUB$_{2}^{?}$ ḫul	Year: "Anšan . . . destroyed"

seal (—)

1.	x-u$_{2}$-x	. . .
2.	nu-banda$_{3}$	captain,
3.	⸢dumu$^{?}$ lugal-gigir$^{?}$⸣	child(?) of Lugal-gigir.

In the next text, No. 60, three or four persons are mentioned. Although it cannot be established beyond doubt, the recipient, Ur-Baba, is probably identical with the person whose seal was rolled on the tablet, Ur-Ababa. However, the text also introduces another party said to have sealed the transaction, E-urbidu (for more on texts mentioning a sealed document, see below).

No. 60. *MS 4715/15 (Adab$^{?}$, IS 2)*

obv.

1.	2(u) še gur	20 gur of barley,
2.	mu ⸢bala⸣-a-še$_{3}$	instead of bala (obligations).
3.	kišib$_{3}^{?}$ ⸢e$_{2}$-ur$_{2}$⸣-bi-du$_{10}$	Sealed tablet of E-urbidu.
4.	ki lu$_{2}$-ma-ma-ta	From Lu-Mama.
5.	ur-ba-ba	Ur-(A)baba

rev.

1.	šu ba-ti	received.
	(seal impression)	
2.	mu en ^{d}inanna unu^{ki} maš$_{2}$ i$_{3}$-pa$_{3}$	Year: "The En-priest of Inanna of Uruk was chosen by omen."

seal (S004738)

1.	ur-^{d}a-ba-ba	Ur-Ababa,
2.	dub-sar	scribe,
3.	dumu a$_{2}$-ur$_{4}$-a	child of A'ur'a.

It is possible to speculate that Ur-Baba and Ur-Ababa are the same person because variation in the writing of names in seal legends and in the texts themselves is not uncommon in Ur III texts. It has even proven helpful to establish variant orthographies of names, and to hypothesise the correct reading of signs. Invariably, the form found in the text of the tablet is the one which would have been the simplest to write (i.e., the one requiring the fewest wedges), whereas the spelling on the seal may be the more complicated. The following text is a clear example of this. Here the name of the recipient and sealing party, Ur-Saga, is written with the sign SIG$_{5}$ in the body of the text and the more complex sign SA$_{6}$ in the seal. The semantic field of both signs (SIG$_{5}$ and SA$_{6}$) overlaps and denotes that something is good or sweet.

TCNU 646 (Umma, ŠS 3)

obv.

1.	1(diš) geš-ur$_{3}$	1 harrow
2.	e$_{2}$ kar-še$_{3}$	for the "house of the harbour."

3.	ki a-du-du-ta	From Adudu.
4.	kišib$_3$ ur-saga(SIG$_5$)	Sealed tablet of Ur-saga.

rev.

1.	mu si-ma-num$_2$^{ki} ba-ḫul	Year: "Simanum was destroyed."

seal (S004663)

1.	ur-sa$_6$-ga	Ur-saga,
2.	dub-sar	scribe,
3.	dumu ur-dingir-ra	child of Ur-dingira.

In rare cases we find a reversal of the standard pattern outlined at the beginning of this chapter (No. 43), where the delivering agent, rather than the recipient or a third party introduced in the text, acts as sealing party. In text No. 61 Namḫani is said to have received the goods (barley) from Ur-Ababa, but the tablet appears to be sealed by that same Ur-Ababa.

No. 61. *MS 4715/18 (Adab?, ŠS 2)*

obv.

1.	1(u) 5(aš) še gur	15 gur of barley,
2.	mu zi$_3$-da bala-a-še$_3$	instead of the flour of the bala (obligation).
3.	ki ur-^{d}a-ba-ba-ta	From Ur-Ababa.
4.	nam-ḫa-ni	Namḫani
5.	šu ba-ti	received.

rev.

1.	še lu$_2$-^{d}nanna	The barley of Lu-Nanna.
	(*seal impression*)	
2.	mu ma$_2$ dara$_3$ abzu ^{d}en-ki-ka ba-ab-du$_8$	Year: "The boat 'Ibex of the Abzu of Enki' was caulked."

seal (—)

1.	ur-^{d}a$^?$-[ba-ba]	Ur-Ababa(?),
2.	dumu x [. . .]	child of [x].

Due to the fragmentary nature of the seal impression this particular example is not absolutely clear. The following text, on the other hand, presents a much clearer example. Of course it remains possible that a third person, bearing the same name as the delivering agent, sealed the transaction. Normally, however, such ambiguity would have led to the identification of the delivering party through an added title or patronymic clearly distinguishing him from his namesake.[268]

It may be important to note that the seal on the following example, where indeed it seems likely that the delivering agent also seals the transaction, is rolled 90° counterclockwise compared to the standard rotation of seals. Whether this rotation is important for our understanding of the order of the participants remains unclear.

---

[268] This is particularly clear in the case of the important Umma administrator Lu-kala, who is never mentioned with a title save for the generic dub-sar, except once when he is found in a text together with his namesake Lu-kala the shepherd. There he is given the title šabra, "chief (household) administrator" (MVN 16, 1294); for a discussion, see Dahl 2007: 105–6.

Aleppo 119 (NMSA 3727) (Umma, Š 35)

obv.

1.	3(geš$_2$) sa gi	180 bundles of reed,
2.	nig$_2$-gu$_7$ di-de$_3$	being said(?) as fodder.
3.	ki ur-^{d}šara$_2$-ta	From Ur-Šara.
4.	ur-zu šu ba-ti	Urzu received.
5.	ša$_3$ bala iti min-eš$_3$	Within the bala (obligation). Month: "Double sanctuary."

rev.

	(seal impression)	
1.	mu us$_2$-sa an-ša-an^{ki} ba-ḫul	Year following: "Anšan was destroyed."

seal (S005355)

1.	ur-^{d}šara$_2$	Ur-Šara,
2.	dub-sar	the scribe,
3.	dumu lugal-ušur$_3$	child of Lugal-ušur,
4.	nu-banda$_3$-gu$_4$ ^{d}šara$_2$	domain-unit administrator of Šara.

In yet other cases, an otherwise unrelated person is found to have rolled his seal on the tablet. Intensive prosopographical studies can sometimes identify the underlying motivations for such discrepancies (see, e.g., Dahl 2007: 80).[269] An example:

Aleppo 122 (NMSA 4156) (Umma, Š 37–vi)

obv.

1.	1(aš) gu$_2$ ^{geš}ma-nu	1 gu$_2$ of willow(?),
2.	1(aš) gu$_2$ gi	1 gu$_2$ of reed.
3.	siskur$_2$ ki ^{d}suen	Offerings of the place of Suen.
4.	ki šeš-a-ni-ta	From Šešani,
5.	ku$_3$-ga-ni	Kugani

rev.

1.	šu ba-ti	received.
2.	iti šu-numun	Month: "Seeding."
3.	mu lugal-e bad$_3$ mu-du$_3$	Year: "The king built the wall."

seal (S003230)

1.	lu$_2$-^{d}nin-tu	Lu-Nintu,
2.	dub-sar	scribe,
3.	dumu en-u$_2$-a	child of Enua.

[269] Note also AAICAB 1/1, pl. 30, 1911-212 where the wife of a certain Ur-Ištaran is mentioned as recipient (without name), but the tablet is sealed by the husband; and AION 31, 175 6 where the seal of a brother of the conveyor is rolled on the tablet instead of that of the recipient or the conveyor (N.B. the location of the Aleppo tablet is today unknown).

Receipts Mentioning a Conveyor (GIRI$_3$)

Some receipts mention another participant. In most cases the exact function of this person remains unclear. Based on the meaning of the Sumerian term introducing this actor, g i r i $_3$ (lit. "foot"), the term is usually translated as a title, "conveyor."[270] In a particular group of receipt tablets discussed below, the conveyor also seals the transactions.

In text No. 62 a very large amount of barley (120 gur or c. 36,000 liters), as replacement for beer of the *bala* (obligation),[271] is received by Ur-Eninnu from Ur-Šulgi. Ur-Baba is introduced as the conveyor. The transaction is said to take place in Adab.

No. 62. *MS 4715/16 (Adab$^?$, IS 2–iv)*

obv.

1.	2(geš$_2$) še gur	120 gur of barley
2.	mu ⸢kaš⸣ bala-a-⸢še$_3$⸣	instead of beer of the bala (obligation).
3.	ki ur-^{d}šul-gi-ta	From Ur-Šulgi.
4.	ur-e$_2$-ninnu	Ur-Eninnu
5.	šu ba-ti	received.

rev.

1.	giri$_3$ ur-ba-ba	Conveyor: Ur-Baba.
2.	ša$_3$ adab^{ki}	Within Adab.
	(seal impression)	
3.	iti u$_5$-bi$_2$-gu$_7$	Month: "Eating the Goose(?)."
4.	mu en ^{d}inanna unu^{ki}-bi maš$_2$-e in-pa$_3$	Year: "The En-priest of Inanna of Uruk was chosen by omen."

seal (S005960)

col. i

1.	^{d}i-bi$_2$-^{d}suen	Ibbi-Suen,
2.	lugal kal-ga	strong king,
3.	lugal uri$_5$^{ki}-ma	king of Ur,
4.	lugal an ub-da limmu$_2$-ba	king of the four quarters (of the world):

col. ii

1.	ur-e$_2$-ninnu	Ur-Eninnu,
2.	dub-sar	scribe,
3.	dumu ur-⸢AB$^?$⸣-[. . .]-ku$_3$-⸢ga$^?$⸣-[. . .]	son of Ur- . . . -kuga- . . . ,
4.	lu$_2$ [. . .]	the man (of? . . . is your slave).

There is no direct indication that the conveyor also physically moved the goods from the delivering agent, here Ur-Šulgi, to the recipient, here Ur-Eninnu, although that is of course possible.

---

270 See Owen 2013: 95 and Heimpel 2009: 27 (also quoted in Owen). Heimpel suggests a meaning "at the feet of the responsible person." For *šēpum* in Old Assyrian documents used of persons who transported goods or tablets, see Michel 1992: 141 ff. See *CAD* Š/2 305, for a meaning "transport" in Old Assyrian, and "routing(?)" in Ur III and Old Babylonian documents, and note Charpin and Ziegler 1997: 245 for the meaning "transporter" similar to the Old Assyrian meaning established by Michel.

271 Despite a recent monograph on the topic, the *bala* (obligations) of the provinces of the Ur III state remains difficult to understand (see Sharlach 2004 with review in Dahl 2006).

In text No. 63, from Umma, an amount of an unknown product is transferred from Lu-uršaga to Ur-Ištaran. The product is destined for an unknown location. The exact role of the conveyor Lugal-zagesi remains unclear.

No. 63. *MS 1947/6 (Umma, ŠS 9)*

obv.

1.	5(aš) gu$_2$ KWU422[272]	5 talents of . . . .
2.	ki lu$_2$-ur$_4$-ša$_3$-ga-ta	From Lu-uršaga.
3.	^{d}suen-dingir-šu-še$_3$[273]	For Suen-ilīšu.
4.	ur-^{d}ištaran	Ur-Ištaran

rev.

1.	šu ba-ti	received.
2.	giri$_3$ lugal-za$_3$-ge-si	Conveyor: Lugal-zagesi.
3.	ša$_3$ bala-a	Within the bala (obligation).
	(*seal impression*)	
4.	mu ^{d}šu-^{d}suen lugal-e e$_2$ ^{d}šara$_2$ umma^{ki} mu-du$_3$	Year: "Šu-Suen, king, built the house of Šara."

seal (S004986)

1.	ur-^{d}ištaran	Ur-Ištaran,
2.	dumu ur-dumu-zi-da	son of Ur-Dumuzida,
3.	dam-gar$_3$	trade-agent.

In a number of texts from Drehem the conveyor (giri$_3$) acts as sealer.[274] Here, this practice seems to be confined to the offices of the ša$_3$-tam and šar$_2$-ra-ab-du, and is frequently found in texts recording weighing of wool.[275]

BIN 3, 356 (Puzriš-Dagan, ŠS 5–vii–28)

obv.

1.	2(aš) gu$_2$ 3(u) ma-na siki GI	2 talents, 30 ma-na of GI[276] wool,

---

[272] The product written with the sign KWU422 (KA × 3(AŠ$_{tenû}$)) is not a hapax, but the only other occurrence known to me is unclear, UCP 09-02-1, 95 rev. ii 4: 4(aš) 2(barig) gur sa$_2$-du$_{11}$ eb-gal KWU422-du.

[273] For a comparable geographical(?) name, see UTI 4, 2579 obv. 3: ^{d}en-lil$_2$-dingir-šu-še$_3$.

[274] See also possibly two Umma texts: AnOr 7, 175, where the conveyor is lugal-nig$_2$-lagar-e and the seal inscription is that of a lugal-si-NE-e, and Nisaba 9, 267 with the seal of a ku$_3$-^{d}nin-ur$_4$-ra appearing as the conveyor in the text (note that no visual documentation is available for the texts published in Nisaba 9).

[275] A number of individuals are attested in this capacity. Nur-Suen the ša$_3$-tam features prominently (e.g., AUCT 3, 209; BPOA 6, 1470 AUCT 3, 324, etc.). Once he is attested as sealing together with Ḫulal the šar$_2$-ra-ab-du (AUCT 3, 324). Ḫulal is independently attested sealing as conveyor (MVN 13, 89). Others are Ur-Baba (BRM 3, 46); Nanna-maba the ša$_3$-tam (MVN 18, 385; PDT 1, 312, PDT 1, 490, PDT 1, 623; Princeton 2, 38); with Dadaya the šar$_2$-ra-ab-du (PDT 2, 1325); Aḫu-waqar the šar$_2$-ra-ab-du (NYPL 119 and NYPL 320); and finally Aḫu-waqar as conveyor but with the seal of Nur-Suen (Princeton 2, 51). In Drehem the offices of šar$_2$-ra-ab-du and ša$_3$-tam were connected to animal herding, whereas in Umma the office of ša$_3$-tam seems related to agriculture (Dahl 2007: 65 and n. 248, 127 and n. 439). For the same office in the Old Babylonian period, see Gallery 1975: 63 ff. and Gallery 1980. The title ša$_3$-tam, probably an Akkadian loanword, occurs in the Old Babylonian period as an administrator's title in its Akkadian form *šatammum*; the title šar$_2$-ra-ab-du is not attested post-Ur III.

[276] Either a color designation (yellow), or denoting the origin of the sheep, here possibly "native" (phonetic for gi$_7$).

2.	[na$_4$] 1(aš) gu$_2$ 2(diš) ma-na-ta	according to the 1 talent, 2 ma-na stone.[277]
3.	[bar udu] mu-ku$_x$(DU)-ra	Fleece of "delivered" sheep.
4.	mu-ku$_x$(DU)	mu-ku$_x$(DU) delivery.[278]
5.	lu$_2$-kal-la	Lu-kala

rev.

1.	šu ba-ti	received.
2.	giri$_3$ nu-ur$_2$-^{d}suen dub-sar	Conveyor: Nur-Suen.
3.	u$_4$ 2(u) 8(diš)-kam	On the 28th day.
4.	iti a$_2$-ki-ti	Month: "Akitu."
5.	mu us$_2$-sa ^{d}šu-^{d}suen lugal uri$_5$^{ki}-ma-ke$_4$ bad$_3$ mar-tu mu-ri-iq-ti-id-ni-im mu-du$_3$	Year following: "Šu-Suen king of Ur built the Amorite wall (called) Muriq-tidnim."

seal (S000563)

col. i

1.	^{d}[šu-^{d}]suen	Šu-Suen,
2.	lugal kal-ga	strong king,
3.	lugal uri$_5$^{ki}-ma	king of Ur,
4.	lugal an ub-da limmu$_2$-ba	king of the four quarters:

col. ii

1.	nu-ur$_2$-^{d}suen	Nur-Suen,
2.	dub-sar	scribe,
3.	dumu [i-di$_3$-er$_3$-ra]	child of Idi(n)-Erra,
4.	ARAD$_2$-[zu]	(is) your slave.

Drehem tablets sealed by the conveyor all deal with wool from delivered animals or with the animals themselves.

Another group of texts, also sealed by the conveyor but from Girsu, deals with the weighing of metal objects. Sometimes multiple conveyors sealed the transaction, and sometimes the recipient sealed together with the conveyors. These texts were probably always encased in envelopes, but envelopes are only preserved in about ten per cent of the probable instances of this procedure. In the following example the texts of the envelope and the tablet are almost identical, except for the occasional difference in line break. The envelope adds a month date.

TLB 3, 157–58 (Girsu, AS 7–vi)

Tablet

obv.

1.	3(u) 5(diš) ^{uruda}ḫa-bu$_3$-da	35 copper hoes,
2.	ki-la$_2$-bi 9(diš) ma-na 1(u) 5(diš) gin$_2$	their weight: 9 ma-na and 15 shekels,

[277] Several Ur III texts record textiles weighed by stones of the same or very similar weights, e.g., the parallel text AoF 29, 18, 3; see comments by Schwemer 2002. See Powell 1987–90: 508 for the textile weight stones, na$_4$ si-sa$_2$, attested in a handful of Pre-Sargonic, Old Akkadian and Lagash II texts.

[278] See the section on mu-ku$_x$(DU) texts below.

3.	ba-zi-ir[279]	(they) were smelted down.
4.	ki lugal-im-ru-a-ta	From Lugal-imrua.
5.	ur-^{d}nin-geš-zi-da	Ur-Ningešzida

rev.

1.	šu ba-ti	received.
2.	giri$_3$ gu$_3$-de$_2$-a ša$_{13}$-dub-ba	Conveyor: Gudea the chief accountant;
3.	giri$_3$ lu$_2$-^{d}nin-gir$_2$-su šabra e$_2$	Conveyor: Lu-Ningirsu the chief administrator.
	(*1 line blank*)	
4.	mu ḫu-uḫ$_2$-nu-ri^{ki} ba-ḫul	Year: "Ḫuḫnuri was destroyed."

Envelope

obv.

1.	3(u) 5(diš) ^{uruda}ḫa-bu$_3$-da	35 copper hoes,
2.	ki-la$_2$-bi 9(diš) ma-na 1(u) 5(diš) gin$_2$	their weight: 9 ma-na and 15 shekels,
3.	ba-zi-ir	(they) were smelted down.
4.	ki lugal-im-ru-a-ta	From Lugal-imrua.
5.	ur-^{d}nin-geš-zi-da šu ba-ti	Ur-Ningešzida received.

rev.

1.	giri$_3$ gu$_3$-de$_2$-a ša$_{13}$-dub-ba	Conveyor: Gudea the chief accountant;
	(*seal impression*)	
3.	giri$_3$ lu$_2$-^{d}nin-gir$_2$-su šabra ⸢e$_2$⸣	Conveyor: Lu-Ningirsu the chief household administrator.
	(*blank line*)	
3.	iti ezem-^{d}dumu-zi	Month: "Festival of Dumuzi"
4.	mu ḫu-uḫ$_2$-nu-ri^{ki} ba-ḫul	Year: "Ḫuḫnuri was destroyed."

seal 1 (S003154)

1.	lu$_2$-^{d}nin-gir$_2$-⸢su⸣	Lu-Ningirsu,
2.	dub-sar	scribe,
3.	dumu ARAD$_2$-mu	child of ARADmu.

seal 2 (S003153)

1.	lu$_2$-^{d}nin-[geš-zi-da]	Lu-Ningešzida,
2.	dumu ur-^{d}nin-geš-[zi-da]	child of Ur-Ningešzida,
3.	ugula [. . .]	overseer of . . .

seal 3 (S002392)

1.	gu$_3$-de$_2$-[a]	Gudea,
2.	ša$_{13}$-dub-ba gir$_2$-su[^{ki}]	accountant of Girsu,
3.	dumu la-ni	child of Lani,

---

[279] The verb ba-zi-ir, "was smelted" (see Joannès 1993: 111) is used by half of the extant texts from this group (Berens 46; DAA 1 127 BM 14661; DAS 30; SAT 1, 358 and 359; TLB 3, 157–58; TCTI 2, 3469), whereas other half uses the verb ba-la$_2$, "was weighed" (DAS 16; ITT 2, 951; TCTI 2, 2563; 2571; 3464; 3932). One text is broken (DAS 17).

4. ša$_{13}$-dub-ba gu-la gir$_2$-su[^{ki}]-⸢ka⸣ chief[280] accountant of Girsu.

In Garšana a conveyor is introduced in texts with very diverse content.[281] And in yet other cases no explanation for the sealing by the conveyor can be given (MVN 2, 68; MVN 5, 230; PDT 1, 103; TCTI 2, 2561; UNT 48; BPOA 6, 802; CST 383). Occasionally, another party was introduced in the text, specifically named as the sealing party.[282] In DC 283 (from ŠS 6 iii), it is explicitly said that PN sealed instead of PN who was the recipient: obv. 5–rev. 9: ki KA-guru$_7$-ta / ad-da-kal-la / šu ba-ti / mu ad-da-kal-la-še$_3$ / kišib$_3$ ur-kin-na-ke$_4$. The document is sealed with the seal of Ur-kinake, the son of Ḫamati.[283] All of these examples appear to be very special cases either originating from rare situations, or from the fringes of the Ur III state.

Unsealed Receipts

Some receipts without seal are explicitly said to be unsealed (kišib$_3$ nu-ra-a[284]).[285] The following text, No. 64, is an example of a receipt using this terminology. Nevertheless, there is a real chance that it was in fact encased in an envelope which was sealed, as suggested by the matching entry in the account Nisaba 6, 26, discussed below.

---

280 Usually, being mentioned with a particular title meant being the chief within that profession (as evidenced by the title ašgab used by the chief of the leather workers of Umma, A(ya)-kala). Here however, the title of the father of the seal owner is qualified by gu-la, presumably making the father the chief accountant. When his son took over the office after his father he likely too became the chief accountant (ša$_{13}$-dub-ba gu-la) but reserved the honorific gu-la for his father in his seal inscription.

281 CUSAS 3, 527 (rations for male and female slaves); CUSAS 3, 545 (compensation for work of hirelings); CUSAS 3, 730 (transfer of textiles); CUSAS 3, 1205 (dates); CUSAS 3, 1338 (bitumen).

282 Aleppo 61 (from Š 34 vii) obv. 5: a-nu-u$_2$-a šu ba-ti, the document is sealed with the seal of Ur-Šara, son of Lugal-usur, the captain of the (plow-)oxen of Šara (ur-^{d}šara$_2$ / dub-sar / dumu lugal-ušur$_3$ / nu-banda$_3$ gu$_4$ ^{d}šara$_2$). AnOr 1, 256 (from AS 6) obv. 4–5: lu$_2$-^{d}en-lil$_2$-la$_2$ šu ba-ti, the document is sealed with the seal of Lugal-si-NE-[e], son of Lugalsaga (lugal-si-ne-[e] / dub-⸢sar⸣ / dumu lugal-⸢sa$_6$⸣-[ga]). CHEU 86 (from Š 39 xi) obv. 5: lu$_2$-i$_3$-zu šu ba-ti, the document is sealed with the seal of Ur-ama, išib-priest of Nin-da-Lagaš (ur-am$_3$-ma / išib ^{d}nin-da-lagaš<ki>). In a few cases the delivering party is also the sealing party, e.g., Aleppo 119, see above, and Aleppo 126 (no date) obv. 2–4: ki lugal-ezem-ta / lugal-a$_2$-zi-da / šu ba-ti, the document is sealed with the seal of Lugal-ezem, scribe, son of Lugal-Emah(e), chief administrator (lugal-ezem / dub-sar / dumu lugal-e$_2$-maḫ-e šabra).

283 See also the parallel text ASJ 19, 220 58 (from ŠS 5 xi), where another (?) son of Ḫamati, Ur-balanga, rolled his seal. See also the similar text AUCT 3, 279 (from AS 7 i).

284 Because there is no apparent difference between the writings with final -a and those without—except perhaps for a slight preference for final -a during the reign of Šulgi—and since writings with final -a are far more numerous than without, I have decided to reconstruct final -a in all cases where it is missing.

285 The compound verb kišib$_3$—ra, "to seal" (lit. "to strike the seal") is predominantly found in the form kišib$_3$ PN(-ak) bi$_2$-ra, "the seal of PN was struck (on the tablet)," i.e., "sealed tablet of PN." Jagersma's translation of l. 3 of the obscure tablet OrSP 47–49, 165 (2010: 327), "Itimu was caused to impress his seal," is problematic due to its lack of discussion of the context of the quote. OrSP 47–49, 165 (Umma, Š33–iv): ša$_3$ še 1(geš$_2$) 7(aš) gur-ta / 1(u) 1(aš) 2(barig) še gur / i-ti-mu-ra kišib$_3$ ba-an-ra // iti nesag / mu a-ra$_2$ 3(diš)-kam-aš si-mu-ru-um^{ki} ba-ḫul mu us$_2$-sa-bi, possibly to be translated "out of each 67 gur of barley, 11 ⅓ were sealed for Itimu. Month: 'First Fruit (Offerings).' Year following: 'Third time Simurum was destroyed.'" i-ti-mu is poorly attested, and known from only three other texts. In one of these texts we find his seal, where he claims to be yet another son of Ur-nigar, the chief cattle-administrator (šuš$_3$) of Umma (BPOA 1, 1642). Perhaps the clue to our text lies in this curious fact. As I speculated in my book on the ruling family of Ur III Umma, members of the family could exit the ordinary state-administration to pursue a career outside its reach, but would occasionally reappear, sealing instead of other members of their family (Dahl 2007: 48, 75–83, 136, but note Pomponio 2013). The above translation assumes that ša$_3$ is used as the Akkadian relative pronoun *ša*, that the "dative" suffix on Itimu's name is used for the Akkadian preposition *ana*, and finally, the "passive" ba-an-ra perhaps stands for Akkadian stative *kanik(ma)*, and that this text follows an Akkadian "model" closely.

No. 64. *MS 1947/12 (Umma, AS 4[286]–xi)*

obv.

1.	4(barig) 4(ban$_2$) 8(diš) sila$_3$ še	4 barig, 4 ban$_2$, 8 sila$_3$ of barley,
2.	nig$_2$-ša$_3$-te ^{d}inanna	for the morning (lit.: cool) (offerings) of Inanna,
3.	a-ša$_3$ la$_2$-maḫ-ta	from the field Lamaḫ,
4.	ki ARAD$_2$-ta	from ARAD(mu).
5.	ur-<geš>gigir sa$_{12}$-du$_5$	Ur-Gigir the surveyor

rev.

1.	šu ba-ti	received.
2.	kišib$_3$ nu-ra-<a>	Unsealed document.
3.	iti pa$_4$-u$_2$-e	Month: "Pa'u'e."
4.	mu en ^{d}nanna maš-e ⸢i$_3$-pa$_3$⸣	Year: "The En-priest of Nanna was chosen by omen."

This receipt is matched in an entry recorded in Nisaba 6, 26 obv. iii 20–21:

20.	4(barig) 4(ban$_2$) 8(diš)![287] sila$_3$ nig$_2$ ša$_3$-te ^{d}inanna	4 barig, 4 ban$_2$, 8 sila$_3$ of barley, for the morning (lit.: cool) (offerings) of Inanna.
21.	kišib$_3$ ur-^{d}en-lil$_2$-la$_2$	Sealed tablet of Ur-Enlila

In the year-end account the receipt No. 64 would most likely have been summarized as a sealed document to either Ur-Enlila (if indeed Nisaba 6, 26 dates to AS 4) or Ur-Gigir, the actual recipient in the document. A seal could also have been rolled on a now lost envelope.

The majority of the instances of kišib$_3$ nu-ra-a come from texts from Umma, and among these a disproportionately high number (more than ten per cent) are said to be deliveries from ARAD(mu), the well-known chief of the granary at Ur III Umma.[288] As is common with deliveries made by ARAD(mu), these are either credited to himself (ki ARAD$_2$-ta) or to his office (ki KA-guru$_7$-ta).[289]

The phrase kišib$_3$ nu-ra-a PN could replace the standard phrase kišib$_3$ PN in lists of deliveries (see, e.g., BPOA 1, 1048) and seems then to refer to a type of document, an "unsealed receipt." A tablet copy could even be said to be of a kišib$_3$ nu-ra-a document (see OrSP 47–49, 367). The following British Museum text is perhaps illustrative of the use of the terminology kišib$_3$ nu-ra-a:

---

[286] The date on No. 64 could be either AS 4 or Š 43, but since the text is closely matched in one of the entries in Nisaba 6, 26 dated by its editors (Al-Rawi and D'Agostino 2005) to AS 5, and a similar account can be expected to have existed from AS 4 based on the surviving primary texts, the receipts, it is more likely that our text should be dated to AS 4 than Š 43, for which the same scenario cannot easily be established.

A few other receipts credited to ARAD(mu) (ki ARAD$_2$-ta) from Amar-Suen 4 can be matched up with entries in Nisaba 6, 26, e.g., BPOA 7, 1862 corresponding to obv. i 14–16; and NYPL 92 probably corresponding to obv. i 41–42 (and summary line obv. ii 1), and note that several other receipts are close but not exact matches, as receipts are sometimes spread across several entries. Note also that parallel receipts exist from AS 5 and 6 and so forth.

[287] Nisaba 6, 26 has 6 (diš) but, unfortunately, no visual documentation exists for the texts published in Nisaba 6.

[288] See also Dahl 2007: 115–21.

[289] Note Steinkeller's reconstruction of the bookkeeping procedures in ARAD(mu)'s office, suggesting that letters were sent out to different locations authorizing deliveries, following which the recipient would bring his sealed document to the office of ARAD(mu) in Umma (Steinkeller 2004). The high number of unsealed documents from ARAD(mu)'s office, however, indicates that documents were made by ARAD(mu)'s office and that they never left Umma. Often, and due to the nature of the activities of ARAD(mu), the sealing party could not be present to seal the tablet documenting the transfer. At the end of the year, ARAD(mu)'s office would line up all of the receipts to document how much of the assets put at his disposal at the beginning of the year had been expended.

MCS 1, 54, BM 113107 (Umma, AS 1–vii)

obv.

1.	1(u) kuš gu$_4$	10 ox hides,
2.	3(diš) kuš anše	3 onager hides.
3.	kišib$_3$ ra-a	Sealed tablet.
4.	2(diš) kuš anše	2 onager hides.
5.	kišib$_3$ nu-ra-a	Unsealed tablet.
6.	kuš gu$_4$ ri-ri-ga	Hides of fallen oxen.

rev.

1.	kišib$_3$ i$_7$-pa-e$_3$	Sealed tablet of I-pa'e.
2.	iti min-eš$_3$	Month: "Double sanctuary."
3.	mu ^{d}amar-^{d}suen lugal	Year: "Amar-Suen (was) king."

seal (S002533)

1.	i$_7$-pa-e$_3$	I-pa'e,
2.	dub-sar	scribe,
3.	dumu lu$_2^{?}$-^{d}šara$_2$	child of Lu-Šara,
4.	sa$_{12}$-du$_5$	surveyor.

Unfortunately, none of these sealed and unsealed documents has been preserved from Amar-Suen year 1. From Amar-Suen year 7 one such possible text has been recovered:

Georgica 1.1.3 (Umma, AS 7)

obv.

1.	2(diš) kuš anše	2 onager hides,
2.	^{geš}apin-na ḪI-la$_2$-de$_3$	. . . .-ing at the plow.
3.	engar-e šu ba-ab-ti	The cultivators received.
4.	kišib$_3$ nam-ša$_3$-tam	Sealed tablet of the nam-šatam[290]

rev.

1.	i$_7$-pa-e$_3$	I-pa'e.
	(*seal impression*)	
2.	mu bi$_2$-⸢tum⸣-[ra]-bi$_2$-[um^{ki} ba-ḫul]	Year: "Bitum-rabium was destroyed."

seal (S002533)

1.	i$_7$-pa-e$_3$	I-pa'e,
2.	dub-sar	scribe,
3.	dumu lu$_2$-^{d}šara$_2$	child of Lu-Šara,
4.	sa$_{12}$-du$_5$	surveyor.

BPOA 1, 408 from the following year improves our understanding of the events behind MS 1, 54, BM 113107. That text lists the hides of "fallen" (ri-ri-ga) plow animals, and the tablet is again sealed by I-pa'e. I-pa'e was an overseer of domain-land (nam-ša$_3$-tam) and therefore responsible for the plow animals allotted to

[290] For the title nam-šatam in Ur III texts, see n. 275.

him during plowing season. Usable parts of any animal that died under his control would have to be recovered and accounted for.

Another text suggestive of an interpretation of kišib$_3$—ra (lit.: "to strike the seal on") as a frozen verbal form, that acts as a noun describing a certain type of administrative document (sealed or unsealed receipt), is CHEU 14:[291]

CHEU 14 (Umma, Š 35–iii)

Tablet

obv.

1.	1(geš$_2$) 1(u) 1(aš) še gur lugal	611 gur of barley (according to the) king('s standard);
2.	1(geš$_2$) 5(u) la$_2$ 3(ban$_2$) dabin gur	650 gur minus 3 ban$_2$ of dabin-flour.
3.	kišib$_3$ ra-a kišib$_3$ nu-ra	Sealed and unsealed documents
4.	lu$_2$ nig$_2$-dab$_5$-ba-ke$_4$-ne	of the . . .[292].

rev.

1.	kišib$_3$ dab$_x$(U$_8$)-ba	. . .[293].
2.	ki ARAD$_2$-ta	From ARAD(mu).
3.	lu$_2$-giri$_{17}$-zal	Lu-Girizal
4.	šu ba-ti	received.
5.	iti še-kar-ra-gal$_2$-la	Month: "Barley is at the quay."
6.	mu us$_2$-sa an-ša-an^{ki} ba-ḫul	Year following: "Anšan was destroyed."

Envelope

obv.

1.	1(geš$_2$) 1(u) 1(aš) še gur lugal	611 gur of barley (according to the) king('s standard);
2.	1(geš$_2$) 3(u) la$_2$ 3(ban$_2$) dabin gur	650 gur minus 3 ban$_2$ of dabin-flour.
3.	kišib$_3$ ra-a kišib$_3$ nu-ra	Sealed and unsealed documents
	(*blank line*)	
4.	lu$_2$ nig$_2$-dab$_5$-ba-ke$_4$-ne	of the . . .
5.	kišib$_3$ dab$_x$(U$_8$)-ba	. . .
6.	ki ARAD$_2$-ta	From ARAD(mu).
7.	lu$_2$-giri$_{17}$-zal šu ba-ti	Lu-Girizal received.

---

[291] See also AUCT 3, 279 discussed below.

[292] The term lu$_2$ nig$_2$-dab$_5$-ba (mostly with the plural ending -ene) describes a social group comparable to the giri$_3$-se$_3$-ga (see, e.g., perhaps MCS 6, 83, BM 105334 where they are paired with giri$_3$-se$_3$-ga dingir-re-ne [rev. i 5], and Ch. 8 below), although possibly of higher social standing. Frequent references to sealed documents of the group exist. See Nisaba 15, 542 for an inventory of a group of lu$_2$ nig$_2$-dab$_5$-ba (from Irisagrig).

[293] The term kišib$_3$ dab$_x$(U$_8$)-ba is also found together with lu$_2$ nig$_2$-dab$_5$-ba in SNAT 429 (rev. 17); see also the pisan-dub-ba text Umma 108.

rev.

1.	iti še-kar-ra-gal$_2$-la	Month: "Barley is at the quay."
	(*blank space*)	
2.	mu us$_2$-sa an-ša-an^{ki} ba-ḫul	Year following: "Anšan was destroyed."
	(*blank space*)	

seal (S002893)

1.	lu$_2$-giri$_{17}$-zal	Lu-Girizal,
2.	dub-sar	scribe,
3.	dumu da-du-mu	child of Dadumu.

It therefore seems most probable that kišib$_3$ PN referred to a sealed document of PN, and kišib$_3$ nu-ra-a to an unsealed document.

Other times it is simply said that the seal of so-and-so was rolled (Sumerian ra, "struck") instead of the seal of so-and-so, suggesting that the variations described above relate to very real practices now largely lost to us. AUCT 3, 279 is an an example of such a text:

AUCT 3, 279 (Umma, AS 7–i)

obv.

1.	1(barig) zu$_2$-lum	1 barig of dates,
2.	še-bi 1(barig) 1(ban$_2$)-⸢ta⸣	its barley: 1 barig, 1 ban$_2$ <<each>>[294].
3.	ki ur$_4$-ša$_3$-ki-du$_{10}$-ta	From Ur-šakidu,
4.	ARAD$_2$-mu	ARADmu
5.	[šu] ba-ti	received.

rev.

1.	mu ARAD$_2$-mu-[še$_3$]	Instead of ARADmu
2.	kišib$_3$ ur-^{d}iškur	the seal of Ur-Iškur
3.	ib$_2$-ra	was rolled (lit. struck).
4.	iti še-sag$_{11}$-ku$_5$	Month: "Harvest."
5.	mu ḫu-ḫu-nu-ri^{ki} ba-ḫul	Year: "Ḫuḫnuri was destroyed."

seal (S004974)

1.	ur-^{d}iškur	Ur-Iškur
2.	[x] x [x]	. . .
3.	ARAD$_2$ lu$_2$-du$_{10}$-ga	slave of Lu-duga.

Texts Nos. 65 and 66 are two small receipts which lack information about the receiving party. An explanation may be that the tablets were originally encased in envelopes supplying this information.

[294] The standard exchange rate between dates and barley was 1 gur of dates to 1 gur and 5 ban$_2$ of barley, or in other words 1 barig of dates equated to 1 barig and 1 ban$_2$ of barley; see, e.g., AUCT 1, 631; 963; and 352. The distributive suffix –ta is obviously superfluous here, but it is frequently found in like situations across the corpus.

No. 65. *MS 1789/1 (Umma, AS 5)*

obv.

1.	1(diš) ½(diš) sila$_3$ i$_3$-nun du$_{10}$-ga	1 ½ sila$_3$ of good ghee,
2.	i$_3$ šu-nir-ra	oil of the emblem
3.	^{d}nin-ur$_4$-ra	of Nin-ura
4.	a-pi$_4$-sal$_4$^{ki}	of Apisal.
5.	ki ur-e$_{11}$-e-ta	From Ur-E'e.

rev.

	(blank space)	
1.	mu en-unu$_6$-gal ^{d}inanna ba-ḫun	Year: "En-unugal of Inanna was installed."
	(blank space)	

The lack of technical terminology aside, the text is unlikely to be a school or practice document as it fits well into the economic reality of Ur III Umma, where indeed Ur-E'e, the chief cattle-administrator, could have supplied some good ghee for an emblem of the god Nin-ura. In fact the sealed tablet Princeton 1, 277 has the almost exact same information from nine years later, but adds the name of the recipient and his seal:

Princeton 1, 277 (Umma, ŠS 5)

obv.

1.	⅔(diš) sila$_3$ la$_2$ 1(diš) gin$_2$	⅔ sila$_3$ minus 1 shekel (= 119 [liquid] shekel)
2.	i$_3$-nun du$_{10}$-ga	of good ghee,
3.	i$_3$ šu-nir-ra	oil of the emblem
4.	^{d}nin-ur$_4$-ra a-pi$_4$-sal$_4$^{ki}	of Nin-ura of Apisal.
5.	ki ur-e$_{11}$-e-ta	From Ur-E'e.

rev.

1.	kišib$_3$ ša$_3$-ku$_3$-ge	Sealed tablet of Šakuge.
	(seal impression)	
2.	mu us$_2$-sa ^{d}šu-^{d}suen lugal-e bad$_3$ mar-tu mu-du$_3$	Year after: "Šu-Suen, king, built the Martu wall."

seal (S004065.2)

1.	ša$_3$-ku$_3$-ge	Šakuge,
2.	dumu ḫe$_2$-sa$_6$-ge	child of Ḫesage,
3.	išib ^{d}šara$_2$-ka$^{?}$	išib-priest of Šara.

Text No. 66 is a receipt for three pieces of pine wood (without any length specified, cf. No. 36 in Ch. 4). Without a receiving party it would be meaningless in the administrative machinery, and again it must be assumed that the tablet was originally encased in an envelope, now lost.

No. 66. *MS 2021/9 (Umma, AS 7–vii)*

obv.

1.	3(diš) ^{geš}u$_3$-suḫ$_5$	3 pieces of pine wood.
2.	ki nig$_2$-lagar-e-ta	From Nig-lagare.
	(blank space)	
3.	iti min-eš$_3$	Month: "Double sactuary."

rev.

1.	mu bi$_2$-tum-ra-bi$_2$-um^{ki} ba-ḫul (*blank space*)	Year: "Bitum-rabium was destroyed."

Text No. 66 is curious for another reason. Whereas the month "Double Sanctuary" is known as month seven in most years of the Ur III dynasty (and used only in Umma), in the period from Amar-Suen's seventh to Šu-Suen's second year, the seventh month in Umma was instead named the "Festival of Amar-Suen (ezem-^{d}amar-^{d}suen).

Sealed Receipts with kišib$_3$ PN

In twelve of the receipts published here the information PN šu ba-ti has been replaced by kišib$_3$ PN. In one text, No. 71, both kišib$_3$ PN and PN šu ba-ti are present. Usually, and in most of these texts, the seal of the person mentioned as a sealing party in the text is also found on the tablet itself.[295]

The first example is a very simple text, No. 67, where the recipient is indicated through the formula "sealed tablet of PN" instead of "PN received":

No. 67. *MS 4686 (Umma, AS 8)*

obv.

1.	1(aš) še gur	1 gur of barley.
2.	ki ur-^{d}šul-pa-⸢e$_3$⸣-ta	From Ur-Šulpa'e.
3.	kišib$_3$ bi$_2$-du$_{11}$-ga	Sealed tablet of Biduga.

rev.

1.	iti še-sag$_{11}$-ku$_5$ (*seal impression*)	Month: "Harvest."
2.	mu en eridu^{ki} ba-ḫun	Year: "The En-priest of Eridu was installed."

seal (S002054)

1.	bi$_2$-du$_{11}$-ga	Biduga,
2.	dub-sar	scribe,
3.	dumu la-a-⸢sa$_6$⸣	child of Layasa(g).

The second example, text No. 68, introduces a conveyor as well, but is otherwise comparable to the regular receipts.

No. 68. *MS 4715/17 (Umma, AS 8)*

obv.

1.	1(aš) 1(barig) 4(ban$_2$) 5(diš) sila$_3$ ninda gur	1 gur, 1 barig, 4 ban$_2$, 5 sila$_3$ of bread,
2.	giri$_3$ lugal-ŠE$_3^?$	Conveyor: Lugal-ŠE.
3.	ki ur-ba-ba-ta	From Ur-Baba.
4.	kišib$_3$ šu-^{d}nin-isin$_2^{si}$	Sealed tablet of Šu-Nin-Isin.

[295] Notable deviations to this rule, involving members of the ruling family of Umma, are discussed in Dahl 2007.

rev.

	(seal impression)	
1.	mu en eridu^{ki} ⸢ba⸣-ḫun	Year: "The En-priest of Eridu was installed."

seal (S004250)

1.	šu-^{d}nin-isin$_{2}^{si}$	Šu-Nin-Isin,
2.	dub-sar	scribe,
3.	dumu i$_3$-x-x	child of I- . . .

The next two texts both deal with rations, the first rations for humans (No. 69), the second for animals (No. 70). Rations for humans were usually termed še-ba, literally "barley given (out)," whereas rations for animals were usually termed ša$_3$-gal, literally "big stomach."[296]

No. 69. *MS 2018/8 (Umma, IS 2–xi to IS 2–xii)*

obv.

1.	1(barig) še-ba	1 barig of barley rations;
2.	iti pa$_4$-u$_2$-e u$_3$	(for) the month "Pa'u'e" and
3.	iti ^{d}dumu-zi	the month "Dumuzi."
4.	4(ban$_2$) 5(diš) sila$_3$ ab-ba-gi-na dumu lugal-en-nun	4 ban$_2$, 5 sila$_3$ (of barley for) Abba-gina, child of Lugal-ennun.
5.	4(ban$_2$) ⸢5(diš)⸣ sila$_3$ ur-^{d}⸢gilgameš$_x$(BIL$_3$.GA.MES)⸣	4 ban$_2$, 4 sila$_3$ (of barley for) Ur-Gilgameš(?).
6.	4(ban$_2$) 5(diš) sila$_3$ lu$_2$-^{d}nin-sun$_2$-ka	4 ban$_2$, 5 sila$_3$ (of barley for) Lu-Ninsunka.
7.	3(ban$_2$) ur-^{d}en-lil$_2$-la$_2$ dumu lu$_2$-ge$_6$-par$_4$	3 ban$_2$ (of barley for) Ur-Enlila, child of Lu-Gepar.

rev.

1.	4(ban$_2$) 5(diš) sila$_3$ sipa anše	4 ban$_2$, 5 sila$_3$ (of barley for) the herders of onagers.
	(blank space)	
	(seal impression)	
2.	šunigin 3(barig) 3(ban$_2$) x[297]	Total: 3 barig, 3 ban$_2$ of. . . .
3.	še-ba	Barley rations
4.	iti ^{d}dumu-zi	(for) the month "Dumuzi."
5.	ki šeš-da-⸢da⸣-ta	From Šeš-dada.
6.	kišib$_3$ ur-saga	Sealed tablet of Ur-saga.
7.	mu en ^{d}inanna unu^{ki} maš$_2$-e i$_3$-pa$_3$	Year: "The En-priest of Inanna was chosen by omen."

Seal (—)[298]

1.	ur-sa$_6$	Ur-sa(ga),
2.	x x	. . .

---

[296] See Dahl 2007: 117.

[297] Erasure.

[298] The seal is damaged and it is not possible to tell whether the first line included a final -ga (as one would expect), and whether the seal has three or two lines.

No. 70. *MS 1947/7 (Umma, Š 44)*

obv.

1.	3(u) 6(aš) še gur	36 gur of barley,
2.	ša$_{3}$-gal anše zi-gu$_{5}$-um	fodder for mules.[299]
3.	ki gu-du-du-ta	From Gududu.
4.	kišib$_{3}$ lu$_{2}$-ba	Sealed tablet of Luba.

rev.

	(*seal impression*)	
1.	mu si-mu-ru-um^{ki} ba-ḫul	Year: "Simurum was destroyed."

seal (S002718)

1.	lu$_{2}$-ba	Luba,
2.	ARAD$_{2}$ ^{d}šara$_{2}$	slave of Šara.

In many instances, however, both notations, PN šu ba-ti and kišib$_{3}$ PN, are found in the same text, indicating that receiving the goods is not the same as sealing the transaction.

In text No. 71 Šu-kabta receives an amount of reed in bundles, but the transaction is said to be sealed by the governor (of Umma) rather than Šu-kabta. The seal impression itself is that of Aya-kala, the governor of Umma.

No. 71. *MS 2018/4 = CUSAS 3, 1514 (Umma/Garšana, ŠS 2)*

obv.

1.	2(geš'u) 2(geš$_{2}$) 3(u) ⸢sa gi⸣	2010 bundles of reed,
2.	gu-nigin$_{2}$-ba 1(u) sa-ta	their bales are 10 bundles each.
3.	šu-kab-te[300]	Šu-kabta
4.	šu ba-ti	received.

rev.

1.	ugula lugal-igi-ḫuš	Overseer: Lugal-igiḫuš.
2.	kišib$_{3}$ ensi$_{2}$-ka	Sealed tablet of the governor.
	(*seal impression*)	
3.	mu us$_{2}$-sa ^{d}šu-^{d}suen lugal	Year following: "Šu-Suen (was) king."

seal (S000033)

col. i

1.	^{d}šu-^{d}suen	Šu-Suen,
2.	lugal kal-ga	strong king,
3.	lugal uri$_{5}$^{ki}-ma	king of Ur,
4.	lugal an ub-da limmu$_{2}$-ba	king of the four corners of heaven:

---

[299] See Heimpel 1990: 604 for the Ur III term zi-gum$_{2}$-ma/zi-gu$_{5}$-um associated with mules.

[300] According to Owen and Mayr 2007: 424 n. 97 this is to be analyzed as šu-kab-ta-e.

col. ii

1.	a-a-kal-la	Aya-kala,
2.	ensi$_2$	governor
3.	umma^{ki}	of Umma,
4.	ARAD$_2$-zu	(is) your slave.

There appear to be two possible interpretations of this transaction. Either the transaction took place in Umma and the governor of that city acted as a guarantor for his colleague in Garšana, or the transaction took place in Garšana or another place, with the amount being debited from the account of the governor of Umma. The delivering agent is not directly specified; however we can infer that the overseer Lugal-igihuš acted as such. Note that the editor of CUSAS 3 (D. Owen) assigned this text to Umma.

This pattern is quite frequent in Ur III documents. In ASJ 19, 215 43, for example, a Lu-Dingira receives an amount of poplar leaves or branches (c. 300 kg.)[301] from Ur-Šara, but the transaction is said to be sealed by A(ya)-kala, whose seal is also found on the tablet:

ASJ 19, 215 43 (Umma, AS 3)

obv.

1.	1(u) gu$_2$ pa ku$_5$ ^{geš}asal$_2$	10 talents of poplar leaves/branches;
2.	5(aš) gu$_2$ ^{geš}u$_2$-bil$_2$-la	5 talents of charcoal.
3.	ki ur-^{d}šara$_2$-ta	From Ur-Šara.

rev.

1.	lu$_2$-dingir-ra	Lu-Dingira
2.	šu ba-ti	received.
3.	kišib$_3$ a-kal-la	Sealed tablet of A(ya)-kala.
	(blank space)	
4.	mu ^{geš}gu-za ^{d}en-lil$_2$-la$_2$ ba-dim$_2$	Year: "The throne of Enlil was fashioned."

seal (S001779)

1.	a-kal-la	A(ya)-kala,
2.	dub-sar	scribe,
3.	dumu ur-nigar^{gar} šuš$_3$	child of Ur-Nigar, chief cattle-administrator.

A less informative receipt also mentioning poplar leaves is text No. 72. It is a simple sealed receipt with kišib$_3$ PN:

No. 72. *MS 2018/3 (Umma, IS 3)*

obv.

1.	1(u) gu$_2$ pa ku$_5$ ^{geš}asal$_x$(A.TU.NIR)	10 talents of poplar leaves/branches.
2.	ki e$_2$-ur$_2$-bi-du$_{10}$-ta	From E-urbidu.

---

[301] Leaves of various trees and palms were collected and counted using the weight measure system. Feathers (pa mušen) were counted using the sexagesimal system (in terms of value one shekel of silver fetched c. 2000 bird feathers, see, e.g., SNAT 490 (from ŠS 4) rev. 4–5; SNAT 365 (from AS 6) obv. ii 3; HUCA 30, 113–14 (from AS 3) obv. 8–9).

rev.

1.	kišib$_3$ mu-ni	Sealed tablet of Muni.
	(*seal impression*)	
2.	mu si-mu-ru-um^{ki} ba-ḫul	Year: "Simurum was destroyed."

seal (S003812)

1.	mu-ni	Muni,
2.	dumu a-kal-la	child of A(ya)-kala,
3.	gudu$_4$ ^{d}nin-ur$_4$-ra	gudu$_4$-priest of Nin-ura.

Receipts of this type, mentioning the sealed tablet of PN (kišib$_3$ PN), are frequent and cover all aspects of bookkeeping. Documents recording the transfer of dead animals frequently take this form, as do receipts of products of animal husbandry.[302]

Text No. 73 is an example of such a simple receipt recording the receipt of a dead animal for the household of the governor of Umma:

No. 73. *MS 2018/2 (Umma, AS 1–x–?)*

obv.

1.	1(diš) u$_8$ ba-uš$_2$ kur-ra	1 ewe, dead, kur (type).
2.	ki ur-ru-ta	From Urru.
3.	kišib$_3$ ensi$_2$-ka	Sealed tablet of the Governor.
4.	iti ezem-^{d}šul-gi	Month: "Festival of Šulgi."

rev.

1.	mu ^{d}amar-^{d}suen ⸢lugal⸣	Year: "Amar-Suen (was) king."
	(*seal impression*)	

seal (S006150)

col. i

1.	^{d}šul-gi	Šulgi,
2.	nita kal-ga	strong king,
3.	lugal uri$_5$^{ki}-ma	king of Ur,
4.	lugal an ub-da limmu$_2$-ba	king of the four corners of heaven:

col. ii

1.	ur-^{d}li$_9$-si$_4$	Ur-Lisi,
2.	ensi$_2$	governor
3.	umma^{ki}	of Umma,
4.	ARAD$_2$-zu	(is) your slave.

Text No. 74 is another example of a simple sealed receipt with kišib$_3$ PN. It records a small number of bundles of reed for a specific storehouse. This transaction is said to take place within the period when Umma

[302] See, e.g., MVN 3, 374 (from Š 38), recording 1 barig of lard from Pada, sealed by Lugal-ezem (obv.: 1(barig) i$_3$ šaḫ$_2$ / ki pa$_3$-da-⸢ta⸣ / kišib$_3$ lugal-ezem / mu us$_2$-sa x ba-[x], rev. blank, seal: lugal-ezem dub-sar / dumu lugal-e$_2$-maḫ-e / šabra). Further, see also JCS 26, 99 1 (from ŠS 1), recording 2 ma-na of wool from Ur-Dumuzida, sealed by Nin-ḫiliya, the wife of A(ya)-kala (obv.: 2(diš) ma-na siki / ki ur-^{d}dumu-zi-da-ta / kišib$_3$ nin$_9$-ḫi-li$_2$-a // iti iti-6(diš) / (blank space) / mu ^{d}šu-^{d}suen lugal, seal: (illegible)).

was obliged to contribute to the central administration through a payment referred to as within the *bala* (obligations):

No. 74. *MS 1723/1 (Umma, IS 3–xi)*

obv.

1.	1(u) 1(diš) sa gi	11 bundles of reed,
2.	e$_2$ ninda geš-aš-še$_3$	for the e$_2$ ninda geš-aš.
3.	ki inim-^{d}šara$_2$-ta	From Inim-Šara.
4.	kišib$_3$ lugal-a$_2$-zi-da	Sealed tablet of Lugal-azida.

rev.

1.	ša$_3$ bala-a	Within the bala (obligation).
2.	u$_4$ 1(u) 1(diš)-kam	On the 11th day.
	(*seal impression*)	
3.	mu si-mu-ru-⸢um⸣^{ki} ba-ḫul	Year: "Simurum was destroyed."

seal (S003341)

1.	⸢lugal-a$_2$-zi-da⸣	Lugal-azida,
2.	dub-sar	scribe,
3.	⸢dumu⸣ [da-da]	child of Dada.

The structure for which the reeds were destined, the e$_2$ ninda geš-aš, is attested in only a little more than one dozen texts, most of which come from the same year as this text, the third year of Ibbi-Suen. Most of the texts record similarly small numbers of bundles of reed,[303] but a few record a special type of basket, the bitumen coated ^{gi}kaskal.[304] The e$_2$ ninda geš-aš is once listed with the e$_2$ uz-tur-ga, and once identified as belonging to, or controlled by, a certain Ur-Baba (BPOA 1, 1341).

Reed was not always counted in bundles, as text No. 75 shows. It is a simple sealed receipt with kišib$_3$ PN:

No. 75. *MS 1723/2 (Umma, IS 3)*

obv.

1.	1(aš) gu$_2$ gi	1 talent of reed.
2.	ki inim-^{d}šara$_2$-ta	From Inim-Šara.
3.	kišib$_3$ mu-ni	Sealed tablet of Muni.

rev.

	(*seal impression*)	
1.	mu si-mu-ru-um^{ki} ba-⸢ḫul⸣	Year: "Simurum was destroyed."

seal (S003813)

1.	mu-ni dub-sar	Muni, scribe,
2.	dumu a-a-kal-la	child of Aya-kala,
3.	gudu$_4$ ^{d}nin-ur$_4$-ra	gudu$_4$-priest of Nin-ura.

---

[303] See BPOA 1, 1023; 1079; 1211; 1452; BPOA 2, 2428; UTI 3, 2231, all from IS 3 and all within the *bala* (obligation). See UTI 6, 3541 for a text recording a very similar delivery but from ŠS 5.

[304] BPOA 1, 1341 (the baskets are further qualified as ^{gi}kaskal ninda geš-aš esir$_2$ su-ba); BPOA 1, 1684; UTI 3, 1601 (ŠS 2).

Text No. 76 also records the receipt of bundles of reeds, and like No. 71 it uses the terminology "sealed tablet of PN" (kišib$_3$ PN), but does not add a recipient (PN šu ba-ti).

No. 76. *MS 1698/2 (Umma, ŠS 1)*

obv.

1.	1(geš'u) 1(geš$_2$) 4(u) sa gi	700 bundles of reed,
2.	gu-nigin$_2$-ba 2(u) 1(diš) sa-⸢ta⸣	their bales are 21 bundles each.
3.	1(geš'u) 3(geš$_2$) 4(u) [sa gi]	810 bundles of reed,
4.	gu-nigin$_2$-⸢ba⸣ [. . . sa-ta]	their bales are . . . .
5.	4(geš$_2$) 5(u) ⸢sa gi⸣	290 bundles (of reed),
6.	gu-nigin$_2$-ba ⸢3(u)⸣ [. . . sa-ta]	their bales are 30(+*n* each).
7.	⸢kišib$_3$⸣ a-[. . .]	Sealed tablet of . . .

rev.

1.	9(geš$_2$) sa ⸢gi⸣	540 bundles of reed.
2.	kišib$_3$ ^{d}šara$_2$-⸢kam⸣	Sealed tablet of Šarakam.
3.	5(geš'u) 5(geš$_2$) sa ^{geš}[ma-nu]	3520 bundles of willow(?),
4.	gu-nigin$_2$-ba 1(u) 5(diš) sa-⸢ta⸣	their bales are 15 bundles each.
	(*seal impression*)	
5.	kišib$_3$ ab-ba-gi-⸢na⸣	Sealed document of Abba-gina.
6.	ki ur-e$_{11}$-e-ta	From Ur-E'e,
7.	kišib$_3$ ur-^{d}nun-[gal]	sealed tablet of Ur-Nungal.
9.	mu ^{d}šu-^{d}suen lugal	Year: "Šu-Suen (was) king."

seal (S000493.1)

1.	ur-^{d}nun-gal	Ur-Nungal,
2.	dub-sar	scribe,
3.	dumu ur-^{d}šara$_2$	child of Ur-Šara,
4.	ša$_{13}$-dub-ba	chief archivist.

It is not entirely clear why Ur-E'e is listed in rev. 6. Perhaps he collected the deliveries which were then receipted by Ur-Nungal, the chief archivist at Umma.

A few other tablets in the Schøyen Collection use the terminology "sealed tablet of PN" (kišib$_3$ PN). The first of these, text No. 77, records a medium-sized amount of barley to be used as barter for bitumen. Unfortunately the seal is largely illegible.

No. 77. *MS 1724 (Umma, Š 46)*

obv.

1.	2(u) 6(aš) še gur lugal	26 gur of barley (according to the) king('s standard).
2.	sa$_{10}$ esir$_2$	To barter for bitumen.
3.	ki ARAD$_2$-ta	From ARAD(mu),
4.	kišib$_3$ lugal-sa$_6$-i$_3$-zu	sealed document of Lugal-sa-izu.

rev.

1.	mu ki-maš^{ki} ba-ḫul	Year: "Kimaš was destroyed."
	(*blank space*)	

seal (—)

1.	[. . .]	
2.	[. . .]	
3.	dumu a-x-[x]	child of A- . . .

The next kišib$_3$ PN document in the collection is also from Umma. However, it is dated using the so-called "Reichkalender," a calendar invented for the administrative center Drehem, but also used in Ur, on whose calendar it was based (Sallaberger 1999a: 235–37). It is one of a group of seven texts all recording deliveries of reed or reed products for a structure or location called gu$_2$-gir-ra. In one other text, UTI 4, 2752, a large number of workers are stationed at or in the gu$_2$-gir-ra and/of the "storeroom of the king" (e$_2$ šu-tum lugal). Most of the other receipts tablets are recorded as falling within the *bala* (obligations) of Umma (ša bala), but not text No. 78. Text No. 78 is otherwise similar in form and function to No. 74.

No. 78. *MS 1725 (Umma AS 7–viii)*

obv.

1.	1(u) 1(aš) esir$_2$ ḫad$_2$ gur	11 gur of dried bitumen.
2.	gu$_2$-gir-ra-še$_3$	For the gu$_2$-gir-ra.
3.	ki ab-ba-gi-na-ta	From Abba-gina.
4.	kišib$_3$ ⌜lugal⌝-ušur$_x$(LAL$_2$.TUG$_2$)	Sealed tablet of Lugal-ušur.

rev.

1	[iti] ⌜šu⌝-eš-ša	Month: "šu'eša"
2.	⌜giri$_3$⌝ inim-^{d}šara$_2$	Conveyor: Inim-Šara.
	(*seal impression*)	
3.	mu ḫu-ḫu-nu-ri^{ki} ba-ḫul	Year: "Ḫuḫnuri was destroyed."

seal (S003732)

1.	lugal-ušur$_4$	Lugal-ušur,
2.	dub-sar	scribe,
3.	dumu a$_2$-an-du-ru	child of A'anduru.

The final kišib$_3$ PN document published here, text No. 79, records the transfer of twenty-six textiles of the quality termed "weaver," probably a low-grade textile associated with the textiles given to the textile weavers themselves (see also the discussion of texts Nos. 46 and 47). The delivering agent is the famous I-kala, responsible for the textile factory in Umma. The recipient is Ušmu, a fuller. It is possible that the textiles were returned for a second walking; they are possibly from the *gun*-tax, but the line (obv. 2) is not clear.

No. 79. *MS 2018/6 (Umma, ŠS 6–x)*

obv.

1.	2(u) 6(diš) tug$_2$ uš-bar	26 textiles, weaver (quality),
2.	tug$_2$ gu$_2$-na iri	textiles of the gu$_2$-na-tax, city (?).

3.	ki i$_3$-kal-la-ta	From I-kala.
4.	⌜kišib$_3$⌝ uš-mu	Sealed tablet of Ušmu.

rev.

1.	iti ezem-^{d}šul-gi	Month: "Festival of Šulgi."
2.	giri$_3$ a-kal-la dumu nam-ḫa-ni (*seal impression*)	Conveyor: A(ya)-kala, child of Namḫani.
3.	mu na-ru$_2$-a maḫ ba-du$_3$	Year: "The lofty stela was built."

seal (S005506)

1.	uš-mu	Ušmu,
2.	lu$_2$ azlag$_2$	(chief) fuller,
3.	dumu lu$_2$-dingir-ra	child of Lu-Dingira.

Another group of receipts that consistently use the kišib$_3$ PN formula, instead of PN šu ba-ti, are those that record the basic provisions of beer and cereals for the household of the governor of Umma. None of these numerous tablets is found in the Schøyen Collection, so MVN 4, 257 is edited here as an example:

MVN 4, 257 (Umma, ŠS 1–8–4 to 5)

obv.

1.	1(ban$_2$) kaš saga	1 ban$_2$ of beer, good (quality).
2.	4(ban$_2$) kaš du	4 ban$_2$ of beer, regular (quality).
3.	u$_4$ 4(diš)-kam	On the 4th day.
4.	1(ban$_2$) kaš saga	1 ban$_2$ of beer, good quality.
5.	3(ban$_2$) 5(diš) sila$_3$ kaš du	3 ban$_2$, 5 sila$_3$ of beer, regular (quality).
6.	u$_4$ 5(diš)-kam	On the 5th day.

rev.

1.	1(diš) dug dida saga 1(ban$_2$) 5(diš) sila$_3$	1 dida jar, good (quality), (holding) 1 ban$_2$, 5 sila$_3$.
2.	1(diš) dug dida du 1(ban$_2$) 5(diš) sila$_3$	1 dida jar, regular (quality), (holding) 1 ban$_2$, 5 sila$_3$.
3.	šu-gid$_2$	šu-gid$_2$ offerings
4.	ki ur-mes-ta	from Ur-Mes.
5.	kišib$_3$ ensi$_2$-ka	Sealed tablet of the governor.
6.	iti e$_2$-iti-6(diš)	Month: "House-month-six."
7.	mu ^{d}šu-^{d}suen lugal	Year: "Šu-Suen (was) king."

seal (S000033)

col. i

1.	^{d}šu-^{d}suen	Šu-Suen,
2.	lugal kal-ga	strong king,
3.	lugal uri$_5$^{ki}-ma	king of Ur,
4.	lugal an ub-da limmu$_2$-ba	king of the four corners of heaven:

col. ii

1.	a-a-kal-la	Aya-kala,
2.	ensi$_2$	governor
3.	umma^{ki}	of Umma,
4.	ARAD$_2$-zu	(is) your slave.

Receipts with Envelopes

As far as can be ascertained, none of the more than seven hundred extant tablets encased in envelopes was originally sealed, whereas all the envelopes were. It follows that we can perhaps propose that when primary receipts were not sealed, they were, in all cases, enclosed in an envelope which was sealed.

There are three tablets with envelopes in the Schøyen Collection, one of which has not been opened and another only partially opened. The first of these three, text No. 80, although not without difficulties, exemplifies well the system of encasing an unsealed receipt in a sealed envelope:

No. 80. *MS 1726 = MVN 5, 202 (Girsu, ŠS 8)*

Tablet

obv.

1.	1(u) gin$_2$ ku$_3$-babbar	10 shekels of silver,
2.	su-ga ab-ab-ba	replacement by the elders(?)[305]
3.	i-šar-ra-ḫi-ke$_4$-ne	of Išaraḫi,[306]
4.	mu u$_3$-ta-saḫar-zi-ga-še$_3$	instead of (those of) Utasaḫarziga.[307]

rev.

1.	lu$_2$-^{d}dumu-zi	Lu-Dumuzi
2.	šu ba-ti	received.
3.	giri$_3$ ur-šu-ga-lam-ma	Conveyor: Ur-Šugalamma.
	(*blank space*)	
4.	mu ^{d}šu-^{d}suen lugal uri$_5^{ki}$-ma-ke$_4$ ma$_2$-gur$_8$ maḫ ^{d}en-lil$_2$ ^{d}nin-lil$_2$-ra mu-ne-dim$_2$	Year: "Šu-Suen, king of Ur, fashioned the lofty barge for Enlil and Ninlil."

---

[305] A translation "elders" for ab-ab-ba is tentative and based on the suggestion that Išarahi is a place. Usually "elders" is written ab-ba; ab-ba iri, "city elders" is attested in a handful of texts only (see Barjamovic 2004 for an overview of local authorities in ancient Mesopotamia).

[306] A PN i-šar-ra-ma-aš (also written i-šar-ra-maš) interpreted as *išar-rāmāšu,* is frequently attested. Similarly a PN i-šar-ra-ḫi, perhaps to be interpreted as *išar-rāḫī,* is well known from the Ur III period. Two other texts have a GN i-šar-ra-ḫi: MVN 9, 9 obv. 5–6: i$_3$-dub an-za-gar$_3$ i-šar-ra-ḫi; MVN 12, 371 rev. 1: i$_3$-dub i-šar-ra-ḫi.

[307] u$_3$-ta-saḫar-zi-ga is not otherwise attested, and it is possible that it should not be interpreted as a place name at all but rather a nominalized verbal phrase comparable to šuku engar-ra nu-u$_3$-ta-zi in ASJ 4, 116 17. That line is interpreted by Maekawa (1982) as meaning that no allotment was expended for the cultivators from a specific field (mentioned in the line above). As such, and emending our text to mu u$_3$-ta-<<IŠ>>-zi-ga-še$_3$, our line may mean "because it was not booked out," or similar. However, it is difficult to interpret that here.

Envelope

obv.

1.	1(u) gin$_2$ ku$_3$-babbar	10 shekels of silver,
2.	su-ga ab-ba-ab-ba	replacement by the elders(?)
3.	i-šar-ra-ḫi^{ki}-ke$_4$-ne	of Išaraḫi,
	(*blank space*)	
4.	mu u$_3$-ta-saḫar-zi-ga-še$_3$	instead of (those of) Utasaḫarziga.
5.	kišib$_3$ lu$_2$-^{d}dumu-zi dumu ma-ni	Sealed tablet of Lu-Dumuzi son of Mani.

rev.

1.	giri$_3$ ur-šu-ga-lam-ma dumu me-an-ne$_2$	Conveyor: Ur-Šugalamma son of Me-Anne.
	(*blank space*)	
2.	mu ^{d}šu-^{d}suen lugal uri$_5$^{ki}-ma-ke$_4$ ma$_2$-gur$_8$ maḫ ^{d}en-lil$_2$ ^{d}nin-lil$_2$-ra mu-ne-dim$_2$	Year: "Šu-Suen, king of Ur, fashioned the lofty barge for Enlil and Ninlil."

seal (S003076a)

1.	lu$_2$-^{d}dumu-zi	Lu-Dumuzi,
2.	dumu ma-ni	child of Mani,
3.	sagi	cupbearer
4.	[^{d}]gu$_3$-de$_2$-a	of Gudea.

The following receipt, No. 81, is still partly encased in its envelope. It presumably recorded the transfer of a few ordinary-quality textiles. The name of the recipient, the only one preserved, and only on the tablet, is otherwise only attested in a recently published tablet from Irisagrig/Al-Šarraki (Nisaba 15, 391).

No. 81. *MS 4971 (Irisagrig?, ŠS 9–x)*

Tablet

obv.

	(*beginning not visible, covered by envelope*)	
1.	[. . .]	
2.	ki [. . . -ta]	From PN.

rev.

1.	šu-^{d}nin-ur$_4$-⸢ra⸣	Šu-Ninura
2.	šu ba-ti	received.
3.	iti ezem-⸢maḫ⸣	Month: "Lofty festival."
4.	mu e$_2$ ^{d}⸢šara$_2$⸣ umma⸢^{ki}-ka mu⸣-[du$_3$]	Year: "The house of Šara of Umma was built."

Envelope

obv.

	(*beginning missing*)	
1'.	[. . .] ⸢4(diš)⸣-kam us$_2$ BAD	(. . . textiles?) 4th class, lesser (quality), x.
2'.	[ki . . .]-ta	From PN.
3'.	[šu-^{d}nin-ur$_4$]-⸢ra⸣	Šu-Nin-ura

rev.

1.	šu ba-ti (*seal impression*)	received.
2.	iti ezem-maḫ	Month: "Lofty festival."
3.	⸢mu ^{d}⸣šu-^{d}suen lugal [uri$_5$]$^{⸢ki⸣}$-ma-ke$_4$ [e$_2$ ^{d}šara$_2$ umma^{ki}]-ka [mu-du$_3$]	Year: "The house of Šara of Umma was built."

seal (*illegible*)

Unfortunately, the envelope of text No. 82 has not been opened, and it is not possible to determine whether Na'u'a, who sealed the tablet, was also mentioned as the recipient in the tablet inside, and whether other abnormalities occurred.

No. 82. *MS 1949/5 (Umma, Š 33–vi)*

Envelope

obv.

1.	3(aš) še ⸢gur⸣ [. . .]	3 gur of barley (. . .).
2.	še-bi mu x-x-[x] (*seal impression*)	The barley, ...
3.	ki ARAD$_2$-ta	From Arad(mu),
4.	na-u$_2$-a šu ba-ti	Na'u'a received.
5.	iti šu-numun	Month: "Seeding."

rev.

1.	mu us$_2$-sa si-mu-ru-um^{ki} a-ra$_2$ 3(diš$_{tenû}$)-kam ba-ḫul (*seal impression*)	Year following: "When Simurum was destroyed for the 3rd time."

seal (S005821)

col. i

1.	na-u$_2$-a	Na'u'a,
2.	dub-sar	scribe,

col. ii

1.	šu ^{d}⸢šara$_2$⸣	dependent(?) of Šara.

In the following example, not from the Schøyen Collection, the person sealing the envelope replaces the recipient mentioned in the tablet:

Amherst 119 (Girsu, AS 9)

Tablet

obv.

1.	8(diš) kuš gu$_4$	8 ox hides,
2.	3(geš$_2$) 5(diš) kuš udu	185 sheep skins.
3.	ki ur-^{d}ḫa-ia$_3$-ta	From Ur-Ḫaya.

4.	kuš ^{kuš}suḫub$_2$-še$_3$	Hides for boots.
5.	ku$_x$(KWU147)-ra-ni-sa$_6$	Kudranisa

rev.

1.	šu ba-ti	received.
2.	giri$_3$ ^{d}šul-gi-da-an-qa$_2$-ta$_2$ (*blank line*)	Conveyor: Šulgi-dān-qāta.
3.	mu en ^{d}nanna kar-zi-da	Year: "The En-priest of Nanna of Karzida."

Envelope

obv.

1.	8(diš) kuš gu$_4$ šu-gi$_4$	8 ox hides, old,
2.	3(geš$_2$) 5(diš) kuš udu	185 sheep skins.
3.	kuš ^{kuš}suḫub$_2$-⸢še$_3$⸣	Hides for boots.
4.	ki ur-^{d}ḫa-ia$_3$-ta	From Ur-Ḫaya.
5.	kišib$_3$ ur-^{d}nanše	Sealed tablet of Ur-Nanše.

rev.

1.	giri$_3$ ^{d}šul-gi-da-an-qa$_2$-ta$_2$ sukkal (*blank space*)	Conveyor: Šulgi-dān-qāta, messenger.
2.	mu en ^{d}nanna kar-<zi>-da ba-ḫun	Year: "The En-priest of Nanna of Karzida was installed."

seal (S005168)

1.	ur-^{d}nanše	Ur-Nanše,
2.	dub-sar	scribe,
3.	dumu ur-^{d}ig-alim	child of Ur-Igalim.

In the accounts this entry would presumably be credited to Ur-Ḫaya and debited to Ur-Nanše. Kudranisa, on the other hand, may simply be a receiving agent in the workshop, perhaps able to roll the seal of his master, Ur-Nanše, on the document.

When the envelope of a receipt is preserved it mostly has only the information of who sealed the transaction, whereas the recipient is mentioned on the tablet alone:

MVN 2, 11 (Girsu, Š 40)

Tablet

obv.

1.	3(geš$_2$) 4(u) 1(aš) 4(barig) 1(ban$_2$) še gur lugal	221 gur, 4 barig, 1 ban$_2$ of barley (according to the) king('s standard).
2.	ma$_2$-a si-ga	Loaded on the boat.
3.	ki sanga ^{d}nin-gir$_2$-su-ta	From the sanga-official of Ningirsu.
4.	ur-^{d}nin-mar^{ki} dumu ⸢lu$_2$⸣-^{d}utu	Ur-Ninmar, child of Lu-Utu,

rev.

1.	šu ba-ti	received.
2.	i$_3$-dub e$_2$-duru$_5$-^{d}nin-mar^{ki}-ta	(The barley is) from the granary of the hamlet of Ninmar.
3.	giri$_3$ igi-lam-lam	Conveyor: Igilamlam.
4.	mu us$_2$-sa e$_2$ puzur$_4$^{iš}-da-gan ba-du$_3$	Year following "The house Puzriš-Dagan was built."

Envelope

obv.

1.	3(geš$_2$) 4(u) 1(aš) 4(barig) 1(ban$_2$) še gur lugal ma$_2$-a si-ga	221 gur, 4 barig, 1 ban$_2$ of barley (according to the) king('s standard). Loaded on the boat.
2.	ki sanga ^{d}nin-gir$_2$-su-ta	From the sanga-official of Ningirsu.
3.	kišib$_3$ ur-^{d}nin-mar^{ki} dumu lu$_2$-^{d}utu	Sealed document of Ur-Ninmar, child of Lu-Utu.

rev.

1.	i$_3$-dub e$_2$-duru$_5$-^{d}nin-mar^{ki}-ta	(The barley is) from the granary of the hamlet of Ninmar.
2.	giri$_3$ igi-lam-lam a-ša$_3$ a-sag-du$_3$-du-ta	Conveyor: Igilamlam, from the field of Asagdudu.
3.	mu us$_2$-sa e$_2$ puzur$_4$^{iš}-da-gan ba-du$_3$	Year following: "The house Puzriš-Dagan was built."

seal (S005787)

col. i

1.	al-la	Alla,
2.	ensi$_2$	governor
3.	lagaš^{ki}	of Lagaš:

col. ii

1.	ur-^{d}nin-mar^{ki}	Ur-Ninmar,
2.	dumu lu$_2$-[^{d}utu]	child of Lu-Utu,
3.	ARAD$_2$-zu	(is) your slave.

A difficult text, No. 83, may be better placed among the Ur III legal texts (see Chapter 12 below), as it concerns the taking of a loan. However, as the text does not contain any legal terminology, nor any list of witnesses, I will edit it here:

No. 83. *MS 1739/2 (—)*

Tablet

obv.

1.	⸢5/6(diš) gin$_2$ ku$_3$$^?$-babbar$^?$⸣	5/6 shekel of silver
2.	maš$_2$ ga$_2$-⸢ga$_2$⸣-[de$_3$]	interest will be placed.
3.	⸢ki⸣ nig$_2$-⸢kal⸣-[la-ta]	From Nig-kala,
4.	a-kal-[la]	A(ya)-kala
5.	⸢šu⸣ [ba-ti]	received.

rev.

1.	nig_2 ku_3 bappir	. . .
2.	u_4 2(u) 8(diš) zal-⸢la⸣	28th day has passed.
	(blank space)	

Envelope

obv.

1.	⸢5/6(diš) gin_2⸣ [ku_3-babbar]	5/6 shekel of silver.
2.	ki nig_2-kal-la-ta	From Nig-kala,
	(seal impression)	
3.	a-kal-la šu ⸢ba⸣-[ti]	A(ya)-kala received.
	(seal impression)	
4.	nig_2 ku_3 bappir	. . .

rev. *(broken)*

seal (S005990)

1.	a-a-kal-la	Aya-kala,
2.	dumu ur-šar	child of Ur-Šar.

Perhaps the most surprising feature of text No. 83 is that the envelope makes no reference to the interest explicitly mentioned on the tablet itself. The purpose of the silver loan, listed in rev. 1 of the tablet and obv. 4 of the envelope, is unclear but potentially related to brewing.

Finally, text No. 84 is a regular, simple, sealed receipt. It appears once to have been encased in an envelope, because cut marks on the edge of the tablet suggest that a saw was used to cut it out of its clay envelope in modern times. There is no other indication, in the text or otherwise, that it was originally encased in an envelope. This should perhaps caution us from drawing sweeping conclusions regarding the practice of sealing, of encasing tablets in envelopes, and so forth. However, it may be simply a unique case. The text originates from Garšana.

No. 84. *MS 4696 = CUSAS 3, 1524 (ŠS 9–iii)*

obv.

1.	1(diš) kuš udu	1 hide of a sheep.
2.	⸢1(diš)⸣ kuš $maš_2$ ⸢gal⸣	1 hide of a large goat.
3.	ki ^{d}iškur-illat-ta	From Adad-tillatī,
4.	a-na-aḫ-i_3-li_2	Anaḫ-Ili,

rev.

1.	šu ba-ti	received.
	(blank space)	
2.	iti ses-da-gu_7	Month: "Eating the piglet."
3.	mu e_2 ^{d}$šara_2$ $umma^{ki}$ ba-du_3	Year: "The house of Šara in Umma was built."

seal *(illegible)*

Unsealed Receipts

The following eight receipts are all unsealed, but none have associated envelopes. Some of the unsealed receipts published below appear to relate to very special circumstances and may never have been encased in envelopes and therefore never sealed. On the other hand others, such as the first four published below (Nos. 85–88), almost certainly once had an envelope with a seal impression.

No. 85. *MS 2021/1 (Umma, Š 37–xii)*

obv.

1.	1(diš) ^{kuš}e-sir$_2$ e$_2$-ba-an eš$_3$ sa gid$_2$-da	1 pair of shoes (with) long laces.
3.	ur-^{d}iškur-ke$_4$	Ur-Iškur
4.	šu ba-ti	received.

rev.

1.	iti dumu-zi	Month: "Dumuzi."
2.	mu bad$_3$ ba	Year: "Wall."
	(*blank space*)	

No. 86. *MS 2021/7 (Umma, Š 47)*

obv.

1.	2(u) ^{geš}dusu	20 dusu-baskets.[308]
2.	ki ur-e$_{11}$-⸢e-ta⸣	From Ur-E'e.
3.	kišib$_3$ ab-ba-⸢gi⸣-na	Sealed document of Abba-gina.
	(*blank space*)	

rev.

	(*blank space*)	
1.	mu us$_2$-sa ki-maš^{ki} ba-ḫul	Year after: "Kimaš was destroyed."
	(*blank space*)	

No. 87. *MS 2019/8 (Umma, IS 2–i)*

obv.

1.	2(diš) ½(diš) sila$_3$ ZU	2 ½ sila$_3$ of . . .
2.	1(diš) ½(diš) sila$_3$ NE ZU	1 ½ sila$_3$ of . . .
3.	^{d}šara$_2$-a-mu ⸢šandana⸣	Šara-a(ya)mu the orchard administrator
4.	šu ba-ti	received.
	(*blank space*)	

rev.

	(*blank space*)	
1.	iti še-sag$_{11}$-ku$_5$	Month: "Harvest."
2.	mu us$_2$-sa ^{d}i-bi$_2$-^{d}suen lugal	Year following: "Ibbi-Suen (was) king."
	(*blank space*)	

[308] Note that d u s u baskets, the baskets traditionally associated with the iconic corvée labour of Babylonia, are written with the determinative for wooden objects and not reed.

No. 88. *MS 2021/4 (Umma, Š 44)*

obv.

1.	2(diš) udu bar gal$_2$	2 sheep, with fleece.
2.	siskur$_2$ ki-su$_7$	Offering of the threshing floor
3.	a-ša$_3$ ^{d}šul-pa-e$_3$	of the field Šul-pa'e.
4.	ki ur-e$_{11}$-e-ta	From Ur-E'e.

rev.

1.	kišib$_3$ lugal-ku$_3$-ga-ni	Sealed tablet of Lugal-kugani.
	(*blank space*)	
2.	mu si-⸢mu⸣-[ru-um]^{ki} lu-⸢lu⸣-[bu-um]	Year: "Simurum and Lulubum."

The next text, No. 89, ostensibly a regular receipt, may also originally have been enclosed in an envelope. However, the close association of the document with the messenger texts leaves other possibilities open.

No. 89. *MS 2021/10 (Umma[309], X–vii)*

obv.

1.	1(diš) udu u$_2$	1 grass(-fed) sheep,
2.	3(diš) dug dida ⸢du⸣ 3(ban$_2$)-ta	3 dida(-jars) of regular (quality), (holding) 3 ban$_2$ each,
3.	2(barig) ninda	2 barig of bread,
4.	2(diš) sila$_3$ i$_3$-geš	2 sila$_3$ of sesame oil.

rev.

1.	elam ⸢šu⸣ ba-ti	Elam[310] received.
2.	giri$_3$ su$_{11}$-⸢ka$_3$⸣-li sukkal	Conveyor: Sukali, messenger.
3.	iti min-eš$_3$	Month: "Double sanctuary."
	(*blank space*)	

Text No. 90 is unfortunately damaged, and it is unclear whether this tablet was ever intended to be encased in an envelope or sealed.

No. 90. *MS 1947/17 (Umma, Š 44–ii)*

obv.

1.	⸢1(geš$_2$)⸣ 1(u) 4(aš) 4(barig) 1(ban$_2$) še ⸢gur lugal$^{?}$⸣	614 gur, 4 barig, 1 ban$_2$ of barley, (according to the) king('s standard).
2.	še numun [. . .] ⸢kišib$_3^{?}$ dab$_5^{?}$-ba⸣ x [x] x-⸢ba⸣	Seed-barley. . . .
3.	ki a-kal-la ⸢dumu⸣ lugal-nesag-e-ta	From A(ya)-kala child of Lugal-nesage.

rev.

1.	a-du-mu	Adumu
2.	šu ba-ti	received.

---

[309] The provenience is a guess, supported only by the occurrence of elam šu ba-ti in another Umma text, MVN 21, 377.

[310] It is not clear whether this is an abbreviated personal name or a geographical designation denoting a person.

	(blank line)	
3.	⸢iti ^{geš}⸣sig$_4$-u$_3$-šub-ba-⸢ga$_2$⸣-ra	Month: "Brick placed in the mold."
4.	mu us$_2$-sa en ^{d}nanna maš$_2$-e i$_3$-pa$_3$	Year following: "The En-priest of Nanna was chosen by omen."

Text No. 91 lists deliveries of large amounts of lard for three consecutive years. It is not an account, and no primary documents directly relating to the amounts have been identified in the corpus. The original purpose of the text therefore remains unclear.

No. 91. *MS 3990 (Umma, Š 48 to AS 1)*

obv.

1.	1(aš) 1(barig) 5(ban$_2$) 7(diš) sila$_3$ 4(diš) gin$_2$ i$_3$-šaḫ$_2$ gur	1 gur, 1 barig, 5 ban$_2$, 7 sila$_3$, 4 (liquid) shekels of lard, (according to the) king('s standard).
2.	mu ki-maš^{ki} ba-ḫul	Year: "Kimaš was destroyed."
3.	1(aš) 2(ban$_2$) gur	12 gur (of lard).
4.	mu us$_2$-sa ki-maš^{ki} ba-ḫul	Year following: "Kimaš was destroyed."
5.	1(aš) 1(barig) 1(ban$_2$) 2(diš) ⅔(diš) sila$_3$ 8(diš) gin$_2$ gur	1 gur, 1 barig, 1 ban$_2$, 2 ⅔ sila$_3$, 8 (liquid) shekels (of lard).

rev.

1.	mu ḫa-ar-ši ki-maš^{ki} ba-ḫul	Year: "Ḫarši (and) Kimaš were destroyed."
2.	ki i$_3$-kal-la-ta	From I-kala.
3.	ur-^{d}šul-pa-e$_3$	Ur-Šulpa'e
4.	šu ba-ti	received.
	(blank space)	

The final receipt without seal impression or envelope is another Garšana text, No. 92. There is no obvious reason why this tablet is unsealed and not encased in an envelope.

No. 92. *MS 4700 = CUSAS 3, 1516 (Garšana, ŠS 7–ii)*

obv.

1.	2(diš) kuš udu niga	2 hides of fattened sheep.
2.	kuš udu sa$_2$-du$_{11}$	Hides of sheep of regular (deliveries).
3.	ki ^{d}iškur-illat-ta	From Adad-tillatī.
4.	a-na-aḫ-i$_3$-li$_2$	Anaḫ-ili
5.	šu ba-an-ti	received.

rev.

1.	iti maš-da$_3$-gu$_7$	Month: "Eating the Gazelle."
2.	mu ^{d}šu-^{d}suen lugal uri$_2$⸢^{ki}⸣-ma-ke$_4$ ma-da za-⸢ab⸣-ša-li^{ki} ⸢mu⸣-ḫul	Year: "Šu-Suen, king of Ur destroyed the territory of Zabšali."

Receipt Copies

Some eight hundred primary documents from the Ur III period include the technical term gaba-ri (kišib$_3$(-ba) PN), "copy (of the sealed document (of) PN)." More than a quarter of these examples originate from the ancient city of Garšana.[311] Syntactically, gaba-ri can be written as a subscript (alone or with kišib$_3$(-ba)), or the full form can appear in front of a personal name (with or without final -ba). When occurring with a personal name, the term is presumably to be understood as "copy of (sealed tablet of) PN." Forms without kišib$_3$ appear to be simple abbreviations of forms with kišib$_3$.[312] The few examples of unsealed tablet copies, and the use of the term gaba-ri kišib$_3$ nu-ra(-a), "copy of unsealed tablet," are powerful evidence that kišib$_3$ here denotes a sealed document.[313]

Two texts add the aforementioned but unexplained term aš-a between gaba-ri kišib$_3$(-ba) and a personal name.[314]

Although the most obvious reason for the existence of tablet copies is the need for central control over local transaction,[315] the fact that the corpus of tablet copies makes up less than one per cent of the entire corpus of Ur III texts, and less than five per cent of the corpus of extant receipts, suggests that tablet copies were written in very special situations only.

Prior to the publication of the Garšana archive, only two pairs of a tablet and its copy had been recognized in a publication (Dahl 2003 discussing MCS 8 97 BM 113102 = Nisaba 9, 152; and UTI 3, 2173 = BPOA 6, 1297). The Garšana archive adds many new sets, including many lacking the terminology gaba-ri; some that testify to the existence of triplicates; and other oddities such as the lack of seals on the originals (Such-Gutiérrez 2011). A majority of the Garšana examples belonged to the household of *Adad-tillatī*, and may not be representative of the Ur III administration as a whole. Other sets of duplicates lacking the terminology gaba-ri (kišib$_3$-ba) are known. Some of these, such as the series documented first by Yoshikawa (1985: 191–92), may in fact be school exercises.

Text No. 93 is very similar to the series of duplicate documents discussed by Yoshikawa. However, it ends with a curious inscription on the left edge, [nu]-gal$_2$ gaba-ri, which probably means "un-existing (tablet) copy." Three further texts from Garšana use the same terminology (CUSAS 3, 880; 1135; 1315); three others have the variant gaba-ri nu-gal$_2$ (CUSAS 3, 1024; 1195; 1214). These texts were discussed by Heimpel (2009: 19–20), who noted that the writing nu-gal$_2$ gaba-ri was only used in ŠS 7.

No. 93. *MS 4424 = CUSAS 3, 1515 (Garšana, ŠS 7–iii–10)*

obv.

1.	[...] ⸢geme$_2$⸣ sag-dub	*n*[316] female dependent workers, full-output slaves.[317]
2.	⸢1(diš)⸣ dumu-mi$_2$	1 female child.
3.	ki puzur$_4$-^{d}en-lil$_2$-ta	From Puzur-Enlil.
4.	^{d}iškur-illat	Adad-tillatī
5.	i$_3$-dab$_5$	seized.

---

[311] Such-Gutiérrez 2011: 392.

[312] It is not entirely clear whether the addition of -ba adds semantic meaning to the expressions. Forms without final -ba are inevitably followed by a personal name, whereas forms with final -ba can appear either as a true subscript immediately before the colophon (date) of the text or before a personal name. The two groups are of approximately the same size.

[313] Such-Gutiérrez 2011: 394, and see, e.g., OrSP 47–49, 367 and UTI 3, 2016.

[314] BJRL 64, 100 no. 11 (Umma, AS 8), and on the edge of CTMMA 1, 27 (l.e. v 2). For kišib$_3$ aš-a, see also n. 23.

[315] Such-Gutiérrez (2011: 394–95) lists evidence for tablet copies placed in special archival containers.

[316] Owen and Mayr 2007: 424 reconstructs [1(diš)]

[317] See nn. 83 and 385.

rev.

1.	iti ses-da-⌜gu$_7$⌝ u$_4$ 1(u) ba-[zal]	Month: "Eating of the piglet." The 10th day has passed.
2.	mu ^{d}šu-^{d}suen lugal uri$_2$^{ki}-ma-ke$_4$ ma-da za-ab-ša-li^{ki} mu-ḫul	Year: "Šu-Suen, king of Ur, destroyed the territory of Zabšali."

left edge

1.	[nu]-gal$_2$ gaba-ri	Un-existing copy (of sealed tablet).

None of the Garšana tablet copies have accompanying envelopes, and all belong to the archive of Adad-tillatī, the chief household-administrator of the governor of Garšana, Šu-kabta (and after Šu-kabta's death, of his widow Simat-Ištaran). For a complete study of the function of tablet copies at Garšana, see the study by Such-Gutiérrez 2011.

The following example, text No. 94, suggests that several tablet copies could be summarized in one sealed document.[318] However, No. 94 is not without problems.

No. 94. *MS 2020/9 (Umma, ŠS 1–v)*

obv.

1.	1(barig) še-ba mu še ar$_3$-ra-še$_3$ guru$_7$-a tak$_4$-a	1 barig of barley rations instead of milled barley. Leveling the granary.
2.	^{d}nanna-ki-ag$_2$	Nanna-ki-ag.
3.	ki igi-peš$_2$-ta	From Igi-peš.
4.	gaba-ri kišib$_3$-ba	Copy of the sealed tablet of

rev.

1.	lu$_2$-^{d}šul-gi-ra	Lu-Šulgira.
2.	iti dal	Month: "Flight."
3.	mu ^{d}šu-^{d}suen lugal	Year: "Šu-Suen (was) king."
	(*blank space*)	

It remains to be explained what function Nanna-ki-ag plays (obv. 2). Ontario 2, 297, dated to one month after text No. 94, repeats much of the information in it. However, text No. 94 is not a copy of Ontario 2, 297.

Ontario 2, 297 (Umma, ŠS 1–vi)

obv.

1.	2(barig) 1(ban$_2$) še-ba	2 barig, 1 ban$_2$ of barley rations,
2.	mu še ar$_3$-ra-ka-še$_3$	instead of milled barley.
3.	guru$_7$-a tak$_4$-a	Leveling the granary.
4.	ki ur-dingir-ra-ta	From Ur-Dingira.

[318] This was also argued by Such-Gutiérrez (2011: 392–93), who pointed to examples listing the numbers of tablet copies (i.e., g a b a - r i 3 (d i š) - k a m in YOS 4, 79), but also noted that the tablet copy only recorded one entry in the sealed document (PDT 1, 322 = AUCT 1, 841 obv. 5).

rev.

1.	kišib$_3$ lu$_2$-^{d}šul-gi-ra	Sealed tablet of Lu-Šulgira.
2.	giri$_3$ ur-^{d}šara$_2$	Conveyor: Ur-Šara.
3.	iti šu-numun	Month: "Seeding."
4.	mu ^{d}šu-^{d}suen lugal	Year: "Šu-Suen (was) king."

seal (S002856)

1.	lu$_2$-e$_2$-maḫ-e	Lu-Emaḫe,
2.	dub-sar	scribe,
3.	dumu ur-^{d}li$_9$-si$_4$-na	child of Ur-Lisi,
4.	ensi$_2$ umma^{ki}-ka	governor of Umma.

The next tablet copy, text No. 95, was previously published as MVN 5, 131. It is a close parallel to another published tablet copy, AUCT 1, 750. Both tablets originate from ancient Puzrish-Dagan but they are not dated to the same day, or the same month.[319]

No. 95. *MS 1653/2 = MVN 5, 131 (Puzriš-Dagan, IS 1–iv–22)*

obv.

1.	2(u) [udu]	20 sheep,
2.	1(u) maš$_2$ gal	10 large goats.
3.	šu-gid$_2$	šu-gid$_2$ offerings
4.	u$_4$ 2(u) 2(diš)-kam	on the 22nd day.
5.	ki a-ba-^{d}en-lil$_2$-gin$_7$-ta	From Aba-Enlilgin.
6.	ur-ku$_3$-nun-na	Ur-Kununna

rev.

1.	i$_3$-dab$_5$	seized.
2.	gaba-ri	Copy
3.	kišib$_3$ ab-ba-kal-la	of the sealed tablet of Abba-kala.
	(*blank space*)	
4.	iti ezem-^{d}nin-a-zu	Month: "Festival of Nin-azu."
5.	mu ^{d}⌜i⌝-[bi$_2$]-⌜suen⌝ [lugal]	Year: "Ibbi-Suen (was) king."

left edge

1.	3(u) udu	(Total:) 30 sheep (and goat).

AUCT 1, 750 (Puzriš-Dagan, IS 1–v–27)

obv.

1.	3(u) 8(diš) udu u$_2$	38 grass (fed) sheep,
2.	2(u) maš$_2$ gal u$_2$	20 grass (fed) large goats.
3.	šu-gid$_2$	šu-gid$_2$ offerings
4.	u$_4$ 2(u) 7(diš)-kam	on the 27th day.
5.	ki a-ba-^{d}en-lil$_2$-gin$_7$-ta	From Aba-Enlil-gin.

[319] For Drehem tablet copies, see Hilgert 2003: 40–42 (table 4.2).

rev.

1.	gaba-ri	Copy
2.	kišib$_3$ ab-ba-kal-la	of the sealed tablet of Abba-kala.
3.	iti ki-siki-^{d}nin-a-zu	Month: "Weaving-place(?) of Ninazu."
4.	mu ^{d}i-bi$_2$-^{d}suen lugal	Year: "Ibbi-Suen (was) king."

left edge

1.	5(u) 8(diš) udu	(Total:) 58 sheep and goats.

Ur-Kununna, who is mentioned in text No. 95 as taking charge of the animals, is not included in AUCT 1, 750. Another parallel text, AnOr 1, 28, introduces a certain Ur-Dagi, unknown to text No. 95:

AnOr 1, 28 (Puzriš-Dagan, IS 1–v)

obv.

1.	[...] 1(diš) udu šu-gid$_2$	[...] and 1 sheep, šu-gid$_2$ offerings,
2.	ki a-ba-^{d}en-lil$_2$-gin$_7$-ta	from Aba-Enlilgin.
3.	gaba-ri	Copy
4.	kišib$_3$ ab-ba-kal-la	of the sealed tablet of Abba-kala.
5.	giri$_3$ ur-da-gi$_4$	Conveyor: Ur-Dagi.

rev.

1.	iti ki-siki-^{d}nin-a-zu	Month: "Weaving-place(?) of Ninazu."
2.	mu ^{d}i-bi$_2$-^{d}suen lugal	Year: "Ibbi-Suen (was) king."

Unfortunately, the originals of the intriguing series of tablets discussed above have not been found.

The originals of the following four tablet copies have also not been found. The first is a sealed tablet of a Lugal-Nirgal, who is with some likelihood identical to Lugal-Nirgal the boat-builder (ma$_2$-gin$_2$), slave (ARAD$_2$) of Šara, whose seal is rolled on thirteen extant tablets (S003649, dated to between Š 42 and AS7), and attested independent of his sealing from Š 43 to AS 7.

No. 96. *MS 1947/9 (Umma, AS[320] 6–ii)*

obv.

1.	4(u) ^{geš}KA×X bir$_3$ u$_3$-suḫ$_5$	40 (pieces of) pine wood for ... yokes,
2.	ki ur-^{d}li$_9$-si$_4$-ta	from Ur-Lisi.
3.	ma$_2$ amar-^{d}suen-še$_3$	For the boat of Amar-Suen.
4.	mar-sa-aš	For the shipyard.[321]

rev.

1.	gaba-ri kišib$_3$	Copy of the sealed tablet
2.	lugal-nir-gal$_2$	of Lugal-Nirgal.

---

[320] The same year-name is also used for Š 42 (in this abbreviated form); however the mention of the boat of Amar-Suen (regardless of the fact that the royal name is not written with the divine determinative) suggests that the text is from AS 6. See also Princeton 1, 208, CTNMC 30, and MVN 5, 162.

[321] Two receipts sealed by Lugal-Nirgal mention the shipyard (mar-sa): OrSP 47–49, 359 and JCS 2, 189 YBC 921, both from the same year as MS 1947/9.

3. iti sig$_4$-^{geš}i$_3$-šub-ga$_2$-ra — Month: "Brick placed in the mold."
4. mu ša-aš-ru-um$^{[ki]}$ ba-ḫul — Year: "Šašrum was destroyed."

Similarly, the original of the next tablet, No. 97, cannot be identified in the published record. Lu-Ursaga of our text is probably identical to Lu-Ursaga, scribe, son of Ur-Gigir, the *mu-sar*, whose seal is found on two tablets (UTI 3, 1798 and Syracuse 192).[322]

No. 97. *MS 2020/6 (Umma, AS 7–xii)*

obv.

1. 5(diš) murgu$_2$ ba — 5 turtle shells;
2. 2(diš) sila$_3$ i$_3$ UD.BU$_3$ gaz — 2 sila$_3$ of good . . .[323] oil.
3. ^{geš}ḫu-um ma$_2$-gur$_8$ lugal-ka-ke$_4$ ba-ab-ak — Was "done" (for) the bench(?)[324] of the barge of the king.
4. ki lu$_2$-kal-la-ta — From Lu-kala.
5. gaba-ri kišib$_3$ lu$_2$-ur$_4$-ša$_3$-ga — Copy of the sealed document of Lu-ur-saga.

rev.

1. iti ^{d}dumu-zi — Month: "Dumuzi."
2. mu ḫu-uḫ$_2$-nu-ri^{ki} ba-ḫul — Year: "Ḫuḫnuri was destroyed."

(*blank space*)

The original of text No. 98 also remains unidentified. It is a receipt for a large number of clay vessels returned from the city Zabala. The vessels are delivered by a certain Ḫuwawa, and received by a certain Duga-zida. Neither of these two can be definitively associated with the main pottery workshop of Umma (Dahl 2010a), although Ḫuwawa may be (he is found as a recipient in MVN 21, 203 obv. vi 12).

No. 98. *MS 2020/8 (Umma, ŠS 4)*

obv.

1. 9(geš$_2$) 4(u) dug sila$_3$ bur-zi — 580 bur-zi[325] bowls holding one sila$_3$,
2. 3(u) 5(diš) dug sila$_3$ sa$_2$-du$_{11}$ — 35 sila$_3$ bowls of the regular (deliveries),
3. zabala$_3$^{ki} gur-ra — returned from Zabala.
4. ki ḫu-wa-wa-ta — From Ḫuwawa.
5. gaba-ri kišib$_3$ du$_{11}$-ga-zi-da — Copy of sealed document of Dugazida.

rev.

(*blank space*)

1. mu-us$_2$-sa si-ma-num^{ki} ba-ḫul — Year following: "Simanum was destroyed."

---

[322] The title mu-sar is connected to the Umma divinity Šara.

[323] Probably the same product found in UTI 3, 2004 together with 3 turtle shells, and perhaps the same as i$_3$ UD.KA found in AR RIM 7, 16 12, see Snell 1982: 154.

[324] ^{geš}ḫu-um is attested in connection with boats in a handful of Ur III texts: see, e.g., BPOA 6, 1436 obv. 1–3: 3(diš) ma-na še-gin$_2$ / ^{geš}ḫu-um ma$_2$ ^{d}gu-la u$_3$ / ^{geš}i$_3$-šub im ar-ḫa ga$_2$-ga$_2$-de$_3$, "3 ma-na of glue for the 'bench' of the boat of Gula, and for the brick-mould for fashioning half-bricks." Note the use of the Akkadian word for half-brick (*arḫu*), and the use of im instead of sig$_4$ (text to be collated); the Sumerian word sig$_4$ ab$_2$ may be a pseudo-ideogram similar to sig$_4$ anše = *amāru* for brick-stack (see Heimpel 2009: 227).

[325] The many variants of bur-zi bowls are well attested in the lexical literature (Sallaberger and Civil 1996).

Text No. 99 is a copy of a receipt sealed by Lu-kala, the chief household-administrator of the governor of Umma between AS 2 and ŠS 9 (Dahl 2007: 105 ff., see also McGuiness 1981: 46ff. and 1982a, and Maeda 1996b). During his tenure Lu-kala sealed hundreds of such receipts concerning one or a few dead sheep or goats. Although Urru is the delivering shepherd in forty-five of these transactions (e.g., text No. 73), no original receipts from AS 8 have been published.

No. 99. *MS 2020/11 (Umma, AS 8–1)*

obv.

1.	1(diš) u$_{8}$ bar su-ga	1 ewe without fleece.
2.	ki ur-ru-ta	From Urru.
3.	gaba-ri <kišib-ba> lu$_{2}$-kal-<la>	Copy of (the sealed tablet of) Lu-kala.
4.	iti še-sag$_{11}$-ku$_{5}$	Month: "Harvest."

rev.

	(blank space)	
1.	mu-us$_{2}$-sa ḫu-uḫ$_{2}$-nu-ri[ki]	Year following: "Ḫuḫnuru was destroyed."

The more complex tablet copy No. 100 was included in David I. Owen's publication of the Garšana texts (CUSAS 3, 494), and discussed again by Brunke (2011b: 54–55). It is presented here without any further comments.

No. 100. *MS 4709 = CUSAS 3, 494 (Garšana, ŠS 8–vi)*

obv.

1.	1(ban$_{2}$) zi$_{3}$-gu saga	1 ban$_{2}$ of gu-flour, good (quality).
2.	1(barig) zi$_{3}$-gu du	1 barig of gu-flour, ordinary (quality).
3.	2(barig) dabin	2 barig of dabin-flour.
4.	1(ban$_{2}$) 1(diš) ½(diš) sila$_{3}$ zi$_{3}$ sig$_{15}$	1 ban$_{2}$, 1 ½ sila$_{3}$ of flour, sig$_{15}$ (quality).[326]
5.	7(diš) sila$_{3}$ nig$_{2}$-ar$_{3}$-ra saga	7 sila$_{3}$ of groats,[327] good (quality).
6.	4(diš) sila$_{3}$ ar-⸢za⸣-na	4 sila$_{3}$ of barley grits.
7.	5(diš) sila$_{3}$ gu$_{2}$-⸢tur⸣ al-⸢us$_{2}$-sa⸣	5 sila$_{3}$ of pureed/mashed (chick)peas/lentils.[328]
8.	u$_{4}$ ⸢7(diš) ⸣-kam	On the 7th day.
9.	1(ban$_{2}$) zi$_{3}$-gu saga	1 ban$_{2}$ of gu-flour, good (quality).
10.	1(barig) 2(ban$_{2}$) zi$_{3}$-gu ⸢du⸣	1 barig, 2 ban$_{2}$ of gu-flour, ordinary (quality).
11.	2(barig) ⸢dabin⸣	2 barig of dabin-flour.
12.	1(ban$_{2}$) [zi$_{3}$] sig$_{15}$	1 ban$_{2}$ of flour, sig$_{15}$ (quality).
13.	⸢5(diš) ⸣ sila$_{3}$ gu$_{2}$-gal al-ar$_{3}$-ra	5 sila$_{3}$ of milled/crushed (broad) beans.[329]

rev.

1.	6(diš) sila$_{3}$ nig$_{2}$-ar$_{3}$-ra saga	6 sila$_{3}$ of groats, good (quality)
2.	2(diš) sila$_{3}$ [ba]-ba zi$_{3}$	2 sila$_{3}$ of flour porridge.[330]

---

[326] Note that Brunke 2011b and *passim* does not use the reading sig$_{15}$ for KAL.

[327] Or bulghur, see Brunke 2011a: 167.

[328] See Brunke 2011a: 168 for chickpeas against the traditional translation "lentils," and crushed or pureed for al-us$_{2}$-sa; compare Bottéro 1981: 195 for brine for al-us$_{2}$-sa.

[329] Or bean meal, German *Bohnenschrot*, see Brunke 2011a: 168.

[330] See Brunke 2011a: 159 ff. who doubted the interpretation of ba-ba as mash or gruel (German *Brei* or *Mehlbrei*).

3.	u$_4$ 8(diš)-kam	On the 8th day.
4.	⸢diri⸣ sa$_2$-du$_{11}$ e$_2$ agrig-še$_3$	Surplus (from) the regular (deliveries) of the house of the steward.
5.	an-ta-lu$_2$ agrig maškim	Antalu the steward was enforcer.
6.	zi-ga šu-kab-ta$_2$	Booked out from Šu-kabta.
7.	ki ^{d}iškur-illat-ta	From the place of Adad-tillatī
8.	ba-zi	booked out.
9.	ša$_3$ gar-ša-⸢an⸣-na^{ki}	Within Garšana.
10.	iti ezem-^{d}nin-a-zu	Month: "Festival of Nin-azu."
11.	mu ^{d}šu-^{d}suen lugal ⸢uri$_5$^{ki}⸣-ma-ke$_4$ ma$_2$-gur$_8$ maḫ ⸢^{d}en-lil$_2$ ^{d}⸣nin-lil$_2$-ra [mu]-ne-dim$_2$	Year: "Šu-Suen, king of Ur, fashioned the lofty barge for Enlil and Ninlil."

left edge

1.	[. . .] 1(aš) 2(barig) 1(diš) ½(diš) sila$_3$ ninda gur gaba-ri	. . . 1 gur, 2 barig, 1 ½ sila$_3$ of bread. Copy.

Two further tablet copies in the Schøyen Collection also originate from the Garšana archive, although they were not previously recognized to be part of it, and thus not included in the publication of the archive (Owen and Mayr 2007 and Owen 2011). Both texts include reference to the chief household-administrator of the governor of Garšana, Adad-tillatī. In the first text, No. 101, he is the recipient of the goods (barley); in the second, No. 102, the goods (dates and an unknown product) are booked out from his account.

No. 101. *MS 4454 (Garšana, ŠS 7–iii)*

obv.

1.	2(u) še gur x	20 gur of barley . . . ,
2.	1(u) 4(aš) še gur x	14 gur of barley . . . ,
3.	ki a-da-⸢lal$_3$$^{?}$ šabra⸣ du$_6$-saḫar-ra-ta	from Adalal, chief administrator of Dusaḫara.
4.	^{d}iškur-illat x	Adad-tillatī, . . .

rev.

1.	šu ba-an-ti	received.
2.	iti šeš-da-gu$_7$	Month: "Eating the piglet."
3.	[mu] ^{d}šu-^{d}suen ⸢lugal⸣ uri$_2$^{ki}-[ma]-ke$_4$ ma-⸢da⸣ [za]-ab-ša-⸢li⸣^{ki} mu-⸢ḫul⸣	Year: "Šu-Suen, king of Ur, destroyed the territory of Zabšali."

left edge

1.	gaba-ri	Copy.

No. 102. *MS 4036 (Garšana$^{?}$, IS 1–xi)*

obv.

1.	2(barig) zu$_2$-lum	2 barig of dates;
2.	1(barig) ^{geš}mer had$_2$	1 barig of dried mer-wood.[331]

---

[331] This product is attested in the unpublished text LB 559 obv. i 6 (see CDLI s.v. P210012), where it is also counted in the capacity system.

3.	šar-ru-su-da-ba-ad[332]	Šarrussu-ṭābat
4.	[. . .]-ti	(received?)
5.	[. . .]-x-um	. . .
6.	[. . .] GAR	. . .

rev.

1.	[ki ^{d}]⌜iškur⌝-illat-ta[333] ba-zi	Booked out from the place of Adad-tillatī.
2.	ša$_3$ gar-ša-an-na^{ki}	Within Garšana.
3.	iti ezen-an-⌜na⌝	Month: "Festival of Heaven."
4.	mu ^{d}i-[bi$_2$]-^{d}suen lugal	Year: "Ibbi-Suen (was) king."

left edge

1.	⌜gaba⌝ -[ri]	Copy.

mu-ku$_x$(DU) Documents

A large number of receipt tablets from all provinces of the Ur III state include the technical term mu-ku$_x$(DU).[334] As is seen from the examples below, mu-ku$_x$(DU) documents are not limited to one or a few products. They were written on all days of all months, from the early years of Šulgi to at least Ibbi-Suen's twelfth year (and are also attested in the early Old Babylonian period).

Although we can translate mu-ku$_x$(DU) as "delivery" (Jagersma 2010: 128), it remains difficult to establish the exact technical meaning of the term, beyond that it denoted a special kind of delivery.[335] Most mu-ku$_x$(DU) deliveries were made by important members of the elite. Administratively, the term functions as the opposite to the term ba-zi, "was booked out,"[336] although grammatically the two are different. For ba-zi documents, see below.

Text No. 103 is a mu-ku$_x$(DU) text documenting the delivery of one dependent worker by the name Adata into the (service) of the main house of the deity Šara in Umma, the Emaḫ. Adata is described as a dedicatee (a-ru-a) of Agua (see Chapter 8 for people designated as dedicatees). He is transferred from a certain Ur-dun, and a certain Ur-Iškur takes responsibility for him.

No. 103. *MS 1916 (Umma, AS 1–v)*

obv.

1.	1(diš) a-da-lal$_3$	One Adata,
2.	a-ru-a a-gu-a	"dedicatee" of Agua.
3.	mu-ku$_x$(DU) e$_2$-maḫ	Delivery for the Emaḫ.
4.	ki ur-dun-ta	From Ur-dun,
5.	ur-^{d}iškur i$_3$-dab$_5$	Ur-Iškur seized.
6.	iti dal	Month: "Flight."

---

[332] See also UET 3, 754 obv. ii 19: a-ru-a šar-ru-su-da-bad$_3$.

[333] Erasure between illat and ta.

[334] For a reading ku$_x$ for DU, see already Krecher 1987, but note that it is still frequently read mu-du or mu-tum$_2$. CDLI lists almost 5000 instances of the term mu-ku$_x$(DU) from the Ur III period.

[335] See the useful summary of interpretations in Waetzoldt 1972: 28 n. 225, and note the Old Babylonian use of the term and Kraus's translation as "eine von der Behörde vorgeschriebene 'Lieferung'" (Kraus 1966: 34).

[336] Englund 1990: 32 n. 108.

rev.

1.	mu ^{d}amar-^{d}suen lugal (*seal impression*)	Year: "Amar-Suen (was) king."

seal (S004972)

1.	ur-^{d}iškur	Ur-Iškur,
2.	ugula nam-[1(u)]	commander of ten,
3.	⸢ARAD$_2$⸣ ^{d}nin-ur$_4$-ra	slave of Nin-Ura.

The next text, No. 104, is a receipt of three mu-ku$_x$(DU) deliveries made by the staff of a divine household. No further details are given apart from the month name. The text is here assigned to Umma based on that month name, although this particular kind of mu-ku$_x$(DU) delivery is most frequent among the extant texts from Drehem.

No. 104. *MS 2021/6 (Umma$^?$, X–ii)*

obv.

1.	1(diš) sila$_4^?$	1 lamb,
2.	nig$_2$-lagar-e gudu$_4$	Nig-lagare, gudu$_4$-priest.
3.	1(diš) maš$_2$	1 billy goat,
4.	dumu lugal-ra-ni gudu$_4$ ^{d}en-ki	Child of Lugalrani, gudu$_4$-priest of Enki.

rev.

1.	1(diš) udu	1 sheep,
2.	erin$_x$(KWU896) ^{d}da-gan (*blank space*)	. . .[337] of Dagan.
3.	mu-ku$_x$(DU)	Deliveries.
4.	iti sig$_4$-^{geš}i$_3$-šub-ba-ga$_2$-⸢ra⸣	Month: "Brick placed in the mold."

A comparable tablet from Drehem is OIP 115, 189:

OIP 115, 189 (Drehem, Š 46–viii–15)

obv.

1.	1(diš) maš-da$_3$	1 gazelle,
2.	da-da u$_3$-kul	(from) Dada, messenger(?).[338]
3.	1(diš) gu$_4$ 7(diš) udu	1 oxen, 7 sheep,
4.	1(diš) sila$_4$ 2(diš) maš$_2$	1 lamb, 2 billy goats,
5.	a-ab-ba-ni gudu$_4$ ^{d}nin-ur$_4$-<ra>	(from) Ayabbani, gudu$_4$-priest of Nin-ura.
6.	1(diš) gu$_4$ niga	1 fattened oxen,

---

[337] For KWU896, see n. 342.

[338] Persons bearing the title u$_3$-kul in Ur III texts are usually found in groups of persons going to or coming from Susa or other localities in the east, and often together with military staff (Dahl 2007: 153–54). The term may be derived from the verbal base kul, "to run," as another, specialized term for a messenger.

rev.

1.	1(u) udu 2(diš) sila$_4$	19 sheep, 2 lambs,
2.	puzur$_4$-^{d}iškur šuš$_3$	(from) Puzur-Adad, chief cattle-administrator.
	(*blank space*)	
3.	mu-ku$_x$(DU)	Deliveries.
4.	iti šu-eš$_5$-ša	Month: "šu'eša."
5.	mu ki-maš^{ki} u$_3$ ḫu-ur$_5$-ti^{ki} ba-ḫul	Year: "Kimaš and Ḫurti were destroyed."

left edge

1.	u$_4$ 1(u) 5(diš)-kam	On the 15th day.

Most such Drehem m u - k u$_x$(D U) documents record deliveries from mid- or high-ranking members of society for specific cultic purposes, as the following example shows:[339]

MVN 5, 98 (Š 44–iii–2)

obv.

1.	1(diš) gu$_4$ niga 1(u) udu	1 fattened ox and 10 sheep,
2.	ensi$_2$ urum$_x$(UR$_2$×U$_2$)^{ki}	(from) the governor of Urum.
3.	1(diš) gu$_4$ 1(u) udu	1 ox and 10 sheep,
4.	^{d}nanna-lu$_2$-du$_{10}$	(from) Nanna-ludu.
5.	1(diš) gu$_4$ 1(u) udu	1 ox and 10 sheep,
6.	du$_{11}$-ga-zi-da	(from) Dugazida.
7.	1(diš) gu$_4$ 1(u) udu	1 ox and 10 sheep,
8.	sanga mar$_2$-da^{ki}	(from) the sanga-official of Marad.

rev.

1.	mu-ku$_x$(DU) a$_2$-ki-ti še-sag$_{11}$-ku$_5$	Deliveries (for) the New Year (following) "Harvest."
2.	1(diš) sila$_4$ niga ensi$_2$ umma^{ki}	1 fattened lamb, (from) the governor of Umma.
3.	1(diš) ^{munus}aš$_2$-gar$_3$ niga ensi$_2$ nibru^{ki}	1 female kid, (from) the governor of Nippur.
4.	1(diš) sila$_4$ niga ensi$_2$ ka-zal-lu^{ki}	1 fattened lamb, (from) the governor of Kazallu.
5.	mu-ku$_x$(DU) u$_5$-bi$_2$-gu$_7$	Deliveries (for the month/festival) "Eating the goose/swan."
6.	mu si-mu-ru-um u$_3$ lu-lu-bu^{ki} a-ra$_2$ 1(u) la$_2$ 1(diš$_{tenû}$)-kam-aš ba-ḫul	Year: "Simurum and Lulubum were destroyed for the 9th time."

left edge

1.	u$_4$ 2(diš)-kam	2nd Day.

The next document records seven individuals listed together with substantial amounts of silver, summarized as the deliveries (m u - k u$_x$(D U)) of the governor, received by Lu-kala. Lu-kala's involvement in collecting field rents (m a š a - š a$_3$ - g a) during his tenure as chief household-administrator of the governor is well documented (Dahl 2007: 111–12; see also Steinkeller 1981 and Ouyang 2013). However, this text is silent as to the origin of the silver amounts. Most, although not all, of the persons can be identified with a great deal of certainty as

339 The text published by Sollberger in MVN 5 (1978) is from the now dispersed Pinches collection. Two tablets from that collection are now in the collection published here: No. 150 (MVN 5, 73) and No. 80 (MVN 5, 202).

high-ranking members of Umma administration, the second being in fact Lu-kala himself, the third perhaps his brother, or another person named Lu-Ḫaya.[340]

No. 105. *MS 2020/4 (Umma, ŠS 3–xiii)*

obv.

1.	1(u) gin$_2$ ku$_3$-babbar	10 shekels silver,
2.	ur-ab-ba-saga	(from) Ur-Abbasaga.
3.	⅓(diš) ma-na lu$_2$-kal-la	⅓ ma-na (of silver, from) Lu-kala.
4.	5(diš) gin$_2$ lu$_2$-^{d}ḫa-ia$_3$	5 shekels (of silver, from) Lu-Ḫaya.
5.	5(diš) gin$_2$ al-la agrig	5 shekels (silver, from) Alla, steward.
6.	5(diš) gin$_2$ ad-da-kal-la gudu$_4$	5 shekels (silver, from) Adda-kala, gudu$_4$-priest.

rev.

1.	2(diš) gin$_2$ ur-^{d}šara$_2$	2 shekels (silver, from) Ur-Šara.
2.	2(diš) gin$_2$ šeš-kal-la dumu tir-gu	2 shekels (silver, from) Šeš-kala, child of Tirgu.
	(*blank space*)	
3.	šunigin ⅚(diš) ma-na la$_2$ 1(diš) gin$_2$ ku$_3$-babbar	Total: ⅚ ma-na minus 1 shekel silver.
4.	mu-ku$_x$(DU) ⸢ensi$_2$⸣-ka	Delivery of the governor.
5.	lu$_2$-kal-la šu ba-ti	Lu-kala received.
6.	iti diri	Month: "Extra."

left edge

1.	mu si-ma-num$_2$^{ki} ba-ḫul	Year: "Simanum was destroyed."

Also objects could be transferred as mu-ku$_x$(DU) deliveries, as evidenced by the following two texts, Nos. 106 and 107:

No. 106. *MS 2021/3 (Umma, AS 7–iv)*

obv.

1.	2(diš) ^{geš}kab	2 pieces of kab-wood,[341]
2.	gid$_2$-bi 5(diš) ½(diš) kuš$_3$	their length: 5 ½ cubit.
3.	e$_2$-a-ab-ba-ta	From the E-abba.
4.	mu-ku$_x$(DU)	Delivery
5.	ma$_2$-gur$_8$ lugal-še$_3$	for the barge of the king.

rev.

1.	ša$_3$ erin$_x$(KWU896)$^?$-dab$_5$-⸢še$_3$$^?$⸣	Within Erindabše.[342]
2.	iti nesag	Month: "First Fruits."

---

[340] Lu-Ḫaya was the brother of Lu-kala, and inherited their father's office as chief cattle-administrator (šuš$_3$), whereas Lu-kala became the chief household-administrator of the governor (see Dahl 2007: 85 ff.)

[341] Note Röllig and Waetzoldt 1995: 327, who suggest that this particular type of wood was used for the foot of a chair or bed (see Akkadian *kablu*). Here, however, the kab-wood is destined for a barge and may be a technical term used in both shipbuilding and furniture.

[342] For this locality or construction, see, e.g., NYPL 10 obv. 2: e$_2$ erin-KU-še$_3$ ku$_x$(KWU147)-ra repeated in MVN 10, 230 obv. ii 19: erin$_x$(KWU896)$^?$-dab$_5$-še$_3$ ku$_x$(KWU147)-ra; Nebraska 75 obv. v 5: erin-dab$_5$-še$_3$-ta. Most examples of this proper noun uses the writing erin, whereas our text, and MVN 10, 230, use the more unusual writing erin$_x$(KWU896).

3.	mu bi$_2$-tum-ra-bi$_2$-um^{ki} *(blank space)*	Year: "Bitum-Rabium."

No delivering agent is found in the next document, nor is any person specified who takes the goods into his possession:

No. 107. *MS 1947/10 (Umma, AS 7–vi)*

obv.

1.	2(diš) ^{geš}a-ra	Two (pieces of) a-ra-wood;
2.	4(diš) ^{geš}a-da	Four (pieces of) a-da-wood.
3.	ma$_2$-⸢gur$_8$⸣[343] ga$_2$-ra	Placing the barge.
4.	^{geš}a-da ma$_2$-gur$_8$ lugal ba-an-gar	The a-da-wood was placed in the barge of the king.
5.	mar-sa-aš!(BAD)-ta	From the shipyard(?).

rev.

1.	mu-ku$_x$(DU)	Delivery.
2.	iti šu-numun	Month: "Seeding."
3.	mu bi$_2$-tum-ra-bi$_2$-um^{ki} ba-ḫul *(blank space)*	Year: "Bitum-Rabium was destroyed."

a-ra and a-da wood are always found together, and always in association with boat-building.[344] SANTAG 6, 68 is one of a few key texts recording the materials and work days required to build a boat.[345] The first pieces of wood recorded in that text are the a-ra and a-da wood.

Text No. 108, another mu-ku$_x$(DU) document, records finished products mostly made of leather but with some wooden objects as well. The only person named in the text is the well-known leather worker Anaḫ-ili. Due to the association with Anaḫ-ili, we may speculate that the special boxes (pisan bur$_2$, perhaps referring to a type of lid) listed in rev. 4–6, were partly made of leather.

No. 108. *MS 4706 (Drehem, ŠS 8–ix)*

obv.

1.	1(geš$_2$) 2(u) ^{kuš}maš-li$_2$-⸢um⸣	80 leather buckets,[346]
2.	2(u) kuš a-ga$_2$-la$_2$	20 leather sacks,
3.	3(u) 3(diš) ^{kuš}⸢ummu$_x$ (EDIN.A.LAL)⸣	33 water skins,
4.	2(diš) kuš AB ⸢u$_2$-ḫab$_2$ kuš⸣ [. . .]	2 hides, x, (treated with) oak apples, hides . . .
5.	3(diš) ^{kuš}suḫub$_2$ mi$_2$ babbar e$_2$-⸢ba-an⸣	3 pairs of shiny women's boots,[347]
6.	1(diš) ^{kuš}suḫub$_2$ mi$_2$ du$_8$-ši-a e$_2$-ba-an	1 pair of turquoise women's boots,[348]

---

[343] We should expect ma$_2$-a ga$_2$-ra for placing in the boat, but although the sign is broken and the beginning may not at first look like gur$_8$ (compared also to the well-preserved gur$_8$ in the following line), on closer examination the horizontal lines of the missing center do extend ever so slightly towards the right of the sign in a way very similar to the well preserved gur$_8$ sign in the following line.

[344] a-ra wood, but not a-da wood, is also found in connection with with boats in a broken section of the Old Babylonian literary text Nanna-suen's Journey (ETCSL 1.5.1: l. 48A).

[345] See Widell 2009 for an overview of boat construction in Ur III.

[346] See CAD M 380 (*mašlû* A).

[347] See also CUSAS 3, 925.

[348] See also CUSAS 3, 932.

7.	2(u) 1(diš) ^{kuš}suḫub$_2$ du e$_2$-ba-an	21 pairs of boots, running (quality),
8.	2(diš) ^{kuš}e-sir$_2$ mi$_2$ šu du$_8$-ši-a e$_2$-ba-an	2 pairs of turquoise women's gloves(?),
9.	2(diš) ^{kuš}e-sir$_2$ mi$_2$ šu du$_8$-a SI$_4$ du$_8$-ši-a e$_2$-ba-an	2 pairs of turquoise women's gloves(?) . . . ,
10.	1(u) x ⸢^{kuš}⸣e-DU e$_2$-ba-an	+10 pairs of . . .

rev.

1.	[. . .] dab$_5$ ḫi uš$_2$	. . .
2.	4(diš) ^{kuš}du$_{10}$-gan ti-bala-a	4 courier's pouch.[349]
3.	2(u) 3(diš) ^{kuš}udu ka-tab	sheep skins, (for) covers,
4.	2(diš) pisan bur$_2$ tab-ba geš$^?$ tab-ba	2 boxes, double flaps, wooden flaps (?),
5.	1(diš) pisan bur$_2$ tab-ba	1 box, double flap,
6.	1(diš) pisan bur$_2$ tur tab-ba	1 box, small double flap,
7.	3(diš) kuš udu ŠE$_3$ ⸢KAŠ$^?$⸣	3 sheep skins, . . .
	(seal impression)	
8.	mu-ku$_x$(DU)	Deliveries
9.	a-na-aḫ-i$_3$-li$_2$ ⸢ašgab⸣	(of) Anaḫ-ili, (chief of the) leather workers
10.	iti ezem-^{d}šu-⸢^{d}suen⸣	Month: "Festival of Šu-Suen."
11.	mu ^{d}šu-^{d}⸢suen⸣ lugal uri$_5$^{ki}-ma-ke$_4$ ⸢ma-da⸣ za-⸢ab⸣-ša-li^{ki} ⸢mu⸣-ḫul	Year: "Šu-Suen, king of Ur, destroyed the territory of Zabšali."

seal (S004199)

1.	šu-kab$_2$-ta$_2$ a-zu	Šu-kabta, physician,
2.	ARAD$_2$ na-ra-am-i$_3$-li$_2$	slave of Naram-Ili:
3.	^{d}iškur-illat	Adad-tillatī,
4.	dub-sar	scribe,
5.	dumu a-bi$_2$-a ARAD$_2$-zu	child of Abiya, (is) your slave.

The final mu-ku$_x$(DU) document published here is a list of deliveries made by three persons found in several of the other Adab texts from this collection: Šu-Mama, Ilaknuid, and Ur-(A)Baba. As discussed above, Šu-Mama may have been the father of Ilaknuid: Ur-(A)Baba, although perhaps not related by blood, interacted with both in the texts published here. All three were probably high-ranking members of the Adab administration. As such this document reinforces the interpretation of mu-ku$_x$(DU) documents recording mostly elite deliveries, probably for specific purposes.

No. 109. *MS 4715/4 (Adab$^?$, X–x)*

obv.

1.	1(aš) 1(barig) 4(ban$_2$) dabin gur	1 gur, 1 barig 4 ban$_2$ of dabin-flour
2.	^{d}x-ba-ni	(from) . . .-bani.
3.	1(barig) 4(ban$_2$) dabin šu-na-gu$_2$	1 barig, 4 ban$_2$ of dabin-flour (from) Šunagu.
4.	1(barig) 3(ban$_2$) ziz$_2$ šu-ma-ma	1 barig, 3 ban$_2$ of emmer-wheat (from) Šu-Mama.
5.	2(aš) dabin gur eš$_{18}$-dar-DA	2 gur of dabin-flour (from) Ištar-DA.

349 See Ferwerda 1985: 7.

6.	3(barig) 2(ban_2) KAL-a ugula dabin	3 barig, 2 ban_2 of . . .[350] (from) the overseer of flour
7.	er_3-ra-ba-ni	Erra-bani.

rev.

	(blank space)	
1.	3(barig) 2(ban_2) zi_3 sig_{15}	3 barig, 2 ban_2 of flour, sig_{15} (quality).
2.	5(aš) 2(barig) 1(ban_2) zi_3 gur	5 gur, 2 barig 1 ban_2 of flour.
3.	mu[351]-ku_x(DU)	Delivery
4.	i-la-ak-nu-id	(of?) Ilaknuid.
5.	$giri_3$ ur-ba-ba	Conveyor: Ur-Baba.
6.	iti ab-e_3	Month: "ab'e."

ba-zi and zi-ga Documents

Another type of receipt carries as a subscript either ba-zi, "was booked out," or zi-ga, "booked out," instead of the standard information šu ba-ti or kišib$_3$. The vast majority of these documents originate from ancient Drehem, where, together with the so-called i$_3$-dab$_5$ documents, they seem to occupy a special position in the bookkeeping of herded animals.

More specifically, ba-zi or zi-ga documents record expenditures from an account. As such, the term is reflected in the technical terminology of the "credits" of the Ur III accounts, which are framed by ša$_3$-bi-ta . . . zi-ga.

Syntactically, zi-ga is usually followed by a personal name, and sometimes by the fuller phrase zi-ga ki PN(-ta), where the ablative –ta is rarely written. ba-zi, on the other hand, usually follows a personal name, and the full phrase ki PN-ta ba-zi is mostly present.

Chronologically, ba-zi documents at Drehem are found primarily from Amar-Suen's first year until the end of Šu-Suen's third year, with some documents dated to Ibbi-Suen's first year. zi-ga documents are found in the Drehem archives throughout the entire period of the Ur III dynasty. At Garšana, both ba-zi and zi-ga documents are found almost exclusively from Šu-Suen's fifth year until the end of records from that site early in Ibbi-Suen's fourth year. At Umma the picture is more complicated, and both ba-zi and zi-ga documents are found during the entire period of the Ur III dynasty. ba-zi documents are unknown at Girsu, whereas zi-ga documents are frequent and attested throughout the period.

The first text, No. 110, a ba-zi document from Garšana, dates to Šu-Suen's ninth year, thus within the chronological boundaries established above:

No. 110. *MS 4702 = CUSAS 3, 1525 (Garšana, ŠS 9–iii)*

obv.

1.	1(u) kuš maš-da_3!(NI) gal ⌜niga⌝	10 hides from large fattened gazelles?
2.	1(diš) kuš a-ga_2-⌜la_2⌝	1 leather sack,
3.	4(u) kuš udu ka-tab e-ri_2-na	40 sheepskins, (for) covers, (treated with) madder (?).[352]
4.	a_2 mu-ku_x(DU)	Delivery of work (?),
5.	ki a-na-aḫ-i_3-li_2-ta	from Anaḫ-ili.

---

[350] KAL is usually read sig$_{15}$ in texts concerning cereals, denoting a superior quality (but note that Brunke 2011a and b did not support this interpretation, see n. 326 above); here however, it is likely to denote a different product.

[351] Erasure after mu.

[352] For e-ri$_2$-na meaning madder, see Stol 1980–83: 535.

rev.

1.	ba-zi	booked out.
	(*seal impression*)	
2.	iti ses-da-gu$_7$	Month: "Eating the piglet."
3.	mu ^{d}šu-^{d}suen lugal uri$_2$^{ki}-ma-ke$_4$ e$_2$ ^{d}šara$_2$ umma^{ki} mu- du$_3$	Year: "Šu-Suen, king of Ur, built the house of Šara in Umma."

seal (S006035)[353]

col. i

1.	^{d}šu-^{d}suen	Šu-Suen,
2.	lugal kal-ga	strong king,
3.	lugal uri$_2$^{ki}-ma-ke$_4$	king of Ur,
4.	lugal an ub-da limmu$_2$$^{?}$-ba	king of the four quarters (of the world),

col. ii

1.	me-^{d}ištaran	Me-Ištaran,
2.	nin ki-ag$_2$-ga$_2$-ni	his beloved queen:
	(*blank space*)	
3.	^{d}iškur-illat	Adad-tillatī,
4.	dumu a-bi$_2$-a	child of Abia,
5.	ARAD$_2$-zu	(is) your slave.
	(*blank space*)	
6.	dub-sar	Scribe.

As is clear from text No. 110, ba-zi documents give no information on the recipient of the goods, only the name of the person from whose account the goods are booked out. In No. 110, the hides and skins are booked out from Anaḫ-ili, a well-known person in the Garšana administration of leather production.[354]

No. 110 is not without problems. Some of the products listed in it are not well attested in the Ur III corpus outside of Garšana, but occur in the chronologically later Isin crafts archive (see Kleinerman 2011 for a comparison of these later archives and the Garšana crafts archives, and see Sallaberger 2011 for the language of texts from Garšana).

In the following Drehem text, Nisaba 8, 314, the destination of the goods, here animals, is clear. The dead animals are delivered to the "Kitchen."[355] A certain Inta'ea, well known from his numerous references, is credited for delivering the animals.

Nisaba 8, 314 (Drehem, AS 7–ix–20)

obv.

1.	1(diš) gu$_4$ 1(diš) ab$_2$	1 oxen, 1 cow,
2.	5(diš) udu	5 sheep,
3.	2(diš) maš$_2$ ga	2 milk-fed goats (~kids).

[353] For a shorter seal of Adad-tillatī, see text No. 108.

[354] Kleinerman 2011.

[355] For the institution known as the "Kitchen" (e$_2$-muhaldim), see Allred 2006. For a reading meḫida instead of muḫaldim, see proto-Ea (Civil 1979: 38, 174).

4.	ba-uš$_2$ e$_2$ muḫaldim-še$_3$	They are dead. For the "Kitchen."
5.	u$_4$ 2(u)-kam	on the 20th day.

rev.

1.	ki in-ta-e$_3$-a-ta ba-zi (*blank space*)	From Inta'ea booked out.
2.	iti ezem-maḫ	Month: "Lofty festival."
3.	mu ḫu-uḫ$_2$-nu-ri^{ki} ba-ḫul	Year: "Ḫuḫnuri was destroyed."

left edge

1.	2(diš) gu$_4$ 7(diš) udu	(Total:) 2 oxen and 7 sheep (and goats).

Text No. 111 is an unopened, sealed envelope. But unusually for a sealed envelope the text uses the terminology ba-zi rather than kišib$_3$ (sealed document) or šu ba-ti (received by). Unfortunately, the seal legend is illegible.

No. 111. *MS 4970 (Umma, ŠS 7–ii)*

Envelope

obv.

1.	1(diš) udu sa$_2$-du$_{11}$	1 sheep, regular (delivery)
2.	⸢^{d}⸣inanna zabala$_4^{ki}$	for Inanna of Zabalam.
3.	1(diš) ⸢maš$_2$⸣ sa$_2$-du$_{11}$	1 goat, regular (delivery)
4.	⸢^{d}šara$_2$⸣ umma^{ki}	for Šara of Umma.
5.	⸢ki⸣ i$_3$-li$_2$-bi-la-ni-ta	From Ili-bilani

rev.

1.	ba-zi (*seal impression*)	booked out.
2.	iti maš-da$_3$-gu$_7$	Month, "Eating the gazelle."
3.	⸢mu⸣ us$_2$-sa ^{d}šu-^{d}suen lugal-e na-ru$_2$-a maḫ [mu-na-du$_3$]	Year following: "Šu-Suen, king, erected the lofty stela."

seal (*illegible*)

The content of text No. 111 agrees well with what is otherwise known about ba-zi documents but not that of sealed envelopes.

Few ba-zi documents from Nippur are known. Text No. 112 is one of fewer than ten such texts known to me. It is similar to NATN 736, but the amounts of barley in our text are much larger.

No. 112. *MS 1740 (Nippur, X–vii)*[356]

obv.

1.	4(u) 3(aš) še gur lu$_2$-^{d}da-mu	43 gur of barley (for) Lu-Damu.
2.	1(aš) 3(barig) gur ma-ba	1 gur, 3 barig (for) Maba.
3.	2(aš) gur ^{d}en-lil$_2$-al-sa$_6$	2 gur (for) Enlil-alsa.

---

[356] Text No. 112 may in fact date to the early Old Babylonian period, although the personal names suggest an Ur III date.

4.	1(aš) gur lugal-bad$_3$ lu$_2$ ur-^{d}en-lil$_2$-la$_2$	1 gur (for) Lugal-bad, the man of Ur-Enlila.
5.	1(aš) gur ur-e-pa$_4$-ra	1 gur (for) Ur-Epara.
6.	2(barig) lugal-ti-da	2 barig (for) Lugal-(i)tida.
7.	1(aš) gur lugal-ku$_3$-zu dumu maš-te	1 gur (for) Lugal-kuzu, child of Mašte.
8.	mu ur-^{d}nin-lil$_2$	Instead (?) of Ur-Ninlil.
9.	1(aš) gur la-ni	1 gur (for) Lani.
10.	1(aš) gur lu$_2$-kal-la	1 gur for Lu-kala.
11.	2(u) gur lugal-engar	20 gur (for) Lugal-engar.

rev.

1.	⸢3(aš)⸣ gur lu$_2$-kal-la	3 gur (for) Lu-kala.
2.	lugal x x NI ra$_?$ ku$_{3?}$	. . .
3.	1(u) 2(aš) gur tul$_2$-ta	12 gur (for) Tulta.
4.	⸢3(u) 1(aš) nam-ḫa-ni⸣	(31 (gur for) Namḫani.)[357]
	(blank space)	
5.	1(geš$_2$) 2(u) 7(aš) gur	(Total:)[358] 87 gur.
z	*(blank space)*	
6.	ba-zi ki lugal-ku$_3$-zu-ta	Booked out from (the account of) Lugal-kuzu.
7.	i$_3$-dub ^{d}ašnan	(From the) granary of Ašnan.
8.	iti du$_6$-ku$_3$ u$_4$ ⸢1(u)⸣ x [. . .]	Month: "Shiny mound." 10 . . .

As mentioned above, the majority of the extant ba-zi documents derive from Drehem, and at least one qurter of them have an inscription on the left edge. About ten per cent of all Drehem ba-zi documents were deliveries made "on behalf of the soldiers" (mu aga$_3$-us$_2$-e-ne-še$_3$). The following previously unpublished document, from the collections of the National Museum of Aleppo,[359] is presented here as an example of that type of text:

NMSA 3895 (Aleppo) (Drehem, AS 9–vi)

obv.

1.	3(diš) x [x]	3 . . . ,
2.	1(u) 5(diš) u$_8$	15 ewes,
3.	2(diš) ud$_5$	2 goats,
4.	šu-gid$_2$ e$_2$ muḫaldim	šu-gid$_2$ offerings of the kitchen.
5.	mu aga$_3$-us$_2$-e-ne-še$_3$	On behalf of the soldiers.
6.	ARAD$_2$-mu maškim	ARADmu (is) enforcer.

rev.

1.	ša$_3$ unu^{ki}-ga	Within Uruk.
2.	u$_4$ 1(u) 6(diš)-kam	On the 16th day.
3.	ki du$_{10}$-ga-ta	from (the account) of Duga,
4.	ba-zi	booked out.
5.	giri$_3$ ^{d}nanna-ma-ba dub-sar	Conveyor: Nana-maba, scribe.

---

357 The line is erased.

358 Excepting the erasure in rev. 4, this line accurately represents the sum total of the amounts listed in the text.

359 A large part of the collection of Ur III tablets in the National Museum of Aleppo was not included in M. Touzalin's 1982 dissertation, and is only published online at the CDLI (transliterations by B. Lafont and J. L. Dahl).

6.	iti a$_2$-ki-ti	Month: "Akitu."
7.	mu en ^{d}nanna kar-zi-da ba-[ḫun]	Year: "The En-priest of Nanna of Karzida was installed."

left edge

1.	2(u)	(Total:) 20 (animals).

The remaining five ba-zi documents kept in the Schøyen Collection were previously published in Owen and Mayr 2007. They are transliterated and translated here as Nos. 113–17 without further comment.

No. 113. *MS 4711 = CUSAS 3, 1517 (Garšana, ŠS 7–vi)*

obv.

1.	2(diš) kuš ⸢udu⸣ pu-⸢us$_2$?⸣ x	2 sheep hides . . .
2.	1(diš) ^{kuš}du$_{10}$-gan ti-[bala-a]	1 carrier's pouch.
3.	1(diš) kuš maš$_2$ gal niga	1 hide of a large fattened goat,
4.	1(diš) kuš maš$_2$ niga	1 hide of a fattened goat,
5.	5(diš) gin$_2$ sa udu	5 shekels of sheep tendons,
6.	^{geš}gu-za nita$_2$ geš tug$_2$? tug$_2$? ba-a-gar	were placed on the throne . . .
7.	1(u) x[360] gin$_2$ kuš gu$_4$ u$_2$-hab$_2$?	10 shekels of hides, oxen, (tanned with) oak apples,
8.	5(diš) gin$_2$ sa udu	5 shekels of sheep tendons,
9.	2(diš) 1/2(diš) gin$_2$ eša	2 ½ (liquid) shekels of fine flour,
10.	x x ezem-da-še ba-a-gar	were placed . . . for the festival.

rev.

1.	1(diš) x kuš udu udu e-ri$_2$-na	1+*n* sheep hides treated with madder,
2.	^{gi}kid? ^{geš}gu-za-še$_3$ ba-a-gar	were placed on the reed mat(?) of the throne.
3.	2(diš) kuš udu	2 sheep hides,
4.	2(diš) kuš šaḫ$_2$ babbar	2 hides of pigs, shiny,
5.	bi$_2$-du-lu-um-še$_3$ ba-a-gar	were placed on the bi$_2$-du-lu-um.
6.	½(diš) kuš udu babbar	½ hide of sheep, shiny,
7.	½(diš) gin$_2$ eša	½ (liquid) shekel of fine flour,
8.	ḫu-im-še$_3$ ba-a-gar	were placed on the ḫu-im.
9.	5(diš) gin$_2$ [kuš] gu$_4$ u$_2$-hab$_2$	5 shekels of ox hide, (tanned with) oak apples,
10.	ib-du-um-še$_3$ ba-a-gar	was placed on the ib-du-um.
11.	ki a-na-aḫ-i$_3$-li$_2$-ta ba-zi	From Anaḫ-ili, booked out.
12.	iti ezem-^{d}nin-a-zu	Month: "Festival of Ninazu."
13.	mu ^{d}šu-^{d}suen lugal-e ma-da za-ab-ša-li^{ki} mu-ḫul	Year: "Šu-Suen, king, destroyed the territory of Zabšali."

seal (*illegible*)

No. 114. *MS 4698 = CUSAS 3, 1518 (Garšana, ŠS 7–xii)*

obv.

1.	1(diš) udu	1 sheep.

---

360 Erasure?

2.	1(diš) maš$_2$	1 goat.
3.	ki i$_3$-li$_2$-bi-la-ni-ta	From Ili-bilani.

rev.

1.	⸢ba⸣-zi	Booked out.
	(*blank space*)	
2.	iti še-sag$_{11}$-ku$_5$	Month: "Harvest."
3.	mu ma$_2$-gur$_8$ maḫ mu-ne$_2$-dim$_2$	Year: "He fashioned for them the lofty barge."

seal (S004199)

1.	[šu-^{d}kab$_2$-ta a-zu]	Šu-kabta, physician,
2.	[dumu na-ra-am]-i$_3$-li$_2$	child of Naram-ili:
3.	[^{d}iškur]-illat	Adad-tillatī,
4.	dub-sar	scribe,
5.	dumu a-bi$_2$-a ARAD$_2$-zu	child of Abia, (is) your slave.

No. 115. *MS 4689 = CUSAS 3, 1521 (Garšana, ŠS 8–iv)*

obv.

1.	4(diš) udu u$_2$	4 sheep, grass(-fed)
2.	1(diš) [. . .]	1 . . .
3.	2(diš) ⸢kuš⸣ [. . .] -še$_3$	2 hides of . . .
4.	[. . .] x-še$_3$	. . .
5.	⸢ki⸣ [i$_3$-li$_2$-bi$_2$]-la-ni-ta	From Ili-bilani

rev.

1.	ba-zi	booked out.
	(*blank space*)	
2.	iti u$_5$-bi$_2$-gu$_7$	Month: "Eating the swan/goose."
3.	mu ma$_2$-gur$_8$ maḫ ^{d}en-lil$_2$ ^{d}nin-lil$_2$-ra mu-ne-dim$_2$	Year: "He fashioned the lofty barge for Enlil and Ninlil."

seal (S004199)

1.	šu-^{d}kab$_2$-ta a-zu	Šu-kabta, physician,
2.	dumu na-ra-am-i$_3$-li$_2$	child of Naram-ili:
3.	^{d}iškur-illat	Adad-tillatī,
4.	dub-sar	scribe,
5.	dumu a-bi$_2$-a ARAD$_2$-zu	child of Abia, (is) your slave.

No. 116. *MS 4690 = CUSAS 3, 1522 (Garšana, ŠS 8–iv)*

obv.

1.	4(diš) udu ⸢u$_2$⸣	4 sheep, grass(-fed).
2.	1(diš) gukkal	1 fat-tailed sheep.
3.	ki i$_3$-li$_2$-bi-la-ni-ta	From Ili-bilani.

rev.

1.	ba-zi (*blank space*)	Booked out.
2.	iti u_5-bi_2-gu_7	Month: "Eating the swan/goose."
3.	mu ma_2-gur_8 maḫ ^{d}en-lil_2 ^{d}nin-lil_2-ra mu-ne-dim_2	Year: "He fashioned the lofty barge for Enlil and Ninlil."

seal (S004199)

1.	šu-^{d}[kab_2-ta a-zu]	Šu-kabta, physician,
2.	dumu [na-ra-am-i_3-li_2]	child of Naram-ili.
3.	^{d}iškur-⸢illat⸣	Adad-tillatī,
4.	dub-sar	scribe,
5.	dumu a-bi_2-[a $ARAD_2$-zu]	child of Abia, (is) your slave.

No. 117. *MS 4650 = CUSAS 3, 1523 (Garšana, ŠS 6–v)*

obv.

1.	1(diš) ⅔(diš) guruš ašgab	1 ⅔ workers, leather worker.
2.	u_4 2(diš)-$še_3$	For 2 days.
3.	a bala-e-de_3 gub-ba	Stationed at/for drawing water.
4.	$^{geš}kiri_6$ $ša_3$ gar-ša-an-na^{ki}	(in/of the) garden of Garšana.

rev.

1.	ki a-na-aḫ-i_3-li_2-ta	From Anaḫ-ili.
2.	ba-zi	Booked out.
3.	iti ⸢ki⸣-siki-^{d}nin-a-zu	Month: "Weaving-place(?) of Ninazu."
4.	mu ^{d}šu-^{d}suen lugal uri_5^{ki}-ma na-ru_2-a maḫ ^{d}en-lil_2 ^{d}nin-lil_2-ka[361] mu-ne-du_3	Year: "Šu-Suen, king of Ur, built the lofty stela for Enlil and Ninlil."

seal (*illegible*)

Most zi-ga texts originate from Drehem, and most concern transfers of animals. zi-ga documents basically fall in two groups. In the first group zi-ga precedes the date of the operation: zi-ga u_4 *n*-kam. In the second group zi-ga precedes the name of the person whose account is being credited with the deduction: zi-ga PN, occasionally zi-ga ki PN(-a). KM 89206, an unpublished Drehem text in the Kelsey Museum, Michigan, will serve as an example of the first group:

KM 89206 (Drehem, Š 46–vii–1)

obv.

1.	1(diš) gu_4 2(diš) udu	1 oxen, 2 sheep,
2.	1(u) 4(diš) u8 1(diš) ud_5	14 ewes, 1 nanny goat,
3.	7(diš) $maš_2$ 1(diš) $sila_4$	7 billy goats, 1 lamb,
4.	šu-gid_2 e_2 muḫaldim	šu-gid_2 offerings of the Kitchen.

---

[361] In a majority of the instances of this year-name, the gods Enlil and Ninlil are suffixed the postposition denoting dative objects, -ra, corresponding to the plural dative prefix, -ne-, of the verb du_3 (perhaps to be read ru_2); however in this and a few other texts the genitive suffix -ak is used instead.

rev.

1.	zi-ga u_4 1(diš)-kam	Booked out on the 1st day.
2.	iti ezem-dšul-gi	Month: "Festival of Šulgi."
3.	mu ki-maški u_3 ḫu-ur_5-tiki ba-ḫul	Year: "Kimaš and Ḫurti were destroyed."

DIA 19.024.13, an unpublished text in the Detroit Institute of Arts, will serve as an example of the second group:

DIA 19.024.13 (Drehem, Š 47–viii–3)

obv.

1.	1(diš) gu_4	1 oxen,
2.	e_2 muḫaldim	(for the) Kitchen.
3.	u_4 3(diš)-kam	On the 3rd day.
4.	zi-ga	Booked out
5.	ki den-lil_2-la_2	from (the account of) Enlila.

rev.

1.	iti šu-eš-ša	Month: "šu'eša."
2.	mu us_2-sa ki-mašški ba-ḫul	Year following: "Kimaš was destroyed."
	(blank space)	

There are five zi-ga documents in the Schøyen Collection. None of them is a typical Drehem animal transfer. The first, text No. 100 from Garšana, was presented above under tablet copies and deals with various flours. The second, text No. 118, is an Umma document recording the transfer of a wooden object. Three other zi-ga tablets, Nos. 119–21, record the daily deliveries of small or medium amounts of foodstuffs.

Text No. 118 is neither from Drehem, nor does it concern animals. Rather it is an Umma text recording the transfer of a piece of wood for a cultic or ceremonial item. It remains unclear why the terminology zi-ga was used in this instance.

No. 118. *MS 2021/8 (Umma, Š 37–xi)*

obv.

1.	1(diš) ad šu-nir gešrig$_2$ ak	1 beam for a . . .[362] emblem.
2.	ki-la_2-bi 1(diš) ⅔(diš) ma-⌜na⌝	Its weight: 1 ⅔ ma-na.
3.	šu-nir $ensi_2$-ka	(It is for) the emblem of the governor.

rev.

1.	zi-ga šeš-kal-la-ta	Booked out from (the account of) Šeš-kala.
2.	iti pa_4-u_2-e	Month: "Pa-u'e."
3.	mu bad_3 ba-du_3	Year: "The wall was built."

Texts Nos. 119–21 are three almost identical zi-ga documents from the same year, concerning the same deliveries of foodstuffs. All three texts use the same key terminology, "booked out daily" (zi-ga a_2-u_4-da), followed by a day number. Unfortunately, the texts do not give a month name or any personal names to help determine their original provenience and archival setting. It may be a mere coincidence that the texts are written on the 6th, 12th and 24th days, or it may suggest that although the expenditures were recorded as being daily, they were in fact only booked "weekly."

362 gešga-rig$_2$—ak, "to comb," is unlikely here.

No. 119. *MS 4708 (X, ŠS 2–?–6)*

obv.

1.	⸢2(aš)⸣ 2(barig) 3(ban$_2$) 6(diš) sila$_3$ kaš saga gur	2 gur, 2 barig, 3 ban$_2$, 6 sila$_3$ of good beer.
2.	n(aš) ⸢3(barig)$^{?}$⸣ 3(ban$_2$) 7(diš) sila$_3$ kaš du gur	*n* gur, 3 barig, 3 ban$_2$, 7 sila$_3$ of regular beer.
3.	1(barig) 3(ban$_2$) kaš dida saga	1 barig, 3 ban$_2$ of beer in dida (jars), good (quality).
4.	3(aš) 2(barig) ⸢3(ban$_2$) 2(diš)⸣ sila$_3$ ninda geš AŠ gur	3 gur, 2 barig, 3 ban$_2$, 2 sila$_3$ of bread, . . . (quality).
5.	1(geš$_2$) 9(aš) ⸢3(barig)⸣ 1(ban$_2$) 1(diš) sila$_3$ ninda du gur	69 gur, 3 barig, 1 ban$_2$, 1 sila$_3$ of bread, regular quality.
6.	3(aš) 2(ban$_2$) 8(diš) sila$_3$ ⸢ninda⸣ [x] gur	3 gur, 2 ban$_2$, 8 sila$_3$ of bread, . . . (quality).
7.	1(aš) 3(barig) 4(ban$_2$) 1(diš) sila$_3$ ninda zi$_3$-gu	1 gur, 3 barig, 4 ban$_2$, 1 sila$_3$ of gu-flour bread.
8.	1(ban$_2$) 5(diš) sila$_3$ zi$_3$ ba-ba saga	1 ban, 5 sila$_3$ of flour porridge, good (quality).
9.	3(ban$_2$) zi$_3$-⸢gu$_2$ ninda⸣	3 ban$_2$ of gu-flour bread.
10.	3(barig) 1(ban$_2$) zi$_3$ sig$_{15}$	3 barig, 1 ban$_2$ of flour, sig$_{15}$ (quality),
11.	5(aš) 1(barig) ⸢4(ban$_2$)$^{?}$⸣ 7(diš) sila$_3$ dabin gur	5 gur, 1 barig, 4 ban$_2$, 7 sila$_3$ dabin-flour.
12.	5(ban$_2$) ⸢eša⸣	5 ban$_2$ of fine flour.

rev.

1.	4(barig) 5(ban$_2$) 8(diš) sila$_3$ nig$_2$-ar$_3$-ra saga	4 barig, 5 ban$_2$, 8 sila$_3$ of groats, good (quality).
2.	2(ban$_2$) ŠIM saga gaz	2 ban$_2$ of resin(?), good (quality), crushed(?)
3.	3(ban$_2$) še	3 ban$_2$ of barley.
4.	še-bi 2(geš$_2$) 2(u) 5(ban$_2$) 5(diš) sila$_3$ gur	Its barley: 140 gur, 5 ban$_2$, 5 sila$_3$.
5.	5(geš'u) 7(diš) sa gi	307 bundles of reed.
6.	1(u) 1(aš) ½(aš) gu$_2$ ^{geš}ma-nu	11 ½ talents of willow(?).[363]
	(*blank space*)	
7.	⸢zi⸣-ga a$_2$ u$_4$-da	Booked out daily,
8.	[u$_4$] 6(diš)-kam	on the 6th day.
9.	⸢mu⸣ ma$_2$-dara$_3$ abzu [^{d}]⸢en⸣-ki ba-ab-du$_8$	Year: "The boat 'Ibex of the Abzu of Enki' was caulked."

No. 120. *MS 4695 (X, ŠS 2–?–12)*

obv.

1.	⸢6(aš)⸣ 4(ban$_2$) kaš saga gur	6 gur and 4 ban$_2$ of beer, good (quality).
2.	⸢3(u) 7(aš)⸣ x x kaš [du] gur	37 gur, ... of beer, ordinary (quality).
3.	4(aš) 2(barig) [. . .] ⸢7(diš)⸣ sila$_3$ ⸢ninda geš⸣ AŠ gur	4 gur, 2 barig, . . . , 7 sila$_3$ of bread, . . . (quality).
4.	⸢7(aš)⸣ [. . .] n(ban$_2$) ninda zi$_3$ IŠ ba-ba gur	
5.	4(u) 1(barig) 2(ban$_2$) ninda du gur	40 gur, 1 barig, 2 ban$_2$ of bread, ordinary (quality).
6.	9(aš) 3(barig) 4(ban$_2$) ninda zi$_3$ gur	9 gur, 3 barig, 4 ban$_2$ of flour bread.
7.	1(aš) 3(barig) 2(ban$_2$) ninda gu gur	5 gur, 3 barig, 2 ban$_2$ of . . . bread.
8.	5(aš) 1(barig) 4(ban$_2$) dabin gur	5 gur, 1 barig, 4 ban$_2$ dabin-flour.
9.	⸢3(ban$_2$)⸣ 2(diš) sila$_3$ eša	3 ban$_2$, 2 sila$_3$ of fine flour.

---

[363] The wood recorded here and the reed recorded in the previous line were likely for use in the bread ovens.

10.	4(barig) 5(ban$_2$) 8(diš) sila$_3$ nig$_2$-ar$_3$-ra saga	4 barig, 5 ban$_2$, 8 sila$_3$ of groats, good (quality).
11.	2(ban$_2$) ŠIM saga gaz	2 ban$_2$ of resin(?), good (quality), crushed(?)
12.	2(aš) 3(ban$_2$) še gur	2 gur, 3 ban$_2$ of barley.
13.	še-bi 2(geš$_2$) 2(u) 1(aš) 5(ban$_2$) ⸢gur⸣	Its barley: 141 gur, 5 ban$_2$.

rev.

1.	4(geš'u) 7(geš$_2$) 2(u) sa ⸢gi⸣	2780 bundles of reed.
2.	1(u) 1(aš) gu$_2$ ^{geš}ma-nu	11 bundles of willow(?).
	(*blank space*)	
3.	zi-ga a$_2$-u$_4$-⸢da⸣	Booked out daily,
4.	u$_4$ 1(u) ⸢2(diš)⸣-kam	on the 12th day.
5.	[mu ma$_2$]-⸢dara$_3$⸣ abzu [ba]-ab-du$_8$	Year: "The boat 'Ibex of the Abzu' was caulked."

No. 121. *MS 4693 (X, ŠS 2–?–24)*

obv.

1.	6(aš) 4(barig) kaš saga ⸢gur⸣	6 gur, 4 barig of good beer.
2.	3(u) 7(aš) 3(barig) 2(ban$_2$) 7(diš) sila$_3$ kaš du gur	37 gur, 3 barig, 2 ban$_2$, 7 sila$_3$ of beer, ordinary (quality).
3.	3(ban$_2$) dug dida saga	3 ban$_2$ of (beer in) dida jars, good (quality).
4.	3(aš) 3(barig) 4(ban$_2$) 8(diš) sila$_3$ ninda geš AŠ gur	3 gur, 3 barig, 4 ban$_2$, 8 sila$_3$ of bread, . . . (quality).
5.	5(u) 5(aš) 4(barig) 1(ban$_2$) ninda ⸢du⸣ gur	55 gur, 4 barig, 1 ban$_2$ of regular bread.
6.	1(aš) ⸢4(barig)⸣ 5(ban$_2$) ninda zi$_3$-gu gur	1 gur, 4 barig, 5 ban$_2$ of gu-flour bread.
7.	2(ban$_2$) zi$_3$ sig$_{15}$	2 ban$_2$ of flour, sig$_{15}$ (quality).
8.	6(aš) 3(ban$_2$) dabin gur	6 gur, 3 ban$_2$ dabin-flour.
9.	3(ban$_2$) 4(diš) sila$_3$ eša	3 ban$_2$, 4 sila$_3$ of fine flour.
10.	4(barig) 5(ban$_2$) 8(diš) sila$_3$ nig$_2$-ar$_3$-<ra> saga	4 barig, 5 ban$_2$, 8 sila$_3$ of groats, good (quality).
11.	2(ban$_2$) 1(u) gin$_2$ ŠIM ⸢saga⸣ [gaz]	2 ban$_2$, 1 (liquid) shekel of resin(?), good (quality), crushed(?)
12.	3(ban$_2$) ⸢še⸣	3 ban$_2$ of barley.

rev.

1.	⸢še-bi 2(geš$_2$)⸣ [2(u) 5(ban$_2$) 5(diš) sila$_3$ gur]	Its barley: 140 gur, 5 ban$_2$, and 5 sila$_3$.
2.	⸢4(geš'u) 5(geš$_2$)$^?$ 2(u)$^?$ sa$^?$⸣ [gi]	2720 bundles of reed.
3.	1(u) 1(aš) ⸢½(aš)$^?$⸣ gu$_2$ $^{⸢\text{geš}⸣}$[ma-nu]	11 talents of willow(?).
	(*blank space*)	
4.	zi-ga [a$_2$ u$_4$-da]	Booked out daily,
5.	u$_4$ 2(u) 4(diš)-⸢kam⸣	on the 24th day.
6.	mu ma$_2$-dara$_3$ abzu ^{d}en-ki ba-ab-⸢du$_8$⸣	Year: "The boat 'Ibex of the Abzu of Enki' was caulked."

i$_3$-dab$_5$ Documents

Another group of primary documents, most frequently found in the Drehem archive, uses the technical terminology PN i$_3$-dab$_5$, "PN seized," instead of PN šu ba-ti or kišib$_3$ PN. These texts seem to be related almost exclusively to live animals, although the term was sometimes also used for workers and occasionally for other objects. There are three i$_3$-dab$_5$ documents in the Schøyen Collection. One, text No. 95, was presented above under tablet copies; the others follow.

Text No. 122 is a standard i$_3$-dab$_5$ document recording the transfer of fifteen animals from Ili-bilani to Adad-tillatī, both well-known members of the Garšana administration:

No. 122. *MS 4385 = CUSAS 3, 1519 (Garšana, ŠS 8–i)*

obv.

1.	1(u) ud$_5$	10 nanny goats;
2.	1(diš) ^{munus}aš$_2$-gar$_3$	1 female kid;
3.	⸢3(diš) maš$_2$ gal⸣	3 large billy goats;
4.	1(diš) ⸢maš$_2$⸣	1 billy goat.
5.	⸢ki⸣ [i$_3$-li$_2$-bi$_2$]-la-[ni]-⸢ta⸣	From Ili-bilani.

rev.

1.	^{d}iškur-illat	Adad-tillatī
2.	i$_3$-dab$_5$	seized.
3.	iti še-sag$_{11}$-ku$_5$	Month: "Harvest."
4.	mu ^{d}šu-^{d}suen lugal uri$_2$^{ki}-ma-ke$_4$ ma$_2$-gur$_8$ maḫ ^{d}en-lil$_2$ ^{d}nin-lil$_2$ mu-ne-dim$_2$	Year: "Šu-Suen, king of Ur, fashioned the lofty barge for Enlil and Ninlil."

Text No. 123 is a more unusual i$_3$-dab$_5$ document, recording the transfer of various metal objects. The objects are said to come from outside of the treasury of Nin-ilduma. None of the persons listed in the text is well known.

No. 123. *MS 1947/2 (Umma, SS 7–viii)*

obv.

1.	1(diš) za-ḫu-um ⸢zabar⸣ [. . .]	One bronze Zaḫum . . . ,
2.	ki-la$_2$-bi [. . .]	Its weight: . . .
3.	1(diš) x [. . .]	One . . . ,
4.	ki-la$_2$-[bi . . .]	Its weight: . . .
5.	1(diš) [. . .]	One . . . ,
6.	ki-[la$_2$-bi . . .]	Its weight: . . .
7.	1(diš) [. . .]	One . . . ,
	(*rest broken*)	

rev.

	(*blank space*)	
1.	gil-sa bar-ta gal$_2$-la	Available from outside of the treasury
2.	^{d}nin-ildu$_2$-ma	of Nin-ilduma.
3.	ki da-lu$_5$-ta	From Dalu.
4.	du-du i$_3$-dab$_5$	Dudu seized.
5.	giri$_3$ ur-e$_2$-maš-ka	Conveyor: Ur-Emaška.
6.	iti e$_2$-iti-6(diš)	Month: "House-month-six."
	(*blank space*)	
7.	⸢mu ^{d}šu⸣-^{d}suen lugal ⸢uri$_5$⸣^{ki}-ma-ke$_4$ ma-da za-ab-ša-li^{ki} mu-ḫul	Year: "Šu-Suen, king of Ur destroyed the territory of Zabšali."

in-la$_2$ Documents

The final group of receipts to be discussed here is concerned with the control of metals and textiles. Instead of the standard terminology for receiving goods found in the primary documents (PN šu ba-ti; kišib$_3$ PN; ki PN-ta ba-zi; zi-ga PN; and PN i$_3$-dab$_5$), these documents use the term PN in-la$_2$, "PN weighed it." The person said to weigh the metals can be shown to represent, structurally, the recipient. In about one quarter of the in-la$_2$ documents, an additional recipient is introduced (PN šu ba-ti). None of the in-la$_2$ documents with an additional recipient is sealed: sealed in-la$_2$ documents always carry the seal of the person weighing the objects. Except for one Garšana text (CUSAS 3, 717), all of the c. 225 preserved in-la$_2$ documents come from Umma. The persons weighing the materials in these texts belonged to a very restricted group, being principally members of the ruling family of Umma and a few other persons, such as I-kala, head of the Umma textile workshop, and Ur-Šara, chief smith of Umma (Dahl 2007: 76 n. 279).

There is only one document in the Schøyen Collection that belongs to this group: text No. 124. It is similar to other Umma in-la$_2$ documents concerning metals.

No. 124. *MS 1722 = MVN 5, 28 (Umma, AS 4–vi)*

obv.

1.	3(u) 7(diš) ^{uruda}ḫa-bu$_3$-da	37 hoes of copper.
2.	ki-la$_2$-bi 1(u) 9(diš) ⅔(diš) ma-na 5(diš) gin$_2$	Their weight: 19 ⅔ ma-na and 5 shekels.
3.	kin til-la	Finished work (tools).
4.	ki lu$_2$-kal-la-ta	From Lu-kala,

rev.

1.	ur-^{d}šara$_2$$^{!}$-ke$_4$	Ur-Šara
2.	in-la$_2$	weighed.
	(seal impression)	
3.	iti šu-numun	Month: "Seeding."
4.	mu en maḫ-gal-an-na en ^{d}nanna ba-ḫun	Year: "En-maḫgalanna, the En-priest of Nanna, was installed."

seal (S005354)

1.	ur-^{d}šara$_2$	Ur-Šara,
2.	dub-sar	scribe,
3.	dumu lugal-ušur$_4$	child of Lugal-ušur.

For the sake of completeness I add from other collections two unsealed in-la$_2$ document concerning textiles and one sealed in-la$_2$ document concerning metal objects:

Princeton 1, 301 (Umma, AS 7–viii)

obv.

1.	4(diš) tug$_2$ guz-za 3(diš)-kam us$_2$	4 guz-za textiles, 3rd class, lesser (quality).
2.	ki-la$_2$-bi 2(u) 2(diš) ma-na	Their weight: 22 ma-na.
3.	2(diš) tug$_2$ nig$_2$-lam$_2$ 3(diš)-kam us$_2$	2 nig$_2$-lam textiles, 3rd class, lesser (quality).
4.	ki-la$_2$-bi 3(diš) ma-na	Their weight: 3 ma-na.
5.	2(diš) tug$_2$ guz-za du	2 guz-za textiles, lesser (quality).
6.	ki-la$_2$-bi 8(diš) ma-na	Their weight: 8 ma-na.

rev.

1.	siki kur-ra ^{geš}ga-rig$_2$ [ak]	Wool of kur sheep, combed.
2.	tug$_2$ ki-la$_2$ tag-ga	Textiles: weight (has been) checked.
3.	ki ur-^{d}nin-tu-ta	From Ur-Nintu.
4.	dingir-ra-ke$_4$ in-la$_2$	Dingira weighed.
5.	iti e$_2$-iti-6(diš)	Month: "House-month-six."
6.	mu ḫu-ḫu-nu-ri^{ki} ba-ḫul	Year: "Ḫuḫunuri was destroyed."

Princeton 1, 308 (Umma, ŠS 2–iv)

obv.

1.	1(diš) tug$_2$ guz-za du	1 guz-za textile, running (quality).
2.	ki-la$_2$-bi 4(diš) ma-na 1(u) gin$_2$	Its weight: 4 ma-na and 10 shekels.
3.	1(u) 4(diš) tug$_2$ gu$_2$ anše	14 textiles for the neck ropes of onagers(?).
4.	ki-la$_2$-bi 3(u) 8(diš) ½(diš) ma-na 1(diš) gin$_2$	Their weight: 38 ½ ma-na and 1 shekel.
5.	tug$_2$ ki-la$_2$ tag-ga	Textiles: weight (has been) checked.

rev.

1.	ki ur-^{d}nin-tu-ta	From Ur-Nintu.
2.	ur-^{d}nun-gal-ke$_4$ in-la$_2$	Ur-Nungal weighed.
3.	uš-mu lu$_2$ azlag$_2$	Ušmu, fuller,
4.	šu ba-ti	received.
5.	iti nesag	Month: "First Fruits."
6.	mu ma$_2$ ^{d}en-ki ba-ab-du$_8$	Year: "The boat of Enki was caulked."

Aleppo 495 (NMSA 4064) (Umma, Š 44)

obv.

1.	1(u) ^{uruda}ḫa-zi-in	10 copper axe(-blades).
2.	ki-la$_2$-bi 8(diš) ½(diš) ma-na	Their weight: 8 ½ ma-na.
3.	kin dub$_2$-ba	Broken (during) work.[364]
4.	ki da-da-ga-ta	From Dadaga.
5.	ur-^{d}šara$_2$-ke$_4$ in-la$_2$	Ur-Šara weighed.

rev.

1.	mu si-mu-ru-um lu-lu-bu a-ra$_2$ 1(u) la$_2$ 1(diš)-kam ba-ḫul	Year: "Simurrum (and) Lulubu(m) were defeated for the 9th time."

seal (S005354)

1.	ur-^{d}šara$_2$	Ur-Šara,
2.	dub-sar	scribe,
3.	dumu lugal-ušur$_4$	child of Lugal-ušur.

---

[364] de Maaijer 2001: 306 n. 45; compare to kin til-la mostly used about plowshares.

8
ADMINISTRATION OF WORK

It seems reasonable to divide the documents concerning the administration of work into four groups, documenting available staff, their rations, and their work. The first group is the inventories and other lists. These texts served a dual purpose: first, as state inventory records tracking which institution or team a worker belonged to, and secondly, they were used for the calculations of rations and other allotments. The second group of texts specifically calculated the outputs of work crews. Receipts make up the third group. The fourth group is the accounts. Accounts summarized the receipts and the texts that calculated the output of work crews.

Inventories

Lists that group workers according to category and institution or team are here classified as inventories. These inventories record the institutional affiliation of the workers, and their rations or allotments. The most famous such text is perhaps the Girsu text HSS 4, 4, which lists the "rations" for all the high-ranking members of an institution and the agricultural workers, but not for non-skilled workers or craftsmen.[365]

Several large tablets listing available staff are present in the Schøyen Collection. Some of these texts record the rations for the staff of various institutions and crews, others the allotments and predicted yields of these, for staff of the same or other institutions.

The two terms used most frequently to specify the association of workers are gir$_3$-se$_3$-ga and a-ru-a. These terms remain poorly understood.

gir$_3$-se$_3$-ga is always used in connection with either a divine name, the name of the household of a deity, the palace, or an associated institution. a-ru-a on the other hand is mostly used with a personal name, and more rarely with the name of an institution. It is likely that gir$_3$-se$_3$-ga represented the permanent staff of a household, whereas people designated as a-ru-a may have been dedicated to or by a certain person or office (by the state or a person) for a specific period of time. Since it is possible that a-ru-a and the Sumerian compound verb a—ru, "to dedicate," are related, and since members of these groups seem to be assigned to others, I have, following Gelb 1972, tentatively translated a-ru-a as "dedicatees." I translate giri$_3$-se$_3$-ga as "(household) staff."[366]

The following text example, TUT 154 (from AS 2–iii), a Girsu text, lists the barley rations for the gir$_3$-se$_3$-ga of the "New Mill." Only the totals are transliterated and translated here.[367]

TUT 154 (Girsu, AS 2–iii)

rev. col. iv

	(blank space)	
1.	šunigin 2(diš) dub-sar 1(barig)-ta	Total: 2 scribes, 1 barig (of barley) each.
2.	šunigin 5(diš) guruš 5(ban$_2$)-ta	Total: 5 workers, 5 ban$_2$ (of barley) each.

---

[365] See Englund 1990: 60–63 for a discussion of that text. It is worth noting that in HSS 4, 4 the office of the land surveyor (sa$_{12}$-sug$_5$) is listed as third in rank, above the chief of the granary (KA-guru$_7$). At Umma the office of land surveyor was not in the hands of the ruling family. Whether this office was important on the level of the city administration, or only within the divine household, is unclear. At Umma the office of chief surveyor belonged throughout the Ur III period to members of the family of Inim-Šara. Most of Inim-Šara's sons seem to have been mid-level agricultural administrators (with the title nu-banda$_3$, gu$_4$, or ugula), which argues against a prominent social position within Umma for the holder of this title.

[366] Gelb's term "personnel" may today sound dated, but covers essentially the same as "staff" here (see Gelb 1965: 242). See also Englund 1990: 160.

[367] Compare to a group of texts studied by Uchitel 1984: 75–98. However, Uchitel did not discuss this text, nor does it belong to the same archive.

3.	šunigin 2(diš) dumu 2(ban$_2$)-ta	Total: 2 children,[368] 2 ban$_2$ (of barley) each.
4.	i$_3$-du$_8$-me	They are doorkeepers.
5.	šunigin 2(diš) guruš 1(barig)-ta	Total: 2 workers, 1 barig (of barley) each.
6.	šunigin 1(diš) guruš 5(ban$_2$)	Total: 1 worker, 5 ban$_2$ (of barley),
7.	ad-kup$_4$-me	They are basketry workers.
8.	šunigin 1(diš) nagar 1(barig)	Total: 1 carpenter, 1 barig (of barley).
9.	šunigin 4(diš) baḫar$_2$ 1(barig)-ta	Total: 4 potters, 1 barig (of barley) each.
10.	šunigin 2(diš) ^{na4}kin$_2$-gul-gul 1(barig)-ta	Total: 2 millstone operators,[369] 1 barig (of barley) each.
11.	šunigin 4(diš) gi-ze$_2$ 1(barig)-ta	Total: 4 reed-cutters(?),[370] 1 barig (of barley) each.
12.	šunigin 3(diš) guruš 1(barig)-ta	Total: 3 workers, 1 barig (of barley) each.
13.	šunigin 1(diš) dumu 1(ban$_2$) 5(diš)	Total: 1 child, 1 ban$_2$ 5 sila$_3$ (of barley).
14.	šunigin 1(diš) dumu 1(ban$_2$)	Total: 1 child, 1 ban$_2$ (of barley).
15.	gu-za-la$_2$-me	They are "throne-bearers."
16.	šunigin 8(diš) ma$_2$-laḫ$_5$ 1(barig)-ta	Total: 8 boatmen, 1 barig (of barley) each.
17.	šunigin 1(u) guruš 1(barig)-ta	Total: 10 workers, 1 barig (of barley) each.
18.	šunigin 2(diš) guruš ½(diš) 4(ban$_2$)-ta	Total: 2 workers, half (output), 4 ban$_2$ (of barley) each.
19.	šunigin 1(diš) dumu 2(ban$_2$)	Total: 1 child, 2 ban$_2$ (of barley).
20.	šunigin 1(diš) dumu 1(ban$_2$) 5(diš)	Total: 1 child, 1 ban$_2$ 5 sila$_3$ (of barley).
21.	ma$_2$ gid$_2$-me	They are boat-hauliers.
22.	šunigin 1(diš) šu dumu 5(ban$_2$)	Total: 1 "old child," 5 ban$_2$ (of barley).
23.	šunigin 1(diš) šitim 1(barig)	Total: 1 builder, 1 barig (of barley).
24.	šunigin 2(aš) guruš 3(ban$_2$)-ta	Total: 2 workers, 3 ban$_2$ (of barley) each.
25.	šunigin 1(diš) guruš šu-gi$_4$ 4(ban$_2$)	Total: 1 worker, old, 4 ban$_2$ (of barley).
26.	še-bi 9(aš) 2(barig) 3(ban$_2$) gur	Its barley: 9 gur, 2 barig, 3 ban$_2$.
27.	šunigin 1(diš) munu$_4$-mu$_2$ nu x[371]	Total: 1 maltster, not (receiving).
	(blank space)	
29.	še-ba giri$_3$-se$_3$-ga e$_2$ kikken$_2$ gibil	Barley rations of the staff of the New Mill.
31.	iti ezem-^{d}li$_9$-si$_4$	Month: "Festival of Lisi."
32.	mu-us$_2$-sa ^{d}amar-^{d}suen lugal	Year after: "Amar-Suen (was) king."

Each institution or household, here a mill, was essentially a self-sufficient unit. The large institutions, such as the households of the major gods or the king, presumably had much larger staffs, but no complete listings of those households are known. The gir$_3$-se$_3$-ga was not the only source of manpower available to the institutions; rather, it represented only the permanent staff concerned with maintaining the basic functions of the household. The Girsu text ASJ 20, 108 7 (from Š 48), listed approximately ten thousand men and women who were categorized as the female textile workers (geme$_2$ uš-bar), fullers (lu$_2$-azlag$_2$), and staff of a textile factory (gir$_3$-se$_3$-ga e$_2$ uš-bar). By far the largest of these three groups were the female textile workers, who were not part of the gir$_3$-se$_3$-ga, and likely constituted a mixed bag of prisoners of war, indentured workers, and other members of the lower echelons of society. The fragmentary Girsu text TUT 147 recorded the staffs of the governor's household, of the household of the "chief administrator" of the governor, of the

---

[368] Here perhaps assistants.

[369] See Uchitel 1984: 78. Perhaps to be read ^{na4}ar$_3$-gul-gul for /nargulgul/.

[370] See Civil 1994: 122.

[371] Erasure?

local section of the royal household, and of the various Girsu divine households.[372] Although no parallel texts from other Ur III centers have been found, we should not suppose that such texts did not exist. The tablet container BRM 3, 179, might imply that the same structure recorded in TUT 147 also applied to the household of the Umma governor, for example.[373]

There are seventeen small, medium, and large size inventories of workers in the Schøyen Collection (Table 1). Some of them include the term giri$_3$-se$_3$-ga (staff), some assign people to various other groups (a-ru-a, dedicatees), and some include the technical term to "inspect," "take inventory" (gurum$_2$—ak).[374]

Seven of the inventories include persons belonging to the staff of some institution (giri$_3$-se$_3$-ga). Three of them are yearly summaries (Nos. 126, 129, and 138), and three others cover shorter time-spans (Nos. 125, 127, and 134). Text No. 140 includes the term staff (giri$_3$-se$_3$-ga) but the colophon is poorly preserved, and it is unclear whether this is a yearly inventory or not. All seven texts presumably originate in the Umma central archive, although No. 127 is an inventory of the fishermen(?) in Apisal.

Nine further texts are grouped with these, although they do not include reference to any staff (giri$_3$-se$_3$-ga). Eight of these list groups of dedicatees (a-ru-a): texts Nos. 128, 130, 131, 132, 133, 135, 136, and 139. The ninth, text No. 141, stands out; it lists forty-eight persons but the administrative purpose of the list is not clear.

Table 1. Overview of the inventories in the Schøyen collection

Text No.	Description	Full transliteration
125	Monthly inventory of staff	This chapter
126	Annual inventory of dedicatees	Appendix
127	Monthly inventory of staff	Appendix
128	Annual inventory of cowherds	Appendix
129	Annual inventory of goatherds and cowherds	Appendix
130	Annual inventory of plow teams	Appendix
131	Annual inventory (of plow teams?)	Appendix
132	Annual(?) inventory of shipyard workers	This chapter
133	Annual inventory of fishermen	Appendix
134	Monthly inventory of staff	This chapter
135	Annual inventory of agricultural workers	Appendix
136	Monthly inventory of workers	This chapter
137	Inventory of sailors(?)	This chapter
138	Annual inventory of agricultural(?) staff	Appendix
139	Annual inventory of agricultural(?) workers	This chapter
140	Annual(?) inventory of agricultural workers	Appendix
141	Monthly(?) inventory of workers(?)	This chapter

---

[372] It is likely that the beginning of (obv.) col. ii, should be reconstructed (ll. 2'–5'): 4(u) la$_2$ ⸢2(diš)$^?$⸣ [. . .] / e$_2$ $^{d?}$ereš-[dingir] / e$_2$ ^{d}ba-[ba$_6$-kam$^?$] / u$_3$ eš$_3$ didli-⸢la$^?$⸣, "*n* workers, (of the) household of the ereš-dingir priestess, (which is the) household of Baba, and the various other households."

[373] BRM 3, 179, is a tablet container holding the inventory tablets (gurum$_2$ ak, see below) for the staff of the palace (the Umma branch), the staff of the governor('s household), and inventory tablets concerning shepherds, cowherds and various other persons (pisan dub-ba / gurum$_2$ ak / giri$_3$-se$_3$-ga lugal / giri$_3$-se$_3$-ga⸢ensi$_2$$^?$-ka⸣ / sipa unu$_3$ // u$_3$ erin$_2$ diri lu$_2$ didli zaḫ$_3$ ugula nu-tuku / i$_3$-gal$_2$ / mu⸢si⸣-mu-ru-[um^{ki}] lu-lu-bu a-⸢ra$_2$⸣ [x-kam-aš] ba-⸢ḫul⸣).

[374] For the reading of gurum$_2$(IGI.GAR), see Steinkeller 1982. Steinkeller translates the verb gurum$_2$—ak as "to muster, to inspect," and the nominalised form gurum$_2$ ak(a) as "inspection."

I classify all these texts as inventories, although the technical term here interpreted as "inventory" (gurum$_2$ ak) is only found in the colophon of five texts: Nos. 127, 129, 130, 133, 136 (and possibly 135). The damaged colophon of No. 125 does not seem to permit space for the term. Texts Nos. 128, 131, 132, and 141 do not seem to include it either. The colophons of Nos. 126, 137, 138, and 140 are broken.

It is not clear whether all the persons mentioned in an inventory listing household staff (giri$_3$-se$_3$-ga) should automatically be considered members of a household, or whether mixed inventories existed.

No. 125. *MS 4324 (Umma, ŠS 7 v)*

Text No. 125 is a monthly inventory from Šu-Suen's seventh year, dated to the fifth month. The text lists various persons with their rations. The colophon summarizes all of these persons as the staff of the mill (rev. col. ii 4: [giri$_3$]-se$_3$-ga ša$_3$ e$_2$ kikken-⸢na⸣). Despite its placement as a summary for the entire text, it is difficult to accept that this text listed the staff of only one particular institution. The first section, ending with the last line of obv. col. i, lists in fact the staff of the governor (giri$_3$-se$_3$-ga ensi$_2$). It is possible to speculate that the staff of the mill of the governor was meant here, but that remains tentative. The text is transliterated and translated in full here.

obv. col. i

1.	⸢2(barig)⸣ 4(ban$_2$) še zi$_3$-gu	2 barig, 4 ban$_2$ of barley and gu-flour.
2.	ad-da	(for) Adda.
3.	2(barig) 5(ban$_2$) KA-guru$_7$	2 barig, 5 ban$_2$ (for the) Chief of the Granary,
4.	lu$_2$-^{d}nanna	Lu-Nanna.
5.	[1(barig)][375] 3(ban$_2$) ur-^{d}suen	1 barig, 3 ban$_2$ (for) Ur-Suen.
6.	[1(barig)] 3(ban$_2$) ur-⸢^{d}⸣ašnan	1 barig, 3 ban$_2$ (for) Ur-Ašnan.
7.	x x x[376]	
	(blank line)	
8.	ugula KA-guru$_7$[377]	Overseer: Chief of the Granary.
9.	1(barig) lu$_2$-dingir-ra sagi	1 barig (for) Lu-dingira, cupbearer.
10.	⸢2(ban$_2$)⸣ dumu am$_3$-ni-li$_2$	2 ban$_2$ (for the), child of Amni-ili.
11.	3(ban$_2$) ⸢la⸣-gi-ip	3 ban$_2$ (for) Laqip.
12.	1(barig) ad-da-kal-la	1 barig (for) Adda-kala.
13.	1(barig) da-da-a	1 barig (for) Dadaya.
14.	1(barig) 2(ban$_2$) ba-saga	1 barig, 2 ban$_2$ (for) Basaga.
15.	3(ban$_2$) ur-^{d}šara$_2$	3 ban$_2$ (for) Ur-Šara.
16.	1(barig) lugal-ba-ra-ab-e$_3$	1 barig (for) Lugal-barabe.
17.	1(barig) lu$_2$-^{d}en-lil$_2$-la$_2$	1 barig (for) Lu-Enlila.
18.	1(barig) lu$_2$-^{d}šara$_2$ dumu lugal-ezem	1 barig (for) Lu-Šara, child of Lugal-ezem.
19.	1(barig) ur-e$_2$-gal	1 barig (for) Ur-Egal.
20.	1(barig) 3(ban$_2$) ḫa-da-da	1 barig, 3 ban$_2$ (for) Ḫadada
21.	1(barig) a-ne$_2$	1 barig (for) Ane.
22.	1(barig) ka$_5$-[x]	1 barig (for) Ka-x.
23.	ugula ^{d}šara$_2$-kam dumu na-⸢u$_2$-a⸣	Overseer: Šarakam, child of Na'u'a.
	(blank space with erasure)	
24.	giri$_3$-se$_3$-ga ensi$_2$	Staff of the governor.

[375] This and the following notation are reconstructed using the totals at the bottom of the column.

[376] Erasure? Perhaps originally: ⸢1(barig)$^{?}$ 3(ban$_2$)$^{?}$ u$_3$$^{?}$-ma$^{?}$-ni$^{?}$⸣.

[377] Adda, Lu-Nanna, and Ur-Suen, are all found in the second section of a similar text, OLP 8, 24 21 (from ŠS 4) I 15–17.

bottom edge

1.	4(aš) 1(barig) 5(u)	(computations:) 4 (gur) 1 barig 50 (sila$_3$).

obv. col. ii

1.	⸢4(barig)⸣ gur$_4$-za-an ⸢muḫaldim⸣	4 barig (for) Gurzan, kitchen administrator.
2.	[x] 4(barig) ⸢lugal⸣-sa$_6$-⸢ga⸣	*n*+4 barig (for) Lugal-saga.
3.	2(aš) 3(barig) gur lu$_2$-du$_{10}$-ga dumu lugal-⸢saga⸣	2 gur, 3 barig (for) Lu-duga, child of Lugal-saga.
4.	2(aš) 1(barig) gur x x	2 gur, 1 barig (for) . . .
5.	4(barig) ḪAR-ḪAR-⸢PA⸣ x x	4 barig (for) . . .
6.	2(aš) 2(barig) ⸢gur⸣ gu$^?$-u$_2$-du-du$^?$	2 gur, 2 sila$_3$ (for) Gu'ududu.
7.	4(aš) 2(barig) 3(ban$_2$) gur ur-si-gar	4 gur, 2 barig, 3 ban$_2$ (for) Ur-sigar.
8.	3(aš) 1(barig) 3(ban$_2$) ^{d}šara$_2$-a-mu	3 gur, 1 barig, 3 ban$_2$ (for) Šara-a(ya)mu.
9.	3(aš) 3(ban$_2$) ⸢e$_2$⸣-ur$_2$-⸢bi⸣-du$_{10}$	3 gur, 3 ban$_2$ (for) E-urbidu.
10.	1(aš) 2(barig) 3(ban$_2$) ⸢a-du-du⸣ x-⸢ga⸣	1 gur, 2 barig, 3 ban$_2$ (for) Adudu, the x.
11.	1(barig) lu$_2$-i$_3$-⸢zu⸣ x	1 barig (for) Lu-izu, the . . . .
12.	4(barig) 3(ban$_2$) ma$_2$-gin$_2$	4 barig 3 ban$_2$ (for) the shipbuilder.
13.	⸢2(barig)⸣ 2(ban$_2$) lu$_2$-du$_{10}$-[ga]	2 barig, 2 ban$_2$ (for) Lu-duga.
14.	x ur-am$_3$-ma x [x]	. . . Ur-amma . . .
15.	x 4(barig) 3⸢(ban$_2$)⸣ gudu$_4$ ^{d}⸢nin$^?$⸣-[. . .]	. . . 4 barig 3 ban$_2$ (for) the gudu$_4$-priests of Nin- . . .
16.	x gudu$_4$ ^{d}gu-la	. . . (for) the gudu$_4$-priests of Gula.
17.	x lugal-me-a ugula	. . . (for) Lugal-mea, overseer.
18.	x ab-ba-kal-la	. . . (for) Abba-kala.
19.	x ḫa-ti	. . . (for) Ḫati.
20.	x ^{d}šara$_2$-a-mu	. . . (for) Šara-a(ya)mu.
21.	1(aš) 2(barig) 5(ban$_2$) e$_2$-nig$_2$-⸢lagar⸣	1 gur, 2 barig, 5 ban$_2$ (for) E-niglagar.
22.	3(ban$_2$) nam-tar-eb$_2$-gu-ul	3 ban$_2$ (for) Namtar-ebgul.
23.	2(barig) 3(ban$_2$) ugula a-gu	2 barig, 3 ban$_2$ (for) the overseer Agu.
24.	8(aš) ⸢3(barig)⸣ gur dumu gudu$_4$ ⸢^{d}šara$_2$⸣ umma^{ki}	8 gur, 3 barig (for) the children of the gudu$_4$-priests of Šara of Umma.
25.	⸢1(barig)$^?$⸣ lu$_2$-^{d}nin-ur$_4$-ra ⸢unu$_3$$^?$⸣	1 barig (for) Lu-Ninura, cowherd(?)
	(*blank space*)	

bottom edge

1.	4(u) ⸢1(aš)⸣ 1(barig) 5(u)	(calculations:) 41 (gur) 1 barig 50 (sila$_3$).

rev. col. i

1.	1(barig) lu$_2$-^{d}nin-ur$_4$-ra muhaldim	1 barig (for) Lu-Ninura, kitchen administrator.
2.	⸢1(barig) lu$_2$⸣-mu-ba-zi-ge KAŠ$_4$	1 barig (for) Lumu-bazige, runner.
3.	[x] 3(ban$_2$) lugal-iti-da	. . . 3 ban$_2$ (for) Lugal-itida.
4.	x lugal-iti-da	. . . Lugal-itida.
5.	[x] lu$_2$-du$_{10}$-ga dumu [x]-x-ba$^?$	. . . Lu-duga, child of x-ba.
6.	x x x sagi	. . . cupbearer.
7.	x lugal-e$_2$-maḫ-e x x	. . . (for) Lugal-Emaḫe . . .
8.	[x] ⸢lugal⸣-ḫe$_2$-gal$_2$ mu-SAR	. . . (for) Lugal-ḫegal, mu-SAR worker.

9.	[x] x a-kal-la ašgab	... (for) A(ya)-kala, leather worker.
10.	[x] x lu$_2$-zabala$_3$⸢^{ki} unu$_3$⸣	... (for) Lu-Zabala, cowherd.
11.	x x lu$_2$-du$_{11}$-ga	... (for) Lu-duga.
12.	x šeš-a-ni x [...]	... (for) Šešani ...
	n lines broken	
15'.	3(ban$_2$) x [x] x	3 ban$_2$ (for) ...
16'.	⸢3(ban$_2$)⸣ [x x]-⸢dumu⸣-zi-⸢da⸣ x	3 ban$_2$ (for) ...-Dumuzida
17'.	1(aš) gur ^{d}⸢šara$_2$⸣-a-mu x	1 gur (for) Šara-ayamu ...
18'.	1(aš) ⸢a-kal-la⸣	... (for) A(ya)-kala.
19'.	4(barig) lugal-^{d}x	4 barig (for) Lugal-x.
20'.	1(barig) 3(ban$_2$) x-x-x	1 barig, 3 ban$_2$ (for) ...
21'.	1(barig) 3(ban$_2$) in-sa$_6$-sa$_6$	1 barig, 3 ban$_2$ (for) Insasa
22'.	2(barig) ur-^{d}šul-pa-e$_3$	2 barig (for) Ur-Šulpa'e
23'.	3(ban$_2$) šeš-a-ni gudu$_4$ ^{d}amar-^{d}suen	3 ban$_2$ (for) Šešani, gudu$_4$-priest of Amar-Suen
24'.	2(ban$_2$) du-du x	2 ban$_2$ (for) Dudu
25'.	4(aš) gur	4 gur (for)
26'.	dumu gudu$_4$ KI.AN^{ki}	child of the gudu$_4$-priest of KIAN
27'.	x ur-^{d}nin-x-x	x Ur-Nin-x
28'.	x NI NI x	...

rev. col. ii

1.	x x a sipa x[378]	...
	(*blank space with computations*: 6(aš) x 3(ban$_2$))	
2.	[...] zi$_3$-gu$^?$ [...] ⸢kikken$_2$-na kišib$_3$⸣ lu$_2$-zabala$_3$^{ki}	... gu-flour .... of the mill; sealed tablet of Lu-Zabala.
	(*blank space*)	
3.	[giri$_3$]-se$_3$-ga ša$_3$ e$_2$ kikken-⸢na⸣[379]	Staff of the mill.
4.	[iti] dal	Month: "Flight."
5.	⸢mu⸣ ma-da za-ab-⸢ša⸣-li^{ki} ba-ḫul	Year: "The territory of Zabšali was destroyed."

Although the staff of the governor's household is listed first it is by no means the largest group in this text, nor do its members receive the largest rations. Unfortunately, the end of the text is badly damaged, and although one may suggest that obv. ii and rev. i listed staff of divine households (as opposed to the household of the governor in obv. i), based on the titles of staff of divine households occurring in this section (gudu$_4$), this cannot be confirmed.

The numerical notations recorded at the bottom of obv. i and ii record the subtotals of barley and gu-flour distributed in that column. The notations are a mixture of positional notations and notations in the traditional capacity system, indicating a transition in mathematical practices between the third and the second millennium BC, when positional notations came to dominate.[380] The numerical notations in the body of the text are entirely in the capacity system, but with the frequent omission of the gur sign in notations of one or more gur.

Total of the disbursements of barley and gu-flour in col. i of the obverse:[381]

---

[378] Line erased?

[379] Alternatively to be read e$_2$ kikken ⸢sumun⸣, and translated "the old mill."

[380] Ouyang and Proust *forthcoming*.

[381] Reconstructing 1(barig) in each of the damaged notations in obv. i 5 and 6.

4(aš) 1(barig) 4(ban$_2$) gur

Subtotal listed at the bottom of col. i:

4(aš) 1(diš) 5(u)

Approximate total of barley and gu-flour in col. ii of the obverse:[382]

4(u) 4(aš) 1(barig) 4(ban$_2$) gur

Subtotal listed at the bottom of col. ii:

4(u) +4(aš) 1(barig) 5(u)

The amounts of barley and gu-flour listed in text No. 125 most likely correspond to monthly rations given to the staff of the mill. Some of these rations appear to be rather generous, others appear to conform rather well with what would be expected for regular dependent workers in a flour mill.[383]

No. 126. *MS 1884 (Umma, X–xii)*

Similar to text No. 125, the inventory No. 126 lists barley rations for individuals. Whereas No. 125 covers one month, No. 126 covers one year, and whereas No. 125 is an inventory of the staff (giri$_3$-se$_3$-ga) of a mill, No. 126 lists rations for numerous groups of dedicatees (a-ru-a). Perhaps unrelated to the different types of staff listed in the two texts, the rations found in No. 126 are considerably smaller than those found in No. 125. Males, females, and children are listed in No. 126.

Table 2. Groups of dedicatees listed in text No. 126

Groups of dedicatees	No. 126	Cf. No. 140
a-ru-a ARAD$_2$ KA-guru$_7$-me	obv. ii 6'	
a-ru-a lu$_2$-dingir-ra-me	obv. ii 9'[384]	
[a-ru-a ur-^{geš}]⸢gigir⸣ nu-banda$_3$ gu$_4$	obv. iii 14'	
a-ru-a pa$_4$-a-nim	obv. iv 8	
a-ru-a inim-ma-ni-zi	obv. iv 18	
a-ru-a ur-^{d}a-šar$_2$	obv. iv 20	
a-ru-a ku-za-an	obv. iv 22	
⸢a-ru⸣-a ARAD$_2$-dam	obv. iv 27	
⸢a-ru-a⸣ ur-^{d}nun-gal	obv. iv 29	
⸢a-ru⸣-[a] edin$^{?}$-la	obv. iv 31	
a-ru-a ur$_2$-mes$^{?}$-ni	obv. v 37	obv. ii 15'(?)
a-ru-a ur-gu$_2$-de$_3$-na	obv. v 39	obv. ii 16'
a-ru-a ur-^{geš}gigir	obv. v 41	obv. ii 18
a-ru-a lugal-geš-ḫur-e	obv. v 43	obv. ii 21'
a-ru-a lugal-TAR	obv. v 45	obv. ii 23'
a-ru-a ukken-ne$_2$	obv. vi 22	rev. i 17
a-ru-a ^{d}šara$_2$ a-pi$_4$-sal$_4$^{ki}	rev. i 27	
a-⸢ru-a⸣ ur-x	rev. ii 37	
⸢a-ru-a⸣ nam-ḫa-ni	rev. iv 21	
⸢a-ru-a⸣ ur-nigar$^{<gar>}$	rev. v 32	

---

382 Without adding anything for col. ii 16.

383 See Englund 2012b for worker-compensation rates during the Ur III period.

384 Further specified as "of the weavers from Ur-Nintu" (ša$_3$ uš-bar ki ur-^{d}nin-tu).

Both the beginning and, more crucially, the end of text No. 126 are missing, and the invaluable information usually found in the colophons of such texts is therefore not available. What remains is a very long list of persons and their monthly rations. The text is therefore dealt with here only in excerpts; a full transliteration is given in the Appendix.

The text is divided into sub-sections according to barley rations allotted each month, rather than according to the different groups of dedicatees (a-ru-a). This is indicated by a blank line followed by a total of the barley given in rations in that month, followed by the month name. The fact that the same groups are not listed each month highlights our failure to understand the intricacies of the Ur III labour systems. The first month found in the text is month five in the Umma calendar (iti dal), but given the broken first and second columns there is good reason to expect the text to have begun with month one (iti še sag/sag$_{11}$-ku$_5$). The last month present is the twelfth month (iti ^{d}dumu-zi). The break on the reverse leaves no room for any additional section for an intercalated month.

In this text, dedicatees (a-ru-a) were assigned to, or by, both individuals and institutions. Six of the groups found in No. 126 are also found in No. 140 (Table 2).

None of these groups can be traced in other documents, and it is possible that membership of a group of dedicatees (a-ru-a) was a fleeting duty. This is partially supported by the first of the two examples from text No. 126 given below. The term sag-dub-ba in obv. iv 12–17 is well attested, and although consensus exists that it denoted (female) workers recorded as full-time output, the meaning and etymology are contested.[385]

Examples of two groups of dedicatees in text No. 126 are the following:

obv. col. iv

9.	4(ban$_2$) 5(diš) ba-an-sa$_6$	4 ban$_2$, 5 (units of . . .) (for) Bansa,
10.	ša$_3$ en-nun	in the "prison,"
11.	ša$_3$ umma^{ki}	within Umma.
12.	1(ban$_2$) ama-nig$_2$-du$_{10}$ šu-gi$_4$-ta sag-dub-ba-še$_3$	1 ban$_2$ (for) Ama-nigdu, from the (register of the) old (people) to the (register of) slaves(?).
13.	1(ban$_2$) nin-ḫe$_2$-gal$_2$ dumu ama-kal-la sag-dub-ba-še$_3$	1 ban$_2$ (for) Nin-ḫegal, child[386] of Ama-kala, to the (register of) slaves.
14.	1(ban$_2$) ḫa-ma-ti sag-dub-ba-še$_3$	1 ban$_2$ (for) Ḫamati, to the (register of) slaves.
15.	1(ban$_2$) dingir-mu-da sag-dub-ba-še$_3$	1 ban$_2$ (for) Dingirmuda, to the (register of) slaves.
16.	1(ban$_2$) nig$_2$-ka sag-dub-ba-še$_3$	1 ban$_2$ (for) Nigka, to the (register of) slaves.
17.	1(ban$_2$) geme$_2$-^{d}a-šar$_2$ sag-dub-ba-še$_3$	1 ban$_2$ (for) Geme-Ašar, to the (register of) slaves.
18.	a-ru-a inim-ma-ni-zi	Dedicatees of Inimani-zi.

obv. col. v

46.	1(ban$_2$) ^{geš}apin-du$_{10}$[387]	1 ban$_2$ (for) Apin-du,
47.	še-ba-e daḫ-ḫa	added to the rations (lists?).
48.	2(ban$_2$) ur-e$_2$-maḫ	2 ban$_2$ (for) Ur-Emaḫ.

---

[385] See Yoshikawa 1985: 191–92 for an overview of the discussion until 1985, centering on an interpretation, "(of) the head of the tablet." But note Heimpel 2009: 85 and n. 50 comparing the terms sag-dub and sag-tag, and interpreting the former "head heaper." Both agree that sag-dub denoted full-output workers. Note further that the genitive (-ba) is expressed in our text (*pace* Heimpel 2009: 85 n. 50). See also n. 83, above, and Gelb 1973 for a general overview of prisoners of war in early Mesopotamia.

[386] Note that dumu is used about both male and female children, here a female child, and therefore translated "child" throughout this study.

[387] Note a ^{geš}apin-du$_{10}$ in the unpublished text USC 6703 (Umma, Š 41), assigned to Šara of Apisal and described as a dedicatee of šu/e-gu-bi.

49. dumu ša$_3$-[ku$_3$]-⸢ge⸣	Child: Ša-kuge.
50. dumu ur-^{d}da-ni	Child: Ur-Dani.
51. ⸢2(ban$_2$) lugal⸣-nesag-e	2 ban$_2$ (for) Lugal-nesage.

obv. col. vi

1. dumu ur-li dumu igi-mu	Child: Ur-li; child: Igimu.
2. 3(ban$_2$) ur-saga	3 ban$_2$ (for) Ur-saga.
3. 3(ban$_2$) giri$_3$-ni-i$_3$-sa$_6$	3 ban$_2$ (for) Girini-isa.
4. dumu ḫu-ti gab$_2$-ra-me	Descendants of Ḫuti, the cowherd.[388]
5. ki a-tu-ta	From Atu.[389]
6. 3(ban$_2$) ur-^{d}šul-pa-e$_3$	3 ban$_2$ (for) Ur-Šulpa'e.
7. 1(ban$_2$) 5(diš) na-ka$_5$-la	1 ban$_2$, 5 (units of . . .) (for) Nakala.
8. dumu e$_2$-e-a-na-ab-ba[390]	Child: Ee-anabba.
9. 3(ban$_2$) lu$_2$-^{d}nin-ur$_4$-ra	3 ban$_2$ (for) Lu-Nin-ura,
10. dumu šeš-kal-la kur-ga$_2$-ra	child of Šeš-kala the kurgara.[391]
11. ki lugal-ma$_2$-gur$_8$-re ugula-ta	From Lugal-magure, overseer.
12. 4(ban$_2$) lu$_2$-^{d}a-zi-a	4 ban$_2$ (for) Lu-Azia.
13. 4(ban$_2$) šeš-kal-la	4 ban$_2$ (for) Šeš-kala.
14. dumu a-ba-zi KWU79-me	They are the children of Abazi the x.[392]
15. gurum$_2$-e tak$_4$-a	(Their rations are) set aside for the sustenance.
16. 3(ban$_2$) lu$_2$-eb-gal	3 ban$_2$ (for) Lu-Ebgal.
17. dumu iri-bar-re i$_3$-du$_8$	Child: Iribarre, doorkeeper.
18. 3(ban$_2$) ur-^{d}šul-pa-e$_3$	3 ban$_2$ (for) Ur-Šulpa'e.
19. 3(ban$_2$) ur-^{d}a-šar$_2$ dumu lugal-a$_2$-zi-da ba-uš$_2$	3 ban$_2$ (for) Ur-Ašar, child of Lugal-azida, dead.
20. ki lu$_2$-^{d}ezem-ta	From Lu-Ezem.
21. 4(ban$_2$) lugal-si-sa$_2$	4 ban$_2$ (for) Lugal-lagabdi.
22. a-ru-a ukken-ne$_2$	Dedicatees of Ukkene.

This second group, the dedicatees of Ukkene, is also found with only minor changes in No. 140 obv. iii 14'–rev. i 17.

The next eight worker inventories list prebend fields and other allotments for members of both household staff (giri$_3$-se$_3$-ga) (Nos. 127, 129, 134, 138, and perhaps 140?) and groups of dedicatees (a-ru-a) (Nos. 128, 130–33, and 135). The persons are mostly recorded in small groups that often are specifically identified as based on familial relationships. Text No. 126 is transliterated in full in the Appendix.

No. 127. *MS 4705 (Umma, AS 5–vii–15)*

According to its colophon, the very damaged text No. 127 is an inventory of fishermen of a certain kind based at the settlement Apisal (rev. iii 1: gurum$_2$-ak šu-ku$_6$ ba$^{?}$-KA$^{?}$-me ša a-pi$_4$-sal$_4$^{ki}), dated to Amar-Suen year 5 (mu en-unu$_6$-gal ^{d}inanna ba-ḫun), month 7, passing of the day 15 (iti min-eš$_3$-ta ⸢u$_4$⸣ 1(u) 5(diš)-am$_3$ ba-ra-zal-la-ta). A line follows the date formula, but it is illegible.

---

[388] For more on the children of Ḫuti, see discussion of text No. 140.

[389] Note that Atu is well known as the chief cattle-administrator in Umma (see Englund 1995 and Stepien 1996: 55–58).

[390] For e$_2$-e-a-na-ba, see ASJ 9, 268 74 from Drehem and ASJ 18, 77 10 from Umma. A person named e$_2$-e-a-na-ba-ak is attested in two texts from Ur (UET 3, 1118 and 1150), and a person named e$_2$-e-na-ba-du$_{11}$ is found in one text from Girsu (ITT 2, 1010 + 5, 6848).

[391] A title of staff associated with the cult of Inanna: see now Peled 2014, with literature.

[392] Abazi is found with the same title(?) in text No. 140 rev. i 4, 8. A person Abazi is not otherwise attested.

Most of the workers recorded in text No. 127 seem to be associated with one of four extant groups of staff (giri$_3$-se$_3$-ga):

⌜giri$_3$⌝-[se$_3$-ga . . .] (obv. ii 10')
giri$_3$-se$_3$-ga x-[x] (obv. iii 24')
giri$_3$-se$_3$-ga ^{d}amar-^{d}suen-me (rev. i 3)
giri$_3$-se$_3$-ga ^{d}⌜gu⌝-[la] (rev. i 24)

A final group is associated with the messenger-service station (e$_2$ kas$_4$, translated "Reisestation" by Sallaberger 1993: 277 ff.) at Apisal:

e$_2$ kas$_4$ a-pi$_4$-sal$_4$^{ki} (rev. ii 14)

This last group, consisting of ten persons including two old people, is not classified as staff. In TCL 5, 6038, where a comparable group is found (rev. iii 17–29), it is, however, classified as staff (giri$_3$-se$_3$-ga). Unsurprisingly, the two groups are not identical: not only are the two texts separated by more than ten years, but where TCL 5, 6038 lists primarily worker capacity (1(diš) or ½(diš)) and occasionally barley rations, text No. 127 lists classification and allotments.

The section listing the staff of the messenger-service station in each text is given here, starting with No. 127:

No. 127 rev. col. ii

1.	½(aš$_c$) GAN$_2$ nimgir-an-ne$_2$ baḫar$_3$	½ (receiving unit of) field, Nimgir-anne, potter.
2.	1(aš) ⌜lugal⌝-nesag-e	1 (receiving unit of . . .) Lugal-nesage.
3.	1(diš) ^{d}šara$_2$-mu-tum$_2$	1 Šara-mutum.
4.	dumu lugal-^{geš}gigir-re baḫar$_3$-me	They are children of Lugal-gigire, potter.
5.	ki lu$_2$-dingir-ra ugula-ta	From Lu-Dingira, overseer.
6.	šu za-ga-gi-na	Old, Zagagina.
7.	1(aš$_c$) 1(barig) 4(diš) ug$_3$ ur-mes dumu-ni <<mu>> u$_2$-IL$_2$	1 (receiving unit of field?) 1 barig, 4 (units of . . .), carrier, Ur-mes, his son, fuel carrier(?).
8.	šu ug$_3$ lugal-bad$_3$	Old, carrier, Lugal-bad.
9.	1(aš$_c$) GAN$_2$ ug$_3$ šeš-kal-la lunga	1 (receiving unit of) field, carrier, Šeš-kala, fuller.
10.	1(aš) lu$_2$-^{d}šul-gi-ra	1 (receiving unit of . . .) Lu-Šulgira.
11.	1(diš) ur-^{d}suen	1 Ur-Suen.
12.	1(diš) lugal-amar-ku$_3$	1 Lugal-amar-ku.
13.	dumu lugal-bad$_3$-me	They are children of Lugal-bad.
14.	e$_2$ kas$_4$ a-pi$_4$-sal$_4$^{ki}	(Staff of) the station of Apisal.

TCL 5, 6038 (Umma, ŠS 7)

rev. col. iii

17.	1(diš) ur-e$_{11}$-e	1 Ur-E'e.
18.	1(diš) a-ab-ba	1 Ayabba.
19.	1(diš) lu$_2$-saga dumu gu$_3$-de$_2$-a	1 Lu-saga, child of Gudea.
20.	1(diš) er$_3$-mu gu-za-la$_2$	1 Ermu, "throne-bearer."
21.	2(diš) lugal-inim-gi-na	2[393] Lugal-inimgina.
22.	1(diš)$^?$ ur-mes dumu za-ga-gi-na	1 Ur-mes, child of Zagigina.

[393] The 2(diš) sign is clear on the tablet. This perhaps suggests that the people listed in this and similar texts are not the ones doing the service but rather the ones delivering workers.

23.	1(diš) nimgir-an-ne$_2$ baḫar$_3$	1 Nimgir-Anne, potter.
24.	1(diš) lugal-nesag-e <<NI>>[394]	1 Lugal-nesage.
25.	1(diš) ^{d}šara$_2$-mu-tum$_2$ dumu-ni-me	1 Šara-mutum, they are his children.
26.	1(diš) šeš-kal-la dumu lugal-bad$_3$	1 Šeš-kala, child of Lugal-bad.
27.	⌜1(diš) ^{d}utu$^{?}$⌝-saga dumu ur-^{d}suen šu-ku$_6$	1 Utu(?)-saga, child of Ur-Suen, fisherman.
28.	½(diš) ^{d}nin-ur$_4$-ra-da dumu šeš-a-ni u$_2$-IL$_2$	½ Nin-Urada, child of Šešani, fuel-carrier(?).
	(*blank space*)	
29.	giri$_3$-se$_3$-ga e$_2$ kas$_4$ a-pi$_4$-sal$_4$^{ki}-me	Staff of the station of Apisal.

Whereas No. 127 is an inventory of fishermen, TCL 5, 6038 includes fishermen (rev. ii 39), but is summarized as a (roster) of troops (erin$_2$) levied (e$_3$-e$_3$) for the *bala* (obligation), (from) within Apisal.

In this text, and in the following inventories, a highly idiosyncratic shorthand is used to indicate the rations and allotments given to the different categories of staff.[395]

Four different allowances can be listed: (a) land allotments, (b) barley rations, (c) textile rations, and very occasionally, and in none of the texts here, (d) rations of fish and other foodstuff; it is not always clear which kind of ration is meant. A shorthand is used throughout these texts.

In texts that include land allotments, the following order is usually adhered to:

Fields (usually 1 (aš$_c$) or ½(aš$_c$) GAN$_2$); barley (*n* gur *n* barig *n* ban$_2$ *n* sila$_3$ (še)); textiles ((*n*) tug$_2$); name of recipient (PN often with familial affiliation).

Steinkeller classed the workers according to which prefix was used, as well as some other indicators (his classes A–N, Steinkeller 1987b). Following Steinkeller (1987b) most workers in the inventories published here would belong to his classes L–N. Steinkeller's suggestion that the classifiers (his A–N) were not directly related to actual allotments of fields or foodstuff seems to presuppose a too advanced system of abstraction.

In a recent article J. N. Reid (2019) publishes an Ur III inventory (SM A.1907.690.65+) where commodities listed in the same way as in for example No. 126 are summarized as ma-na of wool, and where the distribution recorded simply as tug$_2$ (textile) in for example No. 134 and other texts is summarised as a count of textiles. Although that new text makes it almost certain that also the notations without qualifiers in the inventories published here represent amounts of wool, a certain ambiguity in a few instances where two different unqualified counts are listed, has made me hesitate explicitly stating this.

In text No. 135, notations are sometimes written below the line at the place where they were intended, suggesting that the scribe made multiple errors and later corrected them.

Finally, staff not receiving anything are also found in many inventories. Various designations are used for these. Most common are šu and zaḫ$_3$. By comparing the entries of the main body of certain texts and the summaries, it can be shown conclusively that šu is shorthand for šu-gi$_4$, "old" (see text No. 132). Staff who had run away are often listed in these inventories, presumably in the hope of their immanent return (but see No. 140). Usually, the term zaḫ$_3$, "fled," is added after the name of a fugitive worker, but it can also precede it.

The curvilinear numerical notation preceding GAN$_2$ (either 1 (aš$_c$) or ½ (aš$_c$), the latter essentially aš$_c$-*tenû* with an aš going through it), occasionally interchanges with a regular notation (aš) and may indicate the size of the field allotment, or it may simply indicate the category of the worker recorded in that entry. Usually, the head of a group is indicated with 1 (aš$_c$), occasionally with 1 (aš), and in fewer instances with ½ (aš$_c$). Sometimes other members of a group are also indicated in this way, but are mostly simply prefixed with a 1 (diš) sign. In many texts, including No. 127, the head of the group is recorded as belonging to the class of carriers (ug$_3$) as well. The size of the GAN$_2$ allotments cannot be estimated from any of the texts published here.

394 The NI sign is possibly erased.

395 See above all Steinkeller 1987b: 78–80. We saw this already in No. 126, where staff was allotted barley and another commodity. Although this is almost certainly wool and/or textiles, see also Reid 2019; I hesitate to state that here without further evidence.

In both text No. 127 and most of the remaining inventories, small family units are listed together. Usually, the father is listed first, followed by one of more of his sons. Whereas the sons are usually recorded with 1 (diš) (Steinekller's class E), the father is mostly recorded with 1 (aš$_c$), presumably indicating that he was an allotment holder (sometimes indicated by adding a GAN$_2$ sign) (Steinkeller's class A or B). In text No. 127 rev. i 12–17, one such group is listed. Here, the first person, Ur-Nigar, counted with 1 (aš$_c$), was presumably the father of the three persons counted with 1 (diš). The person listed immediately after Ur-Nigar, Lugalnesage, counted with 1 (aš) (*not* curvilinear), may be the brother of Ur-Nigar or a similarly higher-ranking member of the group (Steinkeller's class B).

No. 127 rev. col. i

12.	1(aš$_c$) ur-nigar^{gar}	1 (receiving unit of . . .) Ur-Nigar.
13.	1(aš) lugal-nesag-e	1 (receiving unit of . . .) Lugal-nesage.
14.	1(diš) šeš-kal-la	1 Šeš-kala.
15.	1(diš) lugal-⸢ḫe$_2$-gal$_2$⸣	1 Lugal-ḫegal.
16.	1(diš) lu$_2$-^{d}nin-ur$_4$-ra	1 Lu-Nin-ura.
17.	dumu-ni-me	They are his children.

As seen in the example of the staff of the station in Apisal, even when old and presumably retired from a work-crew to which they could no longer contribute, the father and head of a unit can still be listed at the head of the group.

Text No. 127 is transliterated in full in the Appendix.

No. 128. *MS 2369 (Umma, AS 6)*

Text No. 128, a six-column tablet from Amar-Suen's sixth year, lists the allotments and rations for more than one hundred cowherds supervised by the well-known chief cattle-administrator (šuš$_3$), Atu.[396] The seal of Atu is rolled across the tablet twice(?) on each side.

No. 128 seal (S001829)

1.	a-tu	Atu,
2.	dub-sar	scribe,
3.	dumu šeš-kal-la	child of Šeš-kala.

Most of the staff in text No. 128 are also found in No. 31, an account of plow(?) oxen from Šu-Suen's fourth year. In fact, the list of cowherds and cowhands in these two texts are well known and first discussed in detail by Stepien 1996: 56 ff.

As in the previous text, No. 127, the staff found in No. 128 are organized in small groups, primarily made up of members of the same family. For example the group of Ur-Suda:

No. 128 obv. col. iii

9.	1(aš$_c$) GAN$_2$ ur-^{d}su$_4$-da unu$_3$	1 (receiving unit of) field, Ur-Suda, cowherd.
10.	1(diš) ur-gu$_2$-de$_3$-na	1 Ur-Gudena.
11.	1(diš) inim-^{d}šara$_2$	1 Inim-Šara.
12.	dumu-ni-me	They are his children.

Towards the end of the text we find a number of cowherds and cowhands who are not necessarily organized according to family groups. For example the group seized by Addada:

[396] Not to be confused with a-tu child of ur-e$_2$-an-na in JCS 35, 202 4, or the chief cattle-administrator (šuš$_3$) by the name a-tu found in three Girsu texts (MVN 6, 569; Nisaba 13, 35; and SAT 1, 187).

No. 128 rev. col. i

36.	1(aš$_c$) GAN$_2$ ⸢ad⸣-da-da	1 (receiving unit of) field, Addada.
37.	⸢1(diš)$^?$⸣ giri$_3$-ni-i$_3$-sa$_6$ dumu-ni	1 Girini-isa, his child.
38.	⸢1(aš$_c$)⸣ GAN$_2$ ug$_3$ ur-ge$_6$-par$_4$ x	1 (receiving unit of) field, carrier, Ur-Gepar x.
39.	⸢1(aš$_c$)⸣ GAN$_2$ ug$_3$ lu$_2$-bala-saga	1 (receiving unit of) field, carrier, Lu-bala-saga.
40.	1(aš$_c$) GAN$_2$ ug$_3$ ARAD$_2$-ḫu-la	1 (receiving unit of) field, carrier, ARAD-ḫula.
41.	⸢ad⸣-da-da i$_3$-dab$_5$	Addada seized.

In addition to sealing the text, and being listed in the colophon as responsible for the entire group of cowherds and cowhands found here, Atu is also listed as the first recipient of a land-allotment in the very first section of the text, given below. In the first line of the text he is given the title "chief cattle-administrator, cows" (šuš$_3$ ab$_2$). The next three persons are described as his children (dumu-ni-me). The first of these, Duga-zida, is well known in this capacity,[397] but the next two, Ur-Emaḫ and Šara-galzu are not. Atu's family group is followed by another group, headed by a certain Nabasa, described as "his brother" (šeš-a-ni). In texts Nos. 130 and 131 the second group-leader is referred to with the term šeš-tab-ba (lit. "double brother"), usually translated as "assistant." Quite often such assistants were younger brothers of the group leader himself. Nabasa is not otherwise attested as a brother of Atu. Following this second group, it is stated that the chief cattle-administrator (šuš$_3$), in this case surely Atu, seized (control over them) from the shepherds.

No. 128 obv. col. i

1.	1(aš$_c$) GAN$_2$ a-tu šuš$_3$ ab$_2$	1 (receiving unit of) field Atu, chief cattle-administrator of cows.
2.	1(aš) du$_{11}$-ga-zi-da	1 (receiving unit of . . .) Duga-zida.
3.	1(diš) ur-e$_2$-maḫ	1 Ur-Emaḫ(e).
4.	1(diš) ^{d}šara$_2$-gal-⸢zu$^?$⸣	1 Šara-galzu.
5.	dumu-ni-me	They are his children.
6.	1(aš) na-ba-sa$_6$ šeš-a-ni	1 (receiving unit of . . .) Nabasa, his brother.
7.	1(aš) GAN$_2$$^?$ ur-mes aga$_3$-us$_2$	1 (receiving unit of) field, Ur-mes, soldier.
8.	1(diš) ur-^{d}ur$_3$-bar-tab dumu-ni	1 Ur-Urbartab, his child.
9.	⸢1(aš) GAN$_2$⸣ lugal-ku$_3$-ga-ni dumu inim-^{d}šara$_2$	1 (receiving unit of) field Lugal-kugani, son of Inim-Šara.
10.	sipa-ta	From the shepherds,
11.	šuš$_3$ i$_3$-dab$_5$	the chief cattle-administrator seized.

Atu was responsible for the cattle of the household of Šara in the district of Apisal (Dahl 2007: 100), and this text reflects this. The laconic colophon states:

No. 128 rev. col. iii

	(*blank space with seal impression*)	
1.	unu$_3$ gab$_2$-ra-me	Cowherds and cattle herders.[398]
2.	ugula a-tu	Overseer: Atu.
3.	ša$_3$ a-pi$_4$-sal$_4$^{ki}	In Apisal.
	(*blank space*)	
4.	mu ku$_3$-gu-za ^{d}en-lil$_2$-la$_2$ ba-dim$_2$	Year: "The shiny throne of Enlil was fashioned."
	(*blank space with seal impression*)	

---

[397] See OrSP 47–49, 232.

[398] See Selz 1993a.

The title given to Atu in the colophon, u g u l a, is here used as a descriptive title, probably best translated "overseer." In the text itself Atu was recorded as "chief cattle-administrator (of cows)," š u š$_3$ (a b$_2$), a title he also bears in other texts, including the seal of his son.

Not all the cowherds listed in the text receive allotments: several are recorded as "old," and one as "dead" (rev. i 24: ⌜u š$_2$⌝ l u$_5$-l u$_5$). Others, mostly the junior members of family groups, are not recorded with land allotments but simply listed at the end of the groups (as seen in the example quoted above).

The text is transliterated in full in the Appendix.

No. 129. *MS 1883 (Umma, AS 5)*

According to its very damaged colophon, text No. 129 is an inventory of goatherds and cowherds belonging to the main households of Zabala(?)[399] and Apisal in the Umma province.

No. 129 rev. col. viii

	(blank space)	
1.	⌜gurum$_2$ ak sipa ud$_5$ unu$_3$-de$_3$-ne⌝	Inventory of goatherds and cowherds,
2.	[e$_2$] ⌜^{d}šara$_2$⌝	of the household of Šara,
3.	[e$_2$] ⌜^{d}nin-ur$_4$⌝-[ra e$_2$] ⌜^{d}šul-gi⌝-[ra]	the household of Nin-ura, the household of Šulgi,
4.	[u$_3$$^{?}$ e$_2$] ⌜^{d}inanna$^{?}$⌝	and the household of Inanna.
5.	[ša$_3$] ⌜zabala$_3$$^{?ki}$⌝	In Zabala(?)
6.	[u$_3$] ⌜a-pi$_4$-sal$_4$^{ki}⌝	and Apisal.
	(blank space)	
7.	⌜mu⌝ en-unu$_6$-[gal] ⌜en⌝ ^{d}inanna ba-[ḫun]	Year: "Enunugal the En-priest of Inanna was installed."

This reconstruction leaves no room for the name of the responsible person. At first this may seem unlikely, but the same situation can be observed in the account MVN 13, 618 (Umma, AS 7):

MVN 13, 618 rev. col. vi'

10'.	nig$_2$-ka$_9$ ak ⌜sipa⌝ udu udu eme-gi-ra-ke$_4$-ne	Account concerning the shepherds of native sheep,
11'.	e$_2$ ^{d}šara$_2$	of the household of Šara,
12'.	e$_2$ ^{d}nin-ur$_4$-ra	the household of Nin-ura,
13'.	e$_2$ ^{d}šul-gi-ra	the household of Šulgi,
14'.	e$_2$ ^{d}inanna	the household of Inanna,
15'.	u$_3$ e$_2$ ^{d}gu-la	and the household of Gula.
16'.	mu ḫu-uḫ$_2$-nu-ri^{ki} ba-ḫul	Year: "Ḫuḫnuri was destroyed."

The following divine households are preserved in the body of text No. 129:

Household of Šara (e$_2$ ^{d}š a r a$_2$; obv. vii 9)
Household of Nin-ura(?) (e$_2$ ^{d}⌜n i n⌝-[u r$_4$-r a]; rev. iv 31')
Household of Šulgi (e$_2$ ^{d}š u l-g i; rev. v 12)
Household of Nin-ḫili-suga (e$_2$ ^{d}⌜n i n⌝-[ḫ i] -l i$^{?}$-[s u$_3$]-g a$^{?}$; rev. vi 33')

The extant divine households therefore agree well with the list found in MVN 13, 618, and reconstructed in the colophon of No. 129, except for the final one which seems to give the name of an otherwise unknown

---

399 The reconstruction of z a b a l a$_3$ in rev. viii 5 is not entirely certain from the preserved signs, but strongly indicated from the context.

god, Nin-ḫili-suga(?). This final divine household included two distinct groups, "shepherds and sheep-drovers" (sipa udu-lah$_5$-me; rev. vi 8'); and "administrators of sheep" (šar$_2$-ra-ab-du udu-me; rev. vi 15').

As we shall see below, the final units are not associated with any divine households.

Unfortunately, the first column of the text is almost entirely missing, and with it presumably also the information concerning the most important units in the inventory. From the remaining, better-preserved, sections of the text it is clear that it follows the structure of the inventory of Atu (No. 128).

The first well-preserved units appear at the beginning of col. iii of the obverse.

No. 129 obv. col. iii

2.	1(aš$_c$) GAN$_2$ lugal-ezem unu$_3$	1 (receiving unit of) field, Lugal-ezem, cowherd.
3.	1(aš) ^{d}šara$_2$-i$_3$-zu	1 (receiving unit of . . .) Šara-izu.
4.	1(diš) lu$_2$-dingir-ra	1 Lu-Dingira,
5.	dumu ur-^{d}ma-mi-⸢me⸣	they are the children of Ur-Mami.
6.	1(aš$_c$) GAN$_2$ ug$_3$ ur-^{d}ur$_3$-bar-tab	1 (receiving unit of) field, carrier, Ur-Urbartab.
7.	ur-dingir-ra dumu šeš-kal-la	Ur-Dingira, child of Šeš-kala,
8.	lu$_2$-^{d}da-mu ugula i$_3$-dab$_5$	Lu-Damu, overseer, seized.
9.	1(aš$_c$) GAN$_2$ ug$_3$ lugal-si-x	1 (receiving unit of) field, carrier, Lugal-si-x.
10.	1(diš) lugal-nig$_2$-lagar-e dumu-ni	1 Lugal-niglagare, his child.
11.	1(aš$_c$) GAN$_2$ ug$_3$ gu-u$_2$-gu	1 (receiving unit of) field, carrier, Gu'ugu,
12.	dumu lugal-ma$_2$-gur$_8$-re	child of Lugal-magure.
13.	ki ur-ama-na unu$_3$-ta	From Ur-amana, cowherd.
	(*blank space with computations*: 5(u) 8(diš))	(computations:) "58"
14.	lugal-ezem i$_3$-dab$_5$	Lugal-ezem seized.

The scribe who wrote No. 129 added computations in sexagesimal notations, with regular intervals.[400] Due to the damaged nature of the beginning of the text it is impossible to understand what the notation "58" in the blank space between obv. iii 13 and 14 may refer to. Computations are also found immediately after the next unit:

No. 129 obv. col. iii

15.	1(aš$_c$) GAN$_2$ ^{d}šara$_2$-a-mu unu$_3$	1 (receiving unit of) field, Šara-a(ya)mu, cowherd.
16.	1(aš$_c$) GAN$_2$ ab-ba-gi-na	1 (receiving unit of) field, Abba-gina.
17.	1(aš) ur-^{d}suen	1 (receiving unit of . . .) Ur-Suen,
18.	dumu ARAD$_2$-dam-⸢me⸣	they are the children of ARADdam.
19.	1(aš$_c$) GAN$_2$ ug$_3$ ^{d}šara$_2$-i$_3$-sa$_6$	1 (receiving unit of) field, carrier, Šara-isa.
20.	u$_2$-IL$_2$ ^{d}šara$_2$ a-pi$_4$-sal$_4$^{ki}-ta	From the fuel carriers of Šara of Apisal.
21.	1(aš$_c$) GAN$_2$ ug$_3$ lugal-ga$_2$-na-na	1 (receiving unit of) field, carrier, Lugal-ganana.
22.	a-ru-a ama-lal$_3$-ab-zu	Dedicatee(s) of Amalal-Abzu-unu.
	(*blank space with computations:* 1(geš$_2$) 3(u) 2(diš)	(computations:) "92"
23.	^{d}šara$_2$-a-mu i$_3$-dab$_5$	Šara-a(ya)mu seized.

It is unfortunately not clear how the scribe got from "58" in the space between obv. iii 13 and 14 to "92" in the space between obv. iii 22 and 23. The difference is thirty-four, a number which is difficult to reconcile with the information in the preceding entry.

---

400 Following Proust and Ouyang *forthcoming*, these notations were not intended by the scribe to be positional notations, as indicated by the use of geš'u in some instances.

Following the staff of the divine households (until rev. v 12), a number of additional staff are listed. These are not listed as staff of divine households, rather the first group is listed as the staff of the "steer-house" (rev. vii 7'), and the second group is simply described as "swineherds" (rev. vii 16'). Both sections are very damaged.

No. 129 rev. col. vii

	(start broken)	[. . .].
1'.	1(aš) lugal-gi$^{?}$-na$^{?}$	1 (receiving unit of . . .) Lugal-gina.
2'.	dumu ur-^{d}ba-ba$_6$-me	They are children of Ur-Baba.
2'.	½(aš$_c$) GAN$_2$ nig$_2$-lagar-⸢e⸣ dumu ḫu-un-sa$_6$-sa$_6$	½ (receiving unit of) field, Niglagare, child of Ḫunsasa.
3'.	lu$_2$-sar-ta	From Lu-sar.
4'.	½(aš$_c$) GAN$_2$ da-ga	½ (receiving unit of) field, Daga.
5'.	½(aš$_c$) GAN$_2$ ARAD$_2$-mu dumu en-ma-an-gu-ul	½ (receiving unit of) field, ARADmu, child of Enmangul.
6'.	1(aš$_c$) GAN$_2$ ug$_3$ lu$_2$-eb-gal dumu dingir-ba-an ki nig$_2$-du$_7$-pa-e$_3$-ta	1 (receiving unit of) field, carrier, Lu-Ebgal, son of Dingir-ban. From Nig-dupa'e.
	(blank space)	
7'.	giri$_3$-se$_3$-ga e$_2$ amar-ra-ka-me	They are the staff of the steer-house.
8'.	1(aš$_c$) GAN$_2$ ⸢lugal⸣-ḫe$_2$-gal$_2$	1 (receiving unit of) field, Lugal-ḫegal.
9'.	1(aš) ARAD$_2$-[. . .]	1 (receiving unit of . . .) ARAD-x.
10'.	1(diš) ur-x-x-x	1 Ur-x.
11'.	1(diš) ur-am$_3$-ma	1 Ur-amma.
12'.	dumu-ni-me	They are his children.
	(blank space)	
13'.	ki ur-^{d}da-mu ugula-ta	From Ur-Damu, overseer.
14'.	[x] 3(diš) šaḫ$_2$	. . . 3 pigs.
15'.	lugal-ḫe$_2$-[gal$_2$ i$_3$-dab$_5$]	Lugal-ḫegal seized.
16'.	sipa šaḫ$_2$-⸢me⸣	They are swineherds.

The second group appears to include a count of pigs (rev. vii 14'). No animals are recorded anywhere else in the text and this remains unexplained. For a full transliteration of No. 129, see the Appendix.

No. 130. *MS 4739 (Umma, AS 6–xi)*

The structure of text No. 130, a four-column tablet, is similar to the two previous texts, Nos. 128 and 129. According to its colophon it is an inventory of the plow oxen of Lugal-Ištaran. However, the text lists no plow oxen, and it is clear that staff of regular plow-oxen teams are meant, rather than the animals. The roles of the governor (Ur-Lisi), and the two conveyors mentioned with him in the relatively well-preserved colophon, remain obscure.

No. 130 rev. ii

	(blank space)	
1.	gurum$_2$ ak gu$_4$ ^{geš}apin	Inventory of plow oxen (teams).
2.	ugula lugal-^{d}ištaran	Overseer: Lugal-Ištaran.
3.	ur-^{d}li$_9$-si$_4$ ensi$_2$	Ur-Lisi, governor.
4.	⸢giri$_3$ lu$_2$⸣-du$_{10}$-ga dumu lugal-da-da dub-sar u$_3$ lu$_2$-^{d}nanna dub-sar	Conveyors: Lu-duga, child of Lugal-dada, scribe, and Lu-Nanna, scribe.
5.	⸢iti⸣ ezem-me-ki-⸢gal$_2$⸣	Month: "Festival of Mekigal."
6.	⸢mu⸣ ša-aš-⸢ru^{ki}⸣ a-[ra$_2$ x-kam ba]-ḫul	Year: "Šašrum was destroyed for the nth time."

Lugal-Ištaran, mentioned in the colophon, is also listed at the head of the first group: the first and all subsequent groups are organized according to family units. The first few entries are unfortunately damaged, but both the name and the title can be reconstructed, although a break between the name and title remains difficult to explain.

No. 130 obv. col. i

1.	[1(aš$_c$)$^?$ GAN$_2$$^?$] ⸢lugal$^?$⸣-^{d}ištaran [. . .] nu-banda$_3$ gu$_4$	1 (receiving unit of) field, Lugal-Ištaran [x] captain of (plow) oxen.
2.	[x] ur-⸢^{d}⸣[nin]-sun$_2$	1 Ur-Ninsun.
3.	[x] a-x	[1] A-x.
4.	⸢dumu⸣-ni-⸢me⸣	They are his children.
5.	⸢uš$_2$⸣ lugal-KA	Dead: Lugal-KA.
6.	1(aš$_c$) GAN$_2$ lugal-ezem šeš-tab-ba	1 (receiving unit of) field, Lugal-ezem, assistant.
7.	1(aš) ur-^{d}a-šar$_2$	1 (receiving unit of . . .) Ur-Ašar.
8.	⸢1(diš)⸣ lugal-nesag-e	1 Lugal-nesage.
9.	⸢dumu⸣-ni-me	They are his children.
10.	⸢1(aš)⸣ GAN$_2$ lu$_2$-dingir-ra aga$_3$-us$_2$	1 (receiving unit of) field, Lu-Dingira, soldier.
11.	⸢½(aš$_c$)[401]⸣ GAN$_2$ lu$_2$-eb-gal x[402]	½ (receiving unit of) field, Lu-Ebgal.
12.	uš$_2$ ur-mes dumu-ni	Dead: Ur-mes; his child.
13.	⸢nu-banda$_3$⸣-gu$_4$ i$_3$-dab$_5$	The captain of (plow) oxen seized.

The same structure is found in all of the following groups, as for example this unit:

No. 130 obv. col. i

20.	1(aš$_c$) GAN$_2$ ug$_3$ du$_{11}$-ge	1 (receiving unit of) field, carrier, Duge.
21.	1(diš) e$_2$-ḫi-li	1 E-ḫili.
22.	1(diš) nig$_2$-u$_2$-rum	1 Nig-urum.
23.	dumu-ni-me	They are his children.
24.	⸢lugal⸣-iti-da i$_3$-dab$_5$	Lugal-itida seized.

The person seizing the group, Lugal-itida, is almost certainly the cultivator (engar) mentioned at the head of the previous group (obv. i 15).

The text can be divided into seven units, all but one seized by either the cultivator (engar) or the captain of (plow) oxen (nu-banda$_3$ gu$_4$) heading the group. At least three of these units consist of more than one family group. Only four heads of groups are listed with the title cultivator (engar), although it may be reconstructed in one further instance (rev. i 2). All in all, this agrees fairly well with the standard composition of the staff of half of a domain unit (GAN$_2$ gu$_4$). On average, ten domain units, each managed by a cultivator (engar), and each five cultivators being administered by a captain of (plow) oxen (nu-banda$_3$ gu$_4$), made up a domain unit managed by a domain-unit manager (with the title "scribe of ten oxen," dub-sar gu$_4$-1(u)). In reality, of course, the number of cultivators depended on the actual size of the land under the supervision of the domain-unit manager (dub-sar gu$_4$-1(u)) and his two captains of (plow) oxen. Often these groups were extended families with several generations working together.

In text No. 130 the groups are as follows:

---

401 The ½(aš$_c$) sign is broken, and the remains confusing; three horizontal lines seem to cross the aš$_c$-*tenû*, the top one is probably part of the line ruling, the middle and thickest one is probably the aš sign "halving" the aš$_c$-*tenû*, whereas the bottom horizontal line remains unexplained.

402 Followed by an erasure.

Group 1. Lugal-Ištaran, captain of (plow) oxen (nu-banda$_3$ gu$_4$) (obv. i 1–13). This group consists of four subgroups: Lugal-Ištaran and his own two sons (i 2–4); his assistant (šeš-tab-ba) Lugal-ezem and his two sons (i 6–9); Lu-Dingira the soldier (i 10); and Lu-Ebgal and his deceased son (i 11–12). It is unclear whether the dead Lugal-KA (i 5) was still counted as head of the second group. Lugal-Ištaran is well attested as captain of plow oxen, a title he held from Šulgi's last year until Šu-Suen's first year, a period of just over ten years.

Group 2. Lugal-itida, cultivator (engar) (obv. i 15–24), replacing Me-maškim, listed as dead in obv. i 14. This group consists of three subgroups: Lugal-itida and his son[403] (i 15–16); Ur-Nigar and the son of Me-maškim (i 17–19; see also RA 86, 97–103 1 rev. i 26); and Duge and his two sons (i 20–23).

Group 3. Lu-Lisi, cultivator (engar) (obv. i 25–ii 7). This group consists of three subgroups: Lu-Lisi and his son (i 25–ii 1); Lugal-ezem and his two sons who have been returned from flight (ii 2–5), and Bida (ii 6).

Group 4. Lu-Suen, cultivator (engar) (obv. ii 8–13). This group consists of three small subgroups: Lu-Suen and his son (ii 8–9); Enšu(?) (ii 10); and Ur-Iškur (ii 12). It is difficult to place the person recorded in obv. ii 11 and listed as "old" in any of the subgroups.

Group 5. See below.

Group 6. ARAD$_2$-ḫula, cultivator (engar [restored]) (rev. i 2–10). This group consists of four subgroups, but only one of these, the second, consists of more than one person. Subgroup one consists of only ARAD$_2$-hula (i 2), the second group of Ur-nigḪI-x and his three sons (i 3–7), and the last two groups consists one person each: Lugal-nesage (i 8) and Aba-namtum(?) (i 9).

Group 7. Ur-Gigir, son of Ur-kala, cultivator (engar) (rev. i 11–19). This group again consists of four subgroups: Ur-Gigir and his son (i 11); Ur-Azia (i 13); x-luni (i 14); and Ur-Enir and his two sons (i 14–17).

Occasionally other information is furnished, such as in the following unit where two junior members (sons of Lugal-ezem; see Group 3) are said to have returned from flight.

No. 130 obv. col. i

25.	šu ⌜lu$_2$⌝-^{d}li$_9$-si$_4$ ⌜engar$^{?}$⌝	Old, Lu-Lisi, cultivator.

obv. col. ii

1.	1(aš$_c$) GAN$_2$ lugal-ku$_3$-zu dumu-ni	1 (receiving unit of) field, Lugal-kuzu, his child.
2.	1(aš$_c$) GAN$_2$ lugal-ezem <<ta>>[404]	1 (receiving unit of) field, Lugal-ezem.
3.	1(diš) šeš-kal-la	1 Šeš-kala.
4.	1(diš) ur-sukkal	1 Ur-Sukkal.
5.	dumu-ni-me zaḫ$_3$-ta gur-ra	They are his children; returned from flight.

Only Group 5 does not follow the schema outlined above. This group, listed at the end of obv. ii (ll. 14–23), records the names of individuals and a conveyor (Ka(ya)mu (rev. i 1).

No. 130 obv. col. ii

14.	1(aš$_c$) GAN$_2$ lu$_5$-lu$_5$-⌜mu⌝	1 (receiving unit of) field, Lulumu.
15.	uš$_2$ lu$_2$-gaz-zi-da	Dead, Lu-gazzida.
16.	uš$_2$ lugal-amar-ku$_3$	Dead, Lugal-amar-ku
17.	1(diš) lugal-⌜dub⌝-la$_2$	1 Lugal-dubla.
18.	dumu-ni-me	They are his children.
19.	1(aš$_c$) GAN$_2$ ⌜ur⌝-^{d}nin-x$^{?}$	1 unit of field, Ur-Nin-. . . .

---

403 The notation preceding the name of Lugal-itida's son, Ku-Šara, is unclear. The tablet appears to have 1(aš$_c$-*tenû*) 1(aš) ku$_3$-^{d}šara dumu-ni.

404 ta is partly erased.

20.	1(diš) šeš-a-ni dumu-ni	1 Šešani, his child.
21.	1(aš$_c$) GAN$_2$ ⸢ug$_3$ lugal⸣-x-[. . .]	1 (receiving unit of) field, carrier, Lugal-. . . .
22.	1(aš$_c$) GAN$_2$ ⸢ug$_3$⸣ x x [. . .]	1 (receiving unit of) field, carrier, . . .
23.	1(diš) lu$_2$-^{d}⸢šara$_2$⸣	1 Lu-Šara.

rev. col. i

1.	⸢giri$_3$⸣ ka$_5$-mu [x]	Conveyor: Ka(ya)mu.

Groups 6 and 7, the two final groups, return to the usual schema of the text. Group 7 is headed by the cultivator Ur-Gigir, who also seizes the group.

No. 130 rev. col. i

11.	1(aš$_c$) GAN$_2$ ug$_3$ ur-^{geš}gigir engar dumu ur$^{?}$-kal-la	1 (receiving unit of) field, carrier, Ur-Gigir, cultivator, child of Ur-kala.
12.	1(diš) nu ⸢ur-^{d}iškur$^{?}$⸣ dumu-ni	1 not (receiving) Ur-Iškur, his child.
13.	1(aš$_c$) GAN$_2$ ⸢ug$_3$ ur⸣-^{d}a-zi-a	1 (receiving unit of) field, carrier, Ur-Azia.
14.	1(aš$_c$) GAN$_2$ ⸢ug$_3$⸣ [x]-⸢lu$_2$⸣-ni	1 (receiving unit of) field, carrier, X-luni.
15.	1(aš$_c$) GAN$_2$ ⸢ug$_3$⸣ [ur]-e$_2$-nir$_x$(MIR.ZA)	1 (receiving unit of) field, carrier, Ur-Enir.
16.	1(diš) 2(ban$_2$) 2(diš) ⸢ur-^{d}ur$_3$-bar-tab⸣	1, 2 ban$_2$, 2 (units of . . .), Ur-Urbartab.
17.	1(diš) ⸢ur-^{geš}gigir⸣	1 Ur-Gigir.
18.	dumu-ni-me	They are his children.
19.	ur-^{geš}gigir i$_3$-dab$_5$	Ur-Gigir seized.

The introduction of what appears to be barley rations in this group (for the first of the two sons of Ur-Enir), is hard to explain.

The text is dated to the Drehem month "Festival of Mekigal" (e z e m - m e - k i - g a l$_2$) although it appears to be an Umma text. It is transliterated in full in the Appendix.

No. 131. *MS 4764 (Umma, AS 3–v)*

Text No. 131 is not only shaped like No. 130, but its content is also very similar. Unfortunately, the colophon of No. 131 is broken, and it is difficult to see how the remaining traces could include the expected terminology "inventory (g u r u m$_2$—a k) of plow oxen (team) (g u$_4$- a p i n)."

The first group listed in the text consisted of the captain of (plow) oxen and his family.

No. 131 obv. col. i

1.	[1(aš$_c$) GAN$_2$ lugal]-⸢nesag-e⸣ [nu-banda$_3$ gu$_4$]	1 (receiving unit of) field, Lugal-nesage captain of (plow) oxen.
2.	[1(diš)] ⸢lu$_2$-du$_{10}$-ga⸣	1 Lu-duga.
3.	[1(diš)] ⸢^{d}šara$_2$-i$_3$-zu⸣	1 Šara-izu.
4.	⸢1(diš) lu$_2$-dingir-ra⸣ dumu-ni-⸢me⸣	1 Lu-Dingira. They are his children.
5.	1(aš) GAN$_2$ a-kal-la šeš-tab-ba dumu ⸢ur$^{?}$⸣-^{geš}gigir [x]	1 (receiving unit of) field, A-kala, assistant, child of Ur-Gigir [x].
6.	1(aš) GAN$_2$ ḫa-ba-lu$_5$-ge$_2$ aga$_3$-us$_2$ dumu ^{d}utu-mu	1 (receiving unit of) field, Ḫabaluge, soldier, child of Utu-mu.
7.	⸢1(diš)⸣ ab-ba-gi-na dumu-ni	1 Abba-gina, his child.
8.	nu-banda$_3$ gu$_4$ i$_3$-dab$_5$	The captain of (plow) oxen seized.

All seven units of this text follow the same pattern, with the occasional addition of supplementary information.

No. 131 obv. col. ii

4.	1(aš$_c$) GAN$_2$ a-kal-la ⸢engar$^{?}$⸣	1 (receiving unit of) field, A-kala, cultivator.
5.	1(aš$_c$) GAN$_2$ lugal-⸢a$_2$⸣-zi-⸢da⸣	1 (receiving unit of) field, Lugal-azida.
6.	1(diš) lu$_2$-dingir-⸢ra⸣	1 Lu-Dingira.
7.	dumu-ni-me	They are his children.
8.	1(aš$_c$) ug$_3$ GAN$_2$ ur-^{d}⸢suen⸣	1 (receiving unit of) field, carrier, Ur-Suen.
9.	1(diš) lugal-ma$_2$-gur$_8$-re dumu-ni	1 Lugal-magure, his child.
10.	1(aš$_c$) GAN$_2$ lugal-šu-nir-re	1 (receiving unit of) field. Lugal-šunire.
11.	a-kal-la i$_3$-dab$_5$	A-kala seized.

The seven groups of cultivators are similar in structure to those in text No. 130 but there is no overlap in names and staff:

Group 1. Lugal-nesage, captain of (plow) oxen (nu-banda$_3$ gu$_4$; obv. i 1–8). This group consists of three subgroups: Lugal-nesage and his three sons (i 1–4); the assistant of Lugal-nesage (i 5); and a soldier and his son (i 6–7).

Group 2. Ur-Nigar, cultivator (engar; obv. i 9–ii 2). This group also consists of three subgroups: Ur-Nigar and his sons (i 9–13); a second Ur-Nigar (i 14); and A(ya)-kala (ii 1).

Group 3. A(ya)-kala, cultivator (engar; obv. ii 4–11), replacing the person listed as old in obv. ii 3. This group also consists of three subgroups: A(ya)-kala and his sons (ii 4–7); Ur-Suen and his son (ii 8–9); and Lugal-Šunire (ii 10).

Group 4. Lu-amarku, cultivator (engar; obv. ii 12–rev. i 8). This group consists of two subgroups: Lugal-amar-ku and his sons (ii 13–rev. i 1); and Atu and his sons (i 2–7). It is unclear whether all of the persons listed in the second subgroup were sons of Atu, or whether this section actually consisted of more than one subgroup.

Group 5. Lugal-nesage, cultivator (engar; rev. i 10–ii 1), replacing Lal-u'a, listed as old in rev. i 9 and again as father of the last member of the group. This group consists of two or more subgroups: Lugal-nesage and his three sons (i 10–14); a group of three people whose relationship to each other and to Lugal-nesage is unclear (i 15–17).

Group 6. Lugal-Anne, cultivator (engar; rev. ii 2–10). This group is similar in make-up to Group 5, consisting of two or more subgroups: Lugal-anne and his three sons (ii 2–5); three individuals of unknown relationship to one another (ii 6–8), and a conveyor with unclear purpose.

Group 7. Ur-Guedina, cultivator (engar; rev. ii 11–17). This group, the last, is rather damaged; it consists of at least two subgroups (see below).

The end of the last column and the colophon are damaged. The year-name is inscribed on the left edge of the tablet. It has been assigned to Umma based on the personal names and the month name (iti dal).

The final unit before the colophon includes workers who may have been added to the otherwise closely related groups of kinsmen:

No. 131 rev. col. ii

11.	1(aš$_c$)$^{?}$ GAN$_2$ ur-gu$_2$-edin-na engar	1 (receiving unit of) field, Ur-Guedina, cultivator.
12.	1(aš$_c$) GAN$_2$ da-du ⸢dumu⸣ ur-^{d}nin-tu	1 (receiving unit of) field, Dadu, child of Ur-Nintu.
13.	ša$_3$-saḫar-ra ki ur-lugal-ta	Engineer troops from Ur-Lugal.
14.	⸢1(aš$_c$) GAN$_2$⸣ engar-zi ⸢dumu ur⸣-^{d}nin-tu	1 (receiving unit of) field, Engar-zi, child of Ur-Nintu.
15.	[ARAD$_2$]-⸢mu dumu⸣ a-ḫu-šu-ni	x x-mu, child of Aḫušuni.
16.	[. . .] ⸢lugal-pa⸣-ta	x Lugal-pata.

17. [ur]-gu$_2$-edin-na i$_3$-dab$_5$ — Ur-Guedina seized.
(*blank space*)
18. [ugula$^?$] ⸢lugal⸣-nesag-e — Overseer (?) Lugal-nesage.
19. [iti] dal — Month: "Flight."

left edge

1. [mu ^{geš}]gu-za ^{d}en-lil$_2$-la$_2$ ba-dim$_2$ — Year: "The throne of Enlil was fashioned."

The tablet is sealed with the seal of Lugal-nesage.

No. 131 seal (S003612)

1. lugal-[nesag-e] — Lugal-nesage,
2. dub-sar — scribe,
3. dumu lu$_2$-⸢banda$_3$^{da}⸣ — child of Lu-banda.

The text is transliterated in full in the Appendix.

No. 132. *MS 2015 (Umma, AS 3–v)*

Text No. 132 is an inventory of staff working in the shipyard (mar-sa). It dates to Amar-Suen year 3, month 5. The format of this text is similar to that of the previous two inventory texts (Nos. 130 and 131). However, on three points the texts differ. Firstly, where staff recorded in the inventories of agricultural overseers overwhelmingly were grouped together according to rather small familial units centered around a paternal head, the staff of the shipyard were grouped in a mixture of family units and staff whose familial connections to the heads of units cannot be established, and probably were very loose if at all. Secondly, the text includes a summary of the staff. Finally, high numbers of the staff in the shipyard inventory are categorized as "old" (šu (-gi$_4$)[405]), and receiving barley rations rather than an allotment.

The first two units recorded in text No. 132 consist of eight persons described as "shipbuilders" (ma$_2$-gin$_2$). The head of the shipyard, the scribe of the shipyard (dub-sar mar-sa), Lu-sa-izu, is found in the first line, and is also the one who receives the first group. Lu-sa-izu is presumably also found (perhaps with the title overseer) in the broken colophon. However, he does not seal the tablet.

The text is transliterated in full in the following. The bottom of both the obverse and the reverse is damaged, and the text is further obscured by the rolling of the seal across the length of all four columns.

No. 132 obv. col. i

1. 1(aš$_c$) GAN$_2$ lu$_2$-sa$_6$-i$_3$-zu dub-sar mar-sa — 1 (receiving unit of) field, Lu-sa-izu, scribe of the shipyard.
2. 1(diš) lu$_2$-^{d}nin-a-zu dumu-ni — 1 Lu-Ninazu, his child.
3. 1(aš) GAN$_2$ lu$_2$-saga-mu ⸢šeš⸣-tab-ba — 1 (receiving unit of) field, Lu-sagamu, assistant.
4. šu nig$_2$-lagar-e dub-sar — Old, Nig-lagare, scribe.
5. 1(diš) lu$_2$-dingir-ra dumu-ni — 1 Lu-Dingira, his child.
6. ⸢dub⸣-sar mar-sa i$_3$-dab$_5$ — The scribe of the shipyard seized.
7. 1(aš$_c$) GAN$_2$ lu$_2$-me-lam$_2$ — 1 (receiving unit of) field, Lu-melam.
8. 1(diš) lugal-ma$_2$-gur$_8$-re ⸢dumu-ni⸣ — 1 Lugal-magure, his child.
9. 1(aš) GAN$_2$ inim-^{d}šara$_2$ šeš-tab-ba — 1 (receiving unit of) field, Inim-Šara, assistant.

---

[405] šu is commonly found in these texts as a short hand for šu-gi$_4$, "old." In text No. 132 there is agreement between the workers listed as šu in the main text and those totaled as šu-gi$_4$ in the summary, thus proving the abbreviation.

10.	⸢dumu igi⸣-sa$_6$-ge-me	They are children of Igisage.
11.	⸢ma$_2$⸣-gin$_2$-me	They are shipbuilders.

Although all of the people listed in this section (i 1–10) are summarized as shipbuilders (i 11), the first unit (i 1–6) is summarized on its own in the total, whereas the second unit (i 7–10) is grouped with the next.

The members of the next group of staff (obv. i 12–ii 1) are also grouped in small family units. Terminating the section is the statement "from the shipbuilders" (ma$_2$-gin$_2$-ta). The exact function of this term is unclear.

No. 132 obv. col. i

12.	1(aš$_c$) GAN$_2$ ur-mes dumu lu$_5$-gu	1 (receiving unit of) field, Ur-mes, child of Lugu.
13.	1(aš) GAN$_2$ ur-mes šeš-tab-⸢ba⸣	1 (receiving unit of) field, Ur-mes, assistant.
14.	1(aš$_c$) GAN$_2$ a-kal-la	1 (receiving unit of) field, A-kala.
15.	dumu ur-nigar^{gar}-me	They are children of Ur-nigar.
16.	šu ur-nigar$^{⸢gar⸣}$	Old, Ur-nigar.
17.	1(aš) GAN$_2$ lugal-x-x [šeš-tab-ba]	1 (receiving unit of) field, Lugal-x, assistant.
18.	1(aš) lu$_2$-dingir-⸢ra⸣	1 (receiving unit of field?) Lu-Dingira.
19.	1(diš) lu$_2$-sa$_6$-ga-mu	1 Lu-sagamu.
20.	[dumu]-ni-me	They are his children.
21.	[x x] ⸢4(diš)⸣ ug$_3$ lugal-nir-gal$_2$	x 4 (units of . . .), carrier, Lugal-nirgal.
22.	[. . .] ⸢lu$_2$-eb-gal⸣	x Lu-ibgal.
23.	[. . .]-x-$^{d⸢}$šara$_2$⸣	x x-Šara.

obv. col. ii

1.	dumu-ni-⸢me⸣	They are his children.
2.	ma$_2$-gin$_2$-ta	From the shipbuilders.

Whereas the units found in these two sections (obv. i 1–11 and obv. i 12–ii 2) fairly consistently mirror what we have seen in the previous two texts, the units found in the remainder of the text do not. The remainder of the text can be divided into three sections, the final one being the summary.

The first of the two remaining sections consists of persons summarized as fullers (lu$_2$ azlag$_2$) of Umma, the second of persons summarized as "from the old inventory of the overseer" (egir$_6$ gurum$_2$ ugula-ta). The fullers make up, together with the staff listed in the very first section, what we must assume was the regular staff of the shipyard, since a catch-line summarizing both sections is found immediately below this section, designating all the preceding staff as "they are men of the shipyard" (lu$_2$ mar-sa-me).

The fullers are delivered by the known overseer of the textile mill in Umma, I-kala. Most of these staff members are designated old. A summary line gives the number 11, whereas in fact this section has only 10 and the preceding 2. Instead of allotments, the fullers receive barley rations, units of an unspecified commodity which is almost certainly wool, and textiles, and most are designated as carriers (ug$_3$).

No. 132 obv. col. ii

3.	šu 4(ban$_2$) 3(diš) ug$_3$ ur-^{d}suen	Old, 4 ban$_2$, 3 (units of . . .), carrier, Ur-Suen.
4.	šu 4(ban$_2$) 3(diš) ug$_3$ ur-dingir-ra	Old, 4 ban$_2$, 3 (units of . . .), carrier, Ur-Dingira.
5.	šu 4(ban$_2$) 3(diš) ug$_3$ ukken-ne$_2$	Old, 4 ban$_2$, 3 (units of . . .), carrier, Ukkene.
6.	šu 4(ban$_2$) 3(diš) ug$_3$ lugal-zi-mu	Old, 4 ban$_2$, 3 (units of . . .), carrier, Lugal-zimu.
7.	šu 4(ban$_2$) 3(diš) ug$_3$ ur-^{d}da-mu	Old, 4 ban$_2$, 3 (units of . . .), carrier, Ur-Damu.
8.	šu 4(ban$_2$) 3(diš) ug$_3$ ur-nigar^{gar}	Old, 4 ban$_2$, 3 (units of . . .), carrier, Ur-nigar.
9.	1(diš) 1(ban$_2$) 5(diš) 1(diš) ½(diš) lu$_2$-^{d}en-ki dumu-ni	1, 2 ban$_2$, 5 (units of . . .), 1 ½ (units of . . .), Lu-Enki, his child.

10.	1(aš$_c$) GAN$_2$ KA-u$_2$-ga	1 (receiving unit of) field, KA-uga.
11.	1(aš) GAN$_2$ ur-^{d}ištaran šeš-tab-ba	1 (receiving unit of) field, Ur-Ištaran, assistant.
12.	šu 4(ban$_2$) 3(diš) ug$_3$ ga-za	Old, 4 ban$_2$, 3 (units of . . .), carrier, Gaza.
13.	šu 4(ban$_2$) 3(diš) ug$_3$ gi$_4$-du$_3$-mu	Old, 4 ban$_2$, 3 (units of . . .), carrier, Gidumu.
14.	šu 4(ban$_2$) 3(diš) dumu-gi$_7$ inim-ku$_3$	Old, 4 ban$_2$, 3 (units of . . .), dumu-gi$_7$, Inim-ku.
15.	šu ⸢4(ban$_2$) 3(diš) dumu-gi$_7$⸣ ur-gu$_2$-edin-na	Old, 4 ban$_2$, 3 (units of . . .), dumu-gi$_7$, Ur-gu'edina.
16.	1(aš) 1(barig) 4(diš) ug$_3$ ur-^{d}utu	1 (receiving unit of . . .), 1 barig, 4 (units of . . .), carrier, Ur-Utu.
17.	1(diš) 1(ban$_2$) 5(diš) 1(diš) ½(diš) ur-^{d}iškur	1, 1 ban$_2$, 5 (units of . . .), 1 ½ (units of . . .), Ur-Iškur.
18.	dumu-ni-me	They are his children.
19.	1(aš$_c$) 1(barig) 4(diš) ug$_3$ ur-si-⸢gar⸣	1 (receiving unit of field), 4 (units of . . .), carrier, Ur-sigar.

rev. col. i

1.	1(diš) 1(ban$_2$) 5(diš) 1(diš) ½(diš) lu$_2$-⸢^{d}ma⸣-mi dumu-ni	1, 1 ban$_2$, 5 (units of . . .), 1 ½ (units of . . .), Lu-Mami, his child.
2.	lu$_2$ azlag$_2$ ša$_3$ ⸢umma^{ki}⸣	Fullers of Umma.
3.	ki i$_3$-kal-la-⸢ta⸣ *(blank space)*	From I-kala.
4.	lu$_2$ mar-sa-me	They are the men of the shipyard.
5.	1(u) 1(diš) šu-me	11, they are old (ones).

The final section represent various additions to what we must assume therefore was the regular staff of the shipyard:

No. 132 rev. col. i

6.	⸢šu 4(ban$_2$)⸣ 3(diš) ug$_3$ e$_2$-zi-mu	Old, 4 ban$_2$, 3 (units of . . .), carrier, Ezimu.
7.	⸢ki lugal-mu-ma-ag$_2$⸣-ta	From Lugal-mumag.
8.	šu 4(ban$_2$) 3(diš) ug$_3$ lu$_2$-eb-gal šeš ad-da-mu	Old, 4 ban$_2$, 3 (units of . . .), carrier, Lu-Ibgal, brother of Addamu.
9.	ki lugal-ma$_2$-gur$_8$-re-ta	From Lugal-magure.
10.	šu 4(ban$_2$) 3(diš) ug$_3$ ur-⸢saga⸣	Old, 4 ban$_2$, 3 (units of . . .), carrier, Ur-saga.
11.	ki lugal-ma$_2$-gur$_8$-re min-kam-ta	From Lugal-magure, second time.
12.	šu 4(ban$_2$) 3(diš) ug$_3$ šu-na-mu-gi$_4$	Old, 4 ban$_2$, 3 (units of . . .), carrier, Šuna-mugi.
13.	ki ku$_3$-ga-ni-ta	From Kugani.
14.	šu 4(ban$_2$) 3(diš) ug$_3$ ba-du-du	Old, 4 ban$_2$, 3 (units of . . .), carrier, Badudu.
15.	šu a-kal-la dumu ur-dam?	Old, A(ya)-kala, child of Ur-dam.
16.	1(diš) ad-da-mu dumu-ni	1 Addamu, his child.
17.	ša$_3$-gu$_4$ ki lugal-ku$_3$-zu-ta	Ox-drivers from Lugal-kuzu.
18.	guru$_7$ ⸢šu⸣-[x] dab$_5$-a-ta	From the seizing(?) of the . . . of the granary(?).
19.	½(aš$_c$) GAN$_2$ ur-x-x-an-na x ⸢DU⸣ ma$_2$-gur$_8$-[re]-⸢ta⸣	½ (receiving unit of) field, Ur-x x from Magure(?).

rev. col. ii

1.	⸢1(aš)$^?$ 4(ban$_2$)⸣ ug$_3$ ur-⸢dingir⸣ ku$_3$-ta sa$_{10}$-a ur-⸢nigar^{gar}⸣	1 (receiving unit of field), 4 ban$_2$ (of barley), carrier, Ur-Dingir(?), bartered for silver, Ur-nigar.
2.	⸢šu⸣ 4(ban$_2$) 3(diš) ug$_3$ šu-im-[bi$^?$]	Old, 4 ban$_2$, 3 (units of . . .), carrier, Šu-imbi.
3.	egir$_6$ gurum$_2$ ugula-⸢ta⸣ *(blank space)*	Leftover from the inventory of the overseer.

The summary line to this section describe these individuals as a leftover from the (previous) inventory of the overseer. It is not clear who this overseer is or whether by "overseer" (u g u l a) all of the overseers supplying staff to the shipyard are meant.

Before the colophon, the text gives a detailed summary of the staff of the shipyard, which greatly helps in the interpretation of the various categories of staff and the make-up of the entire crew. Most notably, perhaps, the head of the shipyard, even though he is a scribe, is classified as a g u r u š. Also important to note is that each head of a unit is paired with an assistant (š e š - t a b - b a), although this is not always evident in the text itself. Finally, all of the staff classified as "his child" in the body of the text are listed as "male children" (d u m u n i t a $_2$) in the summary.

One staff member is referred to as g u r u š a $_2$ ½ or "half(-output) worker" in the summary. This worker may, unfortunately, be one originally listed in the broken part of section 2 (obv. i 22–23).

No. 132 rev. col. ii

4.	šunigin 1(aš$_c$) GAN$_2$ guruš [x]	Total: 1 (receiving unit of) field, worker x.
5.	šunigin 1(aš) GAN$_2$ ⸢šeš-tab⸣-ba	Total: 1 (receiving unit of) field, assistant.
6.	šunigin 2(diš) ⸢dumu nita$_2$⸣	Total: 2 male children.
7.	šunigin 1(diš) šu-gi$_4$	Total: 1 old.
8.	dub-sar mar-sa i$_3$-dab$_5$	The scribe of the shipyard seized.
9.	šunigin 4(aš$_c$) GAN$_2$ guruš	Total: 4 (receiving units of) field, workers.
10.	šunigin 4(aš) šeš-⸢tab⸣-ba	Total: 4 (receiving units of field?), assistants.
11.	šunigin 1(diš) guruš a$_2$ ½(diš)	Total: 1 half(-output) worker.
12.	šunigin 1(aš) dumu$^?$ nita$_2$ diri	Total: 1 (receiving unit of field?), male child, extra.
13.	šunigin 3(diš) dumu nita$_2$	Total: 3 male children.
14.	šunigin 1(diš) dumu nita$_2$ 1(ban$_2$) 5(diš) 1(diš) ½(diš)	Total: 1 male child (receiving) 1 ban$_2$, 5 (units of . . .) and 1 ½ (units of . . .).
15.	šunigin 3(diš) šu-gi$_4$ 3(ban$_2$) 3(diš)-ta	Total: 3 old, 3 ban$_2$, 3 (units of . . .) each.
16.	šunigin 2(diš) šu-gi$_4$ nu-dab$_5$	Total: 2 old, not receiving (lit. un-seizing).
17.	erin$_2$-⸢me⸣	They are troops.
18.	šunigin 3(aš$_c$) ug$_3$ guruš 1(barig) 4(diš)-ta	Total: 3 (receiving units of field?), carriers, workers, 1 barig, 4 (units of . . .) each.
19.	šunigin 1(aš) ug$_3$ guruš 4(ban$_2$) 1(diš)	Total: 1 (receiving unit of field), carrier, worker (receiving) 4 ban$_2$, 1 (unit of . . .).
20.	šunigin 2(aš) dumu 2(ban$_2$) 1(diš)-ta	Total: 2 (receiving units of field?), children of workers, 1 barig each.
21.	šunigin 3(diš) dumu nita$_2$ 1(ban$_2$) 5(diš) 1(diš) ½(diš)-ta	Total: 3 male children (receiving) 1 ban$_2$, 4 (units of . . .) and 1 ½ (units of . . .) each.
22.	[šunigin] 1(u) 3(diš) šu-gi$_4$ 4(ban$_2$) 2(diš)-⸢ta⸣ *(blank space)*	Total: 13 old, 4 ban$_2$, 2 (units of . . .) each.

The broken colophon classifies all the staff as shipbuilders:

No. 132 rev. col. ii

22.	[ma_2]- ⸢gin_2⸣-me	They are shipbuilders.
23.	[ugula? lu_2]-sa_6-i_3-zu	Foreman: Lu-sa-izu.
24.	[iti] dal	Month: "Flight."
25.	[mu ^{geš}gu]-za ^{d}en-⸢lil_2⸣-la_2 ba-dim_2	Year: "The throne of Enlil was fashioned."

left edge

1.	$kišib_3$ nig_2-lagar-e [x]	Sealed document of Nig-lagare.

The text is sealed with the seal of Nig-lagare:

No. 132 seal (S000306)

1.	nig_2-lagar-e	Nig-lagare,
2.	dub-sar	scribe,
3.	dumu lugal-gaba	child of Lugal-gaba,
4.	šabra	chief administrator.

The seal of Nig-lagare is found on at least forty tablets from Umma. The content of all these texts relates to the shipyard: they are either receipts for materials (e.g., SAT 2, 688 from AS 1–12, or CTNMC 36 from AS 6–8) or labor (e.g., OrSP 47–49, 323 from AS 2, or BPOA 7, 1649 from AS 3). Why Nig-lagare would seal these texts is unclear, although he may be identical with the Nig-Lagare listed as old in obv. i, 4.

No. 133. *MS 1975 (AS 5 vii–15)*

Text No. 133 is an eight-column inventory of fishermen and associated workers. The well-preserved colophon lists the five kinds of workers inspected in the document:

No. 133 rev. col. iv

1.	$gurum_2$ ak[406]	Inventory
2.	šu-ku_6 geš-gid_2-da	of fishermen, geš-gid-da workers,[407]
3.	⸢engar geš⸣-i_3-ka	sesame cultivators,
4.	ma_2 ⸢du_3 enku⸣	boat-builders of the fishery inspectors,
5.	u_3 ambar-da tuš-a	and those staying in the marsh.
	(*blank space*)	
6.	iti min-$eš_3$-ta u_4 1(u) 5(diš)-am_3 ba-ra-zal-la-ta	From month: "Double-sanctuary," from the 15th day has passed.
7.	mu en-unu_6-gal ^{d}inanna ba-ḫun	Year: "Enunugal (the En-priest of) Inanna was installed."

The last three of these five kinds of workers are clearly identified several times in the body of the text:

ambar-da tuš-a-ta/me, "from/they are those staying in the marsh" (obv. i 5, iv 21, rev. i 16)
engar geš-i_3-ka-$še_3$/me, "for (service as)/they are cultivators of sesame" (obv. i 15, iv 20, rev. ii 10)
ma_2 du_3 enku-$še_3$/ta/me, "for or from (service as)/they are boat-builders of the fishery inspectors" (obv. iv 10, rev. i 24, ii 32)

[406] Erasure after a k.

[407] See Englund 1990: 75 and n. 247. Englund suggests that geš-gid_2 here is a punting pole used for upstream travel, rather than a spear.

The first two groups, on the other hand, the fishermen (šu-ku$_6$) and the geš-gid$_2$-da workers, are not similarly identified, although some are included in the following groups:

šu-ku$_6$ gu$_2$-na-me, "they are fishermen of the 'gun'-duty" (obv. iii 28)

guruš ŠIM a de$_2$-a-ta gur-ra, "workers returning from . . . libations" (obv. iii 22)

šu-ku$_6$-ta gur-ra-me, "they are returning from (duty as) fishermen" (rev. i 20)

šu-ku$_6$-ka e$_2$-gal-še$_3$ ku$_6$ TUM$_3$-me/še$_3$, "for (service as)/they are of the fishermen bringing(?)[408] fish to the palace" (obv. iv 15, rev. iii 4; and obv. i 28)

In a fashion similar to the other inventories published here, the first entry of the text recorded the overseer in charge of the group:

No. 133 obv. col. i

1.	1(aš$_c$) GAN$_2$ ur-^{d}kal-kal ugula šu-ku$_6$	1 (receiving unit of) field, Ur-Kalkal, overseer of the fishermen.
2.	1(diš) nam-sukkal-i$_3$-du$_{10}$	1 Namsukkal-idu.
3.	1(diš) lu$_2$-^{d}šara$_2$	1 Lu-Šara.
4.	dumu-ni-me	They are his children.
5.	ambar-da tuš-a-ta	(Levied) from those staying in the marsh.

Ur-Kalkal is known in a few other texts explicitly related to fisheries (Nisaba 9, 186 [Umma, Š 46] and SAT 2, 471 [Umma, Š 46–i]). In SAT 2, 974 (Umma, AS 6), Ur-Kalkal is given the title ma$_2$-lah$_5$, "sailor." That text is also sealed with his seal, where he is named as son of a certain Ur-[. . .], who also held the title sailor.

Ur-Kalkal and his children are followed by a certain "scribe of salt and alkaline (plants)" (dub-sar mun gazi), called Lugal-niglagare, and his four sons. None of the members of this small family group is listed with rations or allotments. The head of the next small group, ARAD-Šara, is listed with an allotment, but whereas Ur-Kalkal is introduced by a curvilinear aš sign, ARAD-Šara is introduced by a cuneiform aš sign. Both are said to receive an allotment (GAN$_2$). ARAD-Šara is said to be an assistant, presumably that of Ur-Kalkal, as Lugal-niglagare was away on *bala* (obligation). ARAD-Šara is followed by his two children. The section ends with a subscript that can be interpreted as relating to the entire first section of the text. It designates both Ur-Kalkal and his family group as well as the two following groups as cultivators of sesame:

No. 133 obv. col. i

6.	lugal-nig$_2$-lagar-e dumu lugal-saga dub-sar mun gazi bala-še$_3$	Lugal-niglagare, child of Lugal-saga, scribe of salt and alkaline (plant), for the bala (obligation).
7.	ku-li	Kuli.
8.	lu$_2$-bala-saga	Lu-balasaga.
9.	lugal-ušum-gal	Lugal-Ušumgal.
10.	lugal-nir-gal$_2$	Lugal-nirgal.
11.	dumu-ni-me	They are his children.
12.	1(aš) GAN$_2$ ARAD$_2$-^{d}šara$_2$ šu-ku$_6$ šeš-tab-⸢ba⸣	1 (receiving unit of) field ARAD-Šara, fisherman, assistant.
13.	ab-ba-mu	Abbamu.
14.	lu$_2$-na-ru$_2$-a šeš-⸢a⸣-ni	Lu-narua, his brother.
15.	⸢engar⸣ geš-i$_3$-ka-še$_3$	For (service as) cultivators of sesame.
	(*blank space*)	

[408] For TUM$_3$ with the meaning "to bring" in Ur III and earlier, see Attinger 1993: 184–85.

The remainder of the text lists about one hundred and fifty further persons, many without any indication of rations or allotments. Some of the persons are recorded as being old (*šu*: obv. ii 21, 25, iv 22, 25, 29, rev. i 25, 30, 39, ii 3, 12, 27; *šu-gi*$_4$: obv. iii 21), others as being dead (*uš*$_2$: obv. ii 18, 19), and still others as having fled (*zaḫ*$_3$: obv. i 29, rev. i 5).

In the following excerpt two family units are described as all being descendants of Pada, who is listed as old at the head of the first group:

No. 133 obv. col. ii

21.	šu pa$_3$-da	Old, Pada.
22.	1(aš$_c$) eš$_3$-ki-du$_{10}$	1 (receiving unit of field?) Eš-kidu.
23.	1(aš) ur-gu$_2$-de$_3$-na dumu-ni	1 (receiving unit of field?) Ur-Gudea, his child.
24.	1(aš) ur-^{d}gilgames$_3$ šeš-tab-ba	1 (receiving unit of field?) Ur-Gilgameš, assistant.
25.	šu ur-^{d}ab-u$_2$ šeš-tab-ba	Old Ur-Ab'u, assistant.
26.	1(aš$_c$) inim-ku$_3$	1 (receiving unit of field?) Inim-ku.
27.	1(aš) ^{geš}guzza:ni šeš-tab-ba	1 (receiving unit of field?) Guzzani, assistant.
28.	1(diš) ur-^{d}da-ni	1 Ur-Dani.
29.	dumu-ni-me	They are his children.
30.	dumu pa$_3$-da-me	Children of Pada.

In the next example, groups of people with unclear status are listed, in what appears to the modern reader as a rather haphazard way:

No. 133 obv. col. iv

2.	lugal-ku$_3$-zu$^{?}$	Lugal-kuzu.
3.	al-la-zi-ša$_3$-gal$_2$ dumu-ni	Alla-zišagal, his child.
4.	lu$_2$-ki-ku$_3$-ga	Lu-kikuga.
5.	al-ba-ni-du$_{11}$ dumu-ni	Albanidu, his child.
6.	in-u$_9$-u$_9$	In-u'u.
7.	ur-^{d}ḫendur-sag-ka	Ur-Ḫendursagka.
8.	ur-e$_2$-nun-na	Ur-Enuna.
9.	ab-ba-du$_{10}$-ga dumu-ni	Abba-duga, his child.
10.	ma$_2$ du$_3$ enku-še$_3$	For the boat-builders of the fisheries inspectors.
11.	ur-^{d}su$_4$-⸢an-na⸣	Ur-Su'ana.
12.	[lugal]-gu$_4$-en-e	Lugal-gu'ene.
13.	šeš-kal-la dumu-ni	Šeš-kala, his child.
14.	dumu nin$_9$-šem$_5$-a-sag-gal$_2$-la	They are(?) children of Nin-šema-saggala.
15.	šu-ku$_6$-ka e$_2$-gal-še$_3$ ku$_3$ tum$_3$-še$_3$	For (service as)/they are of the fishermen bringing(?) fish to the palace.
16.	ur-^{d}utu i$_3$-dab$_5$	Ur-Utu seized.
17.	ur-^{d}kal-kal	Ur-Kalkal.
18.	nam-sukkal-i$_3$-du$_{10}$ dumu šu-ku$_6$-še$_3$	Namsukkal-nidu, as child of the fishermen.
19.	ku$_3$-ga-ni	Kugani.
20.	engar geš-i$_3$-ka-še$_3$	For the cultivators of sesame.
21.	ambar-da tuš-a-me	They dwell in the marshes.

Only a small subset of the workers are assigned as dedicatees (obv. iii 4–5); others are said to derive from crews under the control of various overseers (such as rev. ii 20: *šar*$_2$*-ra-ab-du-ta*) or originating from other professions (such as rev. ii 2: *ša*$_3$*-saḫar-ra-ta*), and the purpose of the text, therefore, remains largely unclear. The text is transliterated in full in the Appendix.

No. 134. *MS 1846/2 (Umma, AS 3 v)*

Text No. 134 lists the staff of an institution called the e$_2$ maš (rev. ii 9: giri$_3$-se$_3$-ga e$_2$ maš-me). The first person listed in this inventory is named a-ab-ba-mu. It is unfortunately not possible to establish whether this is a variant writing of the name of the person found in the colophon, a-ba-ba-mu, or a simple error, or whether the two are different persons. It cannot also be verified whether the sign MU, in either name, is part of the name or a title, muḫaldim, "kitchen administrator." The most likely solution is, of course, that Ababa(mu) of the colophon and A(ya)bba(mu) of the first entry are one and the same person.

The text is dated to month 5 of Amar-Suen's third year. The text is sealed, but the legend can only be partially read. The final section (rev. i 2–10) is mirrored in the large, but poorly preserved, inventory text SANTAG 6, 384 (rev. iii 3'–10'). Most of the staff members in text No. 134 receive barley rations wool (not explicitly recorded in the text) and textiles (Steinkeller's classes M and N). The staff are counted with either 1 (aš) or 1 (diš), with 1 (diš) reserved for children. The barley rations given to most of the workers, 3 (ban$_2$), is at the lower end of the scale of rations for male workers. Only one worker, Abbamu, receives the full ration of 1 barig of barley (Steinkeller's class M). The additional rations given to him and his son are difficult to interpret.

Unusually for inventories, No. 134 is totalled (rev. ii). The first entry of the total is very damaged; it recapitulates the first member of the staff, A(ya)bba(mu), who was probably also the overseer of the group (obv. i 1). The second entry of the total, listing 21 (written 2(u) 1(aš)) carriers (ug$_3$) receiving 3 (ban$_2$) of barley and cloth rations, summarizes obv. i 3–ii 13 and rev. i 9. Lugal-magure (rev. i 3) and Šara-bazige (rev. i 7) are also summarized as carriers (but using the term IL$_2$) in the third entry of the total. The child of A(ya)bba(mu) (obv. i 2) and the two children of Lugal-magure (rev. i 4–5) are summarized in entry four of the total. Three workers described as GAM$^{?}$[409] (rev. i 2), "old" (šu, for šu-gi$_4$: rev. i 10), and "fled" (zaḫ$_3$: rev. i 11), are summarized in entries 5, 6, and 7 of the total.

Rev. i 2–10 is matched in the broken yearly inventory SANTAG 6, 384 rev. iii 3'–10'. In SANTAG 6, 384 rev. iii 12' the group (which included one "Ur-Gigir, son of Lugal-Gigir, 'additional fuller,'" ur-^{geš}gigir dumu lugal-^{geš}gigir-re lunga$_3$ daḫ-ḫu) is said to be "from A(ya)bba(mu)" (ki a-ab-ba-mu-ta), presumably the same person listed in the first entry and as overseer in our text (regardless of the writing issue discussed above).

Text No. 134 is transliterated in full here:

obv. col. i

1.	⌜1(aš)⌝ 1(barig) 4(diš) ug$_3$ a-ab-⌜ba$^{?}$⌝-mu	1 (receiving unit of field?), 1 barig, 4 (units of . . .), carrier, A(ya)bbamu.
2.	⌜1(diš)⌝ 1(ban$_2$) 5(diš) 1(diš) ½(diš) ^{d}x-x-gal$_2$-x$^{?}$ dumu-ni	1, 1 ban$_2$, 5 (units of . . .), 1 ½ (units of . . .), X-gal-x, his child.
3.	1(aš) 3(ban$_2$) 1(diš) tug$_2$ ur-e$_2$-gal dumu ama-kal-la	1 (receiving unit of field?), 3 ban$_2$, 1 textile, Ur-Egal, child of Ama-kala.
	(*blank space*)	
	(*erasure*)	
4.	[1(aš) 3(ban$_2$)] tug$_2$ ur-^{d}šul-pa-e$_3$	1 (receiving unit of field?), 3 ban$_2$, textile, Ur-Shulpa'e.
5.	[1(aš) 3(ban$_2$)] ⌜tug$_2$⌝ ^{d}šul-gi-zi-mu	1 (receiving unit of field?), 3 ban$_2$, textile, Šulgi-zimu.
6.	1(aš) 3(ban$_2$) tug$_2$ ^{d}šul-gi-iri-mu	1 (receiving unit of field?), 3 ban$_2$, textile, Šulgi-irimu.

[409] Based on the parallel text SANTAG 6, 384 (obv. iii 7', rev. iii 3) this is likely an abbreviation of šu gam-gam, a rare term of unknown meaning.

7.	1(aš) 3(ban$_2$) tug$_2$ ur-^{d}da-mu	1 (receiving unit of field?), 3 ban$_2$, textile, Ur-Damu.
8.	⸢1(aš)⸣ 3(ban$_2$) tug$_2$ lugal-ba-ta-e$_3$	1 (receiving unit of field?), 3 ban$_2$, textile, Lugal-bata'e.
9.	⸢1(aš) 3(ban$_2$)⸣ tug$_2$ ^{d}šul-gi-zi-mu min-kam	1 (receiving unit of field?), 3 ban$_2$, textile, Šulgi-zimu, (the) second.
10.	⸢1(aš) 3(ban$_2$)⸣ tug$_2$ a-ḫu-šu-ni	1 (receiving unit of field?), 3 ban$_2$, textile, Aḫušuni.
11.	1(aš) 3(ban$_2$) tug$_2$ lugal-zi-mu	1 (receiving unit of field?), 3 ban$_2$, textile, Lugal-zimu.
12.	1(aš) 3(ban$_2$) tug$_2$ ur-^{d}suen dumu ḫa-lu$_5$-lu$_5$	1 (receiving unit of field?), 3 ban$_2$, textile, Ur-Suen, child of Ḫalulu.
13.	⸢1(aš)⸣ 3(ban$_2$) tug$_2$ ur-^{d}dumu-zi-da dumu nam-x-tur	1 (receiving unit of field?), 3 ban$_2$, textile, Ur-Dumuzida, child of Nam-x-tur.
14.	[1(aš) 3(ban$_2$)] tug$_2$ a-ḫu-du$_{10}$	1 (receiving unit of field?), 3 ban$_2$, textile, Aḫu-tab.
15.	[. . .] x x	. . .

obv. col. ii

1.	giri$_3$ e$_2$-gal ur-^{d}ašnan	Conveyor (of the) palace: Ur-Ašnan,
2.	dumu lugal-^{geš}gigir-re šim-me	child of Lugal-gigire, brewer(?).[410]
3.	1(aš) 3(ban$_2$) tug$_2$ ur-^{geš}gigir dumu e-zi$_2$-ib-tum	1 (receiving unit of field?), 3 ban$_2$, textile, Ur-Gigir, child of Ezibtum.
4.	giri$_3$ e$_2$-gal lugal-šeš-ku$_3$ dumu geme$_2$-^{d}suen	Conveyor (of the) palace: Lugal-šešku, child of Geme-Suen.
5.	1(aš) 3(ban$_2$) tug$_2$ lugal-ezem dumu nin-kal-la	1 (receiving unit of field?), 3 ban$_2$, textile, Lugal-ezem, child of Nin-kala.
6.	1(aš) 3(ban$_2$) tug$_2$ ur-zabala$_3$^{ki} dumu nin-ur$_2$-ra-ni	1 (receiving unit of field?), 3 ban$_2$, textile, Ur-Zabala, child of Nin-urani.
7.	1(aš) 3(ban$_2$) tug$_2$ lugal-^{geš}gigir-re dumu ša-dur	1 (receiving unit of field?), 3 ban$_2$, textile, Lugal-Gigire, child of Šadur.
8.	giri$_3$$^{?}$ e$_2$-gal ur-^{d}dumu-zi-da	Conveyor (of the) palace: Ur-Dumuzida.
9.	1(aš) 3(ban$_2$) tug$_2$ e$_2$-ki-bi dumu zu-ḫu-ut	1 (receiving unit of field?), 3 ban$_2$, textile, Ekibi, child of Zuḫut.
10.	1(aš) 3(ban$_2$) tug$_2$ i-ra-am-i$_3$-li$_2$ dumu a$_2$-bi-mu	1 (receiving unit of field?), 3 ban$_2$, textile, Iram-ili, child of Abimu.
11.	zaḫ$_3$-ta gur-ra	Returned from flight.
12.	1(aš) 3(ban$_2$) tug$_2$ lu$_2$-^{d}utu dumu AN-gu-gu-um	1 (receiving unit of field?), 3 ban$_2$, textile, Lu-Utu, child of ANgugum.
13.	1(aš) 3(ban$_2$) tug$_2$ lugal-^{d}nin-ur$_4$-ra	1 (receiving unit of field?), 3 ban$_2$, textile, Lugal-Nin-ura,

410 A reading b a p p i r$_2$ is unlikely here given the suffix m e.

rev. col. i

1.	dumu ur-apin-du$_7$	child of Ur-apindu.
2.	GAM$^?$ lu$_2$-^{d}utu	. . . Lu-Utu.
3.	1(aš) 3(ban$_2$) 4(diš) lugal-ma$_2$-gur$_8$-re	1 (receiving unit of field?), 3 ban$_2$, 4 (units of . . .), Lugal-magure.
4.	1(diš) 1(ban$_2$) 5(diš) 1(diš) ½(diš) ur-^{d}dumu-zi-da	1, 1 ban$_2$, 5 (units of . . .), 1 ½ (units of . . .), Ur-Dumuzida.
5.	1(diš) 1(ban$_2$) 5(diš) 1(diš) ½(diš) lugal-ezem	1, 1 ban$_2$, 5 (units of . . .), 1 ½ (units of . . .) Lugal-ezem.
6.	dumu-ni-me	They are his children.
7.	1(aš) 2(ban$_2$) 2(diš) ^{d}šara$_2$-ba-zi-ge	1 (receiving unit of field?), 2 ban$_2$, 2 (units of . . .), Šara-bazige,
8.	dumu lu$_2$-˹kal-la˺ dub-sar	child of Lu-kala, scribe.
9.	1(aš) 3(ban$_2$) tug$_2$ ir-du$_{10}$-ga dumu da-ga-mu	1 (receiving unit of field?), 3 ban$_2$, textile, Ir-duga, child of Dagamu.
10.	šu ug$_3$ ma$_2$-gur$_8$-re	Old: carrier, Magure.
11.	zaḫ$_3$ ug$_3$ a-ḫu-ni dumu-ni	Fled: carrier, Aḫuni, his son.
	(*blank space*)	
12.	ki ba-sa$_6$ ugula-ta	From Basa, overseer.
	(*erasures*)	
	(*blank space*)	

rev. col. ii

	(*blank space*)	
1.	˹šunigin 1(aš)˺ 1(barig) 4(diš) ug$_3$ guruš ugula	Total: 1 (receiving unit of field?), 1 barig, 4 (units of . . .), carrier, worker, overseer(?).
2.	šunigin 2(u) 1(aš) ug$_3$ 3(ban$_2$) tug$_2$	Total: 21 (receiving units of field?) carriers, 3 ban$_2$, textile.
3.	šunigin 2(aš) ˹IL$_2$˺ 1(ban$_2$) 2(diš)	Total: (receiving units of field?) 2 carriers(?),[411] 1 ban$_2$, 2 (units of . . .).
4.	šunigin 3(diš) dumu nita$_2$ 1(ban$_2$) 5(diš) 1(diš) ½(diš)	Total: 3 children, male, 1 ban$_2$, 5 (units of . . .), 1 ½ (units of . . .).
5.	˹šunigin˺ 1(diš) GAM$^?$ guruš	Total 1 GAM worker.
6.	˹šunigin˺ 1(diš) ug$_3$ šu ˹guruš˺	Total: 1 carrier, old, worker.
7.	˹šunigin˺ 1(diš) ug$_3$ zaḫ$_3$ ˹guruš˺	Total: 1 carrier, fled, worker.
	(*blank space*)	
8.	ug$_3$-IL$_2$ tur-tur	Carriers (and) children.
9.	giri$_3$-se$_3$-ga e$_2$ maš-me	They are staff of the Emaš.
10.	ugula a-ba-ba-mu	Overseer: Ababamu.
11.	iti dal	Month: "Flight."
12.	mu ku$_3$ gu-za ^{d}en-lil$_2$ ba-dim$_2$	Year: "The shiny throne of Enlil was fashioned."
	(*blank space*)	

[411] Written with the sign IL$_2$ instead of the more common ug$_3$. ug$_3$ is an abbreviated form of ug$_3$-IL$_2$. Note the possible reading of ga$_6$ for IL$_2$ in Umma (see the many examples of še/u$_2$ ga$_6$-ga$_2$ where one would expect še/u$_2$ IL$_2$, and see Selz 1993b: 556).

seal (—)

1.	lugal-da-[. . .]	Lugal-da-x,
2.	dumu ur-⸢e$_2$⸣-[. . .]	child of Ur-E-x.

No. 135. *MS 1908 (Umma, AS 6)*

Text No. 135 is a large inventory of workers (classified as ša$_3$-saḫar-ra, perhaps "dirt workers" or "engineer troops"[412]) of three important agricultural districts in the province Umma: Apisal, Gudena, and Mušbianna. The governor of Umma, Ur-Lisi, is mentioned in the colophon (rev. viii 5), but the reason for this is unclear. The following line, written on dry clay, is mostly illegible.

No. 135 rev. col. viii

	(beginning blank)	
1.	⸢gurum$_2$⸣ ak ša$_3$-saḫar-ra	Inventory of "engineer troops"
2.	[ša$_3$] a-pi$_4$-sal$_4$^{ki}	of Apisal,
3.	⸢gu$_2$⸣-de$_3$-na	Gudena,
4.	⸢u$_3$ muš⸣-bi-an-na	and Mušbianna.
5.	ur-^{d}li$_9$-si$_4$ ensi$_2$ umma ^{ki}	Ur-Lisi, governor of Umma.
6.	[x] x [x] ⸢lu$_2$-du$_{10}$-ga⸣ [. . .] x u$_3$ [. . .] x-mu[413]	. . . Lu-duga . . . and . . .
7.	[mu ša]-aš-šu$_2$-ru ^{ki} ba-hul	Year: "Šaššuru was destroyed."

Although the workers listed in text No. 135 are organized similarly to the previous texts—in small family groups headed by a senior member—the text does not summarize any of these as staff (giri$_3$-se$_3$-ga). Towards the end of the text, a number of added workers, classified as "dedicatees," are found.

Most of the family units are grouped together into larger units. In several instances a few family groups are said to "be the children of PN." In this regard it is perhaps important to note that unlike the other inventories, where most of the "heads" of family units are listed as 1 (aš$_c$), in text No. 135 the majority are recorded as ½(aš$_c$) workers. In some other cases several small family groups are grouped together and said to be transferred from another person.

It is well known that agricultural workers belonged to family groups, and that several generations were often present in the same domain-land unit (see Dahl 2007: 81 and n. 293, 91 n. 317, discussing the text SAT 2, 77). Unfortunately, none of the groups in this text are found again in any other text.

The following excerpt from text No. 135 lists two small family units consisting of one person and his child only, followed by three allotment holders who are all said to be the children of a certain Lugal-Emaḫ(e).

No. 135 obv. col. ii

17.	½(aš$_c$) GAN$_2$ ur-^{d}šul-pa-e$_3$	½ (receiving unit of) field, Ur-Šulpa'e.
18.	1(diš) ki-ba dumu-ni	1 Kiba, his child.
19.	½(aš$_c$) GAN$_2$ ur-^{d}suen	½ (receiving unit of) field, Ur-Suen.
20.	1(aš) lugal-u$_2$-šim$^{?}$-e dumu-ni	1 (receiving unit of field?), Lugal-ušime, his child.
21.	½(aš$_c$) GAN$_2$ lu$_2$-⸢gu⸣-la	½ (receiving unit of) field, Lu-gula.
22.	½(aš$_c$) GAN$_2$ ur-gu$_2$-de$_3$-na	½ (receiving unit of) field, Ur-gudena.
23.	1(aš) GAN$_2$ ur-^{geš}gigir	1 (receiving unit of) field, Ur-Gigir.
24.	dumu lugal-e$_2$-maḫ-e-me	They are the children of Lugal-Emaḫe.

---

[412] Syntactically, ša$_3$-saḫar-ra is comparable to ša$_3$-gu$_4$, "ox-drivers," a title used of agricultural workers. The ša$_3$-saḫar-ra also worked in agriculture, but presumably not with plowing or sowing.

[413] Line written on dry clay.

The following larger unit, consisting of perhaps only one family group; it is said to have been transferred from a certain Basaga:

No. 135 obv. col. iii

6.	uš$_2$ ARAD$_2$ engar	Dead, ARAD(mu), cultivator.
7.	1(aš$_c$) GAN$_2$ ug$_3$ lu$_2$-lugal-e-i$_3$-zu	1 (receiving unit of) field, carrier, Lu-Lugale-izu.
8.	1(aš) 4(ban$_2$) tug$_2$ ug$_3$ ur-^{d}gu-nu-ra	1 (receiving unit of field?), 4 ban$_2$ (of barley), textile, carrier, Ur-MUŠ-tarra.
9.	1(aš) 3(ban$_2$) tug$_2$ ur-^{d}da-mu	1 (receiving unit of field?), 3 ban$_2$ (of barley), textile, Ur-Damu.
10.	dumu 2(ban$_2$) 2(diš) ur-e$_2$-maḫ	Child (category:) 2 ban$_2$ 2 (units of . . .): Ur-Emah.
11.	dumu-ni-me	They are his children.
12.	ša$_3$-saḫar-ra ki ba-sa$_6$-ga-ta	Engineer troops from Basaga.

In the final example given here, one family group, consisting of Ku-Šara and his two children, is said to be the repaid arrears of Lugal-Kiri:

No. 135 obv. col. ii

12.	½(aš$_c$) GAN$_2$ ku$_3$-^{d}šara$_2$	½ (receiving unit of) field, Ku-Šara.
13.	1(aš) ur-^{d}suen	1 (receiving unit of field?) Ur-Suen.
14.	1(diš) [ARAD$_2$]-mu	1 X-mu.
15.	dumu-ni-me	They are his children.
16.	la$_2$-ia$_3$ su-ga lugal-^{geš}kiri$_6$	Repaid arrears (of) Lugal-Kiri.

The text lists twenty-two units of dedicatees (a-ru-a); all are of the category "1(aš)," receiving barley rations and textiles. Most of the dedicatees are found in the final two columns, especially col. vi on the reverse, which is almost entirely written on already dry clay (from l. 5).

No. 135 rev. col. v

28.	1(aš) 2(ban$_2$) tug$_2$ šeš-kal-la	1 (receiving unit of field?), 2 ban$_2$ (of barley), textiles, Šeš-kala.
29.	a-ru-a ur-ama-⸢na⸣	Dedicatee of Ur-amana.
30.	uš$_2$ ^{d}šara$_2$-⸢a-mu⸣	Dead: Šara-a(ya)mu.
31.	a-ru-a a-tu	Dedicatee of Atu.
32.	1(aš) 2(ban$_2$) tug$_2$ lugal-ezem	1 (receiving unit of field?), 2 ban$_2$ (of barley), textiles, Lugal-ezem.
33.	a-ru-a ur$_2$-nig$_2$-du$_{10}$	Dedicatee of Urnigdu.
34.	1(aš) 3(ban$_2$) tug$_2$ šeš-kal-la	1 (receiving unit of field?), 2 ban$_2$ (of barley), textiles, Šeš-kala.
35.	a-ru-a ur-gu$_2$-de$_3$-na	Dedicatee of Ur-gudena.
36.	1(aš) 2(ban$_2$) tug$_2$ lugal-geš-ḫur-e	1 (receiving unit of field?), 2 ban$_2$ (of barley), textiles, Lugal-gešhure.
37.	a-ru-a ur-^{geš}gigir	Dedicatee of Ur-gigir.
38.	1(aš) 2(ban$_2$) tug$_2$ lugal-ezem	1 (receiving unit of field?), 2 ban$_2$ (of barley), textiles, Lugal-ezem.
39.	a-ru-a lugal-^{geš}gigir-re	Dedicatee of Lugal-gigire.
40.	uš$_2$ nam-eb$_2$-gu-ul	Dead: Nam-ebgul.
41.	1(aš) 2(ban$_2$) tug$_2$ šu-im-⸢bi⸣	1 (receiving unit of field?), 2 ban2 (of barley), textiles, Šu-imbi.

42.	a-ru-a lugal-^{geš}-ḫur-e	Dedicatee of Lugal-gešḫure.
43.	1(aš) 2(ban$_2$) tug$_2$ lugal-ḫe$_2$-gal$_2$	1 (receiving unit of field?), 2 ban$_2$ (of barley), textiles, Lugal-ḫegal,
44.	a-ru-a lugal-mu$^?$	dedicatee of Lugal-mu.

rev. col. vi

1.	x x x i$_3$-dab$_5$	. . . seized.
2.	a-ru-a lu$_2$-^{d}šara$_2$$^?$	Dedicatee of Lu-Šara.
3.	uš$_2$ ur- ^{d}⸢iškur⸣	Dead: Ur-Iškur.
4.	a-ru-a inim-ma-ni-⸢zi⸣	Dedicatee of Inimani-zi.
5.	libir-am$_3$	They are old.
	(*blank space*)	
6.	ugula ⸢ku$_3$-ga-ni⸣	Overseer: Kugani.
7.	x x x ^{d}šara$_2$-za-me x	. . . Šara-zame,
8.	a-ru-a AN-gir$_2$-ra	dedicatee of AN-gira.
9.	1(aš) 2(ban$_2$) lu$_2$- ^{d}nin-šubur	1 (receiving unit of field?), 2 ban$_2$ (of barley), Lu-Ninšubur,
10.	⸢a⸣-ru-a ur-lu$_2$-gu-la	dedicatee of Ur-lugula.
11.	1(aš) 2(ban$_2$) tug$_2$ lugal-ma$_2$-gur$_8$-re	1 (receiving unit of field?), 2 ban$_2$ (of barley), textile, Lugal-magure,
12.	a-ru-a nam-ḫa-ni	dedicatee of Namḫani.
13.	1(aš) 3(ban$_2$) tug$_2$ KA-erin-⸢ma$^?$⸣	1 (receiving unit of field?), 3 ban$_2$ (of barley), textile, KA-erinma,
14.	[a]-⸢ru⸣-a šeš-a-ni	dedicatee of Šešani.
15.	1(aš) 2(ban$_2$) tug$_2$ ^{d}šubur-ba-⸢ra⸣	1 (receiving unit of field?), 2 ban$_2$ (of barley), textile, Šubur-bara,
16.	a-ru-a ⸢ša$_3$-ku$_3$-ge⸣	dedicatee of Ša-kuge.
17.	⸢1(aš) 2(ban$_2$) tug$_2$⸣ engar-⸢du$_{10}$⸣	1 (receiving unit of field?), 2 ban$_2$ (of barley), textile, Engar-du,
18.	a-ru-<a> lugal-⸢nesag$^?$-e$^?$⸣	dedicatee of Lugal-nesage.
19.	1(aš) 2(ban$_2$) tug$_2$ ^{d}utu-saga	1 (receiving unit of field?), 2 ban$_2$ (of barley), textile, Utu-saga,
20.	a-ru-a ur-^{d}ma-mi	dedicatee of Ur-Mami.
21.	1(aš) 3(ban$_2$) tug$_2$ ^{d}šara$_2$-mu-tum$_2$	1 (receiving unit of field?), 3 ban$_2$ (of barley), textile, Šara-mutum,
22.	a-ru-a ab-ba-[gi]-na	dedicatee of Abgadana.
23.	1(aš) 2(ban$_2$) 2(diš) an-ta-lu$_2$ a-ru-a aš-kal	1 (receiving unit of field?), 2 ban$_2$ (of barley), 2 (units of . . .), Antalu(?), dedicatees of Aškal(?).
24.	1(aš) 3(ban$_2$) tug$_2$ lu$_2$-^{d}nin-ur$_4$-ra	1 (receiving unit of field?), 3 ban$_2$ (of barley), textile, Lu-Nin-ura.
25.	1(aš) 3(ban$_2$) tug$_2$ lu$_2$-du$_{10}$-ga	1 (receiving unit of field?), 3 ban$_2$ (of barley), textile, Lu-duga.
26.	dumu- mi$_2$ bappir dumu lugal-TAR-me	They are the daughters(?) of the brewers(?), children of Lugal-TAR.
27.	i$_3$-bi$_2$-za zi$_3$ KA-a	. . .
	(*blank space*)	

28.	daḫ-ḫu-me	They are additions.
29.	ugula ku$_3$-ga-ni (*blank space*)	Overseer: Kugani.
30.	ug$_3$-il$_2$-me	They are carriers.
31.	1(aš$_c$) 1(barig) 1(ban$_2$) 5(diš) 5(diš) ug$_3$ šu-^{d}en-lil$_2$	1 (receiving unit of field), 1 barig, 1 ban$_2$, 5 (units of . . .), 5 (units of . . .), carrier, Šu-Enlil.
32.	1(diš) 1(ban$_2$) 5(diš) 1(diš) ½(diš) a-ta$_2$-na-aḫ	1, 1 ban$_2$, 5 (units of . . .), 1 ½ (units of . . .), Atanaḫ.
33.	1(diš) 1(ban$_2$) 5(diš) 1(diš) ½(diš) šu-kab-ta$_2$	1, 1 ban$_2$, 5 (units of . . .), 1 ½ (units of . . .), Šu-kabta.
34.	dumu-[ni]-⸢me⸣	They are his children.
35.	⸢a-ru-a⸣ ur-^{d}gilgames$_3$ dumu a-ti-ma-ti (*blank space*)	Dedicatees of Ur-Gilgameš, child of Adi-mati.

Text No. 135 is transliterated in full in the Appendix.

No. 136. *MS 1846/1 (Umma, AS 4–vii–15)*

Text No. 136 is, together with No. 137, the shortest of the inventories found in the Schøyen Collection (except the ones treated in the next section, on Smaller Inventories). But whereas text No. 137 lacks all of the crucial bookkeeping information usually contained in the colophon (for it is missing), text No. 136 is complete. No. 136 gives a starting date (the middle of the seventh month, iti min-eš$_3$-ta u$_4$ 1(u) 5(diš)-am$_3$ ba-ra-zal-la-ta, of Amar-Suen's fourth year), but no end date; presumably it would have been the end of the year.

The workers are divided into three groups in the total (rev. 12–14). Each group is counted with aš signs, and each group is classified as carriers (ug$_3$). The translation reflects that. Unfortunately, the sign following ug$_3$, presumably giving the classification of carrier, is broken in all three cases. Nevertheless, it is possible to propose that the groups were classified according to their monthly rations, the first group of sixteen carriers were those receiving 4(ban$_2$) a month, the second group, consisting of eleven carriers, received 3(ban$_2$) monthly, whereas the last group, consisting of only one carrier, most likely received only 2(ban$_2$) monthly. This proposal helps the reconstruction of the broken parts of the end of the obverse and the beginning of the reverse, but some problems remain.

Unfortunately, the distinctions found in the summary are not the same as those emphasized in the body of the text, where the first twenty workers seem to be a regular crew and the remaining nine workers various additions.

Although everyone in this text is summarized as a "carrier" (ug$_3$), only two persons are mentioned with titles in the body of the text: the "overseer" (ugula) and Lugal-ezem the potter (bahar$_3$). Lugal-ezem is not, it seems, included in the summary, and the reason for listing him there is not clear. Lugal-ezem the potter is known from a few documents.[414]

Text No. 136 is closely related to an account from Šu-Suen's second year, MVN 10, 102. Although the two texts are separated by seven years, fourteen people can be found in both texts, including the overseer of the crew in No. 136, Ur-Iškur (Table 3). MVN 10, 102 is in fact an account of "carriers" concerning Ur-Iškur (rev. iii 7–8: [nig$_2$-ka$_9$] ak a$_2$ ug$_3$-IL$_2$ / ur-^{d}iškur ugula).

The texts are so similar that it seems fair to suggest that No. 136 belonged to a yearly series of inventories, used to draw up yearly accounts concerning the "carriers" that Ur-Iškur managed. We do not have the inventory and account from the same year, but in fact having texts separated by some years is useful to show the evolution in work crews over extended periods of time (see also Dahl 2010a).

---

[414] AnOr 1, 88 (AS 5) obv. ii 23; BPOA 1, 820 (AS 7) obv. 2; BPOA 7, 2449 (AS 6) obv. 10; SNAT 487 (ŠS 3 ix) obv. i 2.

Table 3. Persons found in both text No. 136 and MVN 10, 102

Name	No. 136	MVN 10, 102
ur-^{d}iškur	obv. 1, 7	obv. i 4, rev. iii 8
lugal-nir-gal	obv. 3	obv. i 2
a-ta$_2$-na-aḫ	obv. 4	obv. i 4
ur-e$_2$-gal	obv. 5	obv. i 15
lugal-ḫa-ma-ti	obv. 6	obv. i 8
dingir-ba-an/ni	obv. 8	obv. i 13
ur-^{d}en-lil$_2$-la$_2$	obv. 9	obv. i 6
lu$_2$-^{d}suen	obv. 11	obv. i 11
ur-nig$_2$-du$_{10}$	obv. 13	obv. i 7
ku$_3$-^{d}šara$_2$	obv. 14	obv. i 3
a-tu	obv. 19	obv. i 10 (tu-ra)
a-kal-la	rev. 7	obv. i 16
ku$_3$-^{d}šara$_2$	rev. 8	obv. i 17
Lugal-geš-ḫur-e	rev. 10	obv. i 20

Text No. 136 is transliterated here in full.

obv.

1.	ug$_3$ ur-^{d}iškur ugula	Carrier, Ur-Iškur, overseer.
2.	1(diš) ur-$^{⌜geš?⌝}$gigir dumu-ni	1 Ur-Gigir, his child.
3.	1(aš) 4(ban$_2$) tug$_2$ lugal-nir-gal$_2$	1 (carrier, receiving unit of field?), 4 ban$_2$ (of barley), textile, Lugal-nirgal.
4.	1(aš) 4(ban$_2$) tug$_2$ a-ta$_2$-na-aḫ	1 (carrier, receiving unit of field?), 4 ban$_2$ (of barley), textile, Atanaḫ.
5.	1(aš) 3(ban$_2$) tug$_2$ ur-e$_2$-gal	1 (carrier, receiving unit of field?), 3 ban$_2$ (of barley), textile, Ur-Egal.
6.	1(aš) 3(ban$_2$) tug$_2$ lugal-⌜ḫa⌝-ma-ti	1 (carrier, receiving unit of field?), 3 ban$_2$ (of barley), textile, Lugal-ḫamati.
7.	1(aš) 3(ban$_2$) tug$_2$ ur-^{d}iškur	1 (carrier, receiving unit of field?), 3 ban$_2$ (of barley), textile, Ur-Iškur.
8.	1(aš) 3(ban$_2$) tug$_2$ dingir-ba-an[415]	1 (carrier, receiving unit of field?), 3 ban$_2$ (of barley), textile, Dingir-ban,
9.	1(aš) 3(ban$_2$) tug$_2$ ur-^{d}en-lil$_2$-la$_2$[416]	1 (carrier, receiving unit of field?), 3 ban$_2$ (of barley), textile, Ur-Enlila.
10.	1(aš) 3(ban$_2$) tug$_2$ šeš-kal-la	1 (carrier, receiving unit of field?), 3 ban$_2$ (of barley), textile, Šeš-kala.
11.	1(aš) 3(ban$_2$) tug$_2$ lu$_2$-^{d}suen	1 (carrier, receiving unit of field?), 3 ban$_2$ (of barley), textile, Lu-Suen.

[415] Probably identical to Dingir-bani in MVN 10, 102.

[416] Probably the same person recorded as ill in AnOr 7, 201.

12.	1(aš) 3(ban$_2$) tug$_2$ ur-e$_2$-maš	1 (carrier, receiving unit of field?), 3 ban$_2$ (of barley), textile, Ur-Emaš.
13.	1(aš) 3(ban$_2$) tug$_2$ ur$_2$-nig$_2$-du$_{10}$	1 (carrier, receiving unit of field?), 3 ban$_2$ (of barley), textile, Ur-nigdu.
14.	1(aš) 3(ban$_2$) tug$_2$ ku$_3$-^{d}šara$_2$	1 (carrier, receiving unit of field?), 3 ban$_2$ (of barley), textile, Ku-Šara.
15.	1(aš) 3(ban$_2$) tug$_2$ giri$_3$-^{d}šara$_2$-i$_3$-dab$_5$ zaḫ$_3$-ta gur-ra	1 (carrier, receiving unit of field?), 3 ban$_2$ (of barley), textile, Giri-Šara-idab, returned from flight.
16.	1(aš) 3(ban$_2$) tug$_2$ lugal-ḫe$_2$-gal$_2$	1 (carrier, receiving unit of field?), 3 ban$_2$ (of barley), textile, Lugal-ḫegal.
17.	1(aš) 3(ban$_2$) tug$_2$ lugal-bara$_2$-ge-si	1 (carrier, receiving unit of field?), 3 ban$_2$ (of barley), textile, Lugal-barage-si.
18.	1(aš) 3(ban$_2$) tug$_2$ nig$_2$-u$_2$-rum	1 (carrier, receiving unit of field?), 3 ban$_2$ (of barley), textile, Nig-urum.
19.	1(aš) 3(ban$_2$) tug$_2$ a-tu	1 (carrier, receiving unit of field?), 3 ban$_2$ (of barley), textile, Atu.
20.	1(aš) 2(ban$_2$) tug$_2$ ^{d}šara$_2$-kam	1 (carrier, receiving unit of field?), 2 ban$_2$ (of barley), textile, Šarakam.
21.	⸢baḫar$_3$⸣ lugal-ezem	Potter: Lugal-ezem.
22.	[1(aš)] ⸢4(ban$_2$)$^{?}$⸣ tug$_2$ lugal-ezem min-kam	1 (carrier, receiving unit of field?), 4 ban$_2$ (of barley), textile, Lugal-ezem, second time.
23.	[x]-am$_3$	It is . . .
24.	[1(aš) 4(ban$_2$)] tug$_2$ geš-bi dumu⸣ ^{d}nin-šubur-an-dul$_3$	1 (carrier, receiving unit of field?), 4 ban$_2$ (of barley), textile, Ninšubur-andul.

rev.

1.	[1(aš)] ⸢4(ban$_2$) tug$_2$ lu$_2$⸣-ma$_2$-gur$_8$-re dumu ^{d}neraḫ-an-dul$_3$	1 (carrier, receiving unit of field?), 4 ban$_2$ (of barley), textile, Lugal-magure, child of Neraḫ-andul.
2.	⸢geš⸣-ḫur-e[417]	(. . .)
3.	1(aš) 4(ban$_2$) tug$_2$ ARAD$_2$-^{d}šara$_2$ dumu ur-^{d}ašnan	1 (carrier, receiving unit of field?), 4 ban$_2$ (of barley), textile, ARAD-Šara, child of Ur-Ašnan.
4.	1(aš) 3(ban$_2$) tug$_2$ ur-gu$_2$-edin-na dumu bi$_2$-da	1 (carrier, receiving unit of field?), 3 ban$_2$ (of barley), textile, Ur-gu-edina, child of Bida.
	(blank space)	
5.	ki ur-^{d}da-mu ugula-ta	From Ur-Damu, overseer.
6.	1(aš) 4(ban$_2$) tug$_2$ u$_2$-še$_3$-ḫe$_2$-du	1 (carrier, receiving unit of field?), 4 ban$_2$ (of barley), textile, Uše-hedu.
7.	1(aš) 4(ban$_2$) tug$_2$ a-kal-la dumu ḫu-wa-wa[418]	1 (carrier, receiving unit of field?), 4 ban$_2$ (of barley), textile, A(ya)-kala, child of Ḫuwawa.
8.	1(aš) 4(ban$_2$) tug$_2$ ku$_3$-^{d}šara$_2$ <dumu$^{?}$> puzur$_4$-ma-ma	1 (carrier, receiving unit of field?), 4 ban$_2$ (of barley), textile, Ku-Šara, child of Puzur-Mama.

[417] Half of the line, before the three preserved signs, has been erased. It is probable that the line originally contained the personal name Lugal-gešḫur'e.

[418] Mentioned together with Atu (l. 19) and A(ya)kala, child of Ḫuwawa (here rev. 7 and probably not yet a permanent member of the staff), as ill in a document from AS 8 (overseer Ur-Iškur) (MVN 16, 799).

	(*blank space*)	
9.	ki lu$_2$-^{d}šara$_2$ ugula-ta	From Lu-Šara, overseer.
10.	1(aš) 4(ban$_2$) tug$_2$ lugal-geš-ḫur-e	1 (carrier, receiving unit of field?), 4 ban$_2$ (of barley) textile, Lugal-gešḫure.
11.	ki ur-^{d}nin-su-ta	From Ur-Ninsu.
	(*blank space*)	
12.	šunigin 1(u) 1(aš) ug$_3$ [4(ban$_2$)]	Total: 11 carriers, (receiving unit of field?), 4 ban$_2$.
13.	šunigin 1(u) 6(aš) ug$_3$ [3(ban$_2$)]	Total: 16 carriers, (receiving unit of field?), 3 ban$_2$.
14.	šunigin 1(aš) ug$_3$ [2(ban$_2$)]	Total: 1 carrier, (receiving unit of field?), 2 ban$_2$.
15.	gurum$_2$ ak ša$_3$ i$_7$ ⸢lugal⸣	Inventory of those(?) of the "king's canal"(?).
16.	iti min-eš$_3$-ta u$_4$ 1(u) 5(diš)-am$_3$ ba-ra-zal-la-ta	From month: "Double-sanctuary," the 15th day has passed.
17.	mu en-unu$_6$-gal en ^{d}inanna ba-[ḫun]	Year: "Enunugal, the En-priest of Inanna, was installed."

Only ten carriers receiving 4 ban$_2$ of barley (a month) are explicitely listed, but one must assume that the overseer, Ur-Iškur, found in line one of the obverse, also received this monthly ration. His child, Ur-Gigir, apparently did not receive any rations on his own.

No. 137. *MS 4691 (Umma, X)*

Both the begining and the end of text No. 137 are missing, and all that remains is a list of persons, identified as boat-builders (ma$_2$-gin$_2$) and sailors (ma$_2$-laḫ$_5$). A piece of a different tablet has been glued on to the top of MS 4691, giving it the impression of being nearly complete.

Despite its missing colophon, No. 137 can confidently be grouped with the inventories based on the colophon of a closely parallel text, Fs Sigrist 2 (BM 106145). That text is identified as an inventory (rev. 20) of the fifth day (rev. 19), and is dated to Amar-Suen year 7, month 11. No calendrical information is preserved in No. 137. The last group of workers in Fs Sigrist 2 is designated as "of the shipyard" (ša$_3$ mar-sa, rev. 19).

Text No. 137 is transliterated here in full:

obv.

	(*start broken*)	
1'.	[x] x [...]	...
2'.	1(diš) nam-tar-eb$_2$-<gu>-ul	1 Namtar-ebgul.
3'.	1(diš) ur-ḫal-i$_3$-du	1 Ur-Ḫal-idu.
4'.	1(diš) giri$_3$-ni	1 Girini.
5'.	1(diš) lu$_2$-^{d}šara$_2$ dumu-ni	1 Lu-Šara, his child.
6'.	1(diš) ur-sukkal	1 Ur-Sukkal.
7'.	1(diš) e$_2$-ur$_3$-bi	1 E-urbi.
8'.	1(diš) giri$_3$-ni-i$_3$-dab$_5$	1 Girini-idab.
9'.	½(diš) lu$_2$-dingir-ra	½ Lu-dingira.
10'.	½(diš) lu$_2$-eb-gal dumu-ni	½ Lu-Ebgal, his child.
11'.	1(diš) an-ne$_2$-ba-du$_7$	1 Anne-badu.
12'.	½(diš) ur-ama-na dumu-ni	½ Ur-amana, his child.
13'.	½(diš) ku$_3$-^{d}šara$_2$	½ Ku-Šara.
14'.	1(diš) ur-^{d}ašnan	1 Ur-Ašnan.
15'.	1(diš) šeš-ki-ag$_2$	1 Šeš-kiag.
16'.	ma$_2$-laḫ$_5$-me	They are sailors.

rev.

1.	1(diš) lu$_2$-me-lam$_2$	1 Lugal-melam.
2.	1(diš) ur-^{d}su$_4$-an-na	1 Ur-Su'anna.
3.	1(diš) ur-mes	1 Ur-mes.
4.	1(diš) giri$_3$-^{d}šara$_2$-i$_3$-dab$_5$	1 Giri-Šara-idab.
5.	1(diš) lu$_2$-eb-gal	1 Lu-Ebgal.
6.	ma$_2$:gin$_2$-me	They are boat-builders.
7.	1(diš) ur-nigar^{gar}	1 Ur-Nigar.
8.	1(diš) ur-si-gar	1 Ur-Sigar.
9.	1(diš) ur-^{d}suen	1 Ur-Suen.
10.	1(diš) ur-^{d}en-ki	1 Ur-Enki.
11.	1(diš) ur-dingir-ra	1 Ur-Dingira.
12.	1(diš) ⌜lu$_2$⌝-^{d}šara$_2$	1 Lu-Šara.
13.	1(diš) [šu]- ⌜im⌝-bi	1 Šu-Imbi.
14.	1(diš) [lugal-nir]-gal$_2$	1 Lugal-Nirgal.
15.	1(diš) [er$_3$-e]-eb	1 Ereb.
	(*rest broken*)[419]	

Due to the many differences between the crews of the two texts, they are unlikely to come from the same year. However, we can assume that text No. 137 dates to before Fs Sigrist 2 because Ur-amana is listed as a child of Anne-badu in No. 137 and Anne-badu no longer appears in Fs Sigrist 2.

The crews listed in the two texts are set out in Table 4*a*–*c* (see pages 200–201). Persons in Fs Sigrist 2 are given first as it is more complete. The order of the persons in No. 137 is indicated in parentheses after their names.

No. 138. *MS 2012 (Umma, X)*

Text No. 138 would have been, when complete, one of the largest Ur III tablets ever discovered. It lists land allotments for various staff. About two hundred entries are preserved, representing two hundred individuals with their allotments and information about the location of their plots. Originally, the text would have listed more than twice that number.

Although the beginning of the colophon is badly damaged and illegible, the text can be assigned to Umma based on the prosopographical information.

The size of most of the prebend-fields listed in text No. 138 is either 1 eše$_3$ or half of that, namely 3 iku. These areas correspond in modern terms to c. 2.16 ha and 1.08 ha (or 10,800 m^2 and 5,400 m^2). The production recorded from these fields is mostly 6 or 7 gur for the 1 eše$_3$ allotments, and 3 gur for the 3 iku allotments. This agrees well with the yield-ratios of Ur III times, when standard fields would be expected to yield 20 gur to each 1 bur$_3$, when sowing 1 gur to each 1 bur$_3$ (6 gur to 1 eše$_3$ corresponds to a yield of 18 gur to 1 bur$_3$, and 7 gur to 1 eše$_3$ corresponds to 21 gur to 1 bur$_3$; 3 gur to 3 iku corresponds to 18 gur to 1 bur$_3$ as well). The value of these grants, generous as they may seem, does not necessarily represent a real advantage over the rations given to the normal worker (1 barig a month corresponds to a yearly ration of 2 gur and 2 barig), or the "wages" given to the hirelings (6 sila$_3$ a day corresponds to a yearly ration of 7 gur and 1 barig). Detailed prosopographical work is needed to assess whether the land allotments found in these texts were given in addition to rations, and whether the entire family of the allotment holder (in addition to plow oxen) were to be fed from this.

---

419 Perhaps to be reconstructed: [ša$_3$ mar-sa-me]/[gurum$_2$-ak u$_4$-*n*-kam]/[iti . . .]/[mu . . .], "Within the shipyard, inventory of the *n*th day, month: x; year x," following D'Agostino and Santagati 2008.

Table 4a. Sailors in text No. 137 and Fs Sigrist 2

Fs Sigrist 2	No. 137
ša-ad-da	—
ur-lugal	—
ḫu-da-ti	—
ur-^{d}šakkan	—
a-kal-la	—
a-kal-la (min-kam)	—
ur-ḫal-i$_3$-du	ur-ḫal-i$_3$-du (2')
nam-tar-eb$_2$-du$_7$	nam-tar-eb$_2$-du$_7$ (1')
ARAD$_2$-mu	—
ARAD$_2$-dam	—
šeš-ki-ag$_2$	šeš-ki-ag$_2$ (14')
giri$_3$-ni	giri$_3$-ni (3')
lu$_2$-^{d}šara$_2$ (child of giri$_3$-ni)	lu$_2$-^{d}šara$_2$ (child of giri$_3$-ni) (4')
e$_2$-ur$_3$-bi	e$_2$-ur$_3$-bi (6')
giri$_3$-ni-i$_3$-dab$_5$	giri$_3$-ni-i$_3$-dab$_5$ (7')
lu$_2$-dingir-ra	lu$_2$-dingir-ra (8')
lu$_2$-eb-gal (child of lu$_2$-dingir-ra)	lu$_2$-eb-gal (child of lu$_2$-dingir-ra) (9')
ur-^{d}ašnan	ur-^{d}ašnan (13')
ku$_3$-^{d}šara$_2$	ku$_3$-^{d}šara$_2$ (12')
ur-ama-na	ur-ama-na (child of an-ne$_2$-ba-du$_7$) (11')
nig$_2$-u$_2$-rum	—
^{d}šara$_2$-i$_3$-zu	—
ur-sukkal	ur-sukkal (5')
—	an-ne$_2$-ba-du$_7$ (10')

Table 4b. Boat-builders in text No. 137 and Fs Sigrist 2

Fs Sigrist 2	No. 137
a-kal-la	—
lugal-me-e$_3$	lugal-me-lam$_2$ (1)
ur-mes	ur-mes (3)
giri$_3$-^{d}šara$_2$-i$_3$-dab$_5$	giri$_3$-^{d}šara$_2$-i$_3$-dab$_5$ (4)
lu$_2$-eb-gal	lu$_2$-eb-gal (5)
—	ur-^{d}su$_4$-an-na (2)

Sometimes a much higher yield is recorded (e.g., rev. iv 1', 10 gur to 1 eše$_3$ and rev. v 26', 12 gur to 1 eše$_3$), and occasionally a much lower yield (e.g., obv. xi 17', 1 gur to 3 iku). In case of a very low yield, the field is classified as ki-BAD (possibly to be interpreted as "dead" or "bad land"; obv. ix 23'–24'). In one case (obv. x 13') no yield is recorded. This is done by simply writing "not" (nu) in the field where a yield would be expected. This field is also classified as ki-BAD.

The approximately two hundred preserved entries, representing individual allotment holders, are grouped together two or three at the time, and assigned to a location. There are approximately one hundred such locations preserved in the text, each given a field name. The same fields are listed several times across the text

Table 4c. Staff of the shipyard in text No. 137 and Fs Sigrist 2

Fs Sigrist 2	No. 137
lugal-ḫe$_2$-gal$_2$ nagar	—
ur-nigar^{gar}	ur-nigar^{gar} (1)
ur-^{d}suen	ur-^{d}suen (3)
ur-^{d}en-ki	ur-^{d}en-ki (4)
ur-si-gar	ur-si-gar (2)
ur-dingir-ra	ur-dingir-ra (5)
šu-im-bi	šu-im-bi (7)
lu$_2$-^{d}šara$_2$	lu$_2$-^{d}šara$_2$ (6)
lugal-nir-gal$_2$	lugal-nir-gal$_2$ (8)
er$_3$-e-eb	er$_3$-e-eb (9)

(the Ninḫursag field is found fifteen times, and the field "across from" (g a b a) the Ninḫursag field another ten times). Most of the field names are known from other texts.

The names of sixteen fields are preserved in text No. 138.[420] Six of them are also found referenced as "field across from . . ." A further three fields are found only in the form "field across from . . ." These field names are set out in Table 5.

The reason that the same field names recur multiple times throughout the text is that the text is organized along the lines of small family units. However, this is not as visible here as it is in many of the previous texts.

In the first five columns of the obverse, these are the family groups of cultivators (e n g a r). The names of thirteen cultivators are preserved. The section most likely originally contained the names of about twenty cultivators, corresponding to the cultivators assigned to two domain units. The remaining part of the text has various other lower-level overseers.

Apart from the overseers, listed with their titles, it is very difficult to trace any of the people listed in this text in the textual record of Ur III Umma; ordinary people simply did not register beyond lists such as this one, except occasionally, when or if they fell ill, died or ran away.

Two passages exemplify how the people listed in this text were organized in small family units:

No. 138 obv. col. iii

10'.	1(cše$_3$) GAN$_2$ 7(aš) gur	1 eše$_3$ of field, (yielding) 7 gur (of barley),
11'.	ur-^{d}šara$_2$ engar	Ur-Šara, cultivator.
12'.	3(iku) GAN$_2$ 3(aš) gur	3 iku of field, (yielding) 3 gur (of barley),
13'.	lugal-nig$_2$-lagar-e	Lugal-Niglagare.
14'.	3(iku) GAN$_2$ 3(aš) gur	3 iku of field, (yielding) 3 gur (of barley),
15'.	giri$_3$-ni	Girini.
16'.	3(iku) GAN$_2$ 3(aš) gur	3 iku of field, (yielding) 3 gur (of barley),
17'.	lugal-me-lam$_2$	Lugal-melam.
18'.	gaba a-ša$_3$ na-ra-am- ^{d} suen	Across from: Field of Naram-Suen.

Although it is not stated that Ur-Šara is an older relative of Lugal-Niglagare, Girizal, and Lugal-Melam, this is at least highly plausible given the usual organization of such groups.

In the next example, one of the junior members of the group is explicitly said to be a relative of the first and most senior member:

[420] A further seven are broken. See obv. vi 5', obv. xii 18', obv. xiii 10', rev. iii 8', 10', 14', 16'.

Table 5. Names of fields in text No. 138

Field name	Translation	Reference	Across from . . .
a-ša$_3$ ^{d}en-lil$_2$-la$_2$	Field of Enlil	rev. vii 6', vii 11', 14'	
a-ša$_3$ ^{d}nin-ḫur-sag	Field of Ninḫursag	obv. x 25', xi 20', xii 5', rev. ii 16', 19', iv 11', v 5', 12', 18', 33', vi 12', 28', 31', vii 29', viii 15', ix 6'	gaba a-ša$_3$ DN: obv. vi 25', 28', rev. ii 13', iii 19', iv 14', v 10', viii 17'. a-ša$_3$ gaba DN: obv. viii 5', ix 2', rev. iv 33'
a-ša$_3$ ^{d}nin-zabala$_3$^{ki}	Field of Nin-Zabala	obv. xi 5'	
a-ša$_3$ ^{d}šara$_2$-gu$_2$-gal	Field of "Boisterous Šara"[421]	obv. vii 6', viii 12', ix 22', rev. i 19'	
a-ša$_3$ a-bu$_3$-du-du	Field of Abu-dudu	rev. i 4', ii 1', 8'	
a-ša$_3$ a-ni-zu	Field of Anizu	obv. viii 9', 21',[422] rev. viii 8', x, 21'	
a-ša$_3$ a-u$_2$-da	Field of A'uda	rev. iv 5'	obv. vi 16', rev. iii 27', iv 2', 22'
a-ša$_3$ a-ur-im	Field of A'ur'im	rev. ii 11'	
a-ša$_3$ apin-ba-zi	Field of Apinbazi	obv. iii 9', v 15', x 5', 17'	obv. vi 10', rev. iv 17', 30', v 27'
a-ša$_3$ gu$_4$-suḫub$_2$	Field of reclaimed land (lit. "Field of the booted oxen")[423]	obv. viii 18'	obv i 9', vi 22'
a-ša$_3$ gur$_4$-za-an		rev. vi 10', 15', 17', vii 27', viii 20'	rev. ix 9'
a-ša$_3$ na-ra-am-^{d}suen	Field of Naram-Sin	obv. vii 9', viii 24', xiii 1', 4', rev. iv 19', vi 25'	obv. iii 4', 18', rev. vii 20'
a-ša$_3$ tul$_2$-ḫul$_2$- ^{d}utu	Field of the Joyful Well of Utu[424]	obv. ii 16', vii 15', x 12', xiii 7'	
a-ša$_3$ u$_2$-du- ^{d} nin-a-ra-li	Field of the shepherd[425] of Ninarali	obv. vi 19', viii 15', rev. i 17', rev vi 23', x 2'	
a-ša$_3$ u$_2$-du-en-e$_2$-a	Field of the shepherd of En'e'a	obv. vi 7', rev. i 7'	
a-ša$_3$ muru$_{13}$	"Middle" field	obv. vii 4', rev. v 30'	
gaba a-ša$_3$ a-bu$_3$[426]	Across from the Abu field	rev. vii 22', viii 5'	
gaba a-ša$_3$ na-gab$_2$-tum	Across from the Nagabtum field	obv. viii 2'	
gaba a-ša$_3$ šul-pa-e$_3$	Across from the field of Šulpa'e	obv. vii 12'	

[421] Although gu$_2$-gal is also a name of a kind of bean, it is likely here to be a description of Šara.

[422] Note the variant writings a-ša$_3$ a-ni-zu$^!$(BA) in obv. viii 21'.

[423] According to Maekawa (1984: 74, 80 ff., 91) the gu$_4$-suḫub was a type of covering for the hooves of the oxen used when bringing new land under the plow.

[424] Or perhaps phonetic for du$_6$-hul$_2$-^{d}utu, "Joyful hill/mound of Utu," see the DN ^{d}nin-du$_6$-ḫul$_2$-^{d}utu.

[425] Probably phonetic for utul, "shepherd."

[426] The fields a-bu$_3$-du-du and a-bu$_3$ are attested in about 20 texts each, and once in the same text (UTI 4, 2836). Another text has the field a-bu$_3$ together with another field a-ša$_3$ a-bu$_3$-^{d}du-du (BPOA 7, 2342). A field across (gaba) from the a-bu$_3$-du-du is also attested: see UTI 4, 2812 obv. 6.

No. 138 obv. col. iv

11'.	1(eše$_3$) GAN$_2$ 7(aš) gur	1 eše$_3$ of field, (yielding) 7 gur (of barley),
12'.	ur- ^{d}dumu-zi-da	Ur-Dumuzi.
13'.	3(iku) GAN$_2$ 3(aš) gur	3 iku of field, (yielding) 3 gur (of barley),
14'.	a-kal-la šeš-a-ni	A(ya)-kala, his brother.
15'.	GAN$_2$ še-ba	Field of barley rations.
16'.	a-a-lu$_2$-du$_{10}$ ša$_3$-saḫar-ra-ta	From Aya-ludu, engineer troop.
17'.	3(iku) GAN$_2$ 3(aš) gur	3 iku of field, (yielding) 3 gur (of barley),
18'.	ḫa-la- ^{d}iškur	Ḫala-Iškur.

In the following two passages we see that the allotments of individuals could be spread across several different fields:

No. 138 obv. col. vii

3'.	2(iku) ½(iku) GAN$_2$ 2(aš) gur	2 iku of field, (yielding) 2 gur (of barley),
4'.	a-ša$_3$ muru$_{13}$	Field: Muru.
5'.	3(iku) ½(iku) GAN$_2$ 2(aš) gur	3 ½ iku of field, (yielding) 2 gur (of barley),
6'.	a-ša$_3$ ^{d}šara$_2$-gu$_2$-gal	Field of "Boisterous Šara."
7'.	šeš-kal-la nagar	Šeš-kala, carpenter.
8'.	1(eše$_3$) 5(aš) gur	1 eše$_3$ of field, (yielding) 5 gur (of barley),
9'.	a-ša$_3$ na-ra-am-^{d}suen	Field of Naram-Suen.
10'.	ur-^{d}nun-gal tug$_2$-du$_8$	Ur-Nungal, felter.

No. 138 rev. col. iv

9'.	1(eše$_3$) GAN$_2$ 3(aš) gur	1 eše$_3$ of field, (yielding) 3 gur (of barley),
10'.	nig$_2$-du$_7$-pa-e$_3$ dumu dingir-ba-an	Nig-dupa'e, child of Dingir-ban.
11'.	a-ša$_3$ ^{d}nin-ḫur-sag	Field of Ninḫursag.
12'.	3(iku) GAN$_2$ 3(aš) gur	1 eše$_3$ of field, (yielding) 3 gur (of barley),
13'.	lu$_2$-^{d}šara$_2$	Lu-Šara.
14'.	gaba a-ša$_3$ ^{d}nin-ḫur-sag	Across from: Field of Ninḫursag.
15'.	nig$_2$-du$_7$-pa-e$_3$ i$_3$-dab$_5$	Nig-dupa'e seized.
16'.	4(iku) ½(iku) GAN$_2$ 8(aš) gur	4 ½ iku of field, (yielding) 8 gur (of barley),
17'.	gaba a-ša$_3$ apin-ba-zi	Across from: Field of Apinbazi.
18'.	1(bur$_3$) GAN$_2$ 1(aš) 2(barig) 3(ban$_2$) gur	1 bur$_3$ of field, (yielding) 1 gur, 2 barig, 3 ban$_2$ (of barley),
19'.	a-ša$_3$ na-ra-am-^{d}suen	Field of Naram-Suen.
20'.	ur-sila-luḫ na-⌜gada⌝	Ur-silaluḫ, herdsman.
21'.	3(iku) GAN$_2$ 3(aš) gur	3 iku of field, (yielding) 3 gur (of barley),
22'.	a-ša$_3$ gaba a-u$_2$-da	Field across from: (Field of) A'uda.
23'.	^{d}utu-bar-ra	Utu-bara.
24'.	ur-sila-luḫ i$_3$-dab$_5$	Ur-silaluḫ seized.
	(blank space)	
25'.	sipa ud$_5$ nam-en-na	Goat herders of the "lordship (administrative area?)."[427]

[427] nam-en-na is an administrative unit of herded animals in Umma. It is not clear to which household it belongs, or what its relationship is to animal administration in general.

The text is transliterated in full in the Appendix.

No. 139. *MS 4357 (Umma, X)*

Text No. 139 is a fragment from the surface of a large inventory tablet, similar or identical to No. 138. The various staff are listed with allotments of either 3 i k u or 1 e š e$_3$, and with the estimated production from these. As was the case with text No. 138, the production is not identical from similar sized fields, but varies within general bands. In No. 138 some fields were specifically said to have produced very little or nothing. Text No. 139 does not preserve any comparable sections. It is transliterated and translated in full here:

obv. col. i'

	(beginning broken)	
1'.	[. . .] x	. . .
2'.	[. . .]-⸢zi⸣-da	. . .
3'.	[. . .] gur	. . .
4'.	[. . .]-zu	
5'.	[. . .] gur	. . .
6'.	[. . .]-x engar	. . . , cultivator.
7'.	[. . .]-x	. . .
8'.	[. . .] gur	. . .
9'.	[. . .]-ta	. . .
10'.	[. . .]-⸢ḫu⸣	. . .

obv. col. ii'

	(beginning broken)	
1'.	[. . .]	. . . . ,
2'.	[. . .] sipa	shepherd.
3'.	[. . .] ⸢ša$_3$⸣-saḫar-ra-še$_3$	. . . as engineer troops.
4'.	[. . .] GAN$_2$ 3(aš) 2(barig) gur	x units of field, (yielding) 3 gur, 2 barig (of barley),
5'.	⸢lu$_2$⸣-bala-saga ša$_3$-⸢saḫar⸣-ra	Lu-balasaga, the engineer troop,
6'.	ki lugal-ma$_2$-gur$_8$-re mu$_6$-sub$_3$!(GU$_4$)	Place of Lugal-magure, herdsman.
7'.	3(iku) GAN$_2$ 3(aš) 2(barig) gur	3 iku of field, (yielding) 3 gur, 2 barig (of barley),
8'.	lu$_2$-^{d}nin-šubur	Lu-Ninšubur.
9'.	1(eše$_3$) GAN$_2$ 7(aš) gur	1 eše$_3$ of field, (yielding) 7 gur (of barley),
10'.	lu$_2$-^{d}šara$_2$ engar	Lu-Šara, cultivator.
11'.	3(iku) GAN$_2$ 3(aš) gur	3 iku of field, (yielding) 3 gur (of barley),
12'.	ur-^{d}ur$_3$-bar-tab	Ur-Urbartab.
13'.	3(iku) GAN$_2$ 3(aš) 2(barig) gur	3 iku of field, (yielding) 3 gur, 2 barig (of barley),
14'.	an-gal$_2$-ka	Angalka.
15'.	3(iku) GAN$_2$ 3(aš) 2(barig) gur	3 iku of field, (yielding) 3 gur, 2 barig (of barley),

obv. col. iii'

1.	x [. . .]	. . .
2.	lu$_2$-[. . .]	Lu- . . .
3.	1(eše$_3$) GAN$_2$ [. . .]	1 eše$_3$ of field, (yielding)
4.	lugal-[. . .]	. . . . , Lugal-. . . .
5.	1(eše$_3$) GAN$_2$ ⸢6(aš)⸣ [. . . gur]	1 eše$_3$ of field, (yielding) 6 gur and . . .

6.	x-x	. . .
7.	1(eše$_3$) GAN$_2$ 6(aš) gur	1 eše$_3$ of field (yielding) 6 gur (of barley),
8.	ur-nigar^{gar}	Ur-Nigar.
9.	a-ša$_3$ muru$_{13}$	"Middle Field."
10.	1(eše$_3$) GAN$_2$ 6(aš) gur	1 eše$_3$ of field, (yielding) 6 gur (of barley),
11.	lugal-kur-dub$_2$-e	Lugal-kurdube.
12.	1(eše$_3$) GAN$_2$ ⸢6(aš)⸣ gur	1 eše$_3$ of field, (yielding) 6 gur (of barley),
13.	al-⸢la⸣	Alla.
14.	1(eše$_3$) GAN$_2$ 6(aš) ⸢gur⸣	1 eše$_3$ of field, (yielding) 6 gur (of barley),
15.	lu$_5$-u$_2$-⸢lu$_5$⸣	Lu'ulu.

obv. col. iv'

(rest of tablet missing)

No. 140. *MS 4332 (Umma, AS 5–vii–x)*

Text No. 140 is a fragmentary six-column inventory. The colophon is damaged but a reconstruction is possible (see No. 133 for a similar colophon):

No. 140 rev. col. iii

(blank space)

1.	[gurum$_2$] ⸢ak⸣ ug$_3$-[IL$_2$] tur-tur	Inventory of carriers and children.
2.	[iti min]- ⸢eš$_3$⸣-ta [u$_4$ x]-am$_3$ ba-ra-[zal]-⸢la⸣-ta	From month: "Double-sanctuary," from the nth day has passed.
3.	[mu en] ⸢unu$_6$⸣-[gal ^{d}inanna] ⸢ba⸣-ḫun	Year: "Enunugal (the En-priest of) Inanna was installed."

Two groups of staff (g i r i$_3$ - s e$_3$ - g a) and eleven groups of dedicatees (a - r u - a) are present in the preserved parts of the text. Most of the groups of dedicatees are also found in text No. 126, and the members of the groups are largely identical. The groups of staff are not found in that text. It is possible, but difficult to verify, that some of the dedicatees were also members of a group of staff, as can be suggested for the damaged beginning of obv. col. iii:

No. 140 obv. col. iii

1'.	[. . .]	(x rations of x for PN),
2'.	⸢a-ru$^?$⸣-[a$^?$ . . .]	dedicatee of (PN).
3'.	1(aš) ⸢2(ban$_2$)⸣ [. . .]	1 (receiving unit of field?), 2 ban$_2$ (of barley for PN),
4'.	a-ru-a [. . .]	dedicatee of (PN).
5'.	a-ru-a x [. . .]	Dedicatee. . . .
6'.	1(aš) 4(ban$_2$) tug$_2$ šu-[. . .]	1 (receiving unit of field?), 4 ban$_2$ (of barley), textiles, (for) Šu-. . . .
7'.	gurum$_2$-e ⸢tak$_4$$^?$⸣-[a$^?$]	Set aside for sustenance.
8'.	1(aš) 2(ban$_2$) 2(diš) ur-[. . .]-du ⸢dumu⸣ [. . .]	1 (receiving unit of field?), 2 ban$_2$ (of barley), 2 (units of . . .), (for) Ur-x, child of . . .
9'.	⸢1(aš) 2(ban$_2$) 2(diš) ⸣ [. . .]	1 (receiving unit of field?), 2 ban$_2$ (of barley), 2 (units of . . .), . . .
10'.	⸢dumu-ni⸣	(for) his child.
11'.	giri$_3$-se$_3$-ga ^{geš}kiri$_6$-ta	Staff of the garden.

Like the previous texts, No. 140 also arranges much of the staff in small family groups. Two small, well-preserved groups are found in col. i of the reverse:

No. 140 rev. col. i

12.	tu-ra lugal-a$_2$-zi-⸢da⸣	Sick: Lugal-azida.
13.	1(aš) 3(ban$_2$) tug$_2$ ur-^{d}šul-pa-e$_3$	1 (receiving unit of field?), 3 ban$_2$ (of barley), textiles, Ur-Šulpa'e.
14.	1(aš) 3(ban$_2$) tug$_2$ ur-^{d}a-šar$_2$	1 (receiving unit of field?), 3 ban$_2$ (of barley), textiles, Ur-Ašar.
15.	1(diš) lugal-nesag-e	1 Lugal-nesage.
16.	dumu lugal-a$_2$-zi-da-me	They are the children of Lugal-Azida.
17.	1(aš) 3(ban$_2$) tug$_2$ lugal-si-sa$_2$ a-ru-a ukken-ne$_2$	1 (receiving unit of field?), 3 ban$_2$ (of barley), textiles, Lugal-sisa, dedicatee of Ukkene.
18.	1(aš) 3(ban$_2$) tug$_2$ lu$_2$-^{d}nin-ur$_4$-ra	1 (receiving unit of field?), 3 ban$_2$ (of barley), textiles, Lu-Nin-ura,
19.	⸢dumu? šeš⸣-kal-la kur-ga$_2$-ra	child of Šeš-kala, kurgara.
20.	ki lugal-ma$_2$-gur$_8$-re-ta	From Lugal-magure.

For one of these family groups (obv. iii 18'–21'), an extraordinary situation had occurred that needed a longer explanation. In this entry we find a certain Ḫuti, whom we have already encountered in three of the inventories published here (Nos. 126, 128, and 129). From these three texts we learn that Huti had four sons, Ur-saga, Girini-isa, Lu-Inanna, and Basaga, and that he originally belonged to the extended family of Lugal-kuzu, cowherd, son of Ur-E'e. Ḫuti's family group is not recorded in the same way in all three texts and the passages are therefore all given in the table below (Table 6). Both from the title given to Ḫuti in No. 126 (gab$_2$-ra, "cowherd") and from the contexts, it is clear that Ḫuti was a herdsman. He is not found in any other published Ur III text.

Text No. 126 most likely dates to after No. 129, since Lugal-kuzu is not listed any longer. In text No. 140, dating to the same year as No. 129, Ḫuti is no longer found among the members of the group, which now consists of only Ur-saga and Girini-isa. Instead, in No. 140 Ḫuti is said to have been a fugitive for the past ten years:

Table 6. Ḫuti's family group in three different inventories

No. 128 (AS 3) obv. iii	No. 129 (AS 5) obv. iv	No. 126 (–) obv. vi
23. 1(aš$_c$) GAN$_2$ lugal-ku$_3$-zu unu$_3$ dumu ur-e$_{11}$-e 24. 1(aš$_c$) GAN$_2$ ḫu-ti 25. 1(aš) giri$_3$-ni-i$_3$-⸢sa$_6$⸣ 26. 1(diš) ur-sa$_6$ 27. 1(diš) lu$_2$-^{d}inanna 28. dumu-ni-me	5. 1(aš$_c$) GAN$_2$ lugal-ku$_3$-zu unu$_3$ dumu ur-e$_{11}$-e 6. ḫu-ti 7. giri$_3$-ni-i$_3$-sa$_6$ 8. ur-sa$_6$ 9. lu$_2$-^{d}⸢inanna⸣ 10. ba-⸢saga⸣ 11. dumu-ni-me	2. 3(ban$_2$) ur-saga 3. 3(ban$_2$) giri$_3$-ni-i$_3$-sa$_6$ 4. dumu ḫu-ti gab$_2$-ra-me 5. ki a-tu-ta
1 (receiving unit of) field, Lugal-kuzu, cowherd, child of Ur-E'e. 1 (receiving unit of) field, Ḫuti. 1 (receiving unit of field?) Girini-isa. 1 Ur-saga. 1 Lu-Inanna. They are his children.	1 (receiving unit of) field, Lugal-kuzu, cowherd, child of Ur-E'e. Ḫuti. Girini-isa. Ur-saga. Lu-Inanna. Basaga. They are his children.	3 ban$_2$ (of barley), Ur-saga. 3 ban$_2$ (of barley), Girini-isa. They are children of Ḫuti, cowherd. From Atu.

No. 140 obv. col. iii

18'.	1(aš) 3(ban$_2$) tug$_2$ ur-sa$_6$	1 (receiving unit of field?), 3 ban$_2$ (of barley), textile, (for) Ur-sa.
19'.	1(aš) 3(ban$_2$) tug$_2$ giri$_3$-ni-i$_3$-⸢sa$_6$⸣	1 (receiving unit of field?), 3 ban$_2$ (of barley), textile, (for) Girini-isa.
20'.	dumu ḫu-ti-me	They are children of Ḫuti.
21'.	mu 1(u)-am$_3$ ḫu-ti ba-zaḫ$_3$ u$_3$ ur-sa$_6$ dumu-ni gurum$_2$-da ba-da-an-du$_{11}$ ensi$_2$ e$_2$ muḫaldim-ta ba-al-la-še$_3$	For 10 years (when) Ḫuti (had) fled and Ur-sa, his child, (had) received(?) rations from the kitchen of the governor . . .

If the reconstruction of the date of text No. 140 is correct, then we may have here an extraordinary piece of evidence of fraud committed in the ancient world. In No. 129, Ḫuti and his family group are not listed as recipients of rations or allotments. If No. 140 really reveals that Ḫuti had actually been absent for the past ten years, then the information in No. 128, dated to two years before Nos. 140 and 129, is fraudulent. Are the two texts Nos. 140 and 129 trying to set the record straight? Unfortunately, the statement in No. 140 obv. iii 21 presents several grammatical and lexical problems and the exact meaning of the line remains uncertain.

What remains clear, however, is that the state administrators were concerned about the whereabouts of workers for substantial periods of time and with an attention to detail of almost modern proportions: at the time text No. 140 was written, Huti had been a runaway for ten years, yet he is still accounted for in the records. The reason may be that his sons were obliged to serve in his place, as is known from other cases (Reid 2015).

No overseer is named in the colophon of text No. 140, but it is almost certain that the text records the crew of Kugani, mentioned in the first line of obv. i and in the last line of rev. i (l. 23). An almost identical crew, also under the overseer Kugani, is found in text No. 135 rev. iv 42–vi 29. No. 135 is dated to AS 6, the year after No. 140. The only significant difference between the two texts, in the make up of the staff, is the designation in No. 135 of the workers of the first and largest group as libir-am$_3$ (lit. "it is old, previous," probably here "original") and a smaller group as daḫ-ḫu-me (lit. "they are additions"). Whereas the workers listed in No. 135 as original (crew members) almost completely overlap with the workers found in No. 140 obv. i–ii, there is very limited or no overlap between the two texts in the second part (the additions). Both texts assign workers as dedicatees, but only No. 140 groups them according to teams (giri$_3$-se$_3$-ga).

Text No. 140 is transliterated in full in the Appendix.

No. 141. *MS 2017 (Umma, X)*

It is difficult to say much about text No. 141, the last of the larger inventories presented here, since the two lines of key terminology that terminate the text are difficult to understand: inim-ni ba-gen$_3$(KUR)-na and KA-TUG$_2$ PN. The use of the sign KUR as a verbal base, presumably with the reading gen$_3$ (or gin$_3$), is otherwise not attested in Ur III Sumerian. Nor is TUG$_2$ attested with the reading dab or dib in Ur III Sumerian. The two lines are here tentatively translated as "their words (= cases) were confirmed, in the second month; 'KATUG-official' is Lugal-amar-ku, child of Dadagani." The body of the text is a list of forty workers, all presumably having fled (zah$_3$):

obv.

1.	la$_2$-ia$_3$ 1(diš) na-ba-sa$_2$	Deficit: 1 Nabasa.
2.	1(diš) ^{d}šara$_2$-kam dumu ur-^{d}suen	1 Šarakam, child of Ur-Suen.
3.	1(diš) ur-ge$_6$-par$_4$	1 Ur-Gepar.
4.	1(diš) lugal-za$_3$-ge-si	1 Lugal-zage-si.
5.	1(diš) ⸢ur⸣-^{d}šul-pa-e$_3$ dumu ARAD$_2$-ḫu-la	1 Ur-Šulpa'e, child of ARAD-ḫula.
6.	1(diš) ^{d}šara$_2$-kam dumu ur-^{d}iškur	1 Šarakam, child of Ur-Iškur.
7.	1(diš) nam-zi-tar-ra	1 Namzi-tara.

8.	1(diš) ab-ba-gi-⌜na⌝ dumu lu$_2$-du$_{10}$-ga	1 Abbagina, child of Lu-duga.
9.	1(diš) inim- ^{d}šara$_2$ dumu lu$_2$-nig$_2$-lagar-e	1 Inim-Šara, child of Lu-niglagare.
10.	1(diš) lu$_2$-du$_{10}$-ga dumu da-lu$_5$	1 Lu-duga, child of Dalu.
	(*blank space*)	
11.	gudu$_4$ ^{d}šara$_2$-me-še$_3$	They are gudu$_4$-priests of Šara.
12.	1(diš) da-da-mu	1 Dadamu.
13.	1(diš) e$_2$-šuš$_3$-ta	1 Ešušta.
14.	1(diš) lu$_2$-^{geš}gigir-re dumu ur-ša	1 Lu-gigire, child of Urša.
15.	1(diš) lu$_2$- ^{d}šara$_2$ dumu ur-šu-kal-la	1 Lu-Šara, child of Ur-šukala.
16.	⌜gudu$_4$⌝ ^{d}šara$_2$ KI.AN^{ki}-me-še$_3$	They are gudu$_4$-priests of Šara of KI.AN.
17.	1(diš) lu$_2$ ^{d}sukkal-an-ka	1 Lu-Sukkal-anka.
18.	1(diš) igi-^{d}šara$_2$-še$_3$ ARAD$_2$ ur-dun	1 Igi-Šaraše, slave of Ur-dun.
19.	1(diš) ur-dun dumu lu$_2$- ^{d}utu	1 Ur-dub, child of Ur-Šara.
20.	1(diš) lu$_2$- ^{d}⌜šara$_2$⌝ dumu šeš-a-ni	1 Lu-Šara, child of Šešani.
21.	1(diš) ur-e$_2$-maḫ muš-laḫ$_5$	1 Ur-Emaḫ, snake-charmer.
22.	1(diš) ur- ^{d}⌜da-mu⌝ ARAD$_2$ ARAD$_2$	1 Ur-Damu, slave of ARAD(mu).

rev.

1.	1(diš) lu$_2$- ^{d}šara$_2$ dumu šeš-kal-la	1 Lu-Šara, child of Šeš-kala.
2.	1(diš) šeš-a-ni sagi	1 Šešani, cup-bearer.
3.	1(diš) ur-e$_{11}$-e šu-i	1 Ur-E'e, barber.
4.	1(diš) lu$_2$- ^{d}šara$_2$ mušen-du$_3$	1 Lu-Šara, bird-trapper.
5.	1(diš) lugal-a$_2$-zi-da	1 Lugal-azida.
6.	1(diš) ur- ^{d}ašnan	1 Ur-Ašnan.
7.	1(diš) ba-an-sa$_6$ nu-^{geš}kiri$_6$	1 Bansa, gardener.
8.	1(diš) ur- ^{d}ab-u$_2$	1 Ur-Ab'u.
9.	1(diš) ur- ^{d}šul-pa-e$_3$	1 Ur-Šulpa'e.
10.	1(diš) lu$_2$- ^{d}da-ni	1 Lu-Dani.
11.	1(diš) mu-u$_2$-a	1 Mu'ua.
12.	1(diš) ARAD$_2$-mu dumu a-kal-la	1 ARADmu, child of A(ya)-kala.
13.	1(diš) ARAD$_2$- ^{d}šara$_2$	1 ARAD-šara.
14.	1(diš) lugal-^{geš}gigir-re	1 Lugal-gigire.
15.	1(diš) ARAD$_2$-mu dumu saga-kal	1 ARADmu, child of Saga-kal.
16.	1(diš) lugal-e$_2$-maḫ-e	1 Lugal-Emaḫe.
17.	1(diš) ur-balag-ga$_2$ nu-^{geš}kiri$_6$	1 Ur-balaga, gardener.
18.	1(diš) inim- ^{d}šara$_2$ dumu šu-eš$_{18}$-dar	1 Inim-Šara, child of Šu-Eštar.
19.	1(diš) lu$_2$-^{d}šara$_2$ dumu-dumu lu$_2$-kal-la	1 Lu-Šara, grandchild(?) of Lu-kala.
19.	sipa-me-eš$_2$	They are shepherds.
20.	1(diš) lu$_2$- ^{d}a-zi-a ašgab	1 Lu-Agia, leather worker.
	(*blank space*)	
21.	šunigin 4(u) guruš zaḫ$_3$	Total: 40 workers, fled.
22.	ša$_3$ umma^{ki}	Within Umma.
23.	inim-ni ba-gen$_7$-na iti 2(diš)-kam	their words (= cases) were confirmed, in the second month;
24.	KA-TUG$_2$ lugal-amar-ku$_3$ dumu da-da-ga-ni	KATUG-official is Lugal-amar-ku, child of Dadagani.

Many of the persons in text No. 141 are also found in Nisaba 24, 23 (Umma IS 3).

Smaller Inventories

The smaller inventories, texts Nos. 142–47, are published here without extensive comments. A few further lists of persons are found among the miscellaneous texts (Chapter 12). Some of the inventories presented in this section and in Chapter 12 might be understood as practice documents.

The first of the smaller inventories, text No. 142, lists nine individuals, all men, and their rations. The total on the reverse can be reconstructed. The text does not have any calendrical information or any information of the association of the individuals listed. The amounts of barley seems to agree with the monthly rations for various types of workers, but the variation is too large to suggest that they were all necessarily working in the same team.

No. 142. *MS 4756*

obv.

1.	2(barig) 3(ban$_2$) še ab-ba-kal-la	2 barig, 3 ban$_2$ barley (for) Abba-kala.
2.	4(barig) ^{d}nanna-i$_3$-sa$_6$	4 barig (for) Nanna-isa.
3.	2(barig) 3(ban$_2$) lu$_2$-^{d}inanna	2 barig, 3 ban$_2$ (for) Lu-Inanna.
4.	4(ban$_2$) ur-^{d}kal-kal	4 ban$_2$ (for) Ur-Kalkal.
5.	4(ban$_2$) lu$_2$-si-gar	4 ban$_2$ (for) Lu-sigar.
6.	4(ban$_2$) ur:^{d}gibil$_6$	4 ban$_2$ (for) Ur-Gibil.
7.	4(ban$_2$) 2(diš) sila$_3$ ur-engur-ma	4 ban$_2$, 2 sila$_3$ (for) Ur-engurma.
8.	3(barig) lu$_2$-^{d}⸢geštin⸣	3 barig (for) Lu-Geštin.

rev.

1.	4(barig) ur-ku$_3$-nun-na	4 barig (for) Ur-kununna.
	(*blank space*)	
2.	⸢šunigin⸣ [2(aš) 4(barig) 4(ban$_2$)] ⸢2(diš) sila$_3$ gur⸣	Total: 2 gur, 4 barig, 4 ban$_2$, 2 sila$_3$ (of barley).

The next text, No. 143, simply lists three individuals, one cowherd, one *kalû*-priest, and one gardener:

No. 143. *MS 1947/15*

obv.

1.	1(diš) nigar$^{gar!}$-ki-du$_{10}$	1 Nigar-kudu, cowherd.
2.	1(diš) lugal-ezem gala	1 Lugal-ezem, *kalû*(-priest).
3.	1(diš) du$_{10}$-ga nu-^{geš}kiri$_6$	1 Duganu, gardener.

rev. (*blank*)

The next two texts, Nos. 144 and 145, are very short inventories. The reason for writing up these texts is not clear, but they do not appear to be practice texts.

No. 144. *MS 2020/14 (Umma, AS 6–iv)*

obv.

1.	5(diš) guruš	5 workers.
2.	ugula ur-^{d}en-lil$_2$-la$_2$	Overseer: Ur-Enlila.
3.	2(diš) guruš	2 workers.
4.	ugula i$_7$-pa-e$_3$	Overseer: Ipa'e.
5.	gurum$_2$ ak u$_4$ 8(diš)-kam	Inventory of the 8th day.

rev.

1.	⸢ki⸣-su$_7$ ša-ra-ḫu-um-ma-ka gub-ba	Stationed at the threshing floor of the Šaraḫumma (canal).
2.	iti nesag	Month: "First Fruits."
3.	mu us$_2$-sa en-unu$_6$-gal ⸢MUŠ$_3$⸣ ba-<ḫun>	Year after: "Enunugal of Inanna(!) was installed."

No. 145. *MS 2028 (Umma$^?$, X–xii–24)*

obv.

1.	2(diš) ma$_2$-gin$_2$	2 boat-builders.
2.	8(diš) ½(diš) ma$_2$-laḫ$_5$	8 ½ sailors.
3.	3(diš) nagar	3 carpenters.
4.	1(diš) ad-kup$_4$	1 basket-weaver.
5.	8(diš) ša$_3$ mar-sa	8 (workers) of the shipyard.
6.	1(u) 7(diš) ša$_3$ en-nun	17 (workers) of the guard house.

rev.

1.	1(diš) ugula da-du-mu	1 overseer, Dadumu.
	(blank space)	
2.	gurum$_2$ ak u$_4$ 2(u) 4(diš)$^?$-kam	Inventory of the 24th day.
3.	iti ^{d}dumu-zi	Month: "Dumuzi."
	(blank space)	

Text No. 146 is a list of old women (or widows), b u r - š u - m a. However, the five persons listed on the obverse are all male: all of them, except the first, bear well-known personal names from Umma. Presumably therefore these five persons were in charge of one old woman each, in some way or another.

No. 146. *MS 2020/15 (Umma)*

obv.

1.	1(diš) du-ba-ni	1 Dubani.
2.	1(diš) ur-^{geš}gigir	1 Ur-gigir.
3.	1(diš) ur-^{d}ur$_3$-bar-tab	1 Ur-Urbartab.
4.	1(diš) nigar-ki-du$_{10}$ unu$_3$	1 Nigar-kidu, cowherd.
5.	1(diš) lugal-ku$_3$-ga-ni	1 Lugal-kugani.

rev.

	(blank space)	
1.	bur-šu-ma	Old women.
	(blank space)	

Text No. 147 also lists persons, but is totalled and complete with year-name. One of the eleven persons named in the text, Nin-zamen (rev. 4), is recorded as having fled (z a ḫ$_3$) and not included in the total. In the total the scribe classified the persons as mixed slaves (s a g ḫ i - a), because the group included both male and females.

No. 147. *MS 4340 (X, Š 38)*

obv.

1.	1(diš) ur-x-[x]	1 Ur- . . .
2.	1(diš) šu-eš$_{18}$-dar	1 Šu-Eštar.
3.	1(diš) a$_2$-dingir-ga$_2$	1 A-dingirga.
4.	1(diš) dingir-a$_2$-daḫ	1 Dingir-adaḫ.
5.	1(diš) puzur$_4$-i-⸢lu$_2$$^{?}$⸣	1 Puzur-ilu.
6.	1(diš) ma-a-DU	1 Ma'aDU.
7.	1(diš) ^{d}a-ba-ba-al-sa$_6$	1 Ababa-alsa.

rev.

1.	1(diš) dumu nita$_2$	1 male child.
2.	1(diš) dumu mi$_2$-du$_8$	1 female child . . . .
3.	1(diš) GIN$_2$ ⸢peš$^{?}$⸣[428]	1 . . .
4.	⸢zaḫ$_3$$^{?}$⸣ nin-za-me-en	Fled: Nin-zamen.
	(*blank space*)	
5.	šunigin 1(u) sag-ḫi-a	Total: 10 mixed slaves.
6.	mu us$_2$-sa bad$_3$ ma-da ba-du$_3$-a	Year after: "The wall of the land was built."
7.	sag-ba ur-[. . .]	Of the slaves . . .

"Work-Crew Lists"

The inventories discussed above served three purposes: they were used to keep track of the workforce and to record any absence—illness, death or flight; they were used to calculate the rations needed to sustain the workers, and in some cases their supplementary allotments; and finally, they were used, it can be assumed, either for direct entry of work-crews into the "debits" section of accounts of work, or to create lists of the development of work crews over an accounting period for subsequent entry into the "debits" section of accounts of work. This relationship is seen most clearly in the case of the inventory No. 136, which recorded a work crew which can be shown to be closely related to that entered into the "debits" of the account MVN 10, 102. Since these two texts were separated by more than seven years, the match is not exact (see Table 3).

Since lists of work crews, showing their monthly progression, exist, it cannot be ruled out that such texts were always drawn up between the inventories and the accounts. I presented one of these texts in Chapter 3 (MVN 21, 212), when discussing the timekeeping system of the Ur III period.

The first entry of AAICAB 1, 1912-1141,[429] recorded the size of a work crew during the first month of the year. Two categories of female workers were involved: full-time workers receiving three ban of barley each month (c. one liter per day), and half-time workers also receiving three ban of barley each month:

---

[428] One would expect a category of worker less productive than a female child here. p e š, meaning "pregnant," may be suitable, but the first sign, G I N$_2$, is not otherwise attested with p e š, nor is p e š used about human beings in Ur III texts.

[429] See the parallel texts UTI 3, 2282 (from ŠS 3 i to xi), recording the "debits" of the work of females concerning Ur-Nintu, the overseer of the textile factory (rev. 23: s a g - n i g$_2$ - g u r$_{11}$ - r a a$_2$ g e m e$_2$ u r - ^{d}n i n - t u u g u l a u š - b a r), MVN 21, 212 (from Š 42 i to xiii or AS 6 i to xiii) the "debits" of Ur-Nintu, Nebraska 42 (from AS 7 i to xii) the "debits" of the overseer Ur-Nintu, AAS 35 (from IS 1 i to xii) (name of the overseer is lost), PSBA 35, 47 (= AAICAB 1, 1912-1141) (from the 1st to the 12th month, year lost) (name of overseer lost). OrSP 47–49, 401 (from ŠS 1 i to xiii) contains the "debits" of Adu, another known textile worker overseer (rev. 20: s a g - n i g$_2$ - g u r$_{11}$ - r a a - d u ⸢š a b r a⸣ [š a b r a = P A . ⸢A L⸣, collated from photo]), and lastly AnOr 7, 302 (AS 1 i to vi), very fragmentary.

AAICAB 1, 1912-1141

obv.

1.	2(geš$_2$) 3(u) 3(diš) ⸢geme$_2$⸣ [3(ban$_2$)]	153 female workers, (receiving) 3 ban$_2$ (monthly),
2.	9(diš) geme$_2$ ⸢a$_2$⸣ [½(diš) 3(ban$_2$)]	9 female workers, half (output), 3 ban$_2$,
3.	iti še-sag$_{11}$-⸢ku$_5$⸣	month: "Harvest."

The following eleven entries recorded the size of the crew through each of the following eleven months. The size of the team decreased somewhat during the year, making it necessary to calculate an average monthly size of the work crew. This average would later be entered into the "debits" of the account concerning the overseer of the team; we read the totals:

AAICAB 1, 1912-1141

rev.

8.	šunigin 3(geš'u) 1(u) 6(diš) geme$_2$ 3(ban$_2$)	Total: 1,816 female workers, (receiving) 3 ban$_2$ (monthly).
9.	šunigin 1(geš$_2$) 4(u) 8(diš) geme$_2$ a$_2$ ½(diš) 3(ban$_2$)	Total: 48 female workers, half (output), (receiving) 3 ban$_2$ (monthly).
10.	geme$_2$ 3(ban$_2$) igi-1(u) 2(diš)-gal$_2$-bi 2(geš$_2$) 3(u) 1(diš) ⅓(diš)	One 12th of the female workers (receiving) 3 ban$_2$ (monthly): 151 ⅓.
11.	geme$_2$ a$_2$ ½(diš) igi-1(u) 2(diš)-gal$_2$-bi 9(diš)	One 12th of the half (output) female workers: 9.
12.	iti 1(u) 2(diš)-⸢še$_3$⸣	For 12 months,
13.	a$_2$-bi u$_4$ 1(šar'u) 5(šar$_2$) 3(geš'u) ⸢5(geš$_2$)⸣	its work: 56,100 (work-)days.[430]
14.	sag-nig$_2$-gur$_{11}$-ra a$_2$ ⸢geme$_2$⸣	(It is the) debits (of the account concerning) the work of female workers
15.	lu$_2$-kal-[la]	(concerning) Lu-kala[431].
16.	mu [. . .] ⸢lugal?⸣ [. . .]	Year: [. . .]

This total can be compared to the first entry of the "debits" of, for example, the account Aegyptus 21, 159 (from AS 8 i to xi):

Aegyptus 21, 159

obv. col. i

1.	[1(geš$_2$) 4(u)+] ⸢1(u)⸣ 6(diš) ⅓(diš) gin$_2$ ⸢geme$_2$⸣ 3(ban$_2$)	116 and 16 ⅓ shekels (~sixtieths) female workers (receiving) 3 ban$_2$ (monthly).
2.	5(diš) 1(u) 6(diš) ⅓(diš) gin$_2$ geme$_2$ a$_2$ ½(diš)	5 and 16 ⅓ shekels (~sixtieths) female workers, half (output),
3.	⸢iti⸣ 1(u) 1(diš)-še$_3$	for 11 months,
4.	[a$_2$]-bi u$_4$ 9(šar) 5(geš'u) 9(geš$_2$)	its work is 35,940 days.[432]

[430] Calculation: (151 ⅓ + (9÷2)) × 360 = 56,100.

[431] See Dahl 2007: 105 ff.

[432] 106 49/180 × 30 × 11 = 35,069 5/6.
5 49/180 ÷ 2 = 2 229/36 (2 229/360) × 30 × 11 = 869 11/12
35,069 5/6
+869 11/12
= 35,939 ¾ approximated to 35,940.

The decrease in the workforce recorded in our work-crew list AAICAB 1, 1912-1141, presumably caused by the harsh working conditions of the mill or textile-factories, can be easily compared with the information provided by the next text example, UTI 3, 1916. This text recorded the work-capacity of one male worker, named Atu, during the seventh year of Amar-Suen:

UTI 3, 1916

obv.

1.	tu-ra a-tu	Sick: Atu.
2.	iti 8(diš)-še$_{3}$ iti še-sag$_{11}$-ku$_{5}$-ta	For 8 months: from month: "Harvest,"
3.	iti e$_{2}$-iti-6(diš) mu ḫu-ḫu-nu-ri^{ki}-še$_{3}$	to month: "House month six," of year: "Ḫuḫnuri (was destroyed)."
4.	uš$_{2}$ a-tu	Dead: Atu.

rev.

1.	iti e$_{2}$-iti-6(diš) mu ḫu-ḫu-nu-ri^{ki}-ta	From month: "House month six," of year: "Ḫuḫnuri (was destroyed).
2.	ugula da-du-mu	Overseer: Dadumu.
3.	kišib$_{3}$ lugal-e$_{2}$-maḫ-e	Sealed by Lugal-Emaḫe.

seal (S003415)

1.	lugal-e$_{2}$-maḫ-e	Lugal-Emaḫe,
2.	dub-sar	scribe,
3.	dumu lugal-ku$_{3}$-ga-ni	child of Lugal-kugani.

The reason for recording this development lies in the accounting procedures of the "free-days" (a$_{2}$ u$_{4}$-du$_{8}$-a): an overseer who possessed such a document would be ascribed full credit for the work-days of that particular worker. The standard "free-days" of the absent worker would, however, be subtracted, hence they were recorded in the "debits" of the accounts.[433] We lack evidence for any punishment of an overseer losing large numbers of his crew, but we are in possession of a substantial number of texts testifying to the many escapees from the Ur III state, occasionally brought back to the state and enrolled in the production anew.[434]

MVN 14, 2 (from AS 1) is a rare example of an administrative record where the information is substantiated by a legal formulae:

---

[433] Englund 1988: 172 and n. 46. See also Englund 1991: 278, Struve 1969: 138–43. V. Struve, who calculated the monthly time off for the female dependent workers (the geme) as 5 days a month, or 1/6 of their time, gave as a reason for these "days of detachment," as he called them, that they "correspond to the days of the women's usual indisposition when, in accordance with the notions of the Sumerians, women were impure and could not be admitted to any work" (p. 140). As a rule male dependent workers had 1/10 of their time described as a$_{2}$ u$_{4}$-du$_{8}$-a.

[434] See, for example, AnOr 7, 286 (from ŠS 6 viii 21): 5 workers are called "seized fugitives" (lu$_{2}$ zaḫ$_{3}$ dab$_{5}$-ba), living in "prison" (en-nu-ga$_{2}$ ⸢til-la⸣). See also MVN 14, 120 (from Š 46 iii 11), a parallel text. MVN 6, 267 (from X–xii–22), is an inventory of 12 females described as "seized fugitive females of the mill" (geme$_{2}$ kikken$_{2}$ zaḫ$_{3}$ dab$_{5}$-ba-me). TCTI 2, 3591 (from ŠS 2 i), speaks about a "soldier" (lu$_{2}$ ^{geš}tukul) of the king dispatched to seize fugitives (lu$_{2}$ zaḫ$_{3}$-a dab$_{5}$-de$_{3}$ >/lu zaḫ-a dab-ed-e/, i$_{3}$-im-gen-na > /i-b-nen-a/, literally "to seize men who have fled, they went there"). See also RTC 355; Rochester 152; DAS 199; TCTI 2, 4185; DAS 197; RTC 397; TCTI 2, 4161; and RTC 354 (X–xii), where it is specifically said that the messenger (u$_{3}$-kul) shall go to GN (saḫar$^{?}$ ki-ḪAR-^{geš}šinig^{ki}-ka-še$_{3}$) to seize the fugitive females (rev. 4–5: la-gi-pu-um u$_{3}$-kul / saḫar$^{?ki}$-ḪAR-^{geš}šinig^{ki}-ka-še$_{3}$ geme$_{2}$ zaḫ$_{3}$ e$_{2}$-gal dab$_{5}$-dab$_{5}$-de$_{3}$ gen-na). See now above all Reid 2015 for fugitives during the Ur III period.

MVN 14, 2 (AS 1)

obv.

1.	uš$_2$ 1(ban$_2$) ur-ama-na	Ur-amana, 1 ban$_2$ (category), dead.
2.	iti e$_2$-iti-6(diš)	From the month: "House month six."
3.	uš$_2$ 1(ban$_2$) ur-si-gar	Ur-Sigar, 1 ban$_2$ (category), dead.
4.	iti še-sag$_{11}$-ku$_5$-ta	From the month: "Harvest."

rev.

1.	ugula ur-^{d}da-ni-ke$_4$	Ur-Dani is overseer.
2.	zi lugal in-pa$_3$	He swore by the life of the king.
3.	kišib$_3$ lugal-ku$_3$-zu	Sealed tablet of Lugal-kuzu.
4.	mu ^{d}amar-^{d}suen lugal	Year: "Amar-Suen (was) king."

seal (S003565)

1.	lugal-ku$_3$-zu	Lugal-kuzu,
2.	dub-sar	scribe,
3.	dumu ⸢ur⸣-[nigar]$^{⸢*gar⸣}$ [šuš$_3$]	child of Ur-Nigar, the chief cattle-administrator.[435]

Receipts

The Ur III administrators created a system in which work itself had a measurable value and could be transferred like any other movable good. Work, be it agricultural tasks or artisanal production, could be transferred from one person to another, and this transfer would be documented with receipts, in a fashion similar to what was discussed for ordinary goods (Chapter 7). However, most receipts concerning work use the technical terminology "sealed tablet of PN" (kišib$_3$ PN), rather than "PN received" (šu ba-ti). In most cases, receipts of work also include details about the work task.

Receipts of manual labor, mostly field work, sometimes computed the total work-days transferred, but receipts of artisanal production never did. However, most receipts concerning work were very laconic, giving only the minimal information needed. Text No. 148 is an example of such a simple receipt.

No. 148. *MS 2018/7 (Umma, ŠS 3–iv–5)*

obv.

1.	1(diš) ug$_3$ lu$_2$-eb-gal	1 carrier, Lu-Ebgal.
2.	KA-KU-še$_3$	To/for (the place of/service of) KAKU(?).
3.	nibru^{ki}-še$_3$	To Nippur.
4.	iti nesag-ta u$_4$ 5(diš)-am$_3$ ba-a-zal-ta	From the month: "First Fruit," the 5th day has passed.

rev.

1.	ki a-kal-la-ta	From A(ya)-kala.
2.	kišib$_3$ dingir-ra	Sealed tablet of Dingira.
	(*seal impression*)	
3.	mu us$_2$-sa ma$_2$ ^{d}en-ki ba-ab-du$_8$	Year after: "The boat of Enki was caulked."

[435] For this Lugal-kuzu, see Dahl 2007: 124–27.

seal (S002175)

1.	dingir-ra	Dingira,
2.	dub-sar	scribe,
3.	dumu lu$_2$-ga	child of Luga.

Perhaps the most interesting information in text No. 148 is that the work of Lu-Ebgal has a start date but apparently no finish date. It is possible that when the text was drawn up in month 4 it was already known that Lu-Ebgal would not return before the end of the year, resulting in 265 (8×30+25) work-days credited to his overseer, A(ya)-kala, but this remains speculation.

In the following example, text No. 149, three manual tasks are listed together in the same receipt, each assigned to a conveyor:

No. 149. *MS 4707 (Umma, ŠS 9?)*

obv.

1.	1(u) 2(diš) guruš u$_4$ 1(u) še$_3$	12 workers for 10 days,
2.	[du$_6^?$] muru$_{13}$-a-ta	from the Mound at the Muru (field),
3.	i$_7$ du-du-še$_3$	to the Dudu-canal,
4.	ku$_6$ ga$_6$-ga$_2$	carrying fish.
5.	giri$_3$ lugal-ḫe$_2$-gal$_2$	Conveyor: Lugal-ḫegal.
6.	1(u) guruš u$_4$ 5(diš)-še$_3$	10 workers for 5 days,
7.	du$_6$ muru$_{13}$-a-ta a-pi$_4$-sal$_4^{ki}$-še$_3$	from the Mound at the Muru (field), to Apisal,
8.	kid šu$_2$ ma$_2$ ga$_6$-ga$_2$	carrying boat-mats.
9.	6(diš) guruš u$_4$ 4(diš)-še$_3$	6 workers for 4 days,

rev.

1.	umma^{ki}-še$_3$ ma$_2$ kid šu$_2$ gid$_2$-da	punting[436] the boat with mats to Umma.
2.	giri$_3$ inim-ma-ni	Conveyor: Inimani
3.	ugula ARAD$_2$-mu	Foreman: ARADmu,
4.	kišib$_3$ lu$_2$-^{d}ḫa-ia$_3$	Sealed tablet of Lu-Ḫaya.
5.	mu e$_2$ ^{d}šara$_2$ ba-du$_3$	Year: "The house of Šara was built."

seal (S003102)

1.	lu$_2$-^{d}ḫa-ia$_3$	Lu-Ḫaya,
2.	dub-sar	scribe,
3.	dumu ur-e$_{11}$-e	child of Ur-E'e.

The twelve workers working for ten days recorded in the first entry of text No. 149 most likely represent an actual assignment, but entered into an account the fact would most likely be reduced to the number of man-days, here 120. In yet other cases, the final amounts of man-days would not be stated in the receipt, as in the following text, No. 150.

In text No. 150 the "item" being accounted for is an amount of dirt to be excavated. The actual time it took is not recorded, only the equivalence rate with which it was to be excavated. This rate may in fact be a bookkeeping description of the type of dirt more than anything else: "7 ½ shekels dirt," or dirt to be excavated

---

[436] See Englund 2010a.

at a rate of 7 ½ shekels (i.e., c. 2 ¼ m^3)[437] per day by each worker. The two examples both point to the receipts recording actual work tasks, and the accounts converting these tasks into man-days using artificial equivalencies.

No. 150. *MVN 5, 73 = MS 1653/1 (Umma, ŠS 3)*

obv.

1.	9(diš) ⅔(diš) sar saḫar	9 ⅔ sar of dirt,
2.	guruš-e 7(diš) ½(diš) gin$_2$-ta	each worker 7 ½ sixtieth (daily).
3.	a-bur$_2$ a-ša$_3$ la$_2$-tur ša$_3$ da-gu-na	The "aqueduct" of the Latur field of the Daguna[438]
4.	[ba-al]- ⌜la⌝ šu-luḫ ak	excavating and cleaning(?).[439]

rev.

1.	[ugula] i$_7$-pa-e$_3$	Overseer: Ipa'e.
2.	kišib$_3$ da-da-ga	Sealed tablet of Dadaga.
	(*seal impression*)	
3.	mu si-ma-num$_2$^{ki} ba-ḫul	Year: "When Simanum was destroyed."

seal (S002124)

1.	da-da-ga	Dadaga,
2.	dub-sar	scribe,
3.	dumu ur-nigar^{gar} šuš$_3$	child of Ur-Nigar, the chief cattle-administrator.

Text No. 151 records the man-days spent in hoeing a small area of land in the Gula field. However, this text gives an amount of work-days rather than the area of land.

No. 151. *MS 2021/5 (Umma, AS 1–vii)*

obv.

1.	7(diš) guruš u$_4$ 1(diš)-še$_3$	7 workers for one day,
2.	al ak 7(diš) sar-ta	hoeing 7 sar each (each day).
3.	a-ša$_3$ ^{d}gu-la	Field: Gula.
4.	ugula lu$_2$-me-lam$_2$	Overseer: Lu-melam.

rev.

1.	iti min-eš$_3$	Month: "Double-sanctuary."
	(*blank space*)	
2.	mu ^{d}amar-^{d}suen lugal	Year: "Amar-Suen (was) king."

The tablet is not sealed, nor does it give the name of the person to whose account the transaction would be credited, and we must assume that it was once encased in an envelope giving that information. The Gula field is not well attested in the textual record, and two of the other three receipts recording work done on this field are likewise unsealed (MVN 21, 137 from AS 1–v and BIN 5, 219 from AS 1–vii).

---

[437] The basic unit of volume was the sar, understood to be the surface area of one sar × 1 kuš$_3$ high. One sar in surface measure is one ninda, or 12 kuš$_3$, square. One kuš$_3$ is c. ½ meter. The sar could be subdivided into 60 gin$_2$.

[438] See also BPOA 1, 625; BPOA 1, 709; MVN 16, 1310; UTI 4, 2732; UTI 4, 2469.

[439] The term šu-luh—ak is usually used about ritual cleansing, but here and elsewhere in the Ur III record it refers to cleaning a watercourse.

UTI 4, 2660 (from ŠS 3) is a receipt of sixty man-days of hirelings working in the Gula field, transferred to the debits of the account of Lu-duga:

UTI 4, 2660 (Umma, ŠS 3)

obv.

1.	1(geš$_2$) guruš ḫun-ga$_2$ u$_4$ 1(diš)-še$_3$	60 hirelings for one day.
2.	a-ša$_3$ ^{d}gu-la gi ze$_x$(SIG$_7$)-a	Cutting reed in the Gula field.
3.	ugu$_2$ lu$_2$-du$_{10}$-ga ga$_2$-ga$_2$-ra	Placed on the "debits" of Lu-duga.
4.	ugula lugal-nesag-e	Overseer: Lugal-nesage.

rev.

	(blank space)	
1.	mu si-ma-num$_2$^{ki} ba-ḫul	Year: "Simanum was destroyed."

seal (S002813)

1.	lu$_2$-du$_{10}$-ga	Lu-duga,
2.	dub-sar	scribe,
3.	dumu ḫe$_2$-ma-du	child of Ḫemadu.

Given the scarcity and oddities of the available evidence concerning work on the Gula field, it may be prudent to regard text No. 151 as an exceptional case.

Text No. 152 does record the name of the administrator to whom the transaction was credited:

No. 152. *MS 1879 = JCS 37, 108 (Umma, ŠS 4–i)*

obv.

1.	1(u) 3(diš) ⌜geme$_2$⌝ u$_4$ 1(diš)-⌜še$_3$$^?$⌝	13 female workers for one day.
2.	ka i$_7$$^!$(A) kunigara(MUŠ/MUŠ)$^{?a\text{-}ra}$-ka[440] saḫar si-ga	Filling the opening of the Kunigar canal with dirt.
3.	ugula ur-^{d}nin-tu	Overseer: Ur-Nintu.

rev.

1.	kišib$_3$ da-da-ga	Sealed tablet of Dadaga.
2.	iti še-sag$_{11}$-ku$_5$	Month: "Harvest."
3.	mu us$_2$-sa si-ma-num$_2$[^{ki} ba-ḫul]	Year following: "Simanum was destroyed."

seal (S002124)

1.	da-da-ga	Dadaga,
2.	dub-sar	scribe,
3.	dumu ur-[nigar^{gar} šuš$_3$]	child of Ur-Nigar, chief cattle-administrator.

---

440 Following Lee (1985: 108), who took this to be a variant writing of the name of the canal Kunigar(a). That waterway is usually written i$_7$ kun-nagar in Ur III sources, but in Diri III 189 a writing i$_7$ MUŠ/MUŠ is given. Although the Diri source is much later than the date of this text Lee's reading is retained here as no other watercourse written with MUŠ over MUŠ is known to me.

The similar lack of a named recipient in text No. 153 indicates again that it may originally have been encased in an envelope. This text too is unlikely to be a practise or school text, and it can be related to text No. 154. However, some of the terminology of No. 153 is unique and remains difficult to understand.

No. 153. *MS 1741 (Nippur, Š 48–xi)*

obv.

1.	1(u) 3(diš) sar ^{gi}kid maḫ	13 sar of reed mat, large.
2.	5(geš$_2$) ^{gi}gil dagal	300 gil-reed, wide.
3.	3(šar$_2$) ^{gi}gil x	10,000 gil-reed, . . .
4.	a$_2$ ad-kup$_4$-še$_3$ GA$_2$ ⸢KID$^?$ TUM$^?$⸣	For the work of the basketry workers . . .
5.	2(geš'u) 2(geš$_2$) 3(u) 4(diš) geš ur$_3$ hi-a	1354 beams, mixed.
6.	a$_2$ gudu$_4$-še$_3$ GA$_2$ KID TUM ḪAR ⸢u$_4$ 2(diš)$^?$-kam$^?$⸣	For the work of the gudu$_4$-priests . . . for 2 days(?).
7.	e$_2$ ^{d}alim$^?$	House of (the god) Alim.

rev.

1.	ki lugal-a$_2$-zi-da-ta	From Lugal-azida.
2.	iti udru^{durus}	Month: Udru (festival)[441]
3.	mu us$_2$-sa ki-maš^{ki} ba-ḫul mu us$_2$-sa-bi	Year after: "Kimaš was destroyed," year after that.

In essence, such receipts, recording the production of household utensils, tools, and other manufactured products, document the transfer of products from one institution to another. As such they conform to the layout of the regular receipts discussed above (Chapter 7). Receipts concerning the work involved in artisanal production (primarily woodworking, basketry, and pottery), rarely indicated the work-days, but usually only the transfer of the finished products. Exceptions are primarily for fuel-carriers and similar. This may be due to the organization of these workshops and the fact that some level of specialization was involved. These workshops presumably consisted of a permanent crew with a certain level of expertise, and workers were therefore presumably not transferred *ad hoc* from other teams to turn pots and weave baskets. Text No. 154 is therefore slightly unusual in that it describes how a now lost number of workers (g u r u š) assigned as basketry weavers were tasked, for five days, with weaving a particular type of basket or mat (^{gi}g i l - s a m a n$_4$).

No. 154. *MS 1942/11 (Umma, Š 35 vi)*

obv.

1.	n ⸢guruš ad⸣-kup$_4$	*n* workers, basket weavers,
2.	u$_4$ 5(diš)- še$_3$	for 5 days,
3.	^{gi}gil-saman$_4$ sur-de$_3$	weaving gil-saman baskets/mats.
4.	ki lu$_2$-kal-la-ta	From Lu-kala

rev.

1.	kišib$_3$ dingir-ra	Sealed tablet of Dingira.
2.	⸢iti⸣ šu-numun *(seal impression)*	Month: "Seeding."
3.	⸢mu⸣ us$_2$-sa an-ša-an^{ki} ba-ḫul	Year after: "Anšan was destroyed."

[441] Cohen 2015: 256.

seal (S002175)

1. dingir-ra	Dingira,
2. dub-sar	scribe,
3. dumu lu_2-ga	child of Luga.

The sole example of a receipt of finished products from a workshop found in the collection published here was edited above as text No. 153. Below I present a more complete example of a receipt for which a corresponding entry in an account can be found.

The following text, a complex receipt of various reed products, was summarized in the account TCL 5, 6036 obv. vi 25–39.

JCS 2, 187 NBC 3500 (Umma–AS 4)

obv.

1. 3(geš$_2$) sa gi	180 bundles of reed.
2. 3(diš) ^{gi}kid	3 reed mats,
3. ki-la$_2$-bi 1(diš) sar 3(diš) gin$_2$	their size: 1 sar and 3 shekels.
4. ti-um e$_2$-šu-tum nu-banda$_3$-[še$_3$]	For the . . . of the storehouse of the captain.
5. 6(diš) ^{gi}kid šer$_7$-ru-um	6 šerum mats,
6. ki-la$_2$-bi 1(diš) ½(diš) sar	their size: 1 ½ sar.

rev.

1. ⸢siki⸣ ba-ba-ra	For . . . wool,
2. [ša$_3$] e$_2$-kišib$_3$-ba	of the storehouse
3. ensi$_2$-ka	of the governor.
4. 4(diš) ^{gi}kid ki-la$_2$ bi ⅓(diš) sar	4 reed mats, their size: ⅓ sar.
5. ma$_2$ nig$_2$-ba lugal-ka ba-a-dul$_x$(UR×A)	Covering the boat of gifts of the king.
6. kišib$_3$ lu$_2$-kal-la	Sealed tablet of Lu-kala.

left edge

1. [iti x]	[month x].
2. mu en-maḫ-gal-an-na ba-ḫun	Year: "Enmaḫgal-anna was installed."

seal (S002932)

1. lu$_2$-kal-la	Lu-kala,
2. dub-sar	scribe,
3. [dumu ur-e$_{11}$-e šuš3]	child of Ur-E'e, chief cattle-administrator.

This information is combined with information from two further receipts also sealed by Lu-kala, and entered into TCL 5, 6036 obv. vi 25–39:

TCL 5, 6036 (Umma, AS 4–i to AS 4–xiii)

obv. col. vi

25. 3(diš) ^{gi}kid	3 reed mats,
26. ki-la$_2$-bi 1(diš) sar 3(diš) gin$_2$	their size: 1 sar and 3 shekels.
27. ti-um e$_2$ šu-tum nu-banda$_3$-še$_3$	For the . . . of the storehouse of the captain.
28. 2(diš) ^{geš}ig e$_2$ esir$_2$ su-ba	2 doors, coated with bitumen,

29.	gid$_2$-bi 5(diš) kuš$_3$-ta	their length: 5 kuš$_3$ each,
30.	dagal-bi 2(diš) kuš$_3$-ta	their width: 2 kuš$_3$ each,
31.	e$_2$-šu-tum nu-banda$_3$ ba-a-de$_6$	brought into the e$_2$-šu-tum of the captain.
32.	6(diš) ^{gi}kid šer$_7$-ru-um	6 šerum mats,
33.	ki-la$_2$-bi 1(diš) ½(diš) sar	their size: 1 ½ sar.
34.	siki ba-ba-ra	For x
35.	ša$_3$ e$_2$-kišib$_3$-ba ensi$_2$-ka	of the storehouse of the governor.
36.	4(diš) ^{gi}kid šer$_7$-ru-um	4 šerum mats,
37.	ki-la$_2$-bi ⅔(diš) sar	their size: ⅔ sar.
38.	ma$_2$ zi$_3$ nig$_2$-ba lugal ba-še$_{12}$	Covering(?) the flour boat of gifts of the king.
39.	kišib$_3$ 3(diš) lu$_2$-kal-la	3 sealed tablets of Lu-kala.

No work-day equivalences are furnished here, only in the second part of the credits section, when similar products are bundled together is an equivalence value calculated and entered into the account (see below). Note also that the 180 bundles of reed recorded in the receipt are not summarized here. They were perhaps implied in the production, as seen by the summary:

TCL 5, 6036

rev. col. ii

28.	šunigin 1(u) 7(diš) ^{gi}kid šer$_7$-ru-um	Total: 17 šerum mats,
29.	ki-la$_2$-bi 4(diš) ½(diš) sar	their size: 4 ½ sar,
30.	gi-bi 2(geš$_2$) 4(u) 2(diš) sa	their reed: 162 bundles,
31.	a$_2$-bi u$_4$ 2(u) 7(diš)	their work: 27 days.

Many more receipts summarized in the large account TCL 5, 6036 have been recovered, and similar examples from other sections of the production exist (Englund 2003a).

Accounts

Most of the large accounts concerning labor followed the outline described above under accounts (Chapter 4), with the sole exception, that work was used as the main equivalency.[442] Accounts concerning manufacturing, however, had a split "credits" section. The reason for this is the way in which the value of the production was calculated. Whereas the first part of the "credits," as expected, lists the individual receipts, the second part bundles the products together. In this second section, each product is split into its smallest computable components, which are then added together to form a grand total of individual raw materials. The production time for each product is calculated in a similar way.

TCL 5, 6036, a twenty-column tablet among the largest Ur III texts ever discovered, can serve as an example of a complex account concerning the manufacturing of utensils for use in both agriculture and household production. The "debits" section lists the stock of raw materials and work-days available to the overseer of the workshop, Agu.[443] The first part of the "debits" section records a "remainder" from the previous year (obv. i 1–22). The "remainder" consists of large numbers of raw materials of the kind normally used in carpentry and basketry workshops. No equivalencies are used for the raw materials. Following the "remainder" the text

[442] Occasionally, accounts of work would include products such as cereals, or raw materials for production, such as reed, in which case other equivalencies could be applied.

[443] Agu's title in this text is "scribe of the artisans" (dub-sar gašam). For the title gašam, see also ITT 3, 4906 (from AS 8) obv. 1–4: pisan dub-ba / nig$_2$-ka$_9$-ak / a$_2$ gašam-e-ne / i$_3$-gal$_2$; and MVN 6, 303 (no date) rev. iv 3'–5': nig$_2$-ka$_9$-ak / gašam-ke$_4$-ne / ugula a-a-mu šabra.

lists the regular work crew of the workshop. Each member of the crew is mentioned with his work capacity. The crew was made up of two kinds of workers: "carriers" (ug$_3$-IL$_2$) and dumu-gi$_7$. Following the work crew we find minor deliveries of bitumen and reed, among other things. Immediately preceding the total of the debit section, we find the "free-days" deducted, corresponding to the number of sick and disabled workers recorded in the "credits."

The total of the raw materials was computed without using equivalencies. Timber was usually qualified according to its length, indicating that the scarcity of long pieces of lumber was very real (see also the discussion under text No. 36 in Chapter 4). The first entry of the "credits" section lists the "free-days" of the workers. Following these we find the individual entries corresponding to the receipts recording the real production of the workshop.[444]

A good example of the production of the workshop can be found on TCL 5, 6036 obv. vii 23–29, which recorded the delivery of various baskets and mats. The transaction was said to be sealed by Lugal-niglagare:

obv. col. vii

23.	3(u) ^{giš}gur-dub 1(barig)-ta	30 gur-dub (baskets holding) 1 barig each.
24.	4(u) ^{giš}gur-dub 4(ban$_2$) <<1(diš)>>-ta	40 gur-dub (baskets holding) 4 ban$_2$ each.
25.	5(diš) ^{giš}gur 1(barig)-ta	5 gur (baskets holding) 1 barig each.
26.	2(diš) ^{giš}kid šer$_7$-ru-um	2 šerum mats,
27.	ki-la$_2$-bi ⅔(diš) sar	their size: ⅔ sar.
28.	bala-še$_3$	For the bala (obligation).
29.	kišib$_3$ lugal-nig$_2$-lagar-e	Sealed tablet of Lugal-niglagare.

Since this entry consisted of different categories of objects it is summarized in different places in the second part of the credit section. The gur-dub baskets holding one barig are bundled together with two other deliveries. Unfortunately, the total of the three entries of one-barig gur-dub baskets does not add up to the total recorded in rev. iv 30–32 (obv. iv 17 [listing 14 pieces]; vii 38 [listing 2 pieces]); but it seems reasonable to identify a simple copying error in this. The summary of these baskets reads:

rev. col. iv

30.	šunigin 4(u) 8(diš) ^{giš}gur-dub 1(barig)-ta	Total: 48 gur-dub (baskets holding) 1 barig each.
31.	gi-bi 4(u) 8(diš) sa	Their reed: 48 bundles.
32.	a$_2$-bi u$_4$ 8(diš) ½(diš) 6(diš) gin$_2$	Their work-days: 8 ½ and 6 shekels.

One bundle of reed was used to produce one gur-dub basket, and the equivalence in work-days was set at c. 5 ½ gur-dub baskets each day. The 4(ban$_2$) gur-dub baskets are summarized in rev. iv 24–26:

rev. col. iv

24.	šunigin 4(u) ^{giš}gur-dub 4(ban$_2$)-ta	Total: 40 gur-dub (baskets holding) 4 ban$_2$ each.
25.	gi-bi 2(u) 6(diš) ⅔(diš) sa	Their reed: 26 ⅔ bundles.
26.	a$_2$-bi u$_4$ 8(diš)	Their work-days: 8.

It may be interesting to note that these slightly smaller baskets were produced at the slower rate of five per day, but required much less reed for their production.

---

[444] Several of the primary documents have been found in the published record. The first entry in the "credits" was recorded on BIN 5, 273 = TCL 5, 6036 obv. iv 10–26. JCS 2, 187 (NBC 3500) = TCL 5, 6036 obv. v 25–29, 32–38. JCS 2, 187 (YBC 767) = TCL 5, 6036 obv. vi 15–19. MVN 14, 87 = TCL 5, 6036 obv. vii 23–29. SAKF 5 l. 2 = TCL 5, 6036 obv. v 35. UTI, 2770 = TCL 5, 6036 obv. vii 11–19. JCS 28, 121 no. 15 = TCL 5, 6036 obv. vi 12–14.

The gur baskets received by Lugal-niglagare are not further qualified, whereas the summary in TCL 5, 6036 distinguishes between gur baskets coated in bitumen and those classified as EN. Both are summarized in rev. col. iii:

rev. col. iii

36.	šunigin 3(u) ^{gi}gur 1(barig)-ta esir$_2$ su-ba	Total: 30 gur baskets (holding) 1 barig each, coated with bitumen.
37.	gi-bi 3(u) sa	Its reeds: 30 bundles.
38.	esir$_2$-bi 3(ban$_2$)	Its bitumen: 3 ban$_2$.
39.	peš-bi 1(u) murgu$_2$	Its palm ribs: 10.
40.	a$_2$-bi u$_4$ 1(u)	Its work: 10 days.
41.	šunigin 3(geš$_2$) 4(u) la$_2$ 1(diš) ^{gi}gur 1(barig)-ta en	Total: 119 gur (baskets holding) 1 barig each, EN (quality?).
42.	gi-bi 3(geš$_2$) 4(u) la$_2$ 1(diš) sa	Its reeds: 119 bundles.
43.	peš-bi 1(geš$_2$) 1(u) 3(diš) murgu$_2$	Its palm ribs: 73.
44.	a$_2$-bi u$_4$ 1(geš$_2$) 1(u) 3(diš)	Its work: 73 days.

Similarly, all of the the šerum mats produced by Agu's workshop (seventeen in total) were bundled together in the second section of the debits where details about their production were calculated:

rev. col. ii

28.	šunigin 1(u) 7(diš) ^{gi}kid šer$_7$-ru-um	Total: 17 šerum mats,
29.	ki-la$_2$-bi 4(diš) ½(diš) sar	their size: 4 ½ sar,
30.	gi-bi 2(geš$_2$) 4(u) 2(diš) sa	their reed is 162 bundles,
31.	a$_2$-bi u$_4$ 2(u) 7(diš)	its work: 27 days.

The receipt MVN 14, 87 specifies as the delivering agent Agu, the head of the workshop accounted for in TCL 5, 6036. Although it confirms Lugal-niglagare as the recipient (kišib$_3$ lugal-nig$_2$-lagar-e), the seal rolled on the tablet has the name of Lugal-si-NE-e. However, all similar cases have the same discrepancy between the name on the seal and the name in the text (see, e.g., CST 629 and 721), and one can speculate that one was a writing of the other.

MVN 14, 87 (Umma, AS 4–xii)

obv.

1.	3(u) ^{gi}gur-dub 1(barig)	30 gur-dub (baskets holding) 1 barig (each).
2.	4(u) ^{gi}gur-dub 4(ban$_2$)	40 gur-dub (baskets holding) 4 ban$_2$ (each).
3.	5(diš) ^{gi}gur 1(barig)	5 gur (baskets holding) 1 barig (each).
4.	2(diš) ^{giš}šer$_7$-ru-um	2 šerum mats,
5.	ki-la$_2$-bi ⅔(diš) sar	their size: ⅔ sar.
6.	bala-še$_3$	For the bala (obligation).

rev.

1.	ki a-gu-ta	From Agu.
2.	kišib$_3$ lugal-nig$_2$-lagar-e (*seal impression*)	Sealed tablet of Lugal-niglagare.
3.	iti ^{d}dumu-zi	Month: "Dumuzi."
4.	mu en-maḫ-gal ^{d}nanna ba-ḫun	Year: "Enmaḫgal(anna) of Nanna was installed."

seal (S003673)

1.	lugal-si-NE-[e]	Lugal-siNEe,
2.	dub-sar	scribe,
3.	dumu lugal-sa$_6$-ga	child of Lugal-saga.

The accountant who drew up the record concerning Agu used a set of equivalencies specific to the production of baskets and mats to calculate the value of the production. The equivalencies for reed mats were tied to surface metrology, and based on the use of reed and work-days.[445] The other products, such as baskets, were equated to work-days as well, but no clear standard numerical relationship between the products, the labor and the raw-materials has been discovered.

Another branch of the Umma industry, well documented in the extant sources, is the pottery workshop (see Dahl 2010a). This workshop, perhaps connected to the governor's household, produced large quantities of pottery. The format of the accounts concerning pottery production is similar to those of the reed and basketry workshop. However, the second part of the "credits" in the accounts concerning the overseer of the pottery workshop calculated only the work-day equivalencies of the products, since the raw materials that were used in the production of pottery had no economic value.

No. 155. *MS 4712 (Umma, X–ix to X–xii), and* **No. 156.** *MS 4713 (Umma, —)*

There are two, fragmentary, large accounts concerning agricultural work in the Schøyen Collection: texts Nos. 155 and 156, both transliterated in full in the Appendix. Although both accounts are missing their colophons and most of the "debits" section, it can be suggested that they are accounts concerning Lugal-gu'e, an overseer of agricultural workers known from the two key-texts BIN 5, 272 and TCL 5, 5675, published almost one hundred years ago.[446] These two accounts, now in Yale and the Louvre, cover the years AS 3 and 4, and our texts Nos. 155 and 156 are likely to date to the years immediately before or after them.

Neither No. 155 nor No. 156 includes any products other than the work-days of the crew, and the "credits" section is therefore simple compared to the accounts concerning the specialized crews working in the basketry or pottery workshops.

Although both texts are very fragmentary, No. 156 preserves some of the key administrative terminology, including the summary of the "debits" section:

No. 156 obv. col. i

(column broken)

obv. col. ii

	(beginning broken)	
1'.	[. . .] ⌜ug$_3^?$-IL$_2^?$ u$_4$⌝ 1(diš)-še$_3$	. . . work-days of carriers,
2'.	[ki] x-^{d}x-x-ta	from PN$_1$.
3'.	[. . .] x x x tur-[tur . . .] u$_4$ 1(diš)-še$_3$	. . . work-days of children, . . .
4'.	[ki . . .]-dingir-ta	from PN$_2$.
	(blank space)	

---

[445] A worker was expected to weave 1/6 of a sar (ca. 6 m^2) of reed mat (^{gi}kid) each day, using 6 bundles of reed (sa gi) per ⅙ šar. See Englund 1988: 121–85, in particular n. 43, and Goetze 1948: 165–202.

[446] V.V. Struve based some of his most important work on an analysis of BIN 5, 272 and TCL 5, 5675, see Struve 1954.

5'.	[šunigin] ⸢2(šar$_2$)⸣ 5(geš'u) 3(u) [3+n(diš)[447]] ⸢guruš u$_4$ 1(diš)⸣-še$_3$	Total: 10,233+n work-days (of regular dependent workers).
6'.	[šunigin 5(geš$_2$) 1(u)] ⸢8(diš)? ½(diš)?⸣ ug$_3$-IL$_2$ tur-tur u$_4$ 1(diš)-še$_3$	Total: x+ 7 work-days of carriers and children.
	(blank space)	
7'.	⸢sag⸣-nig$_2$-gur$_{11}$-ra-kam	(That) is the "debits."

The first preserved line of col. ii lists all or some of the seven work-days of carriers totalled in l. 5' of the same column. The total of work-days of ordinary workers is almost identical to that found in BIN 5, 272, but smaller than that found in TCL 5, 5675:

No. 156 obv. ii 5': [šunigin] ⸢2(šar$_2$)⸣ 5(geš'u) 3(u) [3+n(diš)] ⸢guruš u$_4$ 1(diš)⸣-še$_3$
BIN 5, 272 obv. ii 1': šunigin 2(šar$_2$) 5(geš'u) 5(geš$_2$) 1(u) 3(diš) ⅔(diš) guruš u$_4$ 1(diš)-še$_3$
TCL 5, 5675 obv. ii 17: šunigin 3(šar$_2$) 1(geš'u) 9(geš$_2$) 2(u) 6(diš) 5/6(diš) guruš u$_4$ 1(diš)-še$_3$

The larger size of the total of TCL 5, 5675 is probably due to the fact that that text covered a year with an intercalation, hence thirteen months. The total of text No. 156 can therefore be estimated to correspond to a work team of about twenty-five workers over a period of twelve months (the team in TCL 5, 5675 consists of twenty-four workers, whereas there seems to be some development in the size of the team of BIN 5, 272, with an average total of twenty-four workers).

The number of carriers and other auxiliary workers recorded in text No. 156 is also smaller than that found in TCL 5, 5675; no such group is found in BIN 5, 272.

The "debits" section of text No. 155 is entirely missing, as is the total of the "credits" and the operating balance, and it is therefore not possible to estimate whether the total of this text would have matched that of No. 156 or TCL 5, 5675. The total of the "credits" of No. 156 is preserved, and it is smaller than the total of the "debits," resulting in a "deficit":

No. 156 rev. col. v

	(blank space)	
5'.	[šunigin] 2(šar$_2$) 3(geš'u) ⸢6(geš$_2$)⸣ 4(u) [n(diš)] ⅔(diš) guruš u$_4$ 1(diš)-še$_3$	Total: 9,400+n ⅔ work-days.
6'.	[šunigin] ⸢5(geš$_2$) 1(u)⸣ 8(diš) ½(diš) ug$_3$-IL$_2$ tur-tur u$_4$ 1(diš)-še$_3$	Total: 318 ½ work-days of carriers and children.
7'.	[zi]-ga-am$_3$	Booked out.
8'.	[la$_2$-ia$_3$] 1(geš'u) 3(geš$_2$) ⸢5(u)⸣ 2(diš) ⅓(diš) ⸢guruš u$_4$ 1(diš)⸣-še$_3$	Deficit: 832 ⅓ work-days.
	(blank space)	
	(rest broken)	

In contrast, both TCL 5, 5675 and BIN 5, 272 balance, and no deficit or surplus is therefore recorded. This is also reflected in TCL 5, 5675, which is the account from the year following that of BIN 5, 272: TCL 5, 5675 has no "deficit" carried over from a previous account. Unfortunately, the beginning of BIN 5, 272 is broken and it cannot be confirmed whether text No. 156 was the account from the year preceding it.

The teams recorded in accounts Nos. 155 and 156 work on some of the same fields as those found in BIN 5, 272 and TCL 5, 5675, helping our reconstructions and aiding the identification of the responsible overseer.

The tasks are similar in the four texts discussed here, and can basically be divided into four main sections. The first section is harvest (š a$_3$ b u r u$_{14}$, "within the harvest"). It is partly preserved in No. 156 (obv. iii 13)

[447] Since the total in rev. v 5' is partially broken it is impossible to reconstruct this notation completely.

but almost entirely missing in No. 155 (see for comparison TCL 5, 5675 obv. iii 6: ša$_3$ buru$_{14}$). The second section involves preparing the soil. It is summarized as "work of harrowing" (a$_2$ geš-ur$_3$-ra; No. 155 obv. v 23), although it also involves plowing (tug$_2$-gur$_x$(ŠE.KIN)). The third, and much shorter, section is summarized as "work of sowing" (a$_2$ numun-na; No. 155 obv. vi 1). The sowing section is not preserved in No. 156, nor is the header "work of harrowing" preserved in that text, although much of the section is. The final section in all of the texts concerns various tasks such as weeding, hoeing, breaking up clods, and miscellaneous other tasks, performed by troops, carriers, hirelings and other auxiliary workers, but not generally the core crew. This section is suffixed "field work" (a-ša$_3$-ge kin-ak) in the two texts published here, but that terminology is absent from the Yale and Louvre texts. A final section, following the four main agricultural tasks, details absence from the work crew. This section is found in all four texts discussed here.

Sections two and three, detailing the work of harrowing and sowing, are divided into work performed on domain units (GAN$_2$ gu$_4$) and work performed on the sustenance fields of the cultivator(s) (šuku engar).

Harvest

A relatively brief section subscripted "(work) within the harvest" (ša$_3$ buru$_{14}$)[448] is found, or can be reconstructed, in all four texts (TCL 5 5675 obv. ii 21–iii 6; BIN 5, 272 obv. ii 4'–iii 2'; No. 155 ending obv. iii 24 [reconstructed]; and No. 156 obv. ii 9'–iii 13). In all texts the header is found following a blank space; it is partly broken in No. 156 and completely reconstructed in No. 155. The well-preserved harvest section from TCL 5, 5675 is given here for comparison:

TCL 5, 5675 obv. col. ii

21.	7(geš$_2$) 2(u) 3(diš) guruš u$_4$ 1(diš)-še$_3$	323 work-days,
22.	še gur$_x$(ŠE.KIN)-a	reaping barley.
23.	3(geš$_2$) 5(diš) guruš u$_4$ 1(diš)-še$_3$	185 work-days,
24.	zar tab-ba šu ur$_3$-ra	sheafing (and) spreading(?).[449]
25.	5(geš$_2$) 3(u) 6(diš) guruš u$_4$ 1(diš)-še$_3$	216 work-days,
26.	ki-su$_7$-ka gub-ba	stationed at the threshing floor
27.	a-ša$_3$ ka-ma-ri$_2$^{ki} u$_3$ a-ša$_3$ lugal	(of) the Kamari field and the Lugal field.

obv. col. iii

1.	[kišib$_3$] šeš-kal-la	Sealed tablet of Šeš-kala.
2.	5(geš$_2$) 4(u) 5(diš) guruš u4 1(diš)-še$_3$	345 work-days,
3.	še gur$_x$(ŠE.KIN)-a zar tab-ba a-ša$_3$ ^{d}šara$_2$ u$_3$ a-ša$_3$ la$_2$-maḫ	reaping barley (and) sheafing, the Šara field and the La-maḫ field.
4.	kišib$_3$ lugal-e$_2$-maḫ-e	Sealed tablet of Lugal-Emaḫe,
5.	⸢šeš⸣ lugal-^{geš}[kiri$_6$]	brother of Lugal-kiri.
	(blank space)	
6.	ša$_3$ buru$_{14}$	(Work) within the harvest.

The harvest section of text No. 156 is less well preserved, but can be shown largely to follow that of TCL 5, 5675:

No. 156 obv. col. ii

9'.	⸢8(geš$_2$)⸣ 1(u) 5(diš) guruš u$_4$ 1(diš)-še$_3$	415 work-days,
10'.	[še] gur$_x$(ŠE.KIN)-a zar$_3$ tab-ba	reaping barley (and) sheafing.

[448] It is possible that ša$_3$ here and elsewhere in the Ur III corpus should be understood as a relative pronoun adopted from Akkadian.

[449] See Civil 1994: 91.

11'.	[n] 4(u) guruš u$_4$ 1(diš)-še$_3$	*n*+40 work-days,
12'.	⸢ki⸣-su$_7$ i$_3$-se$_3$ ki-su$_7$ ^{geš}asal$_2$-du$_3$-a u$_3$ [. . .]-lugal gub-ba	stationed at the threshing floor of Ise, at the threshing floor of Asal-dua, and the threshing floor of x-lugal.
13'.	[n] ⸢4(u)⸣ 4(diš) guruš u$_4$ 1(diš)-še$_3$	*n*+44 work-days,
14'.	ki-su$_7$ a-ša$_3$ ^{d}nin-ur$_4$-ra gub-ba	stationed at the threshing floor of the Ninura field.
15'.	[n] 4(u) guruš u$_4$ 1(diš)-še$_3$	*n*+40 work-days,

bottom

1.	⸢1(geš'u)⸣ [. . .]	(calculations:) 600+*n*

obv. col. iii

1.	ki-su$_7$ ^{d}amar-^{d}suen-^{d}šara$_2$-ki-ag$_2$ gub-ba	stationed at the threshing floor of Amar-Suen-Šara-kiag.
2.	⸢2(geš$_2$)⸣ 5(u) 5(diš) guruš u$_4$ 1(diš)-še$_3$	175 work-days,
3.	⸢ki⸣-[su$_7$] x-BI gub-ba	stationed at the threshing floor of x-BI.
4.	1(geš$_2$) 3(u) 6(diš) ⸢guruš⸣ ⸢u$_4$⸣ 1(diš)-še$_3$	96 work-days,
5.	ki-su$_7$ du$_6$-geš-i$_3$-⸢ka⸣ gub-ba	stationed at the threshing floor of Du-gešika.
6.	3(u) 5(diš) guruš u$_4$ 1(diš)-še$_3$	35 work-days,
7.	ki-su$_7$ ^{d}amar-^{d}suen-^{d}šara$_2$-ki-ag$_2$-ta	from the threshing floor of Amar-Suen-Šara-kiag
8.	ka-ma-ri$_2$-še$_3$ še mar-ta la$_2$-a	to Kamari, . . . the barley(?).
9.	1(geš$_2$) 3(u) guruš u$_4$ 1(diš)-še$_3$	90 work-days,
10.	gu$_4$-e us$_2$-sa	tending the oxen.
11.	1(geš$_2$) 1(u) ⸢2(diš) guruš u$_4$ 1(diš) ⸣-[še$_3$]	72 work days,
12.	[kišib$_3$] ⸢apin?⸣ du x x ⸢ša$_3$? ^{d}šara$_2$⸣ (*blank space*)	. . . .
13.	ša$_3$ buru$_{14}$	(Work) within the harvest.

The harvest section of text No. 155 is much more damaged, and transliterated in the Appendix only.

Plowing and Harrowing

Plowing and harrowing, performed by teams of three, are done on specific units: domain units and sustenance plots. The plowing and harrowing section of TCL 5, 5675 consists of two domain units (GAN$_2$ gu$_4$) and the related sustenance plots of the cultivators (šuku engar), as well as one additional area. The plowing and harrowing section of BIN 5, 272 is damaged and it is not clear if the same organization was in place there. The plowing and harrowing section of text No. 155 is divided into four domain units and corresponding sustenance fields of the cultivators. No. 156 is divided into at least three domain units and sustenance fields.

The subscript "work of harrowing" (a$_2$ geš-ur$_3$-ra) is found in TCL 5, 5675 (obv. v 4) and in text No. 155 (obv. v 22), but it is missing from both No. 156 and BIN 5, 272.

The work of plowing and harrowing, described by Maekawa 1974, and elsewhere, and Maeda 1995, involved gangs of three workers. Usually these gangs would first plow the field before harrowing it. Plowing was done at a rate of c. 1 iku each day, whereas harrowing, mostly thrice, was done on much larger areas, often 1 eše$_3$ each day. All four accounts use the same terminology, except that Nos. 155 and 156 abbreviate the technical term geš-ur$_3$-ra to geš.

No. 156 obv. col. iv

1.	4(bur$_3$) 1(eše$_3$) GAN$_2$ tug$_2$-gur$_x$(ŠE.KIN) ½(iku) ¼(iku) GAN$_2$-ta geš a-ra$_2$ 3(diš$_{tenû}$) 4(iku) ½(iku) GAN$_2$-ta	4 bur$_3$ 1 eše$_3$ of field, plowed, ¾ iku field each (team each day); harrowed thrice, (at a rate of) 4 ½ iku each (team each day).
2.	a$_2$ erin$_2$-na-bi u$_4$ 7(geš$_2$) 4(u) 8(diš)	Its team work-days: 468.[450]
3.	1(bur$_3$) [5(iku) ¼(iku) GAN$_2$] geš a-⸢ra$_2$⸣ [3(diš$_{tenû}$)] ⸢4(iku)⸣ [½(iku) GAN$_2$-ta]	1 bur$_3$ 5 ¼ iku of field, harrowed thrice, (at a rate of) 4 ½ iku each (worker each day).
4.	a$_2$ erin$_2$-na-bi u$_4$ 4(u) 6(diš) ½(diš)	Its team work-days: 46 ½.[451]
5.	GAN$_2$-gu$_4$	Domain unit.
6.	4(iku) ½(iku) GAN$_2$ geš a-ra$_2$ 3(diš$_t$) 4(iku) ½(iku) GAN$_2$-ta	4 ½ iku of field, harrowed thrice, (at a rate of) 4 ½ iku each (worker each day).
7.	a$_2$ erin$_2$-na-bi u$_4$ 1(u) la$_2$ 1(diš$_{tenû}$)	Its team work-days: 9.[452]
8.	šuku engar	Sustenance (plots) of the cultivator(s).
9.	a-⸢ša$_3$ GAN$_2$-ur-gu⸣	Field: GAN-urgu.

Similar operations are found in the other texts discussed here. Only an example from text No. 155 is given:

No. 155 obv. col. iv

19.	1(bur$_3$) GAN$_2$ tug$_2$-gur$_x$(ŠE.KIN) ½(iku) ¼(iku) GAN$_2$ geš a-ra$_2$ 3(dištenû) 4(iku) ½(iku) GAN$_2$-ta	1 bur$_3$ of field, plowed, ¾ iku field each (team each day), harrowed thrice, (at a rate of) 4 ½ iku each (team each day).
20.	a$_2$ erin$_2$-na-bi u$_4$ 1(geš$_2$) ⸢4(u) 8(diš)⸣	Its team work-days: 108.[453]
21.	1(bur$_3$) 2(eše$_3$) 4(iku) ½(iku) GAN$_2$ geš a-ra$_2$ 3(dištenû) 4(iku) ½(iku) GAN$_2$-ta	1 bur$_3$, 2 eše$_3$, 4 ½ iku of field harrowed thrice, (at a rate of) 4 ½ iku each (team each day).
22.	a$_2$ erin$_2$-na-bi u$_4$ 1(geš$_2$) 9(diš)	Its team work-days: 69.[454]
23.	GAN$_2$-gu$_4$	It is a domain unit.
24.	1(eše$_3$) 1(iku) ¼(iku) GAN$_2$ geš ⸢a-ra$_2$⸣ 3(dištenû) 4(iku) ½(iku) ⸢GAN$_2$⸣-ta	1 eše$_3$, 1 ¼ iku field harrowed thrice, (at a rate of) 4 ½ iku each (team each day).
25.	a$_2$ erin$_2$-na-bi u$_4$ ⸢1(u)⸣ 4(diš) ⸢½(diš)⸣	Its team work-days: 14 ½.[455]
26.	šuku engar	Sustenance field of the cultivator(s).
27.	a-ša3 ša-ra-ḫu-um-ma	Field: Šaraḫumma.

Sowing

The next task recorded in the texts, and probably also the next task performed during the agricultural year, is sowing. The technical terminology, "work of sowing" (a$_2$ numun-na), is present in TCL 5, 5675, No. 155, and BIN 5, 272, but has been lost in No. 156: it was probably once to be found in the broken part at the end of obv. v or rev. i.

Text No. 155 lists the domain units in two groups (obv. v 24 and 25), and the sustenance plots of the cultivators in one line (obv. v 27). Since both the total of the sustenance plots and the total work-days are partially broken, the reconstruction here is not certain. The combined area of the sustenance plots is calculated by

[450] Calculation: ((78 × 3) ÷ ¾) + ((78 × 3 × 3) ÷ 4 ½) = 312 + 156 = 468.

[451] Calculation: ((23 ¼ × 3 × 3) ÷ 4 ½) = 46 ½.

[452] Calculation: ((4 ½ × 3 × 3) ÷ 4 ½) = 9.

[453] Calculation: ((18x3) ÷ ¾) + ((18×3×2) ÷ 4 ½) = 72 + 36 = 108.

[454] Calculations: (34 ½ × 3 × 3) ÷ 4 ½ = 69.

[455] Calculations: (7 ¼ × 3 × 3) ÷ 4 ½ = 14 ½.

adding the four plots found in the plowing and harrowing section (obv. iv 6–8, 15–17, 24–26, and v 19–21). The column total found at the the end of col. v validates this reconstruction (assuming that l. 17 of the same column reads: a$_2$ erin$_2$-na-bi u$_4$ ⸢2(geš$_2$) 2(u) 7(diš)⸣). Sowing was done twice, by teams of four people.

No. 155 obv. col. v

24.	2(bur'u) 7(bur$_3$) 2(iku) ½(iku) GAN$_2$	2 bur'u 7 bur$_3$ 2 ½ iku of field;
25.	2(eše$_3$) 4(iku) ½(iku) GAN$_2$ a-ša$_3$ bala	2 eše$_3$ 4 ½ iku of field, the bala (obligation) field.
26.	[GAN$_2$]-gu$_4$	Domain unit(s).
27.	[1(bur$_3$) 1(eše$_3$)] 4(iku) GAN$_2$ šuku engar	1 bur$_3$ 1 eše$_3$ 4 iku of field. Sustenance plots of the cultivators.
28.	⸢uru$_4$⸣-[a] ⸢2(iku)⸣ GAN$_2$-ta	Sown at a rate of a 2 iku field (each team of four, each day).
29.	a$_2$ erin$_2$-na-bi ⸢u$_4$⸣ 1(geš'u) ⸢7(geš$_2$)⸣ [4(u)] ⸢6(diš)⸣	Its team work-days: 1066.[456]

bottom

1.	2(geš'u) 9(geš$_2$) 4(u) [½(diš)]	(computations:) 2380 ½

col. vi

	(blank space)	
1.	a$_2$ numun-na	Work of sowing.

TCL 5, 5675 is formatted slightly different but contains the same information:

TCL 5, 5675 obv. col. v

5.	2(bur'u) 2(bur$_3$) [1(eše$_3$)] 3(iku) ½(iku) GAN$_2$ a-ša$_3$ uru$_4$-a 2(iku) GAN$_2$-ta	2 bur'u, 2 bur$_3$, 1 eše$_3$, 3 ½ iku field plowed (at a rate of a) 2 iku field (each team of four, each day).
6.	a-ša$_3$ a-geštin	Field: A-geštin.
7.	5(bur$_3$) 1(eše$_3$) 2(iku) GAN$_2$ uru$_4$-a 2(iku) GAN$_2$-ta	5 bur$_3$, 1 eše$_3$, 2 iku field plowed (at a rate of a) 2 iku field (each team of four, each day)
8.	a-ša$_3$ ša-ra-ḫu-um-ma	Field: Šaraḫumma.
9.	5(bur$_3$) 1(eše$_3$) 5(iku) GAN$_2$ uru$_4$-a 2(iku) GAN$_2$-ta	5 bur$_3$, 1 eše$_3$, 5 iku (field) plowed (at a rate of a) 2 iku field (each team of four, each day)
10.	a-ša$_3$ lugal	Field of the King.
11.	1(bur$_3$) 5(iku) GAN$_2$ uru$_4$-a 2(iku) GAN$_2$-ta	1 bur$_3$, 5 iku (field) plowed (at a rate of a) 2 iku field (each team of four, each day)
12.	a-ša$_3$ e$_2$-lugal	Field of the house of the king.
13.	a$_2$ erin$_2$-na-bi 2(geš'u) 5(u) 5(diš)	Its team work-days: 1855.[457]
14.	GAN$_2$-gu$_4$	Domain units.
15.	1(eše$_3$) GAN$_2$ šuku uru$_4$-a 2(iku) GAN$_2$-ta	1 eše$_3$ field, sustenance plots (of the cultivators), plowed (at a rate of a) 2 iku field (each team of four, each day).
16.	a$_2$ erin$_2$-na-bi u$_4$ 1(u) 2(diš)	Its team work-days: 12.[458]
17.	a-ša$_3$ a-geštin	Field: A-geštin.
	(blank space)	
18.	a$_2$ numun-na	Work of sowing.

456 Calculation: ((488 ½ + 16 ½ + 28) ÷ 2) × 4 = 1066.

457 Calculation: ((405 ½ + 98 + 101 + 23) ÷ 2) × 4 = 1255.

458 Calculation: (6 ÷ 2) × 4 = 12.

Miscellaneous Field Work

Two organizing principles are at play in this section of all four accounts discussed here. The section is divided according to the category of the workers (hirelings, lu$_2$ ḫun-ga$_2$; ox-drivers, ša$_3$-gu$_4$; team-workers, erin$_2$; carriers, ug$_3$-IL$_2$), and according to the task at hand (cutting reed, gi ze$_x$(SIG$_7$)-a; hoeing, described with the short hand "hoe," al; clearing the furrows of clods, ab-sin$_2$-ta la-ag ri-ri-ga; weeding, ^{geš}diḫ$_3$ ku$_5$-ra, etc.).

In texts Nos. 155 and 156 the section is subtitled "field work" (a-ša$_3$-ge kin-ak); the same terminology is not found in TCL 5, 5675 or BIN 5, 272.

No. 155 obv. col. vi

2.	4(geš'u) sar gi 2(u) sar-ta	2,400 sar of reed, 20 sar (of land) each (worker, each day).
3.	a$_2$-bi u$_4$ 2(geš$_2$)	Its work-days: 120.[459]
4.	1(geš'u) 5(geš$_2$) 3(diš) sar al 6(diš) sar-ta	903 sar (of land to be) hoed, 6 sar of land each (worker, each day).
5.	a$_2$-bi u$_4$ 2(geš$_2$) 3(u) ½(diš)	Its work-days: 150 ½.[460]
6.	a$_2$ lu$_2$ ḫun-ga$_2$ 6(diš) sila$_3$-ta	Work of hirelings at 6 sila$_3$ (of barley) each (day).
7.	1(geš$_2$) 6(diš) sar al 6(diš) sar-ta	66 sar (of land to be) hoed, 6 sar of land each (worker, each day).
8.	a$_2$-bi u$_4$ 1(u) 1(diš)	Its work-days: 11.[461]
9.	a$_2$ ša$_3$-gu$_4$	Work of ox-drivers.
10.	5(u) 4(diš) guruš u$_4$ 1(diš)-še$_3$	54 work-days.
11.	a$_2$ erin$_2$ diri$^?$	Work of surplus team-workers.
12.	4(u) 2(diš) ug$_3$-IL$_2$ u$_4$ 1(diš)-še$_3$	42 work-days of carriers,
13.	ab-sin$_2$-ta la-ag ri-ri-ga	clearing the furrows of clods.
14.	a-ša$_3$ la$_2$-maḫ[462]	Field: Lamaḫ.
15.	1(geš'u) 5(geš$_2$) 2(u) 7(diš) sar al 6(diš) sar-ta	927 sar (of land to be) hoed, 6 sar (of land) each (worker, each day).
16.	⸢a$_2$⸣-bi u$_4$ 2(geš$_2$) 3(u) 4(diš) ½(diš)	Its work-days: 154 ½.[463]
17.	⸢a$_2$ lu$_2$ ḫun-ga$_2$ 5(diš)$^?$⸣ sila$_3$-ta	Work of hirelings at 5 sila$_3$ (of barley) each (day).

We can compare this section to that found in TCL 5, 5675 rev. col. iii 3–18:

TCL 5, 5675 rev. col. iii

3.	7(geš$_2$) 2(u) sar u$_2$ ^{geš}ḫašḫur 1(u) sar-ta	440 sar (of land) weed and apple trees(?), 10 sar (of land) each (worker, each day).
4.	a$_2$-bi u$_4$ 4(u) 4(diš)	Its work-days: 44.[464]
5.	7(geš$_2$) 5(diš) sar gi ze$_x$(SIG$_7$)-a 1(u) sar-ta	425 sar (of land) to cut reed, 10 sar (of land) each (worker, each day).
6.	a$_2$-bi u$_4$ 4(u) 2(diš) ½(diš)	Its work-days: 42 ½.[465]

---

[459] Calculations: 2400 ÷ 20 = 120.

[460] Calculations: 903 ÷ 6 = 150 ½.

[461] Calculations: 66 ÷ 6 = 11.

[462] Erasure after la$_2$-maḫ.

[463] Calculations: 927 ÷ 6 = 154 ½.

[464] Calculation: 440 ÷ 10 = 44.

[465] Calculation: 425 ÷ 10 = 42.5.

7.	4(geš$_2$) sar al 5(diš) sar-ta	240 sar (of land to be) hoed, 5 sar (of land) each (worker, each day).
8.	a$_2$-bi u$_4$ 4(u) 8(diš)	Its work-days: 48.[466]
9.	4(u) sar al 4(diš) sar-ta	40 sar (of land to be) hoed, 4 sar (of land) each (worker, each day).
10.	a$_2$-bi u$_4$ 1(u)	Its work-days: 10.[467]
11.	4(geš$_2$) sar ^{geš}diḫ$_3$ ku$_5$-ra$_2$ 2(u) sar-ta	240 sar (of land) camelthorn to be cut, 20 sar (of land) each (worker, each day).
12.	a$_2$-bi u$_4$ 1(u) 2(diš)	Its work-days: 12.[468]
13.	a-ša$_3$ ša-ra-ḫu-um-ma kišib$_3$ ab-ba-gi-na	Field: Šaraḫumma. Sealed tablet of Abbagina.
14.	4(geš'u) 3(geš$_2$) 2(u) sar ^{u2}kiši$_{17}$ ku$_5$-a 1(geš$_2$) sar-ta	2600 sar (of land) weed to be cut, 60 sar (of land) each (worker, each day).
15.	a$_2$-bi u$_4$ 4(u) 3(diš) ⅓(diš)	Its work-days: 43 ⅓.[469]
16.	a$_2$ 7(diš) sila$_3$-ta	work at 7 sila$_3$ each (hireling, each day).
17.	a-ša$_3$ e$_2$-lugal	Field: House of the king.
18.	kišib$_3$ lugal-a$_2$-zi-da	Sealed tablet of Lugal-azida.

Absence, Other Assignments, and Days Off

The last section of each account lists workers who were absent from the regular crew, for a number of reasons. In text No. 155 the preserved parts of this section document three individual workers who were not available for work, and two transfers of work to other crews signed off by their overseers:

No. 155 rev. col. ii

2.	x lugal-nir	. . . Lugal-nir.
3.	uš$_2$ engar-zi	Dead: Engar-zi.
4.	si$_{12}$-a šeš-kal-la dumu u$_2$-da-ur$_4$-ra	Blind: Šeš-kala, child of Uda-ura,
5.	iti 1(u) 2(diš)-še$_3$	For 12 months.
6.	a$_2$-bi u$_4$ 1(geš'u) 2(geš$_2$)	Its work: 720 days.
7.	iti še-sag$_{11}$-ku$_5$-ta	From month: "Harvest,"
8.	iti ^{d}dumu-zi-še$_3$	to month: "Dumuzi."
9.	1(diš) lugal-zi-mu	One Lugal-zimu,
10.	⌜en⌝-nu-ga$_2$ ti-la	living under guard.
11.	iti 6(diš)-še$_3$	For 6 months.
12.	a$_2$-bi u$_4$ 3(geš$_2$)	Its work: 180 days.
13.	iti min$_3$-eš$_3$-[ta]	From month: "Double-sanctuary"
14.	[iti ^{d}dumu-zi-še$_3$]	to month: "Dumuzi."
15.	x guruš [u$_4$ x-še$_3$]	*n* workers for *n* days.
16.	a$_2$-bi u$_4$ 6(diš)	Its work: 6 days.
17.	a zi-ga gu$_2$ idigna-da gub-ba	Stationed at the rising water of the banks of the Tigris.
18.	1(u) 6(diš) guruš u$_4$ 1(diš)-še$_3$	16 workers for one day,

[466] Calculation: 240 ÷ 5 = 48.

[467] Calculation: 40 ÷ 4 = 10.

[468] Calculation: 240 ÷ 20 = 12.

[469] Calculation: 2600 ÷ 60 = 43.33.

19.	a-pi$_4$-sal$_4$^{ki}-ta umma^{ki}-še$_3$ ku$_6$ il$_2$-la	carrying fish from Apisal to Umma.
20.	4(diš) guruš u$_4$ 1(diš)-še$_3$	4 workers for one day,
21.	a-ša$_3$ la$_2$-mah-<ta> tum-mal$_x$(TUR$_3$)^{ki}-še$_3$ ku$_6$ il$_2$-la	carrying fish from the Lamaḫ field to Tummal.
22.	1(u) guruš u$_4$ 1(diš)-še$_3$	10 workers for one day,
23.	a-ša$_3$ la$_2$-maḫ-ta uri$_5$^{ki}-še$_3$ ku$_6$ il$_2$-la u$_3$ ma$_2$ <<x>>[470] gur-ra	carrying fish from the Lamaḫ field to Ur and returning the boat.
	(*blank space*)	
24.	kišib$_3$ lugal-x-x	Sealed tablet of Lugal-x

bottom

25.	⌜2(geš'u)⌝ 1(geš$_2$) 3(u)	(computations:) 1290

rev. col. iii

1.	1(geš$_2$) 1(u) ⌜7(aš)⌝ [. . .] guruš-e ⌜1(aš)⌝ [. . .]	77 . . . each worker one . . . .
2.	a$_2$ x [. . .]⌜1(u) 8(diš)⌝	its work: +18 days.
3.	⌜du$_8$-du$_8$⌝ ša$_3$-gal udu niga bala$^?$ gal-a	. . . fodder for fattened sheep of the bala (obligation) . . .
4.	a-ša$_3$ ^{d}šara$_2$-ta	From the field: Šara,
5.	e$_2$-gal a-ša$_3$ la$_2$-maḫ-še$_3$ ga$_6$-ga$_2$	to the "palace" of the field: Lamaḫ, to be carried.
6.	kišib$_3$ uš-mu	Sealed tablet of Ušmu.
	(*blank space*)	

bottom

1.	1(geš$_2$) 1(u) 8(diš)	(computations:) 78

The unfortunate Lugal-zimu is listed as living under guard in both text No. 155 and TCL 5, 5675:

TCL 5, 5675 rev. col. v

5.	1(diš) lugal-zi-mu	1 Lugal-zimu,
6.	iti 4(diš)-še$_3$	for 4 months.
7.	a$_2$-bi u$_4$ 2(geš$_2$)[471]	Its work: 120 days.
8.	en-nun-ga$_2$ ti-la	Living under guard.
9.	kišib$_3$ lu$_2$-dingir-ra	Sealed tablet of Lu-Dingira.
10.	6(diš) guruš gu$_4$ us$_2$-sa	6 workers, following the oxen,
11.	6(diš) guruš a-ša$_3$-da tuš-a	6 workers, sitting at the field,
12.	iti 4(diš)-še$_3$	for 4 months.
13.	a$_2$-bi u$_4$ 2(geš'u)! 4(geš$_2$)-kam[472]	Its work: 1440 days.
14.	½(diš) ARAD$_2$-ḫu-la	½ ARAD-ḫula,
15.	½(diš) lu$_2$-^{d}nin-ur$_4$-ra	½ Lu-Nin-ura,
16.	½(diš) lu$_2$-^{d}šara$_2$	½ Lu-Šara,
17.	½(diš) lu$_2$-^{d}inanna	½ Lu-Inanna,
18.	½(diš) lu$_2$-gi-na šu-i	½ Lu-gina, barber,
19.	½(diš) lugal-nesag-e	½ Lugal-nesage

[470] The scribe appears to have begun writing ma$_2$ gid$_2$-da (sailing up stream), before correcting to ma$_2$ gur-ra (returning the boat).

[471] Calculation: 1 × 4 × 30 = 120.

[472] Calculation: 12 × 30 × 4 = 1440.

20.	iti 4(diš)-še$_3$	for 4 months.
21.	a$_2$-bi u$_4$ 6(geš$_2$) a$_2$ u$_4$-du$_8$-a dumu-gi$_7$[473]	Its work: 360 free-days for dumu-gi$_7$ workers.
22.	1(geš$_2$) 1(u) 2(diš) guruš u$_4$ 1(diš)-še$_3$	72 workers for one day,
23.	a$_2$ u$_4$-du$_8$-a ug$_3$-IL$_2$	free-days for carriers,
24.	iti 4(diš)-kam	for 4 months,
25.	iti ezem-^{d}šul-gi-ta	From month: "Festival of Šulgi,"
26.	iti diri-še$_3$	to the "extra" month (~intercalendar month).
27.	1(u) 2(diš) guruš u$_4$ 1(diš)-še$_3$	12 workers for 1 day.
28.	kišib$_3$ lugal-mu-ma-an-ag$_2$	Sealed tablet of Lugal-mumanag.
29.	3(geš'u) 7(geš$_2$) 3(u) sar sa gi	2250 sar of reed bundles.
30.	gu-nigin$_2$-ba 1(u) 2(diš)$^{!}$ sa-ta	Its bales: (made of) 12 bundles each.
31.	gu-nigin$_2$-bi 3(geš$_2$)$^{!}$ 7(diš) ½(diš)[474]	Its bales: 187 ½.
32.	guruš-e gu-nigin$_2$ 2(diš)-ta	Each worker, 2 bales (daily).
33.	a$_2$-bi u$_4$ <1(geš$_2$)> 3(u) 3(diš) ⅔(diš)[475]	Its work: 93 ⅔ days.
34.	en-du$_8$-<du>-ta ga$_2$-nun ku$_x$(KWU147)-ra	From the Endudu (field) brought into the storehouse.
35.	kišib$_3$ a$^{?}$ lugal-a$_2$-zi-da	Sealed tablet of Lugal-azida.
36.	1(u) 4(diš) guruš u$_4$ 5(u) 6(diš)-še$_3$	14 workers for 56 days.
37.	a$_2$-bi u$_4$ 1(geš'u) 3(geš$_2$) 4(diš)![476]	Its work: 784 days.
38.	umma^{ki}-ta nibru^{ki}-še$_3$ ma$_2$-la$_2$-a de$_6$-a da-ab-ru-um-ta nibru^{ki}-še$_3$ ma$_2$-la$_2$-a de$_6$-a u$_3$ bala-a gub-ba	Bringing a cargo boat from Umma to Nippur, bringing a cargo boat from Dabrum to Nippur, and stationed for the bala (obligation).
39.	kišib$_3$ ur-^{d}nu-muš-da	Sealed tablet of Ur-Numušda.

Texts Nos. 155 and 156 are transliterated in full in the Appendix.

Miscellaneous Work Texts

Text No. 157 is a single-column account of a team of workers classed as erin$_2$ and further specified as ka-us$_2$-ka-me. Only one other text is known to use this terminology: MVN 4, 25, which identifies a number of workers as lu$_2$ ka-us$_2$-ka-me. The designation ka-us$_2$-sa is well attested in the Ur III period and is probably another title for a messenger (see n. 523, below). I tentatively reconstruct erin$_2$ ka-us$_2$-<sa>-ka-me, and translate "they are erin$_2$-workers of the ka-us$_2$-sa category."

The text is broken and a fragment of another tablet has been glued onto it.

No. 157. *MS 4699 (Umma)*

obv.

1.	1(geš$_2$) 1(u) 5(diš) guruš	75 workers.
2.	ša$_3$-bi-ta	Out of it,
3.	1(u) 5(diš) ma$_2$ zi$_3$-da-še$_3$	15 (workers) for the flour boat.
4.	giri$_3$ ur-lugal	Conveyor: Ur-Lugal.

[473] Calculation: ½ × 6 × 4 × 30 = 360.

[474] Calculation: 2250 ÷ 12 = 187.5.

[475] Calculation: 187.5 ÷ 2 = 93.75.

[476] Calculation: 14 × 56 = 784.
text has 4(u).

5.	1(diš) ma$_2$ mun gazi$^{?}$	1 (worker) for the salt and alkaline boat.
6.	giri$_3^{?}$ lugal-nig$_2$-lagar-e	Conveyor: Lugal-niglagare.
7.	1(u) 1(diš) šeš-tab-ba šu bar-ra	11 assistants, released(?),
8.	2(u) la$_2$ 1(diš$_{tenû}$) ma$_2$ gi ⸢uri$_5^{ki}$⸣-še$_3$	19 (workers) for the reed boat (going) to Ur.
9.	giri$_3$ e$_2$-gal-e-si	Conveyor: Egale-si.
10.	1(diš) ur-mes ma$_2$ 2(diš) guruš x [. . .]	1 Ur-Mes . . .
11.	1(diš) lu$_2$-me-lam$_2$ ⸢ša$_3$⸣ x [. . .]	1 Lu-melam . . .
12.	1(diš) ur-^{d}šara$_2$ ki a-[. . .]	1 Ur-Šara, from . . .
13.	1(diš) ur-^{geš}gigir-re NI x [. . .]	1 Ur-Gigir . . .
14.	1(diš) gu-u$_2$-gu-[a . . .]	1 Gu'ugua.
	(rest broken)	

rev.

	(beginning broken)	
1'.	1(diš) [. . .]	1 . . .
2'.	1(diš) ⸢ur-^{d}suen⸣ [. . .]	1 Ur-Suen
3'.	ki ⸢du$_6^{?}$⸣ du [. . .]	From . . .
4'.	1(diš) lu$_2$-^{d}šara$_2$ dumu lu$_2$-[. . .]	1 Lu-Šara, child of Lu- . . .
5'.	1(diš) ezem-ba-ni [. . .]	1 Ezem-bani.
6'.	ša$_3$-gu$_4$-[me$^{?}$]	They are ox-drivers.
	(blank space)	
9'.	šunigin 1(geš$_2$) 4(diš) guruš	Total: 64 workers.
10'.	zi-ga-⸢am$_3$⸣	Booked out.
11'.	la$_2$-ia$_3$ 1(u) 1(diš) guruš	Deficit: 11 workers.
	(blank space)	
12'.	erin$_2$ ka-us$_2$-<sa>-ka-me	They are the erin$_2$-workers of the ka-us$_2$-sa$_2$ category.
	(blank space)	

Interestingly, and perhaps indicative of the status of the erin$_2$-workers, text No. 157 does not give the time the workers were enlisted in the services recorded.

A whole new set of accounts concerning work was discovered with the publication of the Garšana archive; these accounts detail work on large "public" building projects within the purview of the household of Šu-kabta, the manager and owner of the estate which comprised Garšana. The only example of this set of accounts in the collection published here, text No. 158, was not included in the publication of the Garšana texts. Texts of this type were discussed in detail by Heimpel (2009) and this example is therefore transliterated and translated without any commentary.

No. 158. *MS 4089 (Garšana, ŠS 6)*

obv.

1.	[n] ⸢guruš⸣ x [. . .]	*n* workers . . .
2.	[n] guruš [. . .]	*n* workers . . .
3.	[. . .] x [. . .]	. . .
4.	[n]⸢geme$_2$⸣ ugula x-[. . .]	*n* female workers, overseer . . .
5.	[x] x x x [. . .]	. . .

	(*blank line*)	
6.	⸢šunigin⸣ n guruš x-x	Total: *n* workers . . .
7.	[šunigin n] guruš [x]	[Total *n*] workers . . .
8.	⸢šunigin⸣ n geme$_2$	Total: *n* female workers.
9.	ša$_3$-bi-ta	Out of it,
10.	⸢2(diš)⸣ guruš šitim [. . .]	2 workers, builders . . .
11.	2(diš) guruš x geme$_2$	2 workers . . . female workers.
12.	šu dim$_2$-⸢ma⸣ gub-⸢ba⸣	Stationed at the . . .
13.	2(diš) ⸢guruš⸣ x NE [. . .]	2 workers . . .
14.	x x x im x x [. . .]⸢gub$^?$-ba$^?$⸣	stationed at the . . .

rev.

1.	n guruš im lu-a gub-⸢ba⸣	*n* workers standing at the clay mixing (and)
2.	al-tar e$_2$-ki-ba-gar-ra ša-at-^{d}kab-ta gub-ba	mixing (the clay), and standing at the replacement house of Šat-Kabta.[477]
3.	1(diš) guruš šitim im-du$_8$-a ^{geš}kiri$_6$ zabala$_4^{ki}$ gub-ba	1 worker, builder, standing at the adobe wall of the garden of Zabala.
4.	šunigin 3(diš) guruš šitim	Total: 3 workers, builders.
5.	šunigin n gurus	Total: *n* workers.
6.	šunigin 8(diš) geme$_2$	Total: 8 female workers.
7.	zi-ga-am$_3$	Booked out.
8.	gurum$_2$ ak	Inventory,
9.	giri$_3$ ^{d}iškur-illat sabra	conveyor: Adad-tillatī, overseer.
10.	ša$_3$ gar-ša-an-na^{ki}	Within Garšana.
11.	iti ezem-me-ki-gal$_2$	Month: "Festival of Mekigal."
12.	mu ^{d}šu-^{d}suen lugal-e na-ru$_2$-a maḫ ^{d}en-lil$_2$ ^{d}nin-lil$_2$-[la] mu-ne-[ru$_2$]	Year: "Šu-Suen, king, erected the lofty stela of Enlil and Ninlil."

left edge

1.	u$_4$ 8(diš)-kam	On the 8th day.

[477] See CUSAS 4: 46.

9
LETTERS

Although neo-Sumerian letters have been dealt with on several occasions they remain difficult to translate.[478] This difficulty is no doubt due to the frequent quotations from everyday language. In addition, letters frequently use unorthographical writings. Similar problems also exist with the legal texts of the period.

Another, less frequently discussed problem is the question of the function of the Ur III letters within the administration.[479] Not one single transaction detailed in one of the now more than 750 published Ur III letters has been shown to relate to a transaction recorded in the ordinary administrative texts.[480] The texts published here are no exception. The reason for this may lie in the very nature of the letters, as also expressed in the exhortations: the letters served to override the rigid structures of the administration in exceptional cases.[481]

Most Sumerian letters from the Ur III period conform to the following simple format, here referred to as Type I letters (for Type II, introducing a sender, and Type III reversing the order of address and message, see below):[482]

No. 159. *MS 4738 = CUSAS 3, 1526 (Garšana, —)*[483]

obv.

1.	šar-ru-um-i_3-li_2	To Šarrum-ili
2.	u_3-na-a-du_{11}	speak:
3.	[nig_2]-gal_2-la [x] e_2-za i_3-gal_2	"Available materials . . . that are in your house,
4.	e_2-ki-ba-gar-ra du_8-de_3	to caulk[484] the replacement house,

rev.

1.	^{d}iškur-illat	to Adad-tillatī,
2.	ḫe_2-na-ab-šum_2-mu	let him give."
3.	a-ba šeš-mu-gin_7	Who is like my brother?

In "Type I" letters, the addressee is mentioned in the first line. When more recipients are mentioned they can be separated by a conjunction, u_3, "and." Following the name(s) of the addressee we find the technical term u_3-na-a-du_{11}, literally translated: "after you have spoken to him/her," which in its nominalized form had by

---

[478] The standard edition of the Sumerian letters is Sollberger 1966. The list of Ur III letters has since been updated by B. Lafont in 1990. In 1993 P. Michalowski published an edition of a number of Sumerian letters in translation (1993: 52–118). Later he published a short discussion of actual Ur III letters (Michalowski 2011: 14–15), making the surprising claim that all letters would transmute into receipts by being enclosed in envelopes (citing Owen 1972: 133-34 [JCS 24, 133 UNC 1] and CUSAS 3 1037, without any further evidence, circumstantial or other). The term letter-order was first applied by Oppenheim (1948: 86 *ad* H 24 *et passim*).

[479] Pointedly noted by Hallo (1969: 171–73) in his review of Sollberger 1966.

[480] Except of course for the tablet mentioned above and published by Owen 1972: 133-34, and note that Steinkeller suggests that many of the regular transactions we find documented in receipts were initiated by a letter-order (2004: 71).

[481] For a different viewpoint, see Allred 2010, who argued that a majority of the letters belonged to the private sphere, outside the official administration.

[482] The typology suggested here is based on Sollberger 1966: 2 ff.

[483] The text is translated in the index of verbs in CUSAS 4: 681: "Say to Šarum-ili that '(?) that is in your house should be given to Adad-tillatī in order to caulk the replacement house. Who is like my brother?'"

[484] Although it is not clear why this house has to be caulked, the other meanings of du_8, "to fill" (du_8(b)), "to open" (du_8(h/r)), "to bake," etc. can be excluded (the relationship between these has not been fully explained in the literature).

the Ur III period become the Sumerian word for "letter."[485] When the Sumerian letter terminology is compared to the Akkadian it is clear that there exists a one-to-one correspondence between the Sumerian PN u$_3$-na-a-du$_{11}$ and the Akkadian *ana PN qibīma*. This has led most scholars to interpret and translate the Sumerian form as an imperative.[486] According to a more traditional view of Sumerian grammar, the modal prefix u$_3$- lends a prospective sense to the verb.[487] In this study the introductory formula is translated as an imperative.

Some letters with multiple recipients express their plurality in the prefix chain of the verb du$_{11}$: u$_3$-ne-e/a-du$_{11}$ ("speak to them").[488] However, although letters No. 164 and No. 163 both have two recipients, the verbal form is not changed in either of them to reflect that plurality.

In a Type I letter the actual message is recorded immediately following the address formula. The message of the vast majority of Ur III letters is a brief order, either to give something to someone, or for someone to perform some singular task (release someone, transfer something, etc.). The most frequently attested verb in the message part of Ur III Sumerian letters is therefore unsurprisingly šum$_2$, "to give."[489] The verb is mostly in the imperfect and with a precative modal prefix, but occasionally in the imperative.

Following the message an exhortation is often written, pledging the recipient to see to the matter of the letter. In the example of a Type I letter published above, the exhortation "Who is like my brother?" is found at the end. The exhortations of Ur III letters may be divided into six categories: (a) urgency of message; (b) invocation of family allegiance; (c) invocation of higher authority; (d) clause against complaints; (e) Akkadian exhortations in Sumerian letters; and (f) miscellaneous.[490]

The most frequent category (a) exhortation is a-ma-ru-kam, "it is urgent" (lit. "it is a flood"). "Quickly," ul$_4$-la-bi, is found in a handful of letters. Reference to the passing of time is found in a few other texts: written u$_4$ na-bi$_2$-ib$_2$-zal-e (ITT 2, 3418; TCS 1, 170), u$_4$ na-bi$_2$-zal-e (ITT 3, 6176), or u$_4$ nu-mu-zal-e (SNAT 222) (all loosely translated "The day must not pass"). "It is an express message," kas$_4$ ḫe$_2$-am$_3$-e, is only found in one letter (MCS 3 1 2 HSM 6339 = TCS 1 252).

The exhortation in the first letter, discussed above, belongs to category (b), invoking the allegiance of a brother ("who is like my brother?"). That is the only category (b) exhortation attested with any significant frequency. "Who is like my mother?" is found in one text (ITT 3, 6511 = TCS 1, 54 = Michalowski 1993 no. 127). "Because of me" is also only found in a few letters (bar-mu-še$_3$ in Michalowski 1993 no. 178; [x]-mu-še$_3$ in TCS 1, 326), whereas "because of my name" is found in a handful (mu-mu-še$_3$ for example BPOA 1, 303).

Category (c) exhortations, invoking a higher authority, are not restricted to letters. Phrases such as inim inim ensi$_2$-ka-ta, "on command of the governor," are also found in regular administrative documents. Most revealing, perhaps, is the use in the text BIN 5, 129 (Umma, AS 2), a receipt recording fallen animals and the meat, hides and wool obtained from them and brought into the palace, without the transaction being sealed (kišib$_3$ nu-tuku[491]),

---

485 See the Akkadian loanword *unneddukku* or *umunnedukku* (*CAD* U–W 161–62).

486 Usually with reference to the Old Sumerian letter formula du$_{11}$-ga-na (an imperative), e.g., the grammars of Jagersma (2010) section 24.2.2 ex. 39 with commentary (but see also below), Foxvog (2014: 107), and Edzard (2003: 122, 12.12.2).

487 See, e.g., Jagersma (2010) section 13.2.4 ex. 39–40 (but note his translation as a polite imperative in 24.2.2 ex. 39 with commentary cited above); also Civil 2005: 38–39; Thomsen 1984: 209–10, with reference to Falkenstein's grammar of the Gudea texts (Falkenstein 1950: II 213). Note also Poebel's question whether u$_3$- is to be compared to the Akkadian enclitic corpula -ma (Poebel 1923: 152–53).

488 See, for example, ITT 5, 6975.

489 See already Hallo 1969a: 172.

490 Akkadian letters may have a short statement at the end with similar purpose, but there are no recognizable patterns of exhortations in Akkadian letters comparable to those found in Sumerian letters of the Ur III period (see, for example, Salonen 1967: 50–51 and Sallaberger 1999b: 159–63).

491 The tablet from the Nies Collection, now in the Yale Babylonian Collection, was copied without regard to a division between obverse and reverse. The lines quoted above are numbers 9 and 10 in that hand copy, presumably found on the reverse.

ut on the command of the governor.[492] In the letters, the king, the governor, the palace, the šabra (JCS 28, 167 3), the sukkal-mah (TCS 1, 230), the accountant (ITT 2, 4145), and one's own authority are invoked.[493]

Clauses against complaints (category [d] exhortations) are very common in Ur III letters, in fact, na-mi-gur-re, "it shall not come up again," is the most frequent exhortation in the entire Ur III letter corpus. It is often found together with other exhortations. In a few cases the exhortation is completed by the addition of either du$_{11}$-ga or inim-bi in front of the verbal chain: du$_{11}$-ga na-mi-ib-gur-re (MCS 3, 2 4 HSM 6337); du$_{11}$-ga nam-mi-ib$_2$-gur-re (TCS 1, 175); ⌈inim⌉-bi na-mi-ib$_2$-gur-re (TCS 1, 154); inim-bi na-ba$^?$-ab-gur-re (AuOr 17–18: 222, 15), and we can presume that the instances without du$_{11}$-ga or inim-bi are abbreviated forms. This exhortation probably served to ensure that the order of the letter was being dealt with regardless of any opposition.

A few Ur III letters were written fully, or partly in Akkadian. In some of these letters we also find exhortations. The exhortation in ASJ 12: 54, *a-wa-tum la i$_3$-tu-ra-am*, is a direct translation of the Sumerian inim-a (or: du$_{11}$-ga) na-mi-gur-e. The common Akkadian exhortation *apputtum* ("please") is also found in one Ur III letter (TCS 1, 371), where it is followed by the request, "do not make him go hungry" ([*la*] *tu-ma-su$_4$, from emēṣu, "to be hungry"*).[494]

In the letter TIM 2, 91 (date uncertain[495]), we find the typical Akkadian exhortation *ma-nu-um ki a-hi-a*, "who is like my brother," immediately following the addressee. This exhortation, which is well known in Old Babylonian and Old Assyrian letters,[496] is identical to the Sumerian a-ba-šeš-mu-gin$_7$ (category [b] exhortation).

Text No. 160 has a unique sarcastic statement as part of the exhortation: "When the field is hoed, may it also be levelled."[497] This is followed by a standard exhortation of family allegiance (category [b] exhortation).

No. 160. *MS 4715/14 (Adab, —)*

obv.

1.	ur-^{d}a-ba-ba-ra	To Ur-Ababa
2.	u$_3$-na-a-du$_{11}$	speak:
3.	a-na-a-aš	"Why
4.	še ḫe$_2$-a ku$_3$-babbar ḫe$_2$-a	barley, as much as there is, and silver as much as there is,

rev.

1.	u$_3$-gu-a	to Ugua,
2.	nu-na-šum$_2$	hasn't he given?
3.	a-ša$_3$ ba-da-al-la	When the field is hoed,
4.	si ḫe$_2$-sa$_2$-e	may it also be leveled!
5.	a-ba šeš-mu-gin$_7$	Who is like my brother?"

---

[492] Garfinkle 2008 discusses the fact that the Ur III state was bureaucratic without a bureaucracy in the Weberian sense. A main argument in Garfinkle 2008 is the existence of local patrician families at the expense of a bureaucratic elite. At a more detailed level, the chains of command, described here and in Dahl 2007: 57–58, serve to further strengthen the reconstruction of the Ur III state as one where family far outranked office.

[493] And possibly "an overseer"; see the uncertain reference in YOS 4, 137.

[494] Michalowski translated "Do not go against him!" (1993: 105).

[495] Sollberger (and Michalowski) added the undated Akkadian language text TCS 1, 370 to the corpus of Ur III letters, although it is difficult to date.

[496] Sallaberger 1999b: 185 ff.

[497] Such statements are not unknown in Ur III Sumerian: note for example also the watercourse name i$_3$-ba-al-nu-ba-al, "is it dug, is it not dug" (see, e.g., MVN 10, 105, referenced also in Woods 2008: 142). That name was probably given to a watercourse that often silted up to the point where it was not obvious that it was dug at all.

The sarcastic statement is curiously close to a proverbial saying, although it is not found among the extant Sumerian proverbs. As with all such expressions from antiquity, great care should be taken with regard to an interpretation. In this case, one can speculate that it serves to emphatically urge the recipient to finish the order of the letter, and not to leave it half done.

Only rarely, and in none of the letters published here, is the sender mentioned. It is likely that the sender was identified by his seal. However, although we can speculate that all letters were encapsulated in envelopes, and that these were sealed, very few envelopes have been preserved.[498]

Text No. 161 also has a unique statement at the end of the text. The message of the letter is not entirely clear but involves a special type of boat (ma-su$_3$, possibly a punt?). The reverse has a statement which juxtaposes two similar constructions with the same object (nig$_2$-gu$_2$-na), the first with the verb gar, "to place," the second with the verb gal$_2$, "to be." The object is most likely to be translated as "utensils/tools" (Akkadian *unūtum*), rather than "tribute/load."[499] A tentative translation is given below.

No. 161. *MS 2020/5 (Girsu?, —)*

obv.

1.	gu$_3$-de$_2$-a	To Gudea,
2.	u$_3$-na-a-du$_{11}$	speak:
3.	ma$_2$ su$_3$ teš$_2$-še$_3$ du	"Go to an empty boat,
4.	ARAD$_2$-ra	to ARAD(mu)
5.	ḫe$_2$-mu-na-ab-šum$_2$-mu	let him give it.

rev.

1.	nig$_2$-gu$_2$-na ḫe$_2$-ma-a-ga$_2$-ga$_2$	Let him place the tools for me in it.
2.	nig$_2$-gu$_2$-na-mu ⸢ki⸣ na-ni-gal$_2$[500]	My tools were not there?"
	(*blank space*)	

Text No. 162 is a rare example of a sealed letter. The seal was rolled directly on the tablet, and no envelope has been preserved. The seal impression, which appears to be unique, is damaged. Nevertheless, it can be reconstructed in its entirety using prosopographical data from the city of Adab, where this tablet originated.[501]

No. 162. *MS 4715/21 (Adab, —)*

obv.

1.	ur-ba-ba	To Ur-Baba:
2.	u$_3$-na-du$_{11}$	speak:
3.	1(aš) še gur	"One gur of barley

---

[498] See TMH NF 1–2, 351 for a rare example of a preserved envelope to an Ur III letter.

[499] nig$_2$-gu$_2$-na is found frequently with different craftsmen: geš-kin-ti, "craftsmen," see, e.g., ASJ 18, 217 n. 3 no. 3 and parallels where workers are assigned different tasks among them caring for the tools of the craftsmen; šitim, "builder," see, e.g., CUNES 52-04-050, where 17 workdays are expended carrying the tools from the harbor to the storehouse (e$_2$-kišib$_3$-ba), the previous four lines lists builders; etc. It can be loaded on boats and transported (SAT 2, 128, Nisaba 23, 131, RA 62, 12 18, etc.), and so forth. When nig$_2$-gu$_2$-na occurs with *bala* (obligation) it may represent simply a load (see, for example, SNAT 293 rev. 1: nig$_2$-gu$_2$-na bala-a ma$_2$-a gar, "placing the load of the *bala* [obligation] on the boat").

[500] For the expression ki na-ni-gal$_2$(-la$_2$), see CUNES 49-02-029 rev. 1. T. Ozaki (pers. comm.) transliterates nig$_2$-gu$_2$-na-mu ki-na i$_3$-gal and translates "My tools(?) are at his (= ARAD's) place (= house)."

[501] See also the introduction. Although the governor of Adab could of course have rolled his seal on tablets from other localities, this text indicates that many, if not all, of the texts in the collection published here that mention a person ur-ba-ba originate from ancient Adab.

4.	mu-ni-maḫ	to Munimaḫ
5.	ḫe$_2$-na-ab-šum$_2$-mu	let him give.

rev.

1.	giri$_3$ lu$_2$-^{d}utu	Conveyor: Lu-Utu.
2.	še šuku ensi$_2$	(It is) the subsistence barley of the Governor."
	(*seal impression*)	
3.	⸢mu⸣ ma$_2$ ⸢dara$_3$⸣ [abzu ^{d}]en-[ki]	Year: "Boat of Enki (called) 'Ibex of the Abzu.'"

seal (S003322)

1.	⸢lu$_2$⸣-^{d}[utu$^{?}$]	Lu-Utu,
2.	[dub$^{?}$]-⸢sar⸣	scribe,
3.	⸢dumu⸣ ur-$^{d\ aš}$ašgi^{gi4}	child of Ur-Ašgi,
4.	⸢ensi$_2$⸣	governor
5.	⸢adab⸣$^{[ki]}$	of Adab.

The Type I letter No. 163 also concerns subsistence barley, but unfortunately includes in front of the word for subsistence a sign (IŠ) which is difficult to interpret.

No. 163. *MS 4715/13 (Adab, —)*

obv.

1.	ur-ba-ba	To Ur-Baba
2.	u$_3$ mu-na-a	and Munaya
3.	u$_3$-na-a-du$_{11}$	speak:
4.	IŠ šuku lu$_2$-dingir-ra	"The . . . of the subsistence of Lu-Dingira

rev.

1.	šu ba-ra-ni	release!"
	(*blank space*)	

When a sender is mentioned in the text of the letter he is usually introduced by the term na-be$_2$-a. Like the term introducing the addressee, this term too presents grammatical problems. It is traditionally analyzed as a syncopated nominalized imperfect (*marû*) form, with a third-person singular dative marker: "he is saying to him" (i-n.na-b-e-a). Syntactically, this term corresponds to the Akkadian formula *um-ma PN-ma*. If the sender is presumed to be of higher rank than the addressee, the order will be inverted and the sender recorded before the addressee. The same can be observed in Akkadian letters. A recently published Ur III letter will serve as an example of the use of the formula na-be$_2$-a (Type II letters), since none is present in the collection published here:

BPOA 1, 1234 (Umma, —)

obv.

1.	lugal-mu	My king[502]
2.	na-be$_2$-a	says:
3.	ensi$_2$ umma^{ki}-ra	To the governor of Umma
4.	u$_3$-na-a-du$_{11}$	speak:
5.	7(aš) 4(barig) 1(ban$_2$) 5(diš) sila$_3$ še gur-ta-am$_3$	"7 gur, 4 barig, 1 ban$_2$, and 5 sila$_3$ (c. 2355 liters) according to the gur,

rev.

1.	iti-da	each month,
2.	lu$_2$ ki-maš^{ki}-ke$_4$	(to/by) the man from Kimaš
3.	ḫa-ba-ab-šum$_2$-mu	let him give it to him."

Occasionally the message precedes the addressee. The reason for this is unknown, but the phenomenon is restricted to texts which include a list of objects or people. Text No. 164 is an example of such a letter (Type III):

No. 164. *MS 2019/3 (Umma, —)*

obv.

1.	1(diš) ur$_2$-ra-ni	1 Urrani.
2.	1(diš) da-da dumu ⸢ur-^{geš}gigir⸣	1 Dada, child of Ur-Gigir.
	(*1 line erased*)	
3.	1(diš) nig$_2$-du$_{11}$-ga-ni	1 Nigdugani.
4.	1(diš) ur-gu$_2$-de$_3$-na dumu lu$_2$-giri$_{17}$-zal$^?$	1 Ur-Gu'edina, child of Lu-girizal.
5.	1(diš) lu$_2$-^{d}nin-ur$_4$-ra dumu šu-eš$_{18}$-dar	1 Lu-Nin-ura, child of Šu-Eštar.

rev.

1.	1(diš) lu$_2$-dingir-ra dumu šeš-kal-la	1 Lu-Dingira, child of Šeš-kala.
2.	1(diš) lugal-ušur$_x$(LAL$_2$.TUG$_2$) dumu ur-dun	1 Lugal-ušur, child of Ur-Šul.
3.	1(diš) šeš-kal-la dumu TE-A-na aga$_3$-us$_2$	1 Šeš-kala, child of TE-A-na, soldier.
4.	dingir-ra	To Dingira
5.	u$_3$ lugal-nir	and Lugal-nir
6.	u$_3$-na-a-du$_{11}$	speak:
7.	ḫe$_2$-em-gi$_4$-gi$_4$[503]	"They shall return them(?)."

The next letter, No. 165, is difficult to understand, and may contain two distinct and unrelated(?) messages. The final line, nu-u$_3$-un-ḫun, remains difficult to interpret, but may in fact be another, new exhortation.

[502] In letters where the addressee is refered to as lugal-mu it is not certain that the actual king is meant. lugal-mu is probably used of someone considered superior (in the sense "my lord"), as well as of the sovereign. Here, however, where the order of addressee and sender has been reversed to indicate the higher status of the sender, we must assume that the king was meant, as the addressee is the governor of Umma.

[503] For ḫe-em-gi$_4$-gi$_4$, see also UET 3, 7 obv. 6.

No. 165. *MS 2020/2 (?, —)*

obv.

1.	lugal-mu-[ra]	To my lord,
2.	u$_3$-na-a-du$_{11}$	speak:
3.	ur-^{d}suen-ra	"For Ur-Suen,
4.	4(diš) kuš ga-ra-ab-šum$_2$	4 hides, I will give you.
5.	ma$_2$-a ga$_2$-ar-ba-a	Place them in the boat!"
6.	a-du-mu	(Secondly:) "Adumu

rev.

1.	u$_3$ lu$_2$-mu diš-am$_3$	and Lumu are united,
2.	en-^{nu}nun-še$_3$	under guard,
3.	ḫe$_2$-eb-du$_3$	let him place (them)."
4.	in-na-a-du$_{11}$	I told him.
5.	nu-u$_3$-un-ḫun	It is not calm.
	(*blank space*)	

There are two further Type I letters in the collection. Both are fragmentary and presented here without further comment.

No. 166. *MS 4730 (Adab, —)*

obv.

1.	šabra	To the chief administrator
2.	u$_3$-na-a-du$_{11}$	speak:
3.	ur-^{d}nin-mug-ke$_4$	Ur-Ninmug
4.	lu$_2$ kin-gi$_4$-a	the messenger
5.	lu$_2$-du$_{10}$-ga-ke$_4$	of Lu-duga,
6.	ba-⸢sa$_6$⸣-[. . .]	[to?] Basa,
	(*rest broken*)	. . .

rev.

	(*start broken*)	. . .
1.	1(diš) ⸢ud$_5$$^{?}$⸣ [. . .]	1 goat,
2.	x [. . .]	. . .
3.	⸢ur-^{d}nin$^{?}$⸣-[mug$^{?}$ . . .]	Ur-Nin[mug?]
4.	⸢in-gi-in$^{?}$⸣	made firm (?).
5.	igi-mu-še$_3$	Because of me.
	(*blank space*)	

No. 167. *MS 4760 (?,—)*

obv.

1.	[. . .]-GAN-e	To x
2.	⸢ki-bi⸣-a	Kibia,
3.	ur-ur	(and) Urur,

4.	u$_3$-na-du$_{11}$	speak:
5.	4(bur$_3$) a-ša$_3$ GAN$_2$	“4 bur$_3$ of field
6.	ḫa-ma-ab-šum$_2$-mu	May he give me
7.	gu$_4$-mu šu ga-ab-us$_2$	Let me lead my oxen.”

rev.

1.	[. . .]-ga	. . .
2.	x ur-bi	. . .
3.	⸢lu$_2$⸣ im-ni-x-da	Man . . .
4.	x-bi ḫa-mu-ni-ib$_2$-tuš-e	The . . . May he sit there (?).
5.	x-ga$_2$-e ki-bi	. . . I . . . the place.
6.	x-sa$_6$-ga [. . .] x za$_3$-ke$_4$	. . . .-good . . . .

10
MESSENGER TEXTS

Most of the letters preserved from the Ur III state, and indeed all of the letters published in the previous chapter, were local exchanges that did not necessarily warrant the use of a messenger service. Only a handful of letters are directed to the king or another high-ranking official (for example BPOA 1, 1234 discussed above).[504] Nevertheless, several thousand texts exist (more than 2200 catalogued by CDLI[505]), that are usually referred to as messenger texts. These texts presumably document the exchange of messengers and officials between the Ur III state and its immediate eastern neighbors. The origin of the extant messenger texts is not the capital Ur, however, but Umma, Girsu, and Irisagrig/Al-Šarraki, a city in eastern Babylonia.

Only in very few instances do the messenger texts refer to written missives being exchanged between southern Babylonia and its eastern neighbors, but we can retain the generic title "messenger texts" since most of the people mentioned with a title in the texts are called messengers (sukkal, more than one thousand times; lu$_2$ kas$_4$, more than three hundred times).

The exact differentiation between the different titles usually translated as "messenger," "envoy," "runner," or similar, remains vague. The following all seem to refer to some type of messenger: sukkal ("messenger"), lu$_2$ kas$_4$ (lit. "man of running," "runner"), lu$_2$ kin-gi$_4$-a (lit. "man of the message"(?)), and ka-us$_2$-sa$_2$ (see n. 523 below). Persons with other titles also appear in the messenger texts. These are mostly military titles such as lu$_2$ ^{geš}tukul (gu-la), "(chief) soldier," ra$_2$-gaba, "rider,"[506] aga$_3$-us$_2$, "soldier," u$_3$-kul, unclear meaning (see also Dahl 2007: 153–54, and n. 338 above). It is also not certain whether messengers served as such for the entire duration of the year, or whether they were simply employed for the specific task at hand (see also Owen 2013: 154).

The geographical division of the corpus between texts from Umma, Girsu and Irisagrig is reflected in the form and content of the texts from the three sites. All of the Umma texts, in previous literature referred to as *Botenlohnurkunden* (Schneider 1931), are very small and almost square with diminutive writing. They list rations for up to about a dozen messengers. The Girsu texts, or "errand" texts (McNeil 1971: 25), on the other hand, are oblong texts listing the rations for very diverse parties traveling between Girsu and the east. The Irisagrig texts, finally, are longer and more complex than any of the messenger texts from the sites of Umma and Girsu.

Messenger texts have not received much attention in the literature, and the unpublished dissertation of McNeil (1970) is the most comprehensive study of their form and content.[507] McNeil's typology is largely followed here, except that no attempt is made at distinguishing between McNeil's eight subgroups of the standard Umma messenger text.[508]

---

[504] Although text No. 165 is addressed to "my king," this is understood to be a referent to the sender's superior rather than the actual king.

[505] According to D'Agostino and Politi 2006: 10, there are 2154 published messenger texts (from Umma?).

[506] Traditionally seen as a horse-rider, but see now Such-Gutiérrez 2015, who convincingly argued that officials by this title travelled by boat (to ride/mount can be used of boats and horses).

[507] See McNeil 1971: 17–20 for the history of research up until 1970. Recent years have seen some renewed interest in the topic with the publication of Sigrist's catalogs of British Museum tablet collections including many messenger texts (Sigrist *et al.* 1996, 2006), and four publications of British Museum messenger texts by D'Agostino and Pomponio (2002 = Nisaba 1), Milone and Spada (2003 = Nisaba 3), D'Agostino and Politi (2006 = Nisaba 16), and D'Agostino and Verdarame (2003, also referred to as UMTBM 3; note that the editors of Nisaba have opted for a secondary series within Nisaba called UMTBM [Umma Messenger Texts in the British Museum], with UMTBM 1 = Nisaba 1; UMTBM 2 = Nisaba 3; UMTBM 4 = Nisaba 16). See now also the long excursus in Owen 2013.

[508] See D'Agostini and Pomponio 2002: 13–17 for a review of McNeil's typology, and the beginning of a refinement of it based on a chronological study of the distribution of the texts. For further work in this direction, see also D'Agostino and Politi 2006: 10–12, and also Notizia 2006 for work on the Girsu "errand" texts.

There are twenty-six messenger texts in the Schøyen Collection. All of them are from Umma, and they can therefore all be classified as *Botenlohnurkunden* in Schneider's terminology (retained by McNeil). Since twenty of these are syntactically very similar, they are here referred to as Type I messenger texts (Nos. 170–89). Type I messenger texts correspond to McNeil's groups A, B, C, D, E, F, H, and M. These texts each list about ten individuals, usually without any reference to title or task, or with at most one presumably higher-ranking messenger, who held a title and received larger rations than the other messengers recorded in the text. If present, this higher-ranking messenger would be listed last. Each individual is recorded after a list of his rations (small amounts of beer and bread, and usually most of the following products: onions, oil, and potash[509]). The texts end with a summary of the products. The texts are usually dated to the day, month and often the year as well, albeit in an extremely abbreviated form.

A subgroup of the standard Umma messenger texts, here referred to as Type I*sub* (McNeil's groups J, K, and L), lists the recipients first and then a list of the products that each of them received (1. PN_1, 2. PN_2, etc. PRODUCTS-ta). Usually, there are two groups of recipients in such texts, receiving slightly different rations. This sub-group is represented by two texts in the current collection (Nos. 190–91).

Three further texts published here are similar to Type I messenger texts, but include more products and the information is again arranged differently on the tablet (Nos. 192–94). In these Type II messenger texts (McNeil's group G), two or three individuals receive amounts of products including fish. The products are listed one or two on each line. The Type II messenger texts in this collection record the title of one of the messengers (sukkal, ka-us$_2$-sa$_2$) and lists three messengers as "crossing back from the other side" (gaba-ta [bala(-a)]).[510] Such comments are common in Type II messenger texts, but not in Type I or I*sub*.

McNeil identifies one further structurally distinct subgroup of the regular Umma messenger texts (1970: I 155–58), where the names of the recipients and their rations are listed in an almost tabular format. No texts from this sub-group are found in the present collection.[511]

In addition, there exists a group of vastly more complex messenger texts, the so-called "errand texts," which record not only the travel directions and the titles of the messengers and other members of the parties, but can refer to messages of high-ranking officials brought by the messengers (for example ICP 1295, see below). This group, here called Type III, is not represented in the current collection, but a few examples from other collections are given at the end of this chapter for the sake of completeness.

Finally, a recently recovered corpus of tablets from the site Irisagrig includes messenger texts that form yet another group. They are here classified as Type IV. Although no messenger texts from Irisagrig are found in the Schøyen Collection, I have included two examples of this group below.

Messenger texts from Umma are always very small. Without proof, but with some indicators such as the absence of a mounted messenger service, one may speculate that the diminutive size of the tablets made their transport by running messengers easier.

Type I Messenger Texts

Monthly summaries of the disbursements listed in the Umma messenger texts were recorded on triangular tags (D'Agostino and Pomponio 2002: 17–18, and Laurito *et al.* 2008: 99–110). Lauritio *et al.* were able to show how the tags were fired after having been used (charred remains of the strings were observed inside the tags), suggesting a complicated administrative progression of events where the tags were first used to seal bags with messenger tablets, after which the tags themselves became archival documents (Laurito *et al.* 2008: 109–10). There are two poorly preserved triangular tags, presumably recording monthly summaries of expenditures for the Umma messengers, in the collection published here, Nos. 168 and 169 (see Chapter 1 for examples of other archival tags).

[509] See Butz 1984: 283–86.

[510] See in particular Yoshikawa 1988: 231–41, D'Agostino and Pomponio 2002: 12.

[511] See, e.g., Nik 2, 354–57.

No. 168. *MS 1942/5 (Umma, date broken)*

surface A

1.	3(aš) 2(barig) [. . .] ⸢gur⸣	3 gur, 2 barig [. . . of good (quality) beer],
2.	3(aš) 3(barig) [. . .] gur	3 gur, 3 barig [. . . . of regular (quality) beer].

(Surfaces 2 and 3 broken)

seal (S005881)

col. i

1.	^{d}amar-^{d}suen	Amar-Suen,
2.	lugal kal-ga	strong king,
3.	lugal uri$_{2}$^{ki}-ma	king of Ur,
4.	lugal an-ub-da limmu-ba	king of the four quarters:

col. ii

1.	a-⸢kal⸣-[la]	A(ya)-kala,
2.	ensi$_{2}$	governor
3.	⸢umma⸣[^{ki}]	of Umma,
4.	ARAD$_{2}$-[zu]	(is) your slave.

No. 169. *MS 1942/9 (Umma, ŠS 6)*

surface A

(missing)

surface B

	(start of surface missing)	
1'.	⸢mu⸣ ^{d}šu-[^{d}]⸢suen lugal⸣ uri$_{2}$^{ki}-ma-ke$_{4}$ ⸢na⸣-[ru$_{2}$]-a maḫ ^{d}en-[lil$_{2}$] ^{d}nin-lil$_{2}$-ra mu-⸢ne-ru$_{2}$⸣	Year: "Šu-Suen, king of Ur, erected the mighty stela for Enlil and Ninlil."
2'.	lu$_{2}$-du$_{10}$-ga u$_{3}$ [. . .]	Lu-duga and . . .

surface C

	(start of surface missing)	
1'.	[. . .] du	. . .
2'.	[. . .] ti	. . .

seal (S000493.2)

1.	ur-^{d}nun-gal	Ur-Nungal,
2.	dub-sar	scribe,
3.	dumu ur-^{d}šara$_{2}$	child of Ur-Šara,
4.	ša$_{13}$-dub-ba-ka	archivist.

All of the summary texts were sealed by a member of the ruling family of Umma (Ur-E'e, Lu-kala, or Ur-Lisi), and most of the tags were sealed by Lu-kala with an additional seal of Ur-Nungal, the chief archivist of Umma.[512]

[512] See Lauritio *et al.* 2008: 106–8, Dahl 2007: 102–3. For Ur-Nungal, see Dahl 2007: 93, in particular n. 326.

In most instances, more than one summary text was written for the messenger texts of one month. Perhaps such multiple summaries were necessary because disbursements happened at various locations. This is well exemplified in month 6 of Šu-Suen's second year, where rations were given to the messengers at an undisclosed location (OrSP 47–49, 405, sa$_2$-du$_{11}$ kas$_4$), in Umma (CST 872, sa$_2$-du$_{11}$ kas$_4$ ša$_3$ umma^{ki}), and at the tower by the Girsu-canal (CST 871, sa$_2$-du$_{11}$ kas$_4$ ša$_3$ an-za-gar$_3$ i$_7$ gir$_2$-su^{ki}). At least six messenger texts from that month have survived, one of them in the Schøyen Collection (text No. 172).[513]

An even greater coverage of the primary documents is found in the fourth month of the same year (Šu-Suen 2), from which at least fourteen messenger texts and two summary texts have survived. Among the messenger texts is text No. 170 (Table 7).

These messenger texts (both Type I and II) would presumably have been kept in bags sealed with the triangular tags discussed above. Two such labels from month 4 of Šu-Suen's second year have survived: MVN 4, 173 and Nik 2, 281. Both date to the thirtieth day of the month, and both record the disbursements as being the regular disbursements for the messengers (while) in Umma. For the sake of completeness MVN 4, 173 is transliterated and translated here:

MVN 4, 173 (Umma, ŠS 2–iv–30)

surface A

1.	1(aš) 2(barig) 3(ban$_2$) 1(diš) sila$_3$ kaš ⸢saga⸣ gur	1 gur, 2 barig, 3 ban$_2$, 1 sila$_3$ of good (quality) beer.
2.	2(aš) 1(barig) 6(diš) sila$_3$ kaš du gur	2 gur, 1 barig, 6 sila$_3$ of regular (quality) beer.
3.	2(diš) dug dida du 1(ban$_2$) 5(diš) sila$_3$	2 dida jars, regular (quality), (holding) 1 ban$_2$, 5 sila$_3$ each.
4.	3(aš) 2(barig) 3(ban$_2$) 6(diš) sila$_3$ ninda du gur	3 gur, 2 barig, 3 ban$_2$, 6 sila$_3$ of regular (quality) bread.

Table 7. Messenger texts from Šu-Suen's year 2 month 4

Text ID	Day
BM 18228 (unpub.)[514]	1
SET 214	3
AAS 032	4
MVN 1, 148	4
No. 170 (MS 1871/2)	5
SET 219	6
AAICAB 1/4, Bod S 379	12
Atiqot 4, pl. 7 no. 37	15
AAICAB 1/4, Bod S 444	16
L'uomo 72	20
AAICAB 1/4, Bod S 514	21
BCT 2, 65	22
SET 216	24
AfO 24, pl. 15	30

---

[513] The others are OrSP 18, pl. 11 31 (day 2); SET 229 (day 23); OrSP 18, pl. 11 32 (day 24); OrSP 18, pl. 12 33 (day 26); SET 218 (day 27).

[514] See Sigrist *et al.* 1996: 100.

5.	1(barig) dabin	1 barig flour.
6.	1(aš) še gur	1 gur barley.
7.	1(ban$_2$) 4(diš) sila$_3$ 1(u) 3(diš) gin$_2$ i$_3$-geš	1 ban$_2$, 4 sila$_3$, 13 shekels of sesame oil.

surface B

1.	2(ban$_2$) 2(diš) ⅓(diš) sila$_3$ 5(diš) gin$_2$ igi-sag šum$_2$ ⸢gaz$_x$(KUM)⸣	2 ban$_2$, 2 ⅓ sila$_3$, 5 shekels of crushed igi-sag[515] onions.
2.	9(diš) sila$_3$ 1(u) gin$_2$ naga gaz$_x$(KUM)	9 sila$_3$, 10 shekels of crushed potash.
3.	sa$_2$-du$_{11}$ kas$_4$ ša$_3$ umma^{ki}	Regular (deliveries) for the messengers (while) in Umma.
4.	giri$_3$ gur$_4$-za-an muḫaldim	Conveyor: Gurzan, kitchen administrator.
5.	kišib$_3$ lu$_2$-kal-la	Sealed (tablet of) Lu-kala.
6.	u$_4$ 3(u)-kam	On the 30th day.

surface C

1.	iti nesag	Month: "First Fruits."
2.	mu ma$_2$ ^{d}en-ki ba-ab-du$_8$	Year: "The boat of Enki was caulked."
	(blank space)	
3.	ur-ge$_6$-par$_4$ u$_3$ lu$_2$-[^{d}]šul-gi ib$_2$-gi-ne$_2$	Ur-Gepar and Lu-Šulgi confirmed it.

seal 1 (S000493.2)

1.	ur-^{d}nun-gal	Ur-Nungal,
2.	dub-sar	scribe,
3.	dumu ur-^{d}šara$_2$	child of Ur-Šara,
4.	ša$_{13}$-dub-ba-ka	archivist.

seal 2 (S002932)

1.	lu$_2$-kal-la	Lu-kala,
2.	dub-sar	scribe,
3.	dumu ur-e$_{11}$-e šuš$_3$	child of Ur-E'e, chief cattle-administrator.

The messengers listed in these different messenger texts do not seem to form one unit. In fact there is very little repetition in the onomasticon of the messenger texts from month four of Šu-Suen's second year. That leads to the somewhat problematic conclusion that several hundred persons in Umma, in any given month, would have received rations for traveling to and from the eastern provinces.

The following text, No. 170 from Šu-Suen's second year, month 4, is one of the documents summarized by the two triangular tags discussed above. Note the substantially larger rations given to the last member of the crew. That person, Agua, is also the only person with a title, here sukkal.

No. 170. *MS 1871/2 (Umma, ŠS 2–iv–5)*

obv.

1.	5(diš) sila$_3$ kaš 5(diš) sila$_3$ ninda 5(diš) gin$_2$ šum$_2$ 3(diš) gin$_2$ i$_3$ 2(diš) gin$_2$ naga	5 sila$_3$ of beer; 5 sila$_3$ of bread; 5 shekels of onions; 3 shekels of oil; 2 shekels of potash.
2.	a$_2$-gal$_2$-nu-tuku	A-gal-nutuku.

---

515 See n. 517 below.

3.	5(diš) sila$_3$ kaš 3(diš) sila$_3$ ninda 5(diš) gin$_2$ šum$_2$ 3(diš) gin$_2$ i$_3$ 2(diš) gin$_2$ naga	5 sila$_3$ of beer; 3 sila$_3$ of bread; 5 shekels of onions; 3 shekels of oil; 2 shekels of potash.
4.	a-kal-la	A(ya)-kala.
5.	5(diš) sila$_3$ kaš 3(diš) sila$_3$ ninda 5(diš) gin$_2$ šum$_2$ 3(diš) gin$_2$ i$_3$ 2(diš) gin$_2$ naga	5 sila$_3$ of beer; 3 sila$_3$ of bread; 5 shekels of onions; 3 shekels of oil; 2 shekels of potash.
6.	bu$_3$-za-ni	Buzani.
7.	5(diš) sila$_3$ kaš 3(diš) sila$_3$ ninda 5(diš) gin$_2$ šum$_2$ 3(diš) gin$_2$ i$_3$ 2(diš) gin$_2$ naga	5 sila$_3$ of beer; 3 sila$_3$ of bread; 5 shekels of onions; 3 shekels of oil; 2 shekels of potash.
8.	eš$_{18}$-bar$^!$(DIŠ)	Ešbar.
9.	5(diš) sila$_3$ kaš 3(diš) sila$_3$ ninda 5(diš) gin$_2$ šum$_2$ 3(diš) gin$_2$ i$_3$ 2(diš) gin$_2$ naga	5 sila$_3$ of beer; 3 sila$_3$ of bread; 5 shekels of onions; 3 shekels of oil; 2 shekels of potash.
10.	ur-^{d}en-lil$_2$-la$_2$	Ur-Enlila.

rev.

1.	3(diš) sila$_3$ kaš 2(diš) sila$_3$ ninda 5(diš) gin$_2$ šum$_2$ 3(diš) gin$_2$ i$_3$ 2(diš) gin$_2$ naga	3 sila$_3$ of beer; 2 sila$_3$ of bread; 5 shekels of onions; 3 shekels of oil; 2 shekels of potash.
2.	ur-šu	Ur-Šu.
3.	3(diš) sila$_3$ kaš 2(diš) sila$_3$ ninda 5(diš) gin$_2$ šum$_2$ 3(diš) gin$_2$ i$_3$ 2(diš) gin$_2$ naga	3 sila$_3$ of beer; 2 sila$_3$ of bread; 5 shekels of onions; 3 shekels of oil; 2 shekels of potash.
4.	ur-^{d}suen	Ur-Suen.
5.	3(diš) sila$_3$ kaš 2(diš) sila$_3$ ninda 5(diš) gin$_2$ šum$_2$ 3(diš) gin$_2$ i$_3$ 2(diš) gin$_2$ naga	3 sila$_3$ of beer; 2 sila$_3$ of bread; 5 shekels of onions; 3 shekels of oil; 2 shekels of potash.
6.	tur-am$_3$-i$_3$-li$_2$	Turam-ili.
7.	2(ban$_2$) 5(diš) sila$_3$ kaš 2(ban$_2$) 5(diš) sila$_3$ ninda 1(u) gin$_2$ i$_3$	2 ban$_2$, 5 sila$_3$ of beer; 2 ban$_2$, 5 sila$_3$ of bread; 10 gin$_2$ of oil.
8.	a-gu-a sukkal	Agua, messenger.
9.	šunigin 5(ban$_2$) 9(diš) sila$_3$ kaš šunigin 4(ban$_2$) 8(diš) sila$_3$ ninda	Total: 5 ban$_2$, 9 sila$_3$ of beer. Total 4 ban$_2$, 8 sila$_3$ of bread.
10.	šunigin ⅔(diš) sila$_3$ šum$_2$ šunigin ½(diš) sila$_3$ 4(diš) gin$_2$ i$_3$ šunigin 1(u) 6(diš) gin2 naga	Total ⅔ sila$_3$ of onions. Total ½ sila$_3$, 4 shekels. Total 16 shekels of potash.

left edge

1.	u$_4$ 5(diš)-kam iti nesag mu ma$_2$ ^{d}en-ki ba-ab-du$_8$	On the 5th day. Month: "First Fruits." Year: "The barge of Enki was caulked."

The products distributed in text No. 170 are: beer (kaš), bread (ninda), onions (šum$_2$), oil (i$_3$), and potash (naga). The summary tablet MVN 4, 173 includes both regular and good quality beer, dida-jars (dug dida), a special type of vessel with a cereal product, possibly a type of beer, flour, and barley. The bread is furthermore qualified as regular quality; the oil as sesame oil(?);[516] the onions as being crushed (gaz) and using the still unsatisfactorily understood term igi-sag;[517] and the potash as being crushed.[518]

The following messengers are listed in text No. 170 (MS 1871/2): a$_2$-gal$_2$-nu-tuku, a-kal-la, bu$_3$-za-ni, eš$_{18}$-bar!(DIŠ), ur-^{d}en-lil$_2$-la$_2$, ur-šu, ur-^{d}suen, tur-am$_3$-i$_3$-li$_2$, a-gu-a.

---

[516] See Waetzoldt 1980–83 for a translation flax-seed oil for geš-i$_3$.

[517] See Englund 1992: 94–95 n. 11 who translated literally as "eye and head."

[518] Nik 2, 281 adds 5 ban$_2$ of regular (quality) chick-pea flour? (zi-gu)(side A l. 5).

Only the last person mentioned in the text is given a title (sukkal, "messenger"). Apart from possibly A(ya)-kala (see below) none of the persons listed in this text is found in the other messenger texts from the same month.

The personal name A-gal-nutuku is found in three further texts (Nisaba 23, 39; SAT 2, 1041; Tavolette 53), but to date never again in another messenger text. The name A(ya)-kala is very frequent in Ur III texts from Umma, and is found in several messenger texts, including perhaps AfO 24, pl. 15 dated to day 30, month 4 of Šu-Suen year 2, although the reading of the name in rev. 14 is not certain.[519] Buzani the soldier (lu$_2$ ^{geš}tukul, lit. "man of weapon") is found in the broken Type II messenger text MVN 5, 288 (no date). The reading of the name Ešbar is inferred from two other instances of the same name in messenger texts from Umma: text No. 171 (from Šu-Suen 2–ii–25) and Nik 2, 360 (from Šu-Suen 6–ix–17). The remaining names, Ur-Enlila,[520] Ur-Šu,[521] Ur-Suen,[522] Turam-ili,[523] and Agua[524] are all well-known names in the Ur III period.

The names found in all three types and subtypes of messenger texts are evenly distributed between Sumerian and Semitic.[525] Some Type III texts mention groups of people from the eastern periphery of Babylonia, but these are rarely named. In a few other instances envoys of foreign rulers are mentioned.

Due to their formulaic and tabular nature the remainder of the standard Umma messenger texts published here will not be discussed in full detail, but difficult or special passages will be noted.

No summary text is preserved for the following messenger text:

No. 171. *MS 1871/5 (Umma, ŠS 2–ii–25)*

obv.

1. [5(diš)] sila$_3$ kaš 3(diš) sila$_3$ ninda 5(diš) gin$_2$ šum$_2$ 3(diš) gin$_2$ i$_3$ 2(diš) gin$_2$ naga
2. da-da-a
3. 5(diš) sila$_3$ kaš 3(diš) sila$_3$ ninda 5(diš) gin$_2$ šum$_2$ 3(diš) gin$_2$ i$_3$ 2(diš) gin$_2$ naga
4. ur-saga
5. 5(diš) sila$_3$ kaš 3(diš) sila$_3$ ninda 5(diš) gin$_2$ šum$_2$ 3(diš) gin$_2$ i$_3$ 2(diš) gin$_2$ naga
6. šu-na-bu-um
7. 5(diš) sila$_3$ kaš 3(diš) sila$_3$ ninda 5(diš) gin$_2$ šum$_2$ 3(diš) gin$_2$ i$_3$ 2(diš) gin$_2$ naga

---

[519] See, e.g., AfO 40–41, 56, 4, a messenger text from ŠS 2–x–18 (rev. 4); Auktionkatalog, Stuttgart, T.2 from ŠS 2–xi–6 (obv. 18); or Nisaba 16, 38 from ŠS 3–iii–28 (rev. 9).

[520] See, e.g., text No. 177 (AS 7–i–2); Nisaba 1, 50 (AS 7–i–30); and Nisaba 16, 165 (ŠS 3–iv–6).

[521] See, e.g., the messenger texts Nisaba 3/1, 144; Nisaba 3/1, 108; and Nisaba 13, 89 (none dated to the year). In Nisaba 13, 89 Ur-Šu is given the title "soldier" (lu$_2$ ^{geš}tukul, obv. 10).

[522] A messenger by the name Ur-Suen is attested in both Girsu and Umma. For Umma texts, see, e.g., Nisaba 1, 159 (no year); Nisaba 16, 162 (no year); and UMTBM 3, 57 (no year).

[523] See, e.g., the messenger texts Nisaba 3/1, 161 (no year); Nisaba 16, 115 (no year), and UMTBM 3, 1 (Amar-Suen 7–viii–9). In several messenger texts a Turam-ili is given the title ka-us$_2$-sa$_2$ (see, e.g., MVN 14, 545 from ŠS 4–x–26), and one letter (BPOA 1, 0592) may mention the same Turam-ili. The title ka-us$_2$-sa$_2$ has not been discussed previously, although it is well attested (more than 100 times) as a title for messengers. The term should not be confused with the term for an agricultural activity ka-us$_2$-sa (see, e.g., Nisaba 16, 15 listed in index pp. 278–79 next to ka-us$_2$-sa$_2$). ka-us$_2$-sa is always found with the verb to place, gar. See, e.g., AAICAB 1/1, pls. 76–77, 1924-1056 obv. ii 13–18: 3(geš$_2$) 1(u) sar ^{u2}kiši$_{17}$ ku$_5$-ra$_2$ 1(u) sar-ta / a$_2$-bi u$_4$ 2(u) la$_2$ 1(diš) / 1(geš$_2$) 5(diš) guruš u$_4$ 1(diš)-še$_3$ / ab-sin$_2$-ta la-ag ri-ri-ga / 4(u) 4(diš) guruš u$_4$ 1(diš)-še$_3$ / ka-us$_2$-sa ga$_2$-ra, "190 sar (of land) cutting weed (at a rate of) 10 sar each. Its work-days: 19. 65 work-days removing clods from the furrows. 44 work-days placing the ka-us$_2$-sa."

[524] A person with the name Agua and the title sukkal is attested in messenger texts from both Umma (Type I and II) and Girsu (Type III).

[525] Note that, as with all other texts published here, no distinction is made in the transliterations or transcriptions of names as to the presumed language of the name.

8. lu$_2$-gu$_3$-de$_2$-a
9. 3(diš) sila$_3$ kaš 2(diš) sila$_3$ ninda 5(diš) gin$_2$ šum$_2$ 3(diš) gin$_2$ i$_3$ 2(diš) gin$_2$ naga
10. nam-ḫa-ni
11. 5(diš) sila$_3$ kaš 3(diš) sila$_3$ ninda 5(diš) gin$_2$ šum$_2$ 3(diš) gin$_2$ i$_3$ 2(diš) gin$_2$ naga
12. ur-e$_2$-babbar$_2$

rev.

1. 5(diš) sila$_3$ kaš 3(diš) sila$_3$ ninda 5(diš) gin$_2$ šum$_2$ 3(diš) gin$_2$ i$_3$ 2(diš) gin$_2$ naga
2. eš$_{18}$-bar
3. 5(diš) sila$_3$ kaš 3(diš) sila$_3$ ninda 5(diš) gin$_2$ šum$_2$ 3(diš) gin$_2$ i$_3$ 2(diš) gin$_2$ naga
4. igi-a-a
5. 2(ban$_2$) kaš 2(ban$_2$) ninda 1(u) 5(diš) gin$_2$ i$_3$
6. NIM ama$^?$-ba-a-⸢a$^?$⸣[526]
7. ⸢šunigin⸣ 5(ban$_2$) 2(diš) sila$_3$ kaš
8. [šunigin] 5(ban$_2$) ninda ⅔(diš) sila$_3$ šum$_2$
9. [šunigin ½(diš)] sila$_3$ 8(diš) gin$_2$ i$_3$
10. [šunigin 1(u)] 6(diš) sila$_3$ naga

left edge

1. ⸢u$_4$⸣ 2(u) 5(diš)-kam iti sig$_4$-^{geš}i$_3$-šub-ba-gar
2. [mu] ⸢us$_2$⸣-sa ^{d}šu-^{d}suen lugal

As mentioned above, the three summary texts CST 871, 872 and OrSP 47–49, 405, from day 30, month 6 of Šu-Suen year 2, summarize, among other texts, the following:

No. 172. *MS 1871/1 (Umma, ŠS 2–vi–20)*

obv.

1. 5(diš) sila$_3$ kaš 3(diš) sila$_3$ ninda 5(diš) gin$_2$ šum$_2$ 3(diš) gin$_2$ i$_3$ 2(diš) gin$_2$ naga
2. i-gu-um
3. 5(diš) sila$_3$ kaš 3(diš) sila$_3$ ninda 5(diš) gin$_2$ šum$_2$ 3(diš) gin$_2$ i$_3$ 2(diš) gin$_2$ naga
4. pu-ḫa-ti
5. 5(diš) sila$_3$ kaš 3(diš) sila$_3$ ninda 5(diš) gin$_2$ šum$_2$ 3(diš) gin$_2$ i$_3$ 2(diš) gin$_2$ naga
6. šar-ru-ba-ni
7. 5(diš) sila$_3$ kaš 3(diš) sila$_3$ ninda 5(diš) gin$_2$ šum$_2$ 3(diš) gin$_2$ i$_3$ 2(diš) gin$_2$ naga
8. lugal-ni-maḫ
9. 5(diš) sila$_3$ kaš 3(diš) sila$_3$ ninda 5(diš) gin$_2$ šum$_2$ 3(diš) gin$_2$ i$_3$ 2(diš) gin$_2$ naga
10. zu$_2$-ga-li
11. 5(diš) sila$_3$ kaš 3(diš) sila$_3$ ninda 5(diš) gin$_2$ šum$_2$ 3(diš) gin$_2$ i$_3$ 2(diš) gin$_2$ naga

---

[526] A person by the name ba-a-a is frequently attested in messenger texts (e.g., NYPL 3 from ŠS 3–xii–9 or Ontario 2, 460 from AS 3–i–14 [with the title ka-us$_2$-sa$_2$]), a ḫu-ba-a-a with less frequency. It is unclear whether ama here is part of the name. nim may stand for the gentilic "Elamite."

12. ḫu-bu-ti-a
13. 3(diš) sila$_3$ kaš 2(diš) sila$_3$ ninda 5(diš) gin$_2$ šum$_2$ ⸢3(diš)⸣ gin$_2$ i$_3$ 2(diš) naga
14. šu-e$_3$-a

rev.

1. 3(diš) sila$_3$ kaš 2(diš) sila$_3$ ninda 5(diš) gin$_2$ šum$_2$ 3(diš) gin$_2$ i$_3$ 2(diš) gin$_2$ naga
2. ur-^{d}utu
3. 3(diš) sila$_3$ kaš 2(diš) sila$_3$ ninda 5(diš) gin$_2$ šum$_2$ 3(diš) gin$_2$ i$_3$ 2(diš) gin$_2$ naga
4. še-le-bu-um
5. 1(ban$_2$) kaš <1(diš)> dug dida 1(ban$_2$) 5(diš) ⸢sila$_3$-ta$^{?}$⸣ 1(ban$_2$) ninda 2(ban$_2$) dabin$^{?}$ 1(u) gin$_2^{?}$ i$_3^{?}$
6. in-za-um
7. šunigin 4(ban$_2$) 9(diš) sila$_3$ kaš 1(diš) dug ⸢dida⸣ 1(u) 5(diš) ⸢sila$_3^{?}$-ta$^{?}$⸣
8. šunigin 3(ban$_2$) 4(diš) sila$_3$ ninda ⸢2(ban$_2$)$^{?}$⸣ 2(ban$_2$) dabin$^{?}$
9. šunigin ⅔(diš) sila$_3$ 5(diš) gin$_2$ šum$_2$ ½(diš) sila$_3$ 6(diš) gin$_2$ i$_3$ 1(u) 8(diš) gin$_2$ naga

left edge

1. u$_4$ 2(u)-kam iti šu-numun
2. mu ma$_2$ ^{d}en-ki ba-an-du$_8$

Only one summary text for the same months as the following document has been recovered (MVN 4, 176).

No. 173. *MS 1871/6 (Umma, ŠS 2–ix–8)*

obv.

1. 5(diš) sila$_3$ kaš saga 5(diš) sila$_3$ ninda 5(diš) gin$_2$ šum$_2$ 3(diš) gin$_2$ i$_3$ 2(diš) gin$_2$ naga
2. tap-pa$_4$-ma
3. 5(diš) sila$_3$ kaš saga 5(diš) sila$_3$ ninda 5(diš) gin$_2$ šum$_2$ 3(diš) gin$_2$ i$_3$ 2(diš) gin$_2$ naga
4. ^{d}utu-mu
5. 5(diš) sila$_3$ kaš saga 5(diš) sila$_3$ ninda 5(diš) gin$_2$ šum$_2$ 3(diš) gin$_2$ i$_3$ 2(diš) gin$_2$ naga
6. lu$_2$-dingir-ra
7. 5(diš) sila$_3$ kaš 5(diš) sila$_3$ ninda 5(diš) gin$_2$ šum$_2$ 3(diš) gin$_2$ i$_3$ 2(diš) gin$_2$ naga
8. AN-x
9. 5(diš) sila$_3$ kaš 5(diš) sila$_3$ ninda 5(diš) gin$_2$ šum$_2$ 3(diš) gin$_2$ i$_3$ 2(diš) gin$_2$ naga
10. puzur$_4$-^{d}er$_3$-ra
11. 5(diš) sila$_3$ kaš 5(diš) sila3 ninda 5(diš) gin$_2$ šum$_2$ 3(diš) gin$_2$ i$_3$ 2(diš) gin$_2$ naga
12. na-na-ku-za
13. 3(diš) sila$_3$ kaš 2(diš) sila$_3$ ninda 5(diš) gin$_2$ šum$_2$ 3(diš) gin$_2$ i$_3$ 2(diš) gin$_2$ naga
14. ḫu-un-bi
15. 3(diš) sila$_3$ kaš 2(diš) sila$_3$ ninda 5(diš) gin$_2$ šum$_2$ 3(diš) gin$_2$ i$_3$ 2(diš) gin$_2$ naga
16. i-di$_3$-a

rev.

1. 3(diš) $sila_3$ kaš 2(diš) $sila_3$ ninda 5(diš) gin_2 $šum_2$ 3(diš) gin_2 i_3 2(diš) gin_2 naga
2. ur-^{d}nanše
3. 3(diš) $sila_3$ kaš 2(diš) $sila_3$ ninda 5(diš) gin_2 $šum_2$ 3(diš) gin_2 i_3 2(diš) gin_2 naga
4. a-ḫu-ni
5. 3(diš) $sila_3$ kaš 2(diš) $sila_3$ ninda 5(diš) gin_2 $šum_2$ 3(diš) gin_2 i_3 2(diš) gin_2 naga
6. i_3-li_2-be-li_2
7. šunigin 1(ban_2) 5(diš) $sila_3$ kaš saga šunigin 3(ban_2) kaš
8. šunigin 4(ban_2) ninda šunigin ⅔(diš) $sila_3$ 5(diš) gin_2 $šum_2$
9. šunigin ½(diš) 3(diš) gin_2 i_3 šunigin ⅓(diš) 2(diš) gin_2 naga
10. iti $^{d}li_9$-si_4
11. [u_4] 8(diš)-kam
12. [mu] ma_2 ^{d}en-ki

There are no summary texts preserved for any of the following four texts.

No. 174. *MS 1871/4 (Umma, ŠS 3–x–12)*

obv.

1. 5(diš) $sila_3$ kaš saga 5(diš) $sila_3$ ninda 5(diš) gin_2 $šum_2$ 3(diš) gin_2 i_3 2(diš) gin_2 naga
2. a-ḫu-a-ti
3. 5(diš) $sila_3$ kaš saga 5(diš) $sila_3$ ninda 5(diš) gin_2 $šum_2$ 3(diš) gin2 i_3 2(diš) gin_2 naga
4. i-šar-la-ni
5. 5(diš) $sila_3$ kaš 5(diš) $sila_3$ ninda 5(diš) gin_2 $šum_2$ 3(diš) gin_2 i_3 2(diš) gin_2 naga
6. dingir-ki-ma-at
7. 5(diš) $sila_3$ kaš 5(diš) $sila_3$ ninda 5(diš) gin_2 $šum_2$ 3(diš) gin_2 i_3 2(diš) gin_2 naga
8. SI-A-a
9. 5(diš) $sila_3$ kaš 5(diš) $sila_3$ ninda 5(diš) gin_2 $šum_2$ 3(diš) gin_2 i_3 2(diš) gin_2 naga
10. ba-riq_2-dingir[527]
11. 5(diš) $sila_3$ kaš 5(diš) $sila_3$ ninda 5(diš) gin_2 $šum_2$ 3(diš) gin_2 i_3 2(diš) gin_2 naga
12. na-x
13. 5(diš) $sila_3$ kaš 5(diš) $sila_3$ ninda 5(diš) gin_2 $šum_2$ 3(diš) gin_2 i_3 2(diš) gin_2 naga

rev.

1. x-bi_2-[x]
2. 3(diš) $sila_3$ kaš 2(diš) $sila_3$ ninda 5(diš) gin_2 $šum_2$ 3(diš) gin_2 i_3 2(diš) gin_2 naga
3. e-mu-lum

---

527 The same name is found in the Girsu messenger text ITT 2, 667; note also that the personal name transliterated ⸢e⸣-zum-dingir in the messenger text Nisaba 16, 98 obv. 2, should be read ⸢ba⸣-riq_2-dingir instead (the end of the middle horizontal wedge of ba is visible on the tablet). The most likely interpretation of the name is *bāriq-ilī,* meaning something like "my god is one who flashes" (from *bāraqu* "to flash," as an epithet of Amurru, see *CAD* B 110). e-zum-dingir resists all attempts at analysis.

4. 3(diš) $sila_3$ kaš 2(diš) $sila_3$ ninda 5(diš) gin_2 $šum_2$ 3(diš) gin_2 i_3 2(diš) gin_2 naga
5. dingir-i_3-zu
6. 3(diš) $sila_3$ kaš 2(diš) $sila_3$ ninda 5(diš) gin_2 $šum_2$ 3(diš) gin_2 i_3 2(diš) gin_2 naga
7. $eš_{18}$-dar-al-šu
8. 3(diš) $sila_3$ kaš 2(diš) $sila_3$ ninda 5(diš) gin_2 $šum_2$ 3(diš) gin_2 i_3 2(diš) gin_2 naga
9. ri-iš-dingir
(blank space)
10. šunigin 1(ban_2) kaš saga šunigin 3(ban_2) 7(diš) $sila_3$ kaš du
11. šunigin 4(ban_2) 3(diš) $sila_3$ ninda šunigin 5/6(diš) $sila_3$ 5(diš) gin_2 $šum_2$
12. šunigin ½(diš) $sila_3$ 3(diš) gin_2 i_3 šunigin ⅓(diš) $sila_3$ 2(diš) gin_2 naga
13. u_4 1(u) 2(diš)-kam iti ezem-^{d}šul-gi
14. mu si-ma-num_2^{ki} ba-ḫul

No. 175. *MS 2022/2 (Umma, ŠS 4–i–18)*

obv.
1. 5(diš) $sila_3$ kaš 3(diš) $sila_3$ ninda 5(diš) gin_2 $šum_2$ 3(diš) gin_2 i_3 2(diš) gin_2 naga
2. ar-ši-aḫ
3. 5(diš) $sila_3$ kaš 3(diš) $sila_3$ ninda 5(diš) gin_2 $šum_2$ 3(diš) gin_2 i_3 2(diš) gin_2 naga
4. eb-ku-ša
5. 5(diš) $sila_3$ kaš 3(diš) $sila_3$ ninda 5(diš) gin_2 $šum_2$ 3(diš) gin_2 i_3 2(diš) gin_2 naga
6. za-ba-ba
7. 5(diš) $sila_3$ kaš 3(diš) $sila_3$ ninda 5(diš) gin_2 $šum_2$ 3(diš) gin_2 i_3 2(diš) gin_2 naga
8. lu_2-^{d}nanna
9. 3(diš) $sila_3$ kaš 2(diš) $sila_3$ ninda 5(diš) gin_2 $šum_2$ 3(diš) gin_2 i_3 2(diš) gin_2 naga
10. ḫu-la-al
11. 3(diš) $sila_3$ kaš 2(diš) $sila_3$ ninda 5(diš) gin_2 $šum_2$ 3(diš) gin_2 i_3 2(diš) gin_2 naga

rev.
1. ḫu-ba-a
2. 3(diš) $sila_3$ kaš 2(diš) $sila_3$ ninda 5(diš) gin_2 $šum_2$ 3(diš) gin_2 i_3 2(diš) gin_2 naga
3. ur-^{d}da-mu
4. 3(diš) $sila_3$ kaš 2(diš) $sila_3$ ninda 5(diš) gin_2 $šum_2$ 3(diš) gin_2 i_3 2(diš) gin_2 naga
5. lu_2-sa_6-ga
6. šunigin 3(ban_2) 2(diš) $sila_3$ kaš šunigin 2(ban_2) ninda
7. šunigin ⅔(diš) $sila_3$ $šum_2$
8. šunigin ⅓(diš) $sila_3$ 4(diš) gin_2 ⸢i_3⸣
9. šunigin 1(u) 6(diš) gin_2 naga

left edge
1. u_4 1(u) 8(diš)-kam iti še-sag_{11}-[ku_5]
2. mu us_2-sa si-ma-num_2^{ki} ba-ḫul

No. 176. *MS 2022/3 (Umma, ŠS 6–ii–8)*

obv.

1. 5(diš) sila$_3$ kaš saga 3(diš) sila$_3$ ninda 5(diš) gin$_2$ šum$_2$
2. 3(diš) gin$_2$ i$_3$ 2(diš) gin$_2$ naga
3. ⸢ur⸣-ba-gara$_2$ sukkal
4. 5(diš) sila$_3$ kaš 3(diš) sila$_3$ ninda 5(diš) gin$_2$ šum$_2$
5. 3(diš) gin$_2$ i$_3$ 2(diš) gin$_2$ naga
6. ^{d}šul-gi-iri-mu
7. 5(diš) sila$_3$ kaš 3(diš) sila$_3$ ninda 5(diš) gin$_2$ šum$_2$
8. 3(diš) gin$_2$ i$_3$ 2(diš) gin$_2$ naga
9. lu$_2$-kal-la
10. 3(diš) sila$_3$ kaš 2(diš) sila$_3$ ninda 5(diš) gin$_2$ šum$_2$
11. 3(diš) gin$_2$ i$_3$ 2(diš) gin$_2$ naga

rev.

1. a-da-lal$_3$
2. šunigin 5(diš) sila$_3$ kaš saga
3. šunigin 1(ban$_2$) 3(diš) sila$_3$ kaš du
4. šunigin 1(ban$_2$) 1(diš) sila$_3$ ninda
5. šunigin ⅓(diš) sila$_3$ šum$_2$
6. šunigin 1(u) 2(diš) gin$_2$ i$_3$
7. ⸢šunigin⸣ 8(diš) gin$_2$ naga
8. u$_4$ 8(diš)-kam
9. iti sig$_4$-^{geš}i$_3$-šub-ba-gar

left edge

1. mu us$_2$-sa bad$_3$ mar-tu ba-du$_3$ mu us$_2$-sa-bi

No. 177. *MS 1871/3 (Umma, AS 7[528]–i–10)*

obv.

1. 5(diš) sila$_3$ kaš 5(diš) sila$_3$ ninda 5(diš) gin$_2$ šum$_2$
2. 3(diš) gin$_2$ i$_3$ 2(diš) gin$_2$ naga
3. ur-^{d}en-lil$_2$-la$_2$
4. 5(diš) sila$_3$ kaš 5(diš) sila$_3$ ninda 5(diš) gin$_2$
5. 3(diš) gin$_2$ i$_3$ 2(diš) gin$_2$ naga
6. nig$_2$-u$_2$-rum

---

528 The year-name, mu us$_2$-sa a-ra$_2$ 2(diš)-kam, is in a very abbreviated form and could refer to several different years. However, several other Umma messenger texts are dated to AS 7 using the slightly longer form of the year-name, mu us$_2$-sa a-ra$_2$ 2(diš)-kam ša-aš-ru-um^{ki} (e.g., Nisaba 1, 282), and this text is therefore assumed to come from that year.

7. 5(diš) sila$_3$ kaš 5(diš) sila$_3$ ninda 5(diš) gin$_2$
8. 3(diš) gin$_2$ i$_3$ 2(diš) gin$_2$ naga
9. ur-^{d}ba-ba$_6$
10. 5(diš) sila$_3$ kaš 5(diš) sila$_3$ ninda 5(diš) gin$_2$
11. 3(diš) gin$_2$ i$_3$ 2(diš) gin$_2$ naga

rev.

1. šeš-a-ni
2. 5(diš) sila$_3$ kaš 5(diš) sila$_3$ ninda 5(diš) gin$_2$
3. maš-maš
4. 3(diš) sila$_3$ kaš 2(diš) sila$_3$ ninda 5(diš) gin$_2$
5. 3(diš) gin$_2$ i$_3$ 2(diš) gin$_2$ naga
6. nu-ur$_2$-^{d}iškur
7. 3(diš) sila$_3$ kaš 2(diš) sila$_3$ ninda 5(diš) gin$_2$
8. 3(diš) gin$_2$ i$_3$ 2(diš) gin$_2$ naga
9. a-ḫu-dingir
10. šunigin 3(ban$_2$) 1(diš) sila$_3$ kaš 3(ban$_2$) la$_2$ 1(aš$_{45}$) sila$_3$ ninda ½(diš) sila$_3$ 6(diš) gin$_2$ šum$_2$
11. šunigin 1(u) 8(diš) gin$_2$ i$_3$ 1(u) 2(diš) gin$_2$ naga

left edge

1. iti še-sag$_{11}$-ku$_5$ u$_4$ 1(u)-kam
2. mu us$_2$-sa a-ra$_2$ ⸢2(diš)-kam⸣

No summary tablets can be matched up with the following Umma messenger texts since none of them preserves a year-name.

The list of messengers in text No. 178 includes one person, Kurbiak, who receives far more than the remainder of the party. This person is probably identical to Kurbiak the soldier (lu$_2$ ^{geš}tukul, lit. "man of weapon") found in an unpublished text in the Institut Catholique, Paris, France.[529] As was seen above, some of the summary tablets include dida-jars, and these also occur in this primary text.

No. 178. *MS 1746 (Umma, X–iv–1)*

obv.

1. 5(diš) sila$_3$ kaš 5(diš) sila$_3$ ninda 2(diš) sa šum$_2$
2. 3(diš) gin$_2$ i$_3$ 2(diš) gin$_2$ naga
3. e-lu-ra-bi$_2$[530]
4. 5(diš) sila$_3$ kaš 5(diš) sila$_3$ ninda 2(diš) sa šum$_2$
5. 3(diš) gin$_2$ i$_3$ 2(diš) gin$_2$ naga
6. ^{d}iškur-ba-ni
7. 2(diš) dug dida 2(ban$_2$)-ta

---

[529] ICP 1272 mentioned in the catalogue of Jean (1922) as no. 78. See the discussion of ICP 1227 below for more on this collection.

[530] One e-lu-ra-pi$_2$(BI?) (tablet not collated) is attested in BM 20552, and a dingir-lu-ra-bi$_2$ in two texts (MVN 21, 369 and Nisaba 16, 212). A bur-lu-ra-bi$_2$ is found in the Nippur text NATN 606.

8. 4(ban$_2$) ninda 2(diš) sa šum$_2$
9. ½(diš) sila$_3$ i$_3$ 2(diš) gin$_2$ naga
10. kur-bi-ak
11. 5(diš) sila$_3$ kaš 5(diš) sila$_3$ ninda 2(diš) sa šum$_2$
12. 3(diš) gin$_2$ i$_3$ 2(diš) gin$_2$ naga
13. lu$_2$-si-gar

rev.

1. 3(diš) sila$_3$ kaš 2(diš) sila$_3$ ninda 2(diš) sa šum$_2$
2. 3(diš) gin$_2$ i$_3$ 2(diš) gin$_2$ naga
3. ur-^{d}nun-gal
4. 3(diš) sila$_3$ kaš 2(diš) sila$_3$ ninda 2(diš) sa šum$_2$
5. 3(diš) gin$_2$ i$_3$ 2(diš) gin$_2$ naga
6. ur-e$_2$-e$_3$
7. 3(diš) sila$_3$ kaš 2(diš) sila$_3$ ninda 2(diš) sa šum$_2$
8. 3(diš) gin$_2$ i$_3$ 2(diš) gin$_2$ naga
9. ⸢nu?⸣-ḫi-dingir
10. 3(diš) sila$_3$ kaš 2(diš) sila$_3$ ninda 2(diš) sa šum$_2$
11. 3(diš) gin$_2$ i$_3$ 2(diš) gin$_2$ naga
12. tu-tu
13. 2(diš) dug dida du ⸢2(ban$_2$)-ta?⸣
14. 2(ban$_2$) 7(diš) sila3 kaš 3(diš) sila$_3$ ninda 1(u) 6(diš) gin$_2$ sa šum$_2$
15. 5/6(diš) sila$_3$ 1(diš) gin$_2$ i$_3$ 1(u) 6(diš) gin$_2$ naga

left edge

1. u$_4$ 1(diš)-kam iti nesag

The totals recorded in rev. 13–15 lack the standard terminology (šunigin). Additionally, rev. 14 erroneously has 3 sila$_3$ of bread instead of 1 barig 1 ban$_2$ and 4 sila.[531]

No. 179. *MS 1871/7 (Umma, X–?–20?)*

obv.

1. 5(diš) sila$_3$ kaš saga 5(diš) sila$_3$ ninda 5(diš) gin$_2$ šum$_2$
2. 3(diš) gin$_2$ i$_3$ 2(diš) gin$_2$ naga
3. x-na-an-ne
4. 5(diš) sila$_3$ kaš saga 5(diš) sila$_3$ ninda 5(diš) gin$_2$
5. 3(diš) gin$_2$ i$_3$ 2(diš) gin$_2$ naga
6. šar-ru-a

---

[531] Errors are perhaps more frequent in messenger texts than in other texts, and it is possible to speculate that the texts, in particular Type I and I*sub*, were not actually meant to be read, as the information was entirely formulaic, and that the presence of the document alone had enough authority to secure the issuing of the amounts listed in it.

7. 5(diš) sila$_3$ kaš saga 5(diš) sila$_3$ ninda 5(diš) gin$_2$
8. 3(diš) gin$_2$ i$_3$ 2(diš) gin$_2$ naga
9. SI-A-a sukkal
10. 5(diš) sila$_3$ kaš 5(diš) sila$_3$ ninda 5(diš) gin$_2$
11. 3(diš) gin$_2$ i$_3$ 2(diš) gin$_2$ naga
12. e$_2$-ni-ib
13. 5(diš) sila$_3$ kaš 5(diš) sila$_3$ ninda 5(diš) gin$_2$
14. 3(diš) gin$_2$ i$_3$ 2(diš) gin$_2$ naga
15. ^{d}suen-ba-ni

rev.

1. 5(diš) [sila$_3$ kaš 5(diš)] sila$_3$ ninda 5(diš) gin$_2$
2. [3(diš) gin$_2$ i$_3$ 2(diš)] gin$_2$ naga
3. AN-x-a
4. 5(diš) sila$_3$ kaš 5(diš) sila$_3$ ninda 5(diš) gin$_2$
5. 3(diš) gin$_2$ i$_3$ 2(diš) gin$_2$ naga
6. ku$_5$-da-a
7. [3(diš)] sila$_3$ kaš 2(diš) sila$_3$ ninda 5(diš) gin$_2$
8. [3(diš)] gin$_2$ i$_3$ 2(diš) gin$_2$ naga
9. [x]-ḪI-num$_2$
10. [3(diš)] sila$_3$ kaš 2(diš) sila$_3$ ninda 5(diš) gin$_2$
11. [3(diš)] gin$_2$ i$_3$ 2(diš) gin$_2$ naga
12. šu-GAN$_2^{?}$
13. šunigin 1(ban$_2$) 5(diš) sila$_3$ kaš saga 2(ban$_2$) 6(diš) ⸢kaš⸣
14. šunigin 4(ban$_2$) n(diš) ⸢sila$_3$ ninda⸣ ⅔(diš) sila$_3$ 5(diš) gin$_2$ [šum$_2$]
15. [. . .] gin$_2$ i$_3$ [. . .] naga

left edge

1. u$_4$ 2(u) [. . .]

No. 180. *MS 1871/8 (Umma, X–ix–23)*

obv.

1. 5(diš) sila$_3$ kaš saga 5(diš) sila$_3$ ninda 5(diš) gin$_2$ šum$_2$
2. 3(diš) gin$_2$ i$_3$ 2(diš) gin$_2$ naga
3. maš-maš
4. 5(diš) sila$_3$ kaš saga 5(diš) sila$_3$ ninda 5(diš) gin$_2$ šum$_2$
5. 3(diš) gin$_2$ i3 2(diš) gin$_2$ naga
6. AN-PA
7. 5(diš) sila$_3$ kaš saga 5(diš) sila$_3$ ninda 5(diš) gin$_2$ šum$_2$
8. 3(diš) gin$_2$ i$_3$ 2(diš) gin$_2$ naga
9. ur-dingir-ra

10. 5(diš) sila$_3$ kaš 5(diš) sila$_3$ ninda 5(diš) gin$_2$ šum$_2$
11. 3(diš) gin$_2$ i$_3$ 2(diš) gin$_2$ naga
12. nu-ur$_2$-geš
13. 5(diš) sila$_3$ kaš 5(diš) sila$_3$ ninda 5(diš) gin$_2$ šum$_2$
14. 3(diš) gin$_2$ i$_3$ 2(diš) gin$_2$ naga
15. da-a-a
16. 5(diš) sila$_3$ kaš 5(diš) sila$_3$ ninda 5(diš) gin$_2$ šum$_2$
17. 3(diš) gin$_2$ i$_3$ 2(diš) gin$_2$ naga
18. a-ḫu-du$_{10}$

rev.

1. 3(diš) sila$_3$ kaš 2(diš) sila$_3$ ninda 5(diš) gin$_2$ šum$_2$
2. 3(diš) gin$_2$ i$_3$ 2(diš) gin$_2$ naga
3. lu$_2$-nin-ga$_2$
4. 3(diš) sila$_3$ kaš 2(diš) sila$_3$ ninda 5(diš) gin$_2$ šum$_2$
5. 3(diš) gin$_2$ i$_3$ 2(diš) gin$_2$ naga
6. ka$_5$-a-mu
7. 3(diš) sila$_3$ kaš 2(diš) sila$_3$ ninda 5(diš) gin$_2$ šum$_2$
8. 3(diš) gin$_2$ i$_3$ 2(diš) gin$_2$ naga
9. a-x-ma
10. 3(diš) sila$_3$ kaš 2(diš) sila$_3$ ninda 5(diš) gin$_2$ šum$_2$
11. 3(diš) gin$_2$ i$_3$ 2(diš) gin$_2$ naga
12. ad-a-a
13. 3(diš) sila$_3$ kaš 2(diš) sila$_3$ ninda 5(diš) gin$_2$ šum$_2$
14. 3(diš) gin$_2$ i$_3$ 2(diš) gin$_2$ naga
15. maš-maš min
16. 3(diš) sila$_3$ kaš 2(diš) sila$_3$ ninda 5(diš) gin$_2$ šum$_2$
17. 3(diš) gin$_2$ i$_3$ 2(diš) gin$_2$ naga
18. šunigin 1(ban$_2$) 5(diš) sila$_3$ kaš saga šunigin 3(ban$_2$) 3(diš) sila$_3$ kaš
19. šunigin 4(ban$_2$) n(diš) sila$_3$ ninda šunigin 1(diš) sila$_3$ 5(diš) gin$_2$ šum$_2$

left edge

1. šunigin ⅔(diš) sila$_3$ la$_2$ 1(aš$_{45}$) gin$_2$ i$_3$ šunigin ⅓(diš) sila$_3$ 6(diš) gin$_2$ naga
2. iti ^{d}li$_9$-si$_4$ u$_4$ 2(u) 3(diš)-kam

No. 181. *MS 1944/1 (Umma, X–iii–14)*

obv.

1. 5(diš) sila$_3$ kaš 5(diš) sila$_3$ ninda 2(diš) sa šum$_2$
2. 3(diš) gin$_2$ i$_3$ 2(diš) gin$_2$ naga
3. nu-ur$_2$-^{d}utu
4. 5(diš) sila$_3$ kaš 5(diš) sila$_3$ ninda 2(diš) sa šum$_2$

5. 3(diš) gin$_2$ i$_3$ 2(diš) gin$_2$ naga
6. bur-ma-am$_3$
7. 5(diš) sila$_3$ kaš 5(diš) sila$_3$ ninda 2(diš) sa šum$_2$
8. 3(diš) gin$_2$ i$_3$ 2(diš) gin$_2$ naga
9. e-lu$_2$-x-ad
10. 1(ban$_2$) kaš 1(ban$_2$) ninda 2(diš) sa!(sila$_3$) šum$_2$
11. da-da-a
12. 5(diš) sila$_3$ kaš 4(diš) sila$_3$ ninda 2(diš) sa šum$_2$
13. 3(diš) gin$_2$ i$_3$ 1(diš) gin$_2$ naga

rev.

1. ur-lugal
2. 5(diš) sila$_3$ kaš 4(diš) sila$_3$ ninda 2(diš) sa šum$_2$
3. 3(diš) gin$_2$ i$_3$ 2(diš) gin$_2$ naga
4. bu$_3$-KA
5. 3(diš) sila$_3$ kaš 2(diš) sila$_3$ ninda 2(diš) sa šum$_2$
6. 3(diš) gin$_2$ i$_3$ 2(diš) gin$_2$ naga
7. ur-ma-ma
8. 3(diš) sila$_3$ kaš 2(diš) sila$_3$ ninda 2(diš) sa šum$_2$
9. 3(diš) gin$_2$ i$_3$ 2(diš) gin$_2$ naga
10. ur-^{d}utu
11. šunigin 4(ban$_2$) 1(diš) sila$_3$ kaš 4(ban$_2$) 1(diš) sila$_3$ ninda 1(u) 6(diš) sa šum$_2$
12. ½(diš) sila$_3$ 1(diš) gin$_2$ ⸢i$_3$⸣ 1(u) 6(diš) gin$_2$ naga

left edge

1. u$_4$ 1(u) 4(diš)-kam iti še-kar-ra ^{ga2}gar

No. 182. *MS 1944/2 (Umma, X–x–17)*

obv.

1. 5(diš) sila$_3$ kaš 3(diš) sila$_3$ ninda 3(diš) gin$_2$ šum$_2$
2. 3(diš) gin$_2$ i$_3$ 2(diš) gin$_2$ naga x-x-x[532]
3. 5(diš) sila$_3$ kaš 3(diš) sila$_3$ ninda 3(diš) gin$_2$ šum$_2$
4. 3(diš) gin$_2$!(sila$_3$) i$_3$ 2(diš) gin$_2$ naga
5. al-la-mu
6. 5(diš) sila$_3$ kaš 3(diš) sila$_3$ ninda 3(diš) gin$_2$ šum$_2$
7. 3(diš) gin$_2$ i$_3$ 2(diš) gin$_2$ naga
8. ša-al-maḫ

---

532 The scribe appears to have squeezed in the name of the recipient of the first entry, possibly after realising that he had already started writing the second entry. See also rev. 4.

rev.

1. 5(diš) sila$_3$ kaš 3(diš) sila$_3$ ninda
2. 3(diš) gin$_2$ šum$_2$ 3(diš) gin$_2$ naga
3. ur-^{d}ba-ba$_6$
4. 3(diš) sila$_3$ kaš 2(diš) sila$_3$ ninda 3(diš) gin$_2$ šum$_2$ 3(diš) gin$_2$ naga ḫu-ba
5. 3(diš) sila$_3$ kaš 2(diš) sila$_3$ ninda 3(diš) gin$_2$ šum$_2$
6. 3(diš) gin$_2$ i$_3$ 2(diš) gin$_2$ ⸢naga⸣
7. ba-za-za
8. šunigin 2(ban$_2$) 6(diš) sila$_3$ kaš
9. šunigin 1(ban$_2$) 6(diš) sila$_3$ ninda
10. šunigin 1(u) 8(diš) gin$_2$ šum$_2$ 1(u) 8(diš) gin$_2$ [i$_3$ 1(u) 2(diš) gin$_2$ naga$^?$]

left edge

1. u$_4$ 1(u) 7(diš)-kam iti$^?$ ezem-^{d}šul-gi

No. 183. *MS 1944/3 (Umma, X–?–18)*

obv.

1. 5(diš) sila$_3$ kaš 5(diš) sila$_3$ ninda
2. 2(diš) gin$_2$ i$_3$ 2(diš) gin$_2$ naga$^?$
3. ma-ma
4. 5(diš) sila$_3$ kaš 5(diš) sila$_3$ ninda x gin$_2$ šum$_2$
5. 3(diš) gin$_2$ i$_3$ 2(diš) gin$_2$ naga
6. ^{d}šara$_2$-kam
7. 1(ban$_2$) kaš 1(ban$_2$) ninda 2(diš) gin$_2$ šum$_2^?$
8. 3(diš) gin$_2$ i$_3$ 2(diš) gin$_2$ naga
9. a-bu-ni
10. 5(diš) kaš 5(diš) ninda 2(diš)$^?$ šum$_2^?$

rev.

1. 3(diš) gin$_2$ i3 2(diš) gin$_2$ šum$_2$
2. la$_2$-la$_2$
3. 1(ban$_2$) kaš 1(ban$_2$) ninda 2(diš) gin$_2$ šum$_2$
4. 3(diš) gin$_2$ i$_3$ 2(diš) gin$_2$ naga
5. IGI-gun$_3$
6. 3(diš) sila$_3$ kaš 2(diš) sila$_3$ ninda 2(diš) gin$_2$ šum$_2$
7. 3(diš) gin$_2$ i$_3$ 2(diš) gin$_2$ naga
8. ur-i$_7$-nun
9. ⸢šunigin⸣ 3(ban$_2$) 8(diš) sila$_3$ kaš 3(ban$_2$) 8(diš)$^?$ sila$_3$ ninda 1(u) 2(diš) gin$_2$ šum$_2$

left edge

1. u$_4$ 1(u) 8(diš)-kam iti e$_2$-⸢iti⸣-6(diš)
   (further traces)

No. 184. *MS 4987 (Umma, —)*

obv.

1. 5(diš) sila$_3$ kaš saga 5(diš) sila$_3$ ninda 5(diš) gin$_2$ šum$_2$ 3(diš) gin$_2$ i$_3$ 2(diš) gin$_2$ naga
2. šu-ma-ma
3. 5(diš) sila$_3$ kaš ⸢saga$^?$⸣ 5(diš) sila$_3$ ninda 5(diš) gin$_2$ šum$_2$ 3(diš) gin$_2$ i$_3$ 2(diš) gin$_2$ naga
4. ⸢suḫuš⸣-gi
5. 5(diš) sila$_3$ kaš ⸢saga$^?$⸣ 5(diš) sila$_3$ ninda [5(diš)] gin$_2$ šum$_2$ 3(diš) gin$_2$ i$_3$ 2(diš) gin$_2$ naga
6. a-[ḫu]-a
7. 5(diš) sila$_3$ kaš 5(diš) sila$_3$ ninda 5(diš) gin$_2$ šum$_2$ 3(diš) gin$_2$ i$_3$ 2(diš) gin$_2$ naga
8. x-ni-a
9. ⸢5(diš)⸣ sila$_3$ kaš 5(diš) sila$_3$ ninda 5(diš) gin$_2$ šum$_2$ 3(diš) gin$_2$ i$_3$ 2(diš) gin$_2$ naga
10. ⸢ḫu⸣-wa-wa
11. ⸢3(diš)⸣ sila$_3$ kaš 3(diš) sila$_3$ ninda 5(diš) gin$_2$ šum$_2$ 3(diš) gin$_2$ i$_3$ 2(diš) gin$_2$ naga

rev.

1. [. . .]-kal
2. [3(diš) sila$_3$ kaš 3(diš) sila$_3$ ninda 5(diš) gin$_2$ šum$_2$ 3(diš)] gin$_2$ i$_3$ 2(diš) gin$_2$ naga
3. [. . .]-ga
4. [3(diš) sila$_3$ kaš 3(diš) sila$_3$ ninda 5(diš) gin$_2$ šum$_2$ 3(diš)] gin$_2$ i$_3$ 2(diš) gin$_2$ naga

(rest broken)

No. 185. *MS 4988 (Umma, —)*

obv.

(beginning broken)

1'. [n(diš) sila$_3$ kaš n(diš) sila$_3$ ninda n(diš) gin$_2$ šum$_2$] n(diš) ⸢gin$_2$ i$_3$⸣ [n(diš) gin$_2$ naga]
2'. [. . .]-⸢a$^?$⸣
3'. [n(diš) sila$_3$ kaš n(diš) sila$_3$ ninda n(diš) gin$_2$ šum$_2$] 3(diš) ⸢gin$_2$ i$_3$⸣ 2(diš) gin$_2$ [naga]
4'. [. . .]-x
5'. [n(diš) sila$_3$ kaš n(diš) sila$_3$ ninda n(diš) gin$_2$] ⸢šum$_2$⸣ 3(diš) ⸢gin$_2$ i$_3$⸣ 2(diš) gin$_2$ [naga]
6'. [. . .]-dam$^?$
7'. [n(diš) sila$_3$ kaš n(diš) sila$_3$ ninda] 5(diš) ⸢gin$_2$ šum$_2$⸣ 3(diš) ⸢gin$_2$ i$_3$⸣ 2(diš) gin$_2$ [naga]
8'. [x]-ba-x
9'. [n(diš) sila$_3$ kaš n(diš) sila$_3$] ⸢ninda⸣ 5(diš) ⸢gin$_2$ šum$_2$⸣ 3(diš) ⸢gin$_2$⸣ [i$_3$ 2(diš) gin$_2$ naga]
10'. [x]-x-ni-x
11'. [n(diš) sila$_3$ kaš n(diš)] ⸢sila$_3$ ninda⸣ 5(diš) ⸢gin$_2$ šum$_2$⸣ 3(diš) ⸢gin$_2$⸣ [i$_3$ 2(diš) gin$_2$ naga]
12'. x-ka-x

rev.

1. [n(diš) sila$_3$ kaš] n(diš) ⸢sila$_3$ ninda⸣ n(diš) ⸢gin$_2$ šum$_2$⸣ [3(diš) gin$_2$ i$_3$ 2(diš) gin$_2$ naga]
2. [. . .]
3. [n(diš) sila$_3$ kaš] n(diš) sila$_3$ ninda 5(diš) gin$_2$ šum$_2$ 3(diš) ⸢gin$_2$⸣ [i$_3$ 2(diš) gin$_2$ naga]

4. [. . .]
5. [n(diš) sila$_3$ kaš] n(diš) sila$_3$ ninda 5(diš) gin$_2$ šum$_2$ 3(diš) gin$_2$ i$_3$ 2(diš) gin$_2$ ⸢naga⸣
6. [x]-eš$_{18}$-dar
7. [n(diš) sila$_3$ kaš] n(diš) sila$_3$ ninda 5(diš) gin$_2$ šum$_2$ 3(diš) gin$_2$ i$_3$ 2(diš) gin$_2$ ⸢naga⸣
8. [x]-ba-[x]
9. [n(diš) sila$_3$ kaš] n(diš) sila$_3$ ninda 5(diš) gin$_2$ šum$_2$ 3(diš) gin$_2$ i$_3$ 2(diš) ⸢gin$_2$ naga⸣
10. [n(diš)] dug dida 1(ban$_2$) 5(diš) ⸢sila$_3$⸣-[ta . . .]

(*rest broken*)

No. 186. *MS 4989 (Umma, —)*

obv.

1. ⸢5(diš)⸣ sila$_3$ kaš 5(diš) sila$_3$ ninda 5(diš) gin$_2$ šum$_2$
2. ⸢3(diš)⸣ gin$_2$ i$_3$ 2(diš) gin$_2$ naga
3. ⸢lugal⸣-šu-nir-e
4. ⸢5(diš)⸣ sila$_3$ kaš 5(diš) sila$_3$ ninda 5(diš) gin$_2$
5. [3(diš)] gin$_2$ i$_3$ 2(diš) gin$_2$ naga
6. [ur$^?$]-da-mu
7. [5(diš) sila$_3$] kaš 5(diš) sila$_3$ ninda 5(diš) gin$_2$
8. [3(diš)] ⸢gin$_2$⸣ i$_3$ 2(diš) gin$_2$ naga
9. [x]-ša-me
10. [5(diš) sila$_3$] kaš 5(diš) sila$_3$ ninda 5(diš) gin$_2$
11. [3(diš)] ⸢gin$_2$⸣ i$_3$ 2(diš) gin$_2$ naga
12. [x]-^{d}en-lil$_2$-la$_2$
13. [5(diš)] ⸢sila$_3$⸣ kaš 5(diš) sila$_3$ ninda 5(diš) gin$_2$
14. [3(diš) gin$_2$] i$_3$ 2(diš) gin$_2$ naga

rev.

1. [x-^{d}]suen
2. [5(diš) sila$_3$] kaš 5(diš) sila$_3$ ninda 5(diš) gin$_2$
3. [3(diš)] ⸢gin$_2$⸣ i$_3$ 2(diš) gin$_2$ naga
4. [x]-am$_3$-i$_3$-li$_2$
5. [3(diš) sila$_3$] kaš 2(diš) sila$_3$ ninda 5(diš) gin$_2$
6. [3(diš)] ⸢gin$_2$⸣ i$_3$ 2(diš) gin$_2$ naga
7. [x]-ba-gi-na
8. [3(diš)] ⸢sila$_3$⸣ kaš 2(diš) sila$_3$ ninda 5(diš) gin$_2$
9. [3(diš)] gin$_2$ i$_3$ 2(diš) gin$_2$ naga
10. ⸢a⸣-ḫu-a-qar
11. 3(diš) sila$_3$ kaš 2(diš) sila$_3$ ninda 5(diš) gin$_2$
12. 3(diš) gin$_2$ i$_3$ 2(diš) gin$_2$ naga
13. a-bu-ni

14. šunigin ⸢4(ban$_2$)⸣ la$_2$ 1(aš$_{45}$) sila$_3$ kaš 3(ban$_2$) 6(diš) sila$_3$ ninda ⅔(diš) sila$_3$ 5(diš) ⸢gin$_2$⸣ šum$_2$
15. šunigin ⅓(diš) sila$_3$ 7(diš) gin$_2$ i$_3$ 1(u) 8(diš) gin$_2$ naga

left edge

1. [. . .] ⸢gal-la$^{?}$⸣

No. 187. *MS 4990 (Umma, X–xi–11)*

obv.

1. 5(diš) ⸢sila$_3$⸣ [kaš 5(diš) sila$_3$ ninda 5(diš) gin$_2$ šum$_2$]
2. 3(diš) ⸢gin$_2$⸣ [i$_3$ 3(diš) gin$_2$ naga]
3. ur-[. . .]
4. 5(diš) ⸢sila$_3$⸣ [kaš 5(diš) sila$_3$ ninda 5(diš) gin$_2$]
5. 3(diš) [gin$_2$ i$_3$ 3(diš) gin$_2$ naga]
6. giri$_3$-[. . .]
7. 5(diš) ⸢sila$_3$ kaš⸣ [5(diš) sila$_3$ ninda 5(diš) gin$_2$]
8. 3(diš) gin$_2$ i$_3$ [3(diš) gin$_2$ naga]
9. ⸢ur-tar$^{?}$⸣-[x]
10. 5(diš) sila$_3$ kaš 5(diš) sila$_3$ ninda [5(diš) gin$_2$]
11. 3(diš) gin$_2$ i$_3$ 2(diš) gin$_2$ naga
12. x-i$_3$-ku-u-⸢bi$_2^{?}$⸣

rev.

1. 5(diš) sila$_3$ kaš ⸢5(diš)⸣ [sila$_3$ ninda x$^{?}$]
2. 3(diš) gin$_2$ i$_3$ [2(diš) gin$_2$ naga]
3. ur-e$_2$-[x]
4. 3(diš) sila$_3$ kaš 2(diš) sila$_3$ ninda 5(diš) gin$_2$
5. 3(diš) gin$_2$ i$_3$ 2(diš) gin$_2$ naga
6. la-ni
7. 3(diš) sila$_3$ kaš 2(diš) sila$_3$ ninda 5(diš) gin$_2$
8. 3(diš) gin$_2$ i$_3$ 2(diš) gin$_2$ naga
9. ba-a-mu
10. šunigin 3(ban$_2$) 1(diš) sila$_3$ kaš 3(ban$_2$) la$_2$ 1(aš$_{45}$) sila$_3$ ninda ½(diš) sila$_3$ 5(diš) gin$_2$ šum$_2$
11. šunigin ⅓(diš) sila$_3$ n(diš) [gin$_2$ i$_3$ n(diš) sila$_3$ n(diš) gin$_2$ naga]

left edge

1. u$_4$ 1(u) 1(diš)-kam iti pa$_4$-<<e>>-u$_2$-e

No. 188. *MS 4992 (Umma, —)*

obv.

(broken)

1'. [. . .] x ⸢sila$_3$ ninda 5(diš) gin$_2$⸣

rev.

1. [3(diš)] gin$_2$ i$_3$ 2(diš) gin$_2$ naga
2. šu-^{d}er$_3$-ra
3. 5(diš) sila$_3$ kaš 5(diš) sila$_3$ ninda 5(diš) gin$_2$
4. 3(diš) gin$_2$ i$_3$ 2(diš) gin$_2$ naga
5. a-⌜ḫu$^?$⌝-a
6. 3(diš) sila$_3$ kaš 2(diš) sila$_3$ ninda 5(diš) gin$_2$
7. 3(diš) gin$_2$ i$_3$ 2(diš) gin$_2$ naga
8. ur-^{d}ba-ba$_6$
9. šunigin 3(ban$_2$) 3(diš) sila$_3$ kaš 3(ban$_2$) 2(diš) sila$_3$ ninda ½(diš) sila$_3$ 5(diš) gin$_2$ šum$_2$
10. šunigin ⅓(diš) sila$_3$ 1(diš) gin$_2$ i$_3$ 1(u) 4(diš) gin$_2$ naga

left edge

(broken: traces of date)

No. 189. *MS 4993 (Umma, —)*

obv.

(broken)

1'. ⌜5(diš)⌝ [...]
2'. 3(diš) gin$_2$ i$_3$ 2(diš) gin$_2$ naga

rev.

1. en-num$_2$-i$_3$-li$_2$
2. 5(diš) sila$_3$ kaš 5(diš) sila$_3$ ninda 5(diš) gin$_2$
3. 3(diš) gin$_2$ i$_3$ 2(diš) gin$_2$ naga
4. gu-gu-a
5. 3(diš) sila$_3$ kaš 2(diš) sila$_3$ ninda 5(diš) gin$_2$
6. 3(diš) gin$_2$ i$_3$ 2(diš) gin$_2$ naga
7. dingir-sukkal
8. 3(diš) sila$_3$ kaš 2(diš) sila$_3$ ninda 5(diš) gin$_2$
9. 3(diš) gin$_2$ i$_3$ 2(diš) gin$_2$ naga
10. a-ḫu-du$_{10}$
11. 3(diš) sila$_3$ kaš 2(diš) sila$_3$ ninda 5(diš) gin$_2$
12. 3(diš) gin$_2$ i$_3$ 2(diš) gin$_2$ naga
13. a-bu-ni
14. šunigin 4(ban$_2$) la$_2$ 1(aš$_{45}$) sila$_3$ kaš ⌜3(ban$_2$)⌝ 6(diš) sila$_3$ ⌜ninda⌝ ⅔(diš) sila$_3$ 5(diš) gin$_2$ šum$_2$
15. šunigin ⅓(diš) sila$_3$ 7(diš) gin$_2$ i$_3$ 1(u) 9(diš) gin$_2$ naga

left edge

(broken: traces of date)

*Type I*sub *Messenger Texts*

There are only two Type I*sub* texts in the Schøyen Collection, Nos. 190 and 191.

No. 190. *MS 2022/1 (Umma, ŠS 6–xi–21)*

obv.

1.	1(diš) a-ḫu-a	1 Aḫua.
2.	1(diš) lu$_2$-gu-la	1 Lu-gula.
3.	1(diš) ur-^{d}iškur	1 Ur-Iškur.
4.	1(diš) lugal-a$_2$-mu	1 Lugal-a(ya)mu.
5.	1(diš) ^{geš}kin$_2$-na-i$_3$-sa$_6$	1 Kina-isa.
6.	1(diš) lu$_2$-^{d}en-ki	1 Lu-Enki.
7.	sukkal-me	They are messengers.
8.	5(diš) sila$_3$ kaš 3(diš) sila$_3$ ninda 5(diš) gin$_2$ šum$_2$ 3(diš) gin$_2$ i$_3$ 2(diš) gin$_2$ naga-ta	5 sila$_3$ of beer; 3 sila$_3$ of bread; 5 shekels of onions; 3 shekels of oil; 2 shekels of potash each.
9.	1(diš) a-gu-a	1 Agua.
10.	1(diš) ba-a-ga	1 Bayaga.
11.	1(diš) lu$_2$-^{d}ba-ba$_6$	1 Lu-Baba.
12.	1(diš) ur-^{d}nun-gal	1 Ur-Nungal.
13.	lu$_2$-^{d}šul-gi-ra	Lu-Šulgira.

rev.

1.	lu$_2$-saga	Lu-saga.
2.	lu$_2$ maškim-me	They are enforcers.
3.	3(diš) sila$_3$ kaš 2(diš) sila$_3$ ninda 5(diš) gin$_2$ šum$_2$ 3(diš) gin$_2$ i$_3$ 2(diš) gin$_2$ naga-ta	3 sila$_3$ of beer; 2 sila$_3$ of bread; 5 shekels of onions; 3 shekels of oil; 2 shekels of potash each.
4.	šunigin 4(ban$_2$) 8(diš) sila$_3$ kaš šunigin 3(ban$_2$) ninda	Total: 4 ban$_2$, 8 sila$_3$ of beer; Total: 3 ban$_2$ of bread;
5.	šunigin 1(diš) sila$_3$ šum$_2$ šunigin ½(diš) sila$_3$ 6(diš) gin$_2$ i$_3$	Total: 1 sila$_3$ of onions; Total: ½ sila$_3$, 6 shekels of oil;
6.	šunigin ⅓(diš) sila$_3$ 4(diš) gin$_2$ naga	Total: ⅓ sila$_3$, 4 shekels of potash.
7.	u$_4$ 2(u) 1(diš)-kam	On the 21st day.
8.	iti pa$_4$-u$_2$-e	Month: "Pa'u'e."
9.	mu na maḫ ba-du$_3$	Year: "Lofty Stele was erected."

The second Type I*sub* messenger text in the collection is similar, so only given in transliteration:

No. 191. *MS 2022/5 (Umma, ŠS 6–xii–13)*

obv.

1. 1(diš) šu-^{d}utu
2. 1(diš) lugal-nin-maḫ
3. 1(diš) x-ta-gul
4. 5(diš) sila$_3$ kaš saga ⌜3(diš)?⌝ sila$_3$ ninda 5(diš) gin$_2$ šum$_2$ 3(diš) gin$_2$ i$_3$ 2(diš) gin$_2$ naga
6. sukkal-me
7. 1(diš) ^{d}šul-gi-dingir-dan$^{?}$

8. 1(diš) ^{d}lamma-aš-da-an
9. 1(diš) ni-ib-^{d}utu
10. 1(diš) du$_{10}$-i$_3$-li$_2$
11. 1(diš) nu-ur$_2$-i$_3$-li$_2$

rev.

1. 3(diš) sila$_3$ kaš ⸢du$^{?}$⸣ n sila$_3$ ninda 3(diš) gin$_2$ šum$_2$ 3(diš) gin$_2$ i$_3$ 2(diš) gin$_2$ naga
2. lu$_2$ maškim-me
3. šunigin 1(ban$_2$) 5(diš) sila$_3$ kaš saga
4. šunigin 1(ban$_2$) 5(diš) sila$_3$ kaš du šunigin ½(diš) sila$_3$ 9(diš) gin$_2$ šum$_2$
5. šunigin ⅔(diš) sila$_3$ x ⅓(diš) sila$_3$ i$_3$
6. šunigin 1(u) 6(diš) gin$_2$ naga
7. iti ^{d}dumu-zi u$_4$ ⸢1(u)⸣ 3(diš)-kam
8. mu na-ru$_2$-a maḫ ba-du$_3$

Type II Messenger Texts

There are only three Type II messenger texts in the collection published here (Nos. 192–94). Type II messenger texts from Umma could also be summarized in the triangular tags discussed at the beginning of this chapter.

No. 192. *MS 1709/1 (Umma, X–vii–23)*

obv.

1.	5(diš) sila$_3$ kaš saga	5 sila$_3$ good (quality) beer.
2.	3(diš) sila$_3$ ninda	3 sila$_3$ of bread.
3.	2(diš) gin$_2$ i$_3$ 2(diš) gin$_2$ naga	2 shekels of oil. 2 shekels of potash.
4.	1(diš) ku$_6$ 1(diš) sa šum$_2$	1 fish. 1 bundle of onions.
5.	^{d}nanna-kam sukkal	Nannakam, messenger.
6.	3(diš) sila$_3$ kaš saga 2(diš) sila$_3$ ninda	3 sila$_3$ of good (quality) beer. 2 sila$_3$ of bread.

rev.

1.	2(diš) gin$_2$ i$_3$ 2(diš) gin$_2$ naga	2 shekels of oil. 2 gin$_2$ of potash.
2.	1(diš) ku$_6$ 1(diš) sa šum$_2$	1 fish. 1 bundle of onions.
3.	tab-ša-la-mu	Tabšalamu.
4.	u$_4$ 2(u) 3(diš)-kam iti min-eš$_3$	The 23rd day. Month: "Double sanctuary."

No. 193. *MS 1709/2 (Umma, X–vi–1)*

obv.

1.	5(diš) sila$_3$ kaš saga	5 sila$_3$ good (quality) beer.
2.	3(diš) sila$_3$ ninda	3 sila$_3$ of bread.
3.	2(diš) gin$_2$ i$_3$ 2(diš) gin$_2$ naga	2 shekels of oil. 2 shekels of potash.
4.	1(diš) ku$_6$ 1(diš) sa šum$_2$	1 fish. 1 bundle of onions.
5.	dingir-ra-bi$_2$ gaba-ta	Ilu-rapi, (crossing back) from the other (side).
6.	3(diš) sila$_3$ kaš 2(diš) sila$_3$ ninda	3 sila$_3$ good (quality) beer. 2 sila$_3$ of bread.
7.	2(diš) gin$_2$ i$_3$ 2(diš) gin$_2$ naga	2 shekels of oil. 2 shekels of potash.

rev.

1.	1(diš) ku$_6$ 1(diš) sa šum$_2$	1 fish. 1 bundle of onions.
2.	i-šar-ki-^{d}utu	Išar-ki-Šamash.
3.	3(diš) sila$_3$ kaš 2(diš) sila$_3$ ninda	3 sila$_3$ good (quality) beer. 2 sila$_3$ of bread.
4.	2(diš) gin$_2$ i$_3$ 2(diš) gin$_2$ naga	2 shekels of oil. 2 shekels of potash.
5.	1(diš) ku$_6$ 1(diš) sa šum$_2$	1 fish. 1 bundle of onions.
6.	a-ḫu-ni gaba-ta	Aḫuni (crossing back) from the other (side).
7.	u$_4$ 1(diš)-kam	On the 1st day.

left edge

1.	iti šu-numun	Month: "Seeding."

A piece of the surface of another tablet has been glued on to tablet No. 194, patching a hole in the obverse.[533]

No. 194. *MS 2022/6 (Umma; X–iii)*

obv.

(beginning missing)

1'.	[. . .] gin$_2$ i$_3$ 2(diš) gin$_2$ naga	. . . shekels of oil, 2 shekels of potash.
2'.	3(diš) ku$_6$ 3(diš) sa šum$_2$	3 fish, 3 bundle of onions.
3'.	la-la-a-a gaba-ta?	Lalaya, (crossing back) from the other (side).

rev.

1.	2(diš) sila$_3$ kaš 2(diš) sila$_3$ ninda	2 sila$_3$ beer, 2 sila$_3$ bread.
2.	2(diš) gin$_2$ i$_3$ 2(diš) gin$_2$ naga	2 shekels of oil, 2 shekels of potash.
3.	1(diš) ku6 1(diš) sa šum$_2$	1 fish, 1 bundle of onions.
4.	a-na-ti ka-us$_2$-[sa]	Anati, . . .
5.	šunigin 2(diš) dug dida du 1(ban$_2$)	Total: 2 dida jars regular (quality), (holding) 1 ban$_2$.
6.	šunigin 5(diš) sila$_3$ kaš saga 5(diš) sila$_3$ kaš [du]	Total: 5 sila$_3$ of beer, good (quality), total: 5 sila$_3$ of beer, regular (quality).
7.	šunigin 2(ban$_2$) 2(diš) sila$_3$ ninda šunigin 6(diš) gin$_2$ i$_3$	Total: 2 ban$_2$, 2 sila$_3$ of bread, total: 6 shekels of oil.
8.	šunigin 6(diš) gin$_2$ naga	Total: 6 shekels of potash.
9.	šunigin 6(diš) ku$_6$ šunigin 7(diš)$^{?}$ sa šum$_2$	Total: 6 fish, total: 7 bundles of garlic.
10.	u$_4$ 1(u) 6(diš)$^{?}$-kam iti še-kar-[ra-gal$_2$-la]	On the 16th day, month "Barley was brought to the harbour."

Type III Messenger Texts

No Type III messenger texts ("errand texts") are found in the Schøyen Collection, and the four examples below are added for the sake of completeness.

[533] The fragment (MS 2022/6A) appears to be from the summary of another messenger text, ll. 1'–4': kur-bi-la-ak gaba-ta / šunigin 1(ban$_2$) kaš šunigin 7(diš) sila$_3$ ninda / šunigin 6(diš) gin$_2$ i$_3$ / šunigin 6(diš) gin$_2$ naga.

Nisaba 22, 59 (Girsu, ŠS 1–vii–14)

obv.

1.	2(diš) sila$_3$ kaš [x] sila$_3$ ninda	2 sila$_3$ beer. n sila$_3$ bread.
2.	1(diš) id-gur$_2$ i$_3$	1 *itquru* of oil.
3.	ša$_3$ iri	(While) in the city.
4.	1(diš) dug dida 5(diš) sila$_3$ dabin	1 dida jar. 5 sila$_3$ of dabin-flour.
5.	kaskal-še$_3$	(While) on campaign.
6.	i$_3$-zu lu$_2$-^{geš}tukul	Izu the soldier.
7.	1(barig) kaš 1(barig) ninda	1 barig beer. 1 barig bread,
8.	1(diš) sila$_3$ i$_3$-geš	1 sila$_3$ sesame(?) oil.
9.	elam ši-ma-aš-gi$_4$^{ki}-me	They are Elamites and Šimašgeans
10.	ši-ma-aš-gi$_4$^{ki}-še$_3$ gen-ne-ne[534]	when they came to Šimašgi.

rev.

1.	u$_3$-na-a-du$_{11}$ sukkal-maḫ	A letter of the Sukkal-maḫ.
2.	giri$_3$ i$_3$-zu lu$_2$-^{geš}tukul	Conveyor: Izu the soldier.
3.	2(diš) sila$_3$ kaš 2(diš) sila$_3$ ninda	2 sila$_3$ of beer. 2 sila$_3$ of bread,
4.	1(diš) id-gur$_2$ i$_3$	1 *itquru* of oil.
5.	ša$_3$ iri	(While) in the city.
6.	1(diš) dug dida 5(diš) sila$_3$ dabin	1 dida jar. 5 sila$_3$ of dabin flour.
7.	kaskal-še$_3$	(While) on campaign.
8.	a-bi$_2$-sa$_6$-sa$_6$ lu$_2$-^{geš}tukul	Abi-sasa the soldier.
9.	šušin^{ki}-še$_3$ gen-ni	when he came to Susa.
10.	iti ezem-^{d}šul-gi u$_4$ 1(u) 4(diš)-kam	Month: "Festival of Šulgi." On the 14th day.
11.	mu ^{d}šu-^{d}suen lugal	Year: "Šu-Suen (was) king."

BPOA 1, 309 (Girsu, AS 1–vi)

obv.

1.	4(u) 4(diš) elam 2(diš) sila$_3$ kaš 2(diš) sila$_3$ ninda-ta	44 "Elamites" 2 sila$_3$ beer, 2 sila$_3$ bread each.
2.	kaš-bi 1(barig) 2(ban$_2$) 8(diš) sila$_3$ lugal	Its beer is 1 barig, 2 ban$_2$, 8 sila$_3$ (according to the) king('s standard).
3.	ninda-bi 1(barig) 2(ban$_2$) 8(diš) sila$_3$	Its bread is 1 barig, 2 ban$_2$, 8 sila$_3$.
4.	elam-me	They are Elamites.
5.	2(diš) ra-gaba 1(ban$_2$) kaš 1(ban$_2$) dabin-ta	2 riders, 1 ban$_2$ beer each 1 ban$_2$ dabin-flour each.

rev.

1.	elam uri$_5$^{ki}-ta	Elamites from Ur
2.	mar-ḫa-ši^{ki}-še$_3$ gen-na	when he came to Marḫaši.

---

534 The description of the movements of the messengers frequently found in the complex messenger texts, using various, for the most part suffixed forms of the verb gen/du, are complicated grammatically. Whereas we would syntactically expect an imperfect, *marû*, form of the verb, translated as "going to" or "coming from," the more complex forms found in the new Irisagrig texts seem to rule this out (*ḫamṭu* plural /ere/ is used in Nisaba 15, 127, for example). I have therefore chosen to treat the suffixed forms as *ḫamṭu* pronominal conjugations (often without nominalising -a?), see Foxvog 2016: 151-152, but note that Foxvog interpreted these as *marû* forms.

3.	giri$_3$ ARAD$_2$-ḫu-la šagina	Conveyor: ARAD-ḫula, the general.
4.	iti ezem-^{d}dumu-zi	Month: "Festival of Dumuzi."
5.	mu ^{d}amar-^{d}suen lugal	Year: "When Amar-Suen (was) king."

The next two texts are part of the collection of the Institute Catholique, Paris, catalogued, transliterated, imaged, and presented online by B. Lafont and J. L. Dahl in 2002. The current state of the collection is unknown to the author.

ICP 1227 (Girsu, X–v)

obv.

1.	3(diš) sila$_3$ kaš du	3 sila$_3$ of beer, regular (quality).
2.	2(diš) sila$_3$ zi$_3$-gu	2 sila$_3$ of gu-flour.
3.	1(diš) id-gur$_2$ i$_3$	1 *itquru*[535] of oil.
4.	gi-na-bi$_2$-li$_2$ lu$_2$ kas$_4$	(For) Kinabi-ili, the runner,
5.	a-dam-šaḫ$_2$^{ki}-ta gen-ni	when he came from Adamšaḫ.
6.	3(diš) sila$_3$ kaš du	3 sila$_3$ of regular quality beer.
7.	2(diš) sila$_3$ zi$_3$-gu	2 sila$_3$ of gu-flour.
8.	1(diš) id-gur$_2$ i$_3$ ša$_3$ iri	1 *itquru* of oil (while) in the city.
9.	1(aš) dug dida du	1 dida jar, regular (quality).
10.	5(diš) sila$_3$ zi$_3$ kaskal-še$_3$	5 sila$_3$ of flour (while) on campaign.
11.	i-di$_3$-er$_3$-ra šu-i$_3$	(For) Idi-erra, barber,
12.	šušin^{ki}-še$_3$ gen-ni	when he came to Susa.
13.	5(diš) sila$_3$ kaš du	5 sila$_3$ of beer, regular (quality).

rev.

1.	5(diš) sila$_3$ zi$_3$-gu	5 sila$_3$ of gu-flour.
2.	1(diš) id-gur$_2$ i$_3$	1 *itquru* of oil.
3.	ḫu-ba šagina$^{?}$	(For) Huba, general,
4.	a-dam-šaḫ$_2$^{ki}-ta gen-ni	when he came from Adamšaḫ.
5.	3(diš) sila$_3$ kaš du	3 sila$_3$ of beer, regular (quality).
6.	2(diš) sila$_3$ zi$_3$-gu	2 sila$_3$ of gu-flour.
7.	1(diš) id-gur$_2$ i$_3$	1 *itquru* of oil.
8.	ku$_3$-^{d}nanna lu$_2$ kas$_4$	(For) Ku-Nanna, runner.
9.	2(diš) sila$_3$ kaš du	2 sila$_3$ of regular quality beer.
10.	2(diš) sila$_3$ zi$_3$-gu	2 sila$_3$ of gu flour.
11.	1(diš) id-gur$_2$ i$_3$	1 *itquru* of oil.
12.	u$_3$-na-NE dumu nu-banda$_3$	(For) UnaNE, child of the captain,
13.	mu lu$_2$-^{d}nin-⸢šubur$^{?}$⸣-še$_3$$^{?}$ gen-na-me	when he came instead of Lu-Ninšubur.

left edge

1.	iti munu$_4$-gu$_7$	Month: "Eating Salt?"

Below is an example of an even more complex Type III messenger text.

---

[535] A container for oil or ointments, see *CAD* I–J 300–302.

ICP 1295 (Girsu, X–vii)

obv.

1.	⸢2(barig) 3(ban$_2$) kaš du lugal⸣	2 barig, 3 ban$_2$ beer, regular, (according to the) king('s standard).
2.	2(barig) ⸢3(ban$_2$)⸣ dabin	3 barig, 3 ban$_2$ dabin flour.
3.	⸢5(diš) sila$_3$⸣ i$_3$-geš	5 sila$_3$ sesame oil.
4.	<ša$_3$> iri	(While) within the city.
5.	i-di$_3$-⸢lum$^?$ šagina⸣	(For) Idi-ilum, general,
6.	u$_3$-na-a-du$_{11}$ sukkal-maḫ-ta	(with a) letter of the Sukkal-mah
7.	šušin^{ki}-še$_3$ gen-ni	when he went to Susa.
8.	4(diš) sila$_3$ kaš 4(diš) sila$_3$ ninda	4 sila$_3$ beer. 4 sila$_3$ bread.
9.	2(diš) id-gur$_2$ i$_3$ ša$_3$ iri	2 *itquru* of oil while in the city.

rev.

1.	1(aš) dug dida du	1 dida jar, regular (quality).
2.	1(ban$_2$) zi$_3$ kaskal-še$_3$	1 ban$_2$ of flour while on campaign.
3.	šu-ku-bu-um lu$_2$ ^{geš}tukul	(For) Šu-kubum, the soldier
4.	u$_3$ eb-ku-ša lu$_2$ ^{geš}tukul	and Ebkuša, the soldier
5.	šušin^{ki}-še$_3$ gen-ne-ne	when they went to Susa.
6.	2(diš) sila$_3$ kaš 2(diš) sila$_3$ ninda	2 sila$_3$ beer. 2 sila$_3$ bread.
7.	1(diš) id-gur$_2$ i$_3$	1 *itquru* of oil.
8.	šu-^{d}utu lu$_2$ ^{geš}tukul	(For) Šu-Šamaš, the soldier
9.	šušin^{ki}-ta gen-ni	when he went from Susa.
	(1 line blank)	
10.	iti ezem-^{d}šul-gi	Month: "Festival of Šulgi."

Type IV Messenger Texts

In the archive from Irisagrig, recently edited by David I. Owen (Owen 2013), is a group of about three hundred texts that broadly can be classified together with the messenger texts discussed in this chapter, although they are much more detailed. Whereas most of the messengers in the Umma and Girsu texts held titles of ordinary messengers, most of the messengers in the Irisagrig texts are royal messengers (lu$_2$ kin-gi$_4$-a lugal); and whereas the Umma and Girsu messengers traveled to and from only the eastern periphery of the Ur III state (including Susa), the Irisagrig messengers traveled exclusively to the north-eastern frontier of the Ur III state (Dēr and Diniktum), and to the western part of Iran.

For the sake of completeness, I include two texts from Irisagrig below.

Nisaba 15, 96 (Irisagrig, AS 8–?–8)

obv.

1.	3(diš) sila$_3$ kaš 2(diš) sila$_3$ ninda	3 sila$_3$ beer, 2 sila$_3$ bread.
2.	puzur$_4$-ḫa-ia$_3$ lu$_2$ kin-gi$_4$-a lugal	(For) Puzur-Ḫaya, royal messenger,
3.	u$_4$ zi-daḫ-ru-um^{ki}-ta	the day he from Zidaḫrum
4.	ki lugal-še$_3$ ba-gen-na-a	to the place of the king came.
5.	3(diš) sila$_3$ kaš 2(diš) sila$_3$ ninda	3 sila$_3$ beer, 2 sila$_3$ bread.
6.	lugal-TUG$_2$-maḫ lu$_2$ kin-gi$_4$-a lugal	(For) Lugal-TUGmaḫ, royal messenger,

rev.

1.	u$_4$ gu$_4$-še$_3$ gi$_4$-[gi$_4$-de$_3$] im-gen-[na-a]	the day he came to return the oxen.
2.	3(diš) sila$_3$ kaš 2(diš) sila$_3$ ⸢ninda⸣	3 sila$_3$ beer, 2 sila$_3$ bread.
3.	bi$_2$-za-za lu$_2$ kin-gi$_4$-a lugal	(For) Bizaza, royal messenger,
4.	u$_4$ ki da-da-ni-še$_3$ im-gen-na-a	the day he came to Dadani's place.
5.	šunigin 9(diš) sila$_3$ kaš	Total: 9 sila$_3$ beer.
6.	šunigin 6(diš) sila$_3$ ninda	Total: 6 sila$_3$ bread.
7.	zi-ga iti ezem-^{d}li$_9$-si$_4$	Booked out (in) month: "Festival of Lisi."
8.	mu en eridu^{ki} ba-ḫun	Year: "The En-priest of Eridu was installed."

left edge

1.	u$_4$ 8(diš)-kam	On the 8th day.

Nisaba 15, 127 (Irisagrig, AS 8–?–1)

obv.

1.	5(diš) sila$_3$ kaš 5(diš) sila$_3$ ninda	5 sila$_3$ beer, 5 sila$_3$ bread.
2.	nu-ḫi-dingir lu$_2$ kin-gi$_4$-a lugal	(For) Nuḫi-ilum, royal messenger.
3.	5(diš) sila$_3$ kaš 5(diš) sila$_3$ ninda	5 sila$_3$ of beer, 5 sila$_3$ of bread.
4.	šu-eš$_{18}$-dar lu$_2$ kin-gi$_4$-a lugal	(For) Šu-Eštar, royal messenger,
5.	u$_4$ zaḫ$_3$ lu$_2$ iri-sag-rig$_7$^{ki} dab$_5$-ba-de$_3$ im-e-re-ša-a	the day they came to catch the fugitives, the men of Irisagrig.
6.	1(ban$_2$) kaš 1(ban$_2$) ninda	1 ban$_2$ of beer, 1 ban$_2$ of bread.
7.	1(diš) sila$_3$ nig$_2$-i$_3$-de$_2$-a	1 sila$_3$ of sweet date paste.[536]
8.	i$_3$-li$_2$-ki-ib-ri$_2$ nu-banda$_3$	(For) Ili-kibri, captain,
9.	u$_4$ udu ur$_4$-de$_3$ im-gen-na-a	the day he came to muster (workers) to sheer/pluck sheep.
10.	5(diš) sila$_3$ kaš 5(diš) sila$_3$ ninda	5 sila$_3$ beer, 5 sila$_3$ bread,
11.	i$_3$-li$_2$-ki-ib-ri$_2$ lu$_2$ kin-gi$_4$-a lugal	(For) Ili-kibri, royal messenger.
12.	u$_4$ udu ur$_4$-de$_3$ zi-zi-de$_3$ im-gen-na-a	the day they came to sheer the sheep and pluck(?)
13.	5(diš) sila$_3$ kaš 5(diš) sila$_3$ ninda	5 sila$_3$ beer, 5 sila$_3$ bread,
14.	1(ban$_2$) kaš 1(ban$_2$) ninda	1 ban$_2$ beer, 1 ban$_2$ bread.
15.	šu-eš$_{18}$-dar sukkal lu$_2$ kin-gi$_4$-a lugal	(For) Šu-Eštar, messenger (sukkal), (and) royal messenger,
16.	u$_4$ BAD$_3$.AN^{ki}-še$_3$ ba-gen-na-a	the day he came to Dēr.
17.	3(diš) sila$_3$ kaš 2(diš) sila$_3$ ninda	3 sila$_3$ beer, 2 sila$_3$ bread.
18.	nu-ur$_2$-^{d}iškur lu$_2$ kin-gi$_4$-a lugal	(For) Nur-Adad, royal messenger;

rev.

1.	3(diš) sila$_3$ kaš 2(diš) sila$_3$ ninda	3 sila$_3$ beer, 2 sila$_3$ bread.
2.	^{d}iškur-illat lu$_2$ kin-gi$_4$-a lugal	(For) Adad-tillatī, royal messenger,
3.	u$_4$ si-maš-ku-um^{ki}-še$_3$ ba-e-re-ša-a	when they went to Simaškum.

[536] Owen 2013: 399.

4.	3(diš) sila$_3$ kaš 2(diš) sila$_3$ ninda	3 sila$_3$ beer, 2 sila$_3$ bread,
5.	ur-^{d}nin-mug lu$_2$ kin-gi$_4$-a lugal	(for) Ur-Ninmug, royal messenger,
6.	u$_4$ ki-maš^{ki}-še$_3$ ba-gen-na-a	when he came to Kimaš.
7.	5(diš) sila$_3$ kaš 5(diš) sila$_3$ ninda	5 sila$_3$ beer, 5 sila$_3$ bread,
8.	a-bil-lum-ma lu$_2$ kin-gi$_4$-a lugal	(for) Apilumma, royal messenger;
9.	3(diš) sila$_3$ kaš 2(diš) sila$_3$ ninda	3 sila$_3$ beer, 2 sila$_3$ bread,
10.	ḫu-wa-wa lu$_2$ kin-gi$_4$-a lugal	(for) Ḫuwawa, royal messenger,
11.	u$_4$ ki da-da-ni-še$_3$ im-e-re-ša-a	when they came to the place of Dadani.
	(*blank space*)	
12.	šunigin 5(ban$_2$) 7(diš) sila$_3$ kaš	Total: 5 ban$_2$, 7 sila$_3$ of beer.
13.	šunigin 5(ban$_2$) 3(diš) sila$_3$ ninda	Total: 5 ban$_2$, 3 sila$_3$ of bread.
14.	šunigin 1(diš) sila$_3$ nig$_2$-i$_3$-de$_2$-a	Total: 1 sila$_3$ of sweet date paste.
15.	zi-ga iti še-sag$_{11}$-ku$_5$	Booked out (in) month: Harvest.
16.	mu en eridu^{ki} ba-ḫun	Year: "The En-priest of Eridu was installed."

left edge

1.	u$_4$ 1(diš)-kam	The 1st day.

One messenger text in the collection, No. 195, is too damaged to be transliterated, and is included in the catalogue only.

11

LEGAL TEXTS

Like the letters, Ur III legal texts are notorious for their high content of everyday language and are thus equally difficult to translate. Although most of the Ur III legal texts are in fact administrative documents probably belonging to the sphere of the state, it is just as difficult to link the legal texts to the daily administrative records as it is to link the letters to them.

Legal texts can usually be identified by the inclusion of one or more witnesses, frequent references to the swearing of an oath, and occasional other technical terminology (such as di til-la introducing finished cases, and references to judges, di-ku$_5$, etc.). The simplest of these texts are the loan documents. Taking an oath is rare in loan documents, but not unknown.

Ur III legal texts were first treated systematically by Falkenstein (1956–57). Most recently M. Molina has devoted several studies to the same body of texts (see in particular Molina 2013). I present the Ur III legal texts in the Schøyen Collection below, with minimal commentary.

Purchase Documents

The first text, No. 196, is a court record concerning the purchase of an ox. The document is complete with witnesses.

No. 196. *MS 1716/2 (Umma$^?$, Š 40)*

obv.

1.	1(diš) gu$_4$ dingir-ra-⸢mu⸣	One ox (belonging to) Dingiramu,
2.	ku$_3$-bi 6(diš) ½(diš) ⸢gin$_2$⸣	its silver is 6 ½ shekels of silver.
3.	inim-bi i$_3$-⸢til⸣	The case is closed.[537]
4.	⸢lugal-ma$_2$-gur$_8$⸣ -re-še$_3$	From Lugal-magure,
5.	a-tu-e in-ši-⸢sa$_{10}$⸣	Atu bought it.
6.	igi lu$_2$-kal-la-[še$_3$]	In front of Lu-kala;
7.	igi bi$_2$-da-še$_3$	in front of Bida;
8.	igi lugal-ku$_3$-zu-še$_3$	in front of Lugal-kuzu;
9.	igi ur-sag$_{10}$	in front of Ur-sag;
10.	igi nimgir-an-ne$_2$	in front of Nimgir-Anne.

rev.

1.	lu$_2$ ki inim-ma-me	They are the witnesses.
2.	mu us$_2$-sa e$_2$ puzur$_4$-da-gan$_3$ ba-du$_3$	Year following: "The house at Drehem was built."
	(blank space)	

The second legal text published here, No. 197, concerns the purchase of a house. The beginning and end of the text are not preserved so it is not clear if any special circumstances led to writing it; the names of the sellers and buyers are also not preserved. The governor of Adab, Ḫabaluge, is mentioned after the oath, but his function in the text is not clear.

The tablet's obverse has been patched with a fragment of an unrelated text not dating to the Ur III period (MS 5010A).

---

[537] See Falkenstein 1956–57: 9 n. 4.

No. 197. *MS 5010 (Adab, —)*

obv.

	(beginning missing)	
1.	[. . .]	
2.	1(diš) lu$_{2}$-lal$_{3}$ dumu ur-⸢e$_{2}$⸣-maḫ	1 Lulal, child of Ur-Emaḫ,
3.	1(diš) ur-an-na-ni-a šeš an-na	1 Ur-Annania, brother of Anna,
4.	1(diš) bu-zu-zu dumu ur-⸢du$_{6}$⸣-ku$_{3}$-ga	1 Buzuzu, child of Ur-Dukuga,
5.	1(diš) giri$_{3}$-ni dumu x-[. . .]	Girini, child of . . . ,
6.	1(diš) ad-da-me ⸢dumu⸣ [. . .] la x [. . .]	Addame, child of . . . ,

rev.

1.	1(diš) ur-^{d}ḫa-⸢ia$_{3}$⸣ [. . .]	1 Ur-Ḫaya,
2.	⸢lu$_{2}$⸣ inim-ma-[bi-me]	They are the witnesses.
3.	igi-bi-še$_{3}$ e$_{2}$ ba-[sa$_{10}$]	In front of them (lit.: it), the house was purchased,
4.	mu lugal ba-[pa$_{3}$]	(and) by the name of the king was sworn.
5.	šu ḫa-ba-lu$_{5}$-[ge$_{2}$]	Hand of Ḫabaluge,
6.	ensi$_{2}$ adab^{ki}	governor of Adab.
	(seal impression)	
	(rest missing)	

seal *(illegible)*

Text No. 198 records the transfer of seven oxen, but mentions no price or associated transaction. The text has been grouped with the legal documents simply because it includes both a list of witnesses and the taking of an oath, and is presented with the purchase documents because it records the transfer of some object.

No. 198. *MS 4096 (Umma?[538] ŠS 4–vi)*

obv.

1.	7(diš) gu$_{4}$ geš	7 breeding oxen
2.	ki a-na-ta	from Ana
3.	mu[539] engar-še$_{3}$	on behalf of the cultivators
4.	za$_{3}^{?}$-mu	Zamu
5.	u$_{3}$ da-a	and Daya
6.	in-⸢dab$_{5}^{?}$⸣[540]-eš	seized it.
7.	igi ad-da-kal-la ⸢šabra⸣ gu$_{4}$	In front of Adda-kala, domain unit overseer,
8.	igi ⸢ur⸣-^{d}a-ba-ba nu-banda$_{3}$ gu$_{4}$	In front of Ur-Ababa, captain of plow oxen,
9.	[1(diš)] ⸢lu$_{2}$⸣-^{d}inanna dub-sar	(In front of) Lu-Inanna, scribe,
10.	1(diš) ur-^{d}dumu-zi-da	1 Ur-Dumuzida,
11.	1(diš) ur-^{d}nin-urta ḫa-za-nu-um	1 Ur-Ninurta, city mayor,

[538] See now Owen 2018, suggesting that this text is from an archive from a settlement called Du-Enlila.

[539] Owen 2018 has nam, but mu seems a better fit both with the preserved wedges and content of the text; it is possible that mu is written over an erasure.

[540] Owen 2018 expects lah$_{4/5}$.

rev.

1.	1(diš) du$_{11}$-⸢ga⸣-ni-zi x [. . .] x	1 Duganizi the . . . ,
2.	1(diš) iz-⸢bu⸣-um nu-$^{\langle geš\rangle}$kiri$_6$	1 Izbum, gardener.
3.	1(diš) du$_{11}$-ga-a dumu ur-sukkal	Dugaya, child of Ur-Sukkal,
4.	1(diš) ug$_3$-IL$_2$ dumu ur-dun	UNIL, child of Ur-Dun,
5.	1(diš) lugal-⸢a$_2$⸣-zi-da dub-sar	Lugal-azida, scribe,
6.	igi-⸢bi⸣-še$_3$ mu ⸢lugal⸣ ba-pa$_3$	In front of them (lit.: it), by the name of the king was sworn.
	(seal impression)	
7.	iti šu-numun-a	Month: "Seeding."
8.	mu us$_2$-sa si-ma-num^{ki} ba-ḫul-a	Year after: "Simanum was destroyed."

seal (S004311)

1.	u$_3$-da-mu	Udamu,
2.	dumu ur-du$_6$-ku$_3$-ga	child of Ur-Dukuga.

Loan Documents

There are three loan documents in the Schøyen Collection. The first of these, text No. 199, is a standard loan document, with an interest rate of twenty per cent for the period of the loan. As is often the case, the period of the loan is not explicitly specified, but it is likely that the common deadline for repayment, harvest, was implicit. That would mean that the amount was to be repaid some four months following the date of the loan.

No. 199. *MS 1743 (Nippur, ŠS 7–viii)*

obv.

1.	2(diš) ½(diš) ⸢gin$_2$ ku$_3$-babbar⸣	2 ½ shekels of silver.
2.	maš$_2$ 5(diš) gin$_2$ 1(diš) ⸢gin$_2$⸣-ta	Interest: (in) five shekels (of silver) one shekel each.
3.	ki ad-da-bi-ta	From Addabi,
4.	lugal-a$_2$-zi-da	Lugal-azida

rev.

1.	šu ba-ti	received.
2.	igi ša$_3$-bi-še$_3$	In front of Šabi.
3.	igi giri$_3$-<ni>-i$_3$-sa$_6$	In front of Girini-isa.
4.	iti ^{geš}apin-du$_8$-<a>	Month: "Releasing the plow."
5.	mu za-ab-ša-li ba-⸢ḫul⸣	Year: "Zabšali was destroyed."

The second loan document in the collection, text No. 200, concerns a loan without interest. Here the loan was taken in the twelfth month and the date of the repayment was stated. The period of the loan was approximately three months.

No. 200. *MS 1745 (Nippur, X–xii)*

obv.

1.	1(aš) 2(ban$_2$) še gur	12 gur of barley,
2.	maš$_2$ nu-ub-tuku	having no interest.
3.	ki dingir-ma-<an>-šum$_2$-ta	From Dingir-manšum.

4.	lu$_2$-<gir>-gi$_4$-lu^{ki}	Lu-Girgilu
5.	šu ba-ti	received.

rev.

1.	iti sig$_4$-ga-a	"In the month of the 'Brick'
2.	gi$_4$-gi$_4$-da	it shall be returned."
3.	mu lugal-bi in-pa$_3$	He swore by the name of the king.
4.	igi ur-^{d}nin-imma$_3$	In front of Ur-Nin-imma.
5.	igi$^{!}$(BAR$^{?}$) a-bu-da	In front of Abuda.
6.	lugal-ezem	(In front of) Luga-ezem.
	(*blank line*)	
7.	lu$_2$ inim-ma-bi	They are the witnesses.
8.	iti še-sag$_{11}$-ku$_5$ u$_4$ ⸢2(u)-kam⸣	The 20th day of month: "Harvest."
9.	mu	Year.

seal (S002889)

1.	lu$_2$-<gir>-gi$_4$-<lu^{ki}>	Lu-Girgilu,
2.	dumu ur-zu	child of Urzu.

The third loan document, text No. 201, specifies both the interest (25%) and the period of the loan (from month 10 to month 2 of the following year; the loan is therefore taken out two months before harvest, to be repaid two months after harvest).

No. 201. *MS 4687 (Nippur, Š 43–x)*

obv.

1.	1(diš) gin$_2$ ku$_3$-babbar	1 shekel of silver.
2.	maš$_2$ 1(diš) gin$_2$ igi 4(diš)-gal$_2$	The interest on 1 shekel: one fourth.
3.	⸢ki ḫu-ni-i-a⸣	From Ḫuniya.
4.	lu$_2$-^{d}ba-⸢ba$_6^{?}$⸣	Lu-Baba,
5.	šu ba-an-ti	received.
6.	⸢iti⸣ gu$_4$-si-su	(In the) month: "Gusisu,"
7.	⸢ḫe$_2^{?}$⸣-la$_2$-e	may he repay it.

rev.

1.	igi e$_2$-a-KU-x	In front of Ea-KU-x.
2.	igi puzur$_4$-^{d}utu dub-sar	In front of Puzur-Šamaš, scribe.
	(*blank space*)	
	(*seal impression*)	
3.	iti ab-ba-e$_3$-a	Month: "Abba-ea."[541]
4.	mu en ^{d}nanna!(UD) maš$_2$-e i$_3$-pa$_3$	Year: "The En-priest of Nanna was chosen by omen."

seal (S003057)

1.	lu$_2$-^{d}ba-⸢ba$_6^{?}$⸣	Lu-Baba,
2.	dumu a-ḫu-ma	child of Aḫuma.

[541] This is a known variant of the Nippur month name ku$_3$-ŠIM, but usually written ab-e$_3$ (see Cohen 2015: 153–56).

Miscellaneous Legal Documents

The remaining texts discussed here are not easily placed within the categories discussed above or generally known for Ur III legal texts. For some, this may be due to the fragmentary state of preservation, for others no good reason can be given at present.

No. 202. *MS 1744 (Nippur, X–iii)*

obv.

1.	mu lugal ur-bi	Year: "The king, Urbi(lum)(?)"
2.	iti sig$_4$-gar-ga	Month: "Brick placed at the mold."
3.	ša$_3$ kišib$_3$-ba nu-zu	Of the sealed tablet, unknown(?).
4.	2(u) 4(aš) še gur ⸢ga⸣-zu	24 gur of barley (for) Gazu(?).
5.	mu NI maḫ	Year: "Lofty . . ."
6.	[x] ⸢lu$_2$⸣-isin$_2$[si]	. . . man of Isin.

rev.

1.	⸢igi⸣ ur-^{d}nin-⸢urta⸣	In front of Ur-Ninurta.
2.	[igi] ⸢lu$_2$⸣-nig$_2$-⸢da⸣-[x]	In front of Lu-nigda-x.
3.	[igi] x x x	In front of . . .
4.	⸢igi a⸣-a-⸢kal-la⸣	In front of Aya-kala.
5.	igi e$_2$-⸢ki⸣-bi	In front of Ekibi.
6.	⸢igi?⸣ a-ad-kal-la	In front of Ada-kala.
7.	⸢lu$_2$ inim⸣-bi-še$_3$	They are the witnesses.

left edge

1.	igi amar-muš-x x	In front of Amar-muš-x.

The next text, No. 203, is difficult to understand, not only because the reverse and parts of the obverse are missing, but also because its context is unknown. The terminology, "it/he is to be examined" (en$_3$-bi tar-re-dam) is not uncommon in Ur III documents, but its exact implications are unclear. The text deals with metal objects and mentions the oath of an otherwise unknown silversmith Nar'u. The text has tentatively been assigned a provenience to Umma, based on the personal names occurring in it.

No. 203. *MS 1946 (Umma?, —)*

obv. col. i

1.	1(u) ^{urudu}šen	10 copper cauldrons.
2.	nar-u$_2$ simug nam-erim$_2$-bi ku$_5$-dam	It is the (declaratory)[542] oath of Nar'u, the silver smith,
3.	1(diš) šu-še$_3$-la$_2$^{urudu} en$_3$-bi tar-re-dam	(that) one copper vessel is to be examined,
4.	ku$_3$-anše dam ur-^{d}er$_3$-ra-ka en$_3$-bi tar-re-dam	(that) Ku-anše, wife of Ur-Errak, is to be examined,
5.	[x] 1(u) gu$_4$ nig$_2$-u$_2$-rum gin$_7$ [x] ma$_2$? en$_3$-bi ku$_5$-dam	(that) +10 oxen (of) Nig'urum . . . are to be examined,

[542] Following Molina (2010) for a translation of the German *promisorische* oath.

6.	[x] ⸢tu⸣-di-da ku$_3$ [ki-la$_2$]-bi 5(diš) gin$_2$	(that) x toggle pins of silver, their weight is 5 shekels,
7.	[. . .]-ki en$_3$-bi tar-re-dam	(of . . .) are to be examined,
8.	[x]-za geme-nigar ⸢dam⸣ lugal-ba-ta-e$_3$	(that) . . . of Geme-nigar, wife of Lugal-bata'e, (and)
9.	[. . . bi$_2$]-za-za ku$_3$-sig$_{17}$	. . . frog(s)[543] of gold,
10.	[x] ⸢dam⸣ da-da ugula	of . . . the wife of Dada, the overseer.
	(*rest of col. 1 blank*)	

obv. col. ii

1.	mu ur-ge$_6$-par$_4$-ka-še$_3$	instead of Ur-Gipar,
2.	en$_3$-bi tar-re-dam	are to be examined.
3.	inim-^{d}inanna ib$_2$-gi-ne$_2$	Inim-Inanna confirmed it.
4.	1(diš) bi$_2$-za-za ku$_3$-babbar u$_2$-gu de$_2$-a	1 frog of silver, was lost.
5.	ur-e$_{11}$-e gudu$_4$ zu nam-erim$_2$-bi ku$_5$-dam	It is the oath of Ur-E'e, the gudu$_4$-zu(?) priest,
6.	3(diš) gin$_2$ ku$_3$ dam a-gi$_4$-gi$_4$-ra en$_3$-bi tar-re-dam	(that) 3 shekels of silver of the wife of Agigi is to be examined.
7.	1(u) 2(diš) gin$_2$ ku$_3$ gir$_2$-su^{ki}	12 shekels of silver of Girsu.
8.	ur-e$_{11}$-e nam-erim$_2$-bi ku$_5$-dam	It is the oath of Ur-E'e, . . .
	(*rest of col. ii blank*)	

rev. (*broken*)

Text No. 204 records a sworn statement concerning the loss of a seal. A few texts reports the loss of a sealed tablet (kišib$_3$(-bi), e.g., OrSP 47–49, 411 or SAT 2, 1167), and fewer yet the loss of an actual seal (only BiMes 6, 55 is known to me, see Hallo 1977). These texts use the verb u$_2$-gu—de$_2$, "to lose," whereas the text below simply says that the seal "was not (present)."

No. 204. *MS 2018/1 (Umma, Š 44–i)*[544]

obv.

1.	kišib$_3$ lu$_2$-^{d}nanna	"The seal of Lu-Nanna
2.	za$_3$ iti še-sag$_{11}$-ku$_3$	since[545] month 'Harvest'
3.	mu us$_2$-sa en ^{d}nanna maš$_2$-e i$_3$-pa$_3$-da-še$_3$	of the year after: 'the En-priest of Nanna was chosen by means of omen,'
4.	ur-^{d}nun-gal-ra	with Ur-Nungal

rev.

1.	nu-un-da-gal$_2$-la	it was not (present)."
2.	mu lugal-bi in-pa$_3$	He swore by the name of the king.

---

543 Although bi$_2$-za-za is usually used as a personal name (e.g., text No. 126 obv. ii 3'), it is also found in CST 54 obv. 4 as an object of silver.

544 The tablet is dated to any date after Š 44 month 1.

545 Lit. "to the edge of the month 'Harvest,' of the year . . ."

seal (S005278)

1.	ur-^{d}nun-gal	Ur-Nungal,
2.	dub-sar	scribe,
3.	dumu lugal-e$_2$-maḫ-e	child of Lugal-Emaḫe.

Text No. 205 is both difficult to translate—it includes a hapax—and difficult to situate in the administrative machinery. The text presumably discusses the future fate of a captured runaway slavegirl by the name Geme-Mami. It uses no legal terminology and has no list of witnesses. Although one could have classified it with the Ur III letters, and it may indeed have served a function similar to a letter, it is also devoid of an addressee or a sender.

No. 205. *MS 2020/7 (Umma?, ŠS 4)*

obv.

1.	1(diš) geme$_2$-^{d}ma-⸢mi⸣	1 Geme-Mami,
2.	geme$_2$ lugal-ma$_2$-gur$_8$-re dumu ur-^{geš}gigir	the slavegirl of Lugal-Magure, child of Ur-Gigir,
3.	ki-su$_7$ a-ša$_3$ ⸢^{d}⸣nin-ur$_4$-ra-ka-ta	from the threshing floor of the Nin-ura field,

rev.

1.	še im-ma-an-du$_{11}$	fled(?).[546]
2.	en-nu-ga$_2$ i$_3$-in-ti-la-am$_3$	She is (now) living in the prison.
3.	lugal na-ba-an-šum$_2$	Shouldn't she be given to the king?
4.	mu us$_2$-sa si-ma-num^{ki} ba-hul	Year after: "Simanum was destroyed."

The beginning of text No. 206 is missing, so although the text appears to be similar to the texts recording finished law cases (the so-called di til-la documents), it is impossible to say for certain what it is.

No. 206. *MS 4997 (Adab, —)*

obv.

	(start of obv. missing)	. . .
1'.	⸢ur-^{d}a-ba-ba-ke$_4$⸣	"Ur-Ababa
2'.	mu-da-an-sir$_2$	checked it,"
3'.	bi$_2$-in-du$_{11}$	he said.
4'.	kišib$_3$ di dab$_5$-ba	The sealed document of the verdict
5'.	lu$_2$-du$_{10}$-ga sanga-ka	of Luduga the sanga-official
6'.	gu$_3$ ba-a-de$_2$	was announced.
7'.	zu-zu nimgir ama-na-⸢ka⸣	Zuzu the town-crier of his mother (?)
8'.	i$_3$-ib$_2$-sar	wrote it.

rev.

1.	ur-^{d}a-ba-ba	Ur-Ababa
2.	ba-dadag^{ag}	was cleared (of charges).
3.	igi šeš-da-da ⸢sanga-še$_3$⸣	In front of Šeš-dada, the sanga-official.
4.	⸢igi⸣ lu$_2$-a$_2$-zi-da sukkal	In front of Lu-azida, messenger.

---

[546] A composite verb še—du$_{11}$ is unknown, and may be a scribal error for kas$_4$ . . . du$_{11}$ "to flee."

5.	[igi] x-gu dumu e$_2$-nam-ti-e	In front of . . . , child of E-namti.
6.	[igi] x-^{d}da-mu ugula kaš	[In front of] x-Damu, overseer of beer.
7.	[igi] ⸢šeš⸣-kal-la ugula šu-ku$_6$	[In front of] Šeš-kala, overseer of the fishermen.
8.	[igi] ⸢ad⸣-da-kal-la dub-sar	[In front of] Adda-kala, the scribe.
9.	[igi ^{d}]en-lil$_2$-da gu-za-la$_2$	[In front of] Enlilda, the "throne-bearer."
10.	[igi] ⸢dingir⸣-i$_3$-li$_2$ ša$_{13}$-dub-<ba>	[In front of] Dingir-ili, the archivist.
11.	⸢lu$_2$⸣ inim-ma-[x]	They are the witnesses.
	(rest of rev. missing)	. . . . . .

Text No. 207 is perhaps to be classified as a purchase document, based on the presence of the phrase, "was received." However, the text is damaged and I have placed it in this section.

No. 207. *MS 4422 (Umma$^{?}$, Š 44)*

obv.

1.	x [. . .] nanna	. . .
2.	nam$^{?}$ [. . .] dingir maḫ	. . .
3.	šu ba-ti-a	was received.
4.	ša-at-ma-mi dumu-mi$_2$ geme$_2$-^{d}nanna	Šat-Mami, the daughter of Geme-Nanna,
5.	nu-ur$_2$-i$_3$-li$_2$	Nur-Ili,
6.	mar-ši-GAR	(and) MaršiGAR,
7.	mu lugal in-pa$_3$	swore by the name of the king.
8.	1(diš) igi-dingir-ba-ni	1 Pan-ili-bani.
9.	1(diš) ba-zi-a	1 Bazia.
10.	1(diš) ur-nigar^{gar}	1 Ur-Nigar.
11.	1(diš) ⸢šu-^{d}⸣utu	1 Šu-Šamaš
12.	1(diš) x-[. . .]-x	1 . . .
	(*rest missing*)	

rev.

	(*start missing*)	
1'.	[. . .]-⸢me$^{?}$⸣	They are . . .
2'.	[. . .]-x	. . .
3'.	1(diš) [. . .]-x	1 . . .
4'.	1(diš) [. . .]-5(diš)	1 . . . five.
5'.	[. . .]-nanna dumu [. . .]-⸢i$_3$⸣-li$_2$	. . .-Nanna, child of . . .-Ili.
6'.	1(diš) me-⸢ba-ba⸣ dam ⸢ku-li⸣	1 Me-Baba, spouse of Kuli.
7'.	1(diš) bu$^{?}$-la-num dub-sar	1 Bulanum, scribe.
8'.	lu$_2$ inim-ma-bi-me	They are the witnesses.
9'.	igi-bi-še$_3$ mu lugal in-pa$_3$	In front of them they swore by the name of the king.
10'.	mu lu-lu-bu-um^{ki} ba-ḫul$^{!}$(ŠE$_3$)	Year: "Lulubum was destroyed."

seal (*illegible*)

The content of the final text is unclear to me. It uses legal terminology and is therefore placed here.

No. 208. *MS 4685 (Umma, ŠS 4)*

obv.

1.	⸢2(aš)⸣ [. . .]	2 gur . . .
2.	kaš aga$_3$-us$_2$	beer (for the) police officer(s).
3.	giri$_3$ ku$_3$-ga-ni	Conveyor: Kugani.
4.	ša$_3$ a$_2$ u$_4$-da	Of the "daily" (delivery?).
5.	kišib$_3$ ḫu-wa-wa-ka	Sealed tablet of Ḫuwawa
6.	tur-re-dam	is to be returned.
7.	kišib$_3$ lu$_2$-kal-la	Sealed tablet of Lu-kala.
8.	mu ^{d}šu-^{d}suen lugal	(of) the year: "Šu-Suen (was) king."
9.	kišib$_3$-bi ki ḫu-wa-wa-ta	Its sealed tablet, from Ḫuwawa

rev.

1.	lu$_2$-kal-la	Lu-kala
2.	šu ba-ti	received.
3.	a$_2$-e$_3$ giri$_3$ lu$_2$ nig$_2$-dab$_5$-ba-ke$_4$-ne-ka	The adoptees, through the nig$_2$-dab$_5$ staff,
4.	igi kar$_2$-kar$_2$-de$_3$	are to be examined.
5.	gaba-ri kišib$_3$ lu$_2$-kal-la	Copy of sealed tablet of Lu-kala.
	(blank line)	
6.	mu bad$_3$ mar-tu ba-du$_3$	Year: "The Martu wall was built."

12
MISCELLANEOUS TEXTS

It is with some disappointment that I have to leave thirty-seven texts in this final chapter under the heading miscellaneous texts.[547] These texts are not necessarily placed here because they are difficult to translate, rather because they do not easily fit into any of the categories of texts established above, or because their broken state does not allow an easy identification. For most of the texts in this chapter comments are therefore minimal.

An Inventory of Date Palms

Although the date palm is today seen as the quintessential Mesopotamian tree, it is not attested in economic records in any great numbers before the Ur III period. A few Old Akkadian inventories of date palms exist,[548] and a good number from the Ur III period. Dates were known much earlier, but the extensive management found in the Ur III documents, where trees were labeled according to yield, is unknown before the Old Akkadian period.

Most of the left edge of text No. 209 is missing, and a piece of another tablet has been glued to it. Too little of that tablet is preserved to make any meaningful interpretation.

No. 209. *MS 4694 (Umma$^?$, AS 7)*

obv.

1.	2(diš) geš 4(ban$_2$)	2 trees, 4 ban$_2$ (each).
2.	1(diš) geš 2(ban$_2$)	1 tree, 2 ban$_2$.
3.	1(diš) geš 1(ban$_2$)	1 tree, 1 ban$_2$.
4.	[x] 4(diš) geš ḫi-a zu$_2$-lum 1(barig) 5(ban$_2$)	4 trees, mixed, (their) dates: 1 barig, 5 ban$_2$.
5.	e$_2$-gal-e-si	(of) Egal-esi.
6.	⸢1(diš)⸣ geš 1(ban$_2$) 5(diš) sila$_3$	1 tree, 1 ban$_2$, 5 sila$_3$.
7.	[3(diš)] geš 5(diš) sila$_3$ 1(diš) geš ⸢ša$_3$ su$_{13}$⸣	3 trees, 5 sila$_3$; 1 tree, fallow.
8.	[x] 4(diš) geš zu$_2$-lum-bi 3(ban$_2$) 5(diš) sila$_3$	4 trees, their dates: 3 ban$_2$, 5 sila$_3$.
9.	uš-⸢dam⸣	(of) Ušdam.
10.	[2(diš)$^?$] geš 1(ban$_2$)	2(?) trees, 1 ban$_2$.
11.	[2(diš)$^?$] geš 5(diš) sila$_3$	2(?) trees, 5 sila$_3$.
12.	[3(diš)] ⸢geš⸣ 2(diš) sila$_3$ 5(diš) geš ša$_3$ su$_{13}$	3 trees, 2 sila$_3$; 5 trees, fallow.
13.	[7(diš)] ⸢geš⸣ ḫi-a zu$_2$-lum-bi 3(ban$_2$) 6(diš) sila$_3$	7 trees, mixed, their dates: 3 ban$_2$, 6 sila$_3$.
14.	[x] ⸢ḪI$^?$ DIN$^?$⸣	. . .
15.	[x] ⸢lu$_2^?$⸣ NI x	. . .

rev.

1.	[n] geš 1(ban$_2$) 5(diš) sila$_3$	*n* trees, 1 ban$_2$, 5 sila$_3$.
2.	[n] geš ša$_3$ su$_{13}$	*n* trees, fallow.
3.	[n] geš	*n* trees.
4.	[4(diš)$^?$] geš 1(ban$_2$) 5(diš) sila$_3$	4(?) trees, 1 ban$_2$, 5 sila$_3$.
5.	[2(diš)$^?$] geš 1(ban$_2$)	2(?) trees, 1 ban$_2$.

[547] Three other texts, classified as miscellaneous in the catalog, have been presented already (Nos. 25, 26, and 38).

[548] See, e.g., the laconic text JCS 35, 211, 3, or the text Lippmann Coll 84 recording trees and yield, or the text MAD 5, 106 listing only trees.

6.	[2(diš)$^{?}$] geš 5(diš) sila$_3$	2(?) trees, 5 sila$_3$.
7.	[6(diš)$^{?}$] geš ša$_3$ su$_{13}$	6(?) trees, fallow.
8.	[n] 1(u) 4(diš) geš ⸢ḫi-<a> zu$_2$⸣-lum-bi 1(barig) 3(ban$_2$)	n+14 trees, mixed, their dates: 1 barig, 3 ban$_2$.
9.	[x] DU-DU x	. . .
	(*blank space*)	. . .
10.	zu$_2$-lum kab$_2$ du$_{11}$-ga	Measured date (palms),
11.	e$_2$ ^{d}nin-⸢ur$_4$-ra⸣	(of the) house of Nin-ura.
12.	mu ḫu-ḫu-nu-ri^{ki} ba-ḫul	Year: "Ḫuḫnuri was destroyed."

An Inventory of Fallen Cattle

Although this text has clear administrative links to other texts concerning cowherds, including the inventories published in Chapter 8, I include it here as it is unclear where in the administrative hierarchy it should be placed, and since it may be more of an occasional text than the inventories discussed in that chapter.

No. 210. *MS 1845 (Umma, AS 6–xii)*

obv. col. i

1.	uš$_2$ 1(diš) gu$_4$ geš	Dead: 1 yoke-ox,
2.	⸢da⸣-du engar	(of) Dadu, cultivator.
3.	1(diš) gu$_4$ ga	1 ox, suckling
4.	⸢lugal⸣-e$_2$-maḫ-e engar	(of) Lugal-Emaḫ(e), cultivator.
5.	ugula ur-^{geš}gigir šabra	Overseer: Ur-Gigir, chief (agricultural) administrator.
6.	1(diš) ⸢gu$_4$[549] geš⸣	1 yoke-ox,
7.	1(diš) ab$_2$ ga	1 cow, suckling,
8.	ša$_3$-igi-na engar	(of) Ša-igina, cultivator.
9.	2(diš) gu$_4$ geš šu-eš$_{18}$-dar engar	2 yoke-oxen, (of) Šu-Eštar, cultivator.
10.	1(diš) šu gu$_4$ 1(diš) gu$_4$ mu 1(aš)	1 old(?) ox, 1 ox, one year old,
11.	1(diš) ab$_2$ ga	1 cow, suckling,
12.	1(diš) gu$_4$ ga	1 ox, suckling,
13.	ur-^{d}utu engar dumu bar-ra an	(of) Ur-Utu, cultivator, child of Barran.
14.	ugula ur-^{geš}gigir nu-banda$_3$-gu$_4$	Overseer: Ur-gigir, captain of plow oxen.
15.	1(diš) gu$_4$ mu 2(aš)	1 ox, two years old,
16.	1(diš) gu$_4$ ga u$_2$-gu de$_2$-a	1 ox, suckling, lost,
17.	ḫa$^{!}$(ZA)-an-da engar	(of) Ḫanda, cultivator.
18.	1(diš) gu$_4$ geš 1(diš) gu$_4$ mu 1(aš)	1 yoke-ox, 1 ox, one year old,
19.	ur-^{d}utu engar	(of) Ur-Utu, cultivator.
20.	1(diš) gu$_4$ ga lu$_2$-^{d}er$_3$-ra	1 ox, suckling, (of) Lu-Erra, cultivator.
21.	ugula lugal-e$_2$-maḫ-e <<1(diš)>>	Overseer: Lugal-Emaḫe.
22.	1(diš) ab$_2$ maḫ$_2$ lu$_2$-kal-la	1 adult cow, (of) Lu-kala.
23.	1(diš) ab$_2$ maḫ$_2$ lugal-^{geš}gigir-re engar	1 adult cow, (of) Lugal-gigire, cultivator.
24.	1(diš) gu$_4$ geš kal-la engar	1 yoke-ox, Kala, cultivator.
25.	⸢ugula⸣ ba-sa$_6$	Overseer: Basa.

[549] Erasure after gu$_4$.

obv. col. ii

1.	1(diš) šu gu$_4$	1 old ox,
2.	1(diš) gu$_4$ mu 1(aš)	1 ox, one year old,
3.	2(diš) ab$_2$ ga	2 cows, suckling,
4.	ur-^{d}nin-zu engar	(of) Ur-Ninzu, cultivator.
5.	1(diš) gu$_4$ geš	1 yoke-ox,
6.	inim-ma-ni-zi engar	(of) Inimani-zi, cultivator.
7.	1(diš) ab$_2$ maḫ$_2$	1 adult cow,
8.	1(diš) gu$_4$ geš	1 yoke-ox,
9.	ur-sukkal engar	(of) Ur-Sukkal, cultivator.
10.	2(diš) eme$_6$ maḫ$_2$	2 adult female onagers,
11.	ur-e$_2$-maḫ	(of) Ur-Emaḫ(e).
12.	1(diš) gu$_4$ geš	1 yoke-ox,
13.	kilim$^?$-u engar	(of) Kilim'u, cultivator.
14.	ugula da-x-mu	Overseer: Da- . . . -mu.
15.	1(diš) eme$_6$ maḫ$_2$	1 adult female onager,
16.	ur-⸢gu$_2$-de$_3$⸣-na engar	(of) Ur-Gudena, cultivator.
17.	ugula lugal-nesag-e	Overseer: Lugal-nesage.
18.	1(diš) gu$_4$ ga	1 ox, suckling,
19.	lugal-^{geš}gigir-re engar	(of) Lugal-Gigire, cultivator.
20.	1(diš) gu$_4$ geš	1 yoke-ox,
21.	lugal-ezem engar	(of) Lugal-ezem, cultivator.
22.	1(diš) eme$_6$ maḫ$_2$	1 adult female onager,
23.	ur-^{d}nun-gal	(of) Ur-Nungal.
24.	ugula lugal-ukken-ne$_2$	Overseer: Lugal-ukkene.
25.	1(diš) ab$_2$ ⸢maḫ$_2$⸣	1 adult cow,

rev. col. i

1.	ur-kišib$_3$-la$_2$ engar	(of) Ur-kišib-la, cultivator.
2.	1(diš) gu$_4$ mu 3(aš)	1 ox, three years old,
3.	1(diš) ab$_2$ ga	1 cow, suckling,
4.	lugal-za$_3$-ge-si engar	(of) Lugal-zage-si, cultivator.
5.	1(diš) dur$_3$ geš	1 yoke-mule(?),[550]
6.	gu-u$_2$-gu-a engar	(of) Gu'ugu'a, cultivator.
7.	1(diš) ab$_2$ maḫ$_2$	1 adult cow,
8.	lugal-me-lam$_2$ engar	(of) Lugal-melam, cultivator.
9.	1(diš) ab$_2$ ga	1 cow, suckling,
10.	ur-⸢saga⸣-mu engar	(of) Ur-sagamu, cultivator.
11.	ugula i$_7$-⸢pa-e$_3$⸣	Overseer: I-pa'e.
12.	1(diš) ⸢eme$_6$⸣ maḫ$_2$	1 adult female onager,
13.	lu$_2$-^{d}x ⸢engar⸣	(of) Lu- . . . , cultivator.
14.	1(diš) ⸢gu$_4$ geš⸣	1 yoke-ox,
15.	gu-na engar	(of) Guna, cultivator.

[550] Here geš may refer to the yoke, or be phonetic for geš$_3$, representing the breeding animal (cf. nn. 31, 74).

16.	1(diš) ⸢gu$_4$ mu⸣ 1(aš)	1 ox, one year old,
17.	1(diš) ab$_2$ ga	1 cow, suckling,
18.	lugal-ezem engar	(of) Lugal-ezem, cultivator.
19.	ugula lugal-ku$_3$-zu	Overseer: Lugal-kuzu.
	(*blank space*)	

rev. col. ii

	(*blank space*)	
1.	gu$_4$ anše ri-ri-ga	Oxen and onagers, fallen,
2.	nu-banda$_3$ gu$_4$-ke$_4$-ne	of the captains of plow-teams.
3.	iti ^{d}dumu-zi	Month: "Dumuzi."
4.	mu ša-aš-ru^{ki} ba-ḫul	Year: "Šašru was destroyed."
	(*blank space*)	

An Inventory of the Treasury of Alim-maḫ

Text No. 211 is an inventory of the treasury of the deity Alim-maḫ. Many of the products remain unknown but are probably names of beads or parts of inlays. It does not make sense to try to translate many of these, and I have only done so when the meaning is certain.

No. 211. *MS 2011 (Umma, AS 7)*

obv. col. i

1.	1(u) 1(diš) tu-di-da ku$_3$-babbar	11 toggle pins, silver.
2.	ki-la$_2$-bi ⅓(diš) ma-na 6(diš) gin$_2$	Their weight: ⅓ ma-na, 6 shekels.
3.	u$_3$	And,
4.	4(diš) tu-di-da ku$_3$-babbar	4 toggle pins, silver.
5.	ki-la$_2$-bi 1(u) 1(diš) gin$_2$ mu-ku$_x$(DU) gibil$^?$	Their weight: 11 shekels. New mu-ku$_x$(DU) delivery.
6.	4(diš) har ku$_3$-babbar	4 rings, silver.
7.	ki-la$_2$-bi ⅔(diš) ma-na 6(diš) gin$_2$	Their weight: ⅔ ma-na, 6 shekels.
8.	1(diš) tu-di-da za-gul sag KWU474 ku$_3$-sig$_{17}$	1 toggle pin, head of carnelian, . . . of gold.
9.	[x] kišib$_3$ za-gin$_3$ ku$_3$-sig$_{17}$ gar	*n* seals, lapis lazuli, set in gold (i.e., with gold caps).
10.	[x] ⸢kišib$_3$⸣ za-gin$_3$ zabar gar	*n* seals, lapis lazuli, set in bronze.
11.	[x] ⸢kišib$_3$⸣ za-gin$_3$	*n* seals, lapis lazuli.
12.	[x] ⸢kišib$_3$ za⸣-gin$_3$ tur	*n* seals, lapis lazuli, small.
13.	[. . .]⸢NE$^?$⸣	. . .
	(*rest broken*)	

obv. col. ii

1.	1(geš$_2$) bur zabar KU-bi uruda	60 bronze bowls, their . . . copper.
2.	ki-la$_2$-bi 5(diš) ma-na 4(diš) gin$_2$	Their weight: 5 ma-na, 4 shekels.
3.	1(u) 6(diš) tu-di-da zabar	16 toggle pins, bronze.
4.	ki-la$_2$-bi 1(diš) ma-na	Their weight: 1 ma-na.
5.	ša$_3$-ba 5(diš) tu-di-da ka-ba ku$_3$ nigin$_2$-na 2(diš) tu-di-da ka-ba an-na nigin$_2$-na i$_3$-in-gal$_2$	Among them are 5 toggle pins, their openings wound with silver; 2 toggle pins, their openings wound with tin.

6.	1(geš$_2$) 3(u) 5(diš) za-gul zalag$_2$	95 (pieces of) carnelian, bright.
7.	1(geš$_2$) 5(u) 3(diš) za-aḫ ku$_3$-sig$_{17}$	113 (pieces of) za-aḫ of gold.
8.	1(geš$_2$) ^{geš}bulug$_3$ za-gin$_3$	60 . . . of lapis lazuli.
9.	2(u) la$_2$ 1(aš) nir$_3$ ka-ba ku$_3$-sig$_{17}$	19 nir$_3$ (stones), their openings of gold.
10.	4(diš) za-tu-tu-bi ku$_3$-sig$_{17}$	4 za-tu-tu-bi of gold.
11.	2(aš) gu$_2$ za-gin$_3$ zalag$_2$	2 talent (sized blocks) of lapis lazuli, bright.
12.	gid$_2$-bi ½(diš) kuš-ta	Their length: ½ cubit each.
13.	1(geš$_2$) nir$_3$ zalag$_2$	60 nir$_3$ (stones), bright.
14.	1(geš$_2$) za-gin$_3$ ka-ba ku$_3$-sig$_{17}$	60 (pieces of) lapis lazuli, their opening of gold.
15.	[. . .] x 4(diš) za-gul	. . . 4 (pieces of) carnelian.
16.	[. . .] x ku$_3$-babbar esir$_2$-a [. . .] i$_3$-gal$_2$	. . . silver, set in bitumen . . .
	(*rest broken*)	

obv. col. iii

1.	2(u) 1(diš) ^{na4}nig$_2$ ki nu gu$_7$	21 nig$_2$ stones, not . . .
2.	9(diš) za-aḫ za-gin$_3$	9 (pieces of) za-aḫ of lapis lazuli.
3.	9(diš) za-aḫ šuba$_3$ ku$_3$-sig$_{17}$	9 (pieces of) za-aḫ of agate(?) (and) gold.
4.	8(diš) KWU543 me-e$_3$	8 . . . .
5.	1(u) 1(diš) za-aḫ al-ga-um	11 (pieces of) za-aḫ of al-ga-um.
6.	2(diš) nir$_3$ igi min	2 nir$_3$ (stones), double eyes.
7.	2(diš) na$_4$ za-gul ze$_2$	2 carnelian stones, cut(?).[551]
8.	5(diš) KWU543 e$_3$ zu$_2$-lum	5 . . . dates . . .
9.	1(u) 6(diš) nir$_3$ umbin	16 nir$_3$ (stones), wheel?
10.	1(u) 4(diš) ^{geš}bulug$_3$ nir$_3$	14 . . . of nir$_3$ (stone)
11.	1(diš) nir$_3$ igi	1 nir$_3$ (stone), eyes.
12.	1(diš) šuba$_3$ ku$_3$-sig$_{17}$ ḫuš-a dim$_2$-ma	1 (piece of) agate(?), fashioned with red gold.
13.	2(u) 8(diš) ^{na4}ša-e$_2$	28 ša-e$_2$ stones.
14.	1(diš) šuba$_3$	1 (piece of) agate(?).
15.	1(diš) za-gul gid$_2$-da	1 (piece of) carnelian, long.
16.	1(diš) ^{na4}x-[. . .]	1 . . . stone
17.	2(geš'u) 2(u) 7(diš) ⸢za⸣-[. . .]	147 . . .
18.	5(diš) ⸢šuba$_3$⸣ [. . .]	5 (pieces of) agate(?) . . .
19.	1(diš) za-aḫ ⸢zabar⸣ [. . .]	1 (piece of) za-aḫ of bronze . . .
20.	1(geš'u) 7(diš) aš x [. . .]	67 . . .
	(*rest broken*)	

rev. col. i

	(*beginning broken*)	
1'.	5(u) ⸢8(diš)⸣ [. . .]	58 . . .
2'.	2(diš) za-aḫ ⸢zabar?⸣ [. . .]	2 (pieces of) za-aḫ of bronze . . .
3'.	1(diš) na$_4$ mušen x [. . .]	1 bird stone(?) . . .
4'.	5(u) 3(diš) za-aḫ za-[gin$_3$ . . .]	53 (pieces of) za-aḫ of lapis lazuli.
5'.	4(diš) nir$_3$ igi [. . .]	4 nir$_3$ (stones), eyes . . .

[551] See n. 370.

6'.	1(u) 5(diš) za-gul KA [. . .]	15 (pieces of) carnelian, . . .
7'.	5(diš) ^{na4}nig$_2$ ki nu [gu$_7^?$]	5 nig$_2$ stones not . . .
8'.	2(u) la$_2$ 1(diš$_{tenû}$) za-aḫ šuba$_3$ [. . .]	19 (pieces of) za-aḫ of agate(?).
9'.	2(diš) ^{geš}bulug$_3$ mušen-du$_3$ ⌜gi$^?$⌝ [. . .]	2 . . . bird trapper . . . reed . . .
10'.	9(diš) KWU543 me-e$_3$	9 . . .
11'.	1(diš) za-gul kun-gir$_2$	1 (piece of) carnelian, "knife-tail."
12'.	7(diš) ^{geš}bulug$_3$ nir$_3$	7 . . . of nir$_3$ (stone).
13'.	1(u) 7(diš) za-aḫ šuba$_3$ ku$_3$-sig$_{17}$	17 (pieces of) za-aḫ of agate(?) (and) gold.
14'.	9(diš) za-aḫ al-ga-um	9 (pieces of) za-aḫ of al-ga-um.
15'.	1(u) 3(diš) ^{na4}ša-e$_2$	13 ša-e$_2$ stones.
16'.	1(diš) ^{geš}bulug$_3$ bur	1 . . .
17'.	4(u) 3(diš) nir$_3$ umbin	43 nir$_3$ (stones), wheel(?).
18'.	2(diš) ^{na4}⌜zu⌝-a	2 zu-a stones.
19'.	1(u) 5(diš) ^{na4}nig$_2$ ki nu-gu$_7$ zalag$_2$	15 nig$_2$ stones, not . . . , bright.
20'.	2(diš) nir$_3$ a$_2$ suh ku$_3$-sig$_{17}$ gar	2 nir$_3$ (stones) . . . set in gold.
21'.	1(geš'u) 1(geš$_2$) 1(u) 3(diš) za-aḫ za-gul zalag$_2$	673 (pieces of) za-aḫ of bright carnelian.
22'.	7(geš$_2$) 2(u) 7(diš) aš x ku$_3$-sig$_{17}$	447 . . . . , gold.
23'.	4(u) 6(diš) nir$_3$ zalag$_2$	46 nir$_3$ (stones), bright.
24'.	1(diš) ^{geš}bulug$_3$ za-gul ku$_3$-sig$_{17}$ gar	1 . . . of carnelian, set in gold.
25'.	1(diš) šuba$_3$ ku$_3$-babbar ḫuš-a dim$_2$-ma	1 (piece of) agate(?), fashioned in red silver.
26'.	1(diš) ḫe$_2$-eb$_2$ za-gin$_3$	1 ḫe$_2$-eb$_2$ of lapis lazuli.

rev. col. ii

	(beginning broken)	
1'.	[. . .] x	. . .
2'.	[. . .] ku$_3$-sig$_{17}$	. . . , gold.
3'.	[. . .]⌜4(u)⌝ nir$_3$ ku$_3$-sig$_{17}$ gar	*n*+40 nir$_3$ (stones), set in gold.
4'.	x gu$_2$ min-a-kam	. . . . , second time.
	(blank space)	
5'.	2(u) 4(diš) tug$_2$ uš-bar	24 textiles, weaver (quality).
6'.	1(u) 2(diš) tug$_2$ nig$_2$-lam$_2$ us$_2$	12 nig$_2$-lam$_2$ textiles, lesser (quality).
7'.	1(diš) tug$_2$ a-zu BAD	1 a-zu textile, BAD (quality).
8'.	2(diš) tug$_2$ guz-za 4(diš)-kam us$_2$	2 guz-za textiles, 4th class, lesser (quality).
9'.	4(diš) tug$_2$ uš-bar ka-aḫ	4 textiles, weaver (quality), . . .
10'.	2(diš) tug$_2$ nig$_2$-lam$_2$ ka-aḫ	2 nig$_2$-lam$_2$ textiles, . . .
11'.	1(diš) tug$_2$ gu$_2$-la$_2$ nig$_2$-eb	1 . . . textiles.
12'.	1(u) la$_2$ 1(diš$_t$) gada du	9 (pieces of) linen, regular (quality).
13.	1(diš) gada maḫ	1 (piece of) linen, large.
14'.	2(diš) gada du BAD	2 (pieces of) linen, regular (quality), BAD.
15'.	7(diš) gada nig$_2$-eb	7 (pieces of) linen, nig$_2$-eb.
16'.	2(diš) tug$_2$ NIG$_2$.MI$_2$.LAL.SAG[552] du	2 headbands (for women), running (quality)
17'.	2(diš) tug$_2$ NIG$_2$ NE zu an	2 . . . . textiles.
	(blank space)	

[552] Possibly to be read b a l l a$_2$: see Al-Mutawalli and Sallaberger 2017: 173.

18'.	2(diš) ḫar zabar	2 rings, bronze,
19'.	ki-la$_2$-bi ⅓(diš) ma-na la$_2$ 1(u) gin$_2$	their weight: ⅓ ma-na minus 10 shekels.
20'.	mu-ku$_x$(DU) gibil	mu-ku$_x$(DU) delivery, new.
	(blank space)	

rev. col. iii

	(beginning broken)	
1'.	[. . .] gal$_2$-la	. . . existing.
2'.	[. . .] x u$_4$ ki-la$_2$-bi igi 4(diš)-gal$_2$	. . . its weight: ¼ (of a ma-na?)
3'.	[. . .] x za gal x ku$_3$-babbar gar	. . . set in silver.
4'.	[. . .] x tu-di-da zabar	. . . toggle pins, bronze.
5'.	[ki-la$_2$]-˹bi˺ 1(diš) ⅓(diš) ma-na	Their weight: 1 ⅓ ma-na.
6'.	[. . .] ˹tu-di-da˺ igi še$_3^?$-a	. . . toggle pins . . .
7'.	x tu-di-da zabar	. . . toggle pins, bronze.
8'.	[ki-la$_2$]-˹bi˺ 1(diš) ⅓(diš) ma-na 4(diš) gin$_2$	Their weight: 1 ⅓ ma-na 4 shekels.
9'.	1(diš) ḫe$_2$-eb$_2$ za-gin$_3$	1 ḫe$_2$-eb$_2$ of lapis lazuli.
	(blank space)	
10'.	mu-ku$_x$(DU) gibil ki ga$_2$-ga$_2$	mu-ku$_x$(DU) deliveries, new, to be placed(?).
	(blank space)	
11'.	gil-sa ^{d}alim-maḫ	Treasury of Alim-mah.
12'.	mu ḫu-uḫ$_2$-nu-ri^{ki} ba-hul	Year: "Ḫuḫnuri was destroyed."

An Exercise Tablet?

Text No. 212 (MS 4898) is complete with month and year-name, but its content is difficult to understand and the text may ultimately be an exercise tablet.

No. 212. *MS 4898 (X, IS 2)*

obv.

1.	1(diš) DAG a-ra$_2$ 1(diš)-kam	1 . . . , for the first time.
2.	4(diš) a-ra$_2$ 2(diš)-kam	4 (. . .), for the second time.
3.	1(diš) a-ra$_2$ 3(diš)-kam	1 (. . .), for the third time.
4.	3(diš) a-ra$_2$ 4(diš)-kam	3 (. . .), for the fourth time.
5.	2(diš) a-ra$_2$ 5(diš)-kam	2 (. . .), for the fifth time.
6.	˹1(diš)˺ a-ra$_2$ 6(diš)-kam	1 (. . .), for the sixth time.
7.	1(diš) a-ra$_2$ 7(diš)-kam	1 (. . .), for the seventh time.
8.	1(diš) a-ra$_2$ 8(diš)-kam	1 (. . .), for the eighth time.
9.	2(diš) a-ra$_2$ 1(u) la$_2$ 1(diš$_{tenû}$)-kam	2 (. . .), for the ninth time.
10.	1(diš) a-ra$_2$ 1(u)-kam	1 (. . .), for the tenth time.

rev.

1.	i$_3$ nar nita$_2$	Oil (for?) male singers.
2.	ki šeš-šeš	From Šeššeš.
3.	gal$_2$-la	Is present.
	(blank space)	

4.	iti še-sag$_{11}$-⸢ku$_5$⸣	Month: "Harvest."
5.	mu us$_2$-sa ^{d}i-bi$_2$-^{d}suen lugal	Year after: "Ibbi-Suen (was) king."

The Volume of Ditches and Canals

This broken text, No. 213, calculates the volume of several ditches or canals. The canals originate at the opening (mouth) of the Barla canal. However, a Barla canal is not otherwise attested. The text gives the name of a conveyor and the year-name.

No. 213. *MS 4715/5 (X, ŠS 3)*

obv.

1.	ka i$_7$ bar-la-ta	From the mouth of the Barla canal.
2.	½(diš) ninda dagal 5(diš) kuš$_3$	½ ninda width, 5 cubits (depth).
3.	5(u) 2(diš) ninda gid$_2$ 4(diš) kuš$_3$ bur$_3$	52 ninda length, 4 cubits depth.
4.	a-ša$_3$-bi 1(geš$_2$) 3(u) 5(diš) ⅓(diš) sar	Its field (~dirt): 95 ⅓ (volume-)sar
5.	4(diš) sar saḫar daḫ-ḫu	4 sar dirt is added.
6.	½(diš) ninda dagal 5(diš) kuš$_3$	½ ninda width, 5 cubits (depth),
7.	4(u) 5(diš) ninda gid$_2$ 6(diš) kuš$_3$ bur$_3$	45 ninda length, 6 cubits depth.
8.	a-ša$_3$ 2(geš$_2$) 3(diš) ⅔(diš) sar 5(diš) gin$_2$	(Its) field (~dirt): 123 ⅔ (volume-)sar and 5 gin$_2$.[553]
9.	½(diš) ninda dagal 5(diš) kuš$_3$	½ ninda width, 5 cubits (depth)
10.	1(geš$_2$) ⸢3(u)⸣ ninda gid$_2$ ⸢5(diš)⸣ ½(diš) kuš$_3$ bur$_3$	90 ninda length, 5 ½ cubits (depth)
	(rest broken)	

rev.

	(beginning broken)	
	(blank space)	
1'.	šunigin 5(geš$_2$) 4(u) ninda gid$_2$	Total: 340 ninda length.
2'.	saḫar-bi 1(geš'u) sar	Its dirt: 600 (volume-)sar.
3'.	saḫar zi-zi i$_7$ bar-la i$_7$ lugal	Dirt lifted (from the) Barla canal (and) the "King's Canal."
4'.	giri$_3$ ur-ba-ba	Conveyor: Ur-Baba.
	(blank space)	
5'.	mu si-ma-num$_2$^{ki} ba-ḫul	Year: "Simanum was destroyed."

A Field Plan Without a Drawing

Text No. 214 gives the area of four fields and their expected yield. Such texts were discussed in Nissen, Damerow and Englund 1993 and again in Friberg 2007. The transliteration here follows the mental map of the calculations rather than the actual line numbering. The measurement and production of each field is written within a box, with the first length measurement written vertically against the left side of the box (here a.1), and the second against the top (a.2). In the case of the first and second fields the length of the third side, the bottom, is inferred from the top of the next field, indicating that the fields were adjacent. The total area and the expected field are written either next to the top length or below it (b.1), followed by the amount of fallow or otherwise unused land (b.2). The name of the person responsible for the field is written next (d), followed

553 Calculation: (½ × 45) × 5 ½ = 123 ¾.

by the total barley produced (c). The bottom length of the third field is written against the bottom line. The reverse gives the total of land and produce.

The fields are reconstructed in the diagram (Fig. 1).

No. 214. *MS 1938/1 (Umma, Š 33)*

obv.

1.a.1.	[4(u)]	40 (nindan).
1.a.2.	[1(geš$_2$) 4(u) 9(diš)]	109 (nindan).
1.b.1.	1(bur$_3$) ⌜1(eše$_3$) ¼(iku) GAN$_2$⌝ [še] ⌜3(barig) 3(ban$_2$) gur-ta⌝	1 bur$_3$, 1 eše$_3$, ¼ iku of field (growing) barley (at a rate of) 3 barig, 3 ban$_2$ each (iku).
1.b.2.	1(eše$_3$) ⌜4(iku) ½(iku) GAN$_2$ su$_3$⌝ [...]	1 eše$_3$, 4 ½ iku of field (which is) inundated ...[554]
1.c.	1(u) 7(aš) še gur	(Producing) 17 gur.[555]
1.d.	x-x-[...]	...
2.a.1.	4(u)	40 (nindan).
2.a.2.	1(geš$_2$) 1(u) 2(diš)	72 (nindan).
2.b.	1(bur$_3$) 1(eše$_3$) 5(iku) ⌜¼(iku)⌝ GAN$_2$ ⌜še 2(aš)⌝ gur-ta	1 bur$_3$, 1 eše$_3$, 5 ¼ iku ... of field (growing) barley (at a rate of) 2 gur each (iku).[556]
2.c.	5(u) 8(aš) 2(barig) ⌜3(ban$_2$)⌝ gur	(Producing) 58 gur, 2 barig, 3 ban$_2$.[557]
2.d.	ba-sa$_6$-ga	Basaga.
3.a.1.	4(u)	40 (nindan).
3.a.2.	1(geš$_2$) 1(u) 4(diš)	74 (nindan).
3.b.1.	1(bur$_3$) ⌜4(iku)⌝ ½(iku) ¼(iku) GAN$_2$ še 2(aš) 3(barig) ⌜gur⌝-[ta]	1 bur$_3$, 4 ¾ iku of field (growing) barley (at a rate of) 2 gur, 3 barig each (iku).
3.b.2.	4(iku) su$_3$ 1(iku) ki?	4 iku (which is) inundated, 1 iku (which is) ...[558]

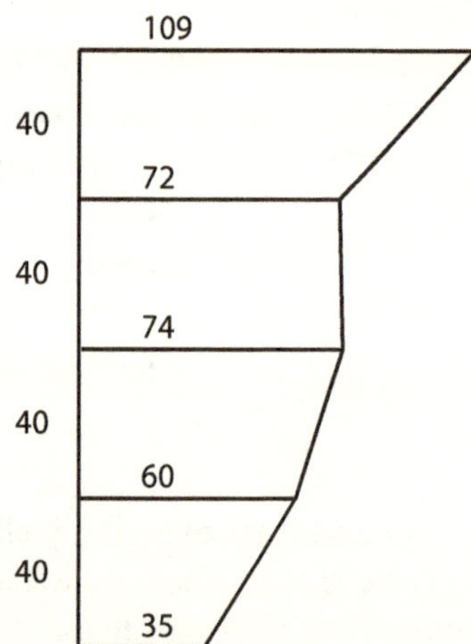

Figure 1: The fields recorded in No. 214

[554] Calculation: 40 × (102 +72)/2 = 3480n = 34.8 iku (text: 34.75); N.B. 72 taken from next field side notation.

[555] Calculation: 24.25 × 210 = 5092.5 = 16;4,5,2 ½ še (text: 17;0,0,0).

[556] Calculation: 40 × (72 + 74)/2 = 2920n = 29.2 iku (text: 29.25).

[557] Calculation: 29.25 × 600 = 17750 = 58;2,3,0 še.

[558] Calculation: 40 × (74 + 60)/2 = 2680n = 26.8 iku (text: 26.75).

3.c.	5(u) 9(aš) ⸢4(ban$_2$)⸣ 5(diš) sila$_3$ ⸢gur⸣	59 gur, 4 ban$_2$, 5 sila$_3$ (of barley).[559]
3.d.	^{geš}guzza-ni-⸢gi⸣	Guzzani.
4.a.1.	⸢4(u) 6(diš)⸣	46 (nindan).
4.a.2.a.	1(geš$_2$)	60 (nindan).
4.a.2.b.	3(u) 5(diš)	35 (nindan).
4.b.1.	1(eše$_3$) 5(iku) ½(iku) GAN$_2$ še 1(aš) 3(barig) gur-[ta]	1 eše$_3$, 5 ½ iku of field (growing) barley (at a rate of) 1 gur, 3 barig each (iku).
4.b.2.	3(iku) bar še	3 iku without barley.
4.b.3.	1(eše$_3$) 1(iku) ½(iku) ⸢su$_3$⸣ [. . .]	1 eše$_3$, 1 ½ iku (which is) inundated . . .[560]
4.c.	2(u) ⸢3(aš)⸣ 1(barig) gur	23 gur (of barley).[561]
4.d.	u$_2$-da-ur$_4$-ra	Udaurra.

rev.

1.	šunigin 5(bur$_3$) ⸢2(iku)$^{?}$⸣ GAN$_2$ [še]	Total: 5 bur$_3$, 2 iku of field (growing) barley.[562]
2.	1(bur$_3$) 3(iku) GAN$_2$ su$_3$ 1(iku) [ki$^?$]	1 bur$_3$, 3 iku of field (which is) inundated, 1 iku . . .[563]
3.	šunigin 2(geš$_2$) 3(u) 7(aš) 4(barig) 1(ban$_2$) 5(diš) [sila$_3$ še gur]	Total: 157 gur, 4 barig, 1 ban$_2$, 5 sila$_3$ of barley.[564]
4.	du$_{10}$-ga-[x]	Duga- . . .
5.	a-ša$_3$ me-en-[kar$_2$]	Field: Menkar.
6.	ugula ur-^{d}nin-⸢su⸣ [. . .]	Overseer: Ur-Ninsu . . . .
7.	giri$_3$ lu$_2$-i$_3$-⸢zu⸣	Conveyor: Lu-izu.
8.	mu a-ra$_2$ 3(diš$_t$)-kam si-mu-[rum^{ki} ba-hul] *(blank space)*	Year: "Third time Simurum was destroyed."

Two field plans with drawings of the fields are present in the Schøyen Collection (MS 1984 and MS 1850). They were published by J. Friberg (2007: 137–42).

Bundles of Reed for the Storehouse of the Edana

This small text, No. 215, lists large amounts of reed bundles for the storehouse of a place named Edana, as part of a *bala* (obligation) of a certain Išarum. The text provides us with the interesting equivalence of one bale of reed (written gu-nigin$_2$) = one talent in weight (written 1(diš) gu$_2$).

No. 215. *MS 2019/9 (Umma, ŠS 9–v)*

obv.

1.	⸢9(šar$_2$)⸣ 3(geš'u) ⸢5(geš$_2$)⸣ [7(diš) sa gi]	34,567 bundles of reed.
2.	gu-nigin$_2$-ba 2(u) 7(diš) ⸢sa⸣-ta	Their bales: 27 bundles each.
3.	gu-nigin$_2$-bi 2(geš'u) 1(geš$_2$) 1(u) 8(diš)	Their bales: 1,278.

---

559 Calculation: 22.75 × 780 = 17745 = 59;0,4,5 še.

560 Calculation: 46 × (60 + 35)/2 = 2185n = 21.85 iku (text: 22).

561 Calculation: 14.5 × 480 = 6960 = 23;1,0,0 še.

562 Calculation: 24.25 + 29.25 + 22.75 + 14.5 = 90.75 = 5b 3/4i (text 5b 2i).

563 Calculation: 10.5 + 4 + 7.5 = 22 = 1b 4i (text 1b 3i ?).

564 Calculation: 17;0,0 + 58;2,3 + 59;0,4,5 + 23;1,0,0 = 157;4,1,5.

4.	9(šar$_2$) ⸢3(geš'u)⸣ sa 2(u) 6(diš) sa-ta	34,200 bundles (of reed). (Their bales:) 26 bundles each.
5.	gu-nigin$_2$-bi 2(geš'u) 1(geš$_2$) 5(u) 5(diš)	Their bales: 1,315.
6.	ki lu$_2$-^{d}en-ki-ta	From Lu-Enki.

rev.

1.	3(geš$_2$) gu$_2$ gi	180 talents of reed.
2.	ki lu$_2$-banda$_3$^{da}-ta	From Lu-banda.
3.	2(geš$_2$) 3(u) gu$_2$ gi	150 talents of reed.
4.	ki a-a-kal-la unu^{ki}-ta *(blank space)*	From Aya-kala, of Uruk.
5.	šunigin 4(geš'u) 8(geš$_2$) 4(u) 3(aš) gu$_2$ gi	Total: 2,923 talents of reed.[565]
6.	ga$_2$-nun e-da-na-ka ku$_x$(KWU636)-ra	Entered into the storehouse of Edana.
7.	ki i-šar-ru-um	From Išarum.
8.	⸢ša$_3$⸣ bala-a	Within the bala (obligation).
9.	iti dal	Month: "Flight."
10.	⸢mu⸣ ^{d}šu-^{d}suen ⸢lugal⸣-e e$_2$ ^{d}⸢šara$_2$ umma^{ki}⸣ mu-⸢du$_3$⸣	Year: "Šu-Suen, king, built the house of Šara in Umma."

left edge

1.	[. . .]-bi$^{?}$ gi en-du$_8$-du [(x)]	. . . reed (of the field:) Endudu . . .

Two Exercises in Cereal Computations

These two texts, Nos. 216 and 217, lack names of agents, and No. 216 even lacks a date. They are likely to be exercise tablets. Both texts deal with various types of cereal.

No. 216. *MS 2019/6 (—)*

obv.

1.	5(u) ⸢3(aš) 2(barig) x zi$_3$⸣ gur	53 gur, 2 barig . . . flour.
2.	1(geš$_2$) 1(aš) 1(barig) 4(ban$_2$) 3(diš) ½(diš) sila$_3$ še gur	61 gur, 1 barig, 4 ban$_2$, 3 ½ sila$_3$ of barley.
3.	a-ra$_2$ 1(diš)-kam	For the first time.
4.	1(u) 6(aš) 3(barig) 2(ban$_2$) zi$_3$ gur	16 gur, 3 barig, 2 ban$_2$ of flour.
5.	2(u) 1(barig) 3(ban$_2$) 6(diš) sila$_3$ še gur	20 gur, 1 barig, 3 ban$_2$, 6 sila$_3$ barley.
6.	a-ra$_2$ 2(diš)-kam	For the second time.
7.	5(u) 2(aš) 3(barig) ⸢4(ban$_2$)⸣ zi$_3$ gur	52 gur, 3 barig, 4 ban$_2$ of four.
8.	3(u) 4(aš) 5(ban$_2$) še gur	34 gur, 5 ban$_2$ of barley.
9.	2(aš) ziz$_2$ gur 1(aš) gig gur	2 gur of emmer wheat. 1 gur of wheat.
10.	1(aš) kaš dida gur	1 gur of beer (in) dida (jars).

---

565 Using a value 1 bale of reeds = 1 talent, addition of the totals of bales of reed (obv. 3, 5) and the two amounts of reed counted in talents (rev. 1, 3) makes the grand total given in this line.

rev.

1.	a-ra$_2$ 3(diš)-kam	For the third time.
2.	3(aš) 3(barig) ⌜4(ban$_2$)⌝ zi$_3$ gur	3 gur, 3 barig, 4 ban$_2$ flour.
3.	1(u) 8(aš) 3(barig) 4(ban$_2$) še gur	18 gur, 3 barig, 4 ban$_2$ barley.
4.	a-ra$_2$ 4(diš)-kam	For the fourth time.
	(blank space)	
5.	šunigin 2(geš$_2$) 6(aš) 3(barig) 3(ban$_2$) zi$_3$ gur	Total: 126 gur, 3 barig, 2 ban$_2$ of flour.
6.	šunigin 2(geš2) 1(u) ⌜4(aš)⌝ 2(barig) 4(ban$_2$) 9(diš) 1/2(diš) sila$_3$ še gur	Total: 134 gur, 2 barig, 4 ban$_2$, 9 ½ sila$_3$ of barley.
7.	šunigin 2(aš) ziz$_2$ gur	Total: 2 gur of emmer wheat.
8.	šunigin 1(aš) gig gur	Total: 1 gur of wheat.
9.	šunigin 1(aš) dug dida gur	Total: 1 gur of (beer in) dida jars.
10.	še-bi 4(geš$_2$) 2(u) 6(aš) 2(barig) 5(ban$_2$) ⌜9(diš) sila$_3$ še⌝ gur	Its barley: 266 gur, 2 barig, 5 ban$_2$, 9 sila$_3$.

No. 217. *MS 1947/3 (Umma?, IS 3)*

obv.

1.	1(aš) 1(barig) 3(ban$_2$) še gur	1 gur, 1 barig, 3 ban$_2$ of barley.
2.	1(aš) 3(barig) 3(ban$_2$) zi$_3$ gur	1 gur, 3 barig, 3 ban$_2$ of flour.
3.	sa$_2$-du$_{11}$ šu-a gi-na	Regular "regular (deliveries)."
4.	iti 1(u) 3(diš)-kam	Of the 13th month.
5.	1(ban$_2$) 4(diš) sila$_3$ zi$_3$ sig$_{15}$	1 ban$_2$, 4 sila$_3$ of sig$_{15}$ (quality) flour.
6.	2(ban$_2$) zi$_3$-gu	2 ban$_2$ of gu-flour.
7.	1(ban$_2$) zu$_2$-lum	1 ban$_2$ of dates.
8.	6(diš) sila$_3$ eša	6 sila$_3$ of fine flour.
9.	4(ban$_2$) kaš du	4 ban$_2$ of regular (quality) beer.
10.	ezem nesag	(For the) First Fruits festival.
11.	1(ban$_2$) 2(diš) sila$_3$ zi$_3$ sig$_{15}$	1 ban$_2$, 2 sila$_3$ of sig$_{15}$ (quality) flour.
12.	2(ban$_2$) zi$_3$-gu	2 ban$_2$ of gu-flour.

rev.

1.	1(ban$_2$) zu$_2$-lum	1 ban$_2$ of dates.
2.	6(diš) sila$_3$ eša	6 sila$_3$ of fine flour.
3.	4(ban$_2$) kaš du	4 ban$_2$ of regular (quality) beer.
4.	ezem e$_2$-iti-6(diš)	(For the) festival "House-month-six."
5.	1(ban$_2$) zi$_3$ sig$_{15}$	1 ban$_2$ of sig$_{15}$ (quality) flour.
6.	1(ban$_2$) 5(diš) sila$_3$ zi$_3$-gu	1 ban$_2$, 5 sila$_3$ of gu-flour.
7.	5(diš) sila$_3$ eša	5 sila$_3$ of fine flour.
8.	1(ban$_2$) zu$_2$-lum	1 ban$_2$ of dates.
9.	[. . .] kaš du	. . . of regular (quality) beer.
10.	⌜ezem⌝ pa$_4$-u$_2$-e	(For the) festival of Pa'u'e.
11.	še-bi [4(aš) 1(ban$_2$)] gur	Its flour: 4 gur 1 ban$_2$.
12.	1(aš) gur sa$_{10}$-am$_3$ udu 2(diš)-kam	1 gur (of barley as) barter for sheep, second time.
13.	šunigin 5(aš) 1(ban$_2$) gur	Total: 5 gur, 1 ban$_2$ (of barley).
14.	^{d}ašnan	Ašnan.

left edge

1.	mu si-mu-ru-um^{ki} ba-ḫul	Year: "Simurum was destroyed."

A Discarded Exercise Tablet?

This difficult text is written on a tablet that appears to have been deliberately destroyed in antiquity (squeezed in the hand perhaps?). It could well be an exercise attesting to the practical education of Ur III scribes.

No. 218. *MS 1942/10 (—)*

obv.

	(blank space)	
1.	[...] 4(geš$_2$) 4(u) 3(aš) 3(barig) 5(ban$_2$) gur	283 gur, 3 barig, 5 ban$_2$.
2.	[ki] x-ḫur-BAD-ta	From ...
3.	[...] ⸢4(aš)⸣ 1(barig) 4(ban$_2$) gur	+4 gur, 1 barig, 4 ban$_2$.
4.	[...]-x-x-ka	...
5.	[ki] ⸢ka⸣-guru$_7$-ta	From the chief of the granary.
6.	[...] 3(aš) 1(ban$_2$) gur	+3 gur, 1 ban$_2$.
7.	[...]⸢ki⸣ ku$_3$-^{d}nin-ur$_4$-ra-ta	... From Ku-Nin-ura.
8.	[x] ki šeš-kal-la-ta	... From Šeš-kala.
9.	⸢šunigin⸣ 5(geš$_2$) 2(u) 9(aš) 3(ban$_2$) gur	Total: 329 gur, 3 ban$_2$.
	(blank space)	

rev. *(broken)*

Animals for Gods

Text No. 219 records a small number of animals given in a certain month to various gods and cultic objects. However, it does not record any agents or households from which the animals derive. The destinations of the animals are similar to those found in the triangular bullae discussed in Chapter 2.

No. 219. *MS 1747 (Umma, AS 5–vii)*

obv.

1.	1(diš) udu niga 1(diš) udu u$_2$ ⸢1(diš)$^{?}$ maš$_2$⸣	1 sheep, fattened; 1 sheep, grass(-fed); 1 goat
2.	u$_4$-sakar u$_4$ 1(u) 5(diš) ^{d}⸢šara$_2$⸣	(for the) Full Moon, the 15th day (of) Šara.
3.	1(diš) maš$_2$	1 goat,
4.	^{d}šul-gi	(for) Šulgi.
5.	1(diš) maš$_2$	1 goat,
6.	^{d}amar- ^{d}suen	(for) Amar-Suen
7.	1(diš) udu u$_2$	1 sheep, grass(-fed)

rev.

1.	bara$_2$ gir$_{13}$-geš^{ki}	(for the) dais of Girgeš.
2.	3(diš) udu niga 1(diš) maš$_2$-gal niga	3 sheep, fattened, 1 large goat, fattened,
3.	2(diš) udu u$_2$ 2(diš) maš$_2$	2 sheep, grass(-fed), 2 goats,
4.	a$_2$ u$_4$-da	daily.
5.	1(diš) maš$_2$	1 goat,

6. balag nu_2-a — (for the) "Harp for the disappearance (of the moon)"
7. iti min-$eš_3$ — of the Month: "Double Sanctuary."
8. mu en-unu_6-gal [d]inanna ba-ḫun — Year: "En-unugal (En-priest) of Inanna was installed."

A Receipt Without Context

This sealed receipt, No. 220, is hard to fit into the administrative system of the Ur III state. It is therefore published here among the miscellaneous texts.

No. 220. *MS 4451 (—)*

obv.

1.	1(barig) 1(ban_2) 2(diš) $sila_3$ še numun	1 barig, 1 ban_2, 2 $sila_3$ of seed-barley.
2.	ugula šu-$eš_{18}$-dar	Overseer, Šu-Eštar.

rev.

(*seal impression*)

seal (*illegible*)

A Receipt of Three Receipts?

Text No. 221 is, judging from both its size and shape, a regular receipt. However, it lists three entries of amounts of cereals as sealed tablets of three named individuals. The text has no other named recipients, and we must assume that these three persons, Ur-amma, Alulu, and Ur-Dun, received the cereals mentioned before their names. The last entry, added in the blank space, may be an addition. Perhaps all the cereals were from the "old mill."

No. 221. *MS 1947/11 (X, ŠS 2–vi)*

obv.

1.	1(aš) ziz_2 gur	1 gur of emmer.
2.	$kišib_3$ ur-am_3-ma	Sealed tablet of Ur-amma.
3.	6(aš) še gur	6 gur of barley.
4.	$kišib_3$ a-lu_5-lu_5	Sealed tablet of Alulu.
5.	1(aš) še gur	1 gur of barley.
6.	sa_2-du_{11} [d]nin-ḫur-sag-gu-la	Regular (deliveries) for Ninḫursag-gula.

rev.

1.	$kišib_3$ ur-dun	Sealed tablet of Ur-Dun.
2.	2(barig) še šuku-ra[?]	2 barig of barley of the sustenance.
	(*blank space*)	
3.	e_2 kikken sumun-ta	From the old mill.
4.	iti šu-numun	Month: "Seeding."
5.	mu ma_2 [d]en-ki ba-ab-du_8	Year: "Boat of Enki was caulked."

Two Inventories of Unknown Purpose

A few other small inventories were published in Chapter 8. Text No. 222 was not included there as it seems to lack most bookkeeping terminology and may instead be an exercise text.

No. 222. *MS 2019/4 (—)*

obv.

1.	1(diš) lu$_2$-^{d}suen agar$_4$-nigin$_2$	One Lu-Suen, "Field Rounder."[566]
2.	1(diš) lu$_2$-^{d}inanna agar$_4$-nigin$_2$	One Lu-Inanna, "Field Rounder."
3.	lu$_2$-e$_2$-a lugal-mu-da-me	. . .
4.	inim sag-ga$_2$-ra-a	. . .

rev. (*blank*)

No. 223. *MS 1742/1 (Nippur, Š 25 or IS 3[567]–X–15)*

obv.

1.	3(u) guruš	30 workers.
2.	nu-banda$_3$ ur-^{d}da-mu	Captain: Ur-Damu.
3.	1(u) 8(diš) ur-$^{d⌜}$en⌝-lil$_2$-la$_2$	18 (workers, captain:) Ur-Enlila.
4.	2(u) lu$_2$-$^{d⌜}$nin-šubur⌝	20 (workers, captain:) Lu-Ninšubur.
5.	6(diš) ^{d}en-lil$_2$-al-sa$_6$	6 (workers, captain:) Enlil-alsa.
6.	2(u) 1(diš) a-ma$^?$-u$_2$	21 (workers, captain:) Ama'u.
7.	1(u) 1(diš) giri$_3$-ni-i$_3$-⌜sa$_6$⌝	11 (workers, captain:) Girini-isa.
8.	šunigin 1(geš$_2$) 4(u) 6(diš) guruš lu$_2$ ḫun-ga$_2$	Total: 106 workers, hirelings.

rev.

1.	1(u) guruš ša$_3$-gu$_4$	10 workers, ox-drivers,
2.	⌜u$_3$⌝ lu$_2$ sig$_4^?$ ⌜gub$^?$-ba$^?$⌝-me	And men stationed at the bricks(?).
3.	nu-banda$_3$ ur-^{d}en-lil$_2$-la$_2$	Captain: Ur-Enlila.
4.	šabra lugal-ku$_3$-⌜zu$^?$⌝	Chief administrator: Lugal-kuzu.
5.	ša$_3^?$[568] iti ku$_3$-<šim>[569] u$_4$ 1(u) 5(diš) ba-zal	Within the month "Shiny fragrance," the 15th day has passed.
6.	mu si-mu-ru-⌜um$^?$⌝^{ki} ⌜ba-hul⌝	Year: "Simurum was destroyed."

Two Fragments Glued Together

Two fragments of similar texts glued together (upside down). Both deal with workers. No. 224a is the larger fragment, 224b the smaller fragment.

---

[566] See Marchesi 2001: 315, suggesting that this title denoted someone who walked rounds in the fields of the governor.

[567] Most Umma texts dated with this year-name ("Simurum was destroyed") belong to Ibbi-Suen's third year and not to the 25th year of Šulgi (four Šulgi years were named after the destruction of Simurum, and although the full forms mentions the count of campaigns, confusion can occur: Šulgi year 27 [rare], the second destruction of Simurum, year 32, the third destruction of Simurum, and year 44, the ninth destruction of Simurum).

[568] For a reading ša$_3$ here, see NRVN 1, 043.

[569] šim partly erased.

No. 224a. *MS 4704/1 (Umma, IS 1–ii)*

obv.

1.	7(diš) guruš gub-⸢ba⸣	7 workers, present.
2.	tu-ra ur-^{d}dumu-zi-da	Sick, Ur-Dumuzida.
3.	ugula lu$_2$-sa$_6$-i$_3$-zu	Overseer, Lu-saizu.
4.	2(diš) guruš gub-⸢ba⸣	2 workers, present.
5.	1(diš) guruš ki ur-im-[. . .]	1 worker, from Ur-Im . . .
6.	⸢2(diš)⸣ guruš nig$_2$ buru$_{14}$ ⸢gaba$^{?}$⸣-[. . .]	2 workers, harvest . . .
	(rest broken)	

rev.

	(start broken)	
1'.	⸢ugula ur-^{d}⸣dumu-zi-[da]	Overseer, Ur-Dumuzida.
2'.	3(u) 9(diš) geme$_2$ uš-bar	39 female workers, weavers.
3'.	ugula i$_3$-kal-la	Overseer, I-kala.
	(blank space)	
4'.	gurum$_2$ ak u$_4$ 6(diš)-kam	Inventory of the 6th day.
5'.	erin$_2$ tab-ba a-ša$_3$ a-ba-gal-gu-la	Supplementary erin$_2$-workers of the field Abagal-gula.
6'.	iti sig$_4$-^{geš}i$_3$-šub-ba-gar	Month: "Brick placed in mold."
7'.	mu ^{d}i-bi$_2$-^{d}suen lugal	Year: "Ibbi-Suen (was) king."

No. 224b. *MS 4704/2 (Umma, IS 1)*

obv.

1.	1(u) 6(diš) guruš gub-ba	16 workers, present.
2.	la$_2$-ia$_3$ 3(diš) guruš	Deficit, 3 workers.
3.	ugula a-gu	Overseer, Agu.
4.	x guruš gu-⸢ba⸣	. . . workers, present.
	(rest broken)	

rev.

	(start broken)	
1'.	⸢iti⸣ še-[. . .]	Month: " . . . "
2'.	⸢mu⸣ ^{d}i-bi$_2$-[^{d}suen] lugal	Year: "Ibbi-Suen (was) king."

Offerings from the Governor

No. 225. *MS 1945 (—)*

obv.

1.	1(u) 4(diš) GA$_2$ u$_2$ ki dagal-⸢la⸣	14 . . .
2.	1(u) 4(aš) še gur	14 gur of barley.
3.	1(u) 4(aš) ziz$_2$ gur	14 gur of emmer wheat.
4.	4(barig) zi$_3$ dub-dub	4 barig of crushed flour.

5.	2(barig) eša	2 barig of fine flour.
6.	1(barig) dig sar	1 barig . . .
7.	2(barig) dug KWU475xBI	2 vessels . . .
8.	5(diš) dug sila$_3$ gin$_2$-bar	5 sila$_3$ vessels . . .
9.	2(u) gu$_2$ gi NE	20 talents of NE reed.
10.	1(u) gu$_2$ ^{geš}ma-nu	10 talents of willow(?).
11.	3(aš) gu$_2$ gug$_4$	3 talents of . . .
	(blank space)	
12.	2(barig) zi$_3$ sig$_{15}$	2 barig of sig$_{15}$ (quality) flour.

rev.

1.	1(barig) ⸢dabin⸣	1 barig of dabin flour.
2.	nig$_2$ siskur$_2$-ra	Items of the offerings.
	(blank space)	
3.	nig$_2$-dab$_5$ e$_2$ ga$_2$-ga$_2$-da	. . .
	(double ruling)	
4.	6(geš$_2$) 3(u) 5(diš) ^{gi}pisan gid$_2$	215 reed-container, long.
	(blank space)	
5.	⸢ki⸣ ensi$_2$-ka-⸢ta⸣	From the governor.

Not a Tag?

Tablet No. 226 may be a tag (see Chapter 2), but the text lacks all technical terminology. It is difficult to see how expensive objects such as bronze plowshares and ax-blades would be accounted for in such a haphazard manner, and the text is therefore edited here as perhaps an exercise tablet.

No. 226. *MS 1947/14 (—)*

obv.

1.	5(diš) ^{uruda}gur$_{10}$	5 plow shares of copper.
2.	2(diš) ^{uruda}ha-⸢zi$^?$⸣-in	2 ax(-blades of bronze).
	(erasure)	. . .

rev. *(blank space)*

Two Notes or Exercise Tablets?

The next two texts, Nos. 227 and 228, could be either notes or exercise tablets. They are published here without any further comments.

No. 227. *MS 2019/7 (—)*

obv.

1.	[x] ⸢1(ban$_2$)⸣ i$_3$ min-a-⸢bi$^?$⸣	*n*+1 ban$_2$ of oil (for) the two (?).
2.	⸢1(barig)⸣ dumu ba-⸢sa$_6$$^?$⸣	1 barig (oil for the) child of Basa.
3.	1(barig) da-⸢da$^?$⸣	1 barig (oil for) Dada.
4.	1(barig) inim-^{d}šara$_2$	1 barig (oil for) Inim-Šara.
	(line erased)	
5.	1(barig) ⸢gudu$_4$⸣ zabala$_3$^{ki}	1 barig (oil for) the gudu$_4$-priest of Zabala.

6.	3(barig) lugal-za$_3$-ge-si	3 barig (oil for) Lugal-zagesi.
	(line erased)	

rev.

	(lines erased)	
	(blank space)	

No. 228. *MS 2021/2 (X, ŠS 3–iii)*

obv.

1.	1(aš) še ur$_5$-ra mu-ku$_x$(DU) gur	1 gur of barley (loan with) interest of the mu-ku$_x$(DU) delivery.
2.	ur-am$_3$-ma agar$_4$-nigin$_2$	Ur-amma, "Field Rounder."
	(blank space)	

rev.

	(blank space)	
1.	iti še-kar-ra-gal$_2$	Month: "Barley brought to the harbor."
2.	mu us$_2$-sa ma$_2$ ^{d}en-ki	Year after: "The boat of Enki."

Receipts or Exercise Tablets?

The following four tablets, Nos. 229–32, could all be exercise tablets as they lack key administrative terminology.

No. 229. *MS 2020/13 (—)*

obv.

1.	1(ban$_2$) šu-ḫal-bi	1 ban$_2$ (for) Šu-Ḫalbi,
2.	dumu nin-e$_2$-šu-⸢bur⸣	child of Nin-ešubur.
	(blank space)	
3.	ki lugal-e$_2$-maḫ-e-⸢ta⸣	From Lugal-Emaḫe.
	(blank space)	

rev. *(blank space)*

No. 230. *MS 2364 (Umma, X–viii)*

obv.

1.	2(diš) gurus	2 workers,
2.	3(u) lu$_2$ a$_2$ ½(diš)	30 "men" working at ½ (capacity),
3.	sig$_4$ <im>-gu$_2$-en-na NE GA$_2$	bricks of river sediment . . .

rev.

	(blank space)	
1.	iti e$_2$-iti-6(diš)	Month: "House-month-six"
	(blank space)	

No. 231. *MS 1947/8 (Umma, ŠS 8–vii)*

obv.

1.	⸢2(barig)⸣ še-ba	2 barig barley rations,
2.	a-ta$_2$-na-aḫ	(for) Atanaḫ.
3.	ki-su$_7$ gub$_3$-temen-na-ta	From the threshing floor of Gub-Temena.
	(blank space)	

rev.

	(blank space)	
1.	iti min-eš$_3$	Month: "Double Sanctuary."
2.	mu ma$_2^!$-gur$_8^!$-maḫ ba-dim$_2$	Year: "The lofty barge was fashioned."

No. 232. *MS 2020/17 (—)*

obv.

1.	1(diš) nig$_2$-bara$_3$	1 nig$_2$-bara$_3$.[570]
2.	lu$_2$-dingir-ra SIG$_7$-a dumu ša$_3$-mu	Lu-Dingira, blind, child of Šamu.
3.	a bala-a	Drawing water at the
4.	ka i$_7$-da	mouth of the river.

rev.

1.	giri$_3$ e$_2$-gal-e-si dumu ur-ku$_3$-ga	Conveyor: Egale-si, child of Ur-kuga.
	(blank space)	

It is possible that these texts were originally encased in envelopes (see Chapter 7), on which was written the missing information such as year-name, recipient, and so forth.

A Broken Account of Foodstuffs

Text No. 233 is most likely a yearly account listing monthly deliveries for messengers. The relationship of the text to the messenger service is based entirely on the types and amounts of products found in the texts, as it fails to mention any persons or titles anywhere in the preserved portions of the text.

No. 233. *MS 4294 (Umma, —)*

obv. col. i

	(beginning broken)	
1'.	[u$_4$] 3(u) la$_2$ 1(diš$_{tenû}$)-kam	On the 29th day.
2'.	⸢iti⸣ še-sag$_{11}$-ku$_5$	Month: "Harvest."
3'.	2(aš) 4(barig) 2(ban$_2$) 5(diš) sila$_3$ kaš du gur	2 gur, 4 barig, 2 ban$_2$, 5 sila$_3$ of beer, regular (quality).
4'.	2(diš) dug dida du 3(ban$_2$)-ta	2 dida jars, regular (quality), (holding) 3 ban$_2$ each.
5'.	2(diš) dug dida du 1(ban$_2$) 5(diš) sila$_3^?$-ta	2 dida jars, regular (quality), (holding) 1 ban$_2$ 5 sila$_3$ each.

[570] See Maekawa 1993: 120–21 for a discussion of tug$_2$-nig$_2$-bara$_3$(DAG) and related terms.

6’.	2(aš) 9(diš) sila$_{3}$ ninda du gur	2 gur, 9 sila$_{3}$ of bread, regular (quality).
7’.	1(barig) 3(ban$_{2}$) dabin	1 barig, 3 ban$_{2}$ of dabin-flour.
8’.	3(ban$_{2}$) še	3 ban$_{2}$ of barley.
9’.	1(diš) udu u$_{2}$	1 sheep, grass(-fed).
10’.	1(ban$_{2}$) 4(diš) ½(diš) 2(diš) gin$_{2}$ i$_{3}$-geš	1 ban$_{2}$ 4 ½ (sila$_{3}$), 2 (liquid) shekels of sesame oil.
11’.	8(diš) 5/6(diš) sila$_{3}$ 6(diš) gin$_{2}$ igi-sag šum$_{2}$$^{?}$ gaz$^{?}$	8 ⅚ sila$_{3}$, 6 (liquid) shekels of igi-sag onions, crushed.
12’.	5(diš) 5/6(diš) sila$_{3}$ 4(diš) gin$_{2}$ naga$^{?}$ gaz$^{?}$	5 ⅚ sila$_{3}$, 4 (liquid) shekels of potash.
	(blank space)	
13’.	u$_{4}$ 3(u) la$_{2}$ 1(diš$_{tenû}$)-kam	The 29th day.
14’.	iti sig$_{4}$-^{geš}i$_{3}$-šub-ba-gar	Month: “Brick placed in the mold.”
15’.	2(barig) kaš saga	2 barig of beer, good (quality).
16’.	3(aš) 2(ban$_{2}$) 4(diš) sila$_{3}$ kaš du gur	3 gur, 2 ban$_{2}$, 4 sila$_{3}$ of beer, regular (quality).
17’.	6(diš) dug dida saga 3(ban$_{2}$)-ta	6 dida jars, good (quality), (holding) 3 ban$_{2}$ each.
18’.	⸢9(diš)$^{?}$⸣ dug dida du 3(ban$_{2}$)-ta	9 dida jars, regular (quality), (holding) 3 ban$_{2}$ each.
19’.	1(diš) dug dida du 2(ban$_{2}$)	1 dida jar, regular (quality), (holding) 2 ban$_{2}$.

obv. col. ii

	(beginning broken)	
1’.	6(diš) sila$_{3}$ 4(diš) gin$_{2}$ ⸢naga$^{?}$ gaz$^{?}$⸣	6 sila$_{3}$, 4 (liquid) shekels of crushed potash.
2’.	1(diš) ^{gi}kaskal	1 road-basket.
	(blank space)	
3’.	u$_{4}$ 3(u) la$_{2}$ 1(diš$_{tenû}$)-kam	On the 31st day.
4’.	iti še-kar-ra-gal$_{2}$-la	Month: “Barley brought to the harbor.”
5’.	2(aš) 4(barig) 3(ban$_{2}$) 5(diš) sila$_{3}$ kaš du gur	2 gur, 4 barig, 3 ban$_{2}$, 5 sila$_{3}$ of beer, regular (quality).
6’.	2(diš) dug dida saga 3(ban$_{2}$)-ta	2 dida jars, good (quality), (holding) 3 ban$_{2}$ each.
7’.	1(u) la$_{2}$ 1(diš$_{tenû}$) dug dida du 3(ban$_{2}$)-ta	9 dida jars, regular (quality), (holding) 3 ban$_{2}$ each.
8’.	3(diš) dug dida du 2(ban$_{2}$)-ta	3 dida jars, regular (quality), (holding) 2 ban$_{2}$ each.
9’.	3(diš) dug dida du 1(ban$_{2}$) 5(diš) sila$_{3}$-ta	3 dida jars, regular (quality), (holding) 1 ban$_{2}$, 5 sila$_{3}$ each.
10’.	1(aš) 4(barig) 2(ban$_{2}$) 3(diš) sila$_{3}$ ninda du gur	1 gur, 4 barig, 2 ban$_{2}$, 3 sila$_{3}$ of bread, regular (quality).
11’.	3(ban$_{2}$) zi$_{3}$-gu saga	3 ban$_{2}$ of gu-flour, good (quality).
12’.	1(barig) 2(ban$_{2}$) zi$_{3}$-gu du	1 barig, 2 ban$_{2}$ of gu-flour, regular (quality).
13’.	1(aš) 4(barig) dabin gur	1 gur, 4 barig of dabin-flour.
14’.	4(diš) udu u$_{2}$	4 sheep, grass(-fed).
15’.	1(diš) maš$_{2}$$^{?}$	1 goat.
16’.	2(ban$_{2}$) 3(diš) sila$_{3}$ 1(u) 1(diš) gin$_{2}$ i$_{3}$-geš	2 ban$_{2}$, 3 sila$_{3}$, 11 (liquid) shekels of sesame oil.
17’.	2(barig) zu$_{2}$-lum	2 barig of dates.
18’.	9(diš) ⅚(diš) sila$_{3}$ 1(diš) gin$_{2}$ šum$_{2}$ gaz	9 ⅚ sila$_{3}$, 1 (liquid) shekel of crushed garlic.
19’.	6(diš) ½(diš) sila$_{3}$ 4(diš) gin$_{2}$ naga gaz	6 ½ sila$_{3}$, 4 (liquid) shekels of crushed potash.
20’.	7(diš) ^{gi}gur-dub 1(barig)-ta	7 gur-dub baskets, (holding) 1 barig each.
	(blank line)	
21’.	u$_{4}$ 3(u)-kam iti nesag	On the 30th day.

obv. col. iii

	(beginning broken)	
1'.	x [. . .]	. . .
2'.	1(barig) ⸢4(ban$_2$)$^{?}$⸣ [. . .]	1 barig, 4 ban$_2$ . . .
3'.	4(aš) ⸢4(barig)$^{?}$⸣ [. . .]	4 gur, 4 barig . . .
4'.	3(diš) ⸢dug⸣ [dida . . .]	3 dida jars . . .
5'.	3(diš) ⸢dug⸣ [dida . . .]	3 dida jars . . .
6'.	8(diš) ⸢dug⸣ [dida . . .]	8 dida jars . . .
7'.	3(diš) ⸢dug⸣ [dida . . .]	3 dida jars . . .
8'.	3(diš) ⸢dug⸣ [dida . . .]	3 dida jars . . .
9'.	2(aš) ⸢1(barig)⸣ [. . .]	2 gur, 1 barig . . .
10'.	4(ban$_2$) [. . .]	4 ban$_2$ . . .
11'.	1(barig) 4(ban$_2$) [. . .]	1 barig, 4 ban$_2$ . . .
12'.	2(ban$_2$) [. . .]	2 ban$_2$ . . .
13'.	3(aš) 1(barig) [. . .]	3 gur, 1 barig . . .
14'.	1(aš) 1(barig) 2(ban$_2$) [. . .]	1 gur, 1 barig, 2 ban$_2$ . . .
15'.	½(diš)$^{?}$ [. . .]	½ . . .
16'.	1(diš) ⸢udu$^{?}$⸣ [. . .]	1 sheep . . .
17'.	4(diš) [. . .]	4 . . .
18'.	1(diš) sila$_3$ [. . .]	1 sila$_3$ . . .
19'.	3(ban$_2$) 4(diš) [sila$_3$ . . .]	3 ban$_2$, 4 sila$_3$ . . .
20'.	1(ban$_2$) 1(diš) [sila$_3$ . . .]	1 ban$_2$, 1 sila$_3$ . . .
21'.	7(diš) ⸢⅚(diš)⸣ [. . .]	7 ⅚ . . .
22'.	3(diš) x [. . .]	3 . . .
	(blank line)	
23'.	u$_4$ ⸢3(u)⸣ [. . .-kam iti . . .]	On the 30th day. (Month: . . .)
24'.	2(aš) 2(barig) [. . .]	2 gur, 2 barig . . .
25'.	1(diš) ⸢dug$^{?}$⸣ [. . .]	1 dida jar . . .

obv. col. iv *(broken)*

rev. *(beginning broken)*

rev. col. i'

	(blank line)	
1.	u$_4$ 3(u) la$_2$ 1(diš$_{tenû}$)-kam	On the 29th day.
2.	iti ^{d}li$_9$-si$_4$	Month: "Lisi."
3.	2(aš)$^{?}$ 2(barig) 4(ban$_2$) [. . .]	2 gur, 2 barig, 4 ban$_2$ . . .
4.	4(ban$_2$) kaš dida saga	4 ban$_2$ of beer (in) dida (jars), good (quality).
5.	1(aš) 2(ban$_2$) 5(diš) sila$_3$ kaš dida du$^{?}$	1 gur, 2 ban$_2$, 5 sila$_3$ of beer (in) dida (jars), regular (quality).
6.	3(ban$_2$) zi$_3$-gu saga	3 ban$_2$ of gu-flour, good (quality).
7.	2(aš) 3(barig) 2(ban$_2$) dabin gur	2 gur, 3 barig, 2 ban$_2$ of dabin-flour.
8.	1(aš) 2(barig) 4(ban$_2$) 1(diš) sila$_3$ ninda du gur	1 gur, 2 barig, 4 ban$_2$, 1 sila$_3$ of bread, regular (quality).
9.	4(diš) udu u$_2$ 1(diš) maš$_2$	4 sheep, grass-(fed), 1 goat.
10.	2(barig) zu$_2$-lum	2 barig of dates.

11.	1(diš) sila$_3$ i$_3$-geš du$_{10}$-ga	1 sila$_3$ of sesame oil, sweet (?).
12.	2(ban$_2$) 2(diš) ½(diš) sila$_3$ la$_2$ 1(diš$_{tenû}$) gin$_2$ i$_3$-geš	2 ban$_2$, 2 ½ sila$_3$ minus 1 (liquid) shekel of sesame oil
13.	8(diš) ⅔(diš) sila$_3$ la$_2$ 1(diš$_{tenû}$) gin$_2$ šum$_2$ ⸢gaz⸣	8 ⅔ sila$_3$ minus 1 (liquid) shekel of crushed garlic.
14.	5(diš) ⸢5/6(diš)?⸣ sila$_3$ 7(diš)? gin$_2$ naga ⸢gaz⸣	5 5/6 sila$_3$, 7 (liquid) shekels of crushed potash.
	(blank line)	
15.	u$_4$ 3(u) la$_2$ 1(diš$_{tenû}$)-kam	On the 29th day.
16.	iti ezem-^{d}šul-gi	Month: "Festival of Šulgi."
17.	3(aš) 4(barig) 4(ban$_2$) kaš du gur	3 gur, 4 barig, 4 ban$_2$ of beer, regular (quality).
18.	1(barig) 3(ban$_2$) kaš dida x	1 barig, 3 ban$_2$ of beer (in) dida (jars), . . .
19.	1(aš) 2(barig) 4(ban$_2$) 5(diš) sila$_3$ kaš ⸢dida?⸣ [. . .]	1 gur, 2 barig, 4 ban$_2$, 5 sila$_3$ of beer (in) dida (jars), . . .
20.	2(aš) 1(barig) ⸢4(ban$_2$)? 4(diš)? sila$_3$⸣ [. . .]	2 gur, 1 barig, 4 ban$_2$, 4 sila$_3$ . . .
21.	3(ban$_2$) i3 [. . .]	3 ban$_2$ . . . oil.
22.	2(aš) ⸢2(barig)?⸣ x [. . .]	2 gur, 2 barig . . .
	(rest broken)	

rev. col. ii'

1.	1(barig) 2(ban$_2$) zi$_3$-gu saga	1 barig, 2 ban$_2$ of gu-flour, good (quality).
2.	2(aš) 2(barig) dabin gur	2 gur, 2 barig of dabin-flour.
3.	5(aš) 1(barig) 2(ban$_2$) še gur	5 gur, 1 barig, 2 ban$_2$ of barley.
4.	1(barig) zu$_2$-lum	1 barig of dates.
5.	1(u) la$_2$ 1(diš$_{tenû}$) udu	9 sheep.
6.	3(diš) maš$_2$	3 goats.
7.	1(diš) sila$_3$ i$_3$-geš du$_{10}$-ga	1 sila$_3$ of sesame oil, sweet.
8.	2(ban$_2$) 9(diš) ½(diš) sila$_3$ 6(diš) gin$_2$ i$_3$-geš	2 ban$_2$, 9 ½ sila$_3$, 6 (liquid) shekels of sesame oil.
9.	1(ban$_2$) 3(diš) sila$_3$ 6(diš) gin$_2$ šum$_2$ gaz	1 ban$_2$, 3 sila$_3$, 6 (liquid) shekels of crushed garlic.
10.	8(diš) ⅔(diš) sila$_3$ 4(diš) gin$_2$ šum$_2$ du	8 ⅔ sila$_3$, 4 (liquid) shekels of garlic, regular (quality).
11.	8(diš) ^{giš}gur-dub 1(barig)	8 gur-dub baskets, (holding) 1 barig (each).
	(blank line)	
12.	u$_4$ 3(u)-kam	On the 30th day.
13.	iti ^{d}dumu-zi	Month: "Dumuzi."
	(blank line)	
14.	šunigin 4(barig) 4(ban$_2$) kaš saga	Total: 4 barig, 4 ban$_2$ of beer, good (quality).
15.	šunigin 4(u) 2(aš) 3(barig) 2(ban$_2$) 3(diš) sila$_3$ kaš du gur	Total: 42 gur, 3 barig, 2 ban$_2$, 3 sila$_3$ of beer, regular (quality).
16.	šunigin 2(aš) 2(barig) 5(ban$_2$) dug dida saga gur	Total: 2 gur, 2 barig, 5 ban$_2$ of (beer in) dida jars, good (quality).
17.	šunigin 1(u) 3(aš) 3(ban$_2$) 5(diš) sila$_3$ dug dida du gur	Total: 13 gur, 3 ban$_2$, 5 sila$_3$ of (beer in) dida jars, regular (quality).
18.	šunigin 2(u) 4(aš) 4(barig) 1(ban$_2$) 2(diš) sila$_3$ ninda du gur	Total: 24 gur, 4 barig, 1 ban$_2$, 2 sila$_3$ of bread, regular (quality).
	(rest broken)	

rev. col. iii'

1.	šunigin 3(u) 4(diš) udu bar gal$_2$	Total: 34 sheep, with fleece.
2.	šunigin 2(u) 4(diš) udu u$_2$ su-su-ga	Total: 24 sheep, grass(-fed), replacements.
3.	šunigin 1(u) 7(diš) maš$_2$	Total: 17 goats.
4.	šunigin 2(barig) 1(ban$_2$) 1(diš) $^5/_6$(diš) sila$_3$ 7(diš) gin$_2$ igi-sag šum$_2$ gaz	Total: 2 barig, 1 ban$_2$, 1 $^5/_6$ sila$_3$, 7 (liquid) shekels of igi-sag onions, crushed.
5.	šunigin 1(barig) 2(ban$_2$) 9(diš) sila3 8(diš) gin$_2$ naga gaz	Total: 1 barig, 2 ban$_2$, 9 sila$_3$, 8 (liquid) shekels of crushed potash.
6.	šunigin 1(aš) duḫ du gur	Total: 1 gur of bran, regular (quality).
7.	šunigin 3(u) 3(diš) ^{gi}gur-dub 1(barig)	Total: 33 gur-dub baskets, (holding) 1 barig (each).
8.	šunigin 1(diš) ^{gi}kaskal	Total: 1 road-basket.
	(blank space)	
	(rest broken)	

Two Broken Accounts

These two broken accounts, Nos. 234 and 235, are edited here as they add little to the discussions above.

No. 234. *MS 4715/11 (Umma?, IS 1)*

obv.

1.	5(u) 4(aš) še gur BA U$_3$	54 gur of barley . . .
2.	a-⌜ša$_3$⌝ 7(bur$_3$) 2(eše$_3$) GAN$_2$	Field: 7 bur$_3$, 2 eše$_3$.
3.	ša$_3$-bi-ta	Out of it,
4.	1(u) 4(aš) gur a-ra$_2$ 1(diš)-kam	14 gur (of barley) for the first time.
5.	1(u) 7(aš) 3(barig) mu la$_2$-ia$_3$ dub-sar gi ^{geš}ma-nu ugula erin$_2$-na-me	17 (gur), 3 barig (of barley), because of the deficit of the scribes of reed and willow(?), the overseers of the erin$_2$-troops,
6.	lu$_2$-du$_{10}$-ga	(from) Lu-duga.
7.	6(aš) gur ki ur-e$_2$-maḫ	6 gur, from Ur-Emaḫ(e).
8.	1(u) 1(aš) gur ki ab-ba-kal-la	11 gur, from Abba-kala.
9.	[. . .] ⌜a$_2$? ḫun? da?⌝	. . .
	(rest broken)	

rev.

	(beginning broken)	
1'.	ki ur-ba-ba i$_3$-gal$_2$	From Ur-Baba is present.
	(blank space)	
2'.	mu ^{d}i-bi$_2$-^{d}suen lugal	Year: "Ibbi-Suen (was) king."

Text No. 235, an original fragment of a large account of agricultural work, has been encased in a bronze fitting, complete with a ring from which it can hang, but upside down. The bronze is very iridized.

No. 235. *MS 4518 (Umma)*

obv. (*beginning broken*)

obv. col. i'

	(*beginning broken*)	
1'.	[. . .] x x ⸢lu$_2$⸣-dingir-ra	. . . Lu-Dingira.
2'.	[x] x ⸢4(diš) sila$_3$⸣ še gur	. . . gur . . . 4 sila$_3$ of barley.
3'.	[. . .] x x x ⸢ur⸣-e$_2$-nun	. . . Ur-Enun.
4'.	[. . .] še giri$_3$-ni-i$_3$-⸢sa$_6$⸣ [. . .] ur-^{d}a-šar$_2$	. . . of barley (for) Girini-isa (child of?) Ur-Ašar.
5'.	[. . .] ⸢zi$_3$⸣ šu-^{d}er$_3$-ra	. . . of flour (for) Šu-Erra.
6'.	[. . . n] 2(barig) še gur ir-ḫa-an	. . . gur, . . . 2 barig of barley (for) Irḫan.
7'.	[. . .]	. . .
	(*rest broken*)	

obv. col. ii'

	(*beginning broken*)	
1'.	[. . .] x NI x	. . .
2'.	2(barig) zi$_3^?$ x x ⸢lugal-ku$_3^?$⸣-[zu$^?$] dumu ⸢ur$^?$⸣-^{d}ḫa-ia$_3$	2 barig of flour . . . (for) Lugal-kuzu, child of Ur-Ḫaya.
3'.	2(barig) zi$_3$ a-a-gi-⸢na⸣	2 barig of flour (for) Aya-gina.
4'.	1(barig)$^?$ še ur$^?$-^{d}⸢utu$^?$⸣ x x nam-⸢ḫa$^?$-ni$^?$⸣	1 barig of barley? (for) Ur-Utu, (child of?) Namḫani.
5'.	1(u) 5(aš) ⸢še$_3$ gur⸣	15 gur of barley.
6'.	še ⸢guru$_7$⸣ x x	barley (of the?) granary . . .
7'.	x dingir x	. . .
8'.	x x x [. . .]	. . .
	(*rest broken*)	

rev. (*broken*)

Two Texts Related to the Messenger Service?

The damaged text No. 236 is included here rather than in Chapter 10 as it is not entirely certain that it is a messenger text, although at least one of the products listed in it is commonly associated with messengers (dug dida).

No. 236. *MS 1792/2 (X, X–iv or vi–20)*

obv.

1.	3(aš) dug ⸢dida⸣ saga	3 gur of (beer in) dida jars, good (quality).
2.	6(aš) dug ⸢dida du⸣	6 gur of (beer in) dida jars, regular (quality).
3.	2(barig) 3(ban$_2$) zi$_3$-⸢gu⸣	2 barig, 3 ban$_2$ of gu-flour.
4.	^{d}nanna-kam	(For) Nannakam.
5.	1(barig) kaš 1(diš) udu niga	1 barig of beer. 1 fattened sheep.

rev.

1.	⸢lu$_2$⸣ ^{geš}gigir-bi 1(u) 2(diš)- ⸢am$_3$⸣	Its men of the chariots/wagons are 12.
2.	⸢lu$_2^?$⸣ ^{geš}⸢gigir⸣ x u$_3$ x x x	Men of the chariots/wagons . . . and . . .
3.	⸢iti⸣ šu-numun u$_4$ 2(diš)-kam	Month: "Seeding." The 2nd day.

No. 237. *MS 2022/4 (X, X–X–20)*

obv.

1.	5(diš) sila$_3$ lugal-i$_3$-sa$_6$	5 sila$_3$ (of barley for) Lugal-isa.
2.	5(diš) sila$_3$ ku$_5$-da	5 sila$_3$ (for) Kuda.
3.	2(diš) sila$_3$ lu$_2$ kin-gi$_4$-<a> ma-ri$_2$<^{ki}>-še$_3$ i$_3$-du	2 sila$_3$ (for) the messenger going to Mari.
4.	2(diš) sila$_3$ lu$_2$ kin-gi$_4$-<a> giri$_3$ lu$_2$-igi-sa$_6$-sa$_6$	2 sila$_3$ (for) the messenger, conveyor Lu-igi-sasa.
5.	1(diš) sila$_3$ lu$_2$ gu-du-du	1 sila$_3$ (for) the man of Gududu.

rev.

1.	1(ban$_2$) 7(diš) ½(diš) sila$_3$ sa$_2$-du$_{11}$	1 ban$_2$, 7 ½ sila$_3$ (for) regular (deliveries).
2.	3(diš) sila$_3$ sa$_2$-du$_{11}$	3 sila$_3$ for regular (deliveries).
3.	1(diš) sila$_3$ eša	1 sila$_3$ of fine flour.
	(blank space)	
4.	šunigin 1(diš) sila$_3$ eša	Total: 1 sila$_3$ of fine flour.
5.	šunigin 1(ban$_2$) zi$_3$-gu saga	Total: 1 ban$_2$ of gu-flour.
6.	šunigin 2(ban$_2$) 7(diš) sila$_3$ še	Total: 2 ban$_2$, 7 sila$_3$ of barley.[571]

left edge

1.	u$_4$ 2(diš)-kam	The second day.[572]

Two Texts of Uncertain Content

No. 238. *MS 2019/5 (Umma, —)*

obv.

1.	1(diš) ½(diš) kuš u$_2$-hab$_2$ ki a-kal-la-ta	1 ½ (pieces of) leather, (treated with) oak apples. From A(ya)-kala.
2.	a-kal-la ra$_2$-gaba	A(ya)-kala, rider,[573]
3.	šu ba-ti	received.
4.	⸢iti⸣ dal	Month: "Flight."
5.	4(diš) kuš ka-ninda 5(diš) sila$_3$	4 (pieces of) leather for "bread mouths," 5 sila$_3$.
6.	2(diš) kuš ka-⸢ninda⸣ 2(diš) sila$_3$	2 (pieces of) leather for "bread mouths," 2 sila$_3$.
7.	^{d}šara$_2^{?}$-kam	Šara-kam
8.	šu ba-ti	*received.*
9.	2(diš) kuš u$_2$-hab$_2$ x šim$^?$	2 (pieces of) leather, (treated with) oak apples, . . .
10.	e$_2$ ensi$_2$-še$_3$	For the house of the governor.
11.	6(diš) kuš ka-ninda 5(diš) sila$_3$	6 (pieces of) leather for "bread mouths," 5 sila$_3$.

rev.

1.	a-a	(From?) Aya.
2.	1(diš) kuš ka-ninda 5(diš) sila$_3$	1 (piece of) leather for a "bread mouth" (holding) 5 sila$_3$.
3.	a$_2$-gal$_2$-nu-tuku	(From?) Agal-nutuku.

---

571 Should be 3 ban$_2$, 7 ½ sila$_3$ of barley.

572 Written over an erasure.

573 See n. 506.

4.	1(diš) ^{kuš}du$_{10}$-gan-ti-bala-a	1 courier's pouch.
5.	lugal-e-pa-⸢ri$^{?}$⸣	(From?) Lugal-epari.
6.	ki a-kal-la-ta	From A(ya)-kala,
7.	⸢zi-ga-am$_{3}$$^{?}$⸣	booked out.
	(rest blank)	

No. 239. *MS 4697 (X, AS 5–?–11)*

obv.

1.	4(ban$_{2}$) zi$_{3}$-gu$_{2}$-na ^{d}šara$_{2}$-ba-an$^{?}$-gi-gi	4 ban$_{2}$ of gu-flour (for) Šara-bangigi.
2.	ki a-gu	From Agu.
3.	3(ban$_{2}$) ninda mu-me-en$_{8}$	3 ban$_{2}$ of bread (for) Mumen.
4.	ki lugal-za$_{3}$-ge-si	From Lugal-zagesi.
5.	5(ban$_{2}$) 4(diš) ½(diš) sila$_{3}$ ur-^{d}ur$_{3}$-bar-tab	5 ban$_{2}$, 4 ½ sila$_{3}$ (for) Ur-Urbartab.
6.	3(diš) ⅓(diš) sila$_{3}$ lu$_{2}$-^{d}⸢šara$_{2}$$^{?}$⸣	3 ⅓ sila$_{3}$ (for) Lu-Šara.
7.	1(ban$_{2}$) lugal-ši-lu$_{5}$	1 ban$_{2}$ (for) Lugal-silu.
8.	⅔(diš) sila$_{3}$ lugal-e$_{2}$-maḫ-e	⅔ sila$_{3}$ (for) Lugal-Emaḫe.
9.	1(diš) sila$_{3}$ lu$_{2}$-eb-gal	1 sila$_{3}$ (for) Lu-Ebgal.
10.	1(barig) lugal-a$_{2}$-zi-da	1 barig (for) Lugal-azida.
11.	3(ban$_{2}$) geme$_{2}$-lugal	3 ban$_{2}$ (for) Geme-Lugal.

rev.

1.	ki ur-^{d}en-lil$_{2}$$^{?}$ ⸢ašgab$^{?}$⸣	From Ur-Enlil, leather worker.
2.	3(ban$_{2}$) ^{d}utu-ba-⸢an⸣-e$_{3}$	3 ban$_{2}$ (for) Utu-bane.
3.	ki ur-ge$_{6}$-par$_{4}$	From Ur-Gepar.
4.	4(diš) ½(diš) sila$_{3}$ šeš-kal-la	4 ½ sila$_{3}$ (for) Šeš-kala.
5.	2(diš) sila$_{3}$ ur-^{d}ma-mi	2 sila$_{3}$ (for) Ur-Mami.
6.	5(diš) sila$_{3}$ ur-AB$^{?}$	5 sila$_{3}$ (for) Ur-AB.
7.	ki a-du-du mu$_{6}$-⸢sub$_{3}$⸣	From Adudu, herdsman.
	(blank space)	
8.	šunigin 3(barig) 3(ban$_{2}$) 1(diš) sila$_{3}$ dabin	Total: 3 barig, 3 ban$_{2}$, 1 sila$_{3}$ of dabin flour.
9.	u$_{4}$ 1(u) 1(diš)-kam	On the 11th day.
10.	mu en ^{d}inanna maš$_{2}$-e i$_{3}$-pa$_{3}$	Year: "The En-priest of Inanna was chosen by omen."

A Very Broken Text

No. 240. *MS 4667 (Umma, Š 25 or 32 or 44–vi)*

obv.

1.	1(aš) 2(barig) 2(ban$_{2}$) 4(diš) sila$_{3}$ dabin gur	1 gur, 2 barig, 2 ban$_{2}$, 4 sila$_{3}$ dabin-flour.
2.	kišib$_{3}$ du$_{11}$-ga	Sealed tablet of Duga.
3.	2(aš) 3(barig) 4(ban$_{2}$) 8(diš) sila$_{3}$ zi$_{3}$ sig$_{15}$ gur	2 gur, 3 barig, 4 ban$_{2}$, 8 sila$_{3}$ of gu-flour.
4.	kišib$_{3}$ ur-^{d}šara$_{2}$	Sealed tablet of Ur-Šara.
5.	1(ban$_{2}$) 5(diš) sila$_{3}$ zi$_{3}$-gu	1 ban$_{2}$, 5 sila$_{3}$ gu-flour.
6.	kišib$_{3}$ ARAD$_{2}$-^{d}šara$_{2}$	Sealed tablet of ARAD-Šara.

7.	4(barig) 2(ban$_2$) 2(diš) sila$_3$ zi$_3$-gu	4 barig, 2 ban$_2$, 2 sila$_3$ gu-flour,
8.	1(ban$_2$) 3(diš) sila$_3$ dabin	1 ban$_2$, 3 sila$_3$ dabin-flour.
9.	kišib$_3$ ^{d}šara$_2$-i$_3$-zu dumu nig$_2$-u$_2$-rum	Sealed tablet of Šara-izu, child of Nig'urum.
	(*blank space*)	
10.	[. . .] x	. . .
	(*rest broken*)	

rev.

	(*beginning broken*)	
	(*blank space*)	
	(*seal impression*)	
1'.	iti ⸢šu⸣-numun	Month: "Seeding."
2'.	mu si-mu-ru-um^{ki} ba-ḫul	Year: "Simurum was destroyed."
	(*blank space*)	

seal (S001768)

1.	a-kal-la	A(ya)-kala,
2.	dub-sar	scribe,
3.	dumu lu$_2$-sa$_6$-ga	child of Lu-saga.

Not an Account?

Although complete with the administrative terminology of an account, it is difficult to see how text No. 241 would have worked as part of the administrative machinery, because it lacks the name of the person or institution whose assets were being counted, among other things.

No. 241. *MS 4701 (Umma, IS 1–i)*

obv.

1.	2(barig) i$_3$ nar nita$_2$	2 barig of oil, (for) male singers.
2.	7(diš) ½(diš) sila$_3$ nar mi$_2$	7 ½ sila$_3$ (of oil, for) female singers.
3.	i$_3$ DAG 1(u) 5(diš)-kam	DAG oil . . . . . .
4.	mu-ku$_x$(DU)	mu-ku$_x$(DU) delivery.
5.	⸢ša$_3$-bi⸣-ta	Out of it,
6.	5(diš) ½(diš) sila$_3$ dumu-gi$_7$ HI-da ib$_2$-KWU896	5 ½ sila$_3$ (of oil, for) dumu-gi$_7$[574] workers, . . .[575]

rev.

1.	a-⸢ra$_2$⸣ 2(diš)-kam	For the second time.
2.	4(diš) sila$_3$ ug$_3$-IL$_2$ dumu-dumu u$_3$ he$_2$-dab$_5$ ib$_2$-KWU896	4 sila$_3$ (of oil, for) carriers, children and . . . .
4.	giri$_3$ gu-du-du	Conveyor: Gududu.
5.	iti še-sag$_{11}$-⸢ku$_5$⸣	Month: "Harvest."
6.	mu ^{d}i-bi$_2$-^{d}suen lugal	Year: "Ibbi-Suen (was) king."
	(*blank line*)	

[574] For the meaning and status of the d u m u - g i$_7$, see most recently Koslova 2008.

[575] KWU896 here presumably not to be read e r i n$_x$, see n. 342.

Not a Letter?

Although text No. 242 includes the command, frequently found in letters, to release someone, it lacks all other terminology typical of letters. Indeed, it could have been placed with the legal texts, as it appears to concern a purchase (with a buyer weighing out [silver]), but it has no witnesses or any other legal terminology.

No. 242. *MS 2772 (—)*

obv.

1.	7(diš) x	7 . . .
2.	⸢lugal$^?$-šu$^?$-ru$^?$-du$^?$-ke$_4$$^?$⸣ in-la$_2$-e	Lugal-Šurudu weighed out.
3.	⸢šu⸣ he$_2$-bar-⸢re⸣	May he release him.

rev.

(blank space)

seal (S006049)

1.	en-um-e$_2$-a	Ennum-Ea,
2.	dub-sar	scribe,
3.	dumu a-dar di-ku$_5$	child of Adar, judge.

Not a Regular Legal Text

The final text edited here is a receipt, but it concerns an unusual loan. Loans were not usually part of the administrative system described above in Chapters 2–8, but fulfilled a purpose of mitigating shortages of grain for small-time farmers at the time before harvest, for example. Few in number, many of these loan texts come from northern Babylonia, where social and political circumstances may have favored private enterprise more than in the old city states constituting the core of the Ur III state.

No. 243. *MS 1742/2 (—)*

obv.

1.	1(aš) še gur ur$_5$-še$_3$	1 gur of barley, as an interest bearing loan.
2.	maš$_2$-bi 1(diš) x[576]	Its interest is 1 x
3.	2(iku) GAN$_2$ gur$_x$(ŠE.KIN)-a	2 iku of field harvested.
4.	ki lu$_2$-dingir-ra-⸢ta⸣	From Lu-Dingira.
5.	ba-bi	Babi

rev.

1.	šu ba-ti	received.
	(blank space)	
2.	iti še-⸢sag$_{11}$⸣-[ku$_5$]	Month: "Harvest."
3.	mu ^{d}[. . .]	Year: . . .

A Damaged Garšana Text

Text No. 244 (MS 2893) was published in CUSAS 3 as no. 550. The reader is directed to that volume for a transliteration and discussion of the text.

---

[576] The sign is similar to kir$_{11}$ (MUNUS-SILA$_4$), a female lamb, which is difficult to make sense of here.

Appendix. Transliterations of Long Texts from Chapter 8: Worker Inventories and Work-Day Accounts

No. 126. *MS 1884 (Umma, ŠS 7–v)*

obv. col. i

(beginning broken)

1'. [. . .] x
2'. [. . .] ki
3'. [. . .]-ra
4'. [. . .] x
5'. [. . .] x

(rest broken)

obv. col. ii

(start broken)

1'. [. . .] ⸢ki⸣ [. . .]-⸢zi⸣-da
2'. [x] ⸢im⸣-ti-dam
3'. *n*(ban$_{2}$) bi$_{2}$-za-za
4'. *n*(ban$_{2}$) nin-en-sa$_{6}$
5'. 1(ban$_{2}$) 5(diš) nin-e$_{2}$-ku$_{3}$-ta
6'. a-ru-a ARAD$_{2}$ KA-guru$_{7}$-me
7'. 3(ban$_{2}$) du-ur$_{2}$-ni
8'. 1(ban$_{2}$) 4(diš) a-ku-a
9'. a-ru-a lu$_{2}$-dingir-ra-me
10'. ša$_{3}$ uš-bar ki ur-^{d}nin-tu
11'. 1(ban$_{2}$) nin-ma$_{2}$-gur$_{8}$-re
12'. dumu nam-nin-i$_{3}$-du$_{10}$
13'. ša$_{3}$ kikken-na ki ur-^{d}suen

(blank space)

14'. [šunigin n] 4(ban$_{2}$) še
15'. [iti] dal
16'. [. . .]-KIN-ša$_{3}$-ga
17'. [. . .]⸢ur⸣-za$_{3}$-ge-si
18'. [. . .]-x-gi-na
19'. [. . .]-x-e$_{2}$-gal-e
20'. [. . .] x-ur$_{4}$-ša$_{3}$-ga
21'. [. . .] geme$_{2}$-^{d}šara$_{2}$
22'. [. . .]⸢geme$_{2}$⸣-^{geš}gigir
23'. [. . .] ^{d}šara$_{2}$-an-dul$_{3}$
24'. [. . .]-x-ḫa-ti
26'. [. . .] ki ur-^{d}nin-tu
27'. [. . .]-ku$_{3}$-zu dumu nin-me-lam$_{2}$
28'. [. . . nig$_{2}$]-u$_{2}$-rum
29'. [. . .] -kalam-sa$_{6}$

obv. col. iii

(start broken)

1'. [. . .] na [. . .] IL$_{2}^{?}$
2'. [. . .] NI DU
3'. [. . .]-⸢DU$^{?}$⸣-e-me
4'. [. . .] sukkal
5'. [. . .]-gi-na
6'. [. . .]-ur$_{4}$-ra
7'. [. . .]-sa-du$_{10}$
8'. [. . .]-gu
9'. [. . .] ARAD$_{2}$-mu
10'. [. . .] ^{d}šara$_{2}$-an-dul$_{3}$
11'. [. . .]⸢ur⸣-^{d}nin-a-zu
12'. [. . .]⸢lu$_{2}^{?}$⸣-bala-saga
13'. [. . .]-x-an-na
14'. [a-ru-a ur-^{geš}]⸢gigir⸣ nu-banda$_{3}$ gu$_{4}$
15'. x [. . .] ga
16'. 1(ban$_{2}$) [. . .]-mu-du
17'. dumu [. . .]-⸢ad⸣-me
18'. ⸢ša$_{3}^{?}$⸣ a-[ru$^{?}$-a . . .]-e$_{3}$

19'. 2(ban$_2$) ur-[. . .]-šu-kal
20'. dumu ur-[. . .]-im
21'. 2(ban$_2$) lugal-ezem
22'. 2(ban$_2$) lu$_2$-⸢ur$_4$⸣-[ša$_3$]-ga
23'. dumu a-ḫu-⸢lugal$^?$⸣-me
24'. ki lugal-⸢ukken⸣-ne$_2$
25'. šu ur-^{d}⸢šakkan⸣
26'. dumu lugal-iti-da
27'. ki ur-^{d}en-lil-[la$_2$]
28'. ša$_3$ umma^{ki}
(*blank space*)
29'. šunigin 1(aš) 3(barig) 2(ban$_2$) gur
30'. iti šu-numun
31'. 1(ban$_2$) sipa-na-pa$_4$-e
32'. dumu nin-šu-gi$_4$-gi$_4$ a-ga-am e$_2$ maš
33'. 1(ban$_2$) lu$_2$-^{d}nin-ur$_4$-ra
34'. dumu geme$_2$-^{d}nun-gal
35'. 1(ban$_2$) ama-gi-na
36'. dumu nin-mu-ma-ag$_2$
37'. ki lu$_2$-tur-tur
38'. 1(ban$_2$) lu$_2$-^{d}nin-ur$_4$-ra
39'. dumu geme$_2$-pu$_2^?$-maḫ
40'. 1(ban$_2$) šeš-a-ni dumu nin-ezem
41'. ki ne-sag-ta

obv. col. iv

1. [. . .]
2. [x] x-^{d}gu-la
3. [x] tur-am$_3$-i$_3$-li$_2$
4. lu$_2$ gu$_2$-du$_8$-a^{ki}
5. 4(ban$_2$) lugal-ukken-ne$_2$ nu-^{geš}kiri$_6$-ta e$_2$ gu$_4$-še$_3$
6. 4(ban$_2$) 5(diš) a-ḫu-ba-qar lu$_2$ ab?-me-lum^{ki}
7. 4(ban$_2$) 5(diš) ^{d}šara$_2$-i$_3$-sa$_6$
8. a-ru-a pa$_4$-a-nim
9. 4(ban$_2$) 5(diš) ba-an-sa$_6$
10. ša$_3$ en-nun
11. ša$_3$ umma^{ki}
12. 1(ban$_2$) ama-nig$_2$-du$_{10}$ šu-gi$_4$-ta sag-dub-ba-še$_3$
13. 1(ban$_2$) nin-ḫe$_2$-gal$_2$ dumu ama-kal-la sag-dub-ba-še$_3$
14. 1(ban$_2$) ḫa-ma-ti sag-dub-ba-še$_3$
15. 1(ban$_2$) dingir-mu-da sag-dub-ba-še$_3$
16. 1(ban$_2$) nig$_2$-ka sag-dub-ba-še$_3$
17. 1(ban$_2$) geme$_2$-^{d}a-šar$_2$ sag-dub-ba-še$_3$
18. a-ru-a inim-ma-ni-zi
19. 1(ban$_2$) igi-ni-da-a sag-dub-ba-še$_3$
20. a-ru-a ur-^{d}a-šar$_2$
21. 1(ban$_2$) nin-^{d}lamma sag-dub-ba-še$_3$
22. a-ru-a ku-za-an
23. šu 2(ban$_2$) igi-e$_2$-ba zaḫ$_3$-ta
24. 5(diš) geme$_2$-ge$_6$-par$_4$ dumu nin-ma$_2$-gur$_8$-re
25. 1(ban$_2$) nin-eb$_2$-gu-ul sag-dub-ba-še$_3$ dumu geme$_2$-^{d}šara$_2$
26. 1(ban$_2$) nin-ezem sag-dub-ba-še$_3$
27. ⸢a-ru⸣-a ARAD$_2$-dam
28. šu ⸢nam$^?$⸣-šeš-ša$_3$ zaḫ$_3$-ta
29. ⸢a-ru-a⸣ ur-^{d}nun-gal
30. ⸢1(ban$_2$) geme$_2$⸣-sukkal sag-dub-ba-še$_3$
31. ⸢a-ru⸣-[a] edin$^?$-la
32. 1(ban$_2$) si$_{12}$-[a] lugal-a$_2$-zi-da
33. dumu [x]-ku$_3$-zu$^?$ si$_{12}$-a
34. sag-⸢dub⸣-ba geme$_2$ kikken-na
35. ki lu$_2$-^{d}inanna-ta
36. ki ⸢šeš⸣-saga
37. 1(ban$_2$) a-x-na$_2$
38. 1(ban$_2$) IGI-x-še$_3$
39. 1(ban$_2$) ^{d}x-x-x
40. 1(ban$_2$) ur-^{d}x-[. . .]
41. 1(ban$_2$) dingir-mu-[. . .]

obv. col. v

1. [x] ku$_3$-^{d}šara$_2$ dumu ama-⸢kal-la⸣
2. 2(ban$_2$) lugal-nesag-e dumu ama-kal-la
3. 1(ban$_2$) a-a-lu-ḫi
4. 1(ban$_2$) ur-li
5. 1(ban$_2$) ba-zi-zi
6. ki za$_3$-mu ugula
7. 1(ban$_2$) šeš-kal-la

8. 1(ban$_2$) ur-^{d}su$_4$-an-na
9. 1(ban$_2$) ^{d}šara$_2$-me-a-DU
10. 1(ban$_2$) lugal-a$_2$-mu
11. še-ba-e daḫ-ḫa
12. 4(ban$_2$) lugal-ku$_3$-ga-ni
13. dumu lugal-ku$_3$-zu si$_{12}$-a
14. 4(ban$_2$) lu$_2$-^{d}šara$_2$
15. dumu ur-tur-tur tug$_2$-du$_8$
16. šuku-e tak$_4$-a
17. 4(ban$_2$) lugal-nig$_2$-lagar-e
18. dumu ur-^{d}si$_4$-an-na ba-uš$_2$
19. dumu diri ki lu$_2$-^{d}da-ni-ta
20. 2(ban$_2$) ur-^{d}šul-pa-e$_3$
21. dumu ^{d}suen-a-a
22. 2(ban$_2$) lugal-ma$_2$-gur$_8$-re
23. dumu nin-⸢nam⸣-ḫa-ni
24. še-ba-e daḫ-⸢ḫa⸣
25. ki ARAD$_2$ ugula
26. 1(ban$_2$) a-a-gi-na
27. 1(ban$_2$) a$_2$-dingir-ga$_2$
28. 1(ban$_2$) ARAD$_2$
29. 1(ban$_2$) ma-an-šum$_2$
30. 1(ban$_2$) ARAD$_2$-^{d}šara$_2$
31. 1(ban$_2$) lu$_2$-^{d}šara$_2$
32. 1(ban$_2$) ^{d}šara$_2$-gal-zu
33. 1(ban$_2$) lugal-amar-ku$_3$
34. 1(ban$_2$) a$_2$-dingir-ga$_2$ min-kam
35. 1(ban$_2$) lu$_2$-lugal dumu lugal-šeš
36. 1(ban$_2$) lugal-ezem
37. a-ru-a ur$_2$-mes$^{?}$-ni
38. 1(ban$_2$) šeš-kal-la
39. a-ru-a ur-gu$_2$-de$_3$-na
40. 5(diš) lugal-geš-ḫur-e
41. a-ru-a ur-^{geš}gigir
42. 5(diš) nam-tar-eb$_2$-gu-ul
43. a-ru-a lugal-geš-ḫur-e
44. 5(diš) lugal-nir-gal$_2$
45. a-ru-a lugal-TAR
46. 1(ban$_2$) ^{geš}apin-du$_{10}$
47. še-ba-e daḫ-ḫa
48. 2(ban$_2$) ur-e$_2$-maḫ
49. dumu ša$_3$-[ku$_3$]-⸢ge⸣
50. dumu ur-^{d}da-ni
51. ⸢2(ban$_2$) lugal⸣-nesag-e

obv. col. vi

1. dumu ur-li dumu igi-mu
2. 3(ban$_2$) ur-saga
3. 3(ban$_2$) giri$_3$-ni-i$_3$-sa$_6$
4. dumu ḫu-ti gab$_2$-ra-me
5. ki a-tu-ta
6. 3(ban$_2$) ur-^{d}šul-pa-e$_3$
7. 1(ban$_2$) 5(diš) na-ka$_5$-la
8. dumu e$_2$-e-a-na-ab-ba
9. 3(ban$_2$) lu$_2$-^{d}nin-ur$_4$-ra
10. dumu šeš-kal-la kur-ga$_2$-ra
11. ki lugal-ma$_2$-gur$_8$-re ugula-ta
12. 4(ban$_2$) lu$_2$-^{d}a-zi-a
13. 4(ban$_2$) šeš-kal-la
14. dumu a-ba-zi KWU79-me
15. šuku-e tak$_4$-a
16. 3(ban$_2$) lu$_2$-eb-gal
17. dumu iri-bar-re i$_3$-du$_8$
18. 3(ban$_2$) ur-^{d}šul-pa-e$_3$
19. 3(ban$_2$) ur-^{d}a-šar$_2$ dumu lugal-a$_2$-zi-da ba-uš$_2$
20. ki lu$_2$-^{d}ezem-ta
21. 4(ban$_2$) lugal-si-sa$_2$
22. a-ru-a ukken-ne$_2$
23. 3(ban$_2$) lu$_2$-an-gu$^{?}$-^{d}utu-da$^{?}$
24. dumu ur-x dumu za$_3$-mu
25. ki lu$_2$-^{d}da-mu-ta
26. daḫ-ḫu-me
27. du$_6$-ku$_3$-ga-ni ugula
28. 5(diš) nig$_2$-u$_2$-rum
29. ki a-kal-la nu-^{geš}kiri$_6$-ta
30. ⸢1(ban$_2$)⸣ lu$_2$-dingir-ra
31. dumu uš-mu

32. 2(ban$_2$) ur-^{d}ḫal-mu-ša$_4$
33. dumu lugal-iti-da
34. ki lu$_2$-^{d}nin-ur$_4$-ra
35. 1(ban$_2$) ^{d}amar-^{d}suen-ḫa-ma-ti
36. dumu da-ga-ga si$_{12}$-a
37. ki na-ba-sa$_6$
38. 1(ban$_2$) a-kal-la
39. dumu ḫu-wa-wa
40. 1(ban$_2$) x-dingir-gal
41. ki lu$_2$-^{d}šara$_2$
42. 1(ban$_2$) geš-bi
43. x ur-^{d}⸢gilgames$_x$(BIL$_3$.GA.MES)⸣
44. dumu ^{d}nin-[. . .]
45. 1(ban$_2$) x [. . .]

obv. col. vii

1. ⸢1(ban$_2$)$^{?}$⸣ MU$^{?}$-x-x-x
2. ⸢1(ban$_2$)$^{?}$ ARAD$_2$-^{d}šara$_2$$^{?}$⸣
3. dumu ur-^{d}⸢ŠE$^{?}$⸣
4. 1(ban$_2$) ur-gu$_2$-de$_3$-na
5. dumu bi$_2$-da
6. 5(diš) ur-^{d}x-x
7. dumu ur-gu$_2$-de$_3$-na
8. še-ba-e daḫ-ḫa
9. 1(ban$_2$) lu$_2$-^{d}nin-šubur
10. dumu lugal-nig$_2$-lagar-e
11. šuku-e ⸢daḫ-ḫa⸣
12. ki ur-^{d}x-mu ugula
13. 3(ban$_2$) lugal-amar-ku$_3$
14. dumu lu$_2$-ge$_6$-par$_4$
15. a$_2$-ba an-ne
16. baḫar$_3$ ^{d}⸢šara$_2$-me$^{?}$⸣
17. 3(ban$_2$) aš$_2$-⸢ka$_5$$^{?}$⸣-x
18. 3(ban$_2$) ur-x-x
19. dumu a-kal-[la$^{?}$]
20. 2(ban$_2$)$^{?}$⸣ ur-x
21. dumu lu$_2$-^{d}⸢inanna$^{?}$⸣
22. dumu šu pa$_3$ nu-x-x
23. a$_2$-ba ab-ne-me
24. ki lu$_2$-dingir-ra
25. 3(ban$_2$) lugal-ku$_3$-⸢zu$^{?}$⸣
26. dumu lu$_2$-⸢saga$^{?}$⸣
27. 3(ban$_2$) ur-^{d}⸢ištaran$^{?}$⸣
28. dumu x-x
29. 3(ban$_2$) an-na-x-[x]
30. dumu lu$_2$-x-x
31. dumu šu kur$_6$ nu-x
32. a$_2$-ba ⸢ab-ne$^{?}$⸣-me
33. ki ARAD$_2$-x
34. 2(ban$_2$) a$_2$-ni-x
35. 2(ban$_2$) ur-gu$_2$-⸢de$_3$$^{?}$⸣-na
36. dumu ^{d}NI-x-x
37. ⸢3(ban$_2$)⸣ ur-e$_2$-⸢maḫ⸣
38. dumu ur-x
39. dumu šu kur$_6$ nu-x-ba$^{?}$
40. ab-ne-[. . .]
41. ur-x a$_2$-ba AN x
42. dumu a-kal-la
43. x-x-x-x
44. šuku-e daḫ-ḫa
45. ⸢šu$^{?}$⸣-e$_2$-a lu$_2$-x-x
46. 3(ban$_2$) nam-tar-eb$_2$-⸢gu-ul⸣
47. dumu lu$_2$-du$_{11}$-ga gab$_2$-ra
48. šu lu-zabala$_3$^{ki}
49. x-[x]- ⸢ur$_4$-ra$^{?}$⸣
50. [. . .]-x
51. [. . .]

rev. col. i

1. [. . .]
2. ki a-[. . .]
3. 2(ban$_2$) lu$_2$-^{d}en-⸢lil⸣
4. 1(ban$_2$) a-da-na-aḫ
5. 1(ban$_2$) lugal-nir-gal$_2$
6. 1(ban$_2$) ur-^{d}x
7. 1(ban$_2$) ^{d}x-x
8. 1(ban$_2$) ^{d}[. . .]
9. 1(ban$_2$) giri$_3$$^{?}$-^{d}[. . .]

10. ki ur-[. . .]
11. ša$_3$ a-⸢pi$_4$⸣-[sal$_4$^{ki}]
    (*blank space*)
12. šunigin 6(aš) ⸢2(barig)⸣ [. . .]
13. iti min-[eš$_3$]
14. 1(ban$_2$) lugal$^?$-x-[x]-x
15. dumu nin-ki-ur$_5$-sa$_6$
16. giri$_3$-se$_3$-ga x-gal
17. 1(ban$_2$) geme$_2$-^{d}nanna
18. dumu geme$_2$-x-KA
19. ki uš-bar ki ur-^{d}nin-tu
20. 1(ban$_2$) lu$_2$-ur$_4$-ša$_3$-ga
21. dumu geme$_2$-^{d}dumu-zi-da
22. ki lugal-e$_2$-maḫ-e
23. 3(ban$_2$) lugal-da-mu
24. ARAD$_2$ lu$_2$-x šabra$^?$
25. ⸢zaḫ$_3$⸣ lu$_2$-^{d}zabala$_3$ e$_2$ dab$_5$$^?$-ta
26. 4(ban$_2$) ur-^{d}PA$^?$-sag-sag
27. a-ru-a ^{d}šara$_2$ a-pi$_4$-sal$_4$^{ki}
28. ki šeš-saga-ta
29. 3(ban$_2$) gu-du-du
30. 3(ban$_2$) za-a-la$_2$
31. 2(ban$_2$) lu$_2$-^{d}nin-šubur
32. dumu-ni
33. ARAD$_2$ e$_2$-gal-me
34. 4(ban$_2$) šu-^{d}ašnan
35. ⸢zaḫ$_3$⸣ [. . .]-šul-gi-ra
36. 3(ban$_2$) [. . .] x
37. zaḫ$_3$ x x x
38. 4(ban$_2$) ur-^{d}iškur
39. 1(diš) x-de$_3$-na
40. dumu x-x-x-mu
41. ki nu-ur$_2$-x-x-ta
42. x-x
43. ša$_3$ umma^{ki}
44. 3(ban$_2$) šeš-kal-la
45. 3(ban$_2$) ur-^{d}šul-pa-e$_3$
46. dumu nam-x-x
47. x-x-x
48. [. . .]

rev. col. ii

1. x x x x x x
   (*blank space*)
2. ⸢šunigin⸣ 1(aš) 2(barig) 1(diš) sila$_3$ gur
3. iti e$_2$-iti-6(diš)
4. 5(diš) nin-gi-na
5. dumu geme$_2$-^{d}suen
6. 5(diš) geme$_2$-e$_2$$^?$-gal
7. dumu tur-tur-ra
8. 1(ban$_2$) maš-gu$^?$-la sag-dub-ba-še$_3$
9. dumu nin-lu-sa$_6$-sa$_6$
10. 1(ban$_2$) nin-zabala$_3$$^{?ki?}$ sag-dub-ba-še$_3$
11. dumu geme$_2$-^{d}nanna
12. 5(diš) nin-da-da
13. dumu geme$_2$-^{d}šara$_2$
14. 1(ban$_2$) nin-e$_2$-ku$_3$-ta
15. sag-dub-ba-še$_3$
16. dumu a-du-ba-bi
17. 5(diš) lu$_2$-ur$_4$-ša$_3$ ga
18. dumu nin-en-sa$_6$
19. 1(ban$_2$) nin-ur-šu-gi$_4$-ta sag-dub-ba-še$_3$
20. 2(ban$_2$) i-mu-na-si
21. šu gi$_4$-ta sag-dub-ba-še$_3$
22. 1(ban$_2$) nin-kal-la sag-dub-ba-še$_3$
23. dumu im-ti-dam
24. 1(ban$_2$) geme$_2$-^{d}nin-ur$_4$-ra sag-dub-ba-še$_3$
25. dumu a-x
26. 5(diš) nin-agrig-zi
27. dumu nin-e$_2$-gal-e
28. 1(ban$_2$) geme$_2$-^{d}suen sag-dub-ba-še
29. dumu geme$_2$-^{geš}gigir
30. ki uš-bar
31. ki ur-^{d}nin-tu
32. 5(diš) geme$_2$-^{d}šul-gi dumu geme$_2$-x-x-x
33. ki lu$_2$-bala-saga
34. 1(ban$_2$) ^{d}amar-^{d}suen-ḫa-ma-ti dumu
    nir-i$_3$-da-gal$_2$

35. 1(ban$_2$) geme$_2$ x x x šu ma$_2$-gur$_8$-re
36. 3(ban$_2$) a-du-x
37. a-⸢ru-a⸣ ur-x
38. ki ur-^{d}⸢suen⸣
39. 5(diš) nin-⸢agrig⸣-zi

rev. col. iii

1. dumu nin-en-sa$_6^{?}$
2. ⸢5(diš)$^{?}$⸣ ṣe-lu-uš-du$_{10}$
3. dumu ⸢nin⸣-pa$_3$-da
4. 5(diš) nin-ezem
5. dumu nin-ur$_2$-ra-ni
6. x geme$_2$-^{d}ma-mi sag-dub-ba-še$_3$
7. dumu nin-x-zi-x
8. 1(ban2) nin-a$^{?}$-ni$^{?}$ dumu ⸢nin⸣-en-sa$_6$
9. 1(ban$_2$) geme$_2$-lugal-ezem sag-dub-ba-še$_3$
   dumu lugal-tur-tur
10. 1(ban$_2$) nin-a-ba-an-sa$_6$ sag-dub-ba-še$_3$
   dumu ša-ad-da-ti
11. 2(ban$_2$) lu$_2$-kal-la
12. [dumu?] igi-tur-tur
13. ki giri$_3$-x-x-^{d}suen
14. 3(ban$_2$) 5(diš) ti-e$_2$-maḫ-ta
15. ARAD$_2$ x-x-a
16. ki x-la$_2$
17. 2(ban$_2$) lu$_2$-^{d}nin-ur$_4$-ra
18. 2(ban$_2$) ur-^{d}⸢en⸣-lil$_2$-la$_2$
19. dumu x-x-ki
20. x-x-me
21. x-x-du$_{11}$-ga-x
22. 1(ban$_2$) 5(diš) lu$_2$-a$_2$-zi-da
23. dumu a-ba-^{d}šara$_2$-gin$_7$ ša$_3$-gu$_4$ šu ur-^{geš}gigir
24. 2(ban$_2$) a-ad-da-ka-KU
25. dumu lu$_2$-^{d}šara$_2$
26. ⸢2(ban$_2$)⸣ ur-am$_3$-ma [. . .] ⸢$^{geš?}$⸣gigir-re x
27. 4(ban$_2$) 5(diš) lugal-^{d}šara$_2$ dumu x-x-TAR
28. 4(ban$_2$) 5(diš) ⸢inim-ma-ni-zi⸣
29. ki in-sa$_6$-sa$_6$
30. 2(ban$_2$) ^{d}šara$_2$-me-a-tum$_2$
31. 1(ban$_2$) 5(diš) ur-e$_2$-maḫ
32. 1(ban$_2$) 5(diš) inim-^{d}šara$_2$
33. dumu šu-x-da-x-me
34. ki er$_2$-dingir
35. 4(ban$_2$) lu$_2$-dingir-ra
36. dumu ur-ki-ama
37. ki umma^{ki}
   (*blank space*)
38. šunigin 1(aš) 4(barig) 5(ban$_2$) 5(diš) sila$_3$ gur

rev. col. iv

1. iti ^{d}[li$_9$-si$_4$]
2. 1(ban$_2$) ur-[. . .]-a
3. dumu [. . .]-x
4. x [. . .] ša$_3$-ga
5. [. . .]-za$_3^{?}$-ge-si$^{?}$
6. [. . .] x x x [dumu . . .]-nin-tu
7. 2(ban$_2$) [dingir]-⸢mu-ma⸣-an-šum$_2$
9. ⸢a$^{?}$-pi$_4^{?}$⸣-sal$_4^{ki}$-še$_3^{?}$
10. ⸢2(ban$_2$) ⸣ ur-^{geš}⸢gigir$^{?}$⸣
11. ⸢dumu lugal⸣-^{geš}gigir-⸢re⸣
12. ⸢šu⸣ a-ab-ba-mu
13. x lu$_2$-^{d}šara$_2$
14. nibru^{ki}-ta
15. ki er$_2$-dingir
16. 1(ban$_2$) ama-šu-ḫal-bi
17. dumu geme$_2$-^{d}šara$_2$
18. ki lugal-e$_2$-maḫ-e
19. ša$_3$ ⸢umma⸣^{ki}
20. x x ma$_2$-gur$_8$-re
21. ⸢a-ru-a⸣ nam-ḫa-ni
22. ki ku$_3$-ga-ni ugula
23. giri$_3$-^{d}šara$_2$-i$_3$-dab$_5$
24. dumu x-tu
25. lu$_2$-^{d}nin-ur$_4$-ra
26. ur-^{d}x
27. dumu ⸢nin⸣-ezem-me
28. [. . .] x x x
29. dumu nin-⸢ma$_2^{?}$-gur$_8^{?}$⸣-re
30. x lugal-⸢nesag$^{?}$-e$^{?}$⸣

31. dumu nin-x-x
32. x x x
(*blank space*)
33. šunigin 2(barig) 5(ban$_2$)
34. iti ezem-^{d}šul-gi
35. 1(ban$_2$) nin-me-dingir-bi dumu geme$_2$-gu$_2$-edin
36. ki uš-bar ki ur-^{d}nin-tu
37. x ^{d}amar-^{d}suen-ḫa-ma-ti
38. [. . .]-ma-mi
39. [. . .]-saga
40. [. . .]-na

rev. col. v

1. 1(ban$_2$) geme$_2$-^{d}šul-pa-e$_3$
2. dumu ama-kal-la
3. 1(ban$_2$) lu$_2$-bala-saga
4. dumu nin-ab-ba-na
5. ki giri$_3$ ki lu$_2$-^{d}nanna
6. ki umma^{ki}
7. x nigar^{gar}-ki-du$_{10}$
8. x lugal-ku$_3$-zu
9. dumu lu$_2$-^{d}utu ba-uš$_2$-me
10. dumu lugal-KA
11. 4(ban$_2$) en-ma-an-gu-ul
12. šu-gi$_4$ šuku nu-dab$_5$-ta
13. 1(ban$_2$) lu-lu-uš-du-še$_3$
14. ki a-pi$_4$-sal$_4^{ki}$
(*blank space*)
15. šunigin 2(barig)
16. iti pa$_4$-u$_2$-[e]
17. 2(ban$_2$) nin-[. . .]
18. 1(ban$_2$) x-[. . .]-x
19. [. . .] x [. . .]-še$_3$
20. [. . .]-x
21. [. . .] x
22. [. . .] x
23. [. . .]-na$^{?}$
24. [. . .]-da
25. [. . .]-^{geš}gigir
26. ⸢ki⸣ [x] e$_2$ maš
27. 2(ban$_2$) ur-^{d}suen dumu ši-mu
28. ki ur-^{geš}gigir nu-banda$_3$ gu$_4$
29. 1(barig) si$_{12}$-a ki x lu$_2$ ša$_3$-gu$_4$-ta
30. 1(barig) si$_{12}$-a e-ma-am$_3$
31. 1(barig) si$_{12}$-a nu-ur$_2$-i$_3$-li$_2$
32. ⸢a-ru-a⸣ ur-nigar$^{\langle gar\rangle}$
33. ša$_3$ x bala-a
34. ki ur-^{d}a-šar$_2$ u$_3$ a-gu-du
35. 1(barig) 1(ban$_2$) 5(diš) lugal-iti-da baḫar$_3^{?}$
(*blank space*)
36. šunigin 1(aš) 1(barig) 5(diš) sila$_3$ gur
37. ⸢iti⸣ ^{d}dumu-zi

rev. col. vi

(*blank*)

rev. col. vii

(*blank space*)
1. [. . .]-x
(*rest broken*)

No. 127. *MS 4705 (Umma, X–xii)*

obv. col. i

(*start missing*)
1′. [x] ur-^{d}[. . .] x x
2′. [x] ⸢lu$_2$⸣-saga
3′. [x] ⸢lu$_2$⸣-du$_{10}$-ga
4′. [x] ⸢šeš⸣-kal-⸢la⸣
5′. [x] x ⸢i$_3$⸣-kal-⸢la⸣
6′. [dumu-ni]-me
7′. [. . .]-⸢ku$_3$-ga⸣
8′. [. . .]-x
9′. [. . .] ⸢lu$_2$⸣-uš-gi-na
10′. [x] ⸢šeš⸣-kal-la
11′. [x] x ⸢ug$_3$⸣-du-du-me
12′. [. . .]-KA-ni
13′. [. . .]-^{d}nin-PA dumu-⸢ni⸣
14′. [. . . ur$^{?}$]-e$_{11}$-e
15′. [. . .] AN GIŠ
16′. [. . .]-x-um dumu-ni

17'. [. . .] ⸢lugal⸣-iti-⸢da⸣

18'. [. . .] x

19'. [. . . x]-^{geš}gigir-re

20'. [. . .]-x-mu

obv. col. ii

(start missing)

1'. [. . .]-na

2'. [x]-x-ur$_4$-ra

3'. [x] ARAD$_2$-^{d}šara$_2$

4'. [x] ur-lugal

5'. x-me

6'. [x] ur-e$_2$-maḫ

7'. a-tu ⸢dumu⸣-ni

8'. 1(aš$_c$) ⸢ur$^?$-^{d}šara$_2{}^?$⸣

9'. [x] a-tu

(blank line)

10'. ⸢giri$_3$⸣-[se$_3$-ga . . .]

11'. x [. . .]

12'. 1(aš$_c$) x-[. . .]

13'. 1(aš$_c$) AB [x]-AN-[x]

(several lines missing)

14'. [. . .]-maḫ

15'. x ⸢AB⸣ ur-^{geš}gigir

16'. 1(aš$_c$) e$_2$-maḫ-ki-bi

17'. dumu-ni-me

obv. col. iii

(start missing)

1'. [giri$_3$]-⸢se$_3$⸣-ga [. . .]

2'. x lugal-⸢^{geš}gigir⸣

3'. 1(aš$_c$) inim-ma-ni dumu-ni

4'. 1(aš$_c$) ur-^{d}⸢ištaran$^?$⸣

5'. 1(aš) šeš-a-ni

6'. 1(diš) ur-^{d}[. . .] ⸢dumu⸣ x

7'. 1(diš) x-[. . .]-x

8'. [. . .]

9'. [. . .]

10'. [. . .]

11'. [. . .]

12'. [. . .]

13'. x ⸢ur$^?$⸣-[. . .]

14'. 1(aš) [. . .]

15'. [. . .]

16'. [. . .]

17'. [. . .]

18'. [. . .]-AN-[x]

19'. [. . .]-gi-ra

20'. [. . .] ug$_3$ x

21'. ⸢1(aš$_c$)⸣ ^{d}šara$_2$-kam dumu x

22'. 1(aš$_c$) na-ba-⸢sa$_6{}^?$⸣

23'. x lu$_2$-x-x

(blank line)

24'. giri$_3$-se$_3$-ga x-[x]

25'. 1(aš$_c$) ⸢ur⸣-[. . .]

26'. [. . .]

rev. col. i

1. 1(aš$_c$) lu$_2$-^{d}šara$_2$

2. dumu lu$_2$-ki-ag$_2$-mu

(blank line)

3. giri$_3$-se$_3$-ga ^{d}amar-^{d}suen-me

4. ⸢1(aš$_c$)⸣ lugal-x-x

5. 1(aš) [. . .]

6. 1(aš$_c$) lugal-ḫi-li

7. 1(aš) lugal-ma$_2$-gur$_8$-re

8. 1(diš) a-kal-la

9. 1(diš) ^{d}šara$_2$-i$_3$-zu

10. 1(diš) lu$_2$-tur-tur-mu

11. dumu-ni-me

12. 1(aš$_c$) ur-nigar^{gar}

13. 1(aš) lugal-nesag-e

14. 1(diš) šeš-kal-la

15. 1(diš) lugal-⸢ḫe$_2$-gal$_2$⸣

16. 1(diš) lu$_2$-^{d}nin-ur$_4$-ra

17. dumu-ni-me

18. 1(aš$_c$) lu$_2$-^{d}EN-[x]

19. 1(aš) ur-e$_2$-⸢maḫ⸣

20. 1(diš) ARAD$_2$-x-x

21. 1(diš) ur-e$_{11}$-⸢e⸣
22. 1(diš) ur-si-gar
23. dumu-ni-me

(*blank space*)

24. giri$_{3}$-se$_{3}$-ga ^{d}⸢gu⸣-[la]

rev. col. ii

(*blank space*)

1. ½(diš$_{c}$) GAN$_{2}$ nimgir-an-ne$_{2}$ baḫar$_{3}$
2. 1(aš) ⸢lugal⸣-nesag-e
3. 1(diš) ^{d}šara$_{2}$-mu-tum$_{2}$
4. dumu lugal-^{geš}gigir-re baḫar$_{3}$-me
5. ki lu$_{2}$-dingir-ra ugula-ta
6. šu za-ga-gi-na
7. 1(aš$_{c}$) 1(diš) 4(barig) ug$_{3}$ ur-mes dumu-ni <<mu>> u$_{2}$-IL$_{2}$
8. šu ug$_{3}$ lugal-bad$_{3}$
9. 1(aš$_{c}$) GAN$_{2}$ ug$_{3}$ šeš-kal-la lunga
10. 1(aš) lu$_{2}$-^{d}šul-gi-ra
11. 1(diš) ur-^{d}suen
12. 1(diš) lugal-amar-ku$_{3}$
13. dumu lugal-bad$_{3}$-me
14. e$_{2}$ kas$_{4}$ a-pi$_{4}$-sal$_{4}^{ki}$

(*rest blank*)

rev. col. iii

(*blank* space)

1. gurum$_{2}$-ak šu-ku$_{6}$ ba$^{?}$-KA$^{?}$-me
2. ša$_{3}$ a-pi$_{4}$-sal$_{4}^{ki}$
3. iti min-eš$_{3}$-ta ⸢u$_{4}$⸣ 1(u) 5(diš)-am$_{3}$ ba-ra-zal-la-ta
4. mu en-unu$_{6}$-gal ^{d}inanna ba-ḫun

(*blank space*)

No. 128. *MS 2369 (Umma, AS 3)*

obv. col. i

1. 1(aš$_{c}$) GAN$_{2}$ a-tu šuš$_{3}$ ab$_{2}$
2. 1(aš) du$_{11}$-ga-zi-da
3. 1(diš) ur-e$_{2}$-maḫ
4. 1(diš) ^{d}šara$_{2}$-gal-⸢zu$^{?}$⸣
5. dumu-ni-me
6. 1(aš) na-ba-sa$_{6}$ šeš-a-ni
7. 1(aš) GAN$_{2}^{?}$ ur-mes aga$_{3}$-us$_{2}$
8. 1(diš) ur-^{d}ur$_{3}$-bar-tab dumu-ni
9. ⸢1(aš) GAN$_{2}$⸣ lugal-ku$_{3}$-ga-ni dumu inim-^{d}šara$_{2}$
10. sipa-ta
11. šuš$_{3}$ i$_{3}$-dab$_{5}$
12. šu lu$_{2}$-zabala$_{3}^{ki}$
13. 1(aš$_{c}$) GAN$_{2}$ lu$_{2}$-^{d}utu ⸢unu$_{3}$⸣
14. 1(aš$_{c}$) GAN$_{2}$ ur-e$_{2}$-maḫ
15. 1(aš) AB lu$_{2}$-eb-gal
16. 1(aš) ur-^{d}ištaran
17. dumu-ni-me
18. 1(aš$_{c}$) GAN$_{2}$ ug$_{3}$ nigar^{gar}-ki-du$_{10}$ dumu ur-^{geš}gigir
19. 1(aš$_{c}$) GAN$_{2}$ lu$_{2}$-eb-gal dumu am$_{3}$-ma na:gada
20. 1(aš$_{c}$) GAN$_{2}$ nigar^{gar}-ki-du$_{10}$ dumu kal-la nar
21. 1(aš$_{c}$) GAN$_{2}$ ug$_{3}$ lugal-kisal
22. 1(aš$_{c}$) GAN$_{2}$ ur-^{d}utu
23. 1(aš$_{c}$) GAN$_{2}$ al-ba-ni-du$_{11}$
24. 1(aš$_{c}$) GAN$_{2}$ ug$_{3}$ lu$_{2}$-du$_{10}$-ga
25. 1(diš) ur-<<AN>>-am$_{3}$-ma
26. 1(diš) ur-^{d}suen
27. ⸢1(diš)⸣ nam-tar-eb$_{2}$-gu-ul
28. dumu-ni-me
29. 1(aš$_{c}$) GAN$_{2}$ lu$_{2}$-^{d}šara$_{2}$ dumu ur-e$_{11}$-e
30. 1(diš) lugal-geš-ḫur-e dumu-ni
31. ⸢1(aš)⸣ 3(ban$_{2}$) 1(diš) tug$_{2}$ lugal-amar-ku$_{3}$ dumu u$_{3}$-ma-⸢ni⸣

obv. col. ii

1. 1(aš$_{c}$) GAN$_{2}$ ⸢ug$_{3}$⸣ [šeš]-⸢kal⸣-la ⸢dumu da⸣-da
2. ki ur-^{d}ba-ba$_{6}$-ta
3. lu$_{2}$-^{d}utu i$_{3}$-dab$_{5}$
4. šu ur-nigar^{gar}
5. 1(aš$_{c}$) GAN$_{2}$ ur-⸢sukkal⸣ unu$_{3}$
6. 1(diš) ^{d}šara$_{2}$-mu-tum$_{2}$ dumu-ni
7. 1(aš$_{c}$) GAN$_{2}$ ab-ba-⸢gi-na⸣
8. 1(aš) AB KA-x-x

9. dumu-ni
10. šu ug$_3$ ⸢ur-nigar^{gar}⸣
11. 1(aš$_c$) GAN$_2$ ug$_3$ ⸢sila⸣-si-⸢ig⸣
12. 1(diš) ⸢lu$_2$-^{d}⸣šara$_2$ dumu-ni
13. 1(aš$_c$) GAN$_2$ ug$_3$ lugal-⸢ab⸣-ba
14. 1(aš) AB ba-zi-na
15. 1(diš) lugal-ku$_3$-⸢zu⸣
16. dumu-ni-me
17. 1(aš$_c$) GAN$_2$ gu-du-du
18. 1(aš$_c$) GAN$_2$ ad-da-⸢kal-la⸣
19. 1(diš) lu$_2$-^{d}šara$_2$
20. 1(diš) ur-igi-gal$_2$
21. ⸢ša$_3$⸣ ka-saḫar-ra⸢$^{ki?}$⸣
22. dumu da-a-da-ga x
23. šu lugal-ku$_3$-ga-ni
24. 1(aš$_c$) GAN$_2$ lugal-šu-nir-re
25. 1(aš) ⸢lugal⸣-ušur$_x$(LAL$_2$.TUG$_2$)
26. 1(diš) ur-⸢^{d}en-lil$_2$-la$_2$⸣
27. 1(diš) lugal-maš-zu
28. dumu-ni-me
29. šu ur-dingir-ra
30. 1(aš$_c$) GAN$_2$ ur-^{d}a-šar$_2$
31. 1(diš) ša$_3$-ku$_3$-ge
32. dumu-ni-me
33. 1(aš$_c$) GAN$_2$ ug$_3$ an-ta-lu$_2^{?}$
34. 1(diš) ^{d}šara$_2$-i$_3$-⸢zu$^{?}$⸣ dumu-ni
35. ur-sukkal i$_3$-dab$_5$
36. 1(aš$_c$) GAN$_2$ lugal-ezem unu$_3$
37. 1(diš) [x]-x-i$_3$-x-tug$_2$
38. [. . . lu$_2$]- ⸢dingir⸣-ra
39. ⸢dumu ur⸣-^{d}ma-mi-me

obv. col. iii

1. 1(aš$_c$) GAN$_2$ ug$_3$ ur-^{d}ur$_3$-bar-tab
2. 1(aš$_c$) GAN$_2$ ur-dingir-ra dumu šeš-kal-la
3. lugal-ezem i$_3$-dab$_5$
4. 1(aš$_c$) GAN$_2$ ^{d}šara$_2$-mu unu$_3$
5. 1(aš$_c$) GAN$_2$ ab-ba-gi-na
6. 1(aš) ur-^{d}suen
7. dumu ARAD$_2$-dam-me
8. ^{d}šara$_2$-a-mu i$_3$-dab$_5$
9. 1(aš$_c$) GAN$_2$ ur-^{d}su$_4$-da unu$_3$
10. 1(diš) ur-gu$_2$-de$_3$-na
11. 1(diš) inim-^{d}šara$_2$
12. dumu-ni-me
13. 1(aš$_c$) GAN$_2$ ug$_3$ ^{d}šara$_2$-pa$_3$-da ⸢dumu⸣ ur-^{d}suen
14. ur-^{d}su$_4$-[da] i$_3$-dab$_5$
15. šu inim-gi
16. 1(aš$_c$) GAN$_2$ ^{d}šara$_2$-kam unu$_3$
17. 1(diš) ur-^{d}šul-⸢pa-e$_3$⸣
18. 1(diš) ⸢lu$_2$⸣-^{d}nin-šubur
19. dumu-ni-me
20. 1(aš$_c$) GAN$_2$ ^{geš}dur$_2$-gar-ni$^{?}$
21. dumu inim-gi-me
22. ^{d}šara$_2$-kam i$_3$-dab$_5$
23. 1(aš$_c$) GAN$_2$ lugal-ku$_3$-zu unu$_3$ dumu ur-e$_{11}$-e
24. 1(aš$_c$) GAN$_2$ ḫu-ti
25. 1(aš) giri$_3$-ni-i$_3$-⸢sa$_6$⸣
26. 1(diš) ur-sa$_6$
27. 1(diš) lu$_2$-^{d}inanna
28. dumu-ni-me
29. 1(aš$_c$) GAN$_2$ giri$_3$-ni-i$_3$-⸢sa$_6$⸣ dumu ur-ki-ag$_2$-mu
30. 1(aš$_c$) 1(barig) 4(diš) ug$_3$ mu-du
31. ⸢1(diš) 3(ban$_2$)⸣ 1(diš) ⸢tug$_2$ ab⸣-ba-kal-la
32. [x] 2(diš) ARAD$_2$-^{d}šara$_2$
33. 1(diš) ⸢2(ban$_2$)⸣ 5(diš) 1(diš) ½(diš) šeš-kal-la
34. ⸢dumu⸣-ni-me
35. lugal-ku$_3$-zu i$_3$-dab$_5$
36. 1(aš$_c$) GAN$_2$ ug$_3$ ⸢lugal⸣-šu-nir-e unu$_3$
37. 1(diš) ur-^{d}a-šar$_2$ dumu-ni
38. x x ug$_3$ lu$_2$-^{d}šara$_2$ dumu ur-su$_4$-su$_4$

rev. col. i

1. ⸢lugal-šu-nir⸣-re i$_3$-dab$_5$
2. 1(aš$_c$) GAN$_2$ uš unu$_3$
3. 1(aš$_c$) GAN$_2$ ur-e$_2$-maḫ
4. 1(aš) ^{d}šara$_2$-ki-ag$_2$

5. dumu-ni-me
6. 1(aš$_c$) GAN$_2$ ug$_3$ lugal-si-sa$_2$
7. 1(diš) lugal-nig$_2$-lagar-e dumu-ni
8. ki ^{d}šara$_2$-kam-ta
9. uš i$_3$-dab$_5$
10. 1(aš$_c$) GAN$_2$ ug$_3$ al-ba-ni-du$_{11}$ unu$_3$
11. 1(diš) lugal-šu-nir-re
12. 1(diš) ^{d}šara$_2$-i$_3$-zu
13. dumu-ni-me
14. šu bu$_3$-du
15. 1(aš$_c$) GAN$_2$ ug$_3$ lu$_2$-^{d}šara$_2$ dumu-ni
16. al-ba-ni-du$_{11}$ i$_3$-dab$_5$
17. 1(aš$_c$) GAN$_2$ ur-ama-na unu$_3$
18. 1(aš) ama-ni-ba-an-sa$_6$
19. 1(diš) ša$_3$-ku$_3$-ge
20. dumu gu-za-la$_2$
21. 1(aš$_c$) GAN$_2$ ⸢ug$_3$ lugal-ma$_2$-gur$_8$⸣-re
22. 1(aš) ⸢gu⸣-u$_2$-gu
23. ⸢1(diš)⸣ a-a-gi-na
24. ⸢uš$_2$⸣ lu$_5$-lu$_5$
25. ⸢1(diš)⸣ ur-^{d}ur$_3$-bar-tab
26. dumu-ni-me
27. ⸢1(aš)$^{?}$⸣ ama lugal-eb$_2$-gu-ul
28. ur-ama-na i$_3$-dab$_5$
29. 1(aš$_c$) GAN$_2$ pu$_3$-du
30. ⸢1(aš$_c$) GAN$_2$⸣ ug$_3$ ur-[x]-da
31. dumu ⸢pu$_3$⸣-du
32. ⸢pu$_3$-du i$_3$-dab$_5$⸣
33. ⸢1(aš$_c$) GAN$_2$ ug$_3$⸣ a-ši-mu$_2$ unu$_3$
34. ⸢1(aš$_c$) GAN$_2$⸣ ug$_3$ ⸢lu$_5$-am$_3$⸣
35. [a]-ši-mu$_2$ i$_3$-dab$_5$
36. 1(aš$_c$) GAN$_2$ ⸢ad⸣-da-da
37. ⸢1(diš)$^{?}$⸣ giri$_3$-ni-i$_3$-sa$_6$ dumu-ni
38. ⸢1(aš$_c$)⸣ GAN$_2$ ug$_3$ ur-ge$_6$-par$_4$ x
39. ⸢1(aš$_c$)⸣ GAN$_2$ ug$_3$ lu$_2$-bala-saga
40. 1(aš$_c$) GAN$_2$ ug$_3$ ARAD$_2$-ḫu-la
41. ⸢ad⸣-da-da i$_3$-dab$_5$

(blank space)

rev. col. ii

(blank space, seal impression)

rev. col. iii

(blank space, seal impression)

1. unu$_3$ gab$_2$-ra-me
2. ugula a-tu
3. ša$_3$ a-pi$_4$-sal$_4^{ki}$

(blank space, seal impression)

4. mu ku$_3$-gu-za ^{d}en-lil$_2$-la$_2$ ba-dim$_2$

seal (S001829)

1. a-tu
2. dub-sar
3. dumu šeš-kal-la

No. 129. *MS 1883*

obv. col. i

(blank space)

1'. [. . .] x
2'. [dumu]-ni-me
3'. [. . .]-^{d}⸢nin⸣-šubur šeš-a-ni
4'. [. . .]-um-ma-ni$^{?}$
5'. [. . .]-x-x x [. . .] ⸢dumu⸣ x-x
6'. [. . .] ku$_3$-ga-ni ⸢dumu⸣ [x]-^{d}x
7'. ⸢ARAD$_2$$^{?}$⸣-mu i$_3$-dab$_5$

(blank space)

8'. x [x] i$_3$-dab$_5$
9'. ⸢šu⸣ [lu$_2$]-zabala$_3^{ki}$
10'. 1(aš$_c$) ⸢lu$_2$⸣-^{d}utu

(rest broken)

obv. col. ii

1. [. . .]
2. [. . .]-na$^{?}$
3. [. . .]-x-ta
4. [1(aš$_c$) GAN$_2$] ⸢ug$_3$⸣ lugal-ma$_2$-gur$_8$-re
5. 1(aš) a-a-gi-na
6. 1(diš) ur-^{d}ur$_3$-bar-tab
7. dumu-ni-me
8. ki ur-ama-na unu$_3$-ta

(blank space with calculations: 3(diš) 2(u) 5(diš))

9. lugal-^{d}utu i$_{3}$-dab$_{5}$
10. šu ur-nigar^{gar}
11. ⸢1(aš$_{c}$)⸣ ur-sukkal
12. 1(diš)$^{?}$ ^{d}šara$_{2}$-mu-tum$_{2}$ dumu-ni
13. 1(aš$_{c}$) GAN$_{2}$ ab-ba-gi-na unu$_{3}$
14. 1(aš$_{c}$) inim-^{d}šara$_{2}$
15. dumu ur-nigar^{gar}-me
16. [x] e$_{2}$-u$_{6}$-e
17. [x] sila-si-ig
18. ⸢lu$_{2}$⸣-^{d}šara$_{2}$ dumu-ni
19. [. . .]-re i$_{3}$-[dab$_{5}^{?}$]
20. [. . . lugal]-⸢ab⸣-ba
21. [. . . ab-ba-gi]-na
22. [. . . lugal]-⸢ku$_{3}$⸣-zu
23. [dumu-ni]-me
24. [. . . gu]-⸢du⸣-du
25. [. . .]
26. [. . .]
27. [. . .] x
28. [. . .] ur-⸢igi⸣-gal$_{2}$

(*blank space*)

29. ⸢gab$_{2}^{?}$-us$_{2}^{?}$ ša$_{3}$⸣ ka-saḫar-ra
30. [dumu] ⸢da⸣-a-da-ga-[me]
31. [šu] ⸢lugal⸣-ku$_{3}$-ga-ni
32. [. . .] ⸢lugal⸣-šu-⸢nir-re⸣ [. . .]
33. [. . .] x [. . .]

(*rest broken*)

obv. col. iii

(*blank space*)

1. ab-ba-gi-na i$_{3}$-dab$_{5}$
2. 1(aš$_{c}$) GAN$_{2}$ lugal-ezem unu$_{3}$
3. 1(aš) ^{d}šara$_{2}$-i$_{3}$-zu
4. 1(diš) lu$_{2}$-dingir-ra
5. dumu ur-^{d}ma-mi-me
6. 1(aš$_{c}$) GAN$_{2}$ ug$_{3}$ ur-^{d}ur$_{3}$-bar-tab
7. ur-dingir-ra dumu šeš-kal-la
8. lu$_{2}$-^{d}da-mu ugula i$_{3}$-dab$_{5}$
9. 1(aš$_{c}$) GAN$_{2}$ ug$_{3}$ lugal-si-x
10. 1(diš) lugal-nig$_{2}$-lagar-e dumu-ni
11. 1(aš$_{c}$) GAN$_{2}$ ug$_{3}$ gu-u$_{2}$-gu
12. dumu lugal-ma$_{2}$-gur$_{8}$-re
13. ki ur-ama-na unu$_{3}$-ta

(*blank space with computations*: 5(u) 8(diš))

14. lugal-ezem i$_{3}$-dab$_{5}$
15. 1(aš$_{c}$) GAN$_{2}$ ^{d}šara$_{2}$-a-mu unu$_{3}$
16. 1(aš$_{c}$) GAN$_{2}$ ab-ba-gi-na
17. 1(aš) ur-^{d}suen
18. dumu ARAD$_{2}$-dam-⸢me⸣
19. 1(aš$_{c}$) GAN2 ug$_{3}$ ^{d}šara$_{2}$-i$_{3}$-sa$_{6}$
20. u$_{2}$-IL$_{2}$ ^{d}šara$_{2}$ a-pi$_{4}$-sal$_{4}^{ki}$-ta
21. 1(aš$_{c}$) GAN$_{2}$ ug$_{3}$ lugal-e$_{2}$-na-na
22. a-ru-a ama-lal$_{3}$-ab-zu

(*blank space with computations:* 1(diš) 3(u) 2(diš))

23. ^{d}šara$_{2}$-a-mu i$_{3}$-dab$_{5}$
24. 1(aš$_{c}$) GAN$_{2}$ ur-^{d}su$_{4}$-da ⸢unu$_{3}$⸣
25. 1(aš$_{c}$) ⸢ur⸣-[gu$_{2}$-de$_{3}$]-na
26. 1(diš) inim-⸢^{d}šara$_{2}$⸣ dumu-ni-me
27. 1(aš$_{c}$) GAN$_{2}$ ug$_{3}$ ^{d}⸢šara$_{2}$⸣-pa$_{3}$-da dumu ur-^{d}suen
28. ⸢1(aš$_{c}$) GAN$_{2}$ ug$_{3}$⸣ ab-ba-⸢kal⸣-[la] ⸢dumu⸣ mu-du
29. [. . .]-ku$_{3}$-zu-ta

(*blank space*)

30. [ur-^{d}su$_{4}$]-da i$_{3}$-dab$_{5}$
31. [du$_{11}$]-gi
32. [1(aš$_{c}$) GAN$_{2}$] ^{d}šara$_{2}$-kam ⸢unu$_{3}$⸣
33. [1(diš)? ur]-^{d}⸢šul⸣-[pa]-⸢e$_{3}$⸣
34. [1(diš)? lu$_{2}$-^{d}]⸢nin⸣-šubur
35. [dumu]-⸢ni⸣-me
36. [1(aš$_{c}$) GAN$_{2}$ ^{geš}dur$_{2}$]-gar-ni

(*rest broken*)

obv. col. iv

1. dumu ⸢du$_{11}$⸣-[ge]-⸢me⸣
2. 1(aš$_{c}$) GAN$_{2}$ x-[. . .]-x-[x]-x
3. a-ru-a [x]-ta$^{?}$

(*blank space with computations*: 5(u) 6(diš))

4. ^{d}šara$_{2}$-kam i$_{3}$-dab$_{5}$
5. 1(aš$_{c}$) GAN$_{2}$ lugal-ku$_{3}$-zu unu$_{3}$ dumu ur-e$_{11}$-e

6. ḫu-ti
7. giri$_3$-ni-i$_3$-sa$_6$
8. ur-sa$_6$-ga
9. lu$_2$-^{d}⸢inanna⸣
10. ba-⸢saga⸣
11. dumu-ni-me
12. e$_2$-a-lu$_2$-bi i$_3$-[dab$_5^?$]
13. 1(aš$_c$) GAN$_2$ giri$_3$-ni-[i$_3$]-sa$_6$ dumu ur-e$_{11}$-e muḫaldim
14. x ug$_3$ mu-du
15. ug$_3$ ab-ba-⸢kal-la⸣
16. ARAD$_2$-^{d}šara$_2$
17. šeš-kal-la
18. dumu-ni-me
19. lu$_2$-^{d}x-x-x
20. 1(aš$_c$) GAN$_2$ lu$_2$-dingir-⸢ra⸣ dumu ur-e$_{11}$-e
21. 1(diš) lugal-geš-ḫur-e dumu-ni
22. ki lu$_2$-zabala$_3^{ki}$-ta
23. 1(aš$_c$) GAN$_2$ peš$_2$-am$_3$
24. ki a-ki-šar-ta
25. 1(aš$_c$) GAN$_2$ lu$_2$-^{d}šara$_2$ dumu ur-su$_4$-su$_4$
26. ki lugal-šu-nir-re-ta
27. 1(aš$_c$) GAN$_2$ ur-dingir-ra dumu ⸢šeš⸣-kal-la
28. ki lugal-ezem-ta

(*blank space with computations*: 1(geš$_2$) 3(u))

29. lugal-ku$_3$-zu i$_3$-dab$_5$
30. 1(aš$_c$) GAN$_2$ ug$_3$ lugal-šu-nir-re unu$_3$
31. 1(aš$_c$) ur-^{d}a-šar$_2$ dumu-ni
32. x lu$_2$-^{d}šara$_2$ dumu ur-su$_4$-su$_4$
33. lugal-ku$_3$-zu i$_3$-dab$_5$

(*blank space with computations*: 2(u) 2(diš))

34. lugal-šu-nir-re i$_3$-dab$_5$
35. 1(aš$_c$) GAN$_2$ uš unu$_3$
36. ⸢1(aš$_c$)⸣ ur-e$_2$-maḫ
37. ⸢dumu ^{d}šara$_2$⸣-ki-⸢ag$_2$⸣

obv. col. v

1. [. . .]
2. [. . .] x x
3. lugal-ezem i$_3$-dab$_5$

(*blank space with computations*: 3(u) 2(diš))

4. uš i$_3$-dab$_5$
5. šu ug$_3$ e$_2$-u$_6$-e
6. 1(aš$_c$) GAN$_2$ ug$_3$ al-ba-ni-du$_{11}$ unu$_3$
7. 1(diš) lugal-šu-nir-re
8. 1(diš) ^{d}šara$_2$-i$_3$-zu
9. ⸢1(diš)⸣ giri$_3$-ni-i$_3$-sa$_6$
10. [dumu]-ni-me
11. [x] ug$_3$ bu$_3$-du
12. [. . .] ⸢ug$_3$ lu$_2$⸣-[^{d}]⸢šara$_2$⸣ dumu-ni

(*blank space*)

13. [al-ba-ni]-du$_{11}$ i$_3$-dab$_5$
14. [. . .] ⸢bu$_3$⸣-du x x
15. [. . .] ug$_3$ ur-^{d}⸢en⸣-[ki]
16. [. . .]
17. ⸢šu$^?$⸣ [. . .]
18. x-[. . .]

(*blank space*)

19. [. . .]
20. x x [. . .]
21. 1(aš$_c$) GAN$_2$ ⸢lugal⸣-[. . .]
22. ug$_3$ x-[. . .]-UD ur-^{d}x-[x]
23. 1(aš$_c$) GAN$_2$ ug$_3$ [. . .] x [. . .]
24. 1(aš$_c$) GAN$_2$ [. . .]
25. a-ru-a [x]
26. sipa gu$_4$-laḫ$_5$-me

(*blank space*)

27. unu$_3$ gab$_2$-ra-me
28. ugula a-tu
29. 1(aš$_c$) GAN$_2$ nig$_2$-du$_7$-pa-e$_3$ na-gada
30. 1(aš) lugal-e$_2$-maḫ-e
31. 1(diš) ur-^{d}x-x-x

obv. col. vi

1. 1(aš$_c$) GAN$_2$ ug$_3$ ^{geš}gigir$^?$-re$^?$
2. 1(aš$_c$) GAN$_2$ ug$_3$ ur-x-x
3. 1(aš$_c$) GAN$_2$ ug$_3$ lu$_2$-^{d}šara$_2$ dumu ^{d}⸢šara$_2^?$⸣-i$_3$-sa$_6$ zaḫ$_3$-ta
4. 1(aš$_c$) GAN$_2$ ug$_3$ ḫa-ba-lu$_5$-ge$_2$ dumu ur-^{d}ma-mi

5. gurum$_2$-e tak$_4$-a
6. 1(aš$_c$) GAN$_2$ ug$_3$ a$^?$-da-da a-ru-a-ta
   (*blank space with computations*: 1(geš'u) 3(geš$_2$) 5(u))
7. nig$_2$-du$_7$-pa-e$_3$ i$_3$-dab$_5$
8. 1(aš$_c$) GAN$_2$ ug$_3$ bi$_2$-da na-gada
9. 1(aš$_c$) ug$_3$ ^{d}šara$_2$-kam
10. dumu ṣil$_2$(MI)-la-šu-me
   (*blank space with computations*: 2(geš$_2$) 4(u))
11. bi$_2$-da i$_3$-dab$_5$
12. 1(aš$_c$) GAN$_2$ ba-zi-ge na-gada
   (*n lines broken*)
13'. [. . . lugal-nig$_2$]-lagar-e [dumu] ša$_3$-ku$_3$-ge
14'. [1(aš$_c$) GAN$_2$] ug$_3$ lugal-[a$_2$]-zi-da dumu šu-na
15'. [x] ka$_5$-a-mu
16'. [x] ur-^{d}šul-pa-e$_3$
17'. [ka$_5$-a]-mu i$_3$-dab$_5$
   (*blank space with computations*: ⸢2(geš$_2$)⸣ 5(diš))
18'. sipa ⸢ud$_5$⸣-ga za-wi ^{d}⸢šara$_2$⸣ [a]-⸢pi$_4$⸣-sal$_4$^{ki} -me
19'. ^{d}x-x
20'. lu$_2$-[. . .]
21'. dumu inim-⸢^{d}⸣[. . .]
22'. ⸢ARAD$_2$⸣-mu i$_3$-[dab$_5$]
23'. 1(aš) 4(ban$_2$) ug$_3$ ur-ge$_6$-⸢par$_4$⸣ dumu lugal-⸢nig$_2$-zu⸣
   (*blank space*)
24'. <sipa> ud$_5$-ga za-wi [. . .]
   (*rest broken*)

obv. col. vii

1. [. . .]
2. [. . .]
3. [sipa udu]-laḫ$_5$-[me]
4. lu$_2$-^{d}⸢da-mu$^?$⸣ i$_3$-⸢dab$_5$⸣
5. 1(aš$_c$) GAN$_2$ ug$_3$ x-x
6. a-ru-a lu$_2$-^{geš}⸢gigir$^?$⸣
   (*blank space with computations*: 2(geš$_2$) 5(diš))
7. ur-^{d}dumu-zi-da i$_3$-dab$_5$
   (*blank space*)
8. sipa ud$_5$ nam-en-na-me
   (*blank space*)
9. e$_2$ ^{d}šara$_2$
10. ugula uš
11. 1(aš$_c$) GAN$_2$ lu$_2$-kal-la šuš$_3$
   (*n lines broken*)
12'. [. . .] ⸢aga$_3$⸣-us$_2$
13'. ⸢1(aš)⸣ AB ab-ba-gi-na
14'. 1(diš) da-da
15'. 1(diš) lu$_2$-^{d}šara$_2$
16'. dumu-ni-me
17'. šuš$_3$ i$_3$-dab$_5$
18'. šu ur-e$_{11}$-e
19'. 1(aš$_c$) GAN$_2$ lugal-iti-da unu$_3$
20'. 1(diš) a-kal-la dumu ur-^{d}nin-šu-ba-na$^?$
21'. uš$_2$ ur-ab-ba dumu igi-^{d}šara$_2$-še$_3$
22'. 1(aš$_c$) GAN$_2$ a$_2$-dingir-ga$_2$
23'. ku$_3$-^{d}x-x-x
24'. 1(aš) ur-^{d}x-x-x
   (*blank space with computations*: 3(u) 6(diš))
25'. [x] ⸢lugal⸣-iti-da i$_3$-dab$_5$
26'. [1(aš$_c$)] ⸢GAN$_2$⸣ šeš-a-ni unu$_3$
27'. 1(aš$_c$) [GAN$_2$$^?$ . . .]-kal-la dumu-ni
   (*rest broken*)

obv. col. viii

1. [. . .]
2. ⸢šeš-a-ni i$_3$-dab$_5$⸣
3. ⸢1(aš$_c$) GAN$_2$⸣ ab-ba-gi-na ⸢unu$_3$⸣
4. [. . .]-da-ga [. . .]
   (*blank space with computations*: 3(u) 4(diš))
5. ab-ba-gi-na i$_3$-dab$_5$
6. šu ukken-ne$_2$
7. 1(aš$_c$) GAN$_2$ la-⸢lu$_5$⸣ unu$_3$
8. 1(diš) ur-li
9. 1(diš) ur-^{d}utu
10. 1(diš) lugal-KA
11. dumu-ni-me
12. ⸢1(aš$_c$)⸣ x igi-in-sa$_6$-sa$_6$

13. 1(aš) AB ur-^{geš}⸢gigir$^{?}$⸣
14. dumu ukken-ne$_2$-me

(*blank space with computations*: 4(u) 1(diš))[577]

15. la-lu$_5$ i$_3$-dab$_5$
16. ⸢šu giri$_3$⸣-[. . .]

(*n lines broken*)

17’. [. . .]-KA-x
18’. 1(diš) ^{d}šara$_2$-kam
19’. 1(diš) ^{d}šara$_2$-mu-tum$_2$
20’. dumu-ni-me
21’. 1(aš$_c$) GAN$_2$ suḫuš-gi
22’. 1(aš) lugal-ur$_2$-ra-ni dumu-ni
23’. 1(aš$_c$) GAN$_2$ ug$_3$ ur-x-x dumu la-a-mu
24’. 1(aš$_c$) GAN$_2$ igi-bi
25’. 1(aš$_c$) GAN$_2$ lu$_2$-x
26’. dumu lugal-x
27’. ⸢1(aš$_c$) lu$_2$⸣-x-[. . .]

(*blank space with erasures*)

28’. šeš-kal-[la$^?$] dumu x-x-[. . .]
29’. ⸢šu$^?$ lu$_2$$^?$⸣-x-[. . .]
30’. ug$_3$ x-[. . .]
31’. li-x-x [. . .]
32’. ugula NI-[. . .]
33’. 1(aš$_c$) GAN$_2$ ⸢ug$_3$⸣ [. . .]
34’. 1(aš$_c$) GAN$_2$ ⸢lugal$^?$⸣-[. . .]
35’. 1(diš) lu$_2$-⸢$^{d?}$nin$^?$⸣-[. . .] ki lugal-⸢ma$_2$-gur$_8$$^?$⸣-[re$^?$-ta$^?$]
36’. 1(aš$_c$) GAN$_2$ [. . .]
37’. 1(aš$_c$) GAN$_2$ [. . .] dumu [. . .]
38’. lugal-[. . .]

(*rest broken*)

rev. col. i

(*start broken*)

1’. 1(aš$_c$) ⸢GAN$_2$⸣ x-[. . .]
2’. 1(aš$_c$) ur$^?$-[. . .]
3’. ⸢si$_{12}$⸣-a ab-⸢ba⸣-[. . .]
4’. 1(aš$_c$) GAN$_2$ lu$_2$-^{d}[. . .]
5’. 1(diš) ^{d}šara$_2$-[. . .]
6’. dumu-ni-me
7’. ab-ba-⸢gi⸣-[na]
8’. ARAD$_2$-mu dumu lugal-me-a
9’. da-uš-še$_3$$^?$
10’. KAŠ$_4$ i$_3$-dab$_5$
11’. 1(aš$_c$) GAN$_2$ lu$_2$-banda$_3$^{da}
12’. 1(aš$_c$) GAN$_2$ ^{d}šara$_2$-i$_3$-zu
13’. dumu ⸢ša$_3$⸣-ku$_3$-ge x-x-me
14’. 1(diš) lugal-dub-la$_2$
15’. dumu lugal-gu$_3$-de$_2$-a
16’. 1(diš) šeš-a-ni dumu-ni
17’. 1(aš$_c$) GAN$_2$ lu$_2$-dingir-ra dumu ur-e$_{11}$-e

(*blank space with computations*: 1(geš’u) 2(geš$_2$) 1(u) 6(diš))

18’. [. . .]-x i$_3$-dab$_5$

(*n lines broken*)

19’. x [. . .]
22’. 1(diš) lu$_2$-[. . .]
23’. dumu-ni-me
24’. 1(aš$_c$) GAN$_2$ lugal-e$_2$-maḫ-e šeš-a-ni
25’. 1(diš) ur-^{d}gu-nu-ra
26’. šeš-kal-la
27’. dumu-ni-me
28’. 1(aš$_c$) GAN$_2$ nig$_2$-du$_7$-pa-e$_3$
29’. ki lugal-ni$_2$-zu-ta
30’. 1(aš$_c$) GAN$_2$ al-ba-ni-du$_{11}$
31’. ki lugal-zabala$_3$^{ki}-ta

(*blank space with computations*: 1(geš’u) 2(u) 5(diš))

32’. ur-^{geš}gigir i$_3$-dab$_5$
33’. 1(aš$_c$) GAN$_2$ lugal-ušur$_x$(LAL$_2$.TUG$_2$) na-gada[578]
34’. 1(aš$_c$) lu$_2$-kal-la
35’. 1(aš) lugal-^{d}⸢šul$^?$⸣-pa-e$_3$
36’. uš$_2$ ur-^{d}suen
37’. dumu-ni-me

---

577 The computations are erased.

578 na-gada written next to Lu-kala, but probably belongs to Lugal-ušur.

38'. 1(aš$_c$) GAN$_2$ ug$_3$ ARAD$_2$ dumu lugal-ezem

39'. 1(aš) lugal-x-x

(*rest broken*)

rev. col. ii

(*start broken*)

1'. ki lu$_2$-⸢^{d}da-mu-ta⸣

(*blank space with calculation*: ⸢1(geš$_2$)⸣ 2(u))

2'. ⸢lugal⸣-ušur$_x$(LAL$_2$.TUG$_2$) i$_3$-dab$_5$

3'. ⸢1(aš$_c$) GAN$_2$⸣ ḫe$_2$-sa$_6$-ge na-gada

4'. [...] ARAD$_2$-^{d}šara$_2$

5'. [...] ⸢lu$_2$⸣-du$_{10}$-ga

6'. [...] lugal-pa-e$_3$

7'. ⸢dumu⸣-ni-me

8'. [...] a-tu

9'. [...] ur-^{d}šul-pa-e$_3$ ⸢dumu⸣ nigar^{gar}-ki-du$_{10}$-me

10'. [aga$_3^?$]-us$_2$ ensi$_2$-ka-še$_3$

11'. [...] ša$_3$-ku$_3$-ge

12'. [...] ^{d}šara$_2$-i$_3$-zu

13'. [...] lugal-šu-nir-re

14'. dumu-ni-me

15'. sipa udu-laḫ$_5$-še$_3$

16'. 1(aš$_c$) GAN$_2$ u$_3$-ma-ni

17'. [...] ur-ki-maḫ dumu-ni

18'. [...]-edin-na

(*n lines broken*)

19'. [1(aš$_c$)] ⸢GAN$_2$ ur$^?$⸣-[...]

20'. 1(aš) lu$_2$-^{d}šul-gi-ra dumu-ni

21'. ki ab-ba-saga-ta

(*blank space with computations*: 1(geš'u) 1(geš$_2$) 3(u) 5(diš))

22'. ḫe$_2$-sa$_6$-ge i$_3$-dab$_5$

23'. šu la-la-mu

24'. 1(aš$_c$) GAN$_2$ ug$_3$ lugal-ni$_2$-zu na-gada

25'. 1(aš$_c$) ug$_3$ ab-ba-gi-na

26'. 1(aš$_c$) GAN$_2$ ug$_3$ lugal-ḫi-li

27'. dumu la-la-mu-me

28'. 1(aš$_c$) GAN$_2$ ur-sukkal

29'. 1(aš$_c$) šeš-kal-la

30'. 1(aš$_c$) ur-^{d}šul-pa-e$_3$

31'. ⸢1(aš$_c$) nam-ḫa⸣-ni dumu-ni-me

32'. [lugal-ni$_2$-zu] ⸢i$_3$-dab$_5$⸣[579]

33'. 1(aš$_c$) GAN$_2$ ug$_3$ ur-sila-luḫ a-ru-a-ta

34'. 1(aš$_c$) GAN$_2$ ug$_3$ a-kal-la daḫ-⸢ḫu-me⸣

35'. ⸢lugal-ni$_2$-zu⸣ i$_3$-dab$_5$

(*blank space with computations*: ⸢5(u)$^?$⸣ 6(diš))

rev. col. iii

1. [1(aš$_c$) GAN$_2$ ur-^{d}šul-pa-e$_3$ na-gada]

2. ⸢1(aš$_c$) lu$_2$-^{d}nin⸣-ur$_4$-ra

3. 1(diš) du-du

4. dumu-ni-me

5. 1(aš$_c$) GAN$_2$ ug$_3$ ur-^{geš}gigir dumu geme$_2$-ge$_6$-par$_4$ nar

6. 1(aš$_c$) GAN$_2$ ur-^{d}šul-pa-e$_3$ dumu lugal-ur$_2$-ra-ni

(*blank space with computations*: 5(geš$_2$) 3(u) 5(diš))

7. ur-^{d}šul-pa-e$_3$ i$_3$-dab$_5$

8. 1(aš$_c$) GAN$_2$ ka$_5$-a-mu na-gada

9. 1(aš$_c$) ur-^{d}dumu-zi-da

10. 1(aš) lu$_2$-du$_{10}$-ga

11. [n] lu$_2$-^{d}šara$_2$

12. 1(diš) ur-^{d}suen

13. 1(diš) ur-^{d}a- šar$_2$

14. dumu-⸢ni-me⸣

15. 2(ban$_2$) ⸢2(diš)⸣ ab-[ba]- ⸢kal⸣-la dumu ur-[...]-x

16. ARAD$_2$-[...]

17. x-[...]

18. KA-[...]

19. ur-⸢^{d}a-šar$_2$⸣

20. [x?] lugal-šuba$_3$

21. [dumu-ni]-me

22. [sipa udu] laḫ$_5$-[še$_3$]

(*n lines broken*)

23'. 1(aš$_c$) [...]

24'. ki lugal-[...]

---

579 Line erased.

25'. 1(aš$_c$) GAN$_2$ [. . .]-x

26'. ki lugal-⸢mu⸣-ma-⸢ag$_2$⸣-ta

(*blank space with computations*: 7(geš$_2$) [n$^?$] 2(diš))

27'. ka$_5$-⸢a⸣-mu i$_3$-dab$_5$

28'. 1(aš$_c$) ⸢GAN$_2$⸣ ^{d}šara$_2$-kam na-gada

29'. 1(aš$_c$) ⸢ur⸣-^{d}geštin-an-ka

30'. ⸢1(diš) lugal⸣-^{geš}gigir-re

31'. [dumu]-ni-me

32'. [1(aš$_c$)] GAN$_2$ zu-zu

33'. ⸢dumu⸣ lugal-an-ne$_2$

(*blank space with computations*: 5(geš2) 3(u))

34'. ^{d}šara$_2$-kam i$_3$-dab$_5$

35'. šu ur-geš-⸢ša$_3$-ga⸣

36'. 1(aš$_c$) GAN$_2$ lugal-ku$_3$-⸢zu⸣ na-⸢gada⸣

37'. 1(diš) lugal-dub-⸢la$_2$⸣ dumu-ni

38'. x ⸢ša$_3$⸣-ku$_3$-⸢ge⸣

39'. ⸢1(diš)$^?$⸣ al-⸢ba-ni-du$_{11}$⸣ dumu-ni$^?$

40'. ARAD$_2$-mu i$_3$-dab$_5$

41'. [. . .]

42'. [. . .]

rev. col. iv

1. [. . .]
2. [. . .] x x
3. dumu ur-^{d}ba-ba$_6$
4. 1(diš) ^{d}šara$_2$-kam
5. 1(diš) lugal-banda$_3{}^{da}$
6. ⸢dumu⸣-ni-me
7. 1(aš$_c$) ⸢GAN$_2$⸣[580] ur-^{geš}gigir dumu a-du-ba-bi
8. ARAD$_2$ ugula i$_3$-dab$_5$
9. 1(aš$_c$) GAN$_2$ igi-tur-tur
10. lu$_2$-šar-x-x[581]-ta
11. 1(aš$_c$) GAN$_2$ lugal-ni$_2$-zu
12. ki lu$_2$-dingir-ra-ta
13. 1(aš$_c$) ma-an-ba dumu ḫu-un-sa$_6$-sa$_6$
14. lu$_2$-^{d}šul-gi-ra dumu-ni
15. ḫe$_2$-sa$_6$-ge-⸢ta$^?$⸣
16. [. . .][582] a-kal-la erin$_2$ ka-ma-ri$_2{}^{ki}$-ke$_4$ ba$^?$-ab-tum$_2$

(*blank space with computations*: 7(geš$_2$) 4(u) 4(diš))

17. ab-ba-saga i$_3$-dab$_5$
18. 1(aš$_c$) GAN$_2$ ur-sila-luḫ na-gada
19. 1(aš$_c$) lu$_2$-^{d}šara$_2$
20. 1(diš) ⸢lugal-ma$_2$-gur$_8$-re⸣

(*n lines broken*)

21'. sipa ud$_5$ nam-[en-na-ke$_4$-ne]

22'. 1(aš$_c$) GAN$_2$ ARAD$_2$-ḫu-la

23'. 1(diš) inim-^{d}šara$_2$

24'. 1(diš) ur-^{d}a-šar2

25'. 1(diš) lugal-šuba$_3$

26'. dumu-ni-me

27'. 1(aš$_c$) GAN$_2$ ug$_3$ ^{d}šara$_2$-a$_2$!-zi-da

28'. ki ARAD$_2$ ugula-ta

(*blank space*)

29'. ARAD$_2$-ḫu-la i$_3$-dab$_5$

(*blank space*)

30'. sipa ud$_5$ laḫ$_5$-me

(*blank space*)

31'. e$_2$-^{d}⸢nin⸣-[ur$_4$-ra]

32'. 1(aš$_c$) GAN$_2$ lu$_2$-[du$_{10}$-ga] na$^!$-[gada]

33'. 1(aš$_c$) lugal-⸢ku$_3{}^?$-zu$^?$⸣

34'. 1(aš$_c$) GAN$_2$ ur-^{d}šara$_2$

35'. ⸢dumu⸣ ur-[^{d}]⸢ištaran⸣-me

36'. (aš$_c$) [ ] ḫa-za-num$_2$ [ ] im-ri-a

37'. [. . .]

(*lost computations!*)

38'. [lu$_2$]- ⸢du$_{10}$-ga⸣ i$_3$-dab$_5$

(*rest broken*)

rev. col. v

1. [1 (aš$_c$) GAN$_2$ šeš-kal-la na-gada] dumu [. . .]
2. 1(aš$_c$) u$_2$-tuku
3. 1(aš$_c$) GAN$_2$ ug$_3$ tug$_2$-nig$_2$-dara$_2$

---

[580] GAN$_2$ erased.

[581] One or two signs erased.

[582] Start of line erased.

(*blank space with computations*: 5(geš$_{2}$) 5(u) 1(diš))

4. šeš-kal-la i$_{3}$-dab$_{5}$
5. 1(aš$_{c}$) GAN$_{2}$ ug$_{3}$ nig$_{2}$-du$_{7}$-pa-e$_{3}$ na-gada
6. 1(aš$_{c}$) ug$_{3}$ lu$_{2}$-^{d}šara$_{2}$
7. lu$_{2}$-eb-gal
8. ⸢e$_{2}$⸣ amar-ra-še$_{3}$
9. dumu dingir-ba-an-me

(*blank space with computations*: 2(geš$_{2}$) 3(u) 6(diš))

10. nig$_{2}$-du$_{7}$-pa-e$_{3}$ i$_{3}$-dab$_{5}$

(*blank space*)

11. sipa ud$_{5}$ ⸢nam⸣-en-⸢na⸣-me

(*blank space*)

12. e$_{2}$ ^{d}šul-gi-ra
13. 1(aš$_{c}$) GAN$_{2}$ ma-ma na-gada
14. 1(aš) u$_{2}$-da-ur$_{4}$-ra dumu-ni
15. 1(aš$_{c}$) GAN$_{2}$ ug$_{3}$ sag-du
16. 1(aš$_{c}$) GAN$_{2}$ ug$_{3}$ giri$_{3}$-ni-i$_{3}$-sa$_{6}$
17. ⸢zaḫ$_{3}$⸣ ug$_{3}$ lugal-ur$_{2}$-ra-ni
18. dumu ⸢la⸣-a-mu-me

(*blank space*)

19. ⸢ma-ma i$_{3}$-dab$_{5}$⸣
20. [. . .]
21. [. . .]
22. uš$_{2}$ nam-ḫa-⸢ni⸣ x
23. 1(aš$_{c}$) GAN$_{2}$ lugal-ur$_{2}$-ra-ni na-gada
24. 1(diš) ur-^{geš}gigir dumu-ni
25. ⸢uš$_{2}$⸣ ur-^{d}utu
26. ⸢1(aš$_{c}$)⸣ ug$_{3}$ a-an-na
27. ka$_{5}$-a-mu i$_{3}$-dab$_{5}$
28. 1(aš) 3(ban$_{2}$) tug$_{2}$ gu-u$_{2}$ dumu ur-engar
29. lugal-ur$_{2}$-ra-ni i$_{3}$-dab$_{5}$
30. 1(aš$_{c}$) GAN$_{2}$ ug$_{3}$ ku$_{3}$-ga-ni na-gada
31. 1(ban$_{2c}$) šeš-kal-la dumu inim-^{d}šara$_{2}$
32. ARAD$_{2}$-mu i$_{3}$-dab$_{5}$

(*blank space*)

33. šu ug$_{3}$ ^{d}šara$_{2}$-an-dul$_{3}$
34. 1(diš) du$_{11}$-ga-zi-da
35. 1(diš) lugal-inim-du$_{10}$-ga
36. dumu-ni-me
37. ku$_{3}$-ga-ni i$_{3}$-dab$_{5}$
38. 1(aš$_{c}$) GAN$_{2}$ ab-ba-gi-na na-gada dumu lugal-bad$_{3}$

(*blank space*)

39. ab-ba-gi-na i$_{3}$-dab$_{5}$
40. ⸢1(aš$_{c}$) GAN$_{2}$⸣ ur-^{d}⸢ištaran⸣
41. ⸢1(diš) ⸣ x x x
42. [. . .]
43. [. . .]

rev. col. vi

(*start broken*)

1. ⸢e$_{2}$⸣ x x x
2. ⸢ur-^{d}ištaran i$_{3}$-dab$_{5}$⸣
3. 1(aš$_{c}$) ⸢GAN$_{2}$ ša$_{3}$-ku$_{3}$⸣-ge ⸢na⸣-gada
4. 1(diš) ^{d}šara$_{2}$-⸢i$_{3}$?⸣-[ ]
5. 1(diš) lugal-šu-[nir]- ⸢re⸣
6. dumu-⸢ni-me⸣
7. 1(aš$_{c}$) GAN$_{2}$ ug$_{3}$ ur-gu$_{2}$-edin-na
8. ša$_{3}$-ku$_{3}$-ge i$_{3}$-dab$_{5}$
9. ki ḫe$_{2}$-sa$_{6}$-ge-ta

(*blank space*)

10. sipa udu-laḫ$_{5}$-me
11. 1(aš$_{c}$) GAN$_{2}$ ug$_{3}$ lugal-dub-la$_{2}$ šar$_{2}$-ra-ab-du ab$_{2}$
12. uš2 du$_{11}$-ga-^{d}šara$_{2}$
13. 1(diš) nig$_{2}$-gur$_{11}$-^{d}šara$_{2}$
14. dumu-ni-me
15. 1(aš$_{c}$) GAN$_{2}$ ur-mes
16. 1(aš$_{c}$) GAN$_{2}$ ur-^{d}šara$_{2}$ dumu ur-ku$_{3}$-nun-na
17. šar$_{2}$-ra-ab-du udu-me[583]
18. uš$_{2}$ inim-sa$_{6}$-sa$_{6}$
19. 1(ban$_{2c}$) GAN$_{2}$ nig$_{2}$-bi
20. uš$_{2}$ ^{d}šara$_{2}$-i$_{3}$-zu
21. ⸢1(diš) lugal-ma$_{2}$⸣-gur$_{8}$-re
22. [. . .]

---

[583] see also TCL 5, 6038 rev. i 34.

23. [. . .]
24. 1(ban$_{2c}$) [. . .]-⸢zi-da⸣
25. 1(aš) ur-^{d}šul-pa-e$_{3}$
26. dumu-ni-me
27. 1(ban$_{2c}$) GAN$_{2}$ ur-^{d}nun-gal
28. 1(aš) bar-ra-an-ni-še$_{3}$
29. dumu a-za-tum tug$_{2}$-du$_{8}$-me
30. 1(ban$_{2c}$) GAN$_{2}$ in-sa$_{6}$-sa$_{6}$
31. ⸢1(ban$_{2c}$)$^{?}$⸣ ba-zi-ge e$_{2}$ KAŠ$_{4}$-še$_{3}$
32. ur-^{d}⸢gilgames$_{x}$(BIL$_{3}$.GA.MES)⸣
33. e$_{2}$ ^{d}nin-[ḫi]- ⸢li⸣-[su]-ga
34. ARAD$_{2}$-mu ⸢i$_{3}$-dab$_{5}$⸣
35. a-NE ⸢šu-gi$_{4}$⸣-ta

(blank space with erasures)

36. ki-ni šeš ur-⸢^{d}⸣šara$_{2}$ ga-il$_{2}$
37. ⸢lu$_{2}$-dingir⸣-ra i$_{3}$-dab$_{5}$
38. ⸢1(aš$_{c}$)⸣ ug$_{3}$ ur-ki-maḫ
39. ⸢ur⸣-^{d}ištaran i$_{3}$-dab$_{5}$
40. šu bar-ra ur-^{d}ḫendur-sag-ka
41. ⸢ka$_{5}$-a-mu⸣
42. ⸢ki ur-^{d}nin-tu⸣
43. ⸢ur-^{d}⸣x-x
44. [. . .] i$_{3}$-dab$_{5}$
45. [. . .]-⸢nam$^{?}$⸣
46. [. . .]

(rest broken)

rev. col. vii

(start broken)

1'. 1(aš) lugal-gi$^{?}$-na$^{?}$
2'. dumu ur-^{d}ba-ba$_{6}$-me
3'. 1(ban$_{2c}$) GAN$_{2}$ ⸢nig$_{2}$-lagar-e⸣ dumu ḫu-un-sa$_{6}$-sa$_{6}$
4'. lu$_{2}$-sar-ta
5'. 1(ban$_{2c}$) GAN$_{2}$ da-ga
6'. 1(ban$_{2c}$) šu ARAD$_{2}$-mu dumu en-ma-an-gu-ul
7'. 1(aš$_{c}$) GAN$_{2}$ ug$_{3}$ lu$_{2}$-eb-gal dumu dingir-ba-an ki nig$_{2}$-du$_{7}$-pa-e$_{3}$-ta

(blank space)

8'. giri$_{3}$-se$_{3}$-ga e$_{2}$-⸢amar-ra⸣-ka-me
9'. 1(aš$_{c}$) GAN$_{2}$ ⸢lugal⸣-ḫe$_{2}$-gal$_{2}$
10'. 1(aš) ARAD$_{2}$-[. . .]
11'. 1(diš) ur-x-x-x
12'. 1(diš) ur-⸢am$_{3}$⸣-ma
13'. dumu-⸢ni⸣-me

(blank space)

14'. ki ur-^{d}da-mu ugula-ta
15'. [. . .] 3(diš) ⸢šaḫ$_{2}$⸣
16'. lugal-ḫe$_{2}$-[gal$_{2}$ i$_{3}$-dab$_{5}$]
17'. sipa šaḫ$_{2}$-⸢me⸣

(blank space)

rev. col. viii

(blank space)

1. ⸢gurum$_{2}$ ak sipa ud$_{5}$ unu$_{3}$-de$_{3}$-ne⸣
2. [e$_{2}$] ⸢^{d}šara$_{2}$$^{?}$⸣
3. [e$_{2}$] ⸢^{d}nin-ur$_{4}$⸣-[ra e$_{2}$] ⸢^{d}šul-gi⸣-[ra]
4. [u$_{3}$$^{?}$ e$_{2}$] ⸢^{d}inanna$^{?}$⸣
5. [ša$_{3}$] ⸢zabala$_{3}$$^{?ki}$⸣
6. [u$_{3}$] ⸢a-pi$_{4}$-sal$_{4}$^{ki}⸣

(blank space)

7. ⸢mu⸣ en-unu$_{6}$-[gal] ⸢en⸣ ^{d}inanna ba-[ḫun]

No. 130. *MS 4739 (Umma, AS 6–xi)*

obv. col. i

1. [1(aš$_{c}$)$^{?}$ GAN$_{2}$$^{?}$] ⸢lugal$^{?}$⸣-^{d}ištaran [. . .] nu-banda$_{3}$ gu$_{4}$
2. [x] ur-^{d}[nin]-sun$_{2}$
3. [x] a-x
4. ⸢dumu⸣-ni-⸢me⸣
5. ⸢uš$_{2}$⸣ lugal-KA
6. 1(aš$_{c}$) GAN$_{2}$ lugal-ezem šeš-tab-ba
7. 1(aš) ur-^{d}a-šar$_{2}$
8. ⸢1(diš)⸣ lugal-nesag-e
9. ⸢dumu⸣-ni-me
10. ⸢1(aš)⸣ GAN$_{2}$ lu$_{2}$-dingir-ra aga$_{3}$-us$_{2}$
11. ⸢½(aš$_{2c}$)⸣ GAN$_{2}$ lu$_{2}$-eb-gal x[584]
12. uš$_{2}$ ur-mes dumu-ni

[584] Followed by an erasure.

13. ⸢nu-banda$_3$⸣-gu$_4$ i$_3$-dab$_5$
14. uš$_2$ me-maškim
15. 1(aš$_c$) GAN$_2$ lugal-iti-da engar
16. 1(aš) ku$_3$-^{d}šara$_2$ dumu-ni
17. 1(aš$_c$) GAN$_2$ ur-nigar^{gar}
18. 1(aš) ur-^{d}šul-pa-e$_3$
19. dumu me-maškim-me
20. 1(aš$_c$) GAN$_2$ ug$_3$ du$_{11}$-ge
21. 1(diš) e$_2$-ḫi-li
22. 1(diš) nig$_2$-u$_2$-rum
23. dumu-ni-me
24. ⸢lugal⸣-iti-da i$_3$-dab$_5$
25. šu ⸢lu$_2$⸣-^{d}li$_9$-si$_4$ ⸢engar$^?$⸣

obv. col. ii

1. 1(aš$_c$) GAN$_2$ lugal-ku$_3$-zu dumu-ni
2. 1(aš$_c$) GAN$_2$ lugal-ezem <<ta>>[585]
3. 1(diš) šeš-kal-la
4. 1(diš) ur-sukkal
5. dumu-ni-me zaḫ$_3$-ta gur-ra
6. 1(aš$_c$) GAN$_2$ ug$_3$ bi$_2$-da
7. lu$_2$-^{d}⸢li$_9$⸣-[si$_4$] i$_3$-dab$_5$
8. 1(aš$_c$) ⸢lu$_2$-^{d}suen⸣ engar
9. 1(diš) ⸢ur$^?$⸣-li dumu-ni
10. 1(aš$_c$) GAN$_2$ ug$_3$ ⸢en$^?$-šu$^?$⸣
11. šu a$_2$-x
12. 1(aš$_c$) GAN$_2$ ug$_3$ ur-^{d}⸢iškur⸣
13. lu$_2$-^{d}suen i$_3$-dab$_5$
14. 1(aš$_c$) GAN$_2$ lu$_5$-lu$_5$-⸢mu⸣
15. uš$_2$ lu$_2$-gaz-zi-da
16. uš$_2$ lugal-amar-⸢ku$_3$⸣
17. 1(diš) lugal-⸢dub⸣-la$_2$
18. dumu-ni-me
19. 1(aš$_c$) GAN$_2$ ⸢ur⸣-^{d}nin-x
20. 1(diš) šeš-a-ni dumu-ni
21. 1(aš$_c$) GAN$_2$ ⸢ug$_3$ lugal⸣-x-[. . .]
22. 1(aš$_c$) GAN$_2$ ⸢ug$_3$⸣ x x [. . .]
23. 1(diš) lu$_2$-^{d}⸢šara$_2$⸣

[585] The final -ta is partly erased.

rev. col. i

1. ⸢giri$_3$⸣ ka$_5$-mu [x]
2. 1(aš$_c$) GAN$_2$ ⸢ARAD$_2$-ḫul$_3$⸣-la [engar?]
3. 1(aš$_c$) GAN$_2$ ⸢ug$_3$⸣ ur$_2$-nig$_2$-du$_{10}$
4. [x] 2(ban$_2$) 2(diš) lugal-^{geš}apin-du$_{10}$
5. 1(diš) x 1(diš) ^{d}šul-gi-ḫa-ma-ti
6. 1(diš) ur-^{d}iškur
7. dumu-ni-me
8. 1(aš$_c$) ⸢GAN$_2$⸣ ug$_3$ lugal-nesag-e
9. 1(aš$_c$) GAN$_2$ ug$_3$ a-ba-nam-tum$_2$
10. ARAD$_2$-ḫul$_3$-la i$_3$-dab$_5$
11. 1(aš$_c$) GAN$_2$ ug$_3$ ur-^{geš}gigir engar dumu ur$^?$-kal-la
12. 1(diš) nu ⸢ur-^{d}iškur$^?$⸣ dumu-ni
13. 1(aš$_c$) GAN$_2$ ⸢ug$_3$ ur⸣-^{d}a-zi-a
14. 1(aš$_c$) GAN$_2$ ⸢ug$_3$⸣ [x]- ⸢lu$_2$⸣-ni
15. 1(aš$_c$) GAN$_2$ ⸢ug$_3$⸣ [ur]-e$_2$-nir$_x$(MIR.ZA)
16. 1(diš) 2(ban$_2$) 2(diš) ⸢ur-^{d}ur$_3$-bar-tab⸣
17. 1(diš) ⸢ur-^{geš}gigir⸣
18. dumu-ni-me
19. ur-^{geš}gigir i$_3$-dab$_5$

(*blank space*)

rev. col. ii

(*blank space*)

1. gurum$_2$ ak gu$_4$ ^{geš}apin
2. ugula lugal-^{d}ištaran
3. ur-^{d}li$_9$-si$_4$ ensi$_2$
4. ⸢giri$_3$ lu$_2$⸣-du$_{10}$-ga dumu lugal-da-da dub-sar u$_3$ lu$_2$-^{d}nanna dub-sar
5. ⸢iti⸣ ezem-me-ki-⸢gal$_2$⸣
6. ⸢mu⸣ ša-aš-⸢ru^{ki}⸣ a-[ra$_2$ x-kam ba]-ḫul

No. 131. *MS 4764 (Umma, AS 3–v)*

obv. col. i

1. [1(aš$_c$) GAN$_2$ lugal]-⸢nesag-e⸣ [nu-banda$_3$ gu$_4$]
2. [1(diš)] ⸢lu$_2$-du$_{10}$-ga⸣
3. [1(diš)] ⸢^{d}šara$_2$-i$_3$-zu⸣
4. ⸢1(diš) lu$_2$-dingir-ra⸣ dumu-ni-⸢me⸣

5. 1(aš) GAN$_2$ a-kal-la šeš-tab-ba dumu ⸢ur$^?$⸣-^{geš}gigir [x]
6. 1(aš) GAN$_2$ ḫa-ba-lu$_5$-ge$_2$ aga$_3$-us$_2$ dumu ^{d}utu-mu
7. ⸢1(diš)⸣ ab-ba-gi-na dumu-ni
8. nu-banda$_3$ gu$_4$ i$_3$-dab$_5$
9. 1(aš$_c$) GAN$_2$ ur-nigar^{gar} engar
10. 1(aš$_c$)? GAN$_2$ lugal-ma$_2$-gur$_8$-re
11. 1(aš) ur-^{geš}gigir
12. 1(diš) šeš-a-ni
13. dumu-ni-me
14. 1(aš$_c$) GAN$_2$ ur-nigar^{gar}

obv. col. ii

1. ⸢1(aš$_c$)$^?$ GAN$_2$⸣ a-⸢kal⸣-[la] dumu u$_3$-ma-[ni$^?$]
2. ur-nigar⸢^{gar} i$_3$⸣-dab$_5$
3. šu lu$_2$-[x]-x
4. 1(aš$_c$) GAN$_2$ a-kal-la ⸢engar$^?$⸣
5. 1(aš$_c$) GAN$_2$ lugal-⸢a$_2$⸣-zi-⸢da⸣
6. 1(diš) lu$_2$-dingir-⸢ra⸣
7. dumu-ni-me
8. 1(aš$_c$) ug$_3$ GAN$_2$ ur-^{d}⸢suen⸣
9. 1(diš) lugal-ma$_2$-gur$_8$-re dumu-ni
10. 1(aš$_c$) GAN$_2$ lugal-šu-nir-re
11. a-kal-la i$_3$-dab$_5$
12. 1(aš$_c$) GAN$_2$ ⸢lugal⸣-amar-⸢ku$_3$⸣ engar
13. 1(aš) šeš-kal-la
14. 1(diš) lu$_2$-dingir-ra
15. nig$_2$ lugal-⸢maš-zu⸣

rev. col. i

1. dumu-ni-me
2. 1(aš$_c$) GAN$_2$ a-tu dumu ^{geš}gigir-re
3. 1(aš$_c$) ug$_3$ GAN$_2$ lugal-⸢ma$_2$⸣-gur$_8$-re
4. 1(aš$_c$) GAN$_2$ ur-zabala$_3^{ki}$
5. 1(aš) šu-^{d}suen
6. 1(diš) a-kal-la
7. dumu-ni-me
8. lugal-amar-ku$_3$ i$_3$-dab$_5$
9. šu ug$_3$ la-al-u$_2$-a
10. 1(aš$_c$) ug$_3$ GAN$_2$ lugal-nesag-e engar
11. 1(aš$_c$) ug$_3$ GAN$_2$ a-kal-la
12. 1(aš) nir-i$_3$-da-gal$_2$
13. 1(diš) lugal-e-ba-an-sa$_6$
14. ⸢dumu⸣-[ni]-me
15. 1(aš$_c$) ⸢ug$_3$ GAN$_2$ lugal⸣-a$_2$-zi-da
16. 1(aš) AB lu$_2$-^{d}šara$_2$
17. 1(aš$_c$) ug$_3$ GAN$_2$ ḫu-wa-⸢wa⸣
18. ⸢dumu⸣ la-al-⸢u$_2$-a⸣

rev. col. ii

1. lugal-nesag-e i$_3$-dab$_5$
2. 1(aš$_c$) ug$_3$ GAN$_2$ lugal-an-ne$_2$ engar
3. 1(diš) lugal-⸢muš⸣-[ḫuš]
4. 1(diš) ur-^{d}da-ni
5. dumu-ni-me
6. 1(aš$_c$) GAN$_2$ ug$_3$ ur-am$_3$-ma
7. 1(aš$_c$) GAN$_2$ ab-ba-gi-na
8. 1(aš$_c$) GAN$_2$ a-kal-la dumu ur-nigar^{gar} ba-BAD
9. giri3 šeš-a-ni dumu ab-ba-gi-na
10. lugal-an-ne$_2$ i$_3$-dab$_5$
11. 1(aš$_c$)$^?$ GAN$_2$ ur-gu$_2$-edin-na engar
12. 1(aš$_c$) GAN$_2$ da-du ⸢dumu⸣ ur-^{d}nin-tu
13. ša$_3$-saḫar-ra ki ur-lugal-ta
14. ⸢1(aš$_c$) GAN$_2$⸣ engar-zi ⸢dumu ur⸣-^{d}nin-tu
15. [ARAD$_2$]-⸢mu dumu⸣ a-ḫu-šu-ni
16. [. . .] ⸢lugal-pa⸣-ta
17. [ur]-gu$_2$-edin-na i$_3$-dab$_5$
   (*blank space*)
18. [ugula$^?$] ⸢lugal⸣-nesag-e
19. [iti] dal

left edge

1. [mu ^{geš}]gu-za ^{d}en-lil$_2$-la$_2$ ba-dim$_2$

seal (S003612)

1. lugal-[nesag-e]
2. dub-sar
3. dumu lu$_2$-⸢banda$_3^{da}$⸣

No. 133. *MS 1975 (Umma, AS 5–vii–15)*

obv. col. i

1. 1(aš$_c$) GAN$_2$ ur-^{d}kal-kal ugula šu-ku$_6$
2. 1(diš) nam-sukkal-i$_3$-du$_{10}$
3. 1(diš) lu$_2$-^{d}šara$_2$
4. dumu-ni-me
5. ambar-da tuš-a-ta
6. lugal-nig$_2$-lagar-e dumu lugal-saga dub-sar mun gazi bala-še$_3$
7. ku-li
8. lu$_2$-bala-saga
9. lugal-ušum-gal
10. lugal-nir-gal$_2$
11. dumu-ni-me
12. 1(aš) GAN$_2$ ARAD$_2$-^{d}šara$_2$ šu-ku$_6$ šeš-tab-⸢ba⸣
13. ab-ba-mu
14. lu$_2$-na-ru$_2$-a šeš-⸢a⸣-ni
15. ⸢engar⸣ geš-i$_3$-ka-še$_3$

    (blank space)
16. 1(aš$_c$) ARAD$_2$
17. x [. . .] ⸢ugula$^?$⸣ nig$_2$-NI
18. ⸢1(diš)⸣ [. . .]-ur$_4$-ra
19. 1(diš) lu$_2$-^{d}nin-šubur
20. dumu-ni-me
21. 1(aš) ur-^{d}ma-mi šeš-tab-ba
22. 1(aš) ab-ba-gi-na dumu-ni
23. 1(aš$_c$) lugal-nam-maḫ-zu
24. 1(aš) du$_{11}$-ge šeš-tab-ba
25. 1(aš$_c$) a-kal-la
26. 1(aš) lugal-inim-gi-na dumu-ni
27. 1(aš) lugal-i$_3$-sa$_6$ šeš-tab-ba
28. nimgir-an-ne$_2$ šu-ku$_6$-ka e$_2$-gal-še$_3$ ku$_6$ tum$_3$-še$_3$ ur-^{d}utu i$_3$-dab$_5$
29. zaḫ$_3$ igi-e$_2$-ba
30. 1(aš) nu tug$_2$ lu$_2$-me-lam$_2$ dumu nin-ki-lu$_5$-la geme$_2$ dingir-ra dumu šeš-kal-la
31. 1(diš) nu tug$_2$ ur-^{d}ḫal-mu-ša$_4$ dumu ḫul-dim$_2$-ma geme$_2$ dingir-ra dumu lugal-ku$_3$-zu
32. 1(aš$_c$) lu$_2$-gu-la
33. 1(aš) ^{geš}guzza-ni dumu ug$_3$-IL$_2$ šeš-tab-ba

obv. col. ii

1. 1(aš$_c$) šeš-e-ma-an-gig$^?$
2. 1(aš) lu$_2$-sukkal-an-ka
3. 1(diš) ur-^{d}ḫendur-sag-ka
4. dumu-ni-me
5. 1(aš) ur-sukkal šeš-tab-ba
6. 1(aš) šeš-kal-la
7. 1(diš) ur-^{d}šul-pa-e$_3$
8. dumu-ni-me
9. 1(aš$_c$) lu$_2$-^{d}nin-šubur
10. dumu ur-^{geš}gigir
11. 1(aš) nu tug$_2$ nam-sukkal-i$_3$-du$_{10}$ dumu-ni
12. 1(aš) amar-ni-nam šeš-tab-ba
13. 1(aš) šeš-ba-tuku dumu-ni
14. ⸢1(aš$_c$)⸣ ša$_3$-ku$_3$-⸢ge⸣ dumu ⸢ug$_3$⸣-[. . .]
15. 1(aš$_c$) ⸢ma$_2$⸣-[. . .]
16. 1(aš$_c$) ur-^{d}dumu-zi-da šeš-tab-ba dumu ur-ab-ba
17. 1(aš$_c$) nu tug$_2$ ur-sukkal
18. uš$_2$ ur-^{d}gilgames$_3$ dumu-ni
19. uš$_2$ šeš-kal-la
20. ⸢1(aš) lu$_2$⸣-um-ma dumu-ni šeš-tab-ba
21. šu pa$_3$-da
22. 1(aš$_c$) eš$_3$-ki-du$_{10}$
23. 1(aš) ur-gu$_2$-de$_3$-na dumu-ni
24. 1(aš) ur-^{d}gilgames$_3$ šeš-tab-ba
25. šu ur-^{d}ab-u$_2$ šeš-tab-ba
26. 1(aš$_c$) inim-ku$_3$
27. 1(aš) ^{geš}guzza:ni šeš-tab-ba
28. 1(diš) ur-^{d}da-ni
29. dumu-ni-me
30. dumu pa$_3$-da-me
31. 1(aš) ša$_3$-ku$_3$-ge dumu ab-e-ki-ag$_2$
32. ur-i$_7$-da-nim

    (blank space)
33. lugal-ezem

obv. col. iii

1. dumu-ni-me
2. ka-gal$_{2}$-la
3. ki ur-ku$_{3}$-nun-na
4. 1(aš) ARAD$_{2}$
5. a-ru-a sig$_{4}$-zi
6. ^{geš}kid-bi
7. ur-^{d}geš-ḫa-mun-na
8. engar geš-i$_{3}$-ka-še$_{3}$
9. ki-lu$_{5}$-la
10. amar-^{d}da-ni
11. sig$_{4}$-zi
12. du-du
13. lu$_{2}$-sukkal-an-ka dumu-ni
14. ur-^{d}suen
15. dumu sig-zi-me
16. ^{d}utu-ba-ni
17. ur-nigar^{gar}
18. lu$_{2}$-kal-la dumu-ni
19. ur-^{d}nin-geš-zi-da
20. šeš sig$_{4}$-zi-me
21. ku$_{5}$-da šu-gi$_{4}$-ta
22. guruš ŠIM$^{?}$ a de$_{2}$-a-ta gur-ra
23. ki nir-i$_{3}$-da-gal$_{2}$
24. 1(aš) ur-^{d}nun-gal nu tug$_{2}$
25. dumu ur-^{d}ma-mi ba-BAD gurum$_{2}$-e daḫ-ḫa
   (*blank space*)
26. 1(ban$_{2c}$) ur-nigar^{gar} ma$_{2}$ du$_{3}$
27. e$_{2}$ kas$_{4}$ gaba-ta
28. šu-ku$_{6}$ gu$_{2}$-na-me
29. ugula ur-^{d}kal-kal
30. 1(aš$_{c}$) GAN$_{2}$ ur-^{d}ba-ba$_{6}$ ugula
31. 1(aš) GAN$_{2}$ nig$_{2}$-gi-na-zu šeš-tab-ba
32. dumu ur-ab-zu
33. 1(diš) lu$_{2}$-^{d}šara$_{2}$ dumu-ni

obv. col. iv

1. ugula i$_{3}$-dab$_{5}$
2. lugal-ku$_{3}$-zu$^{?}$
3. al-la-zi-ša$_{3}$-gal$_{2}$ dumu-ni
4. lu$_{2}$-ki-ku$_{3}$-ga
5. al-ba-ni-du$_{11}$ dumu-ni
6. in-u$_{9}$-u$_{9}$
7. ur-^{d}ḫendur-sag-ka
8. ur-e$_{2}$-nun-na
9. ab-ba-du$_{10}$-ga dumu-ni
10. ma$_{2}$ du$_{3}$ enku-še$_{3}$
11. ur-^{d}su$_{4}$-⸢an-na⸣
12. ⸢lugal⸣-gu$_{4}$-en-e
13. šeš-kal-la dumu-ni
14. dumu nin$_{9}$-šem$_{5}$-a-sag-gal$_{2}$-la
15. šu-ku$_{6}$-ka e$_{2}$-gal-še$_{3}$ ku$_{3}$ tum$_{3}$-še$_{3}$
16. ur-^{d}utu i$_{3}$-dab$_{5}$
17. ur-^{d}kal-kal
18. nam-sukkal-i$_{3}$-du$_{10}$ dumu šu-ku$_{6}$-še$_{3}$
19. ku$_{3}$-ga-ni
20. engar geš-i$_{3}$-ka-še$_{3}$
21. ambar-da tuš-a-me
22. šu na-ba-lu$_{5}$
23. 1(aš$_{c}$) al-ba-ni-du$_{11}$ dumu-ni
24. 1(diš) lu$_{2}$-uš-gi-na dumu-ni
25. šu ur-^{d}nun-gal
26. 1(aš) ḫe$_{2}$-sa$_{6}$-ge šeš-tab-ba
27. 1(aš) ur-sukkal dumu-ni
28. ki ur-ku$_{3}$-nun-na-ta
29. šu lu$_{2}$-ga
30. 1(aš$_{c}$) lugal-dingir-mu
31. 1(aš) lu$_{2}$-dingir-re
32. 1(aš) eš$_{3}$-^{d}nigar-ba-ni
33. 1(diš) ab-in-da-ni
34. dumu-ni-me
35. 1(aš) lu$_{2}$-giri$_{17}$-zal šeš-tab-ba
36. 1(aš$_{c}$) ur-^{d}lamma

rev. col. i

1. 1(aš$_{c}$) ur-^{d}ur$_{3}$-bar-tab
2. dumu ur$_{2}$-maḫ-me
3. 1(aš) šeš-du$_{10}$-ga šeš-tab-ba

4. dumu lu$_2$-ga-me
5. zaḫ$_3$ ur-^{d}šara$_2$
6. 1(aš) ur-nigar^{gar}
7. 1(aš) ša$_3$-ku$_3$-ge dumu-ni
8. 1(aš$_c$) ug$_3$ ur-^{d}iškur
9. dumu geme$_2$-ge$_6$-par$_4$
10. lugal-ka-x-[x]
11. šeš lugal-⸢ku$_3$⸣-ga-⸢ni⸣
12. ka-gal$_2$-la
13. ki gu$_3$-de$_2$-a
14. libir-am$_3$
15. 1(aš$_c$) ⸢ku$_3$⸣-ga-⸢ni⸣
16. ambar-da ⸢tuš⸣-a-ta
17. 1(aš) ^{geš}kid-bi šeš-tab-ba
18. 1(aš$_c$) ug$_3$ ur-^{d}geš-ḫa-mun-na
19. dumu geme$_2$-ge$_6$-par$_4$
20. šu-ku$_6$-ta gur-ra-me
21. 1(aš$_c$) ab-ba-mu
22. 1(aš) lu$_2$-x-du$_3$-a
23. dumu lugal-ku$_3$-ga-ni ba-IGI
24. ma$_2$ du$_3$ enku-ta
25. šu lugal-um-a?
26. gurum$_2$-e tuku-a
27. 1(aš) ur-eš$_3$-du$_{10}$-nun šeš-tab-ba
28. 1(aš$_c$) ḫa-ba-an-sa$_6$-ge
29. 1(diš) giri$_3$-[. . .]-⸢ni$^?$⸣
30. šu lu$_2$-[ga]
31. 1(aš) šeš-du$_{10}$-⸢ga⸣
32. 1(diš) nig$_2$-^{d}⸢inanna⸣-x
33. 1(diš) lu$_2$-^{d}ḫa-ia$_3$
34. 1(diš) ur-^{d}a-šar$_2$
35. dumu-ni-me
36. ⸢1(aš)⸣ lugal-nig$_2$-lagar-e
37. dumu lu$_2$-⸢ga-me⸣
38. ki lu$_2$-dingir-ra ugula-ta
39. šu šeš-a-ni
40. 1(aš$_c$) ab-ba-mu
41. 1(aš) ⸢ur⸣-^{geš}gigir šeš-tab-ba
42. 1(diš) lu$_2$-^{d}nin-šubur
43. dumu-ni-me

rev. col. ii

1. ki lu$_2$-^{d}da-ni ugula-ta
2. ša$_3$-saḫar-ra-ta
3. šu ab$^?$-e-ki-ag$_2$
4. 1(aš) a$_2$ ⅓(diš) ur-ge$_6$-par$_4$
5. ⸢1(diš)⸣ lu$_2$-^{d}nin-šubur
6. 1(diš) šer$_7$-da-ni
7. dumu-ni-me
8. gudu$_4$$^?$ ^{d}nin-mar^{ki}-me
9. ki lu$_2$-^{d}šara$_2$ ugula-ta
   (blank space)
10. engar geš-i$_3$-ka-me
11. ugula ur-^{d}ba-ba$_6$
12. šu ur-^{d}utu
13. 1(aš$_c$) GAN$_2$ ARAD$_2$-ḫu-la za$_3$ ku$_6$
14. 1(aš) lugal-ḫe$_2$-gal$_2$
15. 1(diš) inim-^{d}šara$_2$
16. 1(diš) ⸢lu$_2$⸣-^{d}nin-šubur
17. [x] lu$_2$-^{d}šul-gi-ra
18. 1(diš) ⸢lu$_2$⸣-^{d}nanna
19. dumu-⸢ni-me⸣
20. šar$_2$-ra-ab-du-ta
21. 1(aš$_c$) lugal-[x]-zu
22. al-la-zi-ša$_3$-⸢gal$_2$⸣
23. 1(diš) lu$_2$-^{d}šara$_2$
24. dumu-ni-me
25. 1(aš$_c$) lu$_2$-ki-ku$_3$-ga
26. 1(aš) al-ba-ni-du$_{11}$ dumu-ni
27. šu in-u$_9$-u$_9$
28. 1(aš$_c$) ur-^{d}ḫendur-sag-ka
29. 1(aš$_c$) ⸢ur-e$_2$⸣-nun
30. 1(diš) ab-ba-du$_{10}$-ga dumu-ni
31. [. . .][586]
32. ma$_2$ du$_3$ enku-me
33. 1(aš$_c$) ur-^{d}su$_4$-an-na

[586] Line erased.

34. 1(aš$_c$) lugal-gu$_2$-en-e
35. 1(aš) šeš-kal-la dumu-ni

rev. col. iii

1. dumu dam ur$_4$-a-ka-gal$_2$-la
2. 1(aš$_c$) nimgir-an-ne$_2$
(*blank space*)
3. ⸢ki⸣ ur-^{d}⸢ba⸣-ba$_6$-ta
(*blank space*)
4. šu-ku$_6$ ⸢ka$^?$⸣ e$_2$-gal-še$_3$ ku$_6$ tum$_3$-me
(*blank space*)

rev. col. iv

(*blank space*)
1. gurum$_2$ ak[587]
2. šu-ku$_6$ geš-gid$_2$-da
3. ⸢engar geš⸣-i$_3$-ka
4. ma$_2$ ⸢du$_3$ enku⸣
5. u$_3$ ambar-da tuš-a
(*blank space*)
6. iti min-eš$_3$-ta u$_4$ 1(u) 5(diš)-am$_3$ ba-ra-zal-la-ta
7. mu en-unu$_6$-gal ^{d}inanna ba-ḫun
(*blank space*)

No. 135. *MS 1908 (Umma, AS 6)*

obv. col. i

1. [. . .]
2. [. . .]
3. [. . .]-ra
4. [x] lu$_2$-⸢dingir⸣-ra
5. [x] a-tu
6. [x] lugal-amar-ku$_3$
7. ⸢dumu-ni⸣-me
8. [x x]-da-da
9. [x] lugal-iti-da ⸢šeš⸣-tab-ba
10. [. . .] šeš-a-ni
11. [dumu]-ni-me
12. [. . .] i$_3$-dab$_5$
13. [1(aš$_c$)$^?$] GAN$_2$ [. . .] tug$_2$ ug$_3$ lu$_2$-[^{d}]⸢nin⸣-ur$_4$-ra mu$_6$-sub$_3$
14. [x]-ab dumu lugal-ku$_3$-zu dumu-⸢gi$_7$⸣ ki$^?$ pa$_4$ šu šu la$_2$
15. dumu lugal-nig$_2$-lagar-e-me
16. šu du$_{10}$-ga
17. ½(aš$_c$) GAN$_2$ lu$_2$-^{d}⸢šara$_2$ dumu-ni⸣
18. 1(diš) lu$_2$-ama-na dumu-⸢ni$^?$⸣
19. [x] lugal-e$_2$-maḫ-e dumu-ni
20. ⸢1(diš)⸣ KA-mu
21. ⸢1/2(aš$_c$)⸣ GAN$_2$ lugal-ezem
22. 1(aš) ur-li
23. dumu-ni-me
24. 1(aš$_c$) 1(barig) 1(ban$_2$) ⸢6(diš)⸣ ug$_3$ gu-u$_2$-a
25. x ur-^{d}ur$_3$-bar-tab
26. x ur-⸢e$_2$⸣-maḫ
27. ⸢dumu⸣-ni-me
28. [x] zu-zu
29. [x] ⸢GAN$_2$⸣ ur-nigar^{gar}
30. 1(aš) lu$_2$-^{d}suen
31. 1(diš) ur-^{d}šul-pa-e$_3$
32. 1(diš) lugal-^{geš}gigir-re
33. 1(diš) ib$_2$-ta-ab-e$_3$
34. dumu-ni-me
35. x x dumu šeš-kal-la ki$^?$ pa$_4$
36. dumu zu-zu-me
37. zaḫ$_3$ ug$_3$ ^{d}šara$_2$-mu-tum$_2$
38. ⸢1/2(aš$_c$)⸣ GAN$_2$ lugal-kur-ta
39. 1/2(aš$_c$) GAN$_2$ al-la
40. uš$_2$ lu$_2$-^{d}šara$_2$ dumu-ni
41. dumu ur-^{d}suen-me
42. x GAN$_2$ nimgir-an-ne$_2$ muš-laḫ$_5$
43. ⸢1(diš) ur-^{d}nin-ma⸣-da ⸢dumu-ni⸣

obv. col. ii

1. [. . .]
2. [. . .] x [. . .] x x
3. ½(aš$_c$) GAN$_2$ ug$_3$ [. . .]-ga
4. 1(aš) lu$_2$-[. . .]
5. 1(diš) lu$_2$-^{d}[x dumu]-ni

[587] Erasure after ak.

6. uš$_2$ ^{geš}dur$_2$-⸢gar⸣-ni
7. 1(diš) ur-^{d}utu dumu-ni
8. dumu lu$_2$-^{d}šara$_2$-me
9. ½(aš$_c$) 1(barig) 2(ban$_2$) ⸢8(diš)⸣ ug$_3$ a-kal-la dumu lugal-me-lam$_2$
10. ½(diš) 1(ban$_2$) 5(diš) ½(diš) NE-zi dumu-ni
11. uš$_2$ tir-gu
12. ½(aš$_c$) GAN$_2$ ku$_3$-^{d}šara$_2$
13. 1(aš) ur-^{d}suen
14. 1(diš) [ARAD$_2$]-mu
15. dumu-ni-me
16. la$_2$-ia$_3$ su-ga lugal-^{geš}kiri$_6$
17. ½(aš$_c$) GAN$_2$ ur-^{d}šul-pa-e$_3$
18. 1(diš) ki-ba dumu-ni
19. ½(aš$_c$) GAN$_2$ ur-^{d}suen
20. 1(aš) lugal-u$_2$-šim$^{?}$-e dumu-ni
21. ½(aš$_c$) GAN$_2$ lu$_2$-⸢gu⸣-la
22. ½(aš$_c$) GAN$_2$ ur-gu$_2$-de$_3$-na
23. 1(aš) GAN$_2$ ur-^{geš}gigir
24. dumu lugal-e$_2$-maḫ-e-me
25. ½(aš$_c$) GAN$_2$ ur-gu$_2$-de$_3$-na
26. 1(aš) ku$_3$-^{d}šara$_2$ dumu-ni
27. ½(aš$_c$) GAN$_2$ ab-ba-saga
28. 1(diš) lugal-sa$_{12}$-su$_{18}$ dumu-ni
29. šu GAN$_2$ lu$_2$-eb-gal
30. ½(aš$_c$) GAN$_2$ ur-^{d}šul-pa-e$_3$
31. 1(diš) ur-^{d}a-šar$_2$ dumu-ni
32. ½(aš$_c$) GAN$_2$ ur-sukkal
33. 1(diš) ⸢lugal-banda$_3$^{da}⸣
34. 1(diš) ur-⸢^{d}a-šar$_2$ dumu-ni-me⸣
35. šu lu$_5$-gu
36. 1(aš$_c$) GAN$_2$ lu$_2$-du$_{10}$-ga
37. 1(aš$_c$) GAN$_2$ lu$_2$-^{d}šara$_2$ šeš-tab-ba
38. dumu-ni-m
39. zaḫ$_3$ nam-ḫa-ni dumu ARAD$_2$-dam
40. ⸢½(aš$_c$)$^{?}$⸣ 1(barig) 1(ban$_2$) 5(diš) ug$_3$ ur$_4$-ša$_3$-ki-du$_{10}$
41. 1(aš$_c$) 4(ban$_2$) tug$_2$ u$_2$-še$_3$-ḫe$_2$-du
42. x 1(aš) 2(ban$_2$) lugal-ḫe$_2$-gal$_2$
43. dumu-ni-me
44. x 1(barig) 1(ban$_2$) 5(diš) ug$_3$ lum-ma
45. dumu lu$_2$-^{d}x-x
46. ½(aš$_c$) GAN$_2$ šeš-kal-[la]
47. ½(aš$_c$) GAN$_2$ lu$_2$-^{d} [. . .] x 4(diš) ur-^{d}a-šar$_2$
48. x 1(ban$_2$) ur-^{d}šul-pa-e$_3$ dumu-ni

obv. col. iii

1. libir-am$_3$
2. ½(aš$_c$) GAN$_2$ ur-^{d}a-šar$_2$ dumu da-du-mu
3. 1(diš) ^{d}utu-ba-ni dumu-ni
4. SIG$_7$ šabra
5. ki lu$_2$-^{d}nin-ur$_4$-ra-ta
6. uš$_2$ ARAD$_2$ engar
7. 1(aš$_c$) GAN$_2$ ug$_3$ lu$_2$-lugal-e-i3-zu
8. 1(aš) 4(ban$_2$) tug$_2$ ug$_3$ ur-^{d}gu-nu-ra
9. 1(aš) 3(ban$_2$) tug$_2$ ur-^{d}da-mu
10. dumu 2(ban$_2$) 2(diš) ur-e$_2$-maḫ
11. dumu-ni-me
12. ša$_3$-saḫar-ra ki ba-sa$_6$-ga-ta
13. x x ug$_3$ a-kal-la dumu ḫu-⸢wa-wa⸣
14. ša$_3$-gu$_4$ <ki> ma-an-šum$_2$-ta
15. 1(aš) 4(ban$_2$) tug$_2$ ug$_3$ ku$_3$-^{d}šara$_2$ dumu puzur$_4$-ma-ma
16. ša$_3$-gu$_4$ ki ur-^{d}suen e$_2$-la$_2$-ta
17. iti dal-ta
18. ½(aš$_c$) GAN$_2$ ab-ba-gi-na dumu da-da
19. 1(aš) 1(barig) 1(ban$_2$) 5(diš) 4(diš) ug$_3$ li-bur-ti-a
20. šu ḫe$_2$-sa$_6$-ge
21. ½(aš$_c$) GAN$_2$ šeš-a-ni dumu-ni
22. ½(aš$_c$) GAN$_2$ ukken-ne$_2$
23. 1(diš) lu$_2$-^{d}šara$_2$ dumu-ni
24. ½(aš$_c$) GAN$_2$ lu$_2$-^{d}nin-šubur
25. ⸢šu⸣ nig$_2$-ša$_3$-ge
26. ½(aš$_c$) GAN$_2$ lugal-ni$_2$-zu
27. ½(aš$_c$) GAN$_2$ lugal-ma$_2$-gur$_8$-re
28. 1(diš) ur-^{d}ur$_3$-bar-tab
29. 1(diš) ur-^{d}ḫendur-sag-ka
30. ½(aš$_c$) GAN$_2$ ^{d}x-x-x [dumu]-ni

31. dumu ⸢u$_2$-ta$_2$ nar⸣
32. ½(aš$_c$) GAN$_2$ ur-^{d}da-mu
33. ½(aš$_c$) ⸢GAN$_2$⸣ a-kal-la
34. x x x x dum⸢u-ni⸣
35. dumu-⸢ni-me⸣
36. dumu lu$_2$-me-lam$_2$

obv. col. iv

1. 1(aš$_c$) 1(barig) 1(ban$_2$) 4(diš) 4(diš) ug$_3$ ^{geš}dur$_2$-gar-ni dumu da-a-gu-ni?
2. dumu 1(aš) 2(ban$_2$) 2(diš) šeš-kal-la dumu-ni
3. uš$_2$ ⸢šeš-a-ni⸣ x
4. dumu ur-^{d}šul-pa-e$_3$
5. ½(aš$_c$) GAN$_2$ lugal-ma$_2$-gur$_8$-re mu$_6$-sub$_3$
6. 1(diš) ARAD$_2$
7. 1(diš) lu$_2$-^{d}šara$_2$
8. 1(diš) lugal-⸢nesag⸣-e
9. dumu-ni-me
10. x-x-x[588]

(blank space)

11. šu DI ⸢NI⸣ gurum$_2$ u$_3$ ur$_4^{?}$-ur$_4^{?}$-dam
12. ½(aš$_c$) GAN$_2$ ur-gu$_2$-de$_3$-na daḫ-ḫu dumu gu-du-gu-du
13. ugula lu$_2$-^{d}šara$_2$
14. ⸢šu$^{?}$⸣ ug$_3$ ur-^{d}da-mu
15. 1(aš$_c$) GAN$_2$ ug$_3$ ur-^{d}šul-pa-e$_3$ ugula
16. 1(aš) ur-^{d}šara$_2$
17. dumu-ni-me
18. 1(aš$_c$) 1(barig) 1(ban$_2$) 5(diš) 4(diš) ug$_3$ ⸢^{d}nin⸣-[šubur]-an-⸢dul$_3^{?}$⸣
19. 1(aš) 3(ban$_2$) tug$_2$ geš-bi
20. 4(aš) 1(aš) 2(ban$_2$) 2(diš) ur-^{d}gilgames$_x$(BIL$_3$.GA.MES)
21. dumu-ni-me
22. uš$_2$ ug$_3$ ur-^{d}šara$_2$ šeš lugal-i$_3$-sa$_6$
23. ½(aš$_c$) GAN$_2$ lugal-nig$_2$-lagar-e dumu ur-mes
24. uš$_2$ lugal-⸢amar⸣-ku$_3$ dumu-ni
25. 1(aš$_c$) 1(barig) 1(ban$_2$) 5(diš) ug$_3$ ku$_3$-ga-ni
26. 1(ban$_2$) 1(diš) ur-^{d}⸢šul⸣-pa-e$_3$ ⸢dumu-ni⸣
27. 1(aš$_c$) 1(barig) 1(ban$_2$) 5(diš) 4(diš) ug$_3$ ur-^{d}šul-pa-e$_3$ dumu ur-⸢nigar⸣[^{gar}]
28. 1(ašc) 1(aš) 1(barig) 1(ban$_2$) 5(diš) 4(diš) ug$_3$ ⸢^{d}⸣[šara$_2$-za-me]
29. 1(aš$_c$) 1(barig) 1(ban$_2$) 5(diš) 4(diš) ⸢ug$_3$ ur⸣-[^{d}]⸢nin⸣-zu
30. dumu 1(aš) 2(ban$_2$) a-a-gi-na
31. dumu-ni-me
32. SIG$_7$-a ug$_3$ lugal-^{geš}gigir-re dumu igi-^{d}šara$_2$-še$_3$
33. 1(aš$_c$) 1(barig) 1(ban$_2$) 5(diš) 4(diš) ug$_3$ ⸢lugal-ezem⸣
34. sag i$_3$-bi$_2$-za ⸢anzu$_2^{mušen}$-babbar$_2$⸣
35. ½(aš$_c$) GAN$_2$ a-kal-la dumu a-tu
36. [. . .]

obv. col. v

1. ½(aš$_c$) GAN$_2$ ur-^{d}suen
2. ½(aš$_c$) GAN$_2$ lu$_2$-^{d}šara$_2$ ⸢šeš⸣-a-⸢ni⸣
3. dumu ARAD$_2$-mu-⸢me⸣
4. ½(aš$_c$) GAN$_2$ <du$_{11}$>-ga-ḫe$_2$-sa$_6$-e
5. 1(diš) ama-ni-ba-an-⸢sa$_6$⸣
6. 1(diš) inim-^{d}⸢šara$_2$⸣
7. dumu-ni-me
8. ½(aš$_c$) GAN$_2$ lu$_2$-giri$_{17}$-zal
9. ½(aš$_c$) 1(barig) 4(ban$_2$) 3(diš) tug$_2^{?}$ ^{d}neraḫ-an-dul$_3$
10. uš$_2$ ug$_3$ lugal-ma$_2$-gur$_8$-re dumu-ni
11. ½(aš$_c$) GAN$_2$ gu$_3$-de$_2$-a dumu ur-mes
12. šu ug$_3$ peš$_2$-am$_3$
13. ⸢½(aš$_c$)⸣ ug$_3$ ka$_5$-a-⸢mu⸣ dumu-ni
14. [x] lu$_2$-^{d}nagar-pa-e$_3$ dumu ur-suḫ$^{?}$
15. ⸢1(aš$_c$)$^{?}$⸣ 1(barig) 1(ban$_2$) 5(diš) 4(diš) ug$_3$ ur-gu$_2$-de$_3$-na
16. ⸢dumu⸣ 1(aš) 2(ban$_2$) 2(diš) ur-ama-na
17. 1(barig) ⸢1(ban$_2$) 5(diš)⸣ 1(diš) ½(diš) ur-<^{d}>ur$_3$-bar-tab
18. 1(barig) 1(ban$_2$) ⸢5(diš)⸣ lu$_2$-^{d}nin-ur$_4$-ra
19. dumu-ni-me
20. uš$_2$ ⸢ur⸣-^{d}šul-pa-⸢e$_3$⸣ šeš ka$_5$-a-mu

[588] Line erased.

21. ½(aš$_c$) GAN$_2$ lugal-ku$_3$-ga-ni dumu ur-[^{d}]e$_{11}$-e
22. ⸢šu ur⸣-^{d}a-šar$_2$
23. ½(aš$_c$) ⸢GAN$_2$ ab⸣-[ba$^?$]-⸢kal⸣-la [. . .]
24. 1(diš) ⸢^{geš}dur$_2$-gar-ni⸣
25. dumu-ni-⸢me⸣
26. [x] 5(diš) 4(diš) ug$_3$ ab-ba-gi-na dumu ur-^{d}⸢gilgames$_x$(BIL$_3$.GA.MES)⸣
27. ša$_3$-gu$_4$ ki ur-^{d}nin-zu-ta
28. ½(aš$_c$) GAN$_2$ ur-^{d}dumu-zi-da
29. 1(aš) AB a-kal-la
30. dumu ^{geš}dur$_2$-gar-ni ba-uš$_2$-me
31. ⸢SIG$_7$⸣-a ⸢iri⸣-bar-re
32. uš-mu nu-^{geš}kiri$_6$ i$_3$-dab$_5$
33. [x] GAN$_2$ ur-^{d}lugal-⸢banda$_3$⸣^{da}
34. ⸢½(aš$_c$) GAN$_2$⸣ lu$_2$-^{d}šara$_2$ šeš-a-ni

obv. col. vi

1. ⸢dumu⸣ a-kal-la lu$_2$-[. . .]
2. [. . .] ug$_3$ ⸢gi-na-mu⸣
3. [. . .] x lu-uk-x-x
4. [. . .] x a$_2$-zi-⸢da dumu$^?$ a⸣-tu
5. ⸢ki ur⸣-am$_3$-ma-ta
6. 1(aš) 3(ban$_2$) tug$_2$ ug$_3$ ur-x-⸢maḫ$^?$⸣ dumu ur-sukkal
7. 1(aš) 4(ban$_2$) tug$_2$ ug$_3$ šeš-a-ni
8. dumu gu-u$_2$-du
9. 1(aš) 4(ban$_2$) tug$_2$ ug$_3$ ARAD$_2$-^{d}šara$_2$ dumu ur-^{d}⸢ašnan⸣
10. ša$_3$-gu$_4$ ki a-x-⸢ta⸣
11. šu ur-sa$_6$-⸢sa$_6$-ga⸣
12. 1(aš$_c$) GAN$_2$ nig$_2$-ša$_3$-ge
13. 1(aš) GAN$_2$ ur-am$_3$-⸢ma⸣ šeš-tab-⸢ba⸣
14. dumu-ni-me
15. aga$_3$-us$_2$ ki ur-^{d}nin-zu-ta
16. 1(aš) 4(ban$_2$) tug$_2$ ug$_3$ ur-gu$_2$-de$_3$-na dumu bi$_2$-da
17. ša$_3$-gu$_4$ ki ur-e$_2$-nun-na-ta
18. libir-am$_3$
19. ½(aš$_c$) ⸢GAN$_2$⸣ lu$_2$-^{d}šara$_2$
20. 1(diš) du$_{11}$-ga-zi-da dumu lugal-^{geš}gigir-re
21. dumu ur-^{d}suen
22. aga$_3$-us$_2$ e$_2$-gal-<e>-si-ta
23. uš$_2$ ug$_3$ lu$_2$-x
24. tu ug$_3$ a-a-gi-na
25. x ra gu$_4$$^?$ x x
26. šu x-x-x
27. ⸢½(aš$_c$)⸣ GAN$_2$ x x na x
28. dumu lu$_5$-lu$_5$-mu
29. [x] ur-^{geš}gigir
30. [x] AN x [. . .]
31. [x x] x x
32. [x x] x x
33. [x] x x-ti-x
34. [x] ur-PAP$^?$-da-NI$^?$
35. ⸢1(aš$_c$)⸣ GAN$_2$ ⸢lu$_2$-^{d}da-mu⸣
36. ⸢1(diš) lu$_2$⸣-x dumu-ni
37. 1(aš) GAN$_2$ lu$_2$-du$_{10}$-ga šeš-tab-ba x
38. 1(diš) ur-^{d}su$_4$-da dumu-ni
39. ki šeš-kal-⸢la⸣ nu-banda$_3$^{da} gu$_4$-ta
40. 1(aš$_c$) 1(ban$_2$) 5(diš) ug$_3$ 4(diš) ⸢ur⸣-^{d}ma-iš-ti-su
41. ½(aš$_c$) ⸢GAN$_2$ ur⸣-^{d}[. . .]

obv. col. vii

1. ⸢ki⸣ [. . .]
2. ⸢1(aš$_c$)⸣ GAN$_2$ x [. . .]
3. x 1(ban$_2$) ⸢5(diš)⸣ 4(diš) ug$_3$ ARAD$_2$ [dumu] ur-⸢^{geš}gigir⸣
4. ⸢ki$^?$⸣ ARAD$_2$ ugula-ta
5. uš$_2$ ⸢lugal$^!$-nig$_2$-lagar-e⸣ dumu ur-^{d}su$_4$-an-⸢na⸣
6. ⸢zaḫ$_3$⸣ a-kal-⸢la⸣
7. x x ⸢ug$_3$ lu$_2$⸣-x-x
8. 1(aš$_c$) x x x ⸢ug$_3$$^?$⸣ [. . .]-pa-⸢e$_3$ ra$_2$-gaba$^?$⸣
9. dumu x x lugal-ušur$_x$(LAL$_2$.TUG$_2$)
10. 1(diš) ⸢2(ban$_2$) 1(diš)⸣ lugal-a$_2$-zi-da
12. 1(diš) 1(ban$_2$) 5(diš) ur-^{d}ur$_3$-bar-⸢tab⸣ dumu-ni
13. 1(aš$_c$) 1(barig) 1(ban$_2$) 5(diš) 4(diš) ug$_3$ AN-x-ZA-x

14. [. . .] ⸢ur⸣-^{d}ur$_{3}$-bar-tab

15. x x ur-e$_{2}$-maḫ

16. uš$_{2}$ ^{d}šara$_{2}$-ba-zi-⸢ge⸣

17. 1(diš) 1(ban$_{2}$) 5(diš) 1(diš) ½(diš) ⸢lugal-šu⸣-nir-re

18. dumu-ni-me

19. ½(aš$_{c}$) GAN$_{2}$ ur-sukkal dumu u$_{2}$-a-ti

20. ½(aš$_{c}$) GAN$_{2}$ lu$_{2}$-dingir-ra

21. <ša$_{3}$>-gu$_{4}$ diri ki ba-saga-ta

22. ½(aš$_{c}$) GAN$_{2}$ lu$_{2}$-du$_{10}$-ga dumu lugal-^{geš}gigir-re

23. ki da-a-ga-ta

24. šu ug$_{3}$[589] u$_{3}$-ma-ni

25. 1(aš$_{c}$) 1(barig) 1(ban$_{2}$) 5(diš) ug$_{3}$ 4(diš) ur-da-da dumu-ni

26. ša$_{3}$-gu$_{4}$ ki a-gu-gu-ta

27. 1(aš$_{c}$) 1(barig) 1(ban$_{2}$) 5(diš) ug$_{3}$ 4(diš) inim-^{d}⸢šara$_{2}$⸣

28. 1(aš$_{c}$) 1(barig) 1(ban$_{2}$) ⸢5(diš)⸣ ug$_{3}$ e$_{2}$-ku$_{3}$

29. ki a-ki-⸢šar⸣-ta

30. 1(aš$_{c}$) 1(barig) 1(ban$_{2}$) 5(diš) ug$_{3}$ 4(diš) dingir-ga$_{2}$-i$_{3}$-sa$_{6}$

31. a-ru-a ur-nigar^{gar} unu$_{3}$

32. sipa gu$_{4}$-laḫ$_{4}$-ta

33. ki a-tu-ta

34. 1(aš$_{c}$) 1(barig) 1(ban$_{2}$) 5(diš) 4(diš) ug$_{3}$ x-x

35. x [. . .]

obv. col. viii

1. [. . .]

2. [. . .]

3. [. . .]

4. dumu [. . .]

5. ⸢sipa⸣ [gu$_{4}$]-laḫ$_{4}$-ta

6. ⸢1(aš)⸣ GAN$_{2}$ x x-palil$_{2}$ šeš lugal-ku$_{3}$-zu

7. šu-ku$_{6}$ x ka ur-še$_{3}$-ra-ta

8. [. . .]-⸢^{d}⸣ba-ba$_{6}$-ta

9. [x] ⸢GAN$_{2}$⸣ ur-^{geš}gigir

10. 1(aš) ⸢inim⸣-^{d}x

11. 1(diš) ⸢lugal⸣-^{d}x

12. dumu-ni-me

13. uš$_{2}$ ur-^{d}lugal-banda$_{3}^{da}$

14. uš$_{2}$ x-x-x-⸢NE$^{?}$⸣-ga

15. 1(diš) lu$_{2}$-^{d}nin-⸢šubur$^{?}$⸣ dumu-ni-⸢me⸣

16. x x x

17. ⸢1(diš) lu$_{2}$-^{d}⸣nin-⸢sun$_{2}^{?}$⸣

18. dumu ḫu-⸢un⸣-sa$_{6}$

19. uš$_{2}$ ug$_{3}$ x x x NI KA

20. uš$_{2}$ ug$_{3}$ [. . .]

21. 1(diš) ½(diš) 5(diš) ½(diš) igi-⸢^{d}šara$_{2}^{?}$⸣-[x]

22. ½(aš$_{c}$) GAN$_{2}$ nam-⸢ḫa$^{?}$⸣-[ni$^{?}$] KA-U$_{2}$ [x]

23. šu šeš-a-[ni]

24. ½(aš$_{c}$) GAN$_{2}$ ab-ba-[. . .]

25. ½(aš$_{c}$) ur-x-[. . .]

26. ½(aš$_{c}$) GAN$_{2}$? x x [. . .]

27. uš$_{2}$ lu$_{2}$-^{d}[. . .]

28. 1(diš) ur-sukkal-[. . .]

29. dumu šeš-⸢a⸣-[ni?-me?]

30. ½(aš$_{c}$) GAN$_{2}$ ur-x-[. . .]

31. 1(diš) lu$_{2}$-[. . .]

32. ½(aš$_{c}$) GAN$_{2}$ lu$_{2}$-[. . .]

33. 1(diš) ur-^{d}[. . .]

34. 1(diš) lu$_{2}$-^{d}[. . .]

35. šu ⸢gar$^{?}$⸣-x-x-[. . .]

36. 1(diš) lu$_{2}$-⸢dingir⸣-ra ⸢dumu-ni⸣

37. ½(aš$_{c}$) GAN$_{2}$ x-AN-x

38. 1(diš) lu$_{2}$-^{d}utu dumu-ni

39. ⸢ki⸣ lugal-ma$_{2}$-gur$_{8}$-re-ta

40. ½(aš$_{c}$) GAN$_{2}$ ^{d}šara$_{2}$-kam dumu ur-ab-ba dumu-ni ba-NE

41. uš$_{2}$ ^{d}šara$_{2}$-an-⸢dul$_{3}$⸣ dumu-ni

42. ½(aš$_{c}$) ⸢GAN$_{2}$ ur⸣-^{d}suen dumu lu$_{2}$-me-lam$_{2}$ zaḫ$_{3}$-ta

43. ½(aš$_{c}$) ⸢ur⸣-e$_{2}$-⸢maḫ$^{?}$⸣-e

44. 1(aš) lu$_{2}$-^{d}šara$_{2}$

45. 1(diš) AN-x-[. . .]

46. dumu-ni-[me?]

47. ½(aš$_{c}$) GAN$_{2}$ ⸢ur⸣-[. . .]

[589] Erasure below šu and ug$_{3}$.

48. 1(diš) x-[. . .]
49. 1(diš) ^{d}x-[. . .]
50. ½(aš$_c$) x [. . .]
(*rest broken*)

rev. col. i

(*broken*)

rev. col. ii

(*start broken*)

1'. ½(aš$_c$) GAN$_2$ lu$_2$-[. . .] ⸢dumu-ni⸣
2'. ½(aš$_c$) GAN$_2$ ur$_4$-⸢ša$_3$-ki-du$_{10}$⸣
3'. ½(aš$_c$) GAN$_2$ ur-^{d}[. . .]
4'. uš$_2$ x-[. . .]
5'. dumu lugal-⸢^{geš}⸣[. . .]
6'. ½(aš$_c$) GAN$_2$ MIR-[. . .]
7'. dumu lu$_2$-[. . .]
8'. 1(aš$_c$) 1(barig) 1(ban$_2$) 5(diš) 5(diš) x x
9'. 1(aš$_c$) 1(barig) 1(ban$_2$) 5(diš) 5(diš) x x
10'. ⸢dumu⸣ ka$_5$-[x]
11'. uš$_2$ [. . .]
12'. ½(aš$_c$) GAN$_2$ x-[. . .]
13'. ki x-[. . .]
14'. dumu ur-ab-⸢zu-me⸣
16'. x GAN$_2$ a-[. . .] dumu ur-[. . .]
17'. [. . .]
18'. [. . .]
19'. ⸢1(aš$_c$)⸣ [x] 1(ban$_2$) ⸢5(diš) 5(diš)⸣ [. . .]
20'. uš$_2$ [. . .]
21'. ⸢1(aš$_c$)⸣ [. . .]
22'. [. . .] x [. . .]
23'. [. . .] x [. . .]
24'. dumu-⸢ni⸣-[me?]
25'. 1(aš$_c$) 1(barig) 1(ban$_2$) ⸢ug$_3^{?}$⸣ [x]-^{d}dumu-[. . .]
29'. 1(aš$_c$) 1(barig) 1(ban$_2$) 5(diš) ⸢4(diš)⸣ [. . .]
30'. 1(aš$_c$) 1(barig) 1(ban$_2$) ⸢5(diš) 5(diš) ur-^{d}⸣ [x]
31'. [x x] ug$_3$ x [. . .]
32'. ki ⸢lugal-ma$_2$-gur$_8$⸣-re ⸢ugula⸣-[ta?]
33'. ½(aš$_c$) GAN$_2$ ⸢ur-^{d}⸣ [x]
34'. 1(diš) ⸢lu⸣-[. . .]
35'. [. . .]
36'. dumu [. . .]
37'. [x] ur-x-⸢da$^{?}$⸣-[x]
38'. [. . .]⸢ug$_3^{?}$⸣ [. . .]
(*rest broken*)

rev. col. iii

1. ki nig$_2$-⸢du$_7$⸣-[pa-e$_3$]
2. uš$_2$ ug$_3$ ur-[. . .]
3. 1(barig) 2(ban$_2$) 2(diš) ug$_3$ šeš-a-ni dumu lu$_2$-eb-gal ad-kup$_4$
4. ki a-gu-ta
5. [. . .][590]
6. [. . .][591]
7. ⸢daḫ⸣-ḫu-me[592]
8. ⸢ugula⸣ lu$_2$-dingir-ra
9. 1(aš$_c$) GAN$_2$ ug$_3$ ⸢za$_3$⸣-mu ugula
10. 1(aš) šeš-⸢kal-la dumu⸣-ni
11. 1(aš) 4(ban$_2$) tug$_2$ šeš-⸢kal-la⸣
12. uš$_2$ ^{d}šara$_2$-mu-tum$_2$
13. 1(aš) 4(ban$_2$) tug$_2$ a-du-na$_2$
14. 1(aš) ⸢4(ban$_2$) tug$_2$⸣ x-x-zi-da-mu
15. 1(aš) 3(ban$_2$)[593] ^{d}šara$_2$-za-me
16. 1(aš) 3(ban$_2$) tug$_2$ ⸢giri$_3$⸣-^{d}šara$_2$-i$_3$-dab$_5$
17. [. . .] ⸢tug$_2$⸣ ur$_4$-ša$_3$-ki-du$_{10}$
18. [x] ur-^{d}ur$_3$-bar-tab
19. 1(aš) 3(ban$_2$) tug$_2$ nig$_2$-u$_2$-rum
20. 1(aš) 3(ban$_2$) tug$_2$ ka$_5$-a
21. uš$_2$ igi-dingir-še$_3$
22. 1(aš) 4(ban$_2$) tug$_2$ ^{d}er$_3$-ra-dan
23. 1(aš) 4(ban$_2$) tug$_2$ lugal-ma$_2$-gur$_8$-re zaḫ$_3$-ta
24. 1(aš) 4(ban$_2$) tug$_2$ ur-^{d}ḫal-mu-ša$_4$
25. 1(aš) 3(ban$_2$) tug$_2$ dingir-mu-ma-an-šum$_2$
26. 1(aš) 3(ban$_2$) tug$_2$ nu ku$_3$-^{d}⸢šara$_2$ dumu⸣ ama-[a-ra$_2$-mu$_2$]

---

[590] Line erased.

[591] Line erased.

[592] Line written on dry clay.

[593] Erasure after 3(ban$_2$): tug$_2$.

27. 1(aš) 1(barig) 1(ban$_2$) GAN$_2$ x 5(diš) 3(diš) sila$_3$$^?$ gur$^?$ ⸢lugal-nesag⸣-[e] dumu ama-kal-⸢la⸣
28. 1(aš) 1(barig) 3(ban$_2$) a-a-lu$_2$-du$_{10}$
29. tu 3(ban$_2$) tug$_2$ ur-li[594]
30. libir-am$_3$
31. uš$_2$ ur-[. . .]
32. dumu umbin-ku$_5$
33. ki ba-sa$_6$-ta
34. ⸢uš$_2$ ug$_3$⸣ ^{d}utu-bi$_2$-du$_{11}$
35. ⸢1(aš$_c$)⸣ 3(ban$_2$) tug$_2$ ⸢ur⸣-^{d}šul-pa-e$_3$
36. dumu 1(aš) gur lugal-⸢ku$_3$-zu⸣
37. 1(diš) 2(ban$_2$) 2(diš) giri$_3$-ni-i$_3$-⸢sa$_6$⸣
38. ⸢dumu-ni-me⸣
39. 1(aš) 4(ban$_2$) [. . .]-zi-[x]
40. [. . .]
41. [. . .]
42. ⸢dumu⸣ KA-x-[. . .]

rev. col. iv

1. ki da-a-ga-ta
   (*blank space*)
2. x za$_3$-⸢mu⸣[595]
3. [x] nig$_2$-u$_2$-⸢rum⸣[596]
4. [. . .] x ARAD$_2$ PA
5. [. . .] AN x
6. 1(aš) ⸢3(ban$_2$)⸣ [. . .]-⸢zi⸣
7. 1(aš) ⸢3(ban$_2$)⸣ [. . .] x
8. 1(diš) ^{d}x-x-x-⸢nir⸣
9. 1(diš) ⸢lugal-nig$_2$-lagar⸣-e x
10. uš$_2$ lugal-ezem
11. 1(aš) 4(ban$_2$) tug$_2$ ur-e$_2$-gal
12. uš$_2$ šeš-kal-la
13. 1(aš) 4(ban$_2$) tug$_2$ ^{d}šara$_2$-ba-zi-ge
14. 1(aš) 4(ban$_2$) tug$_2$ ur-^{d}suen
15. 1(aš) 4(ban$_2$) tug$_2$ ba-zi-ge
16. 1(aš$_c$) 1(barig) ⸢tug$_2$ lugal-ma$_2$-gur$_8$⸣-re
17. 1(aš) 4(ban$_2$) ⸢tug$_2$ lugal-ku$_3$-ga⸣-ni
18. ⸢dumu⸣ lugal-x-x-x
19. ½(aš$_c$) x ⸢inim⸣-ma-ni-zi
20. ⸢1(aš) 1(barig) tug$_2$⸣ ur-^{d}šul-pa-e$_3$
21. dumu ^{d}suen-a-a
22. 1(aš) 4(ban$_2$) tug$_2$ ^{d}šara$_2$-ku$_3$-zu
23. 1(aš$_c$) 1(barig) 4(ban$_2$) lu$_2$-dingir-ra
24. uš$_2$ ba-zi-⸢ge⸣
25. 1(aš) 4(ban$_2$) tug$_2$ ^{d}šara$_2$-mu-tum$_2$
26. 1(aš$_c$) 1(barig) tug$_2$ ur-^{d}su$_4$-an-⸢na⸣
27. 1(aš$_c$) 1(barig) tug$_2$ ^{d}šara$_2$-me-a-tum$_2$
28. 1(aš$_c$) 1(barig) tug$_2$ lugal-a$_2$-mu
29. uš$_2$ šeš-a-ra$_2$-nu$_2$
30. 1(aš) 4(ban$_2$) tug$_2$ lugal-eb$_2$-gu-ul
31. SIG$_7$-a [x]-⸢du⸣-du AN KA$^?$ ⸢lu$_2$$^?$⸣ [x] x i$_3$-dab$_5$
32. x [. . .] x-^{d}šara$_2$
33. [. . .] tug$_2$ lugal-nig$_2$-gur$_{11}$-e
34. x x ta
35. 1(aš) 1(barig) tug$_2$ ^{d}šara$_2$-i$_3$-sa$_6$
36. a-ru-a nimgir-ḫe$_2$-du$_7$
37. 1(aš) 4(ban$_2$) tug$_2$ ^{d}šara$_2$-zi-da dumu ur-še-il$_2$-⸢la⸣
38. ki ba-sa$_6$-ta
39. libir-am$_3$[597]
40. 1(aš) 4(ban$_2$) tug$_2$ dumu-gi$_7$ lu$_2$-^{d}šara$_2$ x x dumu x ki lu$_2$-^{d}utu dumu-⸢gi$_7$⸣ x ra[598]
41. ugula ARAD$_2$
42. 1(aš$_c$) GAN$_2$ ug$_3$ ku$_3$-ga-ni ugula
43. e$_2$-gal? lugal-^{geš}gigir-re
44. dumu a-gub-ba-na-me
45. uš$_2$ lugal-^{geš}gigir-re
46. dumu nig$_2$-u$_2$-rum
47. 1(aš) 4(ban$_2$) tug$_2$ a-a-gi-na
48. 1(aš) 3(ban$_2$) tug$_2$ šeš-kal-la
49. 1(aš) 3(ban$_2$) tug$_2$ ki-lu$_5$-la
50. uš$_2$ a$_2$-dingir-ga$_2$

---

594 Line written on dry clay.

595 Line written on dry clay.

596 Line written on dry clay.

597 Line written on dry clay.

598 Line written on dry clay.

rev. col. v

1. 1(aš) 4(ban$_2$) ⸢tug$_2$⸣ ARAD$_2$
2. 1(aš) 1(barig) ⸢tug$_2$?⸣ ma-an-gig
3. ⸢1(aš)⸣ 4(ban$_2$) ⸢tug$_2$⸣ ARAD$_2$-saga
4. 1(aš) 3(ban$_2$) tug$_2$ ur-^{d}x-x dumu ⸢ur⸣-x-[. . .]
5. 1(aš) 4(ban$_2$) tug$_2$ ur-e$_{11}$-e dumu ur-^{d}ab-u$_2$
6. dumu lugal-dalla
7. uš$_2$ ur-^{d}suen dumu a-⸢na$^{?}$⸣-lu$_2$
8. uš$_2$ dingir-mu-ma-an-šum$_2$
9. uš$_2$ šeš-a-ni
10. uš$_2$ ur-^{d}kal-kal
11. tu x lugal-ku$_3$-ga-ni
12. 1(aš) x ⸢tug$_2$⸣ lu$_2$-^{d}šara$_2$
13. 1(aš) ⸢1(ban$_2$) tug$_2$⸣ ^{d}šara$_2$-gal-zu
14. 1(aš) ⸢3(ban$_2$) tug$_2$⸣ lugal-amar-ku$_3$
15. 1(aš) 2(ban$_2$) ⸢tug$_2$⸣ ur-^{d}utu
16. dumu lugal-x-x-me
17. 1(aš) x x [. . .]
18. dumu sag-x-x-x
19. 1(aš) 2(ban$_2$) tug$_2$ lugal-ḫe$_2$-gal$_2$
20. uš$_2$ a$_2$-dingir-ga$_2$
21. uš$_2$ ^{d}šara$_2$-i$_3$-sa$_6$
22. 1(aš) 2(ban$_2$) tug$_2$ lu$_2$-lugal
23. dumu lugal-⸢šeš$^{?}$⸣ ba-uš$_2$-me
24. 1(aš) 3(ban$_2$) tug$_2$ ur$_3$-ra-ni
25. 1(aš) 3(ban$_2$) tug$_2$ inim-^{d}šara$_2$ dumu nig$_2$-u$_2$-rum SIG$_7$-a
26. 1(aš) 2(ban$_2$) tug$_2$ ur-^{d}nin-a-zu
27. dumu ur-še-il$_2$-la
28. 1(aš) 2(ban$_2$) tug$_2$ šeš-kal-la
29. a-ru-a ur-ama-⸢na⸣
30. uš$_2$ ^{d}šara$_2$-⸢a-mu⸣
31. a-ru-a a-tu
32. 1(aš) 2(ban$_2$) tug$_2$ lugal-ezem
33. a-ru-a ur$_2$-nig$_2$-du$_{10}$
34. 1(aš) 3(ban$_2$) tug$_2$ šeš-kal-la
35. a-ru-a ur-gu$_2$-de$_3$-na
36. 1(aš) 2(ban$_2$) tug$_2$ lugal-geš-ḫur-e
37. a-ru-a ur-^{geš}gigir
38. 1(aš) 2(ban$_2$) tug$_2$ lugal-ezem
39. a-ru-a lugal-^{geš}gigir-re
40. uš$_2$ nam-eb$_2$-gu-ul
41. 1(aš) 2(ban$_2$) tug$_2$ šu-im-⸢bi⸣
42. a-ru-a lugal-geš-ḫur-e
43. 1(aš) 2(ban$_2$) tug$_2$ lugal-ḫe$_2$-gal$_2$
44. a-ru-a lugal-mu$^{?}$

rev. col. vi

1. x x x i$_3$-dab$_5$
2. a-ru-a lu$_2$-^{d}šara$_2$$^{?}$
3. uš$_2$ ur- ^{d}⸢iškur⸣
4. a-ru-a inim-ma-ni-⸢zi⸣

   (*rest of col. on dried clay*)

5. libir-am$_3$

   (*blank space*)

6. ugula ⸢ku$_3$-ga-ni⸣
7. x x x ^{d}šara$_2$-za-me x
8. a-ru-a AN-gir$_2$-ra
9. 1(aš) 2(ban$_2$) lu$_2$- ^{d}nin-šubur
10. ⸢a⸣-ru-a ur-lu$_2$-gu-la
11. 1(aš) 2(ban$_2$) tug$_2$ lugal-ma$_2$-gur$_8$-re
12. a-ru-a nam-ḫa-ni
13. 1(aš) 3(ban$_2$) tug$_2$ KA-erin-⸢ma$^{?}$⸣
14. [a]-⸢ru⸣-a šeš-a-ni
15. 1(aš) 2(ban$_2$) tug$_2$ ^{d}šubur-ba-⸢ra⸣
16. a-ru-a ⸢ša$_3$-ku$_3$-ge⸣
17. ⸢1(aš) 2(ban$_2$) tug$_2$⸣ engar-⸢du$_{10}$⸣
18. a-ru-<a> lugal-⸢nesag$^{?}$-e$^{?}$⸣
19. 1(aš) 2(ban$_2$) tug$_2$ ^{d}utu-saga
20. a-ru-a ur-^{d}ma-mi
21. 1(aš) 3(ban$_2$) tug$_2$ ^{d}šara$_2$-mu-tum$_2$
22. a-ru-a ab-ba-[gi]-na
23. 1(aš) 2(ban$_2$) 2(diš) an-ta-lu$_2$ a-ru-a aš-kal
24. 1(aš) 3(ban$_2$) tug$_2$ lu$_2$-^{d}nin-ur$_4$-ra
25. 1(aš) 3(ban$_2$) tug$_2$ lu$_2$-du$_{10}$-ga
26. dumu-mi$_2$ bappir dumu lugal-TAR-me
27. i$_3$-bi$_2$-za zi$_3$ KA-a

   (*blank space*)

28. daḫ-ḫu-me
29. ugula ku$_{3}$-ga-ni
(blank space)
30. ug$_{3}$-il$_{2}$-me
31. 1(aš$_{c}$) 1(barig) 1(ban$_{2}$) 5(diš) 5(diš) ug$_{3}$ šu-^{d}en-lil$_{2}$
32. 1(diš) 1(ban$_{2}$) 5(diš) 1(diš) ½(diš) a-da-na-aḫ
33. 1(diš) 1(ban$_{2}$) 5(diš) 1(diš) ½(diš) šu-kab-ta$_{2}$
34. dumu-[ni]-⸢me⸣
35. ⸢a-ru-a⸣ ur-^{d}gilgames$_{3}$ dumu a-ti-ma-ti
(blank space)

rev. col. vii
(blank)

rev. col. viii
(blank space)
1. ⸢gurum$_{2}$⸣ ak ša$_{3}$-saḫar-ra
2. [ša$_{3}$] a-pi$_{4}$-sal$_{4}$^{ki}
3. ⸢gu$_{2}$⸣-de$_{3}$-na
4. ⸢u$_{3}$ muš⸣-bi-an-na
5. ur- ^{d}li$_{9}$-si$_{4}$ ensi$_{2}$ umma ^{ki}
6. [x] x [x] ⸢lu$_{2}$-du$_{10}$-ga⸣ [. . .] x u$_{3}$ [. . .] x-mu[599]
7. [mu ša]-aš-šu$_{2}$-ru ^{ki} ba-ḫul

No. 138. *MS 2012 (Umma, X)*

obv. col. i
(start broken)
1'. [. . .] ⸢gur$^{?}$⸣
2'. [. . .]-iti-da engar
3'. [. . .] GAN$_{2}$ 3(aš) gur
4'. [x]-nigar^{gar}
5'. [. . .] ⸢GAN$_{2}$⸣ 3(aš) gur
6'. [. . .] ⸢ur$^{?}$-^{d}⸣šul-pa-e$_{3}$
7'. [. . .] ⸢GAN$_{2}$⸣ 3(aš) gur
8'. [. . .]-gi
9'. [gaba$^{?}$] ⸢a-ša$_{3}$⸣ gu$_{4}$-suḫub$_{2}$
10'. [. . .] ⸢GAN$_{2}$⸣ 7(aš) gur
11'. [. . .] x-^{d}li$_{9}$-si$_{4}$ engar
12'. [. . .] x ⸢GAN$_{2}$⸣ 3(aš) gur
13'. ⸢lu$_{2}$⸣-^{d}da-ni
14'. 3(iku) GAN$_{2}$ 3(aš) gur
15'. lugal-ezem lu$_{2}$-tir
16'. 3(iku) GAN$_{2}$ 3(aš) gur
17'. ur-^{d}nin-tu
18'. 1(eše$_{3}$) GAN$_{2}$ 7(aš) gur
19'. lu$_{2}$-^{d}suen engar
20'. [. . .] 3(aš) gur
21'. [. . .]-še$_{3}$
22'. [. . . n] gur
(rest broken)

obv. col. ii
(start broken)
1'. x[. . .] x-x
2'. 3(iku) GAN$_{2}$ 3(aš) gur
3'. giri$_{3}$-ni-i$_{3}$-sa$_{6}$
4'. 3(iku) GAN$_{2}$ 3(aš) gur
5'. ^{geš}gigir-re
6'. ki lugal-^{geš}gigir-re ugula-ta
7'. 1(eše$_{3}$) GAN$_{2}$ 7(aš) gur
8'. du$_{11}$-ga engar
9'. 3(iku) GAN$_{2}$ 3(aš) gur
10'. ⸢lugal⸣-^{d}utu
11'. 3(iku) GAN$_{2}$ 3(aš) gur
12'. lugal-TAR
13'. 3(iku) GAN$_{2}$ 3(aš) gur
14'. lu$_{2}$-kal-la
15'. a-ša$_{3}$ tul$_{2}$-ḫul$_{2}$-^{d}utu[600]
16'. nig$_{2}$-du$_{7}$-pa-e$_{3}$ engar
17'. 1(eše$_{3}$) GAN$_{2}$ 7(aš) gur
18'. giri$_{3}$-ni engar
19'. 3(iku) GAN$_{2}$ 3(aš) gur
20'. ur-^{d}a-šar$_{2}$
21'. 3(iku) GAN$_{2}$ 3(aš) gur
22'. lugal-i-ti

---

[599] Line written on dry clay.

[600] Perhaps phonetic for the well-known field name du$_{6}$-ḫul$_{2}$-^{d}utu.

23'. ⌜3(iku)⌝ GAN_2 3(aš) gur

(*rest broken*)

obv. col. iii

(*start broken*)

1'. x [. . .]

2'. 3(iku) GAN_2 3(aš) gur

3'. ur-^{geš}gigir

4'. gaba a-$ša_3$ na-ra-am-^{d}suen

5'. 3(iku) GAN_2 3(aš) gur

6'. ku_3-$^{d}šara_2$

7'. 3(iku) GAN_2 3(aš) gur

8'. a-kal-⌜la⌝[601]

9'. a-$ša_3$ apin-ba-zi

10'. 1(eše$_3$) GAN_2 7(aš) gur

11'. ur-$^{d}šara_2$ engar

12'. 3(iku) GAN_2 3(aš) gur

13'. lugal-nig_2-lagar-e

14'. 3(iku) GAN_2 3(aš) gur

15'. $giri_3$-zal

16'. 3(iku) GAN_2 3(aš) gur

17'. lugal-me-lam_2

18'. gaba a-$ša_3$ na-ra-am-^{d}suen

19'. 1(eše$_3$) GAN_2 1(u) 2(aš) gur

20'. lu_2-kal-la engar

21'. 3(iku) GAN_2 6(aš) gur

22'. e_2-ki

23'. x ⌜gur⌝ x

(*rest broken*)

obv. col. iv

(*start broken*)

1'. [. . .] x

2'. [. . . n] 2(aš) gur

3'. x [. . .]-su_3-bi$^{?}$-an-na

4'. igi-zi engar

5'. 3(iku) GAN_2 3(aš) gur

6'. nu-du_{10}-il

7'. 3(iku) GAN_2 3(aš) gur

8'. ur-^{d}da-ni

9'. 3(iku) GAN_2 3(aš) gur

10'. ur-^{d}en-ki dumu ur-^{d}iškur

11'. 1(eše$_3$) GAN_2 7(aš) gur

12'. ur-^{d}dumu-zi-da

13'. 3(iku) GAN_2 3(aš) gur

14'. a-kal-la šeš-a-ni

15'. GAN_2 še-ba

16'. a-a-lu_2-du_{10} $ša_3$-saḫar-ra-ta

17'. 3(iku) GAN_2 3(aš) gur

18'. ḫa-la-^{d}iškur

19'. 1(eše$_3$) GAN_2 7(aš) gur

20'. lugal-$ušur_x$(LAL_2.TUG_2) engar

21'. 3(iku) GAN_2 3(aš) gur

22'. ur-^{d}a-$šar_2$

23'. ⌜3(iku) GAN_2⌝ 3(aš) gur

24'. [. . .]-⌜kal⌝-la

25'. [. . .] gur

(*rest broken*)

obv. col. v

(*start broken*)

1'. [. . .] ⌜gur⌝

2'. [. . .]-⌜da$^{?}$⌝-ni

3'. [3(iku)] ⌜GAN_2⌝ 3(aš) gur

4'. ⌜lu_2⌝-^{d}nin-šubur

5'. 3(iku) GAN_2 3(aš) gur

6'. ur-^{d}dumu-zi-da

7'. 1(eše$_3$) GAN_2 7(aš) gur

8'. ur-nigar^{gar} engar

9'. 3(iku) GAN_2 3(aš) gur

10'. ur-^{d}nin-zu

11'. 3(iku) GAN_2 3(aš) gur

12'. ur-^{geš}gigir

13'. ⌜3(iku)⌝ GAN_2 3(aš) gur

14'. lugal-nig_2-lagar-e

15'. a-$ša_3$ apin-ba-zi

16'. 1(eše$_3$) GAN_2 7(aš) gur

17'. lugal-e_2-maḫ-e engar

---

[601] Over erasure: a-$ša_3$ kal-x.

18'. 3(iku) GAN$_2$ 3(aš) gur
19'. inim-ku$_3$
20'. 3(iku) GAN$_2$ 3(aš) gur
21'. ur-^{d}ur$_3$-bar-tab
22'. 3(iku) GAN$_2$ 3(aš) gur
23'. ^{d}šara$_2$-bi$_2$-du$_{11}$
24'. 1(eše$_3$) GAN$_2$ 7(aš) gur
25'. a-lu$_5$-lu$_5$ engar
26'. 3(iku) GAN$_2$ 3(aš) gur
27'. lugal-^{geš}gigir-re
28'. 3(iku) GAN$_2$ 3(aš) gur
29'. ur-^{d}ur$_3$-bar-tab
30'. 3(iku) GAN$_2$ 3(aš) gur
31'. x-[x]-⸢ta-ka⸣-x
32'. [. . .] ⸢^{d}utu⸣
(rest broken)

obv. col. vi
(start broken)
1'. x [. . .]
2'. 1(eše$_3$) [GAN$_2$ n gur]
3'. šeš-⸢kal⸣-[la x]
4'. 4(iku) ½(iku) ⸢GAN$_2$ 2(aš)⸣ [n gur]
5'. a-ša$_3$ x
6'. 1(eše$_3$) GAN$_2$ 3(aš) ⸢gur⸣
7'. a-ša$_3$ u$_2$-du-en-e$_2$-⸢a⸣
8'. ur-ab-ba-saga
9'. 1(eše$_3$) GAN$_2$ 1(u) gur
10'. gaba a-ša$_3$ apin-ba-zi
11'. bi$_2$-li-li
12'. ur-^{d}en-lil$_2$-la$_2$ ša$_3$-saḫar-še$_3$
14'. ARAD$_2$-mu i$_3$-dab$_5$
15'. 1(eše$_3$) GAN$_2$ 4(aš) gur
16'. gaba a-ša$_3$ a-u$_2$-da
17'. lu$_2$-saga
18'. 1(eše$_3$) GAN$_2$ 7(aš) gur
19'. a-ša$_3$ u$_2$-du-^{d}nin-a-ra-li
20'. ^{d}iškur-ba-ni
21'. 1(eše$_3$) GAN$_2$ 1(u) gur
22'. gaba a-ša$_3$ gu$_4$-suḫub$_2$
23'. uš-mu
24'. 1(eše$_3$) GAN$_2$ 1(u) gur
25'. gaba a-ša$_3$ ^{d}nin-ḫur-sag
26'. lu$_2$-du$_{10}$-ga dumu ša$_3$-ku$_3$-ge dumu ^{d}šara$_2$-ga$_2$
27'. 3(iku) GAN$_2$ 3(aš) gur
28'. gaba a-ša$_3$ ^{d}nin-ḫur-sag
29'. lugal-ku$_3$-ga-ni dumu ur-^{d}a-šar$_2$
30'. [x] ⸢GAN$_2$⸣ 1(u) gur
31'. [. . .] x
(rest broken)

obv. col. vii
(start broken)
1'. [. . .]
(blank space)
2'. a-igi-du$_8$-me
3'. 2(iku) ½(iku) GAN$_2$ 2(aš) gur
4'. a-ša$_3$ muru$_{13}$
5'. 3(iku) ½(iku) GAN$_2$ 2(aš) gur
6'. a-ša$_3$ ^{d}šara$_2$-gu$_2$-gal
7'. šeš-kal-la nagar
8'. 1(eše$_3$) 5(aš) gur
9'. a-ša$_3$ na-ra-am-^{d}suen
10'. ur-^{d}nun-gal tug$_2$-du$_8$
11'. 1(eše$_3$) GAN$_2$ 2(u) gur
12'. gaba a-ša$_3$ šul-pa-e$_3$
13'. lu$_2$-dingir-ra šum$_2^{?}$
14'. 1(eše$_3$) GAN$_2$ 1(u) 5(aš) gur
15'. a-ša$_3$ tul$_2$-ḫul$_2$-^{d}utu
16'. ur$_2$-maḫ nagar
17'. ki nir-i$_3$-da-gal$_2$-ta
(blank space)
18'. giri$_3$-se$_3$-ga gu$_4$ ^{geš}apin-me
19'. 1(eše$_3$) 1(iku) ¼(iku) GAN$_2$ 3(aš) gur
(rest broken)

obv. col. viii
(start broken)
1'. 1(eše$_3$) GAN$_2$ 1(u) ⸢gur⸣

2'. gaba a-ša$_3$ na-gab$_2$-tum
3'. lugal-ur$_2$-ra-ni
4'. 1(eše$_3$) GAN$_2$ 7(aš) gur
5'. a-ša$_3$ gaba ^{d}nin-ḫur-sag
6'. na-ba-mu
(blank space)
7'. ugula lugal-^{geš}gigir-re
8'. 2(eše$_3$) GAN$_2$ 1(u) 5(aš) gur
9'. a-ša$_3$ a-ni$^?$-zu
10'. ur-^{d}⸢suen⸣ ugula
11'. 1(eše$_3$) GAN$_2$ 7(aš) gur
12'. a-ša$_3$ ^{d}šara$_2$-gu$_2$-gal
13'. u$_3$ dag-ga-šeš-x
14'. 1(eše$_3$) GAN$_2$ 1(u) gur
15'. a-ša$_3$ u$_2$-du-^{d}nin-a-ra-li
16'. ur-x-x-na
17'. 1(eše$_3$) GAN$_2$ ⸢9(aš)⸣ gur
18'. a-ša$_3$ gu$_2$-suḫub$_2$
19'. lugal-ezem
20'. 1(eše$_3$) GAN$_2$ 6(aš) gur
21'. a-ša$_3$ a-ni-zu!(BA)
22'. a-kal-la
23'. 1(eše$_3$) GAN$_2$ 4(aš) gur
24'. a-ša$_3$ na-ra-am-^{d}suen
(rest broken)

obv. col. ix
(start broken)
1'. ⸢3(iku)⸣ [GAN$_2$ 3(aš) gur]
2'. a-ša$_3$ gaba ^{d}nin-ḫur-sag
3'. ba-zi-ge
4'. 1(eše$_3$) GAN$_2$ 1(u) gur
5'. lugal-ku$_3$-ga-ni
6'. 1(eše$_3$) GAN$_2$ 6(aš) gur
7'. uš šu-ku$_6$
8'. 1(eše$_3$) GAN$_2$ 7(aš) gur
9'. ur-^{d}ma-mi
10'. 1(eše$_3$) GAN$_2$ 7(aš) gur
11'. ur$_4$-ša$_3$-ki-du$_{10}$
12'. 1(eše$_3$) GAN$_2$ 7(aš) gur
13'. lugal-IM-BA
14'. 1(eše$_3$) GAN$_2$ 1(u) gur
15'. ur-^{d}gu$_2$-an-ka
16'. 1(eše$_3$) GAN$_2$ 7(aš) gur
17'. ⸢nimgir⸣-ḫe$_2$-du$_7$
18'. 1(eše$_3$) GAN$_2$ 7(aš) gur
19'. nam-ḫa-ni
20'. 1(eše$_3$) GAN$_2$ 6(aš) gur
21'. ab-ba-mu
22'. a-ša$_3$ ^{d}šara$_2$-gu$_2$-gal
23'. 1(eše$_3$) GAN$_2$ 1(aš) gur
24'. a-ša$_3$ ki-BAD
25'. ur-^{d}šul-pa-e$_3$
26'. 1(eše$_3$) GAN$_2$ 7(aš) gur
27'. ur-^{d}suen dumu gur$_4$-za-an
28'. 1(eše$_3$) GAN$_2$ 6(aš) gur
29'. x [. . .]
(rest broken)

obv. col. x
(start broken)
1'. x [. . .] ⸢lu$_2$-kal-la⸣
2'. 1(eše$_3$) GAN$_2$ 6(aš) gur
3'. ur-^{d}ur$_3$-bar-tab ša$_3$-gu$_4$-ta
4'. 1(eše$_3$) GAN$_2$ 6(aš) gur
5'. a-ša$_3$ apin-ba-zi[602]
6'. ur-li ša$_3$-gu$_4$-ta
7'. ugula ni-pa
8'. 1(eše$_3$) GAN$_2$ 7(aš) gur
9'. x-mu-ba
10'. 1(eše$_3$) GAN$_2$ 8(aš) gur
11'. ARAD$_2$ ugula
12'. a-ša$_3$ tul$_2$-ḫul$_2$-^{d}utu
13'. 1(eše$_3$) 2(iku) GAN$_2$ nu
14'. a-ša$_3$ ki-BAD
15'. ⸢lugal⸣-ma$_2$-gur$_8$$^{!?}$-re
16'. 1(eše$_3$) 1(iku) GAN$_2$ 1(u) 3(aš) gur

602 Written over erasure.

17'. a-ša$_3$ apin-ba-zi
18'. da-da šeš-tab-ba
19'. 1(eše$_3$) GAN$_2$ 1(aš) gur
20'. ḫe$_2$-sa$_6$-ge
21'. 1(eše$_3$) GAN$_2$ 1(aš) gur
22'. ukken-ne$_2$
23'. a-ša$_3$ ki-BAD
24'. 1(eše$_3$) 6(aš) gur
25'. a-ša$_3$ ^{d}nin-ḫur-sag
26'. a-kal-la
27'. [. . . n] ⸢3(aš) gur⸣
(rest broken)

obv. col. xi
(start broken)
1'. x ur-^{d}[x . . .]
2'. ARAD$_2$-mu [x]
(blank space)
3'. ugula lugal-⸢^{geš}gigir-re⸣
4'. 1(eše$_3$) GAN$_2$ 3(aš) gur
5'. a-ša$_3$ ^{d}nin-zabala$_3$^{ki}
6'. du$_{10}$-ga
7'. 1(eše$_3$) GAN$_2$ 2(aš) gur
8'. ur$_4$-ša$_3$-ki-du$_{10}$
9'. ur-an-ne$_2$ muš-laḫ$_5$-še$_3$
10'. 1(eše$_3$) GAN$_2$
11'. a-ša$_3$ ki-BAD
12'. ur-^{d}ur$_3$-bar-tab
13'. 1(eše$_3$) 6(aš) gur
14'. a-ša$_3$ ki-BAD
15'. 1(eše$_3$) GAN$_2$ 6(aš) gur
16'. lugal-ma$_2$-gur$_8$-re
17'. 3(iku) GAN$_2$ 1(aš) gur
18'. a-ša$_3$ ki-BAD
19'. 2(iku) ½(iku) ¼(iku) GAN$_2$ 2(aš) 2(barig) gur
20'. a-ša$_3$ ^{d}nin-ḫur-sag
21'. ur$_5$-ba-a dumu muš-⸢laḫ$_5$⸣
(blank space)
(rest broken)

obv. col. xii
(start broken)
1'. [. . .] ⸢^{d}nin⸣-[x]
2'. ur-sa$_6$-sa$_6$-ga
3'. 1(eše$_3$) GAN$_2$ 4(aš) gur
4'. ur-^{d}utu
5'. a-ša$_3$ ^{d}nin-⸢ḫur⸣-sag
6'. 1(eše$_3$) GAN$_2$ 2(barig)
7'. lu$_2$-dingir-ra
8'. a-ša$_3$ ki-BAD
9'. lu$_2$-gu-lu ba-uš$_2$
(blank space)
10'. ugula ur-^{d}da-ni
(blank space)
11'. ša$_3$-⸢saḫar$^{?}$⸣ gu$_2$-edin-⸢na⸣ u$_3$ muš-⸢bi⸣-[an-na]
12'. lugal-⸢KA⸣-[x]
13'. dumu ur-^{d}x-[x]
14'. ki da-a-⸢gi$_4$⸣-[ta]
15'. 1(eše$_3$) GAN$_2$ 3(aš) [gur]
16'. lugal-ku$_3$-[x]
17'. šar$_2$-ra-ab-[. . .]
18'. a-ša$_3$ [. . .]
(rest broken)

obv. col. xiii
(start broken)
1'. ⸢a-ša$_3$⸣ na-[ra-am ^{d}suen]
2'. lugal-x-[. . .]
3'. 3(iku) GAN$_2$ ⸢2(aš)⸣ [gur]
4'. a-ša$_3$ na-⸢ra⸣-[am-^{d}suen]
5'. gu-du-[. . .]
6'. 3(iku) GAN$_2$ ⸢4(aš)⸣ [gur]
7'. a-ša$_3$ tul$_2$-⸢ḫul$_2$⸣-[^{d}utu]
8'. lugal-x-[. . .]
9'. 3(iku) ⸢GAN$_2$⸣ [3(aš)$^{?}$ gur]
10'. a-⸢ša$_3$⸣ [. . .]
(rest broken)

rev. col. i
(start broken)
1'. 3(iku) [GAN$_2$ 3(aš)$^{?}$ gur]

2’. a-ša$_3$ u$_2$-⸢du⸣-[en-e$_2$-a]

3’. 3(iku) GAN$_2$ 3(aš) ⸢gur⸣

4’. a-ša$_3$ a-bu$_3$-[du-du]

5’. ^{d}utu-saga na-gada

6’. 3(iku) GAN$_2$ 2(aš) gur

7’. a-ša$_3$ u$_2$-du-en-e$_2$-⸢a⸣

8’. a-kal-la dumu ur-^{d}ma-mi

9’. ^{d}utu-saga i$_3$-dab$_5$

10’. 1(eše$_3$) 3(iku) GAN$_2$ 1(u) 2(aš) gur

11’. ge$_6$-par$_4^{?}$-šu-na-[x]

12’. 3(iku) GAN$_2$ ⸢5(aš)⸣ [gur]

13’. ^{d}šara$_2$-x-[x]

14’. 3(iku) GAN$_2$ 5(aš) [gur]

15’. ⸢da⸣-da-⸢ga⸣ [x]

16’. mi-la-šu x

17’. a-ša$_3$ u$_2$-da-[^{d}nin-a-ra-lli]

18’. 1(eše$_3$) 3(iku) GAN$_2$ 8(aš) [n gur]

19’. a-ša$_3$ ^{d}šara$_2$-gu$_2$-[gal]

20’. ba-⸢zi$^{?}$⸣-[. . .]

21’. 3(iku) ⸢GAN$_2$⸣ [3(aš)$^{?}$ gur] A

rev. col. ii

(*start broken*)

1’. a-ša$_3$ a-bu$_3$-⸢du-du⸣

2’. ši-in-nam

3’. 3(iku) GAN$_2$ 3(aš) gur

4’. ur-lagab-ba

5’. 3(iku) GAN$_2$ 3(aš) gur

6’. ki i$_3$-du$_8$-ḫu

7’. šeš ur-^{d}šara$_2$

8’. a-ša$_3$ a-bu$_3$-du-du

9’. la-lu$_5$ i$_3$-dab$_5$

10’. 2(eše$_3$) $_3$ (iku) GAN$_2$ 1(u) 5(aš) gur

11’. a-ša$_3$ a-ur-im

12’. 2(iku) GAN$_2$ 4(aš) gur

13’. gaba a-ša$_3$ ^{d}nin-ḫur-sag

14’. am$_3$-ma na-gada

15’. 3(iku) GAN$_2$ 1(aš) 2(barig) gur

16’. a-ša$_3$ ^{d}nin-ḫur-sag

17’. ur-^{d}ištaran

18’. 3(iku) GAN$_2$ 1(aš) 2(barig) gur

19’. a-ša$_3$ ^{d}nin-ḫur-sag

20’. ^{geš}gigir-gar-NI

21’. ⸢3(aš) GAN$_2$⸣ 4(aš) gur

22’. [. . .]-um

rev. col. iii

(*start broken*)

1’. AN [. . .]

2’. GAL x [. . .]

3’. ⸢1(u)⸣ [. . .]

4’. A [. . .]

(*n lines broken*)

5’. A [. . .]

6’. ⸢3(iku)⸣ [GAN$_2$ . . . gur]

7’. ša$_3$ [. . .]

8’. ⸢a$^{?}$-ša$_3^{?}$⸣ [. . .]

9’. 3(iku) [GAN$_2$ . . . gur]

10’. a-ša$_3$ x [. . .]

11’. u$_3$-ma-[. . .]

12’. ḫe$_2$-sa$_6$-[. . .]

13’. 1(bur$_3$) GAN$_2$ [. . . gur]

14’. a-ša$_3$ ^{d}[. . .]

15’. 1(eše$_3$) ⸢GAN$_2$⸣ [. . . gur]

16’. gaba a-ša$_3$ ^{d}[. . .]

17’. la-la-mu ⸢na⸣-[gada$^{?}$]

18’. 3(iku) GAN$_2$ 2(aš) gur

19’. gaba a-ša$_3$ ^{d}nin-ḫur-sag

20’. ab-ba-gi-na

21’. 3(iku) GAN$_2$ 3(aš) gur

22’. lugal-ḫi-li

23’. 3(iku) GAN$_2$ 3(aš) gur

24’. ⸢lugal⸣-ku$_3$-ga-ni

25’. 3(iku) GAN$_2$ 3(aš) gur

26’. ur-sukkal

27’. gaba a-ša$_3$ a-u$_2$-da

28’. la-la-mu i$_3$-dab$_5$

29’. 2(eše$_3$) GAN$_2$ 2(u) gur

30'. ur-^{d}šul-pa-e$_3$ na-gada
31'. 1(iku) GAN$_2$
32'. a-ša$_3$
33'. zaḫ$_3$ ti-e$_2$-maḫ-ta
34'. 3(iku) GAN$_2$ 5(aš) gur
35'. ur-^{geš}gigir
36'. 3(iku) GAN$_2$ 5(aš) gur
(*rest broken*)

rev. col. iv
(*start broken*)
1'. ⸢1(eše$_3$) GAN$_2$ 1(u) gur⸣
2'. gaba a-ša$_3$ a-u$_2$-da
3'. ab-ba-saga na-⸢gada⸣
4'. 3(iku) GAN$_2$ 3(aš) gur
5'. a-ša$_3$ a-u$_2$-da
6'. igi-tur-tur
7'. ab-ba-saga i$_3$-dab$_5$
(*blank space*)
8'. sipa udu eme-gi-ra-me
9'. 1(eše$_3$) GAN$_2$ 3(aš) gur
10'. nig$_2$-du$_7$-pa-e$_3$ dumu dingir-ba-an
11'. a-ša$_3$ ^{d}nin-ḫur-sag
12'. 3(iku) GAN$_2$ 3(aš) gur
13'. lu$_2$-^{d}šara$_2$
14'. gaba a-ša$_3$ ^{d}nin-ḫur-sag
15'. nig$_2$-du$_7$-pa-e$_3$ i$_3$-dab$_5$
16'. 4(iku) ½(iku) GAN$_2$ 8(aš) gur
17'. gaba a-ša$_3$ apin-ba-zi
18'. 1(bur$_3$) GAN$_2$ 1(aš) 2(barig) 3(ban2) gur
19'. a-ša$_3$ na-ra-am-^{d}suen
20'. ur-sila-luḫ na-⸢gada⸣
21'. 3(iku) GAN$_2$ 3(aš) gur
22'. a-ša$_3$ gaba-a-u$_2$-da
23'. ^{d}utu-bar-ra
24'. ur-sila-luḫ i$_3$-dab$_5$
(*blank space*)
25'. sipa ud$_5$ nam-en-na
26'. 1(eše$_3$) GAN$_2$ 3(aš) gur
27'. a-ša$_3$ ki-BAD
28'. lugal-ḫe$_2$-gal$_2$
29'. 1(eše$_3$) GAN$_2$ 1(u) gur
30'. gaba a-ša$_3$ apin-ba-zi
31'. ša$_3$-ku$_3$-ge
32'. 3(iku) GAN$_2$ 3(aš) gur
33'. a-ša$_3$ gaba ^{d}nin-ḫur-sag
34'. A ⸢AN$^{?}$⸣ [. . .]
(*rest broken*)

rev. col. v
(*start broken*)
1'. [. . .]-e i$_3$-dab$_5$
2'. [sipa$^{?}$ udu$^{?}$] ⸢eme$^{?}$⸣-gi-ra-me
(*blank space*)
3'. ⸢ur$^{?}$⸣-^{d}šul-gi-ra
4'. 3(iku) GAN$_2$ 3(aš) gur
5'. a-ša$_3$ ^{d}nin-ḫur-sag
6'. a-kal-la dumu lugal-ḫa-ma-ti
7'. a-bi$_2$-a i$_3$-dab$_5$
8'. sipa udu ge$_6$-me
9'. 3(iku) GAN$_2$ 4(aš) gur
10'. gaba a-ša$_3$ ^{d}nin-ḫur-sag
11'. 1(eše$_3$) GAN$_2$ 4(aš) gur
12'. a-ša$_3$ ^{d}nin-ḫur-sag
13'. ma-ma$^{?}$ na-gada
14'. 3(iku) GAN$_2$ 2(aš) gur
15'. sag-uš zaḫ$_3$-ta
16'. 3(iku) GAN$_2$ 2(aš) gur
17'. giri$_3$-ni-i$_3$-sa$_6$
18'. a-ša$_3$ ^{d}nin-ḫur-sag
19'. ma-ma i$_3$-dab$_5$
20'. sipa ud$_5$-da-me
(*blank space*)
21'. ⸢e$_2$$^{?}$⸣ x x ⸢RI$^{?}$⸣ x ⸢KI$^{?}$⸣
22'. 1(eše$_3$) GAN$_2$ 4(aš) gur
23'. a-ša$_3$ ki-BAD
24'. da-ga
25'. 1(eše$_3$) GAN$_2$ 1(u) 2(aš) gur

26’. gaba a-ša$_{3}$ apin-ba-zi
27’. ⸢šuku$^{?}$⸣-bi
28’. 1(eše$_{3}$) GAN$_{2}$ 1(u) gur
29’. a-ša$_{3}$ muru$_{13}$
30’. ur-^{d}šara$_{2}$ dumu ur-ku$_{3}$-nun-na
31’. 1(eše$_{3}$) GAN$_{2}$ 2(aš) gur
32’. a-ša$_{3}$ ^{d}nin-ḫur-sag
33’. [. . .] ⸢nig$_{2}$-lagar-e⸣
(*rest broken*)

rev. col. vi
(*start broken*)
1’. [. . .] x [. . .]
2’. [. . .] ⸢4(aš)⸣ [gur]
3’. ⸢lu$_{2}$$^{?}$⸣-x-[. . .]
4’. ⸢lu$_{2}$-ga$^{?}$-šu$^{?}$⸣-UD [. . .] ^{geš}gigir-ra
5’. 1(eše$_{3}$) GAN$_{2}$ 4(aš) gur
6’. ⸢lu$_{2}$⸣-dingir-ra
7’. 1(eše$_{3}$) GAN$_{2}$ 4(aš) gur
8’. lugal-^{d}nin-šubur
9’. ⸢mu u$_{3}$$^{?}$ a$^{?}$⸣ du$_{8}$-du$_{8}$
10’. a-ša$_{3}$ gur$_{4}$-za-an
11’. 1(eše$_{3}$) GAN$_{2}$ ⸢3(aš)$^{?}$⸣ gur
12’. a-ša$_{3}$ ⸢^{d}nin-ḫur⸣-sag
13’. inim-^{d}šara$_{2}$
14’. 1(eše$_{3}$) GAN$_{2}$ ⸢4(aš)⸣ gur
15’. a-ša$_{3}$ gur$_{4}$-za-an
16’. inim-ma-ni-⸢zi⸣ dumu ma-an-šum$_{2}$
17’. a-ša$_{3}$ gur$_{4}$-za-an
18’. nig$_{2}$-lagar IL$_{2}$-me
19’. 1(eše$_{3}$) GAN$_{2}$ 1(u) gur
20’. na-ba-sa$_{6}$ i$_{3}$-du$_{8}$
21’. 1(eše$_{3}$) 3(iku) GAN$_{2}$ 1(u) 2(aš) gur
22’. ša$_{3}$-ku$_{3}$-⸢ge⸣
23’. a-ša$_{3}$ u$_{2}$-du-^{d}nin-a-ra-li
24’. 1(eše$_{3}$) GAN$_{2}$ 1(u) gur
25’. a-ša$_{3}$ na-ra-am-^{d}suen
26’. lu$_{2}$-^{d}šara$_{2}$ kikken$_{2}$
27’. 1(eše$_{3}$) GAN$_{2}$ 2(aš) gur
28’. a-ša$_{3}$ ^{d}nin-ḫur-sag
29’. a-kal-la u$_{2}$-IL$_{2}$
30’. 1(eše$_{3}$) GAN$_{2}$ 3(aš) gur
31’. a-ša$_{3}$ ^{d}nin-ḫur-sag
32’. i$_{7}$ NE-gin$_{7}$-4(u)-šar
33’. [. . .] ⸢1(aš)⸣ gur
(*rest broken*)

rev. col. vii
(*start broken*)
1’. [. . .] x
2’. [. . .] x
3’. [. . . ^{d}]⸢en-lil$_{2}$-la$_{2}$⸣
4’. [. . .] x dumu ⸢lugal⸣-x-x-⸢e$_{2}$⸣
5’. [x] ⸢GAN$_{2}$⸣ 4(aš) ⸢gur⸣
6’. a-ša$_{3}$ ^{d}en-lil$_{2}$-la$_{2}$
7’. ur-lu$_{2}$-gu-la
8’. x GAN$_{2}$ 3(barig)
9’. a-⸢ša$_{3}$⸣ ki-BAD
10’. x ⸢GAN$_{2}$⸣ 2(aš) gur
11’. a-ša$_{3}$ ^{d}en-lil$_{2}$-la$_{2}$
12’. ARAD$_{2}$-^{d}šara$_{2}$
13’. 1(eše$_{3}$) GAN$_{2}$ 4(aš) gur
14’. a-ša$_{3}$ ^{d}en-lil$_{2}$-⸢la$_{2}$⸣
15’. ur-^{d}šakkan-na
16’. 1(eše$_{3}$) GAN$_{2}$ 2(aš) gur
17’. a-ša$_{3}$ ki-BAD
18’. lu$_{2}$-^{d}šara$_{2}$
19’. 5(iku) GAN$_{2}$ 6(aš) gur
20’. gaba a-ša$_{3}$ na-ra-am-^{d}suen
21’. 2(iku) GAN$_{2}$ 1(aš) gur
22’. gaba a-ša$_{3}$ a-bu$_{3}$
23’. lu$_{2}$-^{d}utu
24’. nar$^{?}$ nita$_{2}$$^{?}$-me
25’. 3(iku) GAN$_{2}$ 2(aš) gur
26’. muš-laḫ$_{5}$
27’. a-ša$_{3}$ gur$_{4}$-za-an
28’. 3(iku) GAN$_{2}$ 3(barig)
29’. a-ša$_{3}$ ^{d}nin-ḫur-sag

30'. SI$_4$ SI$_4$ lu$_2$-zi-tuš-da
31'. 1(eše$_3$) GAN$_2$ 6(aš) gur
(rest broken)

rev. col. viii
(start broken)
1'. [. . .] ⸢4(aš)⸣ gur
2'. [^{d}]šara$_2$-ḫe$_2$-gal$_2$
3'. [. . .]-x dumu bar-ra-ni-še$_3$
4'. [x] GAN$_2$ 5(aš) gur
5'. [gaba] a-ša$_3$ a-bu$_3$
6'. ⸢lu$_2$⸣-saga gu-za-la$_2$
7'. 2(iku) GAN$_2$ 2(aš) gur
8'. a-ša$_3$ a-ni-zu
9'. 4(iku) GAN$_2$ 2(aš) gur
10'. a-ša$_3$ ki-BAD
11'. ARAD$_2$-mu lunga$^{?}$
12'. lu$_2$ zaḫ$_3$ dab$_5$-dab$_5$-ba
13'. ur-e$_{11}$-e i$_3$-dab$_5$
14'. 1(eše$_3$) 2(iku) GAN$_2$ 4(aš) gur
15'. a-ša$_3$ ^{d}nin-ḫur-sag
16'. 1(eše$_3$) 4(iku) GAN$_2$ 1(u) gur
17'. gaba a-ša$_3$ ^{d}nin-ḫur-sag
18'. ku$_3$-ga-ni
19'. 1(eše$_3$) GAN$_2$ 4(aš) gur
20'. a-ša$_3$ gur$_4$-za-⸢an⸣
21'. lugal-ezem
(rest broken)

rev. col. ix
(start broken)
1'. [. . .] x
2'. [. . . ^{d}]⸢nin-ḫur-sag⸣
3'. šeš-a-ni dumu ur-e$_{11}$-<e>
4'. 1(eše$_3$) GAN$_2$ 1(aš) 2(barig) gur
5'. a-ša$_3$ ^{d}nin-ḫur-sag
6'. ^{d}en-lil$_2$-a-du-du$_8$
7'. ⸢1(eše$_3$)⸣ GAN$_2$ 4(aš) gur
8'. gaba a-ša$_3$ gur$_4$-za-an
9'. [x]-x-tu-ša-ri$_2$
10'. [. . .]-ta
11'. [x] ⸢GAN$_2$⸣ 1(u) 4(aš) gur
12'. [. . .]-lil$_2$ min-me
13'. [x] GAN$_2$ 1(u) 6(aš) gur
14'. [. . . ^{d}]⸢suen⸣
(rest broken)

rev. col. x
(start broken)
1'. 2(iku) GAN$_2$ 3(aš) ⸢gur⸣
2'. a-ša$_3$ u$_2$-da-^{d}⸢nin⸣-a-ra-li
3'. [. . .] GAN$_2$ 3(aš) gur
4'. [. . .] x x
(rest broken)

rev. col. xi
(blank?)

rev. col. xii
(blank?)

rev. col. xiii
(blank space)
1. . . .
2. . . .
(rest broken)

No. 140. *MS 4332*

obv. col. i
(start broken)
1'. [. . . ku$_3$-ga]-⸢ni⸣ ugula
2'. [. . . lugal]- ⸢^{geš}⸣gigir-re
3'. [. . . a-gub]- ⸢ba⸣-na-me
4'. [. . . a-a]- ⸢gi$^{?}$⸣-na
5'. [. . .] i$_3$-⸢dab$_5$⸣
6'. [. . . šeš]-kal-la
7'. [. . .] i$_3$-dab$_5$
8'. [. . .] tu-ra ki-lu$_5$-la
9'. [. . .] a$_2$-dingir-ga$_2$
10'. [. . .] ARAD$_2$
11'. [. . .] ma-an-šum$_2$
12'. [. . .] ARAD$_2$-^{d}šara$_2$
13'. [. . .]-⸢mu⸣ i$_3$-dab$_5$

14'. [. . .] tug$_2$ tu-ra ur-^{d}ḫal-mu-tum$_2$
15'. [. . .] ⸢ur⸣-^{d}ma-mi
16'. [. . .] ur-e$_{11}$-e
17'. [. . .] ur-^{d}ab-u$_2$
18'. [. . .] ⸢lugal⸣-dalla
19'. [. . .]-mu i$_3$-⸢dab$_5$⸣
20'. [. . .] ⸢3(ban$_2$)⸣ tug$_2$ ur-^{d}suen ⸢dumu$^{?}$ na⸣-lu$_2$
21'. [. . . dingir-mu]-ma-an-šum$_2$
22'. giri$_3$-se$_3$-ga ^{d}šara$_2$-du$_6$-ku$_3$-ge-še$_3$
23'. 1(aš) 3(ban$_2$) tug$_2$ šeš-a-ni
24'. [. . .] ⸢tug$_2$⸣ ur-^{d}lamma
25'. [. . .] ⸢lugal⸣-ku$_3$-ga-ni
26'. [. . .]-gal
27'. [. . . lu$_2$]-^{d}šara$_2$
28'. [. . . ^{d}šara-gal]-zu
29'. [. . . lugal-amar]- ⸢ku$_3$⸣
(*rest broken*)

obv. col. ii

(*start broken*)
1'. 1(aš) [. . .]
2'. dumu ⸢KA$^{?}$⸣-[. . .]
3'. 1(aš) ⸢3(ban$_2$)⸣ [. . .]
4'. 1(aš) 3(ban$_2$) x [. . .]
5'. ^{d}šara$_2$-i$_3$-sa$_6$
6'. gu$_2$-tar i$_3$-dab$_5$
7'. 1(aš) 3(ban$_2$) tug$_2$ lu$_2$-lugal
8'. dumu lugal-šeš-me
9'. 1(aš) 3(ban$_2$) tug$_2$ ur$_2$-ra-ni
10'. 1(aš) 3(ban$_2$) tug$_2$ inim-^{d}šara$_2$
11'. dumu nig$_2$-u$_2$-rum SIG$_7$-a
12'. 1(aš) ur-^{d}nin-a-zu dumu dam ur$_4$-a ^{d}šara$_2$-i$_3$-sa$_6$
13'. 1(aš) 3(ban$_2$) tug$_2$ šeš-kal-la a-ru-a ur-ama-⸢na$^{?}$⸣
14'. 1(aš) 3(ban$_2$) tug$_2$ ^{d}šara$_2$-a-mu a-ru-a a-tu
15'. [. . .] ⸢lugal⸣-ezem a-ru-a ur$_2$-nig$_2$-du$_{10}$
16'. 1(aš) 3(ban$_2$) tug$_2$ šeš-kal-la a-ru-a ur-gu$_2$-de$_3$-na
17'. 1(aš) 2(ban$_2$) 2(diš) lugal-geš-ḫur-e a-ru-a ur-^{geš}gigir
18'. 1(aš) 2(ban$_2$) 2(diš) lugal-ezem a-ru-a lugal-^{geš}gigir-re
19'. 1(aš) 2(ban$_2$) 2(diš) nam-tar-eb$_2$-gu-ul
20'. 1(aš) 2(ban$_2$) tug$_2$ šu-im-bi
21'. a-ru-a lugal-geš-ḫur-e
22'. 1(aš) 2(ban$_2$) 2(diš) lugal-nir-gal$_2$
23'. a-ru-a lugal-TAR
24'. ⸢uš$_2$⸣ giri$_3$-^{d}šara$_2$ i$_3$-dab$_5$
25'. [. . .] lu$_2$-^{d}šara$_2$
26'. [. . .] ⸢ur⸣-^{d}iškur

obv. col. iii

(*start broken*)
1'. [. . .]
2'. ⸢a-ru$^{?}$⸣-[a$^{?}$ . . .]
3'. 1(aš) ⸢2(ban$_2$)⸣ [. . .]
4'. a-ru-a [. . .]
5'. a-ru-a x [. . .]
6'. 1(aš) 4(ban$_2$) tug$_2$ šu-[. . .]
7'. gurum$_2$-e ⸢tak$_4$$^{?}$⸣-[a$^{?}$]
8'. 1(aš) 2(ban$_2$) 2(diš) ur-[. . .]-du ⸢dumu⸣ [. . .]
9'. ⸢1(aš) 2(ban$_2$)⸣ 2(diš)⸣ [. . .]
10'. ⸢dumu-ni⸣
11'. giri$_3$-se$_3$-ga ^{geš}kiri$_6$-ta
12'. 1(aš) 3(ban$_2$) 3(diš) dumu-gi$_7$ ma-na-na
13'. ki lu$_2$-^{d}da-ni ugula-ta
14'. 1(aš) 2(ban$_2$) tug$_2$ ur-e$_2$-maḫ dumu ša$_3$-ku$_3$-ge dumu ur-^{d}da-ni
15'. 1(aš) 2(ban$_2^{!}$) tug$_2$ lugal-nesag-e
16'. dumu ur-li
17'. dumu igi-mu
18'. 1(aš) 3(ban$_2$) tug$_2$ ur-sa$_6$
19'. 1(aš) 3(ban$_2$) tug$_2$ giri$_3$-ni-i$_3$-⸢sa$_6$⸣
20'. dumu ḫu-ti-me
21'. mu 1(u)-am$_3$ ḫu-ti ba-zaḫ$_3$ u$_3$ ur-sa$_6$ dumu-ni gurum$_2$-da ba-da-an-du$_{11}$ ensi$_2$ e$_2$ muḫaldim-ta ba-al-la-še$_3$
22'. 1(aš) 3(ban$_2$) tug$_2$ ur-^{d}x-[x]

rev. col. i
1. 1(barig) 1(ban$_2$) 5(diš) 1(diš) ½(diš) ki [. . .]

2. dumu e$_2$-e-a-na-ab-ba [x]
3. ki lugal-ma$_2$-gur$_8$-re-ta
4. šu a-ba-zi KWU79
5. 1(aš) 3(ban$_2$) tug$_2$ lu$_2$-^{d}a-zi-a
6. 1(aš) 3(ban$_2$) tug$_2$ šeš-kal-la
7. 1(barig) bu$_3$-bu$_3$
8. dumu a-ba-zi KWU79-me
9. gurum$_2$-⸢e tak$_4$-a⸣
10. 1(aš) 3(ban$_2$) tug$_2$ lu$_2$-⸢eb⸣-gal dumu iri-bar-re
11. ur-gu-tir
12. tu-ra lugal-a$_2$-zi-⸢da⸣
13. 1(aš) 3(ban$_2$) tug$_2$ ur-^{d}šul-pa-e$_3$
14. 1(aš) 3(ban$_2$) tug$_2$ ur-^{d}a-šar$_2$
15. 1(diš) lugal-nesag-e
16. dumu lugal-a$_2$-zi-da-me
17. 1(aš) 3(ban$_2$) tug$_2$ lugal-si-sa$_2$ a-ru-a ukken-ne$_2$
18. 1(aš) 3(ban$_2$) tug$_2$ lu$_2$-^{d}nin-ur$_4$-ra
19. ⸢dumu$^?$ šeš⸣-kal-la kur-ga$_2$-ra
20. ki lugal-ma$_2$-gur$_8$-re-ta
21. 1(aš) 3(ban$_2$) tug$_2$ lu$_2$-^{d}gu-⸢du⸣-du dumu ur-suḫ dumu ⸢lugal$^?$⸣-[. . .] SIG$_7$-[a]
22. ki ur-^{d}⸢da-mu$^?$⸣-[ta]
23. ugula ku$_3$-ga-ni [x]

(*blank space*)

rev. col. ii

(*blank space*)

rev. col. iii

(*blank space*)

1. [gurum$_2$]- ⸢ak⸣ ug$_3$-[IL$_2$] tur-tur
2. [iti min]- ⸢eš$_3$⸣-ta [u$_4$ x]- ⸢am$_3$⸣ ba-ra-[zal]- ⸢la⸣-ta
3. [mu en] ⸢unu$_6$⸣-[gal ^{d}inanna] ⸢ba⸣-ḫun

No. 155. *MS 4712 (Umma)*

obv. col. i

(*broken*)

obv. col. ii

(*broken*)

obv. col. iii

1. [. . .] guruš u$_4$ 1(diš)-še$_3$
2. [. . .] zar$_3$ tab-ba ŠE$_3$ x
3. [. . .] x-e x x
4. [. . .] x x [. . .]
5. [. . .] x x [. . .]
6. x ⸢iti$^?$⸣ [. . .] nin-ur$_4$-[ra . . .]
7. [. . .] a-kal-⸢la⸣
8. ⸢ki$^?$-su$_7$$^?$⸣ a-ša$_3$ la$_2$-maḫ x
9. ⸢4(u) 5(diš) guruš u$_4$ 1(diš)-še$_3$⸣
10. x ⸢u$_4$$^?$ ga$^?$ ta$^?$⸣ [. . .]
11. [. . .]-ri$_2$-še$_3$ ⸢še⸣ [. . .]
12. ⸢guruš u$_4$⸣-[n-še$_3$]
13. [. . .]
14. [. . .]
15. [. . .] ⸢guruš u$_4$⸣ 1(diš)- ⸢še$_3$⸣
16. [. . . a-ša$_3$] ⸢geš-i$_3$⸣-ka gub-ba
17. [. . .] ⸢3(geš$_2$)$^?$ 1(u)⸣ [guruš u$_4$] 1(diš)-še$_3$
18. [. . .] x ⸢u$_4$ gub⸣-ba
19. ⸢5(u) $^?$⸣ 5(diš) ⸢guruš⸣ [u$_4$ 1(diš)]-še$_3$
20. [. . .] gub-ba
21. [a-ša$_3$] ka-ma-ri$_2$
22. [. . .] x-še$_3$
23. [. . .] x-x-ma x še$_3$ x-ra

(*blank space*)

24. [ša$_3$ buru$_{14}$]

obv. col. iv

1. 2(bur$_3$) 2(eše$_3$) 2(iku) ⸢½(iku) ¼(iku)⸣ [. . .] x x [. . .] GAN$_2$-ta
2. a$_2$ erin$_2$-na-bi u4 ⸢5(geš$_2$)⸣
3. 2(bur$_3$) 2(eše$_3$) GAN$_2$ geš a-ra$_2$ 3(diš$_{tenû}$) 4(iku) ½(iku) GAN$_2$-ta
4. ⸢a$_2$⸣ erin$_2$⸣-na-⸢bi⸣ u$_4$ 1(geš$_2$) 3(u) 6(diš)
5. [GAN$_2$]-gu$_4$
6. [1(eše$_3$)] GAN$_2$ geš a-ra$_2$ 3(diš$_{tenû}$) ⸢4(iku) ½(iku)⸣ GAN$_2$-ta
7. ⸢a$_2$⸣ erin$_2$-na-bi u$_4$ 1(u) 2(diš)
8. šuku⸣ engar
9. ⸢a⸣-ša$_3$ ⸢ka⸣-ma-ri$_2$

10. ⸢2(bur$_3$)⸣ 3(iku) GAN$_2$ tug$_2$-gur$_x$(ŠE.KIN) [½(iku) ¼(iku)] GAN$_2$ geš a-ra$_2$ 3(diš$_{tenû}$) 4(iku) ½(iku) GAN$_2$-ta
11. ⸢a$_2$⸣ erin$_2$-na-bi u$_4$ 3(geš$_2$) 5(u) 4(diš)
12. 2(bur$_3$) 1(eše$_3$) 5(iku) ½(iku) GAN$_2$ geš a-ra$_2$ 3(diš$_{tenû}$) ⸢4(iku)⸣ ½(iku) GAN$_2$-ta
13. a$_2$ erin$_2$-na-bi ⸢u$_4$⸣ 1(geš$_2$) 3(u) 5(diš)
14. GAN$_2$-gu$_4$
15. 4(iku) GAN$_2$ geš a-ra$_2$ 3(diš$_{tenû}$) 4(iku) ½(iku) GAN$_2$-ta
16. a$_2$ erin$_2$-na-bi u$_4$ 8(diš)
17. ⸢šuku⸣ [engar]
18. a-ša$_3$ i$_3$-⸢se$_3$?⸣
19. 1(bur$_3$) GAN$_2$ tug$_2$-gur$_x$(ŠE.KIN) ½(iku) ¼(iku) GAN$_2$ geš a-ra$_2$ 3(diš$_{tenû}$) 4(iku) ½(iku) GAN$_2$-ta
20. a$_2$ erin$_2$-na-bi u$_4$ 1(geš$_2$) ⸢4(u) 8(diš)⸣
21. 1(bur$_3$) 2(eše$_3$) 4(iku) ½(iku) GAN$_2$ geš a-ra$_2$ 3(diš$_{tenû}$) 4(iku) ½(iku) GAN$_2$-ta
22. a$_2$ erin$_2$-na-bi u$_4$ 1(geš$_2$) 9(diš)
23. GAN$_2$-gu$_4$
24. 1(eše$_3$) 1(iku) ¼(iku) GAN$_2$ geš ⸢a-ra$_2$⸣ 3(diš$_{tenû}$) 4(iku) ½(iku) ⸢GAN$_2$⸣-ta
25. a$_2$ erin$_2$-na-bi u$_4$ ⸢1(u)⸣ 4(diš) ⸢½(diš)⸣
26. šuku engar
27. a-ša$_3$ ša-ra-ḫu-um-ma
28. 1(eše$_3$) GAN$_2$ tug$_2$-gur$_x$(ŠE.KIN) ½(iku) ¼(iku) GAN$_2$ geš a-ra$_2$ 3(diš$_{tenû}$) 4(iku) ½(iku) GAN$_2$-ta
29. ⸢a$_2$⸣ erin$_2$-na-bi u$_4$ 3(u) 6(diš)

bottom edge

1. 1(geš$_2$) 6(geš$_2$) 1(u) 6(diš)

obv. col. v

1. ⸢1(bur$_3$)⸣ 1(iku) GAN$_2$ geš a-ra$_2$ 3(diš$_{tenû}$) 4(iku) ½(iku) GAN$_2$-ta
2. a$_2$ erin$_2$-na-bi u$_4$ 3(u) 8(diš)
3. a-ša$_3$ ^{d}nin-ur$_4$-ra
4. 2(bur$_3$) 2(iku) ¼(iku) GAN$_2$ geš a-ra$_2$ 3(diš$_{tenû}$) 4(iku) ½(iku) GAN$_2$-ta
5. a$_2$ erin$_2$-na-bi u$_4$ 1(geš$_2$) 1(u) 6(diš) ½(diš)
6. 1(bur$_3$) GAN$_2$ geš a-ra$_2$ 2(diš$_{tenû}$) 4(iku) ½(iku) GAN$_2$-ta
7. a$_2$ erin$_2$-na-bi u$_4$ 2(u) 4(diš)
8. a-ša$_3$ la$_2$-maḫ
9. 1(bur$_3$) GAN$_2$ tug$_2$-gur$_x$(ŠE.KIN) ½(iku) ¼(iku) GAN$_2$ geš a-ra$_2$ 3(diš$_{tenû}$) 4(iku) ½ (iku) GAN$_2$-ta
10. a$_2$ erin$_2$-na-bi u$_4$ 1(geš$_2$) 4(u) 8(diš)
11. 2(bur$_3$) 5(iku) ½(iku) ¼(iku) GAN$_2$ geš a-ra$_2$ 3(diš$_{tenû}$) 4(iku) ½(iku) GAN$_2$-ta
12. [a$_2$ erin$_2$]-⸢na⸣-bi u$_4$ 1(geš$_2$) 2(u) 3(diš) ½(diš)
13. a-ša$_3$ igi-e$_2$-maḫ-še$_3$
14. 2(bur$_3$) GAN2 tug$_2$-gur$_x$(ŠE.KIN) ½(iku) ¼(iku) GAN$_2$ geš a-ra$_2$ 3(diš$_{tenû}$) 4(iku) ½(iku) GAN$_2$-ta
15. a$_2$ ⸢erin$_2$-na⸣-bi u$_4$ 3(geš$_2$) 3(u) 6(diš)
16. 4(bur$_3$) ⸢1(iku) ? GAN$_2$⸣ geš a-ra$_2$ 3(diš$_{tenû}$) 4(iku) ½(iku) GAN$_2$-ta
17. a$_2$ erin$_2$-na-bi u$_4$ ⸢2(geš$_2$) 2(u) 7(diš)⸣
18. GAN$_2$-gu$_4$
19. 1(eše$_3$) 4(iku) ½(iku) ¼(iku) GAN$_2$ geš a-ra$_2$ 3(diš$_{tenû}$) 4(iku) ½(iku) GAN$_2$-ta
20. a$_2$ erin$_2$-na-bi u$_4$ 2(u) 1(diš) ½(diš)
21. šuku engar
22. a-ša$_3$ muru$_{13}$

    (*blank space*)

23. a$_2$ geš-ur$_3$-ra
24. 2(bur'u) 7(bur$_3$) 2(iku) ½(iku) GAN$_2$
25. 2(eše$_3$) 4(iku) ½(iku) GAN$_2$ a-ša$_3$ bala
26. [GAN$_2$]-gu$_4$
27. [1(bur$_3$) 1(eše$_3$)] 4(iku) GAN$_2$ šuku engar
28. ⸢uru$_4$⸣-[a] ⸢2(iku)⸣ GAN$_2$-ta
29. a$_2$ erin$_2$-na-bi ⸢u$_4$⸣ 1(geš'u) ⸢7(geš$_2$)⸣ [4(u)] ⸢6(diš)⸣

bottom edge

1. 2(geš'u) 9(geš$_2$) 4(u) [1/2(diš)]

obv. col. vi

(*blank space*)

1. a$_2$ numun-na
2. 4(geš'u) sar gi 2(u) sar-ta

3. a$_2$-bi u$_4$ 2(geš$_2$)
4. 1(geš'u) 5(geš$_2$) 3(diš) sar al 6(diš) sar-ta
5. a$_2$-bi u$_4$ 2(geš$_2$) 3(u) ½(diš)
6. a$_2$ lu$_2$ ḫun-ga$_2$ 6(diš) sila$_3$-ta
7. 1(geš$_2$) 6(diš) sar al 6(diš) sar-ta
8. a$_2$-bi u$_4$ 1(u) 1(diš)
9. a$_2$ ša$_3$-gu$_4$
10. 5(u) 4(diš) guruš u$_4$ 1(diš)-še$_3$
11. a$_2$ erin$_2$ diri$^{?}$
12. 4(u) 2(diš) ug$_3$-IL$_2$ u$_4$ 1(diš)-še$_3$
13. ab-sin$_2$-ta la-ag ri-ri-ga
14. a-ša$_3$ la$_2$-maḫ[603]
15. 1(geš'u) 5(geš$_2$) 2(u) 7(diš) sar al 6(diš) sar-ta
16. ⸢a$_2$⸣-bi u$_4$ 2(geš$_2$) 3(u) 4(diš) ½(diš)
17. ⸢a$_2$ lu$_2$ ḫun-ga$_2$ 5(diš)$^{?}$⸣ sila$_3$-ta
18. [a$_2$ lu$_2$ ḫun]-⸢ga$_2$⸣ x ⸢6(diš)⸣ sila$_3$-ta
19. 1(u) 2(diš) ug$_3$-IL$_2$
20. ab-sin$_2$-ta la-ag ri-ri-ga
21. a-ša$_3$ igi-e$_2$-maḫ-še$_3$
22. giri$_3$ ḫu-wa-wa
23. 3(geš'u) 6(geš$_2$) sar ^{u2}erin$_x$(KWU896)-na ze$_x$(SIG$_7$)-a 1(u) 5(diš) sar-ta
24. a$_2$-bi u$_4$ 2(geš$_2$) 2(u) 4(diš)
25. a$_2$ lu$_2$ ḫun-ga$_2$ 6(diš) sila$_3$-ta
26. 7(geš$_2$) 2(u) 4(diš) sar al 6(diš) sar-ta
27. a$_2$-bi u$_4$ 1(geš$_2$) 1(u) 4(diš)
28. a$_2$ ⸢erin$_2$⸣-x-a
29. 2(geš$_2$) 3(u) ⸢sar$^{?}$⸣ ^{u2}ḫirin$_x$(KWU318)-na ze$_x$(SIG$_7$)-a <<ze$_x$(SIG$_7$)-a>> 5(diš) sar-ta x
30. a$_2$-bi 1(geš$_2$) 3(u)
31. a$_2$ ug$_3$-IL$_2$
32. a-ša$_3$ ša-ra-ḫu-um-ma
33. [. . .] x

(rest broken)

rev. col. i

1. x x x
2. a$_2$-bi u$_4$ 1(geš$_2$) ⸢3(diš)⸣

[603] Erasure after la$_2$-maḫ.

3. a$_2$ lu$_2$ ḫun-ga$_2$ 5(diš) sila$_3$-ta
4. 4(geš$_2$) 1(u) 2(diš) sar al 6(diš) sar-ta
5. a$_2$-bi u$_4$ 4(u) 2(diš)
6. a$_2$ erin$_2$ diri
7. [1(geš'u) 2(geš$_2$)] sar al 6(diš) sar-ta
8. ⸢a$_2$⸣-bi u$_4$ 2(geš$_2$)
9. a$_2$ ša$_3$-gu$_4$
10. 1(geš$_2$) 4(u) 6(diš) ug$_3$-IL$_2$ u$_4$ 1(diš)-še$_3$
11. 2(u) 2(diš) guruš ḫun-ga$_2$ a$_2$ 6(diš) sila$_3$-ta
12. ab-sin$_2$-ta la-ag ri-ri-ga
13. a-ša$_3$ i$_3$-se$_3$$^{?}$
14. giri$_3$ da-du
15. 2(geš'u) sar gi ze$_x$(SIG$_7$)-a 1(u) 5(diš) sar-ta
16. a$_2$-bi u$_4$ 1(geš$_2$) 2(u)
17. a$_2$ lu$_2$ ḫun-ga$_2$ 6(diš) sila$_3$-ta
18. 1(geš'u) 5(geš$_2$) sar gi ze$_x$(SIG$_7$)-a 1(u) 5(diš) sar-ta
19. a$_2$-bi u$_4$ 1(geš$_2$)
20. 6(geš$_2$) sar al 6(diš) sar-ta
21. [a$_2$-bi u$_4$ 1(geš$_2$)]
22. [x x] u$_4$ 1(diš)-še$_3$ ab-sin$_2$-ta la-ag ri-ri-ga
24. a$_2$ erin$_2$ diri
25. 1(geš$_2$) ug$_3$-IL$_2$ u$_4$ 1(diš)-še$_3$
26. ab-sin$_2$-ta la-ag ri-ri-ga
27. a-ša$_3$ ka-ma-ri$_2$
28. giri$_3$ ur-^{d}nu-muš-da
29. 1(geš'u) 6(geš$_2$) sar al 6(diš) sar-ta
30. a$_2$-bi u$_4$ 2(geš$_2$) 4(u)
31. a$_2$ lu$_2$ ḫun-ga$_2$ 5(diš) sila$_3$-ta
32. 1(geš'u) 2(u) 7(diš) sar al 6(diš) sar-ta
33. a$_2$-bi u$_4$ 1(geš$_2$) 4(u) 4(diš) ½(diš)
34. 1(geš'u) 5(geš$_2$) 4(u) 5(diš) sar gi ze$_x$(SIG$_7$)-a 1(u) 5(diš) sar-ta
35. a$_2$-bi u$_4$ 1(geš$_2$) 3(diš)
36. a$_2$ erin$_2$ diri
37. 2(geš$_2$) guruš ša$_3$-gu$_4$ u$_4$ 1(diš)-še$_3$
38. 2(u) 6(diš) ug$_3$-IL$_2$ u$_4$ 1(diš)-še$_3$
39. 2(u) guruš ḫun-ga$_2$ a$_2$ 6(diš) sila$_3$-ta

40. ab-sin$_2$-ta la-ag ri-ri-ga

41. a-ša$_3^?$ muru$_{13}$

42. ⸢giri$_3$ lugal$^?$⸣-me-⸢še$_3^?$⸣[604]

bottom edge

1. 3(geš$_2$) 1(u) 2(diš) ug$_3$

rev. col. ii

(blank space)

1. a-ša$_3$ gi kin-ak

(blank space)

2. x lugal-nir

3. uš$_2$ engar-zi

4. SIG$_7$-a šeš-kal-la dumu u$_2$-da-ur$_4$-ra

5. iti 1(u) 2(diš)-še$_3$

6. a$_2$-bi u$_4$ 1(geš'u) 2(geš$_2$)

7. iti še-sag$_{11}$-ku$_5$-ta

8. iti ^{d}dumu-zi-še$_3$

9. 1(diš) lugal-zi-mu

10. ⸢en⸣-nu-ga$_2$ ti-la

11. iti 6(diš)- še$_3$

12. a$_2$-bi u$_4$ 3(geš$_2$)

13. iti min$_3$-eš$_3$-[ta]

14. [iti ^{d}dumu-zi-še$_3$]

15. x guruš [u$_4$ x-še$_3$]

16. a$_2$-bi u$_4$ 6(diš)

17. a zi-ga gu$_2$ idigna-da gub-ba

18. 1(u) 6(diš) guruš u$_4$ 1(diš)-še$_3$

19. a-pi$_4$-sal$_4^{ki}$-ta umma^{ki}-še$_3$ ku$_6$ il$_2$-la

20. 4(diš) guruš u$_4$ 1(diš)-še$_3$

21. a-ša$_3$ la$_2$-maḫ-<ta> tum-mal$_x$(TUR$_3$)^{ki}-še$_3$ ku$_6$ il$_2$-la

22. 1(u) guruš u$_4$ 1(diš)-še$_3$

23. a-ša$_3$ la$_2$-maḫ-ta uri$_5^{ki}$-še$_3$ ku$_6$ il$_2$-la u$_3$ ma$_2$ <<x>> gur-ra

(blank space)

24. kišib$_3$ lugal-x-x

bottom edge

25. ⸢2(geš'u)⸣ 1(geš$_2$) 3(u)

rev. col. iii

1. 1(geš$_2$) 1(u) ⸢7(aš)⸣ [. . .] guruš-e ⸢1(aš)⸣ [. . .]

2. a$_2$ x [. . .] ⸢1(u) 8(diš)⸣

3. ⸢du$_8$-du$_8$⸣ ša$_3$-gal udu niga bala$^?$ gal-a

4. a-ša$_3$ ^{d}šara$_2$-ta

5. e$_2$-gal a-ša$_3$ la$_2$-maḫ-še$_3$ ga$_6$-ga$_2$

4. kišib$_3$ uš-mu

(blank space)

bottom edge

1. 1(geš$_2$) 1(u) 8(diš)

rev. col. iv

(blank space)

rev. col. v

(start broken)

1'. [. . .] x x x

2'. [. . .] ⸢ur⸣-^{d}nun-gal$^?$ ⸢e$_2^?$⸣-kišib$_3$-ba

3'. [. . .]

4'. [. . .] ⸢4(diš) guruš gu$_4$⸣-e-⸢us$_2$-sa⸣

5'. [. . .]-da ⸢dab$_5$⸣-ba

6'. [. . .] ⸢2(diš)⸣-še$_3$

7'. [. . .] u$_4$ 2(geš'u) x

8'. [. . .] ⸢ur-^{d}⸣[. . .]

9'. ½(diš) ^{d}⸢utu⸣-[. . .]

10'. ½(diš) a-a-[. . .]

11'. ½(diš) ^{d}[. . .]

11'. ½(diš) ⸢šeš$^?$⸣-[. . .]

12'. x [. . .]

(blank space)

13'. [u$_4^?$] ⸢2(diš)⸣-še$_3$

14'. ⸢a$_2$⸣-bi u$_4$ 5(geš$_2$)

15'. a$_2$ u$_4$-du$_8$-a dumu-gi$_7$

16'. ⸢1(geš$_2$)⸣ 1(u) 2(diš) guruš u$_4$ 1(diš)-še$_3$

17'. a$_2$ u$_4$-du$_8$-a ug$_3$-IL$_2$

18'. ⸢iti⸣ ^{d}li$_9$-si$_4$-ta

19'. ⸢iti ^{d}dumu⸣-zi-še$_3$

(blank space)

20'. [. . .] x

(rest broken)

---

[604] Line erased.

rev. col. vi

(*broken*)

No. 156. *MS 4713*

obv. col. i

(*broken*)

obv. col. ii

(*start broken*)

1'. [. . .] ⸢ug$_3$$^?$-IL$_2$$^?$ u$_4$⸣ 1(diš)-še$_3$

2'. [ki] x-^{d}x-x-ta

3'. [. . .] x x x tur-[tur . . .] u$_4$ 1(diš)-še$_3$

4'. [. . .]-dingir-ta

(*blank space*)

5'. [šunigin] ⸢2(šar$_2$)⸣ 5(geš'u) 3(u) [3+n(diš)] ⸢guruš u$_4$ 1(diš)⸣-še$_3$

6'. [šunigin 5(geš$_2$) 1(u)] ⸢8(diš)$^?$⸣ 1/2(diš)$^?$ ug$_3$-IL$_2$ tur-tur u$_4$ 1(diš)-še$_3$

(*blank space*)

7'. ⸢sag⸣-nig$_2$-gur$_{11}$-ra-kam

8'. ⸢ša$_3$⸣-bi-ta

9'. ⸢8(geš$_2$)⸣ 1(u) 5(diš) guruš u$_4$ 1(diš)-še$_3$

10'. [še] gur$_x$(ŠE.KIN)-a zar$_3$ tab-ba

11'. [n] 4(u) guruš u$_4$ 1(diš)-še$_3$

12'. ⸢ki⸣-su$_7$ i$_3$-se$_3$ ki-su$_7$ ^{geš}asal$_2$-du$_3$-a u$_3$ [. . .]-lugal gub-ba

13'. [n] ⸢4(u)⸣ 4(diš) guruš u$_4$ 1(diš)-še$_3$

14'. ki-su$_7$ a-ša$_3$ ^{d}nin-ur$_4$-ra gub-ba

15'. [n] 4(u) guruš u$_4$ 1(diš)-še$_3$

bottom edge

1. ⸢1(geš'u)⸣ [. . .]

obv. col. iii

1. ki-su$_7$ ^{d}amar-^{d}suen-^{d}šara$_2$-ki-ag$_2$ gub-ba
2. ⸢2(geš$_2$)⸣ 5(u) 5(diš) guruš u$_4$ 1(diš)-še$_3$
3. ⸢ki⸣-[su$_7$] x-BI gub-ba
4. 1(geš$_2$) 3(u) 6(diš) ⸢guruš u$_4$⸣ 1(diš)-še$_3$
5. ki-su$_7$ du$_6$-geš-i$_3$-⸢ka⸣ gub-ba
6. 3(u) 5(diš) guruš u$_4$ 1(diš)-še$_3$
7. ki-su$_7$ ^{d}amar-^{d}suen-^{d}šara$_2$-ki-ag$_2$-ta
8. ka-ma-ri$_2$-še$_3$ še mar-ta la$_2$-a
9. 1(geš$_2$) 3(u) guruš u$_4$ 1(diš)-še$_3$
10. gu$_4$-e us$_2$-sa
11. 1(geš$_2$) 1(u) ⸢2(diš) guruš u$_4$ 1(diš)⸣-[še$_3$]
12. [kišib$_3$] ⸢apin$^?$⸣ du x x ⸢ša$_3$$^?$ ^{d}šara$_2$⸣

(*blank space*)

13. ša$_3$ buru$_{14}$

bottom edge

1. 7(geš$_2$) 4(u) 8(diš)

obv. col. iv

1. 4(bur$_3$) 1(eše$_3$) GAN$_2$ tug$_2$-gur$_x$(ŠE.KIN) ½(iku) ¼(iku) GAN$_2$-ta geš a-ra$_2$ 3(diš$_{\text{tenû}}$) 4(iku) ½(iku) GAN$_2$-ta
2. a$_2$ erin$_2$-na-bi u$_4$ 7(geš$_2$) 4(u) 9(diš)
3. 1(bur$_3$) [5(iku) ¼(iku) GAN$_2$] geš a-⸢ra$_2$⸣ [3(aš$_c$)] ⸢4(iku)⸣ [½(iku) GAN$_2$-ta]
4. a$_2$ erin$_2$-na-bi u$_4$ 4(u) 6(diš) ½(diš)
5. GAN$_2$-gu$_4$
6. 4(iku) ½(iku) GAN$_2$ geš a-ra$_2$ 3(diš$_{\text{tenû}}$) 4(iku) ½(iku) GAN$_2$-ta
7. a$_2$ erin$_2$-na-bi u$_4$ 1(u) la$_2$ 1(diš$_{\text{tenû}}$)
8. šuku engar
9. a-⸢ša$_3$ GAN$_2$ ur-gu⸣
10. [3(bur$_3$) 1(eše$_3$) 5(iku)] ⸢GAN$_2$⸣ tug$_2$-gur$_x$(ŠE.KIN) ½(iku) ¼(iku) GAN$_2$-ta geš a-ra$_2$ 3(diš$_{\text{tenû}}$) 4(iku) ½(iku) GAN$_2$-ta
11. a$_2$ erin$_2$-na-bi u$_4$ 6(geš$_2$) 3(u)
12. 3(bur$_3$) 1(eše$_3$) 4(iku) ½(iku) GAN$_2$ geš a-ra$_2$ 3(diš$_{\text{tenû}}$) 4(iku) ½(iku) GAN$_2$-ta
13. a$_2$ erin$_2$-na-bi u$_4$ 2(geš$_2$) 1(u) la$_2$ 1(diš$_{\text{tenû}}$)
14. 2(bur$_3$) 1(eše$_3$) GAN$_2$ geš a-ra$_2$ 2(diš$_{\text{tenû}}$) 4(iku) ½(iku) GAN$_2$-ta
15. a$_2$ erin$_2$-na-bi u$_4$ 5(u) 6(diš)
16. GAN$_2$-gu$_4$
17. 2(eše$_3$) GAN$_2$ geš a-ra$_2$ 2(diš$_{\text{tenû}}$)$^?$ 4(iku) ½(iku) GAN$_2$-ta
18. a$_2$ erin$_2$-na-bi [1(u)$^?$ 6(diš)$^?$]
19. šuku [engar]

(*rest broken*)

obv. col. v

1. 3(bur$_3$) 2(eše$_3$) 3(iku) GAN$_2$ tug$_2$-gur$_x$(ŠE.KIN) ½(iku) ¼(iku) GAN$_2$-ta geš a-ra$_2$ 3(diš$_{tenû}$) 4(iku) ½(iku) GAN$_2$-ta
2. a$_2$ erin$_2$-na-bi u$_4$ ⸢6(geš$_2$)⸣ 5(u) 4(diš)
3. 1(bur$_3$) 4(iku) ½(iku) ¼(iku) GAN$_2$ geš a-ra$_2$ 3(diš$_{tenû}$) 4(iku) ½(iku) GAN$_2$-ta
4. ⸢a$_2$ erin$_2$-na⸣-[bi u$_4$ 4(u) 5(diš) ½(diš)]
5. GAN$_2$-gu$_4$
6. 2(eše$_3$) 2(iku) GAN$_2$ geš a-ra$_2$ 3(diš$_{tenû}$) 4(iku) ½(iku) GAN$_2$-ta
7. a$_2$ erin$_2$-na-bi u$_4$ 2(u) 8(diš)
8. šuku engar
9. a-ša$_3$ ša-ra-ḫu-um-ma
10. [. . .] geš a-⸢ra$_2$⸣ [. . .]
11. a$_2$ erin$_2$-na-⸢bi⸣ u$_4$⸣ [x]
12. 1(bur$_3$) 3(iku) ½(iku) GAN$_2$ geš a-ra$_2$ 3(diš$_{tenû}$) 4(iku) ½(iku) GAN$_2$-ta
13. a$_2$ erin$_2$-na-bi u$_4$ 4(u) 3(diš)
14. a-ša$_3$ ^{d}nin-⸢ur$_4$⸣-ra
15. 2(bur$_3$) 4(iku) ½(iku) GAN$_2$ [geš a]-ra$_2$ 2(diš$_{tenû}$) [4(iku) ½(iku) GAN$_2$-ta]
16. a$_2$ erin$_2$-⸢na⸣-[bi u$_4$ 5(u) 4(diš)]
17. a-ša$_3$ ⸢muru$_{13}$⸣
18. 2(bur$_3$) x [. . .] 4(iku) ½(iku) [. . .]
19. a$_2$ [erin$_2$-na-bi u$_4$ x]
20. ⸢a-ša$_3$⸣ [. . .]

(*rest broken*)

rev. col. i

(*start broken*)

1'. a$_2$-[bi u$_4$ . . .]
2'. 6(geš$_2$) 2(u) ⸢sar⸣ [. . .]
3'. a$_2$-⸢bi⸣ [u$_4$ . . .]
4'. a$_2$ 6(diš) x [. . .]

(*blank space*)

5'. a$_2$ lu$_2$ ḫun-ga$_2$
6'. 5(geš'u) 3(geš$_2$) sar ^{u2}kiši$_{17}$ ku$_5$-a 1(u) 5(diš) sar-ta
7'. ⸢a$_2$⸣-bi u$_4$ 3(geš$_2$) 3(u) 2(diš)
8'. [. . .] 4(u) sar ⸢u$_2$⸣ [. . .] ku$_5$-⸢a⸣ 1(u) [. . .]
9'. a$_2$-bi ⸢u$_4$⸣ [. . .]
10'. 5(u) 6(diš) ug$_3$-IL$_2$ u$_4$ 1(diš)-še$_3$
10'. ab-sin$_2$-ta la-ag ri-ri-ga
11'. a$_2$ erin$_2$-⸢na⸣
12'. a-ša$_3$ GAN$_2$ ur-gu
13'. 2(geš'u) ⸢1(u) 1(diš)⸣ sar al [. . .]
14'. a$_2$-bi u$_4$ [. . .]
15'. [. . .]
16'. [a$_2$]- ⸢bi⸣ u$_4$ 1(geš$_2$)
17'. 5(u) 2(diš) guruš u$_4$ 1(diš)-še$_3$
18'. ab-sin$_2$-ta la-ag ⸢ri-ri⸣-ga
19'. a$_2$ 6(diš) sila$_3$-ta
20'. 4(u) 1(diš) guruš u$_4$ 1(diš)-še$_3$ ab-sin$_2$-ta la-ag ri-ri-ga

top edge

1. 3(geš'u) 7(geš$_2$) ⸢6(u)⸣ 1(diš)
2. 4(u) 7(diš) ug$_3$-IL$_2$

rev. col. ii

1. [. . .]
2. a$_2$-[bi u$_4$ . . .]
3. 1(geš'u) 7(geš$_2$) 2(u) [. . .]-a 1(u) 5(diš) sar-[ta]
4. a$_2$-bi u$_3$ 1(geš$_2$) ⸢9(diš) ⅓(diš)⸣
5. 2(geš$_2$) 2(u) 1(diš) ug$_3$-IL$_2$ ⸢u$_4$ 1(diš)⸣-[še$_3$]
6. 1(geš$_2$) 1(u) guruš ša$_3$-gu$_4$ u$_4$ 1(diš)-še$_3$
7. [x] geme$_2$ u$_4$ 1(diš)-še$_3$
8. ab-sin$_2$-ta la-ag ri-ri-ga
9. ⸢a$_2$⸣ erin$_2$-na
10. ⸢a-ša$_3$⸣ sipa-da
11. 2(geš$_2$) 5(u) 7(diš) sar al 6(diš) sar-ta
12. a$_2$-bi u$_4$ 2(u) 9(diš) ½(diš)
13. 4(u) 5(diš) sar al 6(diš) sar-ta
14. [a$_2$]- ⸢bi⸣ u$_4$ 7(diš) ½(diš)
15. a$_2$ [erin$_2$-na$^?$]
16. [. . .] x TUR
17. ⸢1(geš'u)⸣ 5(geš$_2$) sar gi ze$_x$(SIG$_7$)-a 1(u) 5(diš) sar-ta
18. a$_2$-bi u$_4$ 1(geš$_2$)
19. a$_2$ 5(diš) sila$_3$-ta
20. a$_2$ lu$_2$ ḫun-ga$_2$

21. [. . .] ⸢sar⸣ gi ze$_x$(SIG$_7$)-a [1(u) 5(diš)] sar-ta

22. [a$_2$-bi u$_4$] ⸢2(u) 3(diš) ⅓(diš)⸣

23. 2(u) ⸢6(diš)⸣ [. . .]

24. [ab-sin$_2$-ta la-ag] ⸢ri-ri⸣-[ga]

25. a-ša$_3$ la$_2$-maḫ

26. 1(geš'u) 2(geš$_2$) sar ^{u2}numun guruš:e 1(u) sar-ta

27. ⸢a$_2$⸣-bi u$_4$ ⸢1(geš$_2$)$^?$⸣ 1(u) ⸢2(diš)⸣

top edge

1. ⸢9(geš$_2$)⸣ n(u) n(diš) ⅓(diš) guruš

2. 2(geš$_2$) 2(u) 1(diš) ⸢ug$_3$$^?$⸣

rev. col. iii

1. 1(geš'u) 5(geš$_2$) sar ^{u2}⸢erin$_x$(KWU896)$^?$⸣ ze$_x$(SIG$_7$)-a 1(u) sar-ta

2. a$_2$-bi u$_4$ 1(geš$_2$) 3(u)

3. 1(geš'u) 5(geš$_2$) sar gi ze$_x$(SIG$_7$)-a 1(u) 5(diš) sar-ta

4. [a$_2$]- ⸢bi u$_4$⸣ 1(geš$_2$)

5. 3(geš'u) 9(geš$_2$) sar al 6(diš) sar-ta

6. a$_2$-bi u$_4$ 6(geš$_2$) 3(u)

7. 1(geš$_2$) 5(u) ½(diš) ug$_3$-IL$_2$ tur-tur u$_4$ 1(diš)-še$_3$

8. ab-sin$_2$-ta la-ag ri-ri-ga

9. a-ša$_3$ ša-ra-ḫu-um-⸢ma⸣

10. a$_2$ erin$_2$-na

11. a-ša$_3$ gi kin-ak

(blank space)

12. [. . .] x

13. 1(geš$_2$) 1(u) ⸢8(diš)⸣ [. . .]

14. guruš-e 1(aš) gu-nigin$_2$-ta

15. gi ze$_x$(SIG$_7$)-a u$_3$ ⸢gi⸣ lagab a-ša$_3$ ^{d}šara$_2$-ta e$_2$ udu$^?$ a-ša$_3$ la$_2$-maḫ-še$_3$

16. ⸢a$_2$⸣-bi u$_4$ 1(geš$_2$) 1(u) 8(diš)

17. [. . .] mu

18. [. . .] x

(n lines broken)

19'. [. . .] da-da

20'. [. . .] x

21'. [. . .]-še$_3$

22'. [. . .]-x-kam

23'. [. . .] x x

24'. [. . .] 4(diš)

rev. col. iv

1. x [. . .]

2. a$_2$-bi u$_4$ 4(geš$_2$)

3. bala-še$_3$ gen-na bala-a gub-ba bala-ta gur-ra

4. ⸢giri$_3$⸣ ur-^{d}nun-gal

(blank space)

5. 6(diš) guruš gu$_4$-e us$_2$-sa

6. 6(diš) guruš a-ša$_3$-da tuš-a

7. iti 4(diš)-še$_3$

8. a$_2$-bi u$_4$ 2(geš'u) 4(geš$_2$)

9. iti ^{d}li$_9$-si$_4$-ta

10. iti ^{d}dumu-zi-še$_3$

(blank space)

11. ½(diš) ARAD$_2$-^{d}šara$_2$

12. ½(diš) ur-gu$_2$-de$_3$-na

13. ½(diš) ⸢lu$_2$$^?$⸣-[. . .]

14. ½(diš) lugal-inim-x

15. ½(diš) ur-^{d}ištaran

16. ½(diš) lu$_2$-dingir-ra

17. ½(diš) lu$_2$-du$_{10}$-ga

18. [iti . . .]-še$_3$

19. [. . .]

20. [. . .]-še$_3$

21. [. . .]-⸢še$_3$⸣

(rest broken)

rev. col. v

(start broken)

1'. [. . .] x guruš u$_4$ 1(diš)-še$_3$

2'. [. . .] x e si x

4'. [. . .] x x x x

(blank space)

5'. [šunigin] 2(šar$_2$) 3(geš'u) ⸢6(geš$_2$)⸣ 4(u) [n(diš)] ⅔(diš) guruš u$_4$ 1(diš)-še$_3$

6'. [šunigin] ⸢5(geš$_2$) 1(u)⸣ 8(diš) ½(diš) ug$_3$-IL$_2$ tur-tur u$_4$ 1(diš)-še$_3$

7'. [zi]-ga-am$_3$

8'. [la$_2$-ia$_3$] 1(geš'u) 3(geš$_2$) ⸢5(u)⸣ 2(diš) ⅓(diš) ⸢guruš u$_4$ 1(diš)⸣-še$_3$

References

Allred, L. 2006. "Cooks and Kitchens: Centralized Food Production in Late Third Millennium Southern Mesopotamia." Ph.D. diss., Johns Hopkins University.

———. 2010. "Getting the Word Out: Letter-Orders and the Administration of the Third Dynasty of Ur." Pages 9–13 in *Why Should Someone Who Knows Something Conceal It? Cuneiform Studies in Honor of David I. Owen on His 70th Birthday*. Edited by A. Kleinerman and J. M. Sasson. Bethesda, Md.: CDL Press.

Al-Mutawalli, N. 2010. "Administrative Cuneiform Texts from Umma in the Iraq Museum: Excavation of Shara Temple (1999–2000)." *Sumer* 55:45–86.

Al-Mutawalli, N., and W. Sallaberger. 2017. "The Cuneiform Documents from the Iraqi Excavation at Drehem." *ZA* 107 (2): 151–217.

Alotte de la Fuÿe, F.-M. 1919. "Compte de gestion d'un entrepôt de matériaux à Tummal." *RA* 16:1–20.

Al-Rawi, F., and F. D'Agostino. 2005. *Neo-Sumerian Administrative Texts from Umma Kept in the British Museum, Part One*. Nisaba 6 = NATU I. Messina: Di.Sc.A.M.

Attinger, P. 1993. *Éléments de linguistique sumérienne: La construction de du$_{11}$/e/di "dire."* Fribourg: Éditions Universitaires; Göttingen: Vandenhoeck and Ruprecht.

———. 1998. "Inana et Ebih." *ZA* 88:164–95.

Barjamovic, G. 2004. "Civic Institutions and Self-Government in Southern Mesopotamia in the Mid-First Millennium BCE." Pages 47–98 in *Assyria and Beyond: Studies Presented to Mogens Trolle Larsen*. Edited by J. G. Dercksen. PIHANS 100. Leiden: Nederlands Instituut voor het Nabije Oosten.

Beal, R. H. 1992. "Is KUŠ$_7$ the Reading of IŠ = *kizû*?" *NABU* 1992/48.

Bottéro, J. 1981. "Konservierung von Lebensmitteln." *RlA* 6/3–4:191–97.

Brunke, H. 2011a. *Essen in Sumer: Metrologie, Herstellung und Terminologie nach Zeugnis der Ur III-zeitlichen Wirtschaftsurkunden*. OLZ 107. München: Herbert Utz.

———. 2011b. "Food in the Garšana Texts." Pages 31–65 in *Garšana Studies*. Edited by D. I. Owen. CUSAS 6. Bethesda, Md.: CDL Press.

Butz, K. 1984. "On Salt Again . . . lexikalische Randbemerkungen." *JESHO* 27:272–316.

Calvot, D. 1969. "Deux documents inédits de Ṣelluš-Dagan." *RA* 63:101–14.

Charpin, D., and N. Ziegler. 1997. "Mekum, roi d'Apišal." *MARI* 8:243–47.

Christensen, L. P. 2000. *Raisin Production Manual*. Oakland: University of California, Agriculture and Natural Resources, Communication Services.

Civil, M. 1979. *Materials for the Sumerian Lexicon, XIV. Ea A = nâqu, Aa A = nâqu, with Their Forerunners and Related Texts*. Rome: Pontificium Institutum Biblicum.

———. 1994. *The Farmer's Instructions: A Sumerian Agricultural Manual*. Aula Orientalis Supplementa 5. Sabadell-Barcelona: AUSA.

———. 2000 [2005]. "Modal Prefixes." *ASJ* 22:29–42.

Clancier, Ph., F. Joannès, P. Rouillard, and A. Tenu, eds. 2005. *Autour de Polanyi: Vocabulaires, théories et modalités des échanges: Nanterre, 12–14 juin 2004*. Paris: De Boccard.

Cohen, M. E. 1996. "The Gods of Suburban Umma." Pages 27–36 in *Tablettes et images aus pays de Sumer et d'Akkad: Mélanges offerts a Monsieur H. Limet*. Edited by Ö. Tunca and D. Dehesell. Liege: Université de Liege.

———. 2015. *Festivals and Calendars of the Ancient Near East*. Bethesda, Md.: CDL Press.

D'Agostino, F., and J. Politi. 2006. *Umma Messenger Texts in the British Museum, Part Four*. Nisaba 16 = UMTBM 4. Messina: Di.Sc.A.M.

D'Agostino, F., and F. Pomponio. 2002. *Umma Messenger Texts in the British Museum, Part One*. Nisaba 1 = UMTBM 1. Messina: Di.Sc.A.M.

D'Agostino, F., and E. Santagati. 2008. "BM 106145: Un nuovo testo da Umma che menziona personale del cantiere navale (mar-sa)." Pages 1–9 in *On the Third Dynasty of Ur: Studies in Honor of Marcel Sigrist*. Edited by P. Michalowski. JCS Supplemental Series 1. Boston: American Schools of Oriental Research.

D'Agostino, F., and L. Verderame. 2003. *Umma Messenger Texts in the British Museum, Part Three*. UMTBM 3 = Rivista digli Studiia Orientali 26, Suppl. 2. Pisa: Istituti editoriali e poligafici internazionali.

Dahl, J. L. 2002. "Land Allotments During the Third Dynasty of Ur, Some Observations." *AoF* 29:330–38.

———. 2003. "A Note on Ur III Text Duplicates." *CDLB* 2003:5.

———. 2004. "The Quest for Eternity: Studies in Neo-Sumerian Systems of Succession." Pages 117–36 in *Assyrian and Beyond, Studies Presented to Mogens Trolle Larsen*. Edited by J.-G. Dercksen. PIHANS 100. Leiden: Nederlands Instituut voor het Nabije Oosten.

———. 2006. "Revisiting Bala" (review of Tonia Sharlach, *Provincial Taxation and the Ur III State*). *JAOS* 126 (1): 77–88.

———. 2007. *The Ruling Family of Ur III Umma: A Prosopographical Analysis of an Elite Family in Southern Iraq 4000 Years Ago*. PIHANS 108. Leiden: Nederlands Instituut voor het Nabije Oosten.

———. 2010a. "A Babylonian Gang of Potters." Pages 275–305 in *Proceedings of the 53e Rencontre Assyriologique Internationale*. Edited by L. Kogan et al. Winona Lake, Ind.: Eisenbrauns.

———. 2010b. "Naming Ur III Years." Pages 85–93 in *Why Should Someone Who Knows Something Conceal It? Cuneiform Studies in Honor of David I. Owen on His 70th Birthday*. Edited by A. Kleinerman and J. M. Sasson. Bethesda, Md.: CDL Press.

Dercksen, J. G. 2011. "Weeks, Months and Years in Old Assyrian Chronology." *BiOr* 68:233–44.

Edzard, D. O. 2003. *Sumerian Grammar*. HdO I/71. Boston: Brill.

Englund, R. K. 1988. "Administrative Timekeeping in Ancient Mesopotamia." *JESHO* 31:121–85.

———. 1990. *Organisation und Verwaltung der Ur III-Fischerei*. BBVO 10. Berlin: D. Reimer.

———. 1991. "Hard Work—Where Will It Get You? Labor Management in Ur III Mesopotamia." *JNES* 50:255–80.

———. 1995. "Regulating Dairy Productivity in the Ur III Period." *Or* NS 64:377–429.

———. 2003a. "The Year: 'Nissen Returns Joyous from a Distant Island.'" *CDLJ* 2003:1.

———. 2003b. "Worcester Slaughterhouse Account." *CDLB* 2003:1.

———. 2012a. "Equivalency Values and the Command Economy of the Ur III Period in Mesopotamia." Pages 427–58 in *The Construction of Value in the Ancient World*. Edited by J. Papadopoulos and G. Urton. Los Angeles: UCLA Cotsen Institute of Archaeology Press.

———. 2012b. "Versilberte Arbeit: Äquivalenzenfestsetzung in der Ur-III-Zeit." Pages 121–52 in *Wissenskultur im Alten Orient: Weltanschauung, Wissenschaften, Techniken, Technologien*. Edited by H. Neumann. CDOG 4. Münster: Otto Harrassowitz.

Falkenstein, A. 1949-50. *Grammatik der Sprache Gudeas von Lagaš*. AnOr 28-29. Rome: Pontificium Institutum Biblicum.

———. 1956–57. *Die neusumerischen Gerichtsurkunden*. Bayerische Akademie der Wissenschaften, phil.-hist. Klasse. Abhandlungen NF 39–40. Munich: Beck.

Ferwerda, G. Th. 1985. *A Contribution to the Early Isin Craft Archive*. TLB 5. Leiden: Nederlands Instituut voor het Nabije Oosten.

Firth, R. 2013. "Considering the Finishing of Textiles Based on Neo-Sumerian Inscriptions from Girsu." Pages 140–51 in *Textile Production and Consumption in the Ancient Near East: Archaeology, Epigraphy, Iconography*. Edited by M.-L. Nosch, H. Koefoed, and E. Andersson Strand. Oxford: Oxbow Books.

Firth, R., and M. L. B. Nosch. 2012. "Spinning and Weaving Wool in Ur III Administrative Texts." *JCS* 64:53–70.

Fitzgerald, M. A. 2003. "pisan dub-ba and the Direction of Cuneiform Script." *CDLB* 2003:2.

Foster, B. 1982. *Umma in the Sargonic Period.* Memoirs of the Connecticut Academy of Arts and Science 20. Hamden, Conn.: Archon Books.

Foxvog, D. A. 2016. *Introduction to Sumerian Grammar.* CDLP 2.

Friberg, J. 2007. *A Remarkable Collection of Babylonian Mathematical Texts.* Manuscripts in the Schøyen Collection, Cuneiform Texts I. New York: Springer-Verlag.

Gallery, M. 1975. "The Office of the '*šatammu*' in the Old Babylonian Period." Ph.D. diss., Yale University.

———. 1980. "The Office of the *šatammu* in the Old Babylonian Period." *AfO* 27:1–36.

Garfinkle, S. J. 2008. "Was the Ur III State Bureaucratic? Patrimonialism and Bureaucracy in the Ur III Period." Pages 55-61 in *The Growth of an Early State in Mesopotamia: Studies in Ur III Administration.* Edited by S. J. Garfinkle and J.C. Johnson. BPOA 5. Madrid: Consejo Superior de Investigaciones Científicas.

Gelb, I. J. 1957. *Glossary of Old Akkadian.* MAD 3. Chicago: University of Chicago Press.

———. 1960. "Sumerians and Akkadians in Their Ethno-Linguistic Relationship." *Genava: Revue d'histoire de l'art et d'archéologie* NS 8 (CRRAI 9). 258–71.

———. 1965. "The Ancient Mesopotamian Ration System." *JNES* 24:230–43.

———. 1972. "The Arua Institution." *RA* 66:1–32.

———. 1973. "Prisoners of War in Early Mesopotamia." *JNES* 32:70–98.

———. 1982. "Sumerian and Akkadian Words for 'String of Fruit.'" Pages 67-82 in *Zikir šumim. Assyriological Studies Presented to F. R. Kraus on the Occasion of his Seventieth Birthday.* Edited by G. van Driel, Th. J. H. Krispijn, M. Stol and K. R. Veenhof. Leiden: Brill.

George, A. R., ed. 2011. *Cuneiform Royal Inscriptions and Related Texts in the Schøyen Collection.* CUSAS 17. Bethesda, Md.: CDL Press.

Goetze, A. 1948. "Umma Texts Concerning Reed Mats." *JCS* 2:165–202.

———. 1963. "Šakkanakkus of the Ur III Empire." *JCS* 17:1–31.

Gomi, T. 1981. "Kollationen zu den von T. Fish in Manchester Cuneiform Studies veröffentlichten neusumerischen Texten in Grossbritannien, I." *Orient* 17:19–48.

———. 1984a. "Embolism in the Umma Calendar Under Shulgi of the Ur III Period." *ASJ* 6:1–18.

———. 1984b. "On the Critical Economic Situation at Ur Early in the Reign of Ibbisin." *JCS* 36:211–42.

———. 1985. "Kollationen zu den von T. Fish in Manchester Cuneiform Studies veröffentlichten neusumerischen Texten in Großbritannien, II." *Orient* 20:17–32.

———. 1986. "Kollationen zu den von T. Fish in Manchester Cuneiform Studies veröffentlichten Texten in Großbritannien, III." *Orient* 21:1–9.

Gong, Y. 2000. *Die Namen der Keilschriftszeichen.* AOAT 268. Münster: Ugarit.

Greco, A. 2015. *Garden Administration in the Girsu Province during the Neo-Sumerian Period.* BPOA 12. Madrid: Consejo Superior de Investigaciones Científicas.

Grégoire, J.-P. 1970. *Archives administratives sumériennes* (AAS). Paris: Geuthner.

Hallo, W. W. 1956. "Zariqum." *JNES* 15:220–25.

———. 1966. "The Coronation of Ur-Nammu." *JCS* 20:133–41.

———. 1969. "The Neo-Sumerian Letter-Orders." *BiOr* 26:171–75.

———. 1972. "The House of Ur-Meme." *JNES* 31:87–95.

———. 1977. "Seals Lost and Found." Pages 55–60 in *Seals and Sealing in the Ancient Near East.* Edited by McG. Gibson and R. D. Biggs. Bibliotheca Mesopotamica 6. Malibu: Undena.

———. 2006. "A Sumerian Apocryphon? The Royal Correspondence of Ur Reconsidered." Pages 85–104 in *Approaches to Sumerian Literature: Studies in Honour of Stip (H. L. J. Vanstiphout).* Edited by P. Michalowski and N. Veldhuis. Leiden: Brill.

Hallo, W. W., and J. B. Curtis. 1959. "Money and Merchants in Ur III." *HUCA* 30:103–39.

Halperin, R. 1993. "The Concept of Equivalencies in Economic Anthropology." *Research in Economic Anthropology* 14:255–98.

Hasselbach, R. 2005. *Sargonic Akkadian: A Historical and Comparative Study of the Syllabic Texts.* Wiesbaden: Harrassowitz.

Heimpel, W. 1990. "Maultiere." *RlA* 7:602–5.

———. 1993. "Zu den Bezeichnungen von Schafen und Ziegen in den Drehem- und Ummatexten." *BSA* 7:115–60.

———. 1994. "Towards an Understanding of the Term siKKum." *RA* 88:5–31.

———. 1995. "Plow Animal Inspection Records from Ur III Girsu and Umma." *BSA* 8:71–171.

———. 1997. "Disposition of Households in Ur III and Mari." *ASJ* 19:63–82.

———. 2009. "Blind Workers in the Ur III Texts." *KASKAL* 6:43–48.

———. 2011. "Twenty-Eight Trees Growing in Sumer." Pages 75–152 in *Garšana Studies*. Edited by D. I. Owen. CUSAS 6. Bethesda, Md.: CDL Press.

Hilgert, M. (with a contribution by C. D. Reichel). 2003. *Cuneiform Texts from the Ur III Period in the Oriental Institute 2: Drehem Administrative Documents from the Reign of Amar-Suena*. OIP 121. Chicago: Oriental Institute of the University of Chicago.

———. 2008. "Cuneiform Texts in the Collection of St. Martin Archabbey Beuron." *CDLJ* 2008:2.

Hrozny, F. 1913. *Das Getreide im alten Babylonien*. Vienna: A. Hölder.

Hruška, B. 2005. "Pflug. A. In Mesopotamien." *RlA* 10:510–14.

Huber, F. 2001. "La correspondance royale d'Ur, un corpus apocryphe." *ZA* 91:169–206.

Jacobsen, T. 1953. "The Reign of Ibbisin." *JCS* 7:36–47.

Jagersma, B. 2010. "A Descriptive Grammar of Sumerian." Ph.D. diss., Leiden University.

Joannès, F. 1993. "Metalle und Metallurgie. A. I. In Mesopotamien." *RlA* 8:96–112.

Jones, T., and J. Snyder. 1961. *Sumerian Economic Texts from the Third Ur Dynasty*. SET. Minneapolis: University of Minnesota Press.

Kleinerman, A. 2011. "Craft Production at Garšana: The Leather and Textile Workshops." Pages 183–208 in *Garšana Studies*. Edited by D. I. Owen. CUSAS 6. Bethesda, Md.: CDL Press.

Koslova, N. 2000. *Ur III-Texte der St. Petersburger Eremitage*. SANTAG 6. Wiesbaden: Harrassowitz.

———. 2008. "Bezeichnungen der Arbeitskräfte in Umma der Ur III-Zeit." Pages 149–206 in *The Growth of an Early State in Mesopotamia: Studies in Ur III Administration*. Edited by S. J. Garfinkle and J. C. Johnson. BPOA 5. Madrid: Consejo Superior de Investigaciones Científicas.

Kraus, F. R. 1966. *Staatliche Viehhaltung im altbabylonischen Lande Larsa*. Mededelingen der Koninklijke Nederlandse Akademie van Wetenschappen, Afd. Letterkunde. Nieuwe reeks. Deel 29, No. 5. Amsterdam: Noord-Hollandsche Utgevers Maatschappij.

Krebernik, M. 2004. "[(d)]$Pa_{4/5}$-Ú-e." *RlA* 10:367.

Krecher, J. 1987. "DU = ku_x(-r) 'eintreten,' 'hineinbringen.'" *ZA* 77:7–21.

Kutscher, R. 1968. "Apillaša, Governor of Kazallu." *JCS* 22:63–65.

Lafont, B. 1990. "Nouvelles lettres du temps des roi d'Ur." *RA* 84:165–68.

Landsberger, B. 1967. *The Date Palm and Its By-Products According to the Cuneiform Sources*. Archiv für Orientforschung Beiheft 6. Graz: Weidner.

Langdon, S. 1912. "The Sumerian Expression Sinitum." *Babyloniaca* 6 (1): 41–53.

Larsen, M. 1976. *The Old Assyrian City-State and Its Colonies*. Mesopotamia 4. Copenhagen: Akademisk Forlag.

Laurito, R., A. Mezzasalma, and L. Verderame. 2008. "Texts and Labels: A Case Study from Neo-Sumerian Umma." Pages 99–110 in *Proceedings of the 51st Rencontre Assyriologique Internationale Held at the Oriental Institute of the University of Chicago, July 18–22, 2005*. Edited by R. D. Biggs, J. Mayers, and M. T. Roth. SAOC 62 = CRRAI 51. Chicago: Oriental Institute of the University of Chicago.

Lee, T. G. 1985. "The Canal Name Kunigar." *JCS* 37:108.

Liu Changyu. 2015. "Idadu, Son of the Governor of Egula." *NABU* 2015/90.

Maaijer, R. de. 2001. "Late Third Millennium Identifying Marks." Pages 301–24 in *Veenhof Anniversary Volume: Studies Presented to Klaas R. Veenhof on the Occasion of His Sixty-Fifth Birthday*. Edited by W. H. van Soldt, J. G. Dercksen, N. C. Kouwenberg, and T. J. H. Krispijn. PIHANS 89. Leiden: Nederlands Instituut voor het Nabije Oosten.

Maeda, T. 1995. "Three Men of a Gang for Plowing and Four Men for Sowing." *ASJ* 17:333–37.

———. 1996a. "É-tum = bītum, Not kittum." *ASJ* 18:253.

———. 1996b. "Ruler's Family of Umma and Control over the Circulation of Silver." *ASJ* 18:254–60.

Maekawa, K. 1974. "Agricultural Production in Ancient Sumer." *Zinbun* 13:1–60.

———. 1982. "The Agricultural Texts of Ur III Lagash of the British Museum (II)." *ASJ* 4:85–127.

———. 1984. "Cereal Cultivation in the Ur III Period." *BSA* 1:73–96.

———. 1987. "The Management of Domain Land in Ur III Umma: A Study of BM 110116." *Zinbun* 22:25–82.

———. 1988. "New Texts on the Collective Labor Service of the Erin-People of Ur III Girsu." *ASJ* 10:37–94.

———. 1989. "Rations, Wages and Economic Trends in the Ur III Period." *AoF* 16:42–50.

———. 1993. "The Agricultural Texts of Ur III Lagash of the British Museum (IX)." *ASJ* 15:107–30.

———. 1996a. "Confiscation of Private Properties in the Ur III Period: A Study of édul-la and níg-GA." *ASJ* 18:102–68.

———. 1996b. "The Governor's Family and the 'Temple Households' in Ur III Girsu." Pages 171–79 in *Houses and Households in Ancient Mesopotamia.* Edited by K. Veenhof. CRRAI 40. Istanbul: Nederlands Historisch-Archaeologisch Instituut te Istanbul.

Marchesi, G. 2001. "Alleged SIG_7 = $agar_4$ and Related Matters." *Or* NS 70:313–17.

———. 2002. "On the Divine Name $^{d}BA.U_2$." *Or* NS 71:161–72.

Mayr, R. 1997. "The Seal Impressions of Ur III Umma." Ph.D. diss., Leiden University.

———. n.d. "Seal Impressions on Tablets from Umma." Unpublished manuscript.

McGuiness, D. 1981. "Studies in Neo-Sumerian Administrative Machinery." Ph.D. diss., University of Minnesota.

———. 1982a. "The Family of Giri-Zal." *RA* 76:17–25.

———. 1982b. "Ur III Prosopography: Some Methodological Considerations." *Archív Orientální* 50:324–42.

McNeil, R. C. 1971. "The 'Messenger Texts' of the Third Dynasty of Ur." Ph.D. diss., University of Pennsylvania.

Michalowski, P. 1993. *Letters from Early Mesopotamia.* Atlanta, Ga.: Scholars Press.

———. 2011. *The Correspondence of the Kings of Ur: An Epistolary History of an Ancient Mesopotamian Kingdom.* Winona Lake, Ind.: Eisenbrauns.

———. 2013. "Networks of Authority and Power in Early Mesopotamia." Pages 169–205 in *From the 21st Century BC to the 21st Century AD: Proceedings of the International Conference on Neo-Sumerian Studies Held in Madrid, July 22–24, 2010.* Edited by S. J. Garfinkle and M. Molina. Winona Lake, Ind.: Eisenbrauns.

Michel, C. 1992. "Transporteurs, responsables et propriétaires de convois dans les tablettes paléo-assyriennes. Réflexions sur les expressions *šēp* NP et *ellat* NP." Pages 137–56 in *La circulation des biens, des personnes et des idées dans le Proche-Orient ancien.* Edited by D. Charpin and F. Joannès. CRRAI 37. Paris: Editions Recherche sur les civilisations.

Mieroop, M. Van De. 1999–2000. "An Accountant's Nightmare: The Drafting of a Year's Summary." *AfO* 46/47:111–29.

Milano, L. 1993. "Mehl." *RlA* 8:22–31.

Milone, M. E., and G. Spada. 2003. *Umma Messenger Texts in the British Museum, Part Two.* Nisaba 3 = UMTBM 2. Messina: Di.Sc.A.M.

Molina, M. 2010. "Court Records from Umma," Pages 201 2017 in *Why Should Someone Who Knows Something Conceal It? Cuneiform Studies in Honor of David I. Owen on His 70th Birthday.* Edited by A. Kleinerman and J. M. Sasson. Bethesda, Md.: CDL Press.

———. 2013. "Court Officials at Umma in Ur III Times." *ZA* 103:125–48.

Nelson, R. C. 1976. *Pisan-dub-ba Texts from the Sumerian Ur III Dynasty.* Ann Arbor: University Microfilms.

———. 1979. "Inventory of Ur III pisan-dub-ba Texts." Pages 43-56 in *Studies in Honor of Tom B. Jones.* Edited by M. A. Powell Jr. and R. H. Sack. AOAT 2013. Kevelaer: Verlag Butzon und Bercker; Neukirchen-Vluyn: Neukirchener Verlag.

Neumann, H. 1999. "Ur-Dumuzida and Ur-Dun." Pages 43–53 in *Trade and Finance in Ancient Mesopotamia: Proceedings of the First MOS Symposium (Leiden 1997)*. Edited by J. G. Dercksen. Istanbul: Nederlands Historisch-Archaeologisch Instituut.

Nissen, H. J. 1976. "Geographie." Pages 9–40 in *Sumerological Studies in Honor of Thorkild Jacobsen on His Seventieth Birthday, June 7, 1974*. Edited by S. J. Lieberman. AS 20. Chicago: University of Chicago Press.

Nissen, H. J., P. Damerow, and R. K. Englund. 1993. *Archaic Book-Keeping: Early Writing and Techniques of the Economic Administration in the Ancient Near East*. Translated by P. Larsen. Chicago: University of Chicago Press.

Notizia, P. 2006. "Messenger texts from Ĝirsu: for a new classification." *Or* 75: 317- 333.

Oppenheim, A. Leo. 1948. *Catalogue of the Cuneiform Tablets of the Wilberforce Eames Babylonian Collection*. AOS 32. New Haven, Conn.: American Oriental Society.

Ouyang, X. 2011. "The Merchants Did Supply Gold! Connection Between Two Ur III Tablets YBC 13418 and NBC 6641." *NABU* 2011/3.

———. 2013. *Monetary Role of Silver and Its Administration in Mesopotamia During the Ur III Period (c. 2112–2004 BC): A Case Study of the Umma Province*. BPOA 11. Madrid: Consejo Superior de Investigaciones Científicas.

Ouyang, X., and C. Proust. Forthcoming. "Place Value Notations in the Ur III Period: Marginal Numbers in Administrative Texts." In *Cultures of Computation and Quantification in the Ancient World*. Edited by K. Chemla, A. Keller, and C. Proust.

Owen, D. I. 1972. "A Unique Ur III Letter-Order in the University of North Carolina." *JCS* 24: 133-134.

———, ed. 2011. *Garšana Studies*. CUSAS 6. Bethesda, Md.: CDL Press.

———. 2013. *Cuneiform Texts Primarily from Iri-Saĝrig / Āl-Šarrākī and the History of the Ur III Period*. Nisaba 15. Bethesda, Md.: CDL Press.

———. 2018. "A Neo-Sumerian Contract from Du-Enlila? and Related Texts." Pages 491–506 in *Grenzüberschreitungen: Studien zur Kulturgeschichte des Alten Orients. Festschrift für Hans Neumann zun 65. Geburtstag am 9. Mai 2019*. Edited by K. Kleverm, G. Neumann, and S. Paulus. Dubsar 5. Münster: Zaphon.

Owen, D. I., and R. H. Mayr (with the assistance of A. Kleinerman). 2007. *The Garšana Archives*. CUSAS 3. Bethesda, Md.: CDL Press.

Peled, I. 2014. "*Assinnu* and *kurgarrû* Revisited." *JNES* 73:283–97.

Poebel, A. 1923. *Grundzüge der sumerischen Grammatik*. Rostock: Selbstverlag des Verfassers.

Polanyi, K. 1957. "Marketless Trading in Hammurabi's Time." Pages 12–27 in *Trade and Market in the Early Empires, Economies in History and Theory*. Edited by K. Polanyi et al. Glencoe, Ill.: Free Press and Falcon's Wing Press.

Pomponio, F. 2013. "The Ur III Administration: Workers, Messengers, and Sons." Pages 221–32 in *The Growth of an Early State in Mesopotamia: Studies in Ur III Administration*. Edited by S. J. Garfinkle and J. C. Johnson. BPOA 5. Madrid: Consejo Superior de Investigaciones Científicas.

Powell, M. 1977. "Sumerian Merchants and the Problem of Profit." *Iraq* 39 (CRRAI 23): 23–29.

———. 1984. "Sumerian Cereal Crops." *BSA* 1:48–72.

———. 1987–90. "Masse und Gewichte." *RlA* 7:457–517.

Radner, K. 2004. *Das mittelassyrische Tontafelarchiv von Giricano/Dunnu-ša-Uzibi*. Subartu 14. Turnhout: Brepols.

Reid, J. N. 2015. "Runaways and Fugitive-Catchers During the Third Dynasty of Ur."

———. 2019. "Working for Royal Households and Temples at Girsu During the Third Dynasty of Ur: A New Text." Pages 139–67 in *To Gaul, to Greece and into Noah's Ark: Essays in Honour of Kevin J. Cathcart on the Occasion of His Eightieth Birthday*. Edited by L. Quick, E. E. Kozlova, S. Noll, and P. Y. Yoo. JSSS 44. Oxford: Oxford University Press.

Richter, T. 2004. *Untersuchungen zu den lokalen Panthea Süd- und Mittelbabyloniens in altbabylonischer Zeit*. AOAT 257. Münster: Ugarit-Verlag.

Röllig, W., and H. Waetzoldt. 1995. "Möbel. A. I. In Mesopotamien." *RlA* 8:325–30.

Roth, M. 1997. *Law Collections from Mesopotamia and Asia Minor.* 2d ed. Atlanta, Ga.: Scholars Press.

Rubio, G. 2000 [2005]. "On the Orthography of the Sumerian Literary Texts from the Ur III Period." *ASJ* 22:203–25.

Sallaberger, W. 1989. "Zum Schilfrohr als Rohstoff in Babylonien." Pages 311–30 in *Der orientalische Mensch und seine Beziehungen zur Umwelt.* Edited by B. Scholz. Grazer Morgenländische Studien 2. Graz: RM–Druck and Verlagsgesellschaft.

———. 1993. *Der Kultische Kalender der Ur III-Zeit.* UAVA 7. Berlin: Walter de Gruyter.

———. 1999a. "Ur III-Zeit." Pages 121–390 in *Mesopotamien, Akkade-Zeit und Ur III Zeit.* By W. Sallaberger and A. Westenholz. OBO 160/3. Freiburg: Universitätsverlag Freiburg; Göttingen: Vandenhoeck & Ruprecht.

———. 1999b. *"Wenn Du mein Bruder bist, . . .": Interaktion und Textgestaltung in altababylonischen Alltagsbriefen.* CM 16. Groningen: Styx.

———. 1999c. "Riten und Feste zum Ackerbau in Sumer." Pages 381–91 in *Landwirtschaft im Alten Orient. Ausgewählte Vorträge der XLI. Rencontre Assyriologique Internationale, Berlin, 4.-8.7 1994.* Edited by H. Klengel and J. Renger. BBVO 18. Berlin: D. Reimer.

———. 2011. "Sumerian Language Use at Garšana: On Orthography, Grammar, and Akkado-Sumerian Bilingualism." Pages 335–72 in *Garšana Studies.* Edited by D. I. Owen. CUSAS 6. Bethesda, Md.: CDL Press.

Sallaberger, W., and M. Civil. 1996. *Der babylonische Töpfer und seine Gefäße nach Urkunden altsumerischer bis altbabylonischer Zeit sowie lexikalischen und literarischen Zeugnissen / ḪAR-ra = hubullu: Tablet X dug = karpatu.* UHEM 3. Ghent: University of Ghent.

Salonen, A. 1939. *Die Wasserfahrzeuge in Babylonien nach sumerisch-akkadischen Quellen.* Helsinki: Societas Orientalis Fennica.

———. 1965–66. *Die Hausgeräte der alten Mesopotamier nach sumerisch-akkadischen Quellen 1–2.* AASF B 139, 144. Helsinki: Suomalainen Tiedeakatemia.

———. 1967. *Die Gruss- und Höflichkeitsformeln in babylonisch-assyrischen Briefe.* Helsinki: Societas Orientalis Fennica.

———. 1972–75. "Hausgeräte." *RlA* 4:225–29.

Schneider, A. 1931. "Die Drehem- und Djoha Urkunden der Strassburger Universitaets- und Landesbibliothek." *AnOr* 1:16–21.

Schwemer, D. 2002. "Drei Ur-III-Tafelchen." *AoF* 29:12–18.

Selz, G. 1993a. "*Kapparu(m)*, ein Sumerisches Lehnwort im Akkadischen." *RA* 87:29–45.

———. 1993b. *Altsumerische Wirtschaftsurkunden aus amerikanischen Sammlungen.* Stuttgart: Franz Steiner.

Sharlach, T. 2004. *Provincial Taxation and the Ur III State.* CM 26. Leiden: Brill.

Sigrist, M. 1992. *Drehem.* Bethesda, Md.: CDL Press.

Sigrist, M., H. H. Figulla, and C. B. F. Walker. 1996. *Catalogue of the Babylonian Tablets in the British Museum, Vol. II.* London: British Museum Press.

Sigrist, M., R. Zadok, and C. B. F. Walker. 2006. *Catalogue of the Babylonian Tablets in the British Museum, Vol. III.* London: British Museum Press.

Snell, D. 1977. "The Activities of Some Merchants of Umma." *Iraq* 39 (CRRAI 23): 45–50.

———. 1982. *Ledgers and Prices.* YNER 8. New Haven, Conn.: Yale University Press.

Sollberger, E. 1966. *The Business and Administrative Correspondence Under the Kings of Ur.* TCS 1. Locust Valley, N.Y.: J. J. Augustin.

Steinkeller, P. 1981. "The Renting of Fields in Early Mesopotamia and the Development of the Concept of 'Interest' in Sumerian." *JESHO* 24:113–45.

———. 1982. "On the Reading and Meaning of igi-kár and gúrum (IGI.GAR)." *ASJ* 4. 149–51.

———. 1984. "Sumerian Miscellanea." *Aula Orientalis* 2:137–42.

———. 1987a. "The Administration and Economic Organization of the Ur III State: The Core and the Periphery." Pages 119–41 in *The Organization of Power: Aspects of Bureaucracy in the Ancient Near East.* Edited by McG. Gibson and R. Biggs. SAOC 46. Chicago: Oriental Institute of the University of Chicago.

———. 1987b. "The Foresters of Umma: Toward a Definition of Ur III Labor." Pages 73–115 in *Labor in the Ancient Near East.* Edited by M. Powell. AOS 68. New Haven, Conn.: American Oriental Society.

———. 1988. "The Date of Gudea and His Dynasty." *JCS* 40:47–53.

———. 1995. "Sheep and Goat Terminology in Ur III Sources from Drehem." *BSA* 8:49–70.

———. 1996. "The Organisation of Crafts in Third Millennium Babylonia: The Case of Potters." *AoF* 23:232–53.

———. 2001a. "New Light on the Hydrology and Topography of Southern Babylonia in the Third Millennium." *ZA* 91:22–84.

———. 2001b. "AB-tum = èš-tum/iltu." *NABU* 2001/35.

———. 2004. "The Function of Written Documentation in the Administrative Praxis of Early Babylonia." Pages 65–88 in *Creating Economic Order: Record-Keeping, Standardization, and the Development of Accounting in the Ancient Near East: A Colloquium Held at the British Museum, November 2000.* Edited by M. Hudson and C. Wunsch. Bethesda, Md.: CDL Press.

Stepien, M. 1996. *Animal Husbandry in the Ancient Near East.* Bethesda, Md.: CDL Press.

Stol, M. 1980–83. "Leder(industrie)." *RlA* 6:527–43.

Struve, V. 1954. "The Accounts of Work-Team Overseers on a Royal Estate Under the Third Dynasty of Ur." Pages 43–51 in *Papers Presented by the Soviet Delegation of the 23rd International Congress of Orientalists.* Moskva: Izd-vo Akademii Nauk SSSR.

———. 1969. "Some New Data on the Organization of Labour and on Social Structure in Sumer During the Reign of the Third Dynasty of Ur." Originally written in Russian in 1949. Pages 127–72 in *Ancient Mesopotamia: Socio-economic History: A Collection of Studies by Soviet Scholars.* Edited by I. Diakonoff. Moscow: Nauka.

Such-Gutiérrez, M. 2011. "The gaba-ri Texts of the 'Garšana Archives.'" Pages 391–403 in *Garšana Studies.* Edited by D. I. Owen. CUSAS 6. Bethesda, Md.: CDL Press.

———. 2015. "Das $ra_{(2)}$-gaba-Amt anhand der schriftlischen Quellen des 3. Jahrtausends." *AfO* 53:19–39.

Thomsen, M.-L. 1984. *The Sumerian language: an introduction to its history and grammatical structure.* Copenhagen: Akademisk Forlag.

Touzalin, M. 1982. "L'administration palatiale à l'époque de la troisième dynastie d'Ur: Textes inédites du musée d'Alep." Ph.D. diss., University of Tours.

Tsouparopoulou, C. 2013. "A Reconstruction of the Puzrish-Dagan Central Livestock Agency." *CDLJ* 2013:2.

———. 2017. "'Counter-archaeology:' Putting the Ur III Drehem Archives Back in the Ground.'" Pages 611–30 in *At the Dawn of History: Ancient Near Eastern Studies in Honour of J. N. Postgate.* Edited by Y. Hefron, A. Stone, and M. Worthington. Winona Lake, Ind.: Eisenbrauns.

Uchitel, A. 1984. "Daily Work at the Sagdana Millhouse." *ASJ* 6:75–98.

Volk, K. 2004. "Palme." *RlA* 10:283–92.

Waetzoldt, H. 1970–71. "Thronfolger auch Mitregent?" *Mesopotamia* 5–6:321–23.

———. 1972. *Untersuchungen zur neusumerischen Textilindustrie* (UNT). Rome: Inst. per l'Oriente.

———. 1980–83. "Leinen." *RlA* 6:583–94.

———. 1992. "Rohr und dessen Verwendungsweisen anhand der neusumerischen Texte aus Umma." *BSA* 6:125–46.

Widell, M. 2002. "A Previously Unpublished Lawsuit from Ur III Adab." *CDLJ* 2002:2.

———. 2003. "The Ur III Calendar(s) of Tūram-ilī." *CDLJ* 2003:2.

———. 2009. "Schiff und Boot. A. In sumerischen Quellen." *RlA* 12:158–60.

Wilcke, C. 1973. "Sumerische literarische Texte in Manchester und Liverpool." *AfO* 24:1–18.

Woods. C. 2008. *The grammar of perspective: the Sumerian conjugation prefixes as a system of voice.* Leiden; Boston: Brill.

Yoshikawa, M. 1985. "A New Duplicate of YOS IV, No. 67 // V. Scheil, RA 24/1, No.8c." *ASJ* 7:191–92.

———. 1988. "GABA-aš and GABA-ta in the Ur III Umma Texts." *ASJ* 10:231–41.

———. 1989. "Looking for Tummal." *ASJ* 11:285–91.

———. 1992. "Bītum rabium^{ki} and É-gal." *ASJ* 14:428.

Zettler, R. L. 1989. "Field Plans from the Ur III Temple of Inanna at Nippur." *ASJ* 11: 305-313.

Zettler, R.L. and W. Sallaberger. 2011. "Inana's Festival at Nippur under the Third Dynasty of Ur." *ZA* 101: 1–71.

Indexes

The indexes were produced using the concordance program CasualConc (Imao, Y. (2016). CasualConc (Version 2.0.6) [Computer Software]. Osaka, Japan: Osaka University. Available from https://sites.google.com/site/casualconc/). References to some common words have been left out when these were too numerous. No references are given for metrological units. All texts are available online at the CDLI and new indexes can be generated.

PERSONAL NAMES

DIVINE NAMES AND NAMES OF RULERS

CITIES, VILLAGES, AND DISTRICTS

RIVERS AND CANALS

FIELDS

THRESHING FLOORS

MONTH NAMES

YEAR NAMES

SUMERIAN AND AKKADIAN WORDS

Cornell University Studies in Assyriology and Sumerology
(CUSAS)

David I. Owen, editor-in-chief

CUSAS 1 *The Cornell University Archaic Tablets*
Salvatore Monaco. 2007. Pp. xiv + 370. ISBN 978-1-934309-00-1

CUSAS 2 *Sumerian Proverbs in the Schøyen Collection*
Bendt Alster. 2007. Pp. xvi + 156. ISBN 978-1-934309-01-8

CUSAS 3 *The Garšana Archives*
David I. Owen and Rudolf H. Mayr with the assistance of Alex Kleinerman. 2007. Pp. xii + 528. ISBN 978-1-934309-02-5

CUSAS 4 *Analytical Concordance to the Garšana Archives*
Alexandra Kleinerman and David I. Owen. 2009. Pp. x + 795. ISBN 978-1-934309-03-2

CUSAS 5 *Workers and Construction Work at Garšana*
Wolfgang Heimpel. 2009. Pp. xx + 394. ISBN 978-1-934309-04-9

CUSAS 6 *Garšana Studies*
David I. Owen, ed. 2011. Pp. xii + 457. ISBN 978-1-934309-05-6

CUSAS 8 *A Late Old Babylonian Temple Archive from Dūr-Abiešuḫ*
Karel van Lerberghe and Gabriella Voet. 2009. Pp. xviii + 276. Pl. 22. ISBN 978-1-934309-07-9

CUSAS 9 *Babylonian Tablets from the First Sealand Dynasty in the Schøyen Collection*
Stephanie Dalley. 2009. Pp. xviii + 320. Pl. 182. ISBN 978-1-934309-08-7

CUSAS 10 *Babylonian Literary Texts in the Schøyen Collection*
A. R. George. 2009. Pp. xx + 160. Pl. 62. ISBN 978-1-934309-09-4

CUSAS 11 *Early Dynastic and Early Sargonic Tablets from Adab in the Cornell University Collections*
Giuseppe Visicato and Aage Westenholz. 2010. Pp. xxvi + 124. Pl. 94. ISBN 978-1-934309-10-0

CUSAS 12 *The Lexical Texts in the Schøyen Collection*
Miguel Civil. 2010. Pp. xxii + 308. ISBN 978-1-934309-11-7

CUSAS 13 *Classical Sargonic Tablets Chiefly from Adab in the Cornell University Collections*
Massimo Maiocchi. 2009. Pp. xxii + 334. Pl. 38. ISBN 978-1-934309-12-4

CUSAS 14 *Early Dynastic Cereal Texts in the Cornell University Collections*
Salvatore Monaco. 2011. Pp. xii + 289. ISBN 978-1-934309-39-1

CUSAS 15 *Cuneiform Texts in the Carl A. Kroch Library, Cornell University*
Alhena Gadotti and Marcel Sigrist with the assistance of Nicole M. Brisch and David I. Owen. 2011. Pp. xx + 214. Pl. 29. ISBN 978-1-934309-25-4

CUSAS 16 *Ur III Tablets from the Columbia University Libraries*
S. Garfinkle, H. Sauren, and M. Van De Mieroop. 2010. Pp. xxviii + 341. ISBN 978-1-934309-28-5

CUSAS 17 *Cuneiform Royal Inscriptions and Related Texts in the Schøyen Collection*
A. R. George, ed. 2011. Pp. xxxii + 312. Pl. 101. ISBN 978-1-934309-33-9

CUSAS 18 *Babylonian Divinatory Texts Chiefly in the Schøyen Collection*
A. R. George, 2013. Pp. xxviii + 441. Pl. 100. ISBN 978-1-934309-47-6

CUSAS 19 *Classical Sargonic Tablets Chiefly from Adab in the Cornell University Collections, II*
Massimo Maiocchi and Giuseppe Visicato. 2012. Pp. xx + 208. ISBN 978-1-934309-40-7

CUSAS 20 *Middle Sargonic Tablets Chiefly from Adab in the Cornell University Collections*
Francesco Pomponio and Giuseppe Visicato. 2015. Pp. xxxii + 250. ISBN 978-1-934309-60-5

CUSAS 21 *Archaic Bullae and Tablets in the Cornell University Collections*
Salvatore Monaco. 2014. Pp. xii + 228. ISBN 978-1-934309-55-1

CUSAS 22 *Entrepreneurs and Enterprise in Early Mesopotamia: A Study of Three Archives from the Third Dynasty of Ur*
Steven J. Garfinkle. 2012. Pp. xii + 282. ISBN 978-1-934309-41-4

CUSAS 23 *Miscellaneous Early Dynastic and Sargonic Texts in the Cornell University Collections*
Vitali Bartash. 2013. Pp. xiv + 242. Pl. 23. ISBN 978-1-934309-49-0

CUSAS 24 *The Domestication of Equidae in Third-Millennium BCE Mesopotamia*
Juris Zarins. 2014. Pp. xi + 432. ISBN 978-1-934309-51-3

CUSAS 25 *Hemerologies of Assyrian and Babylonian Scholars*
Alasdair Livingstone. 2013. Pp. viii + 278. ISBN 978-1-934309-52-0

CUSAS 26 *A Third-Millennium Miscellany of Cuneiform Texts*
Aage Westenholz. 2014. Pp. xviii + 238. Pl. 6. ISBN 978-1-934309-56-8

CUSAS 27 *The "Šu-ilisu Archive" and Other Sargonic Texts in Akkadian*
Lucio Milano and Aage Westenholz. 2015. Pp. xii + 322. ISBN 978-1-934309-61-2

CUSAS 28 *Documents of Judean Exiles and West Semites in Babylonia in the Collection of David Sofer*
Laurie Pearce and Cornelia Wunsch. 2014. Pp. xlii + 334. Pl. 105. ISBN 978-1-934309-57-5

CUSAS 29 *A Late Old Babylonian Temple Archive from Dūr-Abiešuh: The Sequel*
Kathleen Abraham and Karel van Lerberghe. 2017. Pp. xviii + 189. Pl. 218. ISBN 978-1-934309-74-2

CUSAS 30 *Middle Babylonian Texts in the Cornell University Collections: I. The Later Kings*
Wilfred van Soldt. 2015. Pp. xii + 585. Pl. 21. ISBN 978-1-934309-62-9

CUSAS 31 *Archaic Cuneiform Tablets from Private Collections*
Salvatore F. Monaco. 2016. Pp. x + 310. ISBN 978-1-934309-65-0

CUSAS 32 *Mesopotamian Incantations and Related Texts in the Schøyen Collection*
A. R. George. 2016. Pp. xiv + 196. Pl. 151. ISBN 978-1-934309-66-7

CUSAS 33 *Early Dynastic and Early Sargonic Administrative Texts Mainly from the Umma Region in the Cornell Cuneiform Collections*
Palmiro Notizia and Giuseppe Visicato. 2016. Pp. xii + 312. ISBN 978-1-934309-70-4

CUSAS 34 *Assyrian Archival Texts in the Schøyen Collection and Other Documents from North Mesopotamia and Syria*
A. R. George, Thomas Hertel, Jaume Llop-Raduà, Karen Radner, and Wilfred H. van Soldt. 2017. Pp. xxii + 136. Pl. 92. ISBN 978-1-934309-71-1

CUSAS 35 *Sumerian Administrative and Legal Documents ca. 2900–2200 BC in the Schøyen Collection*
Vitali Bartash. 2017. Pp. xviii + 536. ISBN 978-1-934309-73-5

CUSAS 36 *Old Babylonian Texts in the Schøyen Collection. Part I: Selected Letters*
A. R. George. 2018. Pp. xiv + 192. Pl. 263. ISBN 978-1-934309-75-9

CUSAS 39 *Ur III Texts in the Schøyen Collection*
Jacob L. Dahl. 2020. Pp. xx + 408. ISBN 978-1-5750-6738-4

CUSAS 40 *Tablets from the Irisaĝrig Archive*
Marcel Sigrist and Tohru Ozaki. 2019. Pp. xiv + 715. ISBN 978-1-57506-726-1